# 75 Readings

*Plus*

# 75 Readings

## *Plus*

Sixth Edition

Santi V. Buscemi
Middlesex County College

Charlotte Smith
Adirondack Community College

Boston   Burr Ridge, IL   Dubuque, IA   Madison, WI   New York
San Francisco   St. Louis   Bangkok   Bogotá   Caracas   Kuala Lumpur
Lisbon   London   Madrid   Mexico City   Milan   Montreal   New Delhi
Santiago   Seoul   Singapore   Sydney   Taipei   Toronto

# McGraw-Hill Higher Education

A Division of The **McGraw-Hill** Companies

75 READINGS PLUS

Published by McGraw-Hill, an imprint of The McGraw-Hill Companies, Inc. 1221
Avenue of the Americas, New York, NY, 10020. Copyright © 2002, 2000, 1998, 1996,
1994, 1992 by The McGraw-Hill Companies, Inc. All rights reserved. No part of this
publication may be reproduced or distributed in any form or by any means, or stored in a
database or retrieval system, without the prior written consent of The McGraw-Hill
Companies, Inc., including, but not limited to, in any network or other electronic storage
or transmission, or broadcast for distance learning.
Some ancillaries, including electronic and print components, may not be available to
customers outside the United States

This book is printed on acid-free paper.

domestic       1 2 3 4 5 6 7 8 9 0 FGR/FGR 0 9 8 7 6 5 4 3 2 1 0 9
international   1 2 3 4 5 6 7 8 9 0 FGR/FGR 0 9 8 7 6 5 4 3 2 1 0 9

ISBN 0-07-237062-9


Editorial director: *Phillip A. Butcher*
Executive editor: *Lisa Moore*
Editorial coordinator: *Victoria Fullard*
Senior marketing manager: *David Patterson*
Associate project manager: *Destiny Rynne*
Production supervisor: *Susanne Riedell*
Freelance design coordinator: *Gino Cieslik*
Interior Designer: *©PhotoDisc*
Associate supplement producer: *Vicki Laird*
Media producer: *Greg Di Lorenzo*
Printer: *Quebecor World Fairfield Inc.*
Typeface: *10/12 Times Roman*
Compositor: *Carlisle Communications, Ltd.*


**Library of Congress Cataloging–in–Publication Data**

75 readings plus / [edited by] Santi V. Buscemi, Charlotte Smith.—6th ed.
    p. cm.
    Includes index.
    ISBN 0-07-237062-9 (alk. paper)
    1. College readers. 2. English language—Rhetoric—Problems, exercises, etc. 3. Report
writing—Problems, exercises, etc. I. Title: Seventy-five readings plus. II. Buscemi, Santi V.
III. Smith, Charlotte.
    PE1417.A14 2002
    808'.0427--dc21                                                          2001030331
Use the Internet and eliminate mail time and postage costs  http://www.mhhe.com

INTERNATIONAL EDITION ISBN 0-07-112093-9
Copyright © 2002. Exclusive rights by The McGraw-Hill Companies, Inc. for manufacture
and export.
This book cannot be re-exported from the country to which it is sold by McGraw-Hill.
The International Edition is not available in North America.

# About the Authors

*SANTI BUSCEMI* teaches reading and writing and chairs the English Department at Middlesex County College in Edison, New Jersey.

*CHARLOTTE SMITH* Teaches English composition and technical writing at Adirondack Community College in Queensbury, New York.

# Contents

Chapter 3
PROCESS ANALYSIS   85

Chapter 4
DEFINITION   121

Chapter 5
CLASSIFICATION AND DIVISION   160

## Chapter 6
## COMPARISON AND CONTRAST     214

## Chapter 7
## EXAMPLE AND ILLUSTRATION     250

## Chapter 8
## CAUSE AND EFFECT    286

## Chapter 9
## ANALOGY    328

# THEMATIC CONTENTS

## Power and Politics

## Problems, Solutions, and Consequences

## Culture and Identity

## The Media and the Arts

## Science and Technology

## Health and Medicine

## Use and Abuses of Language

# To The Instructor

*75 Readings Plus* is an expanded version of *75 Readings*, the popular and inexpensive collection of essays for freshman composition first published in 1987 and now in its eighth edition. The tables of contents for the two texts are identical, but the presentation of instructional materials differs.

Questions for discussion, suggestions for writing, and other instructional apparatus for *75 Readings* are presented in a manual from which teachers may copy materials for students as needed. In *75 Readings Plus*, on the other hand, instructional materials appear in the text. Accompanying each selection are an author biography, a set of discussion questions on content and strategy, and three suggestions for sustained writing. In addition, to help instructors exploit the connection between reading, writing, and critical thinking, *75 Readings Plus* again offers a set of prompts for short writing that are inspired by each essay selection and that appear in a subsection entitled Engaging the Text. These prompts can be used as journal assignments or as warm-up exercises for projects such as those described in Suggestions for Sustained Writing. In some cases, they can even be expanded into assignments for complete essays.

The table of contents of the sixth edition of *75 Readings Plus* contains sixteen new essays. E.B. White's "Once More to the Lake," Joan Didion's "Marrying Absurd," Nancy Mairs's "On Being a Cripple," William Lutz's "Doublespeak," Donna Woolfolk Cross's "Politics: The Art of Bamboozling," Scott Russell Sanders's "The Men We Carry in Our Minds," Barbara Huttman's "Crime of Compassion," Brent Staples's "Black Men and Public Space," Horace Miner's "Body Ritual among the Nacirema," Joseph Pace's "Let's go Veggie!" (with a response by Alan Herscovici: "Where's the Beef?"), Camille Paglia's "Rape and Modern Sex War," Susan Jacoby's "Common Decency," Judy Brady's "Why I Want a Wife," Amy Tan's "Mother Tongue," Jamaica Kincaid's "On Seeing England for the First Time," and Lars Eighner's "On Dumpster Diving."

Chapter 10 is again divided between argument and persuasion, with the argumentative essays listed in pairs under the social and political issues to which they relate. New in this chapter are the essays by Paglia, Jacoby, and Brady.

A feature new to the sixth edition is that selections especially effective in teaching mixed rhetorical strategies are found in a chapter of their own: Chapter 11. Some of these appeared in other chapters in earlier editions, but Chapter 11 also contains three essays that are new to the text: Tan's "Mother Tongue," Kincaid's "On Seeing England for the First Time," and Eighner's "On Dumpster Diving." Another new feature in the sixth edition is that the table of contents indicates related readings to make it easier for teachers and students to identify thematic and rhetorical connections between essays that might otherwise have seemed unrelated.

Special thanks are due to the following colleagues who made suggestions for the sixth edition:

Marion Carroll, *John A. Logan College*

Lou Baltman, *Macomb Community College*

Tim Dillon, *Monroe County Community College*

Corin Kagan, *Normandale Community College*

William Digacomo, *Lehigh Carbon Community College*

Steve Katz, *State Technical Institute at Memphis*

Victor Uszerowicz, *Miami–Dade Community College*

Samuel Goldstein, *Daytona Beach Community College*

Leslie Shipp, *Community College of Southern Nevada*

Diana Zilberman, *Baltimore City Community College*

Deborah L. Kirkman, *University of Kentucky*

Marjorie Lynn, *University of Michigan-Dearborn*

Lisa Tatonetti, *Ohio State University*

Paul Heilker, *Virginia Tech*

Dorthea D. Burkhart, *Davidson County Community College*

Janice Trollinger, *Fort Valley State University*

Anneliese Homan, *State Fair Community College*

LaNelle Daniel, *Floyd College*

Janice Freeman, *University of Winnepeg*

Steve Hecox, *University of Nevada, Reno*

Daniel Lowe, *CCAC-Allegheny*

Stephanie Bertoni, *Butte College*

Mary Ann Peters, *University of Oregon*

Steve Levinson, *City College of San Francisco*

Peter Malik, *Alcorn State University*

Kate H. Parker, *Albuquerque Technical Vocational Institute*

David Blakesley, *Southern Illinois University*

Sandra Smith, *Penn State University*

Joyce Harlow, *Rogue Community College*

Charlotte Hoffman, *Nassau Community College*

Robert Fuhrel, *Community College of Southern Nevada*

Elizabeth Patterson, *Yakima Valley Community College*

We are grateful for the comments and suggestions of colleagues who have used *75 Readings* and *75 Readings Plus* over the last 14 years. We welcome ongoing contributions as we continue to improve these texts and make them even more responsive to the needs of students. We would also like to thank our friends at McGraw-Hill, who encouraged us and helped us continue these projects.

*Santi Buscemi*

*Charlotte Smith*

# Narration

One of the things that defines us as human is the universal desire and ability to create narrative. "Tell me a story," the child implores, and we willingly oblige by reciting an old favorite passed down through the generations or by making up one of our own.

We are naturally curious creatures, wanting to know what happened, when, and to whom—even if none of it is true. Perhaps that is why we feel compelled to create mythologies on the one hand and to report the news or write history on the other.

Some narratives contain long evocative descriptions of setting. Others present fascinating characters whose predicaments rivet our attention or whose lives mirror our own. Still others seem more like plays, heavy with dialogue by which writers allow their characters to reveal themselves. Whatever combination of techniques authors use, all stories—from the briefest anecdotes to the longest novels—have a plot. They recount events in a more or less chronological order. They reveal what happened and, in most cases, allow readers or listeners to draw their own conclusions about the significance of those events.

This is perhaps the chief difference between what you will read in Chapter One and the essays in other parts of this text. While some types of writing are aimed at explaining or persuading, narration dramatizes important human concerns by presenting events that, when taken together, create a world the author wants the reader to share.

Moving from beginning to end by order of time, narration generally relies on a more natural pattern of organization than do other types of writing, but it is no less sophisticated or powerful a tool for explaining complex ideas or for changing readers' opinions than, say, analogy, classification, or formal argument. All storytellers, no matter how entertaining their tales, have something to say about human beings and the world they inhabit. If you have already read selections from the chapters that follow, you know that writers often couple narration with other techniques to develop ideas and support opinions that otherwise might have remained abstract, unclear, or unconvincing. A good story may reveal more about a person or a place than physical description, and it sometimes can help readers understand an important problem or issue beyond our most valiant attempts to explain it "logically."

The point is that writers of narrative are not compelled to underscore the connection between the events in a story and the point it makes. Readers can find their own "theses."

Many of the essays you will read in this chapter are autobiographical: Maya Angelou, Langston Hughes, and James Weldon Johnson show how they confronted difficult situations and, in the process, gained significant insight into themselves, their families, and the human personality. Although very different in content and purpose, Naton Leslie's "Don't Get Comfortable" provides similar insight into the human character, not to mention into a few real characters! The writing of essays like theirs often results from a profound compulsion to find meaning in what once seemed devoid of it, a process that may define the act of narration itself.

The selections by George Orwell and Maxine Hong Kingston might be placed in another category. They point beyond themselves to social and political issues that are universal and perennial.

However the pieces in this chapter seem to be related—and you surely will find connections of your own to talk about—remember that each has been included because it has a poignant story to tell. Read each selection carefully and learn what you can about the techniques of narration. Here's hoping that at least a few will inspire you to narrate a personal vision of the world that will enrich both you and your readers.

# A Hanging

## George Orwell

*George Orwell is the pseudonym of Eric Blair (1903–1950). Born in India, where his father served in the British colonial government, Orwell was educated at Eton. As a young man, he served as a British policeman in Burma (now Myanmar), the setting for this selection. Later, he was wounded while fighting for the Loyalists in the Spanish Civil War, about which he wrote in* Homage to Catalonia. *Orwell despised the "Big Brother" mentalities of both the fascists and the communists, who backed opposing sides in that war. However, he also condemned the crass bureaucracy of the democratic governments of his time. In short, Orwell became an enemy of politics and politicians in general. He is remembered for* Animal Farm *(1946) and* 1984 *(1949), classics of political satire, and for his many essays.*

*First published in 1931, "A Hanging" explores the psychological effects of capital punishment on those who must carry it out. Orwell was against capital punishment, but in this essay he never states his opposition explicitly in an identifiable thesis. Instead, he allows the events of the narrative and well-chosen descriptive details to express his point of view. In the process, he also presents both a social and a political commentary that reflects his opposition to colonialism, particularly British colonialism, which he witnessed firsthand in Burma and India. As such, because this essay is clearly intended to persuade, it illustrates the notion that narration is an extremely versatile tool.*

It was in Burma, a sodden morning of the rains. A sickly light, like yellow ₁
tinfoil, was slanting over the high walls into the jail yard. We were waiting
outside the condemned cells, a row of sheds fronted with double bars, like
small animal cages. Each cell measured about ten feet by ten and was quite
bare within except for a plank bed and a pot of drinking water. In some of
them brown silent men were squatting at the inner bars, with their blan-
kets draped round them. These were the condemned men, due to be
hanged within the next week or two.

One prisoner had been brought out of his cell. He was a Hindu, a puny ₂
wisp of a man, with a shaven head and vague liquid eyes. He had a thick,
sprouting moustache, absurdly too big for his body, rather like the moustache of a comic man in the films. Six tall Indian warders were guarding
him and getting him ready for the gallows. Two of them stood by with rifles and fixed bayonets, while the others handcuffed him, passed a chain
through his handcuffs and fixed it to their belts, and lashed his arms tight
to his sides. They crowded very close about him, with their hands always
on him in a careful, caressing grip, as though all the while feeling him to
make sure he was there. It was like men handling a fish which is still alive
and may jump back into the water. But he stood quite unresisting, yielding his arms limply to the ropes, as though he hardly noticed what was
happening.

Eight o'clock struck and a bugle call, desolately thin in the wet air, ₃
floated from the distant barracks. The superintendent of the jail, who was
standing apart from the rest of us, moodily prodding the gravel with his
stick, raised his head at the sound. He was an army doctor, with a grey
toothbrush moustache and a gruff voice. "For God's sake hurry up, Francis," he said irritably. "The man ought to have been dead by this time.
Aren't you ready yet?"

Francis, the head jailer, a fat Dravidian in a white drill suit and gold ₄
spectacles, waved his black hand. "Yes sir, yes sir," he bubbled. "All iss sat-
isfactorily prepared. The hangman iss waiting. We shall proceed."

"Well, quick march, then. The prisoners can't get their breakfast till ₅
this job's over."

We set out for the gallows. Two warders marched on either side of the ₆
prisoner, with their rifles at the slope; two others marched close against
him, gripping him by arm and shoulder, as though at once pushing and
supporting him. The rest of us, magistrates and the like, followed behind.
Suddenly, when we had gone ten yards, the procession stopped short
without any order or warning. A dreadful thing had happened—a dog,
come goodness knows whence, had appeared in the yard. It came bound-
ing among us with a loud volley of barks, and leapt round us wagging its
whole body, wild with glee at finding so many human beings together. It
was a large woolly dog, half Airedale, half pariah. For a moment it pranced
round us, and then, before anyone could stop it, it had made a dash for the

prisoner, and jumping up tried to lick his face. Everyone stood aghast, too taken aback even to grab at the dog.

7      "Who let that bloody brute in here?" said the superintendent angrily. "Catch it, someone!"

8      A warder, detached from the escort, charged clumsily after the dog, but it danced and gambolled just out of his reach, taking everything as part of the game. A young Eurasian jailer picked up a handful of gravel and tried to stone the dog away, but it dodged the stones and came after us again. Its yaps echoed from the jail walls. The prisoner, in the grasp of the two warders, looked on incuriously, as though this was another formality of the hanging. It was several minutes before someone managed to catch the dog. Then we put my handkerchief through its collar and moved off once more, with the dog still straining and whimpering.

9      It was about forty yards to the gallows. I watched the bare brown back of the prisoner marching in front of me. He walked clumsily with his bound arms, but quite steadily, with that bobbing gait of the Indian who never straightens his knees. At each step his muscles slid neatly into place, the lock of hair on his scalp danced up and down, his feet printed themselves on the wet gravel. And once, in spite of the men who gripped him by each shoulder, he stepped slightly aside to avoid a puddle on the path.

10     It is curious, but till that moment I had never realised what it means to destroy a healthy, conscious man. When I saw the prisoner step aside to avoid the puddle, I saw the mystery, the unspeakable wrongness, of cutting a life short when it is in full tide. This man was not dying, he was alive just as we were alive. All the organs of his body were working—bowels digesting food, skin renewing itself, nails growing, tissues forming—all toiling away in solemn foolery. His nails would still be growing when he stood on the drop, when he was falling through the air with a tenth of a second to live. His eyes saw the yellow gravel and the grey walls, and his brain still remembered, foresaw, reasoned—reasoned even about puddles. He and we were a party of men walking together, seeing, hearing, feeling, understanding the same world; and in two minutes, with a sudden snap, one of us would be gone—one mind less, one world less.

11     The gallows stood in a small yard, separate from the main grounds of the prison, and overgrown with tall prickly weeds. It was a brick erection like three sides of a shed, with planking on top, and above that two beams and a crossbar with the rope dangling. The hangman, a grey-haired convict in the white uniform of the prison, was waiting beside his machine. He greeted us with a servile crouch as we entered. At a word from Francis the two warders, gripping the prisoner more closely than ever, half led, half pushed him to the gallows and helped him clumsily up the ladder. Then the hangman climbed up and fixed the rope round the prisoner's neck.

12     We stood waiting, five yards away. The warders had formed in a rough circle round the gallows. And then, when the noose was fixed, the prisoner

began crying out on his god. It was a high, reiterated cry of "Ram! Ram! Ram! Ram!", not urgent and fearful like a prayer or a cry for help, but steady, rhythmical, almost like the tolling of a bell. The dog answered the sound with a whine. The hangman, still standing on the gallows, produced a small cotton bag like a flour bag and drew it down over the prisoner's face. But the sound, muffled by the cloth, still persisted, over and over again: "Ram! Ram! Ram! Ram! Ram!"

The hangman climbed down and stood ready, holding the lever. Minutes seemed to pass. The steady, muffled crying from the prisoner went on and on, "Ram! Ram! Ram!" never faltering for an instant. The superintendent, his head on his chest, was slowly poking the ground with his stick; perhaps he was counting the cries, allowing the prisoner a fixed number— fifty, perhaps, or a hundred. Everyone had changed colour. The Indians had gone grey like bad coffee, and one or two of the bayonets were wavering. We looked at the lashed, hooded man on the drop, and listened to his cries—each cry another second of life; the same thought was in all our minds: oh, kill him quickly, get it over, stop that abominable noise! 13

Suddenly the superintendent made up his mind. Throwing up his head he made a swift motion with his stick. "Chalo!" he shouted almost fiercely. 14

There was a clanking noise, and then dead silence. The prisoner had vanished, and the rope was twisting on itself. I let go of the dog, and it galloped immediately to the back of the gallows; but when it got there it stopped short, barked, and then retreated into a corner of the yard, where it stood among the weeds, looking timorously out at us. We went round the gallows to inspect the prisoner's body. He was dangling with his toes pointed straight downwards, very slowly revolving, as dead as a stone. 15

The superintendent reached out with his stick and poked the bare body; it oscillated slightly. "*He's* all right," said the superintendent. He backed out from under the gallows, and blew out a deep breath. The moody look had gone out of his face quite suddenly. He glanced at his wrist-watch. "Eight minutes past eight. Well, that's all for this morning, thank God." 16

The warders unfixed bayonets and marched away. The dog, sobered and conscious of having misbehaved itself, slipped after them. We walked out of the gallows yard, past the condemned cells with their waiting prisoners, into the big central yard of the prison. The convicts, under the command of warders armed with lathis, were already receiving their breakfast. They squatted in long rows, each man holding a tin pannikin, while two warders with buckets marched round ladling out rice; it seemed quite a homely, jolly scene, after the hanging. An enormous relief had come upon us now that the job was done. One felt an impulse to sing, to break into a run, to snigger. All at once everyone began chattering gaily. 17

18     The Eurasian boy walking beside me nodded towards the way we had come, with a knowing smile: "Do you know, sir, our friend (he meant the dead man), when he heard his appeal had been dismissed, he pissed on the floor of his cell. From fright. Kindly take one of my cigarettes, sir. Do you not admire my new silver case, sir? From the boxwallah, two rupees eight annas. Classy European style."

19     Several people laughed—at what, nobody seemed certain.

20     Francis was walking by the superintendent, talking garrulously: "Well, sir, all has passed off with the utmost satisfactoriness. It wass all finished—flick! like that. It iss not always so—oah, no! I have known cases where the doctor wass obliged to go beneath the gallows and pull the prisoner's legs to ensure decease. Most disagreeable!"

21     "Wriggling about, eh? That's bad," said the superintendent.

22     "Ach, sir, it iss worse when they become refractory! One man, I recall, clung to the bars of hiss cage when we went to take him out. You will scarcely credit, sir, that it took six warders to dislodge him, three pulling at each leg. We reasoned with him. 'My dear fellow,' we said, 'think of all the pain and trouble you are causing to us!' But no, he would not listen! Ach, he wass very troublesome!"

23     I found that I was laughing quite loudly. Everyone was laughing. Even the superintendent grinned in a tolerant way. "You'd better all come out and have a drink," he said quite genially. "I've got a bottle of whisky in the car. We could do with it."

24     We went through the big double gates of the prison, into the road. "Pulling at his legs!" exclaimed a Burmese magistrate suddenly, and burst into a loud chuckling. We all began laughing again. At that moment Francis's anecdote seemed extraordinarily funny. We all had a drink together, native and European alike, quite amicably. The dead man was a hundred yards away.

*1931*

## QUESTIONS FOR DISCUSSION

### Content

a. Does this narrative essay have a "message," or do you think Orwell deliberately avoided one?

b. Orwell avoids saying anything directly about the English presence in Burma—he neither explains that presence nor states his opinion explicitly. Nevertheless, his opinion is voiced. What is his attitude toward his country's presence in Burma?

c. How would you characterize Orwell's description of the Burmese in this piece? Of the Hindu prisoners? How do these descriptions relate to his attitude toward the British?

d. What details of the hanging does Orwell treat as significant? What are his reasons for including these details? What effect do they have on you?

## Strategy and Style

e. In which paragraphs does Orwell use descriptive details most effectively? What other paragraphs do you find effective? Why?

f. Orwell is careful to tell us the dimensions of the prisoners' cells, the time, the number of people, the distance to the gallows, the distance between the officials and the prisoner, etc. Why are these numerical references important?

g. "A Hanging" is a mature writer's recollection of an earlier time in his life. Does Orwell present himself sympathetically, or does he describe himself with a satiric edge? Point to details that support your answer.

h. How does the use of dialogue affect the tone of the essay? In what way would your reaction have been different if Orwell had not used dialogue?

## Engaging the Text

a. Write a letter to Orwell, telling him what you do not understand about his essay. As best you can, tell him why you do not understand it. Include specific references to the essay.

b. Ask a question (or questions) about this essay, and then try to answer the question(s) by piecing together phrases drawn from the essay itself. Then write your own answer or write a response to Orwell's "answer."

## SUGGESTIONS FOR SUSTAINED WRITING

a. Orwell communicates his feelings about capital punishment and other issues in this essay. Use narration to present an issue about which you feel strongly. Present your opinion(s) implicitly by drawing on Orwell's narrative techniques: the use of dialogue, the detailed descriptions of characters, the chronological sequence of events, and the inclusion of humor, to name a few. In short, imbed your opinion within the framework of a story.

b. In paragraph 10, Orwell writes of an epiphany of sorts: "It is curious, but till that moment I had never realized what it means to destroy a healthy, conscious man. When I saw the prisoner step aside to avoid the puddle, I saw the mystery, the unspeakable wrongness, of cutting a life short. . . ." Something similar happens in "Salvation," an essay by Langston Hughes in this chapter. Write an essay in which you explain how what happens to the narrator of "A Hanging" is similar to what happens to the narrator of "Salvation." In addition, compare and contrast (point out similarities and differences in) the ways these authors approach their subjects. For example, you might focus on stylistic elements such as the use of dialogue and the inclusion of detail to describe setting and character. You also might discuss how each author arrives at his "epiphany" and explain what it says about him.

c. Find out more about the British presence in Burma (now Myanmar) or India by researching at least four academic secondary sources found in your college library or on the Internet. Then write an essay in which you explain the historical background that might support Orwell's opposition to British colonial rule in either of those countries. Make sure to cite information taken from these sources—whether quoted directly, paraphrased, or summarized—in the text of your paper and in an appropriate listing of sources. Ask your instructor about the documentation format he or she wishes you to use.

# Salvation

### Langston Hughes

*Among the chief figures of the Harlem Renaissance in the 1920s, Langston Hughes (1902–1967) is one of the best-known poets and playwrights in America. Born in Joplin, Missouri, he also wrote numerous essays that detail life in the South during the early part of the twentieth century. His novels and his autobiography,* I Wonder as I Wander, *are still read widely. Hughes's poetry was so successful that by the time he reached his thirties, he became known as the "Bard of Harlem." "Salvation" was first published in* The Big Sea, *another autobiographical work, in 1940. Because his parents had separated early in his life, Hughes was raised primarily by his grandparents and by other relatives. "Salvation" captures the trauma and disillusionment he experienced during a childhood incident that occurred while he was living with an aunt.*

1   I was saved from sin when I was going on thirteen. But not really saved. It happened like this. There was a big revival at my Auntie Reed's church. Every night for weeks there had been much preaching, singing, praying, and shouting, and some very hardened sinners had been brought to Christ, and the membership of the church had grown by leaps and bounds. Then just before the revival ended, they held a special meeting for children, "to bring the young lambs to the fold." My aunt spoke of it for days ahead. That night I was escorted to the front row and placed on the mourners' bench with all the other young sinners, who had not yet been brought to Jesus.

My aunt told me that when you were saved you saw a light, and some- 2
thing happened to you inside! And Jesus came into your life! And God was
with you from then on! She said you could see and hear and feel Jesus in
your soul. I believed her. I had heard a great many old people say the same
thing and it seemed to me they ought to know. So I sat there calmly in the
hot, crowded church, waiting for Jesus to come to me.

The preacher preached a wonderful rhythmical sermon, all moans and 3
shouts and lonely cries and dire pictures of hell, and then he sang a song
about the ninety and nine safe in the fold, but one little lamb was left out in
the cold. Then he said: "Won't you come? Won't you come to Jesus? Young
lambs, won't you come?" And he held out his arms to all us young sinners
there on the mourners' bench. And the little girls cried. And some of them
jumped up and went to Jesus right away. But most of us just sat there.

A great many old people came and knelt around us and prayed, old 4
women with jet-black faces and braided hair, old men with work-gnarled
hands. And the church sang a song about the lower lights are burning,
some poor sinners to be saved. And the whole building rocked with prayer
and song.

Still I kept waiting to *see* Jesus.                                      5

Finally all the young people had gone to the altar and were saved, but 6
one boy and me. He was a rounder's son named Westley. Westley and I
were surrounded by sisters and deacons praying. It was very hot in the
church, and getting late now. Finally Westley said to me in a whisper:
"God damn! I'm tired o' sitting here. Let's get up and be saved." So he got
up and was saved.

Then I was left all alone on the mourners' bench. My aunt came and 7
knelt at my knees and cried, while prayers and songs swirled all around
me in the little church. The whole congregation prayed for me alone, in a
mighty wail of moans and voices. And I kept waiting serenely for Jesus,
waiting, waiting—but he didn't come. I wanted to see him, but nothing
happened to me. Nothing! I wanted something to happen to me, but nothing happened.

I heard the songs and the minister saying: "Why don't you come? My 8
dear child, why don't you come to Jesus? Jesus is waiting for you. He
wants you. Why don't you come? Sister Reed, what is this child's name?"

"Langston," my aunt sobbed.                                              9

"Langston, why don't you come? Why don't you come and be saved? 10
Oh, Lamb of God! Why don't you come?"

Now it was really getting late. I began to be ashamed of myself, hold- 11
ing everything up so long. I began to wonder what God thought about
Westley, who certainly hadn't seen Jesus either, but who was now sitting
proudly on the platform, swinging his knickerbockered legs and grinning
down at me, surrounded by deacons and old women on their knees praying. God had not struck Westley dead for taking his name in vain or for

lying in the temple. So I decided that maybe to save further trouble, I'd better lie, too, and say that Jesus had come, and get up and be saved.

12      So I got up.

13      Suddenly the whole room broke into a sea of shouting, as they saw me rise. Waves of rejoicing swept the place. Women leaped in the air. My aunt threw her arms around me. The minister took me by the hand and led me to the platform.

14      When things quieted down, in a hushed silence, punctuated by a few ecstatic "Amens," all the new young lambs were blessed in the name of God. Then joyous singing filled the room.

15      That night, for the last time in my life but one—for I was a big boy twelve years old—I cried. I cried, in bed alone, and couldn't stop. I buried my head under the quilts, but my aunt heard me. She woke up and told my uncle I was crying because the Holy Ghost had come into my life, and because I had seen Jesus. But I was really crying because I couldn't bear to tell her that I had lied, that I had deceived everybody in the church, that I hadn't seen Jesus, and that now I didn't believe there was a Jesus any more, since he didn't come to help me.

*1940*

## QUESTIONS FOR DISCUSSION

### Content

a. What is Hughes's purpose in recalling this event?
b. The author's portrayal of the revival meeting is extremely realistic. What rhetorical techniques make it so?
c. What exactly is a religious revival?
d. What biblical metaphor is Hughes alluding to when he tells the reader that this was to be a special meeting "to bring the young lambs to the fold"?
e. Why does Hughes spend time talking about Westley? How is young Langston different from this boy?
f. What does the author's waiting so long before going up to be "saved" tell you about him?
g. Explain why Langston cries so much after coming home. Is there only one reason behind his tears? What does the last paragraph tell you about the young Langston?

## Strategy and Style

h. The telling of this story is enhanced by the author's description of the church and the members of the congregation. In which paragraphs is Hughes's facility with description most evident?
i. What examples of metaphoric language do you find in this essay? How do such figures of speech help Hughes accomplish his purpose?
j. Hughes often makes use of a childlike perspective to relate the incident at his aunt's church. What details help him create that perspective? Does he use words like those a child might use?
k. What is Hughes's attitude or tone in recalling this incident?

## ENGAGING THE TEXT

a. Write about one of your religious experiences, comparing or contrasting it to that of Hughes. Include specific references to his essay.
b. Write an imaginary interview (both your questions and his answers) with Hughes, asking him about his experiences at the revival meeting. Hughes's answers should be consistent with what he writes in the essay.

## SUGGESTIONS FOR SUSTAINED WRITING

a. At one time or another, we all have been pressured into doing things we did not want to do. Recount such an incident from your experience; make sure to describe your feelings both during that experience and after it occurred. If appropriate, narrate the incident in a letter addressed to the individual or individuals who did the pressuring. In the process, however, make reference to Hughes's experience in "Salvation" and compare or contrast it to your own.
b. Read Sam Pickering's "Faith of the Father" in Chapter 4. Then write an essay in which you compare and/or contrast the views of faith and religion presented in Hughes's and Pickering's essays.
c. Describe a religious ceremony that has or used to have significance for you. As clearly and convincingly as you can, describe the emotional or spiritual benefits you derive or derived from that ceremony. Address your essay to someone who you know is skeptical about the value of religious or social ceremonies and observances. Support your position by including facts, ideas, and opinions about this ceremony or about religious or social ceremonies in general, which you research in at least three secondary sources found in your college library or on the Internet. Make sure to include and cite your research, using a format or style approved by your instructor.

# Grandmother's Victory

Maya Angelou

*Born Marguerita Johnson in 1928, Maya Angelou spent most of her childhood in Stamps, Arkansas, where her family owned the general store that is the setting for this selection. After a difficult youth, Angelou became a dancer, actress, and writer. She has performed all over the world, most notably in the U.S. State Department–sponsored production of* Porgy and Bess, *in the television miniseries "Roots," and in a production of Jean Genet's* The Blacks. *She also has taught dance in Rome and Tel Aviv. Active in the civil rights movement, Angelou was appointed northern director for the Southern Christian Leadership Conference by Martin Luther King, Jr., in the 1960s. In 1970, she published the first volume of her autobiography,* I Know Why the Caged Bird Sings, *of which this selection is the fifth chapter. Three other volumes followed. Angelou has also written several books of poetry, including* And Still I Rise *(1978) and* I Shall Not Be Moved *(1990). Recent works include three autobiographies:* The Heart of a Woman *(1981),* Shaker, Why Don't You Sing? *(1983), and* All God's Children Need Traveling Shoes *(1986). In 1993, Angelou read an original composition at the presidential inauguration.*

*"Grandmother's Victory" is a moving account of a young woman's coming face to face with an especially blatant and demeaning form of racism, which causes her extreme emotional pain. At the same time, she comes to realize that the integrity and spiritual strength displayed by her grandmother during this incident are what is needed to overcome such evil.*

1    "Thou shall not be dirty" and "Thou shall not be impudent" were the two commandments of Grandmother Henderson upon which hung our total salvation.

2    Each night in the bitterest winter we were forced to wash faces, arms, necks, legs, and feet before going to bed. She used to add, with a smirk that unprofane people can't control when venturing into profanity, "and wash as far as possible, then wash possible."

3    We would go to the well and wash in the ice-cold, clear water, grease our legs with the equally cold stiff Vaseline, then tiptoe into the house. We wiped the dust from our toes and settled down for schoolwork, cornbread, clabbered milk, prayers, and bed, always in that order. Momma was famous for pulling the quilts off after we had fallen asleep to examine our feet. If they weren't clean enough for her, she took the switch (she kept one behind the bedroom door for emergencies) and woke up the offender with a few aptly placed burning reminders.

4    The area around the well at night was dark and slick, and boys told about how snakes love water, so that anyone who had to draw water at night and then stand there alone and wash knew that moccasins and rattlers, puff adders, and boa constrictors were winding their way to the well and would arrive just as the person washing got soap in her eyes. But Momma convinced us that not only was cleanliness next to Godliness, dirtiness was the inventor of misery.

**12**

The impudent child was detested by God and a shame to its parents 5 and could bring destruction to its house and line. All adults had to be addressed as Mister, Missus, Miss, Auntie, Cousin, Unk, Uncle, Buhbah, Sister, Brother, and a thousand other appellations indicating familial relationship and the lowliness of the addresser.

Everyone I knew respected these customary laws, except for the 6 powhitetrash children.

Some families of powhitetrash lived on Momma's farm land behind 7 the school. Sometimes a gaggle of them came to the Store, filling the whole room, chasing out the air, and even changing the well-known scents. The children crawled over the shelves and into the potato and onion bins, twanging all the time in their sharp voices like cigar-box guitars. They took liberties in my Store that I would never dare. Since Momma told us that the less you say to whitefolks (or even powhitetrash) the better, Bailey and I would stand, solemn, quiet, in the displaced air. But if one of the playful apparitions got close to us, I pinched it. Partly out of angry frustration and partly because I didn't believe in its flesh reality.

They called my uncle by his first name and ordered him around the 8 Store. He, to my crying shame, obeyed them in his limping dip-straight-dip fashion.

My grandmother, too, followed their orders, except that she didn't 9 seem to be servile because she anticipated their needs.

"Here's sugar, Miz Potter, and here's baking powder. You didn't buy 10 soda last month, you'll probably be needing some."

Momma always directed her statements to the adults, but sometimes, 11 Oh painful sometimes, the grimy, snotty-nosed girls would answer her.

"Naw, Annie . . ."—to Momma? Who owned the land they lived on? 12 Who forgot more than they would ever learn? If there was any justice in the world, God should strike them dumb at once!—"Just give us some extra sody crackers, and some more mackerel."

At least they never looked in her face, or I never caught them doing so. 13 Nobody with a smidgen of training, not even the worst roustabout, would look right in a grown person's face. It meant the person was trying to take the words out before they were formed. The dirty little children didn't do that, but they threw their orders around the Store like lashes from a cat-o'-nine-tails.

When I was around ten years old, those scruffy children caused me the 14 most painful and confusing experience I had ever had with my grandmother.

One summer morning, after I had swept the dirt yard of leaves, 15 spearmint-gum wrappers and Vienna-sausage labels, I raked the yellow-red dirt, and made half-moons carefully, so that the design stood out clearly and mask-like. I put the rake behind the Store and came through the back of the house to find Grandmother on the front porch in her big, wide white apron. The apron was so stiff by virtue of the starch that it could have stood alone. Momma was admiring the yard, so I joined her. It truly looked like a flat redhead that had been raked with a big-toothed comb. Momma didn't say anything but I knew she liked it. She looked over toward the school principal's house and to the right at Mr. McElroy's. She was hoping one of those community pillars would see the design before the day's business wiped it out. Then she looked upward to the school. My head had swung with hers, so at just about the same time we saw a troop of powhitetrash kids marching over the hill and down by the side of the school.

16      I looked to Momma for direction. She did an excellent job of sagging from her waist down, but from the waist up she seemed to be pulling for the top of the oak tree across the road. Then she began to moan a hymn. Maybe not to moan, but the tune was so slow and the meter so strange that she could have been moaning. She didn't look at me again. When the children reached halfway down the hill, halfway to the Store, she said without turning, "Sister, go on inside."

17      I wanted to beg her, "Momma, don't wait for them. Come on inside with me. If they come in the Store, you go to the bedroom and let me wait on them. They only frighten me if you're around. Alone I know how to handle them." But of course I couldn't say anything, so I went in and stood behind the screen door.

18      Before the girls got to the porch I heard their laughter crackling and popping like pine logs in a cooking stove. I suppose my lifelong paranoia was born in those cold, molasses-slow minutes. They came finally to stand on the ground in front of Momma. At first they pretended seriousness. Then one of them wrapped her right arm in the crook of her left, pushed out her mouth and started to hum. I realized that she was aping my grandmother. Another said, "Naw, Helen, you ain't standing like her. This here's it." Then she lifted her chest, folded her arms and mocked that strange carriage that was Annie Henderson. Another laughed, "Naw, you can't do it. Your mouth ain't pooched out enough. It's like this."

19      I thought about the rifle behind the door, but I knew I'd never be able to hold it straight, and the .410, our sawed-off shotgun, which stayed loaded and was fired every New Year's night, was locked in the trunk and Uncle Willie had the key on his chain. Through the fly-specked screen door, I could see that the arms of Momma's apron jiggled from the vibrations of her humming. But her knees seemed to have locked as if they would never bend again.

20      She sang on. No louder than before, but no softer either. No slower or faster.

21      The dirt of the girls' cotton dresses continued on their legs, feet, arms, and faces to make them all of a piece. Their greasy uncolored hair hung down, uncombed, with a grim finality. I knelt to see them better, to re-

member them for all time. The tears that had slipped down my dress left unsurprising dark spots, and made the front yard blurry and even more unreal. The world had taken a deep breath and was having doubts about continuing to revolve.

The girls had tired of mocking Momma and turned to other means of  22 agitation. One crossed her eyes, stuck her thumbs in both sides of her mouth and said, "Look here, Annie." Grandmother hummed on and the apron strings trembled. I wanted to throw a handful of black pepper in their faces, to throw lye on them, to scream that they were dirty, scummy peckerwoods, but I knew I was as clearly imprisoned behind the scene as the actors outside were confined to their roles.

One of the smaller girls did a kind of puppet dance while her fellow  23 clowns laughed at her. But the tall one, who was almost a woman, said something very quietly, which I couldn't hear. They all moved backward from the porch, still watching Momma. For an awful second I thought they were going to throw a rock at Momma, who seemed (except for the apron strings) to have turned into stone herself. But the big girl turned her back, bent down and put her hands flat on the ground—she didn't pick up anything. She simply shifted her weight and did a hand stand.

Her dirty bare feet and long legs went straight for the sky. Her dress fell  24 down around her shoulders, and she had on no drawers. The slick pubic hair made a brown triangle where her legs came together. She hung in the vacuum of that lifeless morning for only a few seconds, then wavered and tumbled. The other girls clapped her on the back and slapped their hands.

Momma changed her song to "Bread of Heaven, Bread of Heaven,  25 feed me till I want no more."

I found that I was praying too. How long could Momma hold out?  26 What new indignity would they think of to subject her to? Would I be able to stay out of it? What would Momma really like me to do?

Then they were moving out of the yard, on their way to town. They  27 bobbed their heads and shook their slack behinds and turned, one at a time:

"'Bye, Annie."                                                                                    28
"'Bye, Annie."                                                                                    29
"'Bye, Annie."                                                                                    30

Momma never turned her head or unfolded her arms, but she stopped  31 singing and said, "'Bye, Miz Helen, 'bye, Miz Ruth, 'bye, Miz Eloise."

I burst. A firecracker July-the-Fourth burst. How could Momma call  32 them Miz? The mean nasty things. Why couldn't she have come inside the sweet, cool store when we saw them breasting the hill? What did she prove? And then if they were dirty, mean, and impudent, why did Momma have to call them Miz?

She stood another whole song through and then opened the screen  33 door to look down on me crying in rage. She looked until I looked up.

Her face was a brown moon that shone on me. She was beautiful. Something had happened out there, which I couldn't completely understand, but I could see that she was happy. Then she bent down and touched me as mothers of the church "lay hands on the sick and afflicted" and I quieted.

34     "Go wash your face, Sister." And she went behind the candy counter and hummed, "Glory, glory, hallelujah, when I lay my burden down."

35     I threw the well water on my face and used the weekday handkerchief to blow my nose. Whatever the contest had been out front, I knew Momma had won.

36     I took the rake back to the front yard. The smudged footprints were easy to erase. I worked for a long time on my new design and laid the rake behind the wash pot. When I came back in the Store, I took Momma's hand and we both walked outside to look at the pattern.

37     It was a large heart with lots of hearts growing smaller inside, and piercing from the outside rim to the smallest heart was an arrow. Momma said, "Sister, that's right pretty." Then she turned back to the Store and resumed, "Glory, glory, hallelujah, when I lay my burden down."

*1970*

## QUESTIONS FOR DISCUSSION

### Content

a. Is this simply a story about bad-mannered children and racism? Or is Angelou's intent more complex?

b. Why does the speaker bother to tell us that she made careful patterns when she raked the yard? Why did Momma admire those designs?

c. Angelou describes a number of outdated social observances such as never looking "right in a grown person's face." What other examples can you find in this selection? Why does she make it a point to include them in this recollection of her childhood?

d. Grandmother Henderson addresses each of the white girls as "Miz." Does her doing so have anything to do with her strange victory over these brats?

e. What details does Angelou use to create this obviously unflattering picture of "powhitetrash children"?

f. What does Angelou mean when she describes her uncle's limping in "dip-straight-dip fashion"?

## Strategy and Style

g. In light of what she says early in the narrative, is it important for her to quote all three of the girls as they leave the store (paragraphs 28 through 30)? In general, what effect does Angelou's extensive use of dialogue create?

h. This selection begins with two rather odd commandments, which both startle and amuse the reader. Why are they important to the rest of the essay?

i. Angelou's use of metaphor is brilliant. In paragraph 18, she tells us that her "paranoia was born in those cold, molasses-slow minutes." What other examples of figurative language can you find?

j. How would you describe the speaker's tone at the beginning of this essay? When, exactly, does this tone change?

## ENGAGING THE TEXT

a. What does victory mean to Angelou's grandmother? Write a definition of *victory* as Angelou's grandmother would define it.

b. Write your own definition of *victory*. In other words, what does this concept mean to you personally? Compare your definition with that of Angelou's grandmother.

## SUGGESTIONS FOR SUSTAINED WRITING

a. Relying on your own experiences, narrate an incident from the life of a relative, friend, or neighbor that illustrates the nobility of his or her character, much in the same way that Angelou illustrates the nobility of her grandmother's character. Through description, dialogue, and action, include details that provide the reader with a vivid picture of the person you are discussing. Address your essay to someone who has never met your subject and/or knows little about him or her.

b. Grandmother Henderson's triumph may well have resided in the fact that she had done a far better job of raising children than had many of her "powhitetrash" neighbors. Analyze Angelou's essay in order to explain this and other sources of Momma's victory. In short, discuss aspects of Momma's character that prompted Angelou to make her the centerpiece of this narrative. Make sure to make direct reference to the essay by quoting, paraphrasing, or summarizing from it.

c. Both Angelou's "Grandmother's Victory" and Kingston's "No Name Woman" address issues having to do with families and their place in a particular community. How do the two communities in these essays differ? How are they alike? How do the two families in these essays differ? How are they alike?

# No Name Woman

Maxine Hong Kingston

*Born in 1940 to recently arrived immigrants from China, Maxine Hong Kingston grew up having to negotiate between two very different cultures. Her gender in a culture that valued males over females created further difficulties. These two issues are the main themes that inform much of Kingston's work, most notably* The Woman Warrior: Memoirs of a Girlhood among Ghosts *(1975), a collection of autobiographical narrative essays through which she seeks to understand her female ancestors and the ways they helped form her own identity. "No Name Woman" is from that collection. The most well known of her other books are* China Men *(1980), a collection of character sketches from real and legendary sources; and* Tripmaster Monkey: His Fake Book *(1989), a novel. She has received over 20 awards, fellowships, and honorary degrees, including a National Book Critics Circle Award for* The Woman Warrior, *an American Book Award for* China Men, *and a PEN West Award in Fiction for* Tripmaster Monkey.*

*Through narration, "No Name Woman" explores a number of differences between two cultures. More important, it touches on profound questions of gender, community, individual responsibility, and family loyalty. In the process, it presents a moving, even wrenching account of the life and death of a woman whose name, Kingston was told, must never be mentioned.*

1   "You must not tell anyone," my mother said, "what I am about to tell you. In China your father had a sister who killed herself. She jumped into the family well. We say that your father has all brothers because it is as if she had never been born.

2   "In 1924 just a few days after our village celebrated seventeen hurry-up weddings—to make sure that every young man who went 'out on the road' would responsibly come home—your father and his brothers and your grandfather and his brothers and your aunt's new husband sailed for America, the Gold Mountain. It was your grandfather's last trip. Those lucky enough to get contracts waved goodbye from the decks. They fed and guarded the stowaways and helped them off in Cuba, New York, Bali, Hawaii. 'We'll meet in California next year,' they said. All of them sent money home.

3   "I remember looking at your aunt one day when she and I were dressing; I had not noticed before that she had such a protruding melon of a stomach. But I did not think, 'She's pregnant,' until she began to look like other pregnant women, her shirt pulling and the white tops of her black pants showing. She could not have been pregnant, you see, because her husband had been gone for years. No one said anything. We did not discuss it. In early summer she was ready to have the child, long after the time when it could have been possible.

4   "The village had also been counting. On the night the baby was to be born the villagers raided our house. Some were crying. Like a great saw,

teeth strung with lights, files of people walked zigzag across our land, tear-ing the rice. Their lanterns doubled in the disturbed black water, which drained away through the broken bunds. As the villagers closed in, we could see that some of them, probably men and women we knew well, wore white masks. The people with long hair hung it over their faces. Women with short hair made it stand up on end. Some had tied white bands around their foreheads, arms, and legs.

"At first they threw mud and rocks at the house. Then they threw eggs 5 and began slaughtering our stock. We could hear the animals scream their deaths—the roosters, the pigs, a last great roar from the ox. Familiar wild heads flared in our night windows; the villagers encircled us. Some of the faces stopped to peer at us, their eyes rushing like searchlights. The hands flattened against the panes, framed heads, and left red prints.

"The villagers broke in the front and the back doors at the same time, 6 even though we had not locked the doors against them. Their knives dripped with the blood of our animals. They smeared blood on the doors and walls. One woman swung a chicken, whose throat she had slit, splat-tering blood in red arcs about her. We stood together in the middle of our house, in the family hall with the pictures and tables of the ancestors around us, and looked straight ahead.

"At that time the house had only two wings. When the men came back, 7 we would build two more to enclose our courtyard and a third one to be-gin a second courtyard. The villagers pushed through both wings, even your grandparents' rooms, to find your aunt's, which was also mine until the men returned. From this room a new wing for one of the younger fam-ilies would grow. They ripped up her clothes and shoes and broke her combs, grinding them underfoot. They tore her work from the loom. They scattered the cooking fire and rolled the new weaving in it. We could hear them in the kitchen breaking our bowls and banging the pots. They over-turned the great waist-high earthenware jugs; duck eggs, pickled fruits, vegetables burst out and mixed in acrid torrents. The old woman from the next field swept a broom through the air and loosed the spirits-of-the-broom over our heads. 'Pig.' 'Ghost.' 'Pig,' they sobbed and scolded while they ruined our house.

"When they left, they took sugar and oranges to bless themselves. They 8 cut pieces from the dead animals. Some of them took bowls that were not broken and clothes that were not torn. Afterward we swept up the rice and sewed it back up into sacks. But the smells from the spilled preserves lasted. Your aunt gave birth in the pigsty that night. The next morning when I went for the water, I found her and the baby plugging up the family well.

"Don't let your father know that I told you. He denies her. Now that 9 you have started to menstruate, what happened to her could happen to you. Don't humiliate us. You wouldn't like to be forgotten as if you had never been born. The villagers are watchful."

10

Whenever she had to warn us about life, my mother told stories that ran like this one, a story to grow up on. She tested our strength to establish realities. Those in the emigrant generations who could not reassert brute survival died young and far from home. Those of us in the first American generations have had to figure out how the invisible world the emigrants built around our childhoods fits in solid America.

The emigrants confused the gods by diverting their curses, misleading them with crooked streets and false names. They must try to confuse their offspring as well, who, I suppose, threaten them in similar ways—always trying to get things straight, always trying to name the unspeakable. The Chinese I know hide their names; sojourners take new names when their lives change and guard their real names with silence.

Chinese-Americans, when you try to understand what things in you are Chinese, how do you separate what is peculiar to childhood, to poverty, insanities, one family, your mother who marked your growing with stories, from what is Chinese? What is Chinese tradition and what is the movies?

If I want to learn what clothes my aunt wore, whether flashy or ordinary, I would have to begin, "Remember Father's drowned-in-the-well sister?" I cannot ask that. My mother has told me once and for all the useful parts. She will add nothing unless powered by Necessity, a riverbank that guides her life. She plants vegetable gardens rather than lawns; she carries the odd-shaped tomatoes home from the fields and eats food left for the gods.

Whenever we did frivolous things, we used up energy; we flew high kites. We children came up off the ground over the melting cones our parents brought home from work and the American movie on New Year's Day—*Oh, You Beautiful Doll* with Betty Grable one year, and *She Wore a Yellow Ribbon* with John Wayne another year. After the one carnival ride each, we paid in guilt; our tired father counted his change on the dark walk home.

Adultery is extravagance. Could people who hatch their own chicks and eat the embryos and the heads for delicacies and boil the feet in vinegar for party food, leaving only the gravel, eating even the gizzard lining— could such people engender a prodigal aunt? To be a woman, to have a daughter in starvation time was a waste enough. My aunt could not have been the lone romantic who gave up everything for sex. Women in the old China did not choose. Some man had commanded her to lie with him and be his secret evil. I wonder whether he masked himself when he joined the raid on her family.

Perhaps she had encountered him in the fields or on the mountain where the daughters-in-law collected fuel. Or perhaps he first noticed her in the marketplace. He was not a stranger because the village housed no strangers. She had to have dealings with him other than sex. Perhaps he worked an adjoining field, or he sold her the cloth for the dress she sewed and wore. His demand must have surprised, then terrified her. She obeyed him; she always did as she was told.

When the family found a young man in the next village to be her hus-   17
band, she had stood tractably beside the best rooster, his proxy, and
promised before they met that she would be his forever. She was lucky that
he was her age and she would be the first wife, an advantage secure now.
The night she first saw him, he had sex with her. Then he left for America.
She had almost forgotten what he looked like. When she tried to envision
him, she only saw the black and white face in the group photograph the
men had had taken before leaving.

The other man was not, after all, much different from her husband.   18
They both gave orders: she followed. "If you tell your family, I'll beat you.
I'll kill you. Be here again next week." No one talked sex, ever. And she
might have separated the rapes from the rest of living if only she did not
have to buy her oil from him or gather wood in the same forest. I want her
fear to have lasted just as long as rape lasted so that the fear could have
been contained. No drawn-out fear. But women at sex hazarded birth and
hence lifetimes. The fear did not stop but permeated everywhere. She told
the man, "I think I'm pregnant." He organized the raid against her.

On nights when my mother and father talked about their life back   19
home, sometimes they mentioned an "outcast table" whose business they
still seemed to be settling, their voices tight. In a commensal tradition,
where food is precious, the powerful older people made wrongdoers eat
alone. Instead of letting them start separate new lives like the Japanese,
who could become samurais and geishas, the Chinese family, faces averted
but eyes glowering sideways, hung on to the offenders and fed them leftovers. My aunt must have lived in the same house as my parents and eaten
at an outcast table. My mother spoke about the raid as if she had seen it,
when she and my aunt, a daughter-in-law to a different household, should
not have been living together at all. Daughters-in-law lived with their husbands' parents, not their own; a synonym for marriage in Chinese is "taking a daughter-in-law." Her husband's parents could have sold her, mort-
gaged her, stoned her. But they had sent her back to her own mother and
father, a mysterious act hinting at disgraces not told me. Perhaps they had
thrown her out to deflect the avengers.

She was the only daughter; her four brothers went with her father,   20
husband, and uncles "out on the road" and for some years became Western men. When the goods were divided among the family, three of the
brothers took land, and the youngest, my father, chose an education. After
my grandparents gave their daughter away to her husband's family, they
had dispensed all the adventure and all the property. They expected her
alone to keep the traditional ways, which her brothers, now among the
barbarians, could fumble without detection. The heavy, deep-rooted
women were to maintain the past against the flood, safe for returning. But
the rare urge west had fixed upon our family, and so my aunt crossed
boundaries not delineated in space.

21      The work of preservation demands that the feelings playing about in one's guts not be turned into action. Just watch their passing like cherry blossoms. But perhaps my aunt, my forerunner, caught in a slow life, let dreams grow and fade and after some months or years went toward what persisted. Fear at the enormities of the forbidden kept her desires delicate, wire and bone. She looked at a man because she liked the way the hair was tucked behind his ears, or she liked the question-mark line of a long torso curving at the shoulder and straight at the hip. For warm eyes or a soft voice or a slow walk—that's all—a few hairs, a line, a brightness, a sound, a pace, she gave up family. She offered us up for a charm that vanished with tiredness, a pigtail that didn't toss when the wind died. Why, the wrong lighting could erase the dearest thing about him.

22      It could very well have been, however, that my aunt did not take subtle enjoyment of her friend, but, a wild woman, kept rollicking company. Imagining her free with sex doesn't fit, though. I don't know any women like that, or men either. Unless I see her life branching into mine, she gives me no ancestral help.

23      To sustain her being in love, she often worked at herself in the mirror, guessing at the colors and shapes that would interest him, changing them frequently in order to hit on the right combination. She wanted him to look back.

24      On a farm near the sea, a woman who tended her appearance reaped a reputation for eccentricity. All the married women blunt-cut their hair in flaps about their ears or pulled it back in tight buns. No nonsense. Neither style blew easily into heart-catching tangles. And at their weddings they displayed themselves in their long hair for the last time. "It brushed the backs of my knees," my mother tells me. "It was braided, and even so, it brushed the backs of my knees."

25      At the mirror my aunt combed individuality into her bob. A bun could have been contrived to escape into black streamers blowing in the wind or in quiet wisps about her face, but only the older women in our picture album wear buns. She brushed her hair back from her forehead, tucking the flaps behind her ears. She looped a piece of thread, knotted into a circle between her index fingers and thumbs, and ran the double strand across her forehead. When she closed her fingers as if she were making a pair of shadow geese bite, the string twisted together catching the little hairs. Then she pulled the thread away from her skin, ripping the hairs out neatly, her eyes watering from the needles of pain. Opening her fingers, she cleaned the thread, then rolled it along her hairline and the tops of her eyebrows. My mother did the same to me and my sisters and herself. I used to believe that the expression "caught by the short hairs" meant a captive held with a depilatory string. It especially hurt at the temples, but my mother said we were lucky we didn't have to have our feet bound when we were seven. Sisters used to sit on their beds and cry together, she said, as their mothers or their slaves removed the bandages for a few min-

utes each night and let the blood gush back into their veins. I hope that the man my aunt loved appreciated a smooth brow, that he wasn't just a tits-and-ass man.

Once my aunt found a freckle on her chin, at a spot that the almanac 26 said predestined her for unhappiness. She dug it out with a hot needle and washed the wound with peroxide.

More attention to her looks than these pullings of hairs and pickings at 27 spots would have caused gossip among the villagers. They owned work clothes and good clothes, and they wore good clothes for feasting the new seasons. But since a woman combing her hair hexes beginnings, my aunt rarely found an occasion to look her best. Women looked like great sea snails—the corded wood, babies, and laundry they carried were the whorls on their backs. The Chinese did not admire a bent back; goddesses and warriors stood straight. Still there must have been a marvelous freeing of beauty when a worker laid down her burden and stretched and arched.

Such commonplace loveliness, however, was not enough for my aunt. 28 She dreamed of a lover for the fifteen days of New Year's, the time for families to exchange visits, money, and food. She plied her secret comb. And sure enough she cursed the year, the family, the village, and herself.

Even as her hair lured her imminent lover, many other men looked at 29 her. Uncles, cousins, nephews, brothers would have looked, too, had they been home between journeys. Perhaps they had already been restraining their curiosity, and they left, fearful that their glances, like a field of nesting birds, might be startled and caught. Poverty hurt, and that was their first reason for leaving. But another, final reason for leaving the crowded house was the never-said.

She may have been unusually beloved, the precious only daughter, 30 spoiled and mirror gazing because of the affection the family lavished on her. When her husband left, they welcomed the chance to take her back from the in-laws; she could live like the little daughter for just a while longer. There are stories that my grandfather was different from other people, "crazy ever since the little Jap bayoneted him in the head." He used to put his naked penis on the dinner table, laughing. And one day he brought home a baby girl, wrapped up inside his brown Western-style greatcoat. He had traded one of his sons, probably my father, the youngest, for her. My grandmother made him trade back. When he finally got a daughter of his own, he doted on her. They must have all loved her, except perhaps my father, the only brother who never went back to China, having once been traded for a girl.

Brothers and sisters, newly men and women, had to efface their sex- 31 ual color and present plain miens. Disturbing hair and eyes, a smile like no other, threatened the ideal of five generations living under one roof. To focus blurs, people shouted face to face and yelled from room to room. The immigrants I know have loud voices, unmodulated to American tones even after years away from the village where they called their friendships out across the fields. I have not been able to stop my mother's screams in public libraries or over telephones. Walking erect (knees straight, toes pointed forward, not pigeon-toed, which is Chinese-feminine) and speaking in an inaudible voice, I have tried to turn myself American-feminine. Chinese communication was loud, public. Only sick people had to whisper. But at the dinner table, where the family members came nearest one another, no one could talk, not the outcasts nor any eaters. Every word that falls from the mouth is a coin lost. Silently they gave and accepted food with both hands. A preoccupied child who took his bowl with one hand got a sideways glare. A complete moment of total attention is due everyone alike. Children and lovers have no singularity here, but my aunt used a secret voice, a separate attentiveness.

32    She kept the man's name to herself throughout her labor and dying; she did not accuse him that he be punished with her. To save her inseminator's name she gave silent birth.

33    He may have been somebody in her own household, but intercourse with a man outside the family would have been no less abhorrent. All the village were kinsmen, and the titles shouted in loud country voices never let kinship be forgotten. Any man within visiting distance would have been neutralized as a lover—"brother," "younger brother," "older brother"— one hundred and fifteen relationship titles. Parents researched birth charts probably not so much to assure good fortune as to circumvent incest in a population that has but one hundred surnames. Everybody has eight million relatives. How useless then sexual mannerisms, how dangerous.

34    As if it came from an atavism deeper than fear, I used to add "brother" silently to boys' names. It hexed the boys, who would or would not ask me to dance, and made them less scary and as familiar and deserving of benevolence as girls.

35    But, of course, I hexed myself also—no dates. I should have stood up, both arms waving, and shouted out across libraries, "Hey, you! Love me back." I had no idea, though, how to make attraction selective, how to control its direction and magnitude. If I made myself American-pretty so that the five or six Chinese boys in the class fell in love with me, everyone else—the Caucasian, Negro, and Japanese boys—would too. Sisterliness, dignified and honorable, made much more sense.

36    Attraction eludes control so stubbornly that whole societies designed to organize relationships among people cannot keep order, not even when they bind people to one another from childhood and raise them together. Among the very poor and the wealthy, brothers married their adopted sisters, like doves. Our family allowed some romance, paying adult brides' prices and providing dowries so that their sons and daughters could marry strangers. Marriage promises to turn strangers into friendly relatives—a nation of siblings.

In the village structure, spirits shimmered among the live creatures, ₃₇ balanced and held in equilibrium by time and land. But one human being flaring up into violence could open up a black hole, a maelstrom that pulled in the sky. The frightened villagers, who depended on one another to maintain the real, went to my aunt to show her a personal, physical representation of the break she had made in the "roundness." Misallying couples snapped off the future, which was to be embodied in true offspring. The villagers punished her for acting as if she could have a private life, secret and apart from them.

If my aunt had betrayed the family at a time of large grain yields and ₃₈ peace, when many boys were born, and wings were being built on many houses, perhaps she might have escaped such severe punishment. But the men—hungry, greedy, tired of planting in dry soil—had been forced to leave the village in order to send food-money home. There were ghost plagues, bandit plagues, wars with the Japanese, floods. My Chinese brother and sister had died of an unknown sickness. Adultery, perhaps only a mistake during good times, became a crime when the village needed food.

The round moon cakes and round doorways, the round tables of grad- ₃₉ uated sizes that fit one roundness inside another, round windows and rice bowls—these talismans had lost their power to warn this family of the law: A family must be whole, faithfully keeping the descent line by having sons to feed the old and the dead, who in turn look after the family. The villagers came to show my aunt and her lover-in-hiding a broken house. The villagers were speeding up the circling of events because she was too shortsighted to see that her infidelity had already harmed the village, that waves of consequences would return unpredictably, sometimes in disguise, as now, to hurt her. This roundness had to be made coin-sized so that she would see its circumference: Punish her at the birth of her baby. Awaken her to the inexorable. People who refused fatalism because they could invent small resources insisted on culpability. Deny accidents and wrest fault from the stars.

After the villagers left, their lanterns now scattering in various direc- ₄₀ tions toward home, the family broke their silence and cursed her. "Aiaa, we're going to die. Death is coming. Death is coming. Look what you've done. You've killed us. Ghost! Dead ghost! Ghost! You've never been born." She ran out into the fields, far enough from the house so that she could no longer hear their voices, and pressed herself against the earth, her own land no more. When she felt the birth coming, she thought that she had been hurt. Her body seized together. "They've hurt me too much," she thought. "This is gall, and it will kill me." With forehead and knees against the earth, her body convulsed and then relaxed. She turned on her back, lay on the ground. The black well of sky and stars went out and out and out forever; her body and her complexity seemed to disappear. She was one of the stars, a bright dot in blackness, without home, without a companion, in eternal cold and silence. An agoraphobia rose in her, speeding higher and higher, bigger and bigger; she would not be able to contain it; there would be no end to fear.

41   Flayed, unprotected against space, she felt pain return, focusing her body. This pain chilled her—a cold, steady kind of surface pain. Inside, spasmodically, the other pain, the pain of the child, heated her. For hours she lay on the ground, alternately body and space. Sometimes a vision of normal comfort obliterated reality: She saw the family in the evening gambling at the dinner table, the young people massaging their elders' backs. She saw them congratulating one another, high joy on the mornings the rice shoots came up. When these pictures burst, the stars drew yet further apart. Black space opened.

42   She got to her feet to fight better and remembered that old-fashioned women gave birth in their pigsties to fool the jealous, pain-dealing gods, who do not snatch piglets. Before the next spasms could stop her, she ran to the pigsty, each step a rushing out into emptiness. She climbed over the fence and knelt in the dirt. It was good to have a fence enclosing her, a tribal person alone.

43   Laboring, this woman who had carried her child as a foreign growth that sickened her every day, expelled it at last. She reached down to touch the hot, wet, moving mass, surely smaller than anything human, and could feel that it was human after all—fingers, toes, nails, nose. She pulled it up on to her belly, and it lay curled there, butt in the air, feet precisely tucked one under the other. She opened her loose shirt and buttoned the child inside. After resting, it squirmed and thrashed and she pushed it up to her breast. It turned its head this way and that until it found her nipple. There, it made little snuffling noises. She clenched her teeth at its preciousness, lovely as a young calf, a piglet, a little dog.

44   She may have gone to the pigsty as a last act of responsibility: she would protect this child as she had protected its father. It would look after her soul, leaving supplies on her grave. But how would this tiny child without family find her grave when there would be no marker for her anywhere, neither in the earth nor the family hall? No one would give her a family hall name. She had taken the child with her into the wastes. At its birth the two of them had felt the same raw pain of separation, a wound that only the family pressing tight could close. A child with no descent line would not soften her life but only trail after her, ghostlike, begging her to give it purpose. At dawn the villagers on their way to the fields would stand around the fence and look.

45   Full of milk, the little ghost slept. When it awoke, she hardened her breasts against the milk that crying loosens. Toward morning she picked up the baby and walked to the well.

Carrying the baby to the well shows loving. Otherwise abandon it.  46
Turn its face into the mud. Mothers who love their children take them
along. It was probably a girl; there is some hope of forgiveness for boys.

"Don't tell anyone you had an aunt. Your father does not want to hear  47
her name. She has never been born." I have believed that sex was unspeakable and words so strong and fathers so frail that "aunt" would do
my father mysterious harm. I have thought that my family, having settled
among immigrants who had also been their neighbors in the ancestral
land, needed to clean their name, and a wrong word would incite the kins-
people even here. But there is more to this silence: They want me to participate in her punishment. And I have.

In the twenty years since I heard this story I have not asked for de-  48
tails nor said my aunt's name; I do not know it. People who can comfort
the dead can also chase after them to hurt them further—a reverse ancestor worship. The real punishment was not the raid swiftly inflicted by
the villagers, but the family's deliberately forgetting her. Her betrayal so
maddened them, they saw to it that she would suffer forever, even after
death. Always hungry, always needing, she would have to beg food from
other ghosts, snatch and steal it from those whose living descendants
give them gifts. She would have to fight the ghosts massed at crossroads
for the buns a few thoughtful citizens leave to decoy her away from village and home so that the ancestral spirits could feast unharassed. At
peace, they could act like gods, not ghosts, their descent lines providing
them with paper suits and dresses, spirit money, paper houses, paper automobiles, chicken, meat, and rice into eternity—essences delivered up
in smoke and flames, steam and incense rising from each rice bowl. In an
attempt to make the Chinese care for people outside the family, Chair
man Mao encourages us now to give our paper replicas to the spirits of
outstanding soldiers and workers, no matter whose ancestors they may
be. My aunt remains forever hungry. Goods are not distributed evenly
among the dead.

My aunt haunts me—her ghost drawn to me because now, after fifty  49
years of neglect, I alone devote pages of paper to her, though not
origamied into houses and clothes. I do not think she always means me
well. I am telling on her, and she was a spite suicide, drowning herself in
the drinking water. The Chinese are always very frightened of the
drowned one, whose weeping ghost, wet hair hanging and skin bloated,
waits silently by the water to pull down a substitute.

*1975*

# QUESTIONS FOR DISCUSSION

## Content

a. Is Kingston's family ashamed of No Name Woman because she committed suicide or because she became pregnant by a man who was not her husband? Is the distinction important?
b. Why doesn't the author ever learn her aunt's name?
c. In what way does the story of No Name Woman cast light on Kingston's claim that her mother is guided "by Necessity" (paragraph 13)?
d. Why does Kingston refer to her aunt as "prodigal" (paragraph 15)? What meanings does she associate with this term?
e. Does she see an affinity between herself and her aunt that is not shared by other members of the family? In what ways is this a defense of No Name Woman? Of all Chinese women? Of all women?
f. "The villagers punished [No Name Woman] for acting as if she could have a private life, secret and apart from them" (paragraph 37). How does this statement shed light on the culture Kingston is describing?
g. What motives does she ascribe to No Name Woman? To the man who raped her? To the villagers? To her family?

## STRATEGY AND STYLE

h. The author uses her mother's voice to relate the story of the villagers' attack. Would she have done better to tell this story from her own point of view?
i. Why does she address Chinese-Americans directly in paragraph 12? Is she writing to a limited audience?
j. Comment on the author's use of verbs in the passage that recalls the attack of the townspeople. What effect does her choice of verbs create?
k. Among other things, "No Name Woman" is an indictment of sexism, intolerance, and violence against women. Is Hong Kingston's tone appropriate? Should she have made her criticism fiercer and more apparent? Should she have focused on this issue alone?
l. How would you describe the function of the writer in this selection? Is she simply a reporter, or does she have other functions? What might they be?

## ENGAGING THE TEXT

a. Find one passage (one or two paragraphs) that intrigues you in some way. Write about that passage, summarizing it and explaining why it intrigues you.

b. Review or reread "No Name Woman." As you do this, record your reactions to the sexism, violence, and intolerance in the culture Kingston
is describing. Can you find examples of such phenomena in your own
environment?

## SUGGESTIONS FOR SUSTAINED WRITING

a. Hong Kingston tells her version of what might have happened to her
aunt in order to lend substance to her memory of this woman and implicitly to explain the cruelty toward women that can be imbedded in a
culture. Collect several personal memories that might illustrate some
unfairness or injustice to you (as a representative of a larger group) or
to a subgroup within your culture or family. Then turn those memories
into a coherent narrative essay. Although you need not make your work
as detailed or complex as Kingston's, try to interweave these memories
closely so as to create a clear and coherent discussion of the injustice you
wish to illustrate.

b. Making reference to the essay, explain why you think Hong
Kingston's family and the villagers reacted as they did to the fact that
her aunt became pregnant by a man who was not her husband. What
do their reactions say about the culture and the time in which this essay is set? In what important ways do that culture and time differ from
our own? To stimulate your thinking, consider how the grandmother
in Angelou's "Grandmother's Victory" (this chapter) might react to
hearing that one of her granddaughters had become pregnant by a
man who was not her husband. How would your family react to such
news?

c. Kingston shows that it is not unusual for conflict and confusion to develop between the cultural mores of immigrants and those of the children they bear and raise in a new land. Focusing on a particular ethnic
group—perhaps your own—explain why a conflict might arise between immigrant parents and their children over strict adherence to a
traditional religion, the rights and roles of women, marriage to someone outside the family's faith or nationality, or another cultural, social,
or political issue. Support your discussion with information from at
least three library or Internet sources.

# Travelling South*

James Weldon Johnson

*"Travelling South" (editors' title) is a chapter from* The Autobiography of an Ex-Colored Man, *a purported account of the early life of James Weldon Johnson (1871–1938). First published anonymously in 1912, the book's discussion of racial issues—especially miscegenation—is both startling and convincing. Although it was a work of fiction, Johnson's* Autobiography *was based on many of his own travels and experiences as a young man. A poet, diplomat, and anthologist of African-American literature, Johnson was one of the founders of the National Association for the Advancement of Colored People (NAACP).* The Autobiography of an Ex-Colored Man *was republished in 1927 under the author's name. "Travelling South" begins as the narrator journeys from New England to Atlanta, where he plans to enroll in a university.*

1   The farther I got below Washington the more disappointed I became in the appearance of the country. I peered through the car windows, looking in vain for the luxuriant semi-tropical scenery which I had pictured in my mind. I did not find the grass so green, nor the woods so beautiful, nor the flowers so plentiful, as they were in Connecticut. Instead, the red earth partly covered by tough, scrawny grass, the muddy straggling roads, the cottages of unpainted pine boards, and the clay daubed huts imparted a "burnt up" impression. Occasionally we ran through a little white and green village that was like an oasis in a desert.

2   When I reached Atlanta my steadily increasing disappointment was not lessened. I found it a big, dull, red town. This dull red color of that part of the South I was then seeing had much, I think, to do with the extreme depression of my spirits—no public squares, no fountains, dingy street-cars, and, with the exception of three or four principal thoroughfares, unpaved streets. It was raining when I arrived and some of these unpaved streets were absolutely impassable. Wheels sank to the hubs in red mire, and I actually stood for an hour and watched four or five men work to save a mule, which had stepped into a deep sink, from drowning, or, rather, suffocating in the mud. The Atlanta of today is a new city.

3   On the train I had talked with one of the Pullman car porters, a bright young fellow who was himself a student, and I told him that I was going to Atlanta to attend school. I had also asked him to tell me where I might stop for a day or two until the University opened. He said I might go with him to the place where he stopped during his "layovers" in Atlanta. I gladly accepted his offer, and went with him along one of those muddy streets until we came to a rather rickety looking frame house, which we entered. The proprietor of the house was a big, fat, greasy looking brown-

*Editor's title.

skinned man. When I asked him if he could give me accommodation he wanted to know how long I would stay. I told him perhaps two days, not more than three. In reply he said, "Oh, dat's all right den," at the same time leading the way up a pair of creaky stairs. I followed him and the porter to a room, the door of which the proprietor opened while continuing, it seemed, his remark, "Oh, dat's all right den," by adding, "You kin sleep in dat cot in de corner der. Fifty cents please." The porter interrupted by saying, "You needn't collect from him now, he's got a trunk." This seemed to satisfy the man, and he went down leaving me and my porter friend in the room. I glanced around the apartment and saw that it contained a double bed and two cots, two wash-stands, three chairs, and a time-worn bureau with a looking glass that would have made Adonis appear hideous. I looked at the cot in which I was to sleep and suspected, not without good reasons, that I should not be the first to use the sheets and pillowcase since they had last come from the wash. When I thought of the clean, tidy, comfortable surroundings in which I had been reared, a wave of homesickness swept over me that made me feel faint. Had it not been for the presence of my companion, and that I knew this much of his history— that he was not yet quite twenty, just three years older than myself, and that he had been fighting his own way in the world, earning his own living and providing for his own education since he was fourteen—I should not have been able to stop the tears that were welling up in my eyes.

I asked him why it was that the proprietor of the house seemed un-   4
willing to accommodate me for more than a couple of days. He informed me that the man ran a lodging house especially for Pullman porters, and as their stays in town were not longer than one or two nights it would interfere with his arrangements to have anyone stay longer. He went on to say, "You see this room is fixed up to accommodate four men at a time. Well, by keeping a sort of table of trips, in and out, of the men, and working them like checkers, he can accommodate fifteen or sixteen in each week, and generally avoid having an empty bed. You happen to catch a bed that would have been empty for a couple of nights." I asked him where he was going to sleep. He answered, "I sleep in that other cot tonight; tomorrow night I go out." He went on to tell me that the man who kept the house did not serve meals, and that if I was hungry we would go out and get something to eat.

We went into the street, and in passing the railroad station I hired a   5
wagon to take my trunk to my lodging place. We passed along until, finally, we turned into a street that stretched away, up and down hill, for a mile or two; and here I caught my first sight of colored people in large numbers. I had seen little squads around the railroad stations on my way south; but here I saw a street crowded with them. They filled the shops and thronged the sidewalks and lined the curb. I asked my companion if all the colored people in Atlanta lived in this street. He said they did not, and assured me

that the ones I saw were of the lower class. I felt relieved, in spite of the size of the lower class. The unkempt appearance, the shambling, slouching gait and loud talk and laughter of these people aroused in me a feeling of almost repulsion. Only one thing about them awoke a feeling of interest; that was their dialect. I had read some Negro dialect and had heard snatches of it on my journey down from Washington; but here I heard it in all of its fullness and freedom. I was particularly struck by the way in which it was punctuated by such exclamatory phrases as "Lawd a mussy!" "G'wan man!" "Bless ma soul!" "Look heah chile!" These people talked and laughed without restraint. In fact, they talked straight from their lungs, and laughed from the pits of their stomachs. And this hearty laughter was often justified by the droll humor of some remark. I paused long enough to hear one man say to another, "W'at's de mattah wid you an' yo' fr'en' Sam?" And the other came back like a flash, "Ma fr'en? He ma fr'en? Man! I'd go to his funeral jes de same as I'd go to a minstrel show." I have since learned that this ability to laugh heartily is, in part, the salvation of the American Negro; it does much to keep him from going the way of the Indian.

6      The business places of the street along which we were passing consisted chiefly of low bars, cheap dry-goods and notion stores, barber shops, and fish and bread restaurants. We, at length, turned down a pair of stairs that led to a basement, and I found myself in an eating-house somewhat better than those I had seen in passing; but that did not mean much for its excellence. The place was smoky, the tables were covered with oil-cloth, the floor covered with sawdust, and from the kitchen came a rancid odor of fish fried over several times, which almost nauseated me. I asked my companion if this were the place where we were to eat. He informed me that it was the best place in town where a colored man could get a meal. I then wanted to know why somebody didn't open a place where respectable colored people who had money could be accommodated. He answered, "It wouldn't pay; all the respectable colored people eat at home, and the few who travel generally have friends in the towns to which they go, who entertain them." He added, "Of course, you could go in any place in the city; they wouldn't know you from white."

7      I sat down with the porter at one of the tables, but was not hungry enough to eat with any relish what was put before me. The food was not badly cooked; but the iron knives and forks needed to be scrubbed, the plates and dishes and glasses needed to be washed and well dried. I minced over what I took on my plate while my companion ate. When we finished we paid the waiter twenty cents each and went out. We walked around until the lights of the city were lit. Then the porter said that he must get to bed and have some rest, as he had not had six hours' sleep since he left Jersey City. I went back to our lodging-house with him.

8      When I awoke in the morning there were, besides my newfound friend, two other men in the room, asleep in the double bed. I got up and

dressed myself very quietly, so as not to awake anyone. I then drew from under the pillow my precious roll of greenbacks, took out a ten dollar bill, and very softly unlocking my trunk, put the remainder, about three hundred dollars, in the inside pocket of a coat near the bottom; glad of the opportunity to put it unobserved in a place of safety. When I had carefully locked my trunk, I tiptoed toward the door with the intention of going out to look for a decent restaurant where I might get something fit to eat. As I was easing the door open, my porter friend said with a yawn, "Hello! You're going out?" I answered him, "Yes." "Oh!" he yawned again, "I guess I've had enough sleep; wait a minute, I'll go with you." For the instant his friendship bored and embarrassed me. I had visions of another meal in the greasy restaurant of the day before. He must have divined my thoughts; for he went on to say, "I know a woman across town who takes a few boarders; I think we can go over there and get a good breakfast." With a feeling of mingled fears and doubts regarding what the breakfast might be, I waited until he had dressed himself.

When I saw the neat appearance of the cottage we entered my fears 9 vanished, and when I saw the woman who kept it my doubts followed the same course. Scrupulously clean, in a spotless white apron and colored head handkerchief, her round face beaming with motherly kindness, she was picturesquely beautiful. She impressed me as one broad expanse of happiness and good nature. In a few minutes she was addressing me as "chile" and "honey." She made me feel as though I should like to lay my head on her capacious bosom and go to sleep.

And the breakfast, simple as it was, I could not have had at any restau- 10 rant in Atlanta at any price. There was fried chicken, as it is fried only in the South, hominy boiled to the consistency where it could be eaten with a fork, and biscuits so light and flaky that a fellow with any appetite at all would have no difficulty in disposing of eight or ten. When I had finished I felt that I had experienced the realization of, at least, one of my dreams of Southern life.

During the meal we found out from our hostess, who had two boys in 11 school, that Atlanta University opened on that very day. I had somehow mixed my dates. My friend the porter suggested that I go out to the university at once and offered to walk over and show me the way. We had to walk because, although the university was not more than twenty minutes distance from the center of the city, there were no street-cars running in that direction. My first sight of the school grounds made me feel that I was not far from home; here the red hills had been terraced and covered with green grass; clean gravel walks, well shaded, led up to the buildings; indeed, it was a bit of New England transplanted. At the gate my companion said he would bid me goodby, because it was likely that he would not see me again before his car went out. He told me that he would make two more trips to Atlanta, and that he would come out and see me; that after his second trip he would leave the Pullman service for the winter and return to school in Nashville. We shook hands, I thanked him for all his kindness, and we said goodby.

12    I walked up to a group of students and made some inquiries. They directed me to the president's office in the main building. The president gave me a cordial welcome; it was more than cordial; he talked to me, not as the official head of a college, but as though he were adopting me into what was his large family, to personally look after my general welfare as well as my education. He seemed especially pleased with the fact that I had come to them all the way from the North. He told me that I could have come to the school as soon as I had reached the city, and that I had better move my trunk out at once. I gladly promised him that I would do so. He then called a boy and directed him to take me to the matron, and to show me around afterwards. I found the matron even more motherly than the president was fatherly. She had me to register, which was in effect to sign a pledge to abstain from the use of intoxicating beverages, tobacco, and profane language, while I was a student in the school. This act caused me no sacrifice; as, up to that time, I was free from either habit. The boy who was with me then showed me about the grounds. I was especially interested in the industrial building.

13    The sounding of a bell, he told me, was the signal for the students to gather in the general assembly hall, and he asked me if I would go. Of course I would. There were between three and four hundred students and perhaps all of the teachers gathered in the room. I noticed that several of the latter were colored. The president gave a talk addressed principally to newcomers; but I scarcely heard what he said, I was so much occupied in looking at those around me. They were of all types and colors, the more intelligent types predominating. The colors ranged from jet black to pure white, with light hair and eyes. Among the girls especially there were many so fair that it was difficult to believe that they had Negro blood in them. And, too, I could not help but notice that many of the girls, particularly those of the delicate brown shades, with black eyes and wavy dark hair, were decidedly pretty. Among the boys, many of the blackest were fine specimens of young manhood, tall, straight, and muscular, with magnificent heads, these were the kind of boys who developed into the patriarchal "uncles" of the old slave régime.

14    When I left the University it was with the determination to get my trunk, and move out to the school before night. I walked back across the city with a light step and a light heart. I felt perfectly satisfied with life for the first time since my mother's death. In passing the railroad station I hired a wagon and rode with the driver as far as my stopping place. I settled with my landlord and went upstairs to put away several articles I had left out. As soon as I opened my trunk a dart of suspicion shot through my heart; the arrangement of things did not look familiar. I began to dig down

excitedly to the bottom till I reached the coat in which I had concealed my treasure. My money was gone! Every single bill of it. I knew it was useless to do so, but I searched through every other coat, every pair of trousers, every vest, and even into each pair of socks. When I had finished my fruitless search I sat down dazed and heartsick. I called the landlord up, and informed him of my loss; he comforted me by saying that I ought to have better sense than to keep money in a trunk, and that he was not responsible for his lodgers' personal effects. His cooling words brought me enough to my senses to cause me to look and see if anything else was missing. Several small articles were gone, among them a black and gray necktie of odd design upon which my heart was set; almost as much as the loss of the money, I felt the loss of my tie.

After thinking for awhile as best I could, I wisely decided to go at once 15 back to the university and lay my troubles before the president. I rushed breathlessly back to the school. As I neared the grounds the thought came across me, would not my story sound fishy? Would it not place me in the position of an impostor or beggar? What right had I to worry these busy people with the results of my carelessness? If the money could not be recovered, and I doubted that it could, what good would it do to tell them about it. The shame and embarrassment which the whole situation gave me caused me to stop at the gate. I paused, undecided, for a moment; then turned and slowly retraced my steps, and so changed the whole course of my life.

If the reader has never been in a strange city without money or friends, 16 it is useless to try to describe what my feelings were; he could not understand. If he has been, it is equally useless, for he understands more than words could convey. When I reached my lodgings I found in the room one of the porters who had slept there the night before. When he heard what misfortune had befallen me he offered many words of sympathy and advice. He asked me how much money I had left, I told him that I had ten or twelve dollars left in my pocket. He said, "That won't last you very long here, and you will hardly be able to find anything to do in Atlanta. I'll tell you what you do, go down to Jacksonville and you won't have any trouble to get a job in one of the big hotels down there, or in St. Augustine." I thanked him, but intimated my doubts of being able to get to Jacksonville on the money I had. He reassured me by saying, "Oh, that's all right. You express your trunk on through, and I'll take you down in my closet." I thanked him again, not knowing then, what it was to travel in a Pullman porter's closet. He put me under a deeper debt of gratitude by lending me fifteen dollars, which he said I could pay back after I had secured work. His generosity brought tears to my eyes, and I concluded that, after all, there were some kind hearts in the world.

I now forgot my troubles in the hurry and excitement of getting my 17 trunk off in time to catch the train, which went out at seven o'clock. I even forgot that I hadn't eaten anything since morning. We got a wagon—the porter went with me—and took my trunk to the express office. My new friend then told me to come to the station at about a quarter of seven, and walk straight to the car where I should see him standing, and not to lose my nerve. I found my rôle not so difficult to play as I thought it would be, because the train did not leave from the central station, but from a smaller one, where there were no gates and guards to pass. I followed directions, and the porter took me on his car, and locked me in his closet. In a few minutes the train pulled out for Jacksonville.

18      I may live to be a hundred years old, but I shall never forget the agonies I suffered that night. I spent twelve hours doubled up in the porter's basket for soiled linen, not being able to straighten up on account of the shelves for clean linen just over my head. The air was hot and suffocating and the smell of damp towels and used linen was sickening. At each lurch of the car over the none too smooth track, I was bumped and bruised against the narrow walls of my narrow compartment. I became acutely conscious of the fact that I had not eaten for hours. Then nausea took possession of me, and at one time I had grave doubts about reaching my destination alive. If I had the trip to make again, I should prefer to walk.

*1912*

## QUESTIONS FOR DISCUSSION

### Content

a. How old is the narrator of this story?

b. What does Johnson mean when he says that laughter is "the salvation of the American Negro; it does much to keep him from going the way of the Indian" (paragraph 5)?

c. Johnson writes about a time when racial segregation was prominent in the South. What evidence of segregation do you see in this selection?

d. Johnson contrasts the narrator's reaction to the people and places in paragraphs 3, 4, 5, 6, and 7 with those in paragraphs 9, 10, and 11. What does this contrast tell us about the narrator's character, upbringing, and lifestyle?

e. The narrator feels "shame and embarrassment" over having lost his money. What might be the cause of that reaction?

f. Why does the narrator decide not to seek help from the university after discovering that he has been robbed? What does his reaction to this incident tell us about the way he views the world? What does it tell us about his character in general?

g. Explain how "Travelling South" might be interpreted as the story of a young person's initiation into adulthood. In your answer, make sure to consider what happens to the narrator on his way to Jacksonville.
h. Does this essay have a thesis? If so, what is it?

## Strategy and Style

i. Why does Johnson use dialect to recreate the language of the proprietor of the boardinghouse and the people on the street? Wouldn't his story have been easier to read had he put their words into standard English?
j. What function does description play in this narrative? Where is it most prominent?
k. Why, in paragraph 3, does the narrator bother to tell us about the life of the young porter who befriends him?
l. Analyze the vocabulary used in paragraph 5. How would you describe the narrator's tone (his attitude toward his subject) in this part of the essay?
m. Where, in paragraph 13 does the author use irony? What effect does this device have on distinguishing the narrator from the author?

## ENGAGING THE TEXT

a. Who do you think stole the narrator's money and necktie? Answer this question with specific reference to the text.
b. Compare and contrast the character of the narrator in this story with that of Sister in Angelou's "Grandmother's Victory," which also appears in this chapter.

## SUGGESTIONS FOR SUSTAINED WRITING

a. Recall an incident in which you had to face a serious setback, difficulty, or reversal such as the one confronting the narrator of "Travelling South." Explain how you faced that setback. Then, as a way to give focus and purpose to your essay, explain what your reaction revealed about your character and personality at the time. Make direct reference to Johnson's essay to show that your experience and his were similar in some way or ways. You might quote directly, paraphrase, or summarize from this essay.
b. Write a letter to the narrator of "Travelling South" as a hypothetical attempt to persuade him to return to Atlanta and the university. Begin your assignment by rereading the essay and making notes in the margins to help you gather details that will make your writing convincing.

As you draft your letter, refer to the text by paraphrasing and including direct quotations. In addition, anticipate and answer the objections the narrator might use to respond to your arguments. Make sure to respond to these objections convincingly. Before you begin, however, read Gail Sheehy's "Predictable Crises of Adulthood" in Chapter 5. It might provide insights that you can pass along in your letter.

c. Research the founding of Grambling College, Howard University, or another institution dedicated to providing educational opportunities for African-Americans. Focus on the early history of this institution, its curriculum, the faculty, the student body, and other aspects that would provide insight into the specific purposes for which this institution was founded. Use at least four library or Internet sources.

# Don't Get Comfortable

Naton Leslie

*Naton Leslie teaches at Siena College in Loudonville, New York. He has published essays and poetry in the* North American Review, *the* Ohio Review, *and the* Kansas Quarterly, *among other periodicals in the United States. "Don't Get Comfortable" is from his collection entitled* Places Cursed by John Brown and Other Essays on History. *It is an autobiographical essay with philosophical overtones about how tenuous human existence can be.*

1   This story is about a railroad detective named Charley Best. Best worked in the 1920s on the narrow-gauge lines between Pittsburgh and the lumber and mining hill towns of northwestern Pennsylvania. My father tells this story and said his father told it to him, having known Best or known others who knew him. Or maybe my grandfather rode those rails to work in the camps; I know he worked for the railroad, lighting kerosene lamps on the bridge over the Allegheny River and during winter breaking ice from cables that hoisted lanterns high above the girders.

2   My father tells that story too, how when he was five years old his father would take him out at night when he made his rounds on the bridge over the Allegheny in Mahoning, Pennsylvania. His father would climb over the side, hanging on to the slick catwalk while he broke cables free after an ice storm. The night would be filled with frigid gusts, and the wind was particularly strong that high above the river. On the swaying iron bridge my grandfather ordered my father to "take a holt" of the side railing. He was never frightened during these trips because his father was so strong, sure-footed, and careful. It must have been like watching an athlete, my grandfather climbing catlike over the rail, hitting the ice-bound

cables with steady blows from the ball-peen. He was a compact man, and every movement, every swing of the hammer, seemed to come from the center of his body.

This was 1934, and my grandfather was lucky to have this bit of a job, ₃ this small paycheck, in the mountains of Pennsylvania where no farm made it, where the mines had begun to play out. So, though the job was dangerous and hard, he did it, and because I remember my grandfather as a meticulous man, I'm sure he did it well. Why he took my father along is less clear, though my grandmother may have asked him to get him out of her hair for a while, not realizing the danger, or perhaps my grandfather assumed his son would have to do the job someday. He'd been taught how to plant, to shoe horses, to make medicines, and to build outbuildings by his own father on the homestead farm. Perhaps my grandfather was teaching his son about the railroad.

Once, as my father tells it, a train crossed the bridge while they were ₄ on it. It was a bitterly cold, moonless night, and the lanterns seemed to light only the barest arc of the old iron bridge. My grandfather was hanging from a side rail, breaking ice and edging a cable through the pulley, when the headlamp of the train broke the darkness. He hollered to my father to hop over the side of the bridge and hold on, to "get a purchase and don't let go no matter what." Then, as the train caused the bridge to quake and sway, my father felt his father's arm around him and his own weight release from his arms as his father held them both by one arm, sixty feet above the icy Allegheny. "Imagine," my father says when he tells the story, "a five-year-old boy and I wasn't even scared," though I wonder if he says that in tribute to his naive courage or in acknowledgment of trusting his father so utterly that fear never occurred to him.

I don't know where my grandfather heard of Charley Best. The area was ₅ sparsely populated; it had been homesteaded in the mid-nineteenth century and remained wholly wilderness until the first oil well in the nation, the Drake Well, was drilled in Titusville. Those who worked in the lumber and mining camps, and later in oil fields and railroad yards, were all like Charley Best and my grandfather, raised on hardscrabble farms in the Allegheny Mountains, farms now part of the Allegheny National Forest, a mixed old-growth-second-growth wilderness replacing their hard-won clearings and plantings. They were coarse, often violent people for whom fighting was merely another kind of work. For Charley Best, his work became violence. Best had a fierce reputation, and my father, who used to see him at Walker's store in Mahoning, said he looked the part. The railroad detective bought cigars at Walker's, and even there he carried a sidearm, what my father thought was an enormous Colt. He was a big man, and my father also remembers his wide hat, the high leather boots with the pant cuffs tucked inside, and the huge chain stretched across his chest, Prince Albert style, upon which hung a nickel-plated railroad watch my father thought was as big as an alarm clock. Mostly, though, he remembers that handgun and a handle-bar mustache Best had cultivated to curl around his wide face. My father poses as Best as he tells the story, striding the catwalks and tops of railcars, wind whipping his mustache back like flames. But it's the same picture he paints of his grandfather, Doc, one of the original homesteaders in Forest County. We have a photograph of him, published in a volume of local history, his reportedly immense size diminished by a team of oxen behind him, that same mustache flaring like horns.

6        My father heard a story about Doc at the funeral of one of his uncles, and in it his mustache and oxen are part of the scenery. Doc Leslie had taken cattle into Brookville, Pennsylvania, to sell. Later, while he was having a drink at the Sigel Hotel, one of the men from town said, "Aren't you scared traveling all the way back to Blue Jay Ridge with that much money on you, Doc?"

7        My father doesn't say what Doc said back—some grunt or mumble through his mustache—but later, on Blood Road in his oxcart, Doc was jumped by three men wearing bandannas, like the outlaws they had read about in dime novels.

8        It was only a joke. These were friends of Doc's, out only to put a scare in him, but when one of them said "Stick 'em up," Doc replied, "Stick 'em up, hell. There'll be feet up and shit flying," as he leaped from the cart, scattering the men with his bullwhip. When my father tells it, he pantomimes rolling up one sleeve to signify the fight, his eyes fierce and fixed. The story is frozen at that point: Doc poised for action, the flight of the men inevitable.

9        Part of Charley Best's story is arrested as well. Best patrolled the tops of railcars as they sped across the hills toward the coal fields. My father said those who hopped trains rode Charley's line only twice: the first time you were warned, and if you took Detective Best's warning with humility, you got where you wanted to go. But Best remembered, and the second time he caught you riding free, you were off.

10        "Off?" I once asked, interrupting my father for once as he told the story. His irritation was clear.

11        "Yeah, *off*," he said, his arms poised in the act of grabbing someone by the scruff of the neck and back of the trousers. I remembered a postcard drawn by Wobbly leader Joe Hill, a comic portrait of himself being booted from a train, and had less admiration for Best and more sympathy for the hoboes who just wanted a ride and ended up flying.

12        I could see them soaring, sprawling like skydivers over the empty air of the railroad cut, over the sixty-foot drop from the bridge in Mahoning. I've always been hesitant about heights—not actually frightened, only concerned and reluctant about climbing, a controllable vertigo. Not that I have suffered many spectacular falls. Once I fell off, or more accurately, ran off, the top of an extension ladder when a wasp landed on my nose. I

simply turned around, stepped off the top of the ladder, and began to run, heading straight down to a gravel parking lot of the car dealership where I was working. I was pretty skinned up, landing on my forearms to protect my face from the gravel, and my coworker, a young biker named Rocky, said, "Man, did you crash 'n' burn!" Perhaps I got this timidity from my mother, who also shied from heights. I remember my father, mother, older sister, and myself climbing a fire tower in the Allegheny Mountains. My mother and I made it about halfway up when the open sides and the lack of a railing sent me back down. My father and sister made it to the top, and I watched from the ground as they laughed and climbed impossibly higher.

My sister trusted my wild and unpredictable father and would follow 13 him, while my trust in him had limits. Probably he had learned not to fear heights from his father on that railroad bridge; he even took a job as a tree-topper for a lumber company and later as a lineman for the power company. When he was sixteen he got a job as a ground hand, or "ground squirrel," as they called the young boys who dragged limbs by the butt to the burn pile. He grew to love the work, part of the postwar rural electrification program, and when not piling brush he watched the men high in trees worrying off limbs with bow saws.

Finally he got his own climbing gear: long hooks like bayonets that 14 strapped to his high-topped boots and a wide leather belt to wrap around tree trunks. He got so good he'd climb a tree, and eventually a utility pole, with only his hooks and hands on the trunk, using the belt only when he reached the top. He said he loved heights; on top of a tree on a mountain he said he could see all of Forest County, see deer move in herds and bears trailing cubs on the ridge miles away. Working for the power company, my father climbed poles on wide rights of way cut across the mountains, high power lines carrying thousands of volts from transformer substations to light lamps in a farmhouse on remote Blue Jay Ridge.

But he fell. Twice. The first time, he says, they were putting up new 15 lines on poles in residential Brookville. Poles were originally treated with creosote to prevent decay, a dark, oil-based coating that smelled vaguely of kerosene and urine, now outlawed in favor of a pressure treatment with brine. These were old poles, put up at the turn of the century during the first wave of utility construction, and that morning my father climbed the first one. He says he had just hooked on his belt and was looking up at the late autumn sky, a mix of clouds and high blue. He thought, "Those clouds sure are moving fast," and then he realized it was he who was moving, not the clouds, as the pole was falling, breaking off at the rotten base. He tells how he managed to take off his belt and scamper to the other side, riding the pole to the ground as it bent, then snapped.

The other time he fell was more dangerous, and more miraculous. He 16 was at the top of a forty-five-foot pole, and according to the newspaper article from the *Oil City Derrick* his belt snapped and he pitched backward. My father says that after he felt the belt give he reached for the crossarm. His fingertips barely reached the glass insulators on his right, but he was unable to grasp them or the wooden beam, and he fell. He flipped backward twice in the air, landed on his feet, bounced, and fell on his side. He stood up, apparently unhurt, but when he tried to unbuckle his tool harness he found the fingers on his left hand would not work; he had broken his wrist in two places. Later he would develop severe back problems and would suffer years of pain, caused I'm sure by that jarring fall, though he never seemed to connect the two.

17   He doesn't tell either of those stories often. You don't tell stories that could have ended so finally. I heard him once admit to waking up in the middle of the night, years later, a dream of fingertips grazing the crossarm tearing him into sweaty wakefulness. And these stories are among the few illustrating a point or a moral. My father would sometimes say, after telling one of these stories, that there's only one thing you need to know to do "high work": "Don't get comfortable." What he means goes beyond the commonplace "Keep your wits about you." It's the lesson I forgot when I ran off the top of that ladder—whenever doing anything high up, do it with the knowledge of where you are. I use this advice whenever I work on ladders or roofs—whenever I am moving about and stop thinking about being up high, I force myself to remember, I stop and say aloud, "Don't get comfortable."

18   Charley Best would not have told his own story either. Perhaps that's why others told the story for him. My father claims he grew mean and that his father did not like Best, not because he threw men off trains but because he shot a twelve-year-old boy in the back for stealing coal from the railyard at night. The boy, a homeless child the railroad workers called Hard Rock Pete, hung around the railyards, and the gandy dancers and switch operators often shared their lunches with him, casually adopting him. My grandfather said he was shy and weak, and they all assumed he slept in abandoned work shacks or boxcars in the yard. Best, my grandfather claimed, saw the boy at night, stooping over and pulling lumps of coal into a shirt hooped to make a sack. Best claimed at the investigation that he couldn't tell it was Hard Rock Pete—the boy was tall and wore bulky clothes that late fall evening, hiding his frail frame. When he stood up and lit a cigarette, Best saw him, and when the detective's menacing voiced called out, the boy ran. That's when Charley Best shot him with the big Colt.

19   But that's not the story of Charley Best my father often tells; that's another story, or actually part of the longer version of the story, because it shows how mean Best got afterward, how what happened changed him. I remember once my father was telling the story at my grandmother Harnish's house, a gathering of men in his mother-in-law's parlor listening,

among them Sam, her second husband, who in the last year had been forced to sit on the couch with an oxygen tank beside him, alternately reaching for the hose and mask to give him the oxygen black lung denied him and bending over, panting with effort, to spit tobacco juice into a plastic bucket.

My father began telling the story sitting down, but was standing by 20 the time he began describing Best, the Harnish men listening closely though they had heard the story before, while I sat watching the story being retold as I leaned forward in the straight-backed chair moved into the room and parked near the television. I had recently turned thirteen and was splitting my time between the room where adult men sat, talking slowly, and the cousins outside exploring the forty-acre farm I had already mapped over the years of visits. Sam's son Warren had finally finished a long-winded story that made my father edgy and restless, and how he had managed to get to the story of Charley Best I'm not sure, but the story was well under way.

Best had been assigned jurisdiction, lacking any other police, over sev- 21 eral mining camps in northwestern Pennsylvania, and was sent to arrest a miner in Chickasaw, near the New York border, who was accused of stealing. My father added that he probably only had stolen coal from the railyard, as everyone did in the 1930s. Warren interrupted briefly to tell how he and his brothers stole coal from the Clarion yards, but my father skillfully steered the conversation back to Best.

"Chickasaw was a rough mining camp, just up the river from Mahon- 22 ing, and Charley Best was sent there, where there was no other law, to arrest that miner," he began again, and everyone leaned comfortably back into the story, glad Warren had been stopped. He explained how Best arrived in town, Colt revolver displayed prominently, cigar under his ample mustache, and how he walked over to the tavern, a slapped-up, long and low shed affair, where he assumed he would find the thief. The men inside sat on rough stools, and the ceiling of plank was held up with twelve-inch rough-cut beams. "One of them eyes Best, and Best figured that was him and that he'd have to slug it out with the miner to take him." My father's eyes grew narrow and menacing.

I'd heard this story many times and knew the men in the room had 23 heard it too; they were sitting through the telling as though it were a ritual, a stage in their conversation they always reached, and passed. But then an unexpected reaction from Sam drew their attention from my father, who was perched on his knees at the end of the story. Sam did not speak much in those last years because speech was breath, and each breath was bought with larger portions of his strength. Yet there in the room filled with his sons and the husbands of his daughters, he pushed out a hurried "Yes," and quickly drawing on the oxygen as the heads of the men turned to him, added, "I drove those miners to Chickasaw every day in an old buckboard—they were usually drunk. A rough, wild bunch," he said, spitting a brown stream and reaching for the hose again. "Yes, that's how it happened."

24   My father never worked in the mines, so was spared the black lung from which Sam and so many others suffered, but he often spoke of the mines as though he had worked there, as he had lived among the miners, played with their children, fought with their sons, and eventually drunk and laughed with them after work on the power lines. In his father's day the miners began forming unions, and these hardened men formed even harder coal-black clumps of strikers. One of them, Piercy MacIntyre, was an organizer and therefore was even rougher than most. The bosses in Chickasaw claimed he had been sent in from the outside, an agitator, but some of the men said he came from around Blue Jay Ridge, from a hill farm so far back "the owls carried knapsacks."

25   My father had met Piercy MacIntyre, but he knew his son Jackie better. The miners said Piercy had been a boxer in France during World War I, and whether true or not, he did teach his son Jackie how to box. He'd take the boy, eight or nine years old, down to Walker's store, and men would clear a makeshift ring in the corner, moving stock to form a rough square. Walker would then hold the bets as Jackie's opponent, usually an older boy of twelve or so, was announced. My father claims Jackie beat all comers, and my father, younger by two or three years, always rooted for him as fervently as he did for Joe Louis when his father would struggle to pick up Louis's fights through the static on KDKA radio. He tells how Louis knocked out Max Schmeling, the Nazi superman, so quickly that once they got the station in, all they heard was the count to ten.

26   Twenty-five years later, after my father had moved one hundred miles away to work in the mills of Ohio, he ran into Jackie MacIntyre at Republic Steel. He spoke to him, and though Jackie, now John, didn't remember him as one of his youngest fans among the dozens or more who had watched him fight as a kid, my father said they talked briefly of people they knew, even about Charley Best. My father said he was puzzled to see how the guys in the mill picked on him, and MacIntyre didn't seem to care. My father thought, "You guys don't know who you're dealing with."

27   Although my father had moved to the edge of the industrial Midwest, the mountains and forests remained home to him, and we went back every weekend to visit. And he hunted in Pennsylvania, not along the industrial riverbanks of Ohio. My father liked only two sports, boxing and hunting, and he tried to teach me both. I never caught on to boxing, partly because my father couldn't coach me while we sparred without beginning to fight in earnest, burying me in a flurry of open-palmed combinations and jabs. I liked the fluidity of the movements, the backpedaling, the duck-and-jab; however, I was not destined to be a boxer. I have a glass jaw, a nerve positioned in my face that makes a knockout a matter of one punch. My father

found this fatal flaw one day while we sparred in the living room. One quick jab to my left jaw and I felt nothing—I saw pinpoints of light and awoke to my father shaking his head and saying, "The kid's got a glass jaw." As a boxer I was finished.

But hunting was another matter. Early on, my father declared I was a 28 natural good shot, that I had a "good eye" that made up, I suppose, for my bad jaw. I cold pick off pennies at twenty-five yards with a .22 caliber rifle, and after I got a shotgun, a 16-gauge, my father spent one long afternoon throwing clay pigeons, which I shot out of the air. He threw more than seventy, and I missed two. I enjoyed target shooting not only because I was good at it but because I did it without thinking. I simply knew when I was on target and then pulled the trigger. I guess it was instinct or something reflexive.

Yet, by age eighteen, I had pretty much lost interest in hunting. Ani- 29 mals made poor targets; they were hard to find, but when found, too big and easy. For a target shooter, walking all day for one shot at an easy target was not much of a thrill. I still went hunting with my father when in my teens, but I had no real enthusiasm for the sport, as he did. I tried to find it; I remember not eating one day, thinking that it would make me a keener hunter, but it only made me a hungry one. What I liked was the evening, getting comfortable down at Archie's camp, near his stone fireplace, listening to hunting stories.

The last time I went hunting with my father I was eighteen. I hadn't 30 been deer hunting that last fall because the season fell during final exam week at college, and it was with some relief that I realized this would happen every year. However, I went hunting for turkey that spring. I think I liked turkey hunting most because the hunt occurred in midautumn and midspring, the two most beautiful times of the year to be in the forest. You also could go deeper into the woods because, unlike a deer, once a turkey was shot it was not hard to pull it out of the woods. Dragging a hundred pounds of deer carcass over several miles of rough terrain quickly dampened the thrill of the hunt.

It was a cold April in the mountains that year; patches of snow still 31 clung to rocks and roots in the forest, and springs remained frozen, even in the bright sunshine. My father led the way through the woods we hunted north of Brookville, stepping around the icy stones and fallen limbs with sure-footed grace and speed. Every hour or so we would stop and cradle our shotguns, and my father would bring out the wooden turkey call, a cedar box with a top that wagged loosely when shaken, chalk between box and lid giving off a decent gobble.

The turkey call was a new addition to our hunting gear. My father had 32 never gone in for gimmicks as a hunter, although he thought my aunt Clair's trick of rubbing apple cores on her boots to attract deer might account for her yearly success. However, in the over twenty-five years he had been hunting, he had never bagged a wild turkey. He was well known among the locals for regularly bringing out a deer. He'd have a deer within the first couple of hours of the opening day of the season and could be found down at Archie's camp or at the Sigel Hotel by early afternoon, telling how the deer, never a trophy buck but respectable, would have risen from his bed twenty-five yards from my father's stand at first light. But turkeys had always eluded him, so he bought the call and had been practicing for months, brief chirps and throaty gobbles rising from our basement ever since September.

33      That day we had walked farther into the woods than usual, so far that we found ourselves on Windfall Ridge, or so it was called on my father's topo map. The ridge was steep and treeless, and the North Fork Creek ran noisily below. My father had noticed a stand of beech, and knowing turkey like beechnuts, we had stopped to look for signs. Sure enough, my father found a large patch where turkey had been scratching the winter-decayed leaves, a large flock probably discovered and broken up by other hunters earlier in the morning. The turkeys would still be in the area, scattered over Windfall, calling out to regroup. We stood and listened, but all I heard was the icy North Fork and a high wind in the trees.

34      So my father decided to try calling them in, making first a few hesitant chirps, then a long and short gobble that he'd heard was the turkey equivalent of "I'm over here."

35      And a turkey answered. The bird sounded like it was on the edge of the ridge, about fifty yards in front of us, but neither of us could see it. We walked cautiously toward the sound, my heart pounding for my father, hoping he'd at long last get a shot at the turkey. As we reached the ridge we split, my father wandering to the right of a tall pine growing in the fragile earth of the rim of the ridge, I to the left. The turkey flew out of the tree in a great bluster of wings. It flew left and was clearly my shot.

36      I snapped up my shotgun and found him quickly, flying high but in range. Then I thought about it. I wished the bird had flown right, to give my father the shot, wished it was not flying over the icy-filmed North Fork into which I would surely have to wade, waist high, to retrieve the bird. And I knew I did not want to kill the turkey; I had no need of it.

37      So I shot behind it, the bird's wings flapping comically faster after the sound echoed over the ridge. The turkey flew higher, out of range of another shot from me or my father, not landing until it reached the next ridge. I turned to look at my father, who said, "How'd you miss him?"

38      "Jerked the trigger, I think," I said, still looking over at the ridge where the bird had disappeared. "Or I choked; I don't know," I added.

39      "Hell, a good shot like you must have hit him," he said. "Maybe he went down with a few shot in him."

"Nah, he was too high up, out of range," I answered, not wanting to 40 have to wade the creek anyway and hike the next ridge looking for the bird.

But we did cross the creek, over the back of a windfallen tree, and af- 41 ter searching for the bird for a while decided we had had our shot for the day and gave up. It was midafternoon, and it was a long way back, and I, having slipped into the North Fork on the return crossing, wearily tramped behind my father, one boot sloshing with creek water.

By the time we arrived at the Sigel Hotel my father was convinced I 42 had hit the gobbler but that, as he said, "death is invisible, while life can be seen." A slain animal is still, and the natural camouflage is perfect. He believed we didn't find a dead turkey because it blended in with the rocks and undergrowth.

At the Sigel Hotel we sat at the long bar, adding our hunting outfits 43 of red wool caps and canvas game vests to those of other hunters gathered there. My father began telling the story of our hunt to the man at his right elbow, and eventually to two or three down the counter. "The boy here got a shot, and I know he hit him—you should have seen the feathers fly! This kid is a great wingshot," he continued, telling of my slaughter of clay pigeons.

The other men answered his story with others, and through that, 44 through the progress of stories to the next, he began telling the story of Charley Best. "He walked into this bar, a smoky place with a low ceiling supported by big, twelve-inch rough-cut posts," he said, his hands surrounding one in the air, "rough like everything else in those camps."

Best looked around the smoky room, and when he spotted the man 45 eyeing him he said, "You'd better finish that drink, because you're coming with me. You're under arrest."

The man sat with his stool tipped backward against a post, and when 46 Best approached he said, "Well, I guess you're going to have to pull that big revolver, because I'm not going anywhere." Best was standing over him, and my father was on his feet in the Sigel Hotel, doing his best to look down at me as Best must have glared at the miner.

Then my father said, "The guy suddenly pulls a knife, cuts Best across 47 the gut, and slips behind the thick post." My father's knees buckle.

Best was not used to working in the camps, so he was out of his ele- 48 ment and forgot to watch himself. He was too comfortable, my father would say, and should have reminded himself that Chickasaw was a rough mining camp and that the man he sought could be armed and was drunk, that he was not simply approaching a frightened hobo on top of a rushing train. At this point my father's voice became a little squeezed, imitating the pain of the knife wound, but he continued, "He cut Best clear across the stomach, and his guts bulged and began to spill. With his left arm Best reached down and pulled his own guts back in, and with the right drew his gun and shot the miner." My father was fully on his knees now, his arm and hand holding in intestines, his other arm raising a Colt revolver.

49     "He hit him in the mouth. Killed him deader than hell."

50     This is where the story of Charley Best generally ends, though sometimes my father tells how they took him by train to a hospital in Brookville, how he got mean after that. But with my father on his knees, clutching his stomach in agony, this is when Charley Best appeared, or should have. He could have been a little fellow, age having shrunken him, a glass of clay-colored liquor in front of him at the bar, his mustache trimmed to a salt-and-pepper line under his nose. He'd sit near the opposite end of the counter, listening to but not telling his own story.

51     Best wouldn't wear hunting clothes. He'd stand up and, pulling out his flannel shirttails, say, "That's just the way it happened." Then he'd raise his shirt quickly, and we'd see the brutish pucker circling his waist. When Best sat back down he would drain the liquor in front of him, no one noticing that his left arm rested across his lap and against his body, holding the organs in, still trying to get comfortable with the wound.

*1996*

## QUESTIONS FOR DISCUSSION

### Content

a. In paragraph 3, the author tells us that in 1934 his grandfather was lucky to have a job. To what circumstances or period is he referring?

b. What does Charley Best's story have in common with other stories in this essay?

c. In what way was Charley Best similar to the author's grandfather and great-grandfather and their contemporaries? Begin your answer by referring to paragraph 5.

d. The narrator tells us a great deal about his father, grandfather, and great-grandfather. Explain what he also reveals about his own character.

e. Discuss the relationship that the narrator had with his father.

f. Does Charley Best really appear in the Sigel Hotel? Why does the author suggest that he does?

g. The thesis of this essay is expressed concisely in its three-word title. Citing details from the text, expand on that statement by explaining Leslie's point and purpose in this essay.

## Strategy and Style

h. Why does the author tell about his and his father's falling from heights? How do these stories help the reader understand Charley Best? How do they help develop the essay's thesis?

i. The introduction and conclusion of this essay seem to reflect some uncertainty. Explain how and why the author expresses that uncertainty.

j. "Don't Get Comfortable" uses an introduction different from those found in other selections of this type. The essay begins by mentioning Charley Best and then quickly moves to stories about the author's father and grandfather before returning to Best in paragraph 5. What is it about the first four paragraphs that holds our attention?

k. Unlike the other narratives in this chapter, "Don't Get Comfortable" does not follow a conventional plot line (events proceeding from beginning to end without interruption). The story of Charley Best is interrupted several times with other interesting tales, which apparently have nothing to do with it. Take a few minutes to outline the plot of this story; then explain why the author has inserted these tales.

l. Where does the author use humor? What function does it serve in this essay?

m. In what way is the structure of this essay (not its contents) reflective of its title and thesis?

n. What does the author's tone reveal about the audience for this essay?

## ENGAGING THE TEXT

a. Explain the title. What does it mean to not get comfortable? Why should we not get comfortable?

b. Compare the plot, purpose, or tone of "Don't Get Comfortable" with David Quammen's "Alias Benowitz Shoe Repair" in Chapter 2 or Sam Pickering's "Faith of the Father" in Chapter 4. In what ways are the essays similar? In what ways are they different?

## SUGGESTIONS FOR SUSTAINED WRITING

a. Using your own experiences and/or the experiences of people you know well, write an essay that develops the same thesis as Leslie's "Don't Get Comfortable." You might choose a number of short tales or anecdotes to illustrate your thesis, or you might tell one longer story in full. Either way, make sure that all the details that you include relate directly to your thesis. Finally, state the thesis in an introduction that, like Leslie's, captures and holds the reader's attention.

b. Write an essay that compares (points out similarities between) this selection and the content or structure of Pickering's "Faith of the Father" (Chapter 4) and Sanders's "The Men We Carry in Our Minds" (Chapter 6).

c. Narrate an exciting, frightening, or tragic event in the history of your community, state, or country. Focus on a specific incident. For example, you might recall the Johnstown (Pennsylvania) Flood of 1889, the San Francisco earthquake in 1989, a specific event during the Holocaust, the World Trade Center terrorist bombing, the Oklahoma City bombing, Hurricane Hugo (or another major storm), or even a military operation. However you choose to approach this assignment, make your story exciting. Try using the kind of language and detail Leslie uses to recreate the incident in which his father and grandfather nearly fell off a railroad bridge or the one in which Charley Best was knifed by a miner. In addition, make sure to include research on the incident from library or Internet sources.

Chapter

# Description

Description makes for diversity. The people, places, and things described in the six selections that follow vary as widely as the distinctive styles and perspectives of their authors. Nonetheless, each essay is a portrait sketched in details that are at once concrete, specific, and vivid.

Good description is never hurried; it is crafted with carefully chosen details that *show* the reader something. Take "The Way to Rainy Mountain," for example, in which N. Scott Momaday paints a vivid picture of the harshness of nature:

> The hardest weather in the world is there. Winter brings blizzards, hot tornadic winds arise in the spring, and in summer the prairie is an anvil's edge. The grass turns brittle and brown, and it cracks between your feet. . . . At a distance in July or August the steaming foliage seems almost to write in fire. Great green-and-yellow grasshoppers are everywhere in the tall grass, popping up like corn to sting the flesh. . . .

Appealing to the senses—in this case sight, hearing, and touch—is fundamental to the process of describing. Some writers rely almost solely on vision and hearing as sources of descriptive detail, but the authors in this chapter teach us that we can use the other senses as well—taste, smell, and touch—to guide readers through our private worlds. Perhaps one of the best examples appears in E. B. White's "Once More to the Lake":

> . . . I remembered clearest of all the early mornings, when the lake was cool and motionless, remembered how the bedroom smelled of the lumber it was made of and of the wet woods whose scent entered through the screen. The partitions in the camp were thin and did not extend clear to the top of the rooms, and as I was always the first up I would dress softly so as not to wake the others, and sneak out into the sweet outdoors and start out in the canoe, keeping close along the shore in the long shadows of the pines. I remembered being very careful never to rub my paddle against the gunwale for fear of disturbing the stillness of the cathedral.

The excerpt from "The Way to Rainy Mountain" above also shows that writers of description exploit techniques often associated with narration, especially the use of verbs that are informative and evocative. More important, Momaday's use of figurative language—"the prairie is an anvil's edge," for example—reminds us that invoking facts and images from the knowledge we share with readers is a good way to show them something new. But flashes of brilliance appear throughout the chapter. Virginia

Woolf's reference to the "narrow and intricate corridors" of her brain, for example, and James Baldwin's reminder that the residents of the ghetto "must struggle stolidly, incessantly, to keep [a] sense [of honor] alive in themselves in spite of the insults, the indifference, and the cruelty they are certain to encounter in their working day" testify to the power and clarity with which they invest their writing.

While relying heavily on physical description, none of the essays collected here is a purely sensate record of its subject. More often than not, describing is a means to an end. It is hard to read a narrative, for example, without stumbling over details that reveal setting and character. Even writers of scientific prose use information that appeals to the senses as a way to discuss the lives of plants and animals or to explore the workings of machines and processes.

Like the other writers in this chapter, Joan Didion and N. Scott Momaday remind us that discussing the people who inhabit a place is a way to reveal its soul. David Quammen, on the other hand, describes the natural splendor of the Rockies to help reveal the passion and energy of a man who is determined to save it. Finally, in recalling the death of a moth Virginia Woolf engages a seemingly banal subject not simply to describe an exterior reality but to tell us about herself, the real subject of her essay. Of course, something of this can also be said of Momaday and White.

As always, you are invited to make your own comparisons and to draw conclusions as you see fit. What makes the selections in this chapter so enjoyable is that each reveals the strong and distinctive voice of its author. Enjoy the artists behind the subjects they describe. They will teach you that your personal commitment to a subject—the "wonder" with which it fills you, Woolf might say—is worth sharing with others.

# Fifth Avenue, Uptown

## James Baldwin

*James Baldwin (1924–1987) was born in Harlem. In 1927 his mother married David Baldwin, a minister who had moved to New York from New Orleans and who preached in a storefront church. With both of his parents working, James became the caretaker of his eight siblings and balanced his time between tending to them and going to school. His teachers at DeWitt Clinton High School encouraged his literary talent, and he began writing poems, stories, plays, and essays while editing the school's literary magazine. At age 14 he had a religious awakening and began preaching, becoming increasingly popular while his stepfather's congregation decreased. But his religious calling was short-lived, and Baldwin, becoming disillusioned with Christianity, stopped preaching after three years. In 1942 he moved to New Jersey but returned to New York a year later when his father was dying. After his father's death, he moved to Greenwich Village to focus on his literary career; after five difficult years he published his first work in 1947, book reviews for the* Nation *and the* New Leader. *In 1948 he received a fellowship and left the United States to live in France. There he wrote his most famous works:* Go Tell It on the Mountain *(1953), a novel about a boy's religious awakenings;* Giovanni's Room *(1956), a novel about a young homosexual man living in Paris; and* Notes of a Native Son *(1955), a nonfiction work about racism in American society. In 1957 he returned to the United States and became active in the civil rights movement, publishing* Another Country *(1962) and* The Fire Next Time *(1963). His other works include novels, nonfiction, essays, and plays. Disillusioned by the assassinations of Martin Luther King, Jr., and Malcolm X, he returned to France, where he spent the rest of his life.*

*The title of this selection is somewhat ironic. Baldwin plays on the fact that "Fifth Avenue" normally is associated with lives of wealth and luxury. The same connotation is often applied to the word* uptown. *However, the area Baldwin describes is very different; it is the inner city, Harlem to be exact. Thus, even the title of the essay prepares us for the rather well-honed edge that the author imparts to this account of his neighborhood, and we learn that this essay is more than simply a verbal photograph of a place. It is the character of this place and its people—perhaps the soul of an inner city—that is being revealed here.*

There is a housing project standing now where the house in which we grew up once stood, and one of those stunted city trees is snarling where our doorway used to be. This is on the rehabilitated side of the avenue. The other side of the avenue—for progress takes time—has not been rehabilitated yet and it looks exactly as it looked in the days when we sat with our noses pressed against the windowpane, longing to be allowed to go "across the street." The grocery store which gave us credit is still there, and there can be no doubt that it is still giving credit. The people in the project certainly need it—far more, indeed, than they ever needed the project. The last time I passed by, the Jewish proprietor was still standing among his shelves, looking sadder and heavier but scarcely any older. Farther down the block stands the shoe-repair store in which our shoes were repaired until reparation became impossible and in which, then, we bought all our "new" ones. The Negro proprietor is still in the window, head down, working at the leather. 1

These two, I imagine, could tell a long tale if they would (perhaps they would be glad to if they could), having watched so many, for so long, struggling in the fishhooks, the barbed wire, of this avenue. 2

The avenue is elsewhere the renowned and elegant Fifth. The area I am describing, which, in today's gang parlance, would be called "the turf," is bounded by Lenox Avenue on the west, the Harlem River on the east, 135th Street on the north, and 130th Street on the south. We never lived beyond these boundaries; this is where we grew up. Walking along 145th Street—for example—familiar as it is, and similar, does not have the same impact because I do not know any of the people on the block. But when I turn east on 131st Street and Lenox Avenue, there is first a soda-pop joint, then a shoeshine "parlor," then a grocery store, then a dry cleaners', then 3 the houses. All along the street there are people who watched me grow up, people who grew up with me, people I watched grow up along with my brothers and sisters; and, sometimes in my arms, sometimes underfoot, sometimes at my shoulder—or on it—their children, a riot, a forest of children, who include my nieces and nephews.

4      When we reach the end of this long block, we find ourselves on wide, filthy, hostile Fifth Avenue, facing that project which hangs over the avenue like a monument to the folly, and the cowardice, of good intentions. All along the block, for anyone who knows it, are immense human gaps, like craters. These gaps are not created merely by those who have moved away, inevitably into some other ghetto; or by those who have risen, almost always into a greater capacity for self-loathing and self-delusion; or yet by those who, by whatever means—World War II, the Korean war, a policeman's gun or billy, a gang war, a brawl, madness, an overdose of heroin, or, simply, unnatural exhaustion—are dead. I am talking about those who are left, and I am talking principally about the young. What are they doing? Well, some, a minority, are fanatical churchgoers, members of the more extreme of the Holy Roller sects. Many, many more are "moslems," by affiliation or sympathy, that is to say that they are united by nothing more—and nothing less—than a hatred of the white world and all its works. They are present, for example, at every Buy Black streetcorner meeting—meetings in which the speaker urges his hearers to cease trading with white men and establish a separate economy. Neither the speaker nor his hearers can possibly do this, of course, since Negroes do not own General Motors or RCA or the A & P, nor, indeed, do they own more than a wholly insufficient fraction of anything else in Harlem (those who *do* own anything are more interested in their profits than in their fellows). But these meetings nevertheless keep alive in the participators a certain pride of bitterness without which, however futile this bitterness may be, they could scarcely remain alive at all. Many have given up. They stay home and watch the TV screen, living on the earnings of their parents, cousins, brothers, or uncles, and only leave the house to go to the movies or to the nearest bar. "How're you making it?" one may ask, running into them along the block, or in the bar. "Oh, I'm TV-ing it"; with the saddest, sweetest, most shamefaced of smiles, and from a great distance. This distance one is compelled to respect; anyone who has traveled so far will not easily be dragged again into the world. There are further retreats, of course, than the TV screen or the bar. There are those who are simply sitting on their stoops, "stoned," animated for a moment only, and hideously, by the approach of someone who may lend them the money for a "fix." Or by the approach of someone from whom they can purchase it, one of the shrewd ones, on the way to prison or just coming out.

5      And the others, who have avoided all of these deaths, get up in the morning and go downtown to meet "the man." They work in the white

man's world all day and come home in the evening to this fetid block. They struggle to instill in their children some private sense of honor or dignity which will help the child to survive. This means, of course, that they must struggle, stolidly, incessantly, to keep this sense alive in themselves, in spite of the insults, the indifference, and the cruelty they are certain to encounter in their working day. They patiently browbeat the landlord into fixing the heat, the plaster, the plumbing; this demands prodigious patience; nor is patience usually enough. In trying to make their hovels habitable, they are perpetually throwing good money after bad. Such frustration, so long endured, is driving many strong, admirable men and women whose only crime is color to the very gates of paranoia.

One remembers them from another time—playing handball in the 6 playground, going to church, wondering if they were going to be promoted at school. One remembers them going off to war—gladly, to escape this block. One remembers their return. Perhaps one remembers their wedding day. And one sees where the girl is now—vainly looking for salvation from some other embittered, trussed, and struggling boy—and sees the all-but-abandoned children in the streets.

*1958*

## QUESTIONS FOR DISCUSSION

### Content

a. What is the image of Harlem that Baldwin creates in your mind? How does that image mesh with or conflict with other images you may have of Harlem?
b. What do the metaphors "fishhooks" and "barbed wire" in paragraph 2 mean? What other metaphors would make the same point?
c. How does Baldwin feel about Harlem? Where in the essay is this feeling revealed?
d. What are the main landmarks along the way? What does Baldwin see as significant about each one?
e. Why have many of the people in Harlem "given up"?
f. Why does Baldwin choose Fifth Avenue as the street to describe?

## STRATEGY AND STYLE

g. Besides the fishhooks and barbed wire metaphors in paragraph 2, what other metaphors does Baldwin use, and why?

h. This essay is from a book written in the 1950s. What do you find in the sentence style or word choice that recalls that time?
i. This is an excerpt from a longer work. From what this essay leads you to expect, what does Baldwin most likely describe immediately before and after the piece? What about this piece sets up those expectations?
j. How does Baldwin sequence this essay? In what order does he take us along this street in Harlem?
k. Baldwin uses a literary tone—calm, dispassionate, evenly paced. What sentences and words in particular create this tone?

## ENGAGING THE TEXT

a. Rewrite a paragraph or short passage from Baldwin's essay to create a different tone, such as one of excitement, anger, romance, or nostalgia. Keep a list of the words you remove from Baldwin and explain, in writing, why you changed those words.
b. Summarize "Fifth Avenue, Uptown," as it is described in this essay.

## SUGGESTIONS FOR SUSTAINED WRITING

a. Reread paragraph 5, where Baldwin reveals much about the struggles of the inhabitants of his former neighborhood. Then, using this paragraph as a point of reference, write an extended description that uses sensory details to explain the problems faced by people living in inner-city apartments. For example, you might use details associated with sight, sound, smell, and touch to expand upon Baldwin's statement, "In trying to make their hovels habitable, they are perpetually throwing good money after bad." Rely on what you have learned about poverty from the media or from your own observations to provide information. You might also read Jo Goodwin Parker's "What Is Poverty?" (Chapter 4) and Jonathan Kozol's "Distancing the Homeless" (Chapter 11) for additional information and insights.
b. Compare or contrast the picture of poverty in this essay with what you see in two other pieces in this text: James Weldon Johnson's "Travelling South" (Chapter 1) and Parker's "What Is Poverty?" (Chapter 4). Make sure to consider the setting and the people the authors describe, but also comment on their use of narrative and especially tone.
c. Research Baldwin's life. (The brief biographical headnote provided here does not begin to describe the author's interesting life.) Write a biographical essay, focusing on the aspect of his life you find most significant. Include at least four secondary sources from your library or the Internet.

# The Death of the Moth

Virginia Woolf

*The daughter of the British essayist and scholar Leslie Stephen, Virginia Woolf (1882–1941) was at the center of the Bloomsbury Group, a circle that included Lytton Strachey and John Maynard Keynes as well as several other important intellectuals, poets, and artists. With her husband, Leonard, Woolf founded the Hogarth Press and published the work of brilliant young writers such as T. S. Eliot and E. M. Forster. Her fiction is important because of her experimentation with the stream-of-consciousness technique and her ability to expose the psychology of her characters in a way that is at once subtle and vivid. Among her most memorable novels are* Mrs. Dalloway *(1925),* To the Lighthouse *(1927),* Orlando *(1928), and* The Waves *(1931). Her nonfiction works include* A Room of One's Own *(1929) and* The Death of the Moth *(1942).*

*The following selection has been interpreted in many ways, but it is clear that Woolf is talking about more than the death of an insect. Indeed, several analogies have been suggested, including one that sees this essay as a statement of feminist ideology. In any event, it is clear that Woolf sees the life force as a common thread among creatures and that she may in fact be grieving over her own mortality.*

Moths that fly by day are not properly to be called moths; they do not excite that pleasant sense of dark autumn nights and ivy-blossom which the commonest yellow-underwing asleep in the shadow of the curtain never fails to rouse in us. They are hybrid creatures, neither gay like butterflies nor sombre like their own species. Nevertheless the present specimen, with his narrow hay-coloured wings, fringed with a tassel of the same colour, seemed to be content with life. It was a pleasant morning, mid-September, mild, benignant, yet with a keener breath than that of the summer months. The plough was already scoring the field opposite the window, and where the share had been, the earth was pressed flat and gleamed with moisture. Such vigour came rolling in from the fields and the down beyond that it was difficult to keep the eyes strictly turned upon the book. The rooks too were keeping one of their annual festivities; soaring round the tree tops until it looked as if a vast net with thousands of black knots in it had been cast up into the air; which, after a few moments sank slowly down upon the trees until every twig seemed to have a knot at the end of it. Then, suddenly, the net would be thrown into the air again in a wider circle this time, with the utmost clamour and vociferation, as though to be thrown into the air and settle slowly down upon the tree tops were a tremendously exciting experience.

The same energy which inspired the rooks, the ploughmen, the horses, and even, it seemed, the lean bare-backed downs, sent the moth fluttering from side to side of his square of the windowpane. One could not help watching him. One was, indeed, conscious of a queer feeling of pity for

him. The possibilities of pleasure seemed that morning so enormous and
so various that to have only a moth's part in life, and a day moth's at that,
appeared a hard fate, and his zest in enjoying his meagre opportunities to
the full, pathetic. He flew vigorously to one corner of his compartment,
and, after waiting there a second, flew across to the other. What remained
for him but to fly to a third corner and then to a fourth? That was all he
could do, in spite of the size of the downs, the width of the sky, the far-off
smoke of houses, and the romantic voice, now and then, of a steamer out
at sea. What he could do he did. Watching him, it seemed as if a fibre, very
thin but pure, of the enormous energy of the world had been thrust into
his frail and diminutive body. As often as he crossed the pane, I could
fancy that a thread of vital light became visible. He was little or nothing
but life.

3        Yet, because he was so small, and so simple a form of the energy that
was rolling in at the open window and driving its way through so many
narrow and intricate corridors in my own brain and in those of other human beings, there was something marvellous as well as pathetic about
him. It was as if someone had taken a tiny bead of pure life and decking it
as lightly as possible with down and feathers, had set it dancing and zig-
zagging to show us the true nature of life. Thus displayed one could not
get over the strangeness of it. One is apt to forget all about life, seeing it
humped and bossed and garnished and cumbered so that it has to move
with the greatest circumspection and dignity. Again, the thought of all that
life might have been had he been born in any other shape caused one to
view his simple activities with a kind of pity.

4        After a time, tired by his dancing apparently, he settled on the window
ledge in the sun, and, the queer spectacle being at an end, I forgot about
him. Then, looking up, my eye was caught by him. He was trying to re-
sume his dancing, but seemed either so stiff or so awkward that he could
only flutter to the bottom of the windowpane; and when he tried to fly
across it he failed. Being intent on other matters I watched these futile attempts for a time without thinking, unconsciously waiting for him to re-
sume his flight, as one waits for a machine, that has stopped momentarily,
to start again without considering the reason of its failure. After perhaps a
seventh attempt he slipped from the wooden ledge and fell, fluttering his
wings, on to his back on the window sill. The helplessness of his attitude
roused me. It flashed upon me that he was in difficulties; he could no
longer raise himself; his legs struggled vainly. But, as I stretched out a pencil, meaning to help him to right himself, it came over me that the failure
and awkwardness were the approach of death. I laid the pencil down
again.

5        The legs agitated themselves once more. I looked as if for the enemy
against which he struggled. I looked out of doors. What had happened
there? Presumably it was midday, and work in the fields had stopped.

Stillness and quiet had replaced the previous animation. The birds had taken themselves off to feed in the brooks. The horses stood still. Yet the power was there all the same, massed outside, indifferent, impersonal, not attending to anything in particular. Somehow it was opposed to the little hay-coloured moth. It was useless to try to do anything. One could only watch the extraordinary efforts made by those tiny legs against an oncoming doom which could, had it chosen, have submerged an entire city, not merely a city, but masses of human beings; nothing, I knew, had any chance against death. Nevertheless after a pause of exhaustion the legs fluttered again. It was superb this last protest, and so frantic that he succeeded at last in righting himself. One's sympathies, of course, were all on the side of life. Also, when there was nobody to care or to know, this gigantic effort on the part of an insignificant little moth, against a power of such magnitude, to retain what no one else valued or desired to keep, moved one strangely. Again, somehow, one saw life, a pure bead. I lifted the pencil again, useless though I knew it to be. But even as I did so, the unmistakable tokens of death showed themselves. The body relaxed, and instantly grew stiff. The struggle was over. The insignificant little creature now knew death. As I looked at the dead moth, this minute wayside triumph of so great a force over so mean an antagonist filled me with wonder. Just as life had been strange a few minutes before, so death was now as strange. The moth having righted himself now lay most decently and uncomplainingly composed. O yes, he seemed to say, death is stronger than I am.

*1942*

## QUESTIONS FOR DISCUSSION

### Content

a. Woolf's essay is obviously a serious discussion of the inevitability of death. Why does she rely on the death of so inconsequential a creature to convey her impressions? Why did she not describe the death of a human being instead?

b. To what is Woolf referring in paragraph 2 when she says, "The same energy which inspired the rooks, the ploughmen, the horses . . . sent the moth fluttering . . ."?

c. In the same paragraph, Woolf indicates that the moth was "little or nothing but life." Yet, by paragraph 5, the insect has died. Did the same power that gave him life strike him down?

d. What connection does Woolf draw between the moth and the world of living things outside her window? Why is it appropriate that the moth die at midday?

## STRATEGY AND STYLE

e. Throughout the first three paragraphs, Woolf refers to herself in the third person ("one"). In paragraphs 4 and 5, however, she uses the more familiar first-person pronoun ("I"). Does this change indicate a change in tone?
f. What other differences do you notice between the first three paragraphs and the last two in regard to both content and rhetorical strategy?
g. At the end of paragraph 1, Woolf uses an extended metaphor. What other interesting uses of figurative language can you identify?

## ENGAGING THE TEXT

a. Why is a moth's death a significant topic for an essay, especially a philosophical essay such as this one? Explain, referring to Woolf's essay.
b. Study Woolf's opening paragraph, looking at the way she structures each sentence, the way she uses punctuation, and the subject matter of each sentence. Then, focusing on an animal other than a moth, write an opening paragraph of your own in Woolf's style.

## SUGGESTIONS FOR SUSTAINED WRITING

a. Woolf's perspective on the death of the moth is, for the most part, subjective. As such, it is a perfect example of the extent to which our personal vision of the world can color our perceptions of natural objects and events. Spend some time observing the night sky, a field of corn in autumn, a newborn calf, the backyard outside your bedroom window, a potted geranium, or another natural subject. Write two short essays about it. In the first, be objective. Describe things accurately and scientifically. Use factual details only and make reference to exact sizes, shapes, and colors. In the second, flex the muscles of your imagination by writing a subjective description. Let your emotions color your perceptions. If possible, use metaphors and other figures of speech to convey your personal impressions of the subject.
b. One of the subthemes of this essay has to do with the fragility of life. Other essays in this text touch on this issue as well; among them is Orwell's "A Hanging" (Chapter 1). Write an essay in which you compare

and contrast these essays in terms of the ways they approach this question. Make sure to address style and strategy as well as content.

c. Woolf proves that even a creature as insignificant as a moth is an appropriate subject for an essay that explores significant human questions. Consider a much more advanced form of animal life such as a chimpanzee, a lion, a wolf, or even a dog. Research this animal in your college library and/or on the Internet in preparation for the writing of a paper that draws similarities between the instincts, habits, behavior, and/or social structure of this species and those of human beings.

# The Way to Rainy Mountain

## N. Scott Momaday

*Half Kiowan and part Cherokee, N. Scott Momaday (b. 1934) was born in Lawton, Oklahoma, and grew up on Navajo, Apache, and Pueblo reservations in northern New Mexico. However, his writing also owes much to the folklore of the Kiowas, who live in Oklahoma. A distinguished writer and a professor of English at Arizona State University, Momaday is also an accomplished painter, photographer, and tribal dancer. His prose, poetry, illustrations, and photographs celebrate the culture of Native Americans and their reverence for the land. Momaday is best known for* The Way to Rainy Mountain *(1969), a book that grew from an autobiographical essay, "The Journey of Tai-me," published two years earlier. But his works are many and varied. In 1968, he won the Pulitzer Prize for* House Made of Dawn, *a novel. He has written two volumes of poetry:* Angle of Geese and Other Poems *(1973) and* The Gourd Dancer *(1976). A second autobiographical work,* The Names: A Memoir, *appeared in 1977. In 1982, he coauthored a pictorial history entitled* American Indian Photographic Images 1868–1931. *Momaday published* In the Presence of the Sun, *a collection of poems and short fiction, in 1992. He is also the author of* The Man Made of Words: Essays, Stories, Passages *(1997).*

*As you read this essay, try to appreciate the skill with which Momaday interweaves the description of a natural space with a discussion of the life and character of his grandmother. Then consider how well he presents this combination against a history of the Kiowas.*

A single knoll rises out of the plain in Oklahoma, north and west of the Wichita Range. For my people, the Kiowas, it is an old landmark, and they gave it the name Rainy Mountain. The hardest weather in the world is there. Winter brings blizzards, hot tornadic winds arise in the spring, and in summer the prairie is an anvil's edge. The grass turns brittle and brown, and it cracks beneath your feet. There are green belts along the rivers and creeks, linear groves of hickory and pecan, willow and witch hazel. At a distance in July or August the steaming foliage seems almost to writhe in fire. Great green-and-yellow grasshoppers are everywhere in the tall grass, popping up like corn to sting the flesh, and tortoises crawl about on the red earth, going nowhere in the plenty of time. Loneliness is an aspect of the land. All things in the plain are isolate; there is no confusion of objects in the eye, but *one* hill or *one* tree or *one* man. To look upon that landscape in the early morning, with the sun at your back, is to lose the sense of proportion. Your imagination comes to life, and this, you think, is where Creation was begun.

2    I returned to Rainy Mountain in July. My grandmother had died in the spring, and I wanted to be at her grave. She had lived to be very old and at last infirm. Her only living daughter was with her when she died, and I was told that in death her face was that of a child.

3    I like to think of her as a child. When she was born, the Kiowas were living that last great moment of their history. For more than a hundred years they had controlled the open range from the Smoky Hill River to the Red, from the headwaters of the Canadian to the fork of the Arkansas and Cimarron. In alliance with the Comanches, they had ruled the whole of the southern Plains. War was their sacred business, and they were among the finest horsemen the world has ever known. But warfare for the Kiowas was preeminently a matter of disposition rather than of survival, and they never understood the grim, unrelenting advance of the U.S. Cavalry. When at last, divided and ill-provisioned, they were driven onto the Staked Plains in the cold rains of autumn, they fell into panic. In Palo Duro Canyon they abandoned their crucial stores to pillage and had nothing then but their lives. In order to save themselves, they surrendered to the soldiers at Fort Sill and were imprisoned in the old stone corral that now stands as a military museum. My grandmother was spared the humiliation of those high gray walls by eight or ten years, but she must have known from birth the affliction of defeat, the dark brooding of old warriors.

4    Her name was Aho, and she belonged to the last culture to evolve in North America. Her forebears came down from the high country in western Montana nearly three centuries ago. They were a mountain people, a mysterious tribe of hunters whose language has never been positively classified in any major group. In the late seventeenth century they began a long migration to the south and east. It was a long journey toward the dawn, and it led to a golden age. Along the way the Kiowas were befriended by the Crows, who gave them the culture and religion of the Plains. They acquired horses, and their ancient nomadic spirit was suddenly free of the ground. They acquired Tai-me, the sacred Sun Dance doll, from that moment the object and symbol of their worship, and so shared in the divinity of the sun. Not least, they acquired the sense of destiny, therefore courage and pride. When they entered upon the southern Plains, they had been transformed. No longer were they slaves to the simple necessity of survival; they were a lordly and dangerous society of fighters

and thieves, hunters and priests of the sun. According to their origin myth, they entered the world through a hollow log. From one point of view, their migration was the fruit of an old prophecy, for indeed they emerged from a sunless world.

Although my grandmother lived out her long life in the shadow of 5 Rainy Mountain, the immense landscape of the continental interior lay like memory in her blood. She could tell of the Crows, whom she had never seen, and of the Black Hills, where she had never been. I wanted to see in reality what she had seen more perfectly in the mind's eye, and traveled fifteen hundred miles to begin my pilgrimage.

Yellowstone, it seemed to me, was the top of the world, a region of 6 deep lakes and dark timber, canyons and waterfalls. But, beautiful as it is, one might have the sense of confinement there. The skyline in all directions is close at hand, the high wall of the woods and deep cleavages of shade. There is a perfect freedom in the mountains, but it belongs to the eagle and the elk, the badger and the bear. The Kiowas reckoned their stature by the distance they could see, and they were bent and blind in the wilderness.

Descending eastward, the highland meadows are a stairway to the 7 plain. In July the inland slope of the Rockies is luxuriant with flax and buckwheat, stonecrop and larkspur. The earth unfolds and the limit of the land recedes. Clusters of trees and animals grazing far in the distance cause the vision to reach away and wonder to build upon the mind. The sun follows a longer course in the day, and the sky is immense beyond all comparison. The great billowing clouds that sail upon it are shadows that move upon the grain like water, dividing light. Farther down, in the land of the Crows and Blackfeet, the plain is yellow. Sweet clover takes hold of the hills and bends upon itself to cover and seal the soil. There the Kiowas paused on their way; they had come to the place where they must change their lives. The sun is at home on the plains. Precisely there does it have the certain character of a god. When the Kiowas came to the land of the Crows, they could see the dark lees of the hills at dawn across the Bighorn River, the profusion of light on the grain shelves, the oldest deity ranging after the solstices. Not yet would they veer southward to the caldron of the land that lay below; they must wean their blood from the northern winter and hold the mountains a while longer in their view. They bore Tai-me in procession to the east.

A dark mist lay over the Black Hills, and the land was like iron. At the 8 top of a ridge I caught sight of Devil's Tower upthrust against the gray sky as if in the birth of time the core of the earth had broken through its crust and the motion of the world was begun. There are things in nature that engender an awful quiet in the heart of man; Devil's Tower is one of them. Two centuries ago, because they could not do otherwise, the Kiowas made a legend at the base of the rock. My grandmother said:

Eight children were there at play, seven sisters and their brother. Suddenly the boy was struck dumb; he trembled and began to run upon his
hands and feet. His fingers became claws, and his body was covered with
fur. Directly there was a bear where the boy had been. The sisters were
terrified; they ran, and the bear after them. They came to the stump of a
great tree, and the tree spoke to them. It bade them climb upon it, and as
they did so, it began to rise into the air. The bear came to kill them, but
they were just beyond its reach. It reared against the tree and scored the
bark all around with its claws. The seven sisters were borne into the sky,
and they became the stars of the Big Dipper.

From that moment, and so long as the legend lives, the Kiowas have kinsmen in the night sky. Whatever they were in the mountains, they could be
no more. However tenuous their well-being, however much they had suffered and would suffer again, they had found a way out of the wilderness.

9      My grandmother had a reverence for the sun, a holy regard that now
is all but gone out of mankind. There was a wariness in her, and an ancient
awe. She was a Christian in her later years, but she had come a long way
about, and she never forgot her birthright. As a child she had been to the
Sun Dances; she had taken part in those annual rites, and by them she had
learned the restoration of her people in the presence of Tai-me. She was
about seven when the last Kiowa Sun Dance was held in 1887 on the
Washita River above Rainy Mountain Creek. The buffalo were gone. In order to consummate the ancient sacrifice—to impale the head of a buffalo
bull upon the medicine tree—a delegation of old men journeyed into
Texas, there to beg and barter for an animal from the Goodnight herd. She
was ten when the Kiowas came together for the last time as a living Sun
Dance culture. They could find no buffalo; they had to hang an old hide
from the sacred tree. Before the dance could begin, a company of soldiers
rode out from Fort Sill under orders to disperse the tribe. Forbidden without cause the essential act of their faith, having seen the wild herds slaughtered and left to rot upon the ground, the Kiowas backed away forever
from the medicine tree. That was July 20, 1890, at the great bend of the
Washita. My grandmother was there. Without bitterness, and for as long
as she lived, she bore a vision of deicide.

10     Now that I can have her only in memory, I see my grandmother in the
several postures that were peculiar to her: standing at the wood stove on
a winter morning and turning meat in a great iron skillet; sitting at the
south window, bent above her beadwork, and afterwards, when her vision
had failed, looking down for a long time into the fold of her hands; going
out upon a cane, very slowly as she did when the weight of age came upon
her; praying. I remember her most often at prayer. She made long, rambling prayers out of suffering and hope, having seen many things. I was
never sure that I had the right to hear, so exclusive were they of all mere
custom and company. The last time I saw her she prayed standing by the

side of her bed at night, naked to the waist, the light of a kerosene lamp moving upon her dark skin. Her long, black hair, always drawn and braided in the day, lay upon her shoulders and against her breasts like a shawl. I do not speak Kiowa, and I never understood her prayers, but there was something inherently sad in the sound, some merest hesitation upon the syllables of sorrow. She began in a high and descending pitch, exhausting her breath to silence; then again and again—and always the same intensity of effort, of something that is, and is not, like urgency in the human voice. Transported so in the dancing light among the shadows of her room, she seemed beyond the reach of time. But that was illusion; I think I knew then that I should not see her again.

*1969*

## QUESTIONS FOR DISCUSSION

### Content

a. Is this essay the description of a place, of a person, or of both? What other purpose does Momaday have in writing this piece?
b. In what way does describing what he saw on his 1,500-mile journey help Momaday tell us about his grandmother?
c. Who is Tai-me, and what function does he serve in this essay?
d. What is the "deicide" that Momaday talks about near the end of this essay? How does this event help him explain the consciousness of his grandmother? What does it tell us about the Kiowas?
e. What is Momaday's point in telling us that his grandmother was born when "the Kiowas were living that last great moment of their history" (paragraph 3)?
f. The earth, for Momaday, is a redemptive force. What signs of this belief do you find in "The Way to Rainy Mountain"?

## STRATEGY AND STYLE

g. In what way does the Kiowa myth about the eight children help us understand the author's grandmother and her culture?
h. Momaday uses concrete details to describe the landscape he sees. What devices does he use to describe his grandmother?
i. Why is it important for the reader to learn about developments in Kiowan history?

j. Comment on the author's use of figurative language. Where, for example, does he use similes and metaphors? What is the effect of such language?
k. Momaday's prose often has a rhythmic beauty. In paragraph 5, for example, he says that his grandmother "could tell of the Crows, whom she had never seen, and of the Black Hills, where she had never been." What other examples of parallelism and balance do you find in this selection?

## ENGAGING THE TEXT

a. Good description relies heavily on the use of concrete and specific nouns. Find a paragraph or two that illustrates Momaday's reliance on both common and proper names to make his writing believable. Explain why these names make his writing believable.
b. Near the end of this selection, the author tells us about the sound of his grandmother's voice. Other parts of the essay appeal to our sense of touch. Reread Momaday's essay, paying close attention to references to the five senses. Write a brief essay explaining where and how Momaday uses sensory details.

## SUGGESTIONS FOR SUSTAINED WRITING

a. Go through your family albums and select a series of photographs that "tell the story" of one member of your family or one of your ancestors. If you can, take out the photos and arrange them in their "storytelling" sequence. Then write the story they tell, adding your own memories of your subject as you do so. Momaday does something similar in his book *The Way to Rainy Mountain;* you might want to find a copy in your library and use it as a source for ideas.
b. Read another essay in this text that describes the author's family. For example, you might choose Kingston's "No Name Woman" (Chapter 1), Leslie's "Don't Get Comfortable" (Chapter 1), or Noda's "Growing Up Asian in America" (Chapter 5). Then write a comparison/contrast essay in which you point out similarities and differences between this essay and Momaday's. Focus on purpose, thesis, and techniques for describing character. Also consider the reasons for which one or both of these authors describe setting (time and place) to develop their essays. If possible, also comment on the authors' tone.
c. Research the folklore, culture, or history of the Kiowa, Navajo, Apache, Pueblo, or another Native American people. Then write a paper that uses description to discuss a limited aspect of their culture, such as a religious ceremony, a harvest festival, a hunting ritual, or their agriculture. If you are interested in architecture, you might even describe the

longhouses of the Iroquois, the cliff dwellings of the prehistoric inhabitants of northern Arizona, the temples of the Aztec, or the ball courts of the Maya.

# Alias Benowitz Shoe Repair

David Quammen

*David Quammen (b. 1948) has taken degrees at Oxford and Yale universities and has been a Rhodes scholar and Guggenheim fellow. At age 22, he published his first novel,* To Walk the Line *(1970), which was based on his work in a Chicago ghetto. Other fiction by Quammen includes* Stories of Fathers and Sons *(1987) and two political thrillers:* The Zolta Configuration *(1983) and* The Soul of Victor Tronko *(1987). Though not a scientist, Quammen writes "Natural Acts," a regular column on science, nature, and the environment for* Outside *magazine. Collected in* Natural Acts: A Sidelong View of Science and Nature *(1985) and* The Flight of the Iguana: A Sidelong View of Science and Nature *(1988), these essays ask probing, often humorous questions about the natural world and the way we see it. "Alias Benowitz Shoe Repair," one such column, first appeared in 1985.*

*Like "The Way to Rainy Mountain," this essay can be seen as the description of both a personality and a landscape. As the subtitles of his two nonfiction works imply, Quammen is not typical of nature writers in that he interweaves personal insight with objective observation. The result can be somewhat challenging, and it can generate a variety of responses and interpretations from readers. However, Quammen's "sidelong" views are always fascinating, entertaining, and thought-provoking.*

I first heard about George Ochenski from a friend of mine who happens to be president of the Montana River-Snorkelers Association. We were in a fancy restaurant, as I recall, and there was wine involved. Ochenski had come to my friend's attention in the course of his (the friend's) presidential duties, which are in strict point of fact nonexistent. I should explain that the MRSA presidency is a purely honorary title, self-bestowed actually, because the MRSA is a mythical organization. This is all quite different, please note, from labeling the organization itself nonexistent. Certainly the Montana River-Snorkelers Association does exist (mainly over wine and beer at various bars and restaurants, occasionally also around a campfire); it just isn't *real*. An actual mythical entity, then, the MRSA, of roughly the same ontological status as the NCAA national championship in football, or the domino theory of international relations. You should look into this fellow Ochenski, my friend told me. He can be reached care of Benowitz Shoe Repair, in a tiny town called Southern Cross, up in the Flint Mountains above Anaconda. Have some more cabernet, I said. But

1

sure enough it turned out to be true. Benowitz Shoe Repair is another mythical entity, existent in its own way but not real. George Ochenski is both mythical and real. Are you with me so far?

2   George Ochenski must certainly be the preeminent river-snorkeler in the Rocky Mountains. He has talent, commitment, infectious enthusiasm, broad experience, state-of-the-art equipment, and a measure of lunatic daring. He has precious little competition. Most important, he has self-abnegating dedication to a larger purpose.

3   Sometimes you have to snorkel a river, Ochenski believes, in order to save it.

4   So dedicated is George Ochenski, and so scornful of risk, that—if necessary to make a point—he is willing even to snorkel the Clark Fork River downstream from the Anaconda smelter.

5   Now a river-snorkeler (in case this isn't self-evident) is someone who swims downstream in a river with his face under water, enjoying the ride, watching the scenery, breathing through his little tube. A lazy, hypnotic pastime best practiced on pellucid trout streams in midsummer. A few of us have been toying at it for years.

6   But George Ochenski does not toy. He jimmies himself into a full wet suit, adds fins and a hood and neoprene gloves and a fanny pack holding three cans of beer, pulls a pair of skateboarding knee pads into place, defogs his mask, and jumps into rivers. Gentle rivers and raging whitewater monsters. Last year, for instance, he did thirty-eight miles of the Salmon in Idaho without benefit of a boat. Also last year, he leapt into the Quake Lake trench—an earthquake-contorted stretch of the Madison River famous for biting kayaks in half—and nearly died. On that run his mask was ripped off six times while he tumbled head over teakettle through a garden of sharp boulders; the trench, George admits today, was a miscalculation. In Montana this kind of behavior does not pass unnoticed. By word, and more discreetly by the looks on their faces, people frequently tell him: *Son, you must be out of your everlovin' skull.* But they said that to Orville Wright, and they were wrong. Then again, they said it to Evel Knievel, and they were right. George Ochenski figures somewhere in between.

7   He has an enduring though ambivalent attraction to what he himself classifies "death sports." Huge squinting grin from George as he acknowledges this ambivalence. Mountaineering. Iceclimbing. Scuba. Never a major injury, never a bad accident—unless you count the time he fell 600 feet down a steep rock slope in the Alaska Range and did a self-arrest on his nose. Back in those years he traveled exotically for serious climbing, with generous sponsorship from the equipment people, and took part in the first successful ascent of the west face of Alaska's Mt. Hayes. Scaled some breathtaking frozen waterfalls. Around the same time, a consummate autodidact, he turned himself into an expert cobbler, because he wasn't satisfied with the professional repair work on his climbing boots; be-

fore long he was doing work for his friends too, and they had rechristened him, whimsically and metonymically, "Benowitz Shoe Repair." Today he mostly stays close to the little wood-heated cabin at Southern Cross, in the front room of which stands a bass fiddle. The fiddle is a logical switch from tuba, which he played for thirteen years. Benowitz is a man of many skills.

Several years ago, in response to pressure both internal and external, he gave up the glorious climbing, thanked the sponsors, and settled down to being useful politically. He had come to feel that he owed something back to the mountains and rivers; meanwhile there happened to be a certain crisis brewing near home. He now makes his living as an editorial assistant to an author of textbooks on environmental science. The cabin is filled ceiling-high with an eclectic library. On one wall is a quote from Congressman Ron Dellums: "Democracy is not about being a damn spectator against the backdrop of tapdancing politicians swinging in the winds of expediency." By disposition, George is certainly no spectator. Some people, particularly of the opposition, might still take him on first impression for a wild-haired, good-timing, reckless flake. They would be grievously mistaken. George Ochenski has an excellent brain, he has chutzpah, he has focus. 8

And in a small trailer up the hill behind his own cabin, where the ash from his cook stove can't fuddle its circuits, he has an Apple II computer, its floppy discs full of damning information concerning the Anaconda Minerals Company. 9

On September 29, 1980, the Anaconda Company announced that it was closing its copper-smelting operations at the town of Anaconda. This came as a severe shock to the 1,000 smelter workers suddenly unemployed, and marked the end of a century of awesome environmental pillage. For one hundred years the Company had cut down forests, poisoned streams, smelted copper, piled up vast mounds of slag, and filled the air of the country with a sulfurous smog, in exchange for the regular paychecks dispensed. Now the economics of copper had shifted. Goodbye, thanks for everything. "The Company thought they could just lock the doors and walk away," says George Ochenski. 10

He and a few other Anaconda folk, some of them former smelter workers, think otherwise. They are after the Company like a fierce dog after a bear. They have formed an enraged-citizens' organization, pressured the governor, pressured the senators, pressured the EPA. They want more than goodbyes. They want reclamation. They want accountability. At very least they want precise information about the nature and magnitude of the poisonous mess left behind. 11

With sulfur dioxide no longer pouring from the smelter stack, the chief concern now is over toxic metals: lead, cadmium, mercury, zinc, copper itself, and especially arsenic. One hundred years of copper-smelting have left various concentrations of some or all of these in the waters, in the plants, in the soil, in the animals of the county. George Ochenski and his 12 compatriots want to know: *How much?* How much was dumped in the ponds, how much was buried, how much is still blowing free off the smelter site? How much is already in our lungs and our bones? How much is ingested with each brown trout from the Clark Fork River, if a person should be so lucky as to catch one of the surviving fish, and so foolhardy as to eat it?

13    How much lead? How much cadmium? How much arsenic? The Anaconda Company, no doubt, devoutly wishes that these questions would go away.

14    Sometimes you have to snorkel a river in order to save it. Guided by this dictum, George Ochenski loaded his gear into the back of my car. It was late in the season, Labor Day weekend, with the air already growing cool. We paused briefly, where the gravel lane down from Southern Cross joined the larger road, to check the Benowitz Shoe Repair mailbox. Then George led me off on a pair of brief but illuminating tours.

15    We went to the Big Hole River, across the Continental Divide from Anaconda and clear of the war zone over heavy metals. The Big Hole is still a pellucid trout stream. We jimmied ourselves into wet suits, added fins and hoods and neoprene gloves; I pulled George's one extra skateboarding pad into position over my favorite knee. Masks were defogged, snorkels adjusted, and we jumped in.

16    The view was beautiful. Trout and whitefish looked me in the eye, aghast, and skittered away. Sculpins darted discreetly for cover. I observed the differences in underwater behavior among three different species of stonefly. I gazed at the funnel webs of *Arctopsyche* caddisfly larvae, down between rocks in the fast water, that I had read about often but never before seen. I found a mayfly nymph equipped with an elephantine pair of tusks. We passed through a few modest sets of rapids, where the current abruptly accelerated and the boulders came at me like blitzing linebackers who must be straight-armed away. After two hours of cruising we were nearly hypothermic, but the experience had been delightful.

17    Our second tour was to the Clark Fork River, downstream from the settling ponds into which the Anaconda Company has voided its years of industrial offal. "We're off to snorkel the Clark Fork," George told a friend as we pulled out of town. The friend looked puzzled. Huge squinting grin from George. "Then we'll come back and glow in the dark."

18    We snorkeled a long section of the Clark Fork. Here the water was turbid, visibility was poor. The rocks of the stream bed were largely cemented together with silt, leaving no habitat for stoneflies or *Arctopsyche*. I didn't see a single fish. I didn't see a single insect. Some people claim that the Clark Fork today is actually much improved over its sorry condition two decades ago, before the Company adopted certain technical measures to mitigate the toxicity of its releases. Maybe those people are right. But I remain skeptical. The river I was swimming through, with my eyes open and

my nose very close to the bottom, was definitely no basis for passing out congratulations.

This dramatic lack of vitality proves nothing, of course, about what 19 causal role the smelter wastes, and the erosion from denuded hillsides around Anaconda, may or may not still be playing. It simply correlates. Consider it, if you wish to, purest coincidence. It is not, however, mythical. It is real.

Later Benowitz and I were careful to shower ourselves down with 20 clean water. "River-snorkeling," he told me, and he should know, "is not supposed to be a death sport."

*1985*

## QUESTIONS FOR DISCUSSION

### Content

a. This is as much a description of a person as it is of a place. What does the environment in which "Benowitz" has chosen to live tell us about him?
b. What is *chutzpah*? How does Quammen prove that "Benowitz" has this quality and that he "has focus" (paragraph 8)?
c. Behavior reveals personality. What does the author tell us about "Benowitz's" behavior and lifestyle that provides clues to his personality?
d. Why does Quammen entitle this piece "Alias . . . "? Why didn't he just call it "George Ochenski"?

## STRATEGY AND STYLE

e. Description can be put to many uses. What has Quammen set out to do in this essay?
f. Why does he spend so much time explaining the difference between "mythical" and "real"? Is the distinction important to his purpose?
g. Why does he mention Orville Wright and Evel Knievel when trying to describe "Benowitz"?
h. Is this essay aimed solely at scientific readers? What can we assume about the educational background, interests, and values of Quammen's intended audience?
i. What examples of figurative language can you find in this essay? Is figurative language appropriate to "scientific" writing? Why or why not?

j. Find examples of irony. How do they affect the tone of this essay? Is this tone appropriate to scientific writing?

k. Although Quammen is not a scientist, his writing is convincing. How does the author establish his expertise?

## ENGAGING THE TEXT

a. Write briefly about someone you know who has "chutzpah" or "focus." Try to record the kinds of details that you might later use in a clear and convincing character sketch of this individual. Compare this person to George Ochenski.

b. Reread the essay, recording your thoughts about George Ochenski or about his environmental activism. Explain what drives Ochenski. What are his motives? Do you have a similar drive to do good?

## SUGGESTIONS FOR SUSTAINED WRITING

a. Write a character sketch about a person whom you admire greatly and whom you met recently. Or write about a person in your community who is well known and whose ways of getting things done are considered a bit eccentric. You can use the method Quammen chose by narrating your own experiences with the person, or you can experiment with other methods, such as using the third-person point of view or relying on fragmented descriptions rather than narration. Whatever method you choose, like Quammen, make the sketch detailed, informative and entertaining.

b. Find a copy of Quammen's "The Flight of the Iguagna," an essay in a collection by the same name. Summarize that essay and then compare it to "Alias Benowitz Shoe Repair." In what way(s) are both essays "sidelong" views of nature? What similarities do you see among the purposes, contents, and techniques in these two essays? If this assignment doesn't interest you, summarize "Sex, Drugs, Disasters, and the Extinction of Dinosaurs" by Stephen Jay Gould in Chapter 11 of this text. In addition, explain in what ways Quammen's "sidelong" view of nature compares and/or contrasts with Gould's view.

c. Write an essay about an environmental problem that focuses on a particular person or organization involved in solving or creating the problem. If the former, explain how that person or organization has worked to find a solution; if the task has been difficult, explain the struggle your subject has endured. Get your readers to sympathize with your subject or even to join in the struggle. If the latter, show your readers why you think your subject has caused the problem and explain what can be done to solve it. This assignment requires library and/or Internet research. Include information and insights from at least three secondary sources.

# Once More to the Lake

## E. B. White

*A regular contributor to the* New Yorker *and* Harper's *magazines, E(lwyn) B(rooks) White (1899–1985) was one of the best-known American essayists of the twentieth century. He was born in Mount Vernon, New York, but lived much of his life in Maine. After serving with the U.S. Army in World War I, White worked as a journalist for the United Press and the* Seattle Times, *then began writing for the* New Yorker. *In 1938, he launched "One Man's Meat," a regular column for* Harper's. *Among his friends were important writers such as Dorothy Parker, Stephen Leacock, and Robert Benchley. With his good friend James Thurber, White collaborated on a work with the intriguing title* Is Sex Necessary? (1929). *His most famous collections include* One Man's Meat (1942), The Points of My Compass (1962), *and* Poems and Sketches (1981). *Among his other works are several books for children, such as* Stuart Little (1945), Charlotte's Web (1952), *and* The Trumpet of the Swan (1970). *He was also responsible for revising the classic* Elements of Style, *written by William Strunk, one of his professors at Cornell University. White was the recipient of the Presidential Medal of Freedom and of a citation from the Pulitzer Prize Committee. In 1939, he took up permanent residence in Brookline, Maine, where he produced the bulk of his writings.*

   *"Once More to the Lake," a classic essay that is often anthologized, recalls his many boyhood vacations in Maine. Without a doubt, the continued popularity of this selection arises from its skillful use of concrete, sensory details to paint a verbal portrait of both a place and an experience. However, "Once More to the Lake" tells us far more about a camp in Maine; it also provides valuable insights into aspects of its speaker's character.*

## AUGUST 1941

One summer, along about 1904, my father rented a camp on a lake in   1
Maine and took us all there for the month of August. We all got ringworm from some kittens and had to rub Pond's Extract on our arms and legs night and morning, and my father rolled over in a canoe with all his clothes on; but outside of that the vacation was a success and from then on none of us ever thought there was any place in the world like that lake in Maine. We returned summer after summer—always on August 1 for one month. I have since become a salt-water man, but sometimes in summer there are days when the restlessness of the tides and the fearful cold of the

sea water and the incessant wind that blows across the afternoon and into the evening make me wish for the placidity of a lake in the woods. A few weeks ago this feeling got so strong I bought myself a couple of bass hooks and a spinner and returned to the lake where we used to go, for a week's fishing and to revisit old haunts.

2      I took along my son, who had never had any fresh water up his nose and who had seen lily pads only from train windows. On the journey over to the lake I began to wonder what it would be like. I wondered how time would have marred this unique, this holy spot—the coves and streams, the hills that the sun set behind, the camps and the paths behind the camps. I was sure that the tarred road would have found it out, and I wondered in what other ways it would be desolated. It is strange how much you can remember about places like that once you allow your mind to return into the grooves that lead back. You remember one thing, and that suddenly reminds you of another thing. I guess I remembered clearest of all the early mornings, when the lake was cool and motionless, remembered how the bedroom smelled of the lumber it was made of and of the wet woods whose scent entered through the screen. The partitions in the camp were thin and did not extend clear to the top of the rooms, and as I was always the first up I would dress softly so as not to wake the others, and sneak out into the sweet outdoors and start out in the canoe, keeping close along the shore in the long shadows of the pines. I remembered being very careful never to rub my paddle against the gunwale for fear of disturbing the stillness of the cathedral.

3      The lake had never been what you would call a wild lake. There were cottages sprinkled around the shores, and it was in farming country although the shores of the lake were quite heavily wooded. Some of the cottages were owned by nearby farmers, and you would live at the shore and eat your meals at the farmhouse. That's what our family did. But although it wasn't wild, it was a fairly large and undisturbed lake and there were places in it that, to a child at least, seemed infinitely remote and primeval.

4      I was right about the tar: it led to within half a mile of the shore. But when I got back there, with my boy, and we settled into a camp near a farmhouse and into the kind of summertime I had known, I could tell that it was going to be pretty much the same as it had been before—I knew it, lying in bed the first morning smelling the bedroom and hearing the boy sneak quietly out and go off along the shore in a boat. I began to sustain the illusion that he was I, and therefore, by simple transposition, that I was my father. This sensation persisted, kept cropping up all the time we were there. It was not an entirely new feeling, but in this setting it grew much stronger. I seemed to be living a dual existence. I would be in the middle of some simple act, I would be picking up a bait box or laying down a table fork, or I would be saying something and suddenly it would be not I but my father who was saying the words or making the gesture. It gave me a creepy sensation.

We went fishing the first morning. I felt the same damp moss covering ₅ the worms in the bait can, and saw the dragonfly alight on the tip of my rod as it hovered a few inches from the surface of the water. It was the arrival of this fly that convinced me beyond any doubt that everything was as it always had been, that the years were a mirage and that there had been no years. The small waves were the same, chucking the rowboat under the chin as we fished at anchor, and the boat was the same boat, the same color green and the ribs broken in the same places, and under the floorboards, the same fresh water leavings and debris—the dead hell-grammite, the wisps of moss, the rusty discarded fishhook, the dried blood from yesterday's catch. We stared silently at the tips of our rods, at the dragonflies that came and went. I lowered the tip of mine into the water, tentatively, pensively dislodging the fly, which darted two feet away, poised, darted two feet back, and came to rest again a little farther up the rod. There had been no years between the ducking of this dragonfly and the other one—the one that was part of memory. I looked at the boy, who was silently watching his fly, and it was my hands that held his rod, my eyes watching. I felt dizzy and didn't know which rod I was at the end of.

We caught two bass, hauling them in briskly as though they were ₆ mackerel, pulling them over the side of the boat in a businesslike manner without any landing net, and stunning them with a blow on the back of the head. When we got back for a swim before lunch, the lake was exactly where we had left it, the same number of inches from the dock, and there was only the merest suggestion of a breeze. This seemed an utterly enchanted sea, this lake you could leave to its own devices for a few hours and come back to, and find that it had not stirred, this constant and trustworthy body of water. In the shallows, the dark, water-soaked sticks and twigs, smooth and old, were undulating in clusters on the bottom against the clean ribbed sand, and the track of the mussel was plain. A school of minnows swam by, each minnow with its small individual shadow, doubling the attendance, so clear and sharp in the sunlight. Some of the other campers were in swimming, along the shore, one of them with a cake of soap, and the water felt thin and clear and unsubstantial. Over the years there had been this person with the cake of soap, this cultist, and here he was. There had been no years.

Up to the farmhouse to dinner through the teeming dusty field, the ₇ road under our sneakers was only a two-track road. The middle track was missing, the one with the marks of the hooves and the splotches of dried, flaky manure. There had always been three tracks to choose from in choosing which track to walk in; now the choice was narrowed down to two. For a moment I missed terribly the middle alternative. But the way led past the tennis court, and something about the way it lay there in the sun reassured me; the tape had loosened along the backline, the alleys were green with plantains and other weeds, and the net (installed in June and removed in

September) sagged in the dry noon, and the whole place steamed with midday heat and hunger and emptiness. There was a choice of pie for dessert, and one was blueberry and one was apple, and the waitresses were the same country girls, there having been no passage of time, only the illusion of it as in a dropped curtain—the waitresses were still fifteen; their hair had been washed, that was the only difference—they had been to the movies and seen the pretty girls with the clean hair.

8      Summertime, oh, summertime, pattern of life indelible with fade-proof lake, the wood unshatterable, the pasture with the sweetfern and the juniper forever and ever, summer without end; this was the background, and the life along the shore was the design, the cottages with their innocent and tranquil design, their tiny docks with the flagpole and the American flag floating against the white clouds in the blue sky, and little paths over the roots of the trees leading from camp to camp and the paths leading back to the outhouses and the can of lime for sprinkling, and at the souvenir counters at the store the miniature birch-bark canoes and the postcards that showed things looking a little better than they looked. This was the American family at play, escaping the city heat, wondering whether the newcomers in the camp at the head of the cove were "common" or "nice," wondering whether it was true that the people who drove up for Sunday dinner at the farmhouse were turned away because there wasn't enough chicken.

9      It seemed to me, as I kept remembering all this, that those times and those summers had been infinitely precious and worth saving. There had been jollity and peace and goodness. The arriving (at the beginning of August) had been so big a business in itself, at the railway station the farm wagon drawn up, the first smell of the pine-laden air, the first glimpse of the smiling farmer, and the great importance of the trunks and your father's enormous authority in such matters, and the feel of the wagon under you for the long ten-mile haul, and at the top of the last long hill catching the first view of the lake after eleven months of not seeing this cherished body of water. The shouts and cries of the other campers when they saw you, and the trunks to be unpacked, to give up their rich burden. (Arriving was less exciting nowadays, when you sneaked up in your car and parked it under a tree near the camp and took out the bags and in five minutes it was all over, no fuss, no loud wonderful fuss about trunks.)

10      Peace and goodness and jollity. The only thing that was wrong now, really, was the sound of the place, an unfamiliar nervous sound of the outboard motors. This was the note that jarred, the one thing that would sometimes break the illusion and set the years moving. In those other summertimes all motors were inboard; and when they were at a little distance, the noise they made was a sedative, an ingredient of summer sleep. They were one-cylinder and two-cylinder engines, and some were make-and-break and some were jump-spark, but they all made a sleepy sound across the lake. The one-lungers throbbed and fluttered, and the twin-cylin-

der ones purred and purred, and that was a quiet sound, too. But now the
campers all had outboards. In the daytime, in the hot mornings, these motors made a petulant, irritable sound; at night in the still evening when the
afterglow lit the water, they whined about one's ears like mosquitoes. My
boy loved our rented outboard, and his great desire was to achieve single-
handed mastery over it, and authority, and he soon learned the trick of
choking it a little (but not too much), and the adjustment of the needle
valve. Watching him I would remember the things you could do with the
old one-cylinder engine with the heavy flywheel, how you could have it
eating out of your hand if you got really close to it spiritually. Motorboats
in those days didn't have clutches, and you would make a landing by shut-
ting off the motor at the proper time and coasting in with a dead rudder.
But there was a way of reversing them, if you learned the trick, by cutting
the switch and putting it on again exactly on the final dying revolution of
the flywheel, so that it would kick back against compression and begin reversing. Approaching a dock in a strong following breeze, it was difficult to
slow up sufficiently by the ordinary coasting method, and if a boy felt he
had complete mastery over his motor, he was tempted to keep it running
beyond its time and then reverse it a few feet from the dock. It took a cool
nerve, because if you threw the switch a twentieth of a second too soon you
would catch the flywheel when it still had speed enough to go up past center, and the boat would leap ahead, charging bull-fashion at the dock.

We had a good week at the camp. The bass were biting well and the 11
sun shone endlessly, day after day. We would be tired at night and lie
down in the accumulated heat of the little bedrooms after the long hot day
and the breeze would stir almost imperceptibly outside and the smell of
the swamp drifted in through the rusty screens. Sleep would come easily
and in the morning the red squirrel would be on the roof, tapping out his
gay routine. I kept remembering everything, lying in bed in the mornings—the small steamboat that had a long rounded stern like the lip of a
Ubangi, and how quietly she ran on the moonlight sails, when the older
boys played their mandolins and the girls sang and we ate doughnuts
dipped in sugar, and how sweet the music was on the water in the shining
night, and what it had felt like to think about girls then. After breakfast we
would go up to the store and the things were in the same place—the minnows in a bottle, the plugs and spinners disarranged and pawed over by
the youngsters from the boys' camp, the Fig Newtons and the Beeman's
gum. Outside, the road was tarred and cars stood in front of the store. Inside, all was just as it had always been, except there was more Coca-Cola
and not so much Moxie and root beer and birch beer and sarsaparilla. We
would walk out with the bottle of pop apiece and sometimes the pop
would backfire up our noses and hurt. We explored the streams, quietly,
where the turtles slid off the sunny logs and dug their way into the soft
bottom; and we lay on the town wharf and fed worms to the tame bass.

Everywhere we went I had trouble making out which was I, the one walking at my side, the one walking in my pants.

One afternoon while we were at that lake, a thunderstorm came up. It was like the revival of an old melodrama that I had seen long ago with childish awe. The second-act climax of the drama of the electrical disturbance over a lake in America had not changed in any important respect. This was the big scene, still the big scene. The whole thing was so familiar, the first feeling of oppression and heat and a general air around camp of not wanting to go very far away. In mid-afternoon (it was all the same) a curious darkening of the sky, and a lull in everything that had made life tick; and then the way the boats suddenly swung the other way at their moorings with the coming of a breeze out of the new quarter, and the premonitory rumble. Then the kettle drum, then the snare, then the bass drum and cymbals, then crackling light against the dark, and the gods grinning and licking their chops in the hills. Afterward the calm, the rain steadily rustling in the calm lake, the return of light and hope and spirits, and the campers running out in joy and relief to go swimming in the rain, their bright cries perpetuating the deathless joke about how they were getting simply drenched, and the children screaming with delight at the new sensation of bathing in the rain, and the joke about getting drenched linking the generations in a strong indestructible chain. And the comedian who waded in carrying an umbrella.

When the others went swimming my son said he was going in, too. He pulled his dripping trunks from the line where they had hung all through the shower and wrung them out. Languidly, and with no thought of going in, I watched him, his hard little body, skinny and bare, saw him wince slightly as he pulled up around his vitals the small, soggy, icy garment. As he buckled the swollen belt, suddenly my groin felt the chill of death.

*1939*

## QUESTIONS FOR DISCUSSION

### Content

a. In paragraph 6, White calls the lake "an enchanted sea . . . a constant and trustworthy body of water." What evidence does he provide in this and other paragraphs to support this view?

b. Given a quick, cursory reading, "Once More to the Lake" might suggest that change is not inevitable. Can you point to passages that indicate just the opposite?

c. Ostensibly, White returns to the lake to seek "the placidity of a lake in the woods." What else is he seeking? What else does he discover?

d. What is the significance of the line with which this essay ends?

## STRATEGY AND STYLE

e. Why does White mention some of the mishaps on his first visit to the lake in the first paragraph?

f. Early in the essay, the author creates a brilliant metaphor by comparing the lake to a cathedral. What other metaphors does he use? What do they help him achieve as he describes the lake and recalls his youth?

g. In what paragraphs does White make especially good use of sensory details?

h. In what paragraphs does he list concrete details in quick succession to create a kind of verbal photograph?

i. Read paragraphs 4 and 5 again. What function do they serve in the essay?

j. Although this essay is heavy in description, it might also be used to teach students techniques relevant to comparison/contrast. Explain.

## ENGAGING THE TEXT

a. Respond to the tone of White's essay, especially to the tone at the end. Why does the tone become darker at the end of the essay?

b. Compare White's experiences to your own on a family vacation, a reunion, or a return to an old haunt. How are your experiences similar to or different from those of White?

## SUGGESTIONS FOR SUSTAINED WRITING

a. As you recall from the Questions for Discussion, White calls the lake "an enchanted sea . . . a constant and trustworthy body of water" (paragraph 6). Write a paper that begins with a paragraph or two supporting White's claim. Make frequent and direct reference to the text as you develop this part of your paper. Then, following White's lead, describe a favorite refuge of your own—a spot where you can relax, unwind, or even make important decisions without distraction. Like the author of "Once More to the Lake," use concrete, sensory details to explain what about this place draws you back to it time and again.

b. Is there a difference between White's perceptions of the lake as a child and as an adult? Why does he bother to give us both views? Write an es-

say in which you contrast your recollection of a spot you once frequented with the present reality of that place. Make your essay interesting by including as many specific, concrete, and vivid details as you
can. For further inspiration, read Pickering's "Faith of the Father"
(Chapter 4), which uses descriptive detail for purposes that are in some
ways similar to those of White.

c. Write an essay about a place that might serve as the basis for a travel
brochure. In other words, try to convince your readers that this is an interesting, enjoyable, or even important place to visit. Focus on a limited
space, such as a particular government building or monument, a war
memorial, a stretch of beach, a town or city center, or a museum. You
might want to write about a place you have seen firsthand, but you can
also write about a place you would like to visit. Either way, include researched material from at least three library and/or Internet sources.

# Marrying Absurd

Joan Didion

*Born in Sacramento, California, Didion (b. 1934) earned a BA from the University of Cal-
ifornia at Berkeley and went on to serve as an associate feature editor for* Vogue *magazine,
as a columnist for the* Saturday Evening Post, *and as a contributing editor to the* National Review. *Her essays are subtle portraits of the American experience, which she scru-
tinizes carefully and recreates with both incisiveness and irony. Her major works include
novels:* Play It As It Lays *(1971),* A Book of Common Prayer *(1977),* Democracy
*(1984), and* The Last Thing He Wanted *(1996); collections of essays:* Slouching Toward
Bethlehem *(1968) and* The White Album *(1979); and nonfiction:* Salvador *(1983) and*
Miami *(1987). She is the coauthor of several screenplays, including* The Panic in Needle
Park *(1971),* A Star Is Born *(1976), and* True Confessions *(1981).*

*"Marrying Absurd" appears in* Slouching Toward Bethlehem. *Didion allows her
voice to come through the essay. Indeed, its title warns us that it will be filled with biting
irony. However, for the most part, Didion allows the facts to speak for themselves, and the
tone of the piece is almost journalistic in its detachment.*

1   To be married in Las Vegas, Clark County, Nevada, a bride must swear that
she is eighteen or has parental permission and a bridegroom that he is
twenty-one or has parental permission. Someone must put up five dollars
for the license. (On Sundays and holidays, fifteen dollars. The Clark
County Courthouse issues marriage licenses at any time of the day or
night except between noon and one in the afternoon, between eight and
nine in the evening, and between four and five in the morning.) Nothing

else is required. The State of Nevada, alone among these United States, demands neither a premarital blood test nor a waiting period before or after the issuance of a marriage license. Driving in across the Mojave from Los Angeles, one sees the signs way out on the desert, looming up from that moonscape of rattle-snakes and mesquite, even before the Las Vegas lights appear like a mirage on the horizon: "GETTING MARRIED? Free License Information First Strip Exit." Perhaps the Las Vegas wedding industry achieved its peak operational efficiency between 9:00 PM and midnight of August 26, 1965, an otherwise unremarkable Thursday which happened to be, by Presidential order, the last day on which anyone could improve his draft status merely by getting married. One hundred and seventy-one couples were pronounced man and wife in the name of Clark County and the State of Nevada that night, sixty-seven of them by a single justice of the peace, Mr. James A. Brennan. Mr. Brennan did one wedding at the Dunes and the other sixty-six in his office, and charged each couple eight dollars. One bride lent her veil to six others. "I got it down from five to three minutes," Mr. Brennan said later of his feat. "I could've married them *en masse,* but they're people, not cattle. People expect more when they get married."

What people who get married in Las Vegas actually do expect—what,   2 in the largest sense, their "expectations" are—strikes one as a curious and self-contradictory business. Las Vegas is the most extreme and allegorical of American settlements, bizarre and beautiful in its venality and in its devotion to immediate gratification, a place the tone of which is set by mobsters and call girls and ladies' room attendants with amyl nitrite poppers in their uniform pockets. Almost everyone notes that there is no "time" in Las Vegas, no night and no day and no past and no future (no Las Vegas casino, however, has taken the obliteration of the ordinary time sense quite so far as Harold's Club in Reno, which for a while issued, at odd intervals in the day and night, mimeographed "bulletins" carrying news from the world outside); neither is there any logical sense of where one is. One is standing on a highway in the middle of a vast hostile desert looking at an eighty-foot sign which blinks "STARDUST" or "CAESAR'S PALACE." Yes, but what does that explain? This geographical implausibility reinforces the sense that what happens there has no connection with "real" life; Nevada cities like Reno and Carson City are ranch towns, Western towns, places behind which there is some historical imperative. But Las Vegas seems to exist only in the eye of the beholder. All of which makes it an extraordinarily stimulating and interesting place, but an odd one in which to want to wear a candlelight satin Priscilla of Boston wedding dress with Chantilly lace insets, tapered sleeves and a detachable modified train.

And yet the Las Vegas wedding business seems to appeal to precisely   3 that impulse. "Sincere and Dignified Since 1954," one wedding chapel advertises. There are nineteen such wedding chapels in Las Vegas, intensely competitive, each offering better, faster, and, by implication, more sincere services than the next: Our Photos Best Anywhere, Your Wedding on A Phonograph Record, Candlelight with Your Ceremony, Honeymoon Accommodations, Free Transportation from Your Motel to Courthouse to Chapel and Return to Motel, Religious or Civil Ceremonies, Dressing Rooms, Flowers, Rings, Announcements, Witnesses Available, and Ample Parking. All of these services, like most others in Las Vegas (sauna baths, payroll-check cashing, chinchilla coats for sale or rent) are offered twenty-four hours a day, seven days a week, presumably on the premise that marriage, like craps, is a game to be played when the table seems hot.

4     But what strikes one most about the Strip chapels, with their wishing wells and stained-glass paper windows and their artificial bouvardia, is that so much of their business is by no means a matter of simple convenience, of late-night liaisons between show girls and baby Crosbys. Of course there is some of that. (One night about eleven o'clock in Las Vegas I watched a bride in an orange minidress and masses of flame-colored hair stumble from a Strip chapel on the arm of her bridegroom, who looked the part of the expendable nephew in the movies like *Miami Syndicate*. "I gotta get the kids," the bride whimpered. "I gotta pick up the sitter, I gotta get to the midnight show." "What you gotta get," the bridegroom said, opening the door of a Cadillac Coupe de Ville and watching her crumple on the seat, "is sober.") But Las Vegas seems to offer something other than "convenience"; it is merchandising "niceness," the facsimile of proper ritual, to children who do not know how else to find it, how to make the arrangements, how to do it "right." All day and evening long on the Strip, one sees actual wedding parties, waiting under the harsh lights at a crosswalk, standing uneasily in the parking lot of the Frontier while the photographer hired by The Little Church of the West ("Wedding Place of the Stars") certifies the occasion, takes the picture: the bride in a veil and white satin pumps, the bridegroom usually in a white dinner jacket, and even an attendant or two, a sister or a best friend in hot-pink *peau de soie*, a flirtation veil, a carnation nosegay. "When I Fall in Love It Will Be Forever," the organist plays, and then a few bars of *Lohengrin*. The mother cries; the stepfather, awkward in his role, invites the chapel hostess to join them for a drink at the Sands. The hostess declines with a professional smile; she has already transferred her interest to the group waiting outside. One bride out, another in, and again the sign goes up on the chapel door: "One moment please—Wedding."

5     I sat next to one such wedding party in a Strip restaurant the last time I was in Las Vegas. The marriage had just taken place; the bride still wore her dress, the mother her corsage. A bored waiter poured out a few swallows of pink champagne ("on the house") for everyone but the bride, who was too young to be served. "You'll need something with more kick than that," the bride's father said with heavy jocularity to his new son-in-law;

the ritual jokes about the wedding night had a certain Panglossian character, since the bride was clearly several months pregnant. Another round of pink champagne, this time not on the house, and the bride began to cry. "It was just as nice," she sobbed, "as I hoped and dreamed it would be."

*1967*

## QUESTIONS FOR DISCUSSION

### Content

a. On the surface, Didion's purpose is to expose the "absurdity" of getting married in Las Vegas. What else is she trying to accomplish?
b. Didion calls what goes on in Las Vegas a "wedding business." How does she support this view?
c. What does Didion's description of setting contribute to her essay? What does she mean by the "geographical implausibility" of Las Vegas?
d. How do you interpret the first sentence of paragraph 2? How does Didion support this idea?
e. What does she mean by telling us that "Las Vegas seems to exist only in the eye of the beholder" (paragraph 2)?
f. In paragraph 4, the author mentions the "baby Crosbys." These were the sons of singer/actor Bing Crosby, who died in 1977. What other references to past people, events, and phenomena do you find in this essay? Do such references date the essay and thereby make it less effective?
g. Who or what is *Lohengrin* (paragraph 4)? Who or what is Pangloss (paragraph 5)? Look up the answers in a good all-purpose encyclopedia or another library reference text. How do these allusions help Didion advance her point?

### STRATEGY AND STYLE

h. How would you characterize the essay's tone?
i. The author's voice is fairly obvious in this essay. To what end has Didion made her presence felt?
j. To what end were the direct quotations in this essay chosen?
k. Comment on the length of the essay's introduction. Is it appropriate? Why or why not?
l. What technique(s) does Didion use in her conclusion?

## Engaging the Text

a. Reread Didion's essay. List specific details she includes to describe the Las Vegas–style wedding. Explain why she sees the Las Vegas wedding as reflecting American culture.

b. Didion focuses on her personal reactions to what she witnesses. Reread the essay and make a list of her personal, subjective responses to Las Vegas and the Las Vegas wedding. Use the list to inspire a personal description of your own of a place you have visited.

## SUGGESTIONS FOR SUSTAINED WRITING

a. Like Didion, describe a religious, social, academic, or community ritual or ceremony that you know well. When you write the first draft, pretend you are producing a multisensory documentary by describing what you have heard, seen, felt, tasted, and smelled. In other words, be as objective as possible; do not include personal responses to what you have experienced. As you develop subsequent drafts, however, be more subjective. Adopt a distinctive voice and add details that will reveal your attitude or attitudes about what you are describing.

b. Read another satire on the superficiality of contemporary American life: Nicols Fox's "Gawk Shows" in Chapter 9. Write an essay that begins by explaining what this selection and Didion's essay say about the superficiality of contemporary American society. Make direct reference to both selections in the form of direct quotations or paraphrases. Then, relying on your own insights and personal observations, explain why you agree or disagree with Didion and/or Fox.

c. Write a research essay in which you explain several of the traditions associated with a typical American wedding. For example, you might explain why the bride wears white; why her father "gives her away"; why the groom should not see the bride on their wedding day until she walks down the aisle; or why the bride carries "something old, something new, something borrowed, something blue." If this assignment does not interest you, describe the typical wedding of people from a culture very unlike our own. In either case, research your topic in the library and/or on the Internet. Rely on at least four secondary sources.

**3**

# Process Analysis

Often thought of as a way to develop scientific papers, process analysis can be used with a variety of topics and in combination with many of the other methods of development illustrated in this text. It is the type of writing used to convey instructions—how to change a tire, write a research paper, take someone's temperature, cook a carp, or paint a fresco! Process analysis also can explain how something happens or happened—the birth of a planet, the way you persuaded your boss to give you a raise, or even the manner in which laws are enacted.

Like narratives, essays on such topics generally follow a chronological order, with each step in the process likened to events in a well-developed plot. Much use is made of transitional words and phrases to keep the reader on the right track. "First," Euell Gibbons tells us, "instead of merely scaling the fish [my brother] skinned them." And like any good storyteller, the writer of process analysis usually begins at the beginning and follows through to the end, sometimes listing steps by number but always providing sufficient detail to help the reader picture the activity accurately and concretely.

Sometimes writers of process analysis infuse their work with vivid, if not unnerving, description like the kind we find in Jessica Mitford's "Behind the Formaldehyde Curtain." More often than not, however, process papers also explain the relationship of causes and effects, as in Alexander Petrunkevitch's "The Spider and the Wasp."

Nonetheless, the purpose of process analysis is instructive in the most practical sense: narration and description may show *what* happens, causal analysis may explain *why* it happens, but process analysis always focuses on *how* it happens. The most important aspect of any process essay therefore is clarity. Readers will not follow unless your explanations are complete, your language is familiar, and your organization is simple. Take your lead from Richard Marius, who lists important advice and information about writing in easy-to-follow steps. And whenever you give instructions, pay your readers the courtesy of preparing them for the task by mentioning required tools, materials, and expectations, as Adam Goodheart does in "How to Paint a Fresco."

Of course, explaining a process does not give you license to produce prose that is dull. Goodheart's essay flashes with wit and color; Mitford's

"Behind the Formaldehyde Curtain" uses just the right degree of engaging satire to address a serious and delicate subject; and Sue Hubbell's "Honey Harvest" offers comic relief while explaining a process that is potentially painful and dangerous.

Like selections in other parts of this text, those that appear here represent a variety of subjects, approaches, and styles. But there is a common denominator. As you might expect, the selections that follow are models of clarity, but their authors never seem cold and detached even when explaining what might first seem recondite or abstract. The committed, sometimes impassioned, voice of the writer always comes through. That is probably why we read these sometimes "technical" pieces with alacrity. Each selection has something important to teach us, but the lesson has relatively little to do with the process its author describes. What we learn here is a need to respect the reader, to understand our attitude toward the subject, and to believe that what we have to say is important.

# The Spider and the Wasp

Alexander Petrunkevitch

*Alexander Petrunkevitch (1875–1964) arrived in the United States around the turn of the twentieth century after having studied in Russia, his native country, and in Germany. A world-famous zoologist, Petrunkevitch taught at several American universities, including Harvard and Yale. As an expert on spiders, he published what is now a standard reference in the field:* Index Catalogue of Spiders of North, Central and South America. *Like James C. Rettie (Chapter 9), Claudia Glenn Dowling (Chapter 4), and Stephen Jay Gould (Chapter 11), Petrunkevitch writes scientific prose that, while accurate and well documented, is colorful, exciting, and accessible to readers with little scientific training. "The Spider and the Wasp" first appeared in* Scientific American *in 1952. It is an excellent example of scientific writing that explains how a natural process occurs.*

1   To hold its own in the struggle for existence, every species of animal must have a regular source of food, and if it happens to live on other animals, its survival may be very delicately balanced. The hunter cannot exist without the hunted; if the latter should perish from the earth, the former would, too. When the hunted also prey on some of the hunters, the matter may become complicated.

2   This is nowhere better illustrated than in the insect world. Think of the complexity of a situation such as the following: There is a certain wasp, *Pimpla inquisitor,* whose larvae feed on the larvae of the tussock moth. *Pimpla* larvae in turn serve as food for the larvae of a second wasp, and the lat-

ter in their turn nourish still a third wasp. What subtle balance between fertility and mortality must exist in the case of each of these four species to prevent the extinction of all of them! An excess of mortality over fertility in a single member of the group would ultimately wipe out all four.

This is not a unique case. The two great orders of insects, Hymenoptera and Diptera, are full of such examples of interrelationship. And the spiders (which are not insects but members of a separate order of anthropods) also are killers and victims of insects. 3

In the feeding and safeguarding of their progeny the insects and spiders exhibit some interesting analogies to reasoning and some crass examples of blind instinct. The case I propose to describe here is that of the tarantula spiders and their arch-enemy, the digger wasps of the genus *Pepsis*. It is a classic example of what looks like intelligence pitted against instinct—a strange situation in which the victim, though fully able to defend itself, submits unwittingly to its destruction. 4

5

A fertilized female tarantula lays from 200 to 400 eggs at a time; thus it is possible for a single tarantula to produce several thousand young. She takes no care of them beyond weaving a cocoon of silk to enclose the eggs. After they hatch, the young walk away, find convenient places in which to dig their burrows and spend the rest of their lives in solitude. Tarantulas feed mostly on insects and millipedes. Once their appetite is appeased, they digest the food for several days before eating again. Their sight is poor, being limited to sensing a change in the intensity of light and to the perception of moving objects. They apparently have little or no sense of hearing, for a hungry tarantula will pay no attention to a loudly chirping cricket placed in its cage unless the insect happens to touch one of its legs.

But all spiders, and especially hairy ones, have an extremely delicate sense of touch. Laboratory experiments prove that tarantulas can distinguish three types of touch: pressure against the body wall, stroking of the body hair, and riffling of certain very fine hairs on the legs called trichobothria. Pressure against the body, by a finger or the end of a pencil, causes the tarantula to move off slowly for a short distance. The touch excites no defensive response unless the approach is from above where the spider can see the motion, in which case it rises on its hind legs, lifts its front legs, opens its fangs and holds this threatening posture as long as the object continues to move. When the motion stops, the spider drops back to the ground, remains quiet for a few seconds and then moves slowly away. 6

The entire body of a tarantula, especially its legs, is thickly clothed with hair. Some of it is short and woolly, some long and stiff. Touching this body hair produces one of two distinct reactions. When the spider is hungry, it responds with an immediate and swift attack. At the touch of a cricket's antennae the tarantula seizes the insect so swiftly that a motion picture taken at the rate of 64 frames per second shows only the result and not the process of capture. But when the spider is not hungry, the stimulation of its hairs 7 merely causes it to shake the touched limb. An insect can walk under its hairy belly unharmed.

8      The trichobothria, very fine hairs growing from disklike membranes on the legs, were once thought to be the spider's hearing organs, but we now know that they have nothing to do with sound. They are sensitive only to air movement. A light breeze makes them vibrate slowly without disturbing the common hair. When one blows gently on the trichobothria, the tarantula reacts with a quick jerk of its four front legs. If the front and hind legs are stimulated at the same time, the spider makes a sudden jump. This reaction is quite independent of the state of its appetite.

9      These three tactile responses—to pressure on the body wall, to moving of the common hair and to flexing of the trichobothria—are so different from one another that there is no possibility of confusing them. They serve the tarantula adequately for most of its needs and enable it to avoid most annoyances and dangers. But they fail the spider completely when it meets its deadly enemy, the digger wasp *Pepsis*.

10     These solitary wasps are beautiful and formidable creatures. Most species are either a deep shiny blue all over, or deep blue with rusty wings. The largest have a wing span of about four inches. They live on nectar. When excited, they give off a pungent odor—a warning that they are ready to attack. The sting is much worse than that of a bee or common wasp, and the pain and swelling last longer. In the adult stage the wasp lives only a few months. The female produces but a few eggs, one at a time at intervals of two or three days. For each egg the mother must provide one adult tarantula, alive but paralyzed. The tarantula must be of the correct species to nourish the larva. The mother wasp attaches the egg to the paralyzed spider's abdomen. Upon hatching from the egg, the larva is many hundreds of times smaller than its living but helpless victim. It eats no other food and drinks no water. By the time it has finished its single gargantuan meal and becomes ready for wasphood, nothing remains of the tarantula but its indigestible chitinous skeleton.

11     The mother wasp goes tarantula-hunting when the egg in her ovary is almost ready to be laid. Flying low over the ground late on a sunny afternoon, the wasp looks for its victim or for the mouth of a tarantula burrow, a round hole edged by a bit of silk. The sex of the spider makes no difference, but the mother is highly discriminating as to species. Each species of *Pepsis* requires a certain species of tarantula, and the wasp will not attack the wrong species. In a cage with a tarantula which is not its normal prey the wasp avoids the spider, and is usually killed by it in the night.

12     Yet when a wasp finds the correct species, it is the other way about. To identify the species the wasp apparently must explore the spider with her antennae. The tarantula shows an amazing tolerance to this exploration. The wasp crawls under it and walks over it without evoking any hostile response. The molestation is so great and so persistent that the

tarantula often rises on all eight legs, as if it were on stilts. It may stand this way for several minutes. Meanwhile the wasp, having satisfied itself that the victim is of the right species, moves off a few inches to dig the spider's grave. Working vigorously with legs and jaws, it excavates a hole 8 to 10 inches deep with a diameter slightly larger than the spider's girth. Now and again the wasp pops out of the hole to make sure that the spider is still there.

When the grave is finished, the wasp returns to the tarantula to complete her ghastly enterprise. First she feels it all over once more with her antennae. Then her behavior becomes more aggressive. She bends her abdomen, protruding her sting, and searches for the soft membrane at the point where the spider's leg joins its body—the only spot where she can penetrate the horny skeleton. From time to time, as the exasperated spider slowly shifts ground, the wasp turns on her back and slides along with the aid of her wings, trying to get under the tarantula for a shot at the vital spot. During all this maneuvering, which can last for several minutes, the tarantula makes no move to save itself. Finally the wasp corners it against some obstruction and grasps one of its legs in her powerful jaws. Now at last the harassed spider tries a desperate but vain defense. The two contestants roll over and over on the ground. It is a terrifying sight and the outcome is always the same. The wasp finally manages to thrust her sting into the soft spot and holds it there for a few seconds while she pumps in the poison. Almost immediately the tarantula falls paralyzed on its back. Its legs stop twitching; its heart stops beating, yet it is not dead, as is shown by the fact that if taken from the wasp it can be restored to some sensitivity by being kept in a moist chamber for several months.

After paralyzing the tarantula, the wasp cleans herself by dragging   14 her body along the ground and rubbing her feet, sucks the drop of blood oozing from the wound in the spider's abdomen, then grabs a leg of the flabby, helpless animal in her jaws and drags it down to the bottom of the grave. She stays there for many minutes, sometimes for several hours, and what she does all that time in the dark we do not know. Eventually she lays her egg and attaches it to the side of the spider's abdomen with a sticky secretion. Then she emerges, fills the grave with soil carried bit by bit in her jaws, and finally tramples the ground all around to hide any trace of the grave from prowlers. Then she flies away, leaving her descendant safely started in life.

In all this the behavior of the wasp evidently is qualitatively different   15 from that of the spider. The wasp acts like an intelligent animal. This is not to say that instinct plays no part or that she reasons as man does. But her actions are to the point; they are not automatic and can be modified to fit the situation. We do not know for certain how she identifies the tarantula—probably it is by some olfactory or chemo-tactile sense—but she does it purposefully and does not blindly tackle a wrong species.

16    On the other hand, the tarantula's behavior shows only confusion. Evidently the wasp's pawing gives it no pleasure, for it tries to move away. That the wasp is not simulating sexual stimulation is certain, because male and female tarantulas react in the same way to its advances. That the spider is not anesthetized by some odorless secretion is easily shown by blowing lightly at the tarantula and making it jump suddenly. What, then, makes the tarantula behave as stupidly as it does?

17    No clear, simple answer is available. Possibly the stimulation by the wasp's antennae is masked by a heavier pressure on the spider's body, so that it reacts as when prodded by a pencil. But the explanation may be much more complex. Initiative in attack is not in the nature of tarantulas; most species fight only when cornered so that escape is impossible. Their inherited patterns of behavior apparently prompt them to avoid problems rather than attack them. For example, spiders always weave their webs in three dimensions, and when a spider finds that there is insufficient space to attach certain threads in the third dimension, it leaves the place and seeks another, instead of finishing the web in a single plane. This urge to escape seems to arise under all circumstances, in all phases of life and to take the place of reasoning. For a spider to change the pattern of its web is as impossible as for an inexperienced man to build a bridge across a chasm obstructing his way.

18    In a way the instinctive urge to escape is not only easier but often more efficient than reasoning. The tarantula does exactly what is most efficient in all cases except in an encounter with a ruthless and determined attacker dependent for the existence of her own species on killing as many tarantulas as she can lay eggs. Perhaps in this case the spider follows its usual pattern of trying to escape, instead of seizing and killing the wasp, because it is not aware of its danger. In any case, the survival of the tarantula species as a whole is protected by the fact that the spider is much more fertile than the wasp.

*1952*

## QUESTIONS FOR DISCUSSION

### Content

a. In paragraph 1, Petrunkevitch claims that for some species, "survival may be very delicately balanced." How does this statement relate to the rest of the essay?

b. How does the word *complicated* (paragraph 1) prepare the reader for what is to follow?

c. Based on your reading of this essay, in what way(s) is process analysis similar to narration?

d. Petrunkevitch makes it a point to describe a number of significant differences between the spider and the wasp. Identify a few of them. Why are they significant?

e. As you probably inferred from the two questions before this one, a variety of techniques, including narration and contrast, can be used to explain a process. What function does description play in this essay?

f. What, according to Petrunkevitch, may account for the tarantula's unwitting acceptance of its own destruction?

## Strategy and Style

g. Outline Petrunkevitch's major points in an attempt to trace the organization of the essay.

h. Given the fact that this selection was first published in *Scientific American*, it is probably safe to assume that Petrunkevitch was writing for a highly educated reader but one who may not have had formal training in zoology. Comment on his use of technical language. Why does the author stop to define unfamiliar words?

i. Petrunkevitch's tone is typically scientific—detached and objective—through most of this selection. At times, however, his language seems highly emotional and charged with excitement. Analyze his choice of words in these instances. What are the connotations of words such as *desperate* and *ghastly*? What images does Petrunkevitch evoke with phrases such as "she pumps in the poison"?

## ENGAGING THE TEXT

a. Summarize the battle between the spider and the wasp in one short paragraph.

b. Reread the essay and make a list of Petrunkevitch's descriptive techniques. Using his techniques, closely observe a pet, if you have one, or another animal and describe its behavior.

## SUGGESTIONS FOR SUSTAINED WRITING

a. As the author points out, nature can be cruel and terrifying. Write a description of a natural process that you find frightening, painful, or unpleasant. Be as specific as you can in conveying an objective picture of the process but, like Petrunkevitch, do not hesitate to allow your emotions to influence your writing.

b. Read other scientific essays in this text by Dowling (Chapter 4), Rettie (Chapter 9), Eiseley (Chapter 9), and Gould (Chapter 11). Then compare and/or contrast Petrunkevitch's essay to one or more of these selections in terms of purpose, audience, and style. Make direct reference to each of the works you are discussing by quoting directly from the text or by paraphrasing.

c. Write an explanation (process analysis) about the way in which an animal undertakes a task necessary to its survival or the survival of its species. Topics to choose from might include how a beaver constructs a dam, how ants build colonies, how deer forage for food, and how birds care for their young. In addition to observing animals firsthand, research this topic in your college library or on the Internet.

# How to Cook a Carp

## Euell Gibbons

*Euell Gibbons (1911–1975) was born and raised in Clarkesville, Texas, but left home when he was 15. He worked in Texas and New Mexico as a harvest hand, a cowboy, a carpenter, and a trapper before joining the army in 1934. After his discharge in 1936, he moved to Washington, where he continued working odd jobs. He joined the Communist party but resigned when the Soviet Union attacked Finland in 1939. During World War II, he worked for the U.S. Navy as a civilian boat builder. After the war, he moved to Hawaii and turned beachcomber, living in a thatched hut for two years and subsisting entirely on wild food. He entered the University of Hawaii as a freshman at the age of 36. Shortly thereafter, he began a career of teaching, writing, and lecturing about wild foods. His books on foraging for wild foods combine detailed "how-to" instructions and recipes with delightfully entertaining narrative. Among his best-known works are* Stalking the Wild Asparagus *(1962), from which "How to Cook a Carp" is taken;* Stalking the Blue-Eyed Scallop *(1964);* Stalking the Healthful Herbs *(1966); and* Euell Gibbons's Beachcomber's Handbook *(1967).*

*Another classic essay, this selection illustrates an interesting way to give the reader instructions. Unlike instructions for completing a scientific or technical procedure, however, "How to Cook a Carp" often resembles a narrative. But don't be fooled. It is Gibbons's purpose that defines this as a process piece. The fact that his presence and the presence of other characters are so prominent serves only to add color and interest. Indeed, without the personal voice we hear throughout the essay, it might have become a lifeless recitation on how to catch and cook fish, much like what we find in a fishing manual or cookbook.*

When I was a lad of about eighteen, my brother and I were working on a  1
cattle ranch in New Mexico that bordered on the Rio Grande. Most Americans think of the Rio Grande as a warm southern stream, but it rises
among the high mountains of Colorado, and in the spring it is fed by melting snows. At this time of the year, the water that rushed by the ranch was
turbulent, icy-cold and so silt-laden as to be semisolid. "A little too thick
to drink, and a little too thin to plow" was a common description of the
waters of the Rio Grande.

A few species of fish inhabited this muddy water. Unfortunately, the  2
most common was great eight- to ten-pound carp, a fish that is considered
very poor eating in this country, although the Germans and Asiatics have
domesticated this fish, and have developed some varieties that are highly
esteemed for the table.

On the ranch where we worked, there was a drainage ditch that ran  3
through the lower pasture and emptied its clear waters into the muddy Rio
Grande. The carp swimming up the river would strike this clear warmer
water and decide they preferred it to the cold mud they had been inhabiting. One spring day, a cowhand who had been riding that way reported
that Clear Ditch was becoming crowded with huge carp.

On Sunday we decided to go fishing. Four of us armed ourselves with  4
pitchforks, saddled our horses and set out. Near the mouth of the ditch, the
water was running about two feet deep and twelve to sixteen feet wide.
There is a saying in that part of the country that you can't get a cowboy to
do anything unless it can be done from the back of a horse, so we forced
our mounts into the ditch and started wading them upstream, four
abreast, herding the carp before us.

By the time we had ridden a mile upstream, the water was less than a  5
foot deep and so crystal clear that we could see our herd of several hundred carp still fleeing from the splashing, wading horses. As the water continued to shallow, our fish began to get panicky. A few of the boldest ones
attempted to dart back past us and were impaled on pitchforks. We could
see that the whole herd was getting restless and was about to stampede
back downstream, so we piled off our horses into the shallow water to
meet the charge. The water boiled about us as the huge fish swirled past
us and we speared madly in every direction with our pitchforks, throwing
each fish we managed to hit over the ditch bank. This was real fishing—
cowhand style. The last of the fish herd was by us in a few minutes and it
was all over, but we had caught a tremendous quantity of fish.

Back at the ranch house, after we had displayed our trophies, we be-  6
gan wondering what we were going to do with so many fish. This started
a series of typical cowboy tall tales on "how to cook a carp." The best of
these yarns was told by a grizzled old *vaquero*, who claimed he had made
his great discovery when he ran out of food while camping on a tributary
of the Rio Grande. He said that he had found the finest way to cook a carp

was to plaster the whole fish with a thick coating of fresh cow manure and bury it in the hot ashes of a campfire. In an hour or two, he said, the casing of cow manure had become black and very hard. He then related how he had removed the fish from the fire, broken the hard shell with the butt of his Winchester and peeled it off. He said that as the manure came off the scales and skin adhered to it, leaving the baked fish, white and clean. He then ended by saying, "Of course, the carp still wasn't fit to eat, but the manure in which it was cooked tasted pretty good."

7     There were also some serious suggestions and experiments. The chief objection to the carp is that its flesh is full of many forked bones. One man said that he had enjoyed carp sliced very thin and fried so crisp that one could eat it, bones and all. He demonstrated, and you really could eat it without the bones bothering you, but it was still far from being an epicurean dish. One cowboy described the flavor as "a perfect blend of Rio Grande mud and rancid hog lard."

8     Another man said that he had eaten carp that had been cooked in a pressure cooker until the bones softened and became indistinguishable from the flesh. A pressure cooker is almost a necessity at that altitude, so we had one at the ranch house. We tried this method, and the result was barely edible. It tasted like the poorest possible grade of canned salmon flavored with a bit of mud. It was, however, highly appreciated by the dogs and cats on the ranch, and solved the problem of what to do with the bulk of the fish we had caught.

9     It was my brother who finally devised a method of cooking carp that not only made it fit for human consumption, but actually delicious. First, instead of merely scaling the fish, he skinned them. Then, taking a large pinch, where the meat was thickest, he worked his fingers and thumb into the flesh until he struck the median bones, then he worked his thumb and fingers together and tore off a handful of meat. Using this tearing method, he could get two or three goodsized chunks of flesh from each side of the fish. He then heated a pot of bland vegetable shortening, rubbed the pieces of fish with salt and dropped them into the hot fat. He used no flour, meal, crumbs or seasoning other than salt. They cooked to a golden brown in a few minutes, and everyone pronounced them "mighty fine eating." The muddy flavor seemed to have been eliminated by removing the skin and the large bones. The forked bones were still there, but they had not been multiplied by cutting across them, and one only had to remove several bones still intact with the fork from each piece of fish.

10     For the remainder of that spring, every few days one or another of the cowboys would take a pitchfork and ride over to Clear Ditch and spear a mess of carp. On these evenings, my brother replaced the regular *cocinero* and we enjoyed some delicious fried carp.

11     The flavor of carp varies with the water from which it is caught. Many years after the above incidents I attended a fish fry at my brother's house.

The main course was all of his own catching, and consisted of bass, catfish and carp, all from Elephant Butte Lake farther down the Rio Grande. All the fish were prepared exactly alike, except that the carp was pulled apart as described above, while the bass and catfish, being all twelve inches or less in length, were merely cleaned and fried whole. None of his guests knew one fish from another, yet all of them preferred the carp to the other kinds. These experiences have convinced me that the carp is really a fine food fish when properly prepared.

Carp can, of course, be caught in many ways besides spearing them 12 with pitchforks from the back of a horse. In my adopted home state, Pennsylvania, they are classed as "trash fish" and one is allowed to take them almost any way. They will sometimes bite on worms, but they are vegetarians by preference and are more easily taken on dough balls. Some states allow the use of gill nets, and other states, because they would like to reduce the population of this unpopular fish, will issue special permits for the use of nets to catch carp.

A good forager will take advantage of the lax regulations on carp fish- 13 ing while they last. When all fishermen realize that the carp is really a good food fish when prepared in the right way, maybe this outsized denizen of our rivers and lakes will no longer be considered a pest and will take his rightful place among our valued food and game fishes.

*1962*

## QUESTIONS FOR DISCUSSION

### Content

a. What do you think is Gibbons's goal in writing this essay? How successful is he in reaching that goal?
b. How would you describe Gibbons's ideal reader? If you were that reader, what use would this essay be to you?
c. Is there an argument implied in this essay? If so, how would you phrase the argument? What would the counterargument be?
d. Carp is common throughout North America. Besides the obvious reason that the essay is based on personal experience, why would Gibbons set his narrative in the ranch country along the Rio Grande and not in some other locale? How would the essay be different if it were set in, for example, Gibbons's "adopted home state, Pennsylvania"?

## Strategy and Style

e. Although Gibbons titles his essay "How to Cook a Carp," he does not actually describe the process until paragraph 9. What does he do first, and what are his reasons for providing this long introduction?

f. Gibbons was an expert on foraging for and cooking wild plants and game, and this essay appears in one of his popular books about foraging. Why, then, does he describe so many failed attempts at cooking carp? Do these accounts add to or detract from his authority as an expert?

g. How do anecdotes such as the account of catching carp with pitchforks or the tale of the "old *vaquero*" (paragraphs 5 and 6) affect the essay? What purpose do they serve other than entertaining the reader?

h. What metaphors does Gibbons use to describe carp and the process of catching them? What effect do these metaphors have on the essay? On you?

## ENGAGING THE TEXT

a. Write a recipe for an inedible, or seemingly inedible, dish. Use Gibbons's organization and style to write humorous instructions for collecting, preparing, and serving the dish.

b. What passages in the essay made you feel queasy (or delighted you)? Explain why the passages disgusted or delighted you.

## SUGGESTIONS FOR SUSTAINED WRITING

a. Write a narrative essay that explains how you accomplished a common but important task. Limit your essay to a simple process that can be explained fully in three or four typewritten pages. For example, explain how you learned to hang wallpaper, cook a Thanksgiving turkey, load software into a home computer, do laundry, set up an aquarium, change the oil in a car, or plant a vegetable patch. Put your comments in the form of a letter to a friend or classmate who has asked for instructions about a process you know well. Assume that your reader knows little about the process.

b. In some ways, Gibbons's essay resembles Hubbell's "Honey Harvest" (this chapter), which explains how something was done, more than an essay that gives instructions, such as Marius's "Writing Drafts" or Goodheart's "How to Paint a Fresco" (this chapter). In what ways is Gibbons's essay like those of these other authors? In what ways is it different? As you write your essay, focus on purpose, style, and organization. Quote directly from or paraphrase the text as often as is necessary.

c. Write an essay in which you explain how to do something that requires technical expertise. Scientific subjects will work well, but so will many other types. For example, you might explain how to cauterize a wound, determine latitude by using a telescope, or solve a calculus problem. Then again, you might explain how to construct a brick wall, build a model-train layout, or create a Web site. Address your instructions to a novice and make sure to include material you have researched in books, manuals, articles, and other print sources as well as on the Internet.

# Behind the Formaldehyde Curtain

Jessica Mitford

*Born in Great Britain to parents who were members of the nobility, Jessica Mitford (1917–1996) immigrated to the United States in 1939. In 1960, she published the first volume of her autobiography,* Daughters and Rebels, *in which she described what it is like to grow up in an aristocratic English household and to receive one's education at home. The title of that book was to prove prophetic, for much of Mitford's later work is social criticism. For instance,* The American Way of Death *(1963; 1998), from which this selection is taken, is an indictment of morticians and their profession as well as of American funeral customs in general. In* Kind and Unusual Punishment: The Prison Business *(1973), Mitford exposes the scandal of the U.S. corrections system. In 1977, Mitford published the second part of her autobiography,* A Fine Old Madness. *Since then, she has published* Faces of Philip: A Memoir of Philip Toynbee *(1984) and* Grace Had an English Heart: The Story of Grace Darling *(1988). Mitford's last book is* The American Way of Birth *(1992).*

The drama begins to unfold with the arrival of the corpse at the mortuary.   1

Alas, poor Yorick! How surprised he would be to see how his counter-   2
part of today is whisked off to a funeral parlor and is in short order sprayed, sliced, pierced, pickled, trussed, trimmed, creamed, waxed, painted, rouged and neatly dressed—transformed from a common corpse into a Beautiful Memory Picture. This process is known in the trade as embalming and restorative art, and is so universally employed in the United States and Canada that the funeral director does it routinely, without consulting corpse or kin. He regards as eccentric those few who are hardy enough to suggest that it might be dispensed with. Yet no law requires embalming, no religious doctrine commends it, nor is it dictated by considerations of health, sanitation, or even of personal daintiness. In no part of the world but in Northern America is it widely used. The purpose of embalming is to

make the corpse presentable for viewing in a suitably costly container; and here too the funeral director routinely, without first consulting the family, prepares the body for public display.

3        Is all this legal? The processes to which a dead body may be subjected are after all to some extent circumscribed by law. In most states, for instance, the signature of next of kin must be obtained before an autopsy may be performed, before the deceased may be cremated, before the body may be turned over to a medical school for research purposes; or such provision must be made in the decedent's will. In the case of embalming, no such permission is required nor is it ever sought. A textbook, *The Principles and Practices of Embalming*, comments on this: "There is some question regarding the legality of much that is done within the preparation room." The author points out that it would be most unusual for a responsible member of a bereaved family to instruct the mortician, in so many words, to *"embalm"* the body of a deceased relative. The very term "embalming" is so seldom used that the mortician must rely upon custom in the matter. The author concludes that unless the family specifies otherwise, the act of entrusting the body to the care of a funeral establishment carries with it an implied permission to go ahead and embalm.

4        Embalming is indeed a most extraordinary procedure, and one must wonder at the docility of Americans who each year pay hundreds of millions of dollars for its perpetuation, blissfully ignorant of what it is all about, what is done, how it is done. Not one in ten thousand has any idea of what actually takes place. Books on the subject are extremely hard to come by. They are not to be found in most libraries or bookshops.

5        In an era when huge television audiences watch surgical operations in the comfort of their living rooms, when, thanks to the animated cartoon, the geography of the digestive system has become familiar territory even to the nursery school set, in a land where the satisfaction of curiosity about almost all matters is a national pastime, the secrecy surrounding embalming can, surely, hardly be attributed to the inherent gruesomeness of the subject. Custom in this regard has within this century suffered a complete reversal. In the early days of American embalming, when it was performed in the home of the deceased, it was almost mandatory for some relative to stay by the embalmer's side and witness the procedure. Today, family members who might wish to be in attendance would certainly be dissuaded by the funeral director. All others, except apprentices, are excluded by law from the preparation room.

6        A close look at what does actually take place may explain in large measure the undertaker's intractable reticence concerning a procedure that has become his major *raison d'être*. It is possible he fears that public information about embalming might lead patrons to wonder if they really want this service? If the funeral men are loath to discuss the subject outside the trade, the reader may, understandably, be equally loath to go on reading at

this point. For those who have the stomach for it, let us part the formaldehyde curtain. . . .

The body is first laid out in the undertaker's morgue—or rather, Mr.  7
Jones is reposing in the preparation room—to be readied to bid the world
farewell.

The preparation room in any of the better funeral establishments has  8
the tiled and sterile look of a surgery, and indeed the embalmer-restorative
artist who does his chores there is beginning to adopt the term "dermasurgeon" (appropriately corrupted by some mortician-writers as "demisurgeon") to describe his calling. His equipment, consisting of scalpels,
scissors, augers, forceps, clamps, needles, pumps, tubes, bowls, and
basins, is crudely imitative of the surgeon's, as is his technique, acquired
in a nine- or twelve-month post-highschool course in an embalming
school. He is supplied by an advanced chemical industry with a bewil-
dering array of fluids, sprays, pastes, oils, powders, creams, to fix or
soften tissue, shrink or distend it as needed, dry it here, restore the moisture there. There are cosmetics, waxes and paints to fill and cover features,
even plaster of Paris to replace entire limbs. There are ingenious aids to
prop and stabilize the cadaver: A Vari-Pose Head Rest, the Edwards Arm
and Hand Positioner, the Repose Block (to support the shoulders during
the embalming), and the Throop Foot Positioner, which resembles an old-
fashioned stock.

Mr. John H. Eckels, president of the Eckels College of Mortuary Sci-  9
ence, thus describes the first part of the embalming procedure: "In the
hands of a skilled practitioner, this work may be done in a comparatively
short time and without mutilating the body other than by slight incision—
so slight that it scarcely would cause serious inconvenience if made upon
a living person. It is necessary to remove the blood, and doing this not only
helps in the disinfecting, but removes the principal cause of disfigure-
ments due to discoloration."

Another textbook discusses the all-important time element: "The  10
earlier this is done, the better, for every hour that elapses between death
and embalming will add to the problems and complications encountered. . ." Just how soon should one get going on the embalming? The
author tells us, "On the basis of such scanty information made available
to this profession through its rudimentary and haphazard system of
technical research, we must conclude that the best results are to be obtained if the subject is embalmed before life is completely extinct—that
is, before cellular death has occurred. In the average case, this would
mean within an hour after somatic death." For those who feel that there
is something a little rudimentary, not to say haphazard, about this advice, a comforting thought is offered by another writer. Speaking of fears
entertained in early days of premature burial, he points out, "One of the
effects of embalming by chemical injection, however, has been to dispel

fears of live burial." How true; once the blood is removed, chances of live burial are indeed remote.

11     To return to Mr. Jones, the blood is drained out through the veins and replaced by embalming fluid pumped in through the arteries. As noted in *The Principles and Practices of Embalming*, "every operator has a favorite injection and drainage point—a fact which becomes a handicap only if he fails or refuses to forsake his favorites when conditions demand it." Typical favorites are the carotid artery, femoral artery, jugular vein, subclavian vein. There are various choices of embalming fluid. If Flextone is used, it will produce a "mild, flexible rigidity. The skin retains a velvety softness, the tissues are rubbery and pliable. Ideal for women and children." It may be blended with B. and G. Products Company's Lyf-Lyk tint, which is guaranteed to reproduce "nature's own skin texture . . . the velvety appearance of living tissue." Suntone comes in three separate tints: Suntan; Special Cosmetic Tint, a pink shade "especially indicated for female subjects"; and Regular Cosmetic Tint, moderately pink.

12     About three to six gallons of a dyed and perfumed solution of formaldehyde, glycerin, borax, phenol, alcohol and water is soon circulating through Mr. Jones, whose mouth has been sewn together with a "needle directed upward between the upper lip and gum and brought out through the left nostril," with the corners raised slightly "for a more pleasant expression." If he should be bucktoothed, his teeth are cleaned with Bon Ami and coated with colorless nail polish. His eyes, meanwhile, are closed with flesh-tinted eye caps and eye cement.

13     The next step is to have at Mr. Jones with a thing called a trocar. This is a long, hollow needle attached to a tube. It is jabbed into the abdomen, poked around the entrails and chest cavity, the contents of which are pumped out and replaced with "cavity fluid." This done, and the hole in the abdomen sewn up, Mr. Jones's face is heavily creamed (to protect the skin from burns which may be caused by leakage of the chemicals), and he is covered with a sheet and left unmolested for a while. But not for long—there is more, much more, in store for him. He has been embalmed, but not yet restored, and the best time to start the restorative work is eight to ten hours after embalming, when the tissues have become firm and dry.

14     The object of all this attention to the corpse, it must be remembered, is to make it presentable for viewing in an attitude of healthy repose. "Our customs require the presentation of our dead in the semblance of normality . . . unmarred by the ravages of illness, disease or mutilation," says Mr. J. Sheridan Mayer in his *Restorative Art*. This is rather a large order since few people die in the full bloom of health, unravaged by illness and unmarked by some disfigurement. The funeral industry is equal to the challenge: "In some cases the gruesome appearance of a mutilated or disease-ridden subject may be quite discouraging. The task of restoration may seem impossible and shake the confidence of the embalmer. This is the time for intestinal

fortitude and determination. Once the formative work is begun and affected tissues are cleaned or removed, all doubts of success vanish. It is surprising and gratifying to discover the results which may be obtained."

The embalmer, having allowed an appropriate interval to elapse, re- 15
turns to the attack, but now he brings into play the skill and equipment of sculptor and cosmetician. Is a hand missing? Casting one in plaster of Paris is a simple matter. "For replacement purposes, only a cast of the back of the hand is necessary; this is within the ability of the average operator and is quite adequate." If a lip or two, a nose or an ear should be missing, the embalmer has at hand a variety of restorative waxes with which to model replacements. Pores and skin texture are simulated by stippling with a little brush, and over this cosmetics are laid on. Head off? Decapitation cases are rather routinely handled. Ragged edges are trimmed, and head joined to torso with a series of splints, wires and sutures. It is a good idea to have a little something at the neck—a scarf or a high collar—when time for viewing comes. Swollen mouth? Cut out tissue as needed from inside the lips. If too much is removed, the surface contour can easily be restored by padding with cotton. Swollen necks and cheeks are reduced by removing tissue through vertical incisions made down each side of the neck. "When the deceased is casketed, the pillow will hide the suture incisions  . . as an extra precaution against leakage, the suture may be painted with liquid sealer."

The opposite condition is more likely to present itself—that of emaci- 16
ation. His hypodermic syringe now loaded with massage cream, the embalmer seeks out and fills the hollowed and sunken areas by injection. In this procedure the backs of the hands and fingers and the under-chin area should not be neglected.

Positioning the lips is a problem that recurrently challenges the inge- 17
nuity of the embalmer. Closed too tightly, they tend to give a stern, even disapproving expression. Ideally, embalmers feel, the lips should give the impression of being ever so slightly parted, the upper lip protruding slightly for a more youthful appearance. This takes some engineering, however, as the lips tend to drift apart. Lip drift can sometimes be remedied by pushing one or two straight pins through the inner margin of the lower lip and then inserting them between the two front upper teeth. If Mr. Jones happens to have no teeth, the pins can just as easily be anchored in his Armstrong Face Former and Denture Replacer. Another method to maintain lip closure is to dislocate the lower jaw, which is then held in its new position by a wire run through holes which have been drilled through the upper and lower jaws at the midline. As the French are fond of saying, *il faut souffrir pour être belle.*

If Mr. Jones has died of jaundice, the embalming fluid will very likely 18
turn him green. Does this deter the embalmer? Not if he has intestinal fortitude. Masking pastes and cosmetics are heavily laid on, burial garments and casket interiors are color-correlated with particular care, and Jones is

displayed beneath rose-colored lights. Friends will say "How *well* he looks." Death by carbon monoxide, on the other hand, can be rather a good thing from the embalmer's viewpoint: "One advantage is the fact that this type of discoloration is an exaggerated form of a natural pink coloration." This is nice because the healthy glow is already present and needs but little attention.

19     The patching and filling completed, Mr. Jones is now shaved, washed and dressed. Cream-based cosmetic, available in pink, flesh, suntan, brunette and blond, is applied to his hands and face, his hair is shampooed and combed (and, in the case of Mrs. Jones, set), his hands manicured. For the horny-handed son of toil special care must be taken; cream should be applied to remove ingrained grime, and the nails cleaned. "If he were not in the habit of having them manicured in life, trimming and shaping is advised for better appearance—never questioned by kin."

20     Jones is now ready for casketing (this is the present participle of the verb "to casket"). In this operation his right shoulder should be depressed slightly "to turn the body a bit to the right and soften the appearance of lying flat on the back." Positioning the hands is a matter of importance, and special rubber positioning blocks may be used. The hands should be cupped slightly for a more life-like, relaxed appearance. Proper placement of the body requires a delicate sense of balance. It should lie as high as possible in the casket, yet not so high that the lid, when lowered, will hit the nose. On the other hand, we are cautioned, placing the body too low "creates the impression that the body is in a box."

21     Jones is next wheeled into the appointed slumber room where a few last touches may be added—his favorite pipe placed in his hand or, if he was a great reader, a book propped into position. (In the case of little Master Jones a Teddy bear may be clutched.) Here he will hold open house for a few days, visiting hours 10 AM to 9 PM.

22     All now being in readiness, the funeral director calls a staff conference to make sure that each assistant knows his precise duties. Mr. Wilber Kriege writes: "This makes your staff feel that they are a part of the team, with a definite assignment that must be properly carried out if the whole plan is to succeed. You never heard of a football coach who failed to talk to his entire team before they go on the field. They have drilled on the plays they are to execute for hours and days, and yet the successful coach knows the importance of making even the bench-warming third-string substitute feel that he is important if the game is to be won." The winning of *this* game is predicated upon glass-smooth handling of the logistics. The funeral director has notified the pallbearers whose names were furnished by the family, has arranged for the presence of clergyman, organist, and soloist, has provided transportation for everybody, has organized and listed the flowers sent by friends. In *Psychology of Funeral Service* Mr. Edward A. Martin points out: "He may not always do as much as the family

thinks he is doing, but it is his helpful guidance that they appreciate in knowing they are proceeding as they should. . . . The important thing is how well his services can be used to make the family believe they are giving unlimited expression to their own sentiment."

The religious service may be held in a church or in the chapel of the fu-  23 neral home; the funeral director vastly prefers the latter arrangement, for not only is it more convenient for him but it affords him the opportunity to show off his beautiful facilities to the gathered mourners. After the clergyman has had his say, the mourners queue up to file past the casket for a last look at the deceased. The family is *never* asked whether they want an open-casket ceremony; in the absence of their instruction to the contrary, this is taken for granted. Consequently well over 90 percent of all American funerals feature the open casket—a custom unknown in other parts of the world. Foreigners are astonished by it. An English woman living in San Francisco described her reaction in a letter to the writer:

> I myself have attended only one funeral here—that of an elderly fellow worker of mine. After the service I could not understand why everyone was walking towards the coffin (sorry, I mean casket), but thought I had better follow the crowd. It shook me rigid to get there and find the casket open and poor old Oscar lying there in his brown tweed suit, wearing a suntan makeup and just the wrong shade of lipstick. If I had not been extremely fond of the old boy, I have a horrible feeling that I might have giggled. Then and there I decided that I could never face another American funeral—even dead.

The casket (which has been resting throughout the service on a Clas-  24 sic Beauty Ultra Metal Casket Bier) is now transferred by a hydraulically operated device called Porto-Lift to a balloon-tired, Glide Easy casket carriage which will wheel it to yet another conveyance, the Cadillac Funeral Coach. This may be lavender, cream, light green—anything but black. Interiors, of course, are color-correlated, "for the man who cannot stop short of perfection."

At graveside, the casket is lowered into the earth. This office, once the  25 prerogative of friends of the deceased, is now performed by a patented mechanical lowering device. A "Lifetime Green" artificial grass mat is at the ready to conceal the sere earth, and overhead, to conceal the sky, is a portable Steril Chapel Tent ("resists the intense heat and humidity of summer and the terrific storms of winter . . . available in Silver Grey, Rose or Evergreen"). Now is the time for the ritual scattering of earth over the coffin, as the solemn words "earth to earth, ashes to ashes, dust to dust" are pronounced by the officiating cleric. This can today be accomplished "with a mere flick of the wrist with the Gordon Leak-Proof Earth Dispenser. No grasping of a handful of dirt, no soiled fingers. Simple, dignified, beautiful, reverent! The modern way!" The Gordon Earth Dispenser (at $5) is of nickel-plated brass construction. It is not only "attractive to the eye and long wearing"; it is also "one of the 'tools' for building better public relations" if presented as "an appropriate non-commercial gift" to the clergyman. It is shaped something like a saltshaker.

26     Untouched by human hand, the coffin and the earth are now united.

27     It is in the function of directing the participants through this maze of gadgetry that the funeral director has assigned to himself his relatively new role of "grief therapist." He has relieved the family of every detail, he has revamped the corpse to look like a living doll, he has arranged for it to nap for a few days in a slumber room, he has put on a well-oiled performance in which the concept of *death* has played no part whatsoever—unless it was inconsiderately mentioned by the clergyman who conducted the religious service. He has done everything in his power to make the funeral a real pleasure for everybody concerned. He and his team have given their all to score an upset victory over death.

*1963*

## QUESTIONS FOR DISCUSSION

### Content

a. What is Mitford's purpose? Do you agree that "public information about embalming might lead patrons to wonder if they really want this service" (paragraph 6)?

b. In what ways does this selection resemble a narrative? What aspects are arranged in chronological order? How does Mitford indicate the passage of time?

c. According to Mitford, why is it odd that embalming remains so secretive a business? What can we infer about the reasons for the persistence of embalming as a widespread practice only in this part of the world?

d. Do you know of any important differences between funeral practices in North America and those in other parts of the world? Why does Mitford bother to mention such differences at the start of this essay?

e. The beginning of paragraph 2 alludes to Shakespeare's *Hamlet*. Who was Yorick, and why has Mitford chosen to include him in her introduction?

f. Why does the author make it a point to mention the brand names of the supplies and equipment used by undertakers?

## Strategy and Style

g. Mitford's use of detail seems to be accurate and thorough. Is it too thorough? Could she have achieved her purpose without being so detailed?

h. Mitford relies heavily on the use of quoted material from embalming textbooks to develop her indictment of morticians. Explain how these citations help her achieve her purpose.

i. In paragraph 6, before parting "the formaldehyde curtain," Why does Mitford warn us about what is to follow.

j. What other interesting metaphors does Mitford use? Do they help "enliven" her prose?

k. What is ironic about her calling the embalming procedure the mortician's *raison d'être*? Identify other examples of irony in this selection.

l. Look up the roots of the term *dermasurgeon* in a good dictionary. What do their meanings suggest? Now look up *demi*. What does the corruption *demisurgeon* tell you about Mitford's view of undertakers? What does Mitford mean by "grief therapist" (paragraph 27)? Why does she say that funeral directors have "assigned" themselves this role?

m. How would you describe Mitford's tone? Analyze at least one paragraph closely (paragraph 13, 14, or 15 would be a good choice). How does her use of language make her attitude about the subject clear?

n. When does irony turn to sarcasm? Reread paragraph 25. What makes Mitford's treatment of graveside ceremonies so caustic?

## ENGAGING THE TEXT

a. To what sections of the essay did you react most strongly? Quoting the essay, explain why these passages affected you as they did.

b. Address a response to Mitford. Tell her what you think of her essay and why.

## SUGGESTIONS FOR SUSTAINED WRITING

a. Write out and review your answers to the Questions for Discussion, which appear above. Then write an essay that analyzes Mitford's "strategy and style" in this essay based on your responses to questions *g* through *n*.

b. Mitford's "Behind the Formaldehyde Curtain" and Nicols Fox's "Gawk Shows" (Chapter 9) focus on two very different subjects, but they both satirize contemporary American behavior. Write an essay in which you compare and/or contrast the authors' purposes and styles. The essay by

Horace Miner (Chapter 9) might make an additional or alternate choice
for comparison.

c. Do you agree with Mitford's assessment of the undertaker's profession?
If not, write an essay in which you refute her by explaining the important role current funeral customs and practices play. Address your essay to Mitford directly, perhaps in the form of a letter. If this assignment
doesn't interest you, write an essay in which you explain the funeral
rites used in another culture. Focus on a culture that is very different
from our own. Whichever option you choose, support your thesis with
library and/or Internet research.

# Writing Drafts

## Richard Marius

*A native of Tennessee, Richard Marius (1933–1999) took his bachelor's degree in journalism
at the University of Tennessee and his master's and doctorate in history at Yale University.
He also holds a BD from Southern Baptist Theological Seminary. Marius is the author of sev-
eral historical studies and received wide acclaim for his full-length biographies of Martin
Luther and Thomas More. He has also written three novels, including* The Coming of Rain
*(1969) and* Bound for the Promised Land *(1976). A director of the Expository Writing
Program at Harvard University, Marius has published several books on writing, including*
The McGraw-Hill College Handbook, *which he coauthored with Harvey Wiener, and* A
Short Guide to Writing about History *(1987). "Writing Drafts" first appeared in* The
Writer's Companion *(1985), his splendid guide for both novice and experienced writers.*

*The essay that follows provides practical advice for any writer no matter what his or
her purpose or topic. Equally important, it is an example of the kind of clear and engaging
writing that is sure to keep the reader's interest and communicate important information
about how to perform a complex cognitive procedure.*

1   Finally the moment comes when you sit down to begin your first draft. It
is always a good idea at the start to list the points you want to cover. A list
is not as elaborate as a formal outline. In writing your first list, don't bother
to set items down in the order of importance. List your main points and
trust your mind to organize them. You will probably make one list, study
it, make another, study it, and perhaps make another. You can organize
each list more completely than the last. This preliminary process may save
you hours of starting and stopping.

2       Write with your list outline in front of you. Once you begin to write,
commit yourself to the task at hand. Do not get up until you have written
for an hour. Write your thoughts quickly. Let one sentence give you an idea

to develop in the next. Organization, grammar, spelling, and even clarity of sentences are not nearly as important as getting the first draft together. No matter how desperate you feel, keep going.

Always keep your mind open to new ideas that pop into your head as    3 you write. Let your list outline help you, but don't become a slave to it. Writers often start an essay with one topic in mind only to discover that another pushes the first one aside as they work. Ideas you had not even thought of before you began to write may pile onto your paper, and five or six pages into your first draft you may realize that you are going to write about something you did not imagine when you started.

If such a revelation comes, be grateful and accept it. But don't imme-    4 diately tear up or erase your draft and start all over again. Make yourself keep on writing, developing these new ideas as they come. If you suddenly start all over again, you may break the train of thought that has given you the new topic. Let your thoughts follow your new thesis, sailing on that tack until the wind changes.

When you have said everything you can say in this draft, print it out if    5 you are working on a computer. Get up from your desk and go sit in a chair somewhere else to read it without correcting anything. Then put it aside, preferably overnight. If possible, read your rough draft just before you go to sleep. Many psychological tests have shown that our minds organize and create while we sleep if we pack them full before bedtime. Study a draft just before sleep, and you may discover new ideas in the morning.

Be willing to make radical changes in your second draft. If your thesis    6 changed while you were writing your first draft, you will base your second draft on this new subject. Even if your thesis has not changed, you may need to shift paragraphs around, eliminate paragraphs, or add new ones. Inexperienced writers often suppose that revising a paper means changing only a word or two or adding a sentence or two. This kind of editing is part of the writing process, but it is not the most important part. The most important part of rewriting is a willingness to turn the paper upside down, to shake out of it those ideas that interest you most, to set them in a form where they will interest the reader, too.

I mentioned earlier that some writers cut up their first drafts with a    7 pair of scissors. They toss some paragraphs into the trash; others they paste up with rubber cement in the order that seems most logical and coherent. Afterward they type the whole thing through again, smoothing out the transitions, adding new material, getting new ideas as they work. The translation of the first draft into the second nearly always involves radical cutting and shifting around. Now and then you may firmly fix the order of your thoughts in your first draft, but I find that the order of my essays is seldom established until the second draft.

With the advent of computers the shifting around of parts of the essays    8 has become easy. We can cut and paste electronically with a few strokes of the keyboard. We can also make back-up copies of our earlier drafts so we can go back to them if we wish. But as I said earlier, computers do not remove from us the necessity to think hard about revising.

9    Always be firm enough with yourself to cut out thoughts or stories that have nothing to do with your thesis, even if they are interesting. Cutting is the supreme test of a writer. You may create a smashing paragraph or sentence only to discover later that it does not help you make your point. You may develop six or seven examples to illustrate a point and discover you need only one.

10   Now and then you may digress a little. If you digress too often or too far, readers will not follow you unless your facts, your thoughts, and your style are so compelling that they are somehow driven to follow you. Not many writers can pull such digressions off, and most editors will cut out the digressions even when they are interesting. In our hurried and harried time, most readers get impatient with the rambling scenic route. They want to take the most direct way to their destination. To appeal to most of them, you must cut things that do not apply to your main argument.

11   In your third draft, you can sharpen sentences, add information here and there, cut some things, and attend to other details to heighten the force of your writing. In the third draft, writing becomes a lot of fun (for most of us). By then you have usually decided what you want to say. You can now play a bit, finding just the right word, choosing just the right sentence form, compressing here, expanding there.

12   I find it helpful to put a printed draft down beside my keyboard and type the whole thing through again as a final draft, letting all the words run through my mind and fingers one more time rather than merely deleting and inserting on the computer screen. I wrote four drafts of the first edition of this book; I have preserved the final draft of that edition on computer diskettes. But I am writing this draft by propping the first edition up here beside me and typing it all over again. By comparing the first draft and the second draft, one can see how many changes I have made, most of them unforeseen until I sat down here to work.

13   I have outlined here my own writing process. It works for me. You must find the process that works for you. It may be different from mine. A friend tells me that his writing process consists of writing a sentence, agonizing over it, walking around the room, thinking, sitting down, and writing the next sentence. He does not revise very much. I think it unnecessarily painful to bleed out prose that way, but he bleeds out enough to write what he needs to write. Several of my friends tell me they cannot compose at a typewriter; they must first write with a pencil on a yellow pad. These are the people most likely to cut up their drafts with scissors and paste them together in a different form. They also tend to be older. Most young writers are learning to compose at a keyboard, and they can-

not imagine another way to write. Neither can I—though on occasion yet I go back to my pencil for pages at a time.

The main thing is to keep at it. B. F. Skinner has pointed out that if you 14 write only fifty words a night, you will produce a good-sized book every two or three years. That's not a bad record for any writer. William Faulkner outlined the plot of his Nobel Prize–winning novel *A Fable* on a wall inside his house near Oxford, Mississippi. You can see it there to this day. Once he got the outline on the wall, he sat down with his typewriter and wrote, following the outline to the end. If writing an outline on a kitchen wall does the trick for you, do it. You can always repaint the wall if you must.

Think of writing as a process making its way toward a product— 15 sometimes painfully. Don't imagine you must know everything you are going to say before you begin. Don't demean yourself and insult your readers by letting your first draft be your final draft. Don't imagine that writing is easy or that you can do it without spending time on it. And don't let anything stand in your way of doing it. Let your house get messy. Leave your magazines unread and your mail unanswered. Put off getting up for a drink of water or a cup of tea. (Never mix alcohol with your writing; true, lots of writers have become alcoholics, but it has not helped their writing.) Don't make a telephone call. Don't straighten up your desk. Sit down and write. And write, and write, and write.

*1988*

## QUESTIONS FOR DISCUSSION

### Content

a. Marius advises using a list outline, but he cautions us not to follow it slavishly. Why not?

b. "Cutting is the supreme test of a writer," the author tells us in paragraph 9. What does he mean?

c. How is rewriting different from simple editing?

d. In what way is writing the second draft different from writing the first? In what way is writing the third draft different from writing the second?

e. How does Marius's suggested process compare with the way you usually write a paper? Which of his suggestions have you tried with success? Which without success? Which suggestions might you try for your next paper?

f. Are there any suggestions in "Writing Drafts" with which you disagree? What is the basis of your disagreement?

## Strategy and Style

g.  The author's personal voice can be heard clearly and distinctly through-out this selection. Is this subjective approach appropriate to writing that instructs?

h.  If the writing process Marius follows may not work for you, why does he explain that process in careful detail?

i.  Marius draws on several metaphors to help him describe the drafting process. One is the sailing metaphor at the end of paragraph 4: "Let your thoughts follow your new thesis, sailing on that tack until the wind changes." What connection does he want us to see between writing and sailing? What other metaphors can you find in the essay?

j.  How does including personal experience, as in paragraph 13, help the author achieve his purposes? Why does he make reference to the experiences of well-known writers such as B. F. Skinner and William Faulkner?

k.  Marius writes directly to you, the student. What was your reaction to this technique when you first read the essay? Why did he choose this technique?

## ENGAGING THE TEXT

a.  Quickly, and without looking back at Marius's essay, list the steps he suggests in writing drafts. Check what you have written against Marius's essay.

b.  What piece of advice in "Writing Drafts" did you find most helpful? Explain how that advice will help you improve your writing.

## SUGGESTIONS FOR SUSTAINED WRITING

a.  Outline your own writing process. You may want to use as an example the last academic paper you wrote. Then, roughly following Marius's essay as a model, describe your *ideal* process for writing papers. As you complete this assignment, keep in mind techniques and practices you might try out with your *next* academic paper.

b.  Write an essay similar to Marius's in which you set forth a set of sequenced suggestions for doing something other than writing drafts for an academic paper. The task you explain could be another kind of writing—poetry or short stories, for instance—or it might be any activity that people often find intimidating. Either way, make the activity seem both unintimidating and fruitfully challenging.

c. Marius explains how to draft an essay. But what about other parts of the writing process? Research the process of writing by reading further in Marius's *The Writer's Companion* or in the other works mentioned in the short biography above. However, focus on a stage in the writing process other than drafting. For example, read about how to gather information, to revise, or to edit/proofread. Then do some more research by consulting the works of composition experts such as Peter Elbow, William Zinsser, and Donald Murray. You can also find information on the Web sites of college and university writing centers. Turn your notes into instructions that will help a fellow student learn how to complete the stage of the writing process you are explaining.

# Honey Harvest*

## Sue Hubbell

*Born in 1935 in Kalamazoo, Michigan, Hubbell attended Swarthmore College and the University of Michigan before getting a bachelor's degree from the University of Southern California in 1956 and a master's degree from Drexel Institute in 1963. She worked as a bookstore manager in New Jersey and as a school librarian in New Jersey and Rhode Island before boldly changing careers in 1973 to become a commercial beekeeper in the Ozark Mountains. In 1985 she added writing to beekeeping when she began writing* A Country Year: Living the Questions *(1986), a collection of essays on life and nature. Since then she has published two books about insects,* A Book of Bees: . . . and How to Keep Them *(1988) and* Broadsides from the Other Orders: A Book of Bugs *(1993), which prompted a book reviewer to call her "one of the two or three best writers-about-bugs now living." She has also published collections of her essays,* On This Hilltop *(1991) and* Far Flung Hubbell *(1995), and she contributes regularly to magazines such as the* New Yorker, Smithsonian, Time, *and* Harper's. *She currently splits her time between her 18 million bees in Missouri and her husband in Washington, D.C. "Honey Harvest" is taken from* A Country Year.

I keep twenty hives of bees here in my home beeyard, but most of my hives 1 are scattered in outyards across the Ozarks, where I can find the thickest stands of wild blackberries and other good things for bees. I always have a waiting list of farmers who would like the bees on their land, for the clover in their pastures is more abundant when the bees are there to pollinate it.

   One of the farmers, a third-generation Ozarker and a dairyman with a 2 lively interest in bees, came over today for a look at what my neighbors call

_____
*Editor's Title.

my honey factory. My honey house contains a shiny array of stainless-steel tanks with clear plastic tubing connecting them, a power uncapper for slicing open honey comb, an extractor for spinning honey out of the comb, and a lot of machinery and equipment that whirs, thumps, hums, and looks very special. The dairyman, shrewd in mountain ways, looked it all over carefully and then observed, "Well . . . ll . . . ll, wouldn't say for sure now, but it looks like a still to me."

3      There have been droughty years and cold wet ones when flowers refused to bloom and I would have been better off with a still back up here on my mountain top, but the weather this past year was perfect from a bee's standpoint, and this August I ran 33,000 pounds of honey through my factory. This was nearly twice the normal crop, and everything was overloaded, starting with me. Neither I nor my equipment is set up to handle this sort of harvest, even with extra help.

4      I always need to hire someone, a strong young man who is not afraid of being stung, to help me harvest the honey from the hives.

5      The honey I take is the surplus that the bees will not need for the winter; they store it above their hives in wooden boxes called supers. To take it from them, I stand behind each hive with a gasoline-powered machine called a bee-blower and blow the bees out of the supers with a jet of air. Meanwhile, the strong young man carries the supers, which weigh about sixty pounds each, and stacks them on pallets in the truck. There may be thirty to fifty supers in every outyard, and we have only about half an hour to get them off the hives, stacked and covered before the bees get really cross about what we are doing. The season to take the honey in this part of the country is summer's end, when the temperature is often above ninety-five degrees. The nature of the work and the temper of the bees require that we wear protective clothing while doing the job: a full set of coveralls, a zippered bee veil and leather gloves. Even a very strong young man works up a considerable sweat wrapped in a bee suit in hot weather hustling sixty-pound supers—being harassed by angry bees at
6 the same time.

     This year my helper has been Ky, my nephew, who wanted to learn something about bees and beekeeping. He is a sweet, gentle, cooperative giant of a young man who, because of a series of physical problems, lacks
7 confidence in his own ability to get on in the world.

     As soon as he arrived, I set about to desensitize him to bee stings. The first day, I put a piece of ice on his arm to numb it; then, holding the bee carefully by her head, I placed her abdomen on the numbed spot and let her sting him there. A bee's stinger is barbed and stays in the flesh, pulling loose from her body as she struggles to free herself. Lacking her stinger, the bee will live only a short time. The bulbous poison sac at the top of the stinger continues to pulsate after the bee has left, its muscles pumping the venom and forcing the barbed stinger deeper into the flesh.

I wanted Ky to have only a partial dose of venom that first day, so af-   8
ter a minute I scraped the stinger out with my fingernail and watched his
reaction closely. A few people—about one percent of the population—are
seriously sensitive to bee venom. Each sting they receive can cause a more
severe reaction than the one before, reactions ranging from hives, difficulty
in breathing and accelerated heartbeat, to choking, anaphylactic shock,
and death. Ky had been stung a few times in his life and didn't think he
was seriously allergic, but I wanted to make sure.

The spot where the stinger went in grew red and began to swell. This   9
was a normal reaction, and so was the itchiness that Ky felt the next day.
That time I let a bee sting him again, repeating the procedure, but leaving
the stinger in his arm a full ten minutes, until the venom sac was emptied.
Again the spot was red, swollen and itchy, but had disappeared the next
day. Thereafter Ky decided that he didn't need the ice cube any more, and
began holding the bee himself to administer his own stings. I kept him at
one sting a day until he had no redness or swelling from the full sting, and
then had him increase to two stings daily. Again the greater amount of
venom caused redness and swelling, but soon his body could tolerate
them without an allergic reaction. I gradually had him build up to ten full
stings a day with no reaction.

To encourage Ky, I had told him that what he was doing might help   10
protect him from the arthritis that runs in our family. Beekeepers generally
believe that getting stung by bees is a healthy thing, and that bee venom
alleviates the symptoms of arthritis. When I first began keeping bees, I
supposed this to be just another one of the old wives' tales that make beekeeping such an entertaining occupation, but after my hands were stung
the pain in my fingers disappeared and I too became a believer. Ky was polite, amused and skeptical of what I told him, but he welcomed my taking
a few companionable stings on my knuckles along with him.

In desensitizing Ky to bee venom, I had simply been interested in   11
building up his tolerance to stings so that he could be an effective helper
when we took the honey from the hives, for I knew that he would be stung
frequently. But I discovered that there had been a secondary effect on Ky
that was more important: He was enormously pleased with himself for
having passed through what he evidently regarded as a rite of initiation.
He was proud and delighted in telling other people about the whole
process. He was now one tough guy.

I hoped he was prepared well enough for our first day of work. I have   12
had enough strong young men work for me to know what would happen
the first day: He would be stung royally.

Some beekeepers insist that bees know their keeper—that they won't   13
sting that person, but *will* sting a stranger. This is nonsense, for summertime bees live only six weeks and I often open a particular hive less frequently than that, so I am usually a stranger to my bees; yet I am seldom

stung. Others say that bees can sense fear or nervousness. I don't know if this is true or not, but I do know that bees' eyes are constructed in such a way that they can detect discontinuities and movement very well and stationary objects less well. This means that a person near their hives who moves with rapid, jerky motions attracts their attention and will more often be blamed by the bees when their hives are being meddled with than will the person whose motions are calm and easy. It has been my experience that the strong young man I hire for the honey harvest is always stung unmercifully for the first few days while he is new to the process and a bit tense. Then he learns to become easier with the bees and settles down to his job. As he gains confidence and assurance, the bees calm down too, and by the end of the harvest he usually is only stung a few times a day.

14       I knew that Ky very much wanted to do a good job with me that initial day working in the outyards. I had explained the procedures we would follow in taking the honey from the hives, but of course they were new to him and he was anxious. The bees from the first hive I opened flung themselves on him. Most of the stingers could not penetrate his bee suit, but in the act of stinging a bee leaves a chemical trace that marks the person stung as an enemy, a chemical sign other bees can read easily. This sign was read by the bees in each new hive I opened, and soon Ky's bee suit began to look like a pincushion, bristling with stingers. In addition, the temperature was starting to climb and Ky was sweating. Honey oozing from combs broken between the supers was running down the front of his bee suit when he carried them to the truck. Honey and sweat made the suit cling to him, so that the stingers of angry bees could penetrate the suit and he could feel the prick of each one as it entered his skin. Hundreds of bees were assaulting him and finally drove him out of the beeyard, chasing him several hundred yards before they gave up the attack. There was little I could do to help him but try to complete the job quickly, so I took the supers off the next few hives myself, carried them to the truck and loaded them. Bravely, Ky returned to finish the last few hives. We tied down the load and drove away. His face was red with exertion when he unzipped his bee veil. He didn't have much to say as we drove to the next yard, but sat beside me gulping down ice water from the thermos bottle.

15       At the second yard the bees didn't bother Ky as we set up the equipment. I hoped that much of the chemical marker the bees had left on him had evaporated, but as soon as I began to open the hives they were after him again. Soon a cloud of angry bees enveloped him, accompanying him to the truck and back. Because of the terrain, the truck had to be parked at an odd angle and Ky had to bend from the hips as he loaded it, stretching the fabric of the bee suit taut across the entire length of his back and rear, allowing the bees to sting through it easily. We couldn't talk over the noise of the beeblower's engine, but I was worried about how he was taking

hundreds more stings. I was removing the bees from the supers as quickly as I could, but the yard was a good one and there were a lot of supers there.

In about an hour's time Ky carried and stacked what we later weighed 16 in as a load of 2500 pounds. The temperature must have been nearly a hundred degrees. After he had stacked the last super, I drove the truck away from the hives and we tied down the load. Ky's long hair was plastered to his face and I couldn't see the expression on it, but I knew he had been pushed to his limits and I was concerned about him. He tried to brush some of the stingers out of the seat of his bee suit before he sat down next to me in the truck in an uncommonly gingerly way. Unzipping his bee veil, he tossed it aside, pushed the hair back from his sweaty face, reached for the thermos bottle, gave me a sunny and triumphant grin and said, "If I ever get arthritis of the ass, I'll know all that stuff you've been telling me is a lot of baloney."

*1983*

## QUESTIONS FOR DISCUSSION

### Content

a. In your own words, explain this essay's thesis.
b. What about beekeeping does Hubbell find particularly appealing?
c. What are supers, and what is their function in the process of collecting honey?
d. What is the process for being desensitized to bee venom, and how does it work?
e. How does harvesting honey benefit Hubbell's nephew, Ky?
f. What are some of the theories explaining why bees sting some people who work with bees more than others?

### Strategy and Style

g. What is the ideal audience for this essay? What in the essay indicates this audience?
h. Why does Hubbell describe the process of being stung by a bee in such detail (paragraph 7)? What purpose does this gruesome description serve?
i. What rhetorical strategies does Hubbell use to discuss the beekeeping process?

j. Where does Hubbell use humor? How does humor help her get her thesis across?

## ENGAGING THE TEXT

a. List the steps in collecting honey, as Hubbell describes them.
b. Briefly explain a "rite of initiation" (paragraph 11) of your own, of your family, or of any group to which you belong. Explain how your rite of initiation is similar to Ky's, as described by Hubbell.

## SUGGESTIONS FOR SUSTAINED WRITING

a. Using your answers to the questions listed under "Strategy and Style" above, write an essay that analyzes the rhetorical strategies and style that Hubbell uses. Make sure to consider audience, purpose, and tone when you write this essay.
b. Hubbell refers to Ky's becoming desensitized to bee venom as a "rite of initiation" (paragraph 11). Write an essay in which you explain what she means. Then explain the steps one must take in another rite of initiation. You might want to focus on a process such as learning how to drive or applying for college. If you are more ambitious, try researching a particular initiation rite practiced in a culture far different from our own.
c. Research a hobby, sport, or career that you might like to undertake. Explain how the hobby, sport, or career is pursued. Include information from at least three secondary sources in your paper.

# How to Paint a Fresco

Adam Goodheart

*An associate editor of* Civilization, *the magazine of the Library of Congress, Adam Goodheart (b. 1970) has written "Lost Arts," a regular column which contains essays on how to master arts that have passed into history. Among these fascinating process essays are "How to Bleed a Patient," "How to Elect a Holy Roman Emperor," "How to Fight a Duel," "How to Hunt a Woolly Mammoth," "How to Mummify a Pharaoh," and "How to Paint a Fresco," which appeared in 1995. He is also the author of travel and cultural essays published in* Civilization *and other periodicals. Based in Washington, D.C., Goodheart has contributed to* Civilization *since 1994.*

*Goodheart, who was born in Philadelphia, attended Harvard University and has studied history and archaeology in Italy. The essay that follows is a brief but accurate account of how to create a fresco, which requires that the artist apply paint to a plaster-covered wall or ceiling while the plaster is still wet. Perhaps the most famous example of a fresco is Michelangelo's painting on the ceiling of the Vatican's Sistine Chapel in Rome. Goodheart's favorite Renaissance frescoes are those on the life of Pope Pius II by Pintoricchio. They can be found in Sienna's cathedral library.*

Although it must be painted in a very short time, a fresco will last a very ₁ long time—that is its great advantage. Many of the masterpieces of the golden age of fresco (from the 14th through the 18th centuries) are as brilliant now as when they were first painted. If you want to fresco a cathedral or palazzo today, you may have a few problems—papal and ducal commissions are scarcer than they once were, and the great Renaissance masters are no longer accepting applications for apprenticeships. Fortunately, a few of their trade secrets have come down to us through the ages.

## EQUIPMENT

*Lime* ₂

*Sand*

*Water*

*A trowel*

*Paper*

*A needle*

*A small bag of charcoal dust*

*The bristles of a white hog*

*The hair of bears, sables and martens*

*The quills of vultures, geese, hens and doves*

*Ocher, burnt grapevines, lapis lazuli*

*Egg yolks*

*Goat's milk*

1.  **Preparing the wall.** Cennino Cennini, a Tuscan master, advised pupils in ₃ 1437 to "begin by decking yourselves with this attire: Enthusiasm, Reverence, Obedience, and Constancy." You'd do better to deck yourself with some old clothes, though, since the first stage of the process is quite messy. Soak the wall thoroughly and coat it with coarse plaster, two parts sand to one part lime, leaving the surface uneven. (Andrea Pozzo, a 17th-century expert, recommended hiring a professional mason to do this, since "the lime makes a foul odor, which is injurious to the head.")

4  2.  *Tracing your design.* You should already have extensive drawings for
       your fresco—these will be much sought by scholars and collectors in
       centuries to come. Make a full-size sketch, on sturdy paper, of a sec-
       tion of the fresco that you can paint in a day. Then go over the draw-
       ing with a needle, pricking holes along every line. Lay a coat of fine
       plaster on a section of the wall corresponding to the location, size,
       and shape of the sketch, and press the sketch against the plaster. Fill
       a loosely woven bag with charcoal dust and strike it lightly all over
       the surface of the paper. Now peel the sketch off. Your design will be
       outlined in black dots on the wet plaster, giving you a guide for the
       day's work.

5  3.  *Painting.* Time is of the essence: You must paint the plaster while it is
       wet, so that the pigments bind chemically with the lime. That gives
       you about six hours, although some painters had tricks to prolong dry-
       ing. (Piero della Francesca packed the plaster with wet rags; problem
       was, this left indentations that are still visible after 500 years.) Use top-
       quality brushes. One 17th-century Flemish master recommended
       those made of "fish hair" (he probably meant seal fur), but most
       painters made brushes from bear, marten, or sable hairs inserted in
       hollow quills. Cennini suggested the bristles of a white hog for the
       coarser work. As for paints, every artist had his own favorite recipes,
       but all agreed that mineral pigments such as ocher or ground stone
       mixed with water were best. Avoid white lead. One 14th-century Um-
       brian used it to paint a nursing infant; the lime turned the white black
       and the milky babe into a "devilish changeling." A few pigments, such
       as dark blue azurite (often used for the Virgin Mary's mantle), must be
       mixed with egg yolk or goat's milk and added after the fresco is dry.
       Such colors will prove less durable.

6          Money is a consideration in choosing materials. When Michelan-
       gelo frescoed the Sistine ceiling, expenses came out of his fee, so he
       used cheap blue smalt for the sky. Twenty years later, when he did the
       *Last Judgment,* Michelangelo used semiprecious lapis lazuli for blue,
       since the pope was paying for the paint. (He made up for it by using
       burnt grapevines for black.)

7  4.  *Casualties of style.* Realism, while a worthy goal, has its perils.
       Spinello Aretino, a 14th-century Tuscan, is said to have painted a
       fresco that depicted Lucifer with such hideous accuracy that the Evil
       One himself came to the artist in a dream and demanded an explana-
       tion. Spinello went half-mad with fear and died shortly thereafter. On
       the other hand, a Florentine woodcut from 1500 depicts a painter who
       has portrayed the Virgin so skillfully that when he falls off the scaffold,
       she reaches out of the fresco and saves him.

## WARNING

Frescoing ceilings can be rough on your back. While working on the Sis- 8
tine Chapel, Michelangelo wrote a poem complaining: "I've already
grown a goiter at this drudgery . . . With my beard toward heaven . . . I am
bent like a bow." Don't be discouraged, though. Bad posture is a small
price to pay for immortality.

*1995*

## QUESTIONS FOR DISCUSSION

### Content

a. What are some of the problems painters of frescoes faced?
b. Why, according to Goodheart, would an artist want to attempt a fresco?
c. Why is time "of the essence" in painting a fresco?
d. What does the quotation from Cennini (paragraph 3) tell us about the
   art of the fresco? What use, other than explanation, does Goodheart
   make of it?
e. Where is Tuscany? Where and what is the Sistine Chapel?

### Style and Strategy

f. What is the effect of Goodheart's listing the equipment needed in a separate paragraph? Why didn't he simply mention tools and supplies in
   the course of explaining the process?
g. Explain the organizational logic behind this essay.
h. The author includes several examples (illustrations) in this essay. Where
   do they appear, and what is their function?
i. Where does Goodheart use comparison and contrast? To what end?
j. What kind of audience does this essay address? Explain your answer
   with reference to both style and content.
k. Identify important transitional devices—common to narrative and
   process analysis—in Goodheart's essay. Then discuss other ways in
   which this essay resembles a narrative.

## ENGAGING THE TEXT

a. Summarize the process of painting a fresco. To what other activities is this process similar? How?
b. Notice that "How to Paint a Fresco" contains a warning at the end. From what you have learned about the art of the fresco, what might you add to this warning?

## SUGGESTIONS FOR SUSTAINED WRITING

a. Using the four steps that Goodheart follows in "How to Paint a Fresco," write a full-length process paper that explains how to complete a task with which you are familiar. Do some freewriting first to gather information that you will put into your paper. After writing the first draft, make sure that you have included enough information to give your reader a clear picture of how to proceed. If you need to gather more information, try brainstorming with a friend or complete some library or Internet research on your subject.
b. In your college library, research a "lost art" that interests you. Take notes from at least three sources. Then write a process paper on this activity. For example, as Goodheart has, you might explain how to fight a duel or hunt a woolly mammoth. Then again, you can explain how to complete a cave painting, build a drawbridge, shoot a crossbow, weave a tapestry, smoke meat, make medicines from herbs, or build a Roman aqueduct. Make sure to give your sources credit by including internal citations as appropriate and a works-cited or references page.
c. Write a research paper in which you discuss a style or method of painting (other than the one Goodheart writes about) or of any other art form. For example, you might define Impressionism or explain the steps involved in creating fine vases.

# Definition

Generally speaking, definitions fall into three broad categories: lexical, stipulative, and extended. The dictionary is of course the best place to begin familiarizing yourself with new concepts, but lexical definitions tend to be abstract, for they sometimes explain terms without reference to particular contexts. And stipulative definitions, while practical, are by their very nature limited to special purposes. Say you were writing a paper on the advantages and disadvantages of being a part-time student. You might *stipulate* that for the purposes of your essay, "a part-timer is someone enrolled for less than 12 credits." Thus, while both lexical and stipulative definitions have their uses, extended definitions are the type used most often to explain complex topics such as those discussed in this chapter.

The many practical uses to which extended definition can be applied make it a powerful tool for exposition. In the hands of writers like Claudia Glenn Dowling and Susan Sontag, it becomes a systematic way to grapple with social, moral, or even scientific questions. It can correct common, sometimes dangerous, misconceptions, as in Gloria Steinem's "Erotica and Pornography," Nancy Mairs's "On Being a Cripple," or Jo Goodwin Parker's "What Is Poverty?" And it can even explain something as delicate as one's relationship to his or her faith, as in Sam Pickering's hilarious "Faith of the Father."

Like process essays, extended definitions are developed by using a number of methods. Among the most common are analogy and comparison/contrast. Sontag discusses differing notions of beauty in Catholic and Protestant countries, and Pickering contrasts a religion of "soft feeling" to one of "sharp thought."

As a matter of fact, many techniques can be used to develop extended definitions. The examples and anecdotes (brief, illustrative stories) Parker uses to define poverty are powerful and incisive tools for correcting social myopia. Mairs uses a wide variety of methods, including narration, description, analogy, contrast, and cause/effect, to show us the effects multiple sclerosis has had on her body, her psyche, and her family.

Approaches to the process of defining, then, are as varied as the authors who use them. Sontag launches her discussion of beauty by tracing its etymology from the Greeks to the present. Sontag and Steinem rely on lexical and etymological information to introduce or clarify specific points in a larger context.

You can learn a great deal more about techniques for writing extended definitions by considering the Questions for Discussion and by addressing the Engaging the Text and Suggestions for Sustained Writing sections that follow each selection in this chapter. Another good way to learn the skills of definition is to read each of the essays in this chapter twice. On your first pass, simply make sure you understand each selection thoroughly and accurately. The second time around, ask yourself how you might define the term being explained, whether you agree with the author's perception, or if you can add information to make the definition even more credible. The method described above might require more time than you had planned to spend on this chapter, but it is the kind of mental exercise that will strengthen your analytical muscles and help you use definition as a powerful tool whenever you need to explain complex ideas.

# Women's Beauty: Put Down or Power Source?

## Susan Sontag

*Susan Sontag (b. 1933) took her BA at the University of Chicago and her MA at Radcliffe College. She also studied at Oxford University. She is an accomplished novelist, film director, and writer of screenplays. Through her essays, which have been published in magazines and journals across the country, Sontag has established a reputation as a critic of modern culture. She will probably be best remembered, however, for her contribution to the theory of aesthetics. In her best-known work,* Against Interpretation *(1966), Sontag enunciates a theory of art based on a reliance on the senses and not the intellect. Her place of authority in the contemporary world of art criticism was confirmed when, in 1976, she published* On Photography. *Her novels include* The Benefactor *(1964),* Death Kit *(1967), and* Volcano Lover *(1992). She has also written senveral plays and screen plays for film. Sontag's nonfiction—*Trip to Hanoi *(1969),* Styles of Radical Will *(1969),* Vudu Urbano *(1985), and* AIDS and Its Metaphors *(1989)—demonstrate her ability to address current social and political realities with the same incisiveness with which she approaches questions of art. In "Women's Beauty," which she first published in* Vogue *in 1975, Sontag provides us with a feminist interpretation of the uses and misuses of beauty throughout history.*

1      For the Greeks, beauty was a virtue: A kind of excellence. Persons then were assumed to be what we now have to call—lamely, enviously—*whole* persons. If it did occur to the Greeks to distinguish between a person's "inside" and "outside," they still expected that inner beauty would be matched by beauty of the other kind. The well-born young Athenians who gathered around Socrates found it quite paradoxical that their hero was so intelligent, so brave, so honorable, so seductive—and so ugly. One of Socrates'

main pedagogical acts was to be ugly—and teach those innocent, no doubt splendid-looking disciples of his how full of paradoxes life really was.

They may have resisted Socrates' lesson. We do not. Several thousand 2 years later, we are more wary of the enchantments of beauty. We not only split off—with the greatest facility—the "inside" (character, intellect) from the "outside" (looks); but we are actually surprised when someone who is beautiful is also intelligent, talented, good.

It was principally the influence of Christianity that deprived beauty of 3 the central place it had in classical ideals of human excellence. By limiting excellence (*virtus* in Latin) to *moral* virtue only, Christianity set beauty adrift—as an alienated, arbitrary, superficial enchantment. And beauty has continued to lose prestige. For close to two centuries it has become a convention to attribute beauty to only one of the two sexes: The sex which, however Fair, is always Second. Associating beauty with women has put beauty even further on the defensive, morally.

A beautiful woman, we say in English. But a handsome man. "Hand- 4 some" is the masculine equivalent of—and refusal of—a compliment which has accumulated certain demeaning overtones, by being reserved for women only. That one can call a man "beautiful" in French and in Italian suggests that Catholic countries—unlike those countries shaped by the Protestant version of Christianity—still retain some vestiges of the pagan admiration for beauty. But the difference, if one exists, is of degree only. In every modern country that is Christian or post-Christian, women *are* the beautiful sex—to the detriment of the notion of beauty as well as of women.

To be called beautiful is thought to name something essential to 5 women's character and concerns. (In contrast to men—whose essence is to be strong, or effective, or competent.) It does not take someone in the throes of advanced feminist awareness to perceive that the way women are taught to be involved with beauty encourages narcissism, reinforces dependence and immaturity. Everybody (women and men) knows that. For it is "everybody," a whole society, that has identified being feminine with caring about how one *looks*. (In contrast to being masculine—which is identified with caring about what one *is* and *does* and only secondarily, if at all, about how one looks.) Given these stereotypes, it is no wonder that beauty enjoys, at best, a rather mixed reputation.

It is not, of course, the desire to be beautiful that is wrong but the oblig- 6 ation to be—or to try. What is accepted by most women as a flattering idealization of their sex is a way of making women feel inferior to what they actually are—or normally grow to be. For the ideal of beauty is administered as a form of self-oppression. Women are taught to see their bodies in *parts*, and to evaluate each part separately. Breasts, feet, hips, waistline, neck, eyes, nose, complexion, hair, and so on—each in turn is submitted to an anxious, fretful, often despairing scrutiny. Even if some pass muster, some will always be found wanting. Nothing less than perfection will do.

7      In men, good looks is a whole, something taken in at a glance. It does not need to be confirmed by giving measurements of different regions of the body, nobody encourages a man to dissect his appearance, feature by feature. As for perfection, that is considered trivial—almost unmanly. Indeed, in the ideally good-looking man a small imperfection or blemish is considered positively desirable. According to one movie critic (a woman) who is a declared Robert Redford fan, it is having that cluster of skin-colored moles on one cheek that saves Redford from being merely a "pretty face." Think of the depreciation of women—as well as of beauty—that is implied in that judgment.

8      "The privileges of beauty are immense," said Cocteau. To be sure, beauty is a form of power. And deservedly so. What is lamentable is that it is the only form of power that most women are encouraged to seek. This power is always conceived in relation to men; it is not the power to do but the power to attract. It is a power that negates itself. For this power is not one that can be chosen freely—at least, not by women—or renounced without social censure.

9      To preen, for a woman, can never be just a pleasure. It is also a duty. It is her work. If a woman does real work—and even if she has clambered up to a leading position in politics, law, medicine, business, or whatever—she is always under pressure to confess that she still works at being attractive. But in so far as she is keeping up as one of the Fair Sex, she brings under suspicion her very capacity to be objective, professional, authoritative, thoughtful. Damned if they do—women are. And damned if they don't.

10      One could hardly ask for more important evidence of the dangers of considering persons as split between what is "inside" and what is "outside" than that interminable half-comic, half-tragic tale, the oppression of women. How easy it is to start off by defining women as caretakers of their surfaces, and then to disparage them (or find them adorable) for being "superficial." It is a crude trap, and it has worked for too long. But to get out of the trap requires that women get some critical distance from that excellence and privilege which is beauty, enough distance to see how much beauty itself has been abridged in order to prop up the mythology of the "feminine." There should be a way of saving beauty *from* women—and *for* them.

*1975*

## QUESTIONS FOR DISCUSSION

### Content

a. What is Sontag's thesis?

b. Sontag makes it a point to explain the differences between the connotations of the word *handsome* and those of *beautiful*. How does this contrast help her develop her thesis? In what other ways does she use contrast as a method of development?

c. Is Sontag's message aimed at a predominantly female audience? At a predominantly male audience? At a mixed audience?

d. Consult appropriate sources in the reference section of your college library. Who are Socrates and Cocteau? Why does Sontag mention them (paragraphs 1 and 8, respectively)?

e. What was it that caused beauty to "lose prestige" (paragraph 3)? How does our conception of beauty differ from the one the Greeks had?

f. To what is Sontag referring when she talks about countries that are "post-Christian" (paragraph 4)?

g. If beauty is "a form of power" (paragraph 8), what about it is "lamentable"?

h. What does Sontag mean when she claims that women are "Damned if they do. . . . And damned if they don't" (paragraph 9)?

## Strategy and Style

i. Sontag launches the essay by spending considerable time discussing notions of beauty through history. Is such a long introduction justified? Why or why not?

j. Does the essay's conclusion echo its introduction? Explain.

k. In some instances, Sontag seems to be addressing the reader directly. Find a few such instances and explain their effect on you.

l. Analyze the author's style. What is the effect of her insistence on varying sentence length and structure?

m. Overall, how would you describe Sontag's tone?

## ENGAGING THE TEXT

a. Rewrite Sontag's essay as song lyrics. An easy way to do this is to use the melody of a well-known song for the structure of your lyrics. Try to remain true to what you believe to be Sontag's meaning.

b. Write a short definition of *ugliness*. Is it the antithesis of beauty, or do beauty and ugliness share some of the same characteristics?

## SUGGESTIONS FOR SUSTAINED WRITING

a. In paragraph 5, the author claims that "the way women are taught to be involved with beauty encourages narcissism, reinforces dependence and immaturity." Think about some relevant television or magazine advertisements for beauty products. Is Sontag correct? Write an analytical essay in which you explain how such ads define *beauty* and evaluate them against Sontag's claim. If this assignment doesn't interest you, ask yourself if there is such a thing as *inner beauty* as distinguished from one's physical appearance. Then write your own definition of *inner beauty*, but make sure to illustrate it with concrete details about a person or persons you know quite well.

b. After reading Gloria Steinem's "Erotica and Pornography," which appears in this chapter, write an essay that explains Sontag's essay from Steinem's point of view. In other words, explain in what ways Steinem might interpret, agree with, or disagree with Sontag. Make direct reference to both essays. Then respond to Sontag's ideas from your own vantage point.

c. In the first paragraph Sontag states that for the Greeks, "beauty was a virtue." Reread this paragraph. Then write an essay that, using library or Internet research, explains the Greek notion of physical beauty or artistic beauty. If this doesn't interest you, write a research paper in which you create a definition of physical beauty or artistic beauty as seen by a culture different from our own. You might focus on a contemporary culture. On the other hand, it might be fun to learn how beauty was defined by some past civilization.

# What Is Poverty?

Jo Goodwin Parker

*This first-person account of what it means to suffer extreme poverty was first published in 1971 in a collection of essays entitled* America's Other Children: Public Schools Outside Suburbia. *Parker presents a startling and moving definition of poverty by explaining both the causes and the effects of a reality that has kept her and her children in misery for years. The author has requested that no biographical information be provided.*

1   You ask me what is poverty? Listen to me. Here I am, dirty, smelly, and with no "proper" underwear on and with the stench of my rotting teeth near you. I will tell you. Listen to me. Listen without pity. I cannot use your pity. Listen with understanding. Put yourself in my dirty, worn out, ill-fitting shoes, and hear me.

2        Poverty is getting up every morning from a dirt- and illness-stained mattress. The sheets have long since been used for diapers. Poverty is living in a smell that never leaves. This is a smell of urine, sour milk, and

spoiling food sometimes joined with the strong smell of long-cooked onions. Onions are cheap. If you have smelled this smell, you did not know how it came. It is the smell of the outdoor privy. It is the smell of young children who cannot walk the long dark way in the night. It is the smell of the mattresses where years of "accidents" have happened. It is the smell of the milk which has gone sour because the refrigerator long has not worked, and it costs money to get it fixed. It is the smell of rotting garbage. I could bury it, but where is the shovel? Shovels cost money.

Poverty is being tired. I have always been tired. They told me at the hospital when the last baby came that I had chronic anemia caused from poor diet, a bad case of worms, and that I needed a corrective operation. I listened politely—the poor are always polite. The poor always listen. They don't say that there is no money for iron pills, or better food, or worm medicine. The idea of an operation is frightening and costs so much that, if I had dared, I would have laughed. Who takes care of my children? Recovery from an operation takes a long time. I have three children. When I left them with "Granny" the last time I had a job, I came home to find the baby covered with fly specks, and a diaper that had not been changed since I left. When the dried diaper came off, bits of my baby's flesh came with it. My other child was playing with a sharp bit of broken glass, and my oldest was playing alone at the edge of a lake. I made twenty-two dollars a week, and a good nursery school costs twenty dollars a week for three children. I quit my job.

Poverty is dirt. You can say in your clean clothes coming from your clean house, "Anybody can be clean." Let me explain about housekeeping with no money. For breakfast I give my children grits with no oleo or corn-bread without eggs and oleo. This does not use up many dishes. What dishes there are, I wash in cold water and with no soap. Even the cheapest soap has to be saved for the baby's diapers. Look at my hands, so cracked and red. Once I saved for two months to buy a jar of Vaseline for my hands and the baby's diaper rash. When I had saved enough, I went to buy it and the price had gone up two cents. The baby and I suffered on. I have to decide every day if I can bear to put my cracked sore hands into the cold water and strong soap. But you ask, why not hot water? Fuel costs money. If you have a wood fire it costs money. If you burn electricity, it costs money. Hot water is a luxury. I do not have luxuries. I know you will be surprised when I tell you how young I am. I look so much older. My back has been bent over the wash tubs every day for so long, I cannot remember when I ever did anything else. Every night I wash every stitch my school age child has on and just hope her clothes will be dry by morning.

Poverty is staying up all night on cold nights to watch the fire knowing one spark on the newspaper covering the walls means your sleeping child dies in flames. In summer, poverty is watching gnats and flies devour your baby's tears when he cries. The screens are torn and you pay so little rent you know they will never be fixed. Poverty means insects in your food, in your nose, in your eyes, and crawling over you when you sleep. Poverty is hoping it never rains because diapers won't dry when it rains and soon you are using newspapers. Poverty is seeing your children forever with runny noses. Paper handkerchiefs cost money and all your rags you need for other things. Even more costly are antihistamines. Poverty is cooking without food and cleaning without soap.

6       Poverty is asking for help. Have you ever had to ask for help, knowing your children will suffer unless you get it? Think about asking for a loan from a relative, if this is the only way you can imagine asking for help. I will tell you how it feels. You find out where the office is that you are supposed to visit. You circle that block four or five times. Thinking of your children, you go in. Everyone is very busy. Finally, someone comes out and you tell her that you need help. That never is the person you need to see. You go see another person, and after spilling the whole shame of your poverty all over the desk between you, you find that this isn't the right office after all—you must repeat the whole process, and it never is any easier at the next place.

7       You have asked for help, and after all it has a cost. You are again told to wait. You are told why, but you don't really hear because of the red cloud of shame and the rising cloud of despair.

8       Poverty is remembering. It is remembering quitting school in junior high because "nice" children had been so cruel about my clothes and my smell. The attendance officer came. My mother told him I was pregnant. I wasn't, but she thought that I could get a job and help out. I had jobs off and on, but never long enough to learn anything. Mostly I remember being married. I was so young then. I am still young. For a time, we had all the things you have. There was a little house in another town, with hot water and everything. Then my husband lost his job. There was unemployment insurance for a while and what few jobs I could get. Soon, all our nice things were repossessed and we moved back here. I was pregnant then. This house didn't look so bad when we first moved in. Every week it gets worse. Nothing is ever fixed. We now had no money. There were a few odd jobs for my husband, but everything went for food then, as it does now. I don't know how we lived through three years and three babies, but we did. I'll tell you something, after the last baby I destroyed my marriage. It had been a good one, but could you keep on bringing children in this dirt? Did you ever think how much it costs for any kind of birth control? I knew my husband was leaving the day he left, but there were no goodbys between us. I hope he has been able to climb out of this mess somewhere. He never could hope with us to drag him down.

9       That's when I asked for help. When I got it, you know how much it was? It was, and is, seventy-eight dollars a month for the four of us; that is all I ever can get. Now you know why there is no soap, no needles and

thread, no hot water, no aspirin, no worm medicine, no hand cream, no shampoo. None of these things forever and ever and ever. So that you can see clearly, I pay twenty dollars a month rent, and most of the rest goes for food. For grits and cornmeal, and rice and milk and beans. I try my best to use only the minimum electricity. If I use more, there is that much less for food.

Poverty is looking into a black future. Your children won't play with 10 my boys. They will turn to other boys who steal to get what they want. I can already see them behind the bars of their prison instead of behind the bars of my poverty. Or they will turn to the freedom of alcohol or drugs, and find themselves enslaved. And my daughter? At best, there is for her a life like mine.

But you say to me, there are schools. Yes, there are schools. My chil- 11 dren have no extra books, no magazines, no extra pencils, or crayons, or paper and most important of all, they do not have health. They have worms, they have infections, they have pink-eye all summer. They do not sleep well on the floor, or with me in my one bed. They do not suffer from hunger, my seventy-eight dollars keeps us alive, but they do suffer from malnutrition. Oh yes, I do remember what I was taught about health in school. It doesn't do much good. In some places there is a surplus com- modities program. Not here. The county said it cost too much. There is a school lunch program. But I have two children who will already be dam- aged by the time they get to school.

But, you say to me, there are health clinics. Yes, there are health clinics 12 and they are in the towns. I live out here eight miles from town. I can walk that far (even if it is sixteen miles both ways), but can my little children? My neighbor will take me when he goes; but he expects to get paid, *one way or another*. I bet you know my neighbor. He is that large man who spends his time at the gas station, the barbershop, and the corner store complain- ing about the government spending money on the immoral mothers of il- legitimate children.

Poverty is an acid that drips on pride until all pride is worn away. 13 Poverty is a chisel that chips on honor until honor is worn away. Some of you say that you would do *something* in my situation, and maybe you would, for the first week or the first month, but for year after year after year?

Even the poor can dream. A dream of a time when there is money. 14 Money for the right kinds of food, for worm medicine, for iron pills, for toothbrushes, for hand cream, for a hammer and nails and a bit of screen- ing, for a shovel, for a bit of paint, for some sheeting, for needles and thread. Money to pay *in money* for a trip to town. And, oh, money for hot water and money for soap. A dream of when asking for help does not eat away the last bit of pride. When the office you visit is as nice as the offices of other governmental agencies, when there are enough workers to help you quickly, when workers do not quit in defeat and despair. When you have to tell your story to only one person, and that person can send you for other help and you don't have to prove your poverty over and over and over again.

15　　I have come out of my despair to tell you this. Remember I did not come from another place or another time. Others like me are all around you. Look at us with an angry heart, anger that will help you help me. Anger that will let you tell of me. The poor are always silent. Can you be silent too?

*1971*

## QUESTIONS FOR DISCUSSION

### Content

a. How would you define the author's purpose? Besides paragraph 15, in what parts of the essay is that purpose most apparent?

b. Why does the speaker address her audience directly, especially in paragraphs 4 and 10? How would you describe that audience?

c. What is the speaker's attitude toward her estranged husband? Do you find it curious? What does it tell you about her? What does it tell you about Parker's purpose?

d. In paragraph 8, the speaker seems to describe a cycle of poverty into which the poor are born and in which they remain. Explain. In what other sections of the essay does she allude to this cycle?

e. How does she account for her inability to keep her family clean? Why is it futile for her to seek a job?

f. What is the distinction between "hunger" and "malnutrition" that she makes in paragraph 11? Why does she deny the usefulness of school lunch programs?

g. The speaker relates incidents in which she has had to endure both public and private humiliation in order to obtain help for her family. What is the source of such humiliation? How does Parker's inclusion of these incidents help her define *poverty*?

### Strategy and Style

h. Often, the speaker makes sure to anticipate and discuss opposing arguments. What is the effect of her doing so? How does this practice help illuminate her character?

i. Parker has organized the essay by having her speaker enunciate a series of characteristics that define poverty. What is the effect of her beginning several paragraphs with "Poverty is . . ."?

j. Comment on the author's use of illustrations. To what physical senses does she appeal most often? What use does she make of metaphor?

k. Parker has created a "persona" or speaker who tells her story by using the first-person pronoun ("I"). How would you describe this "persona"?

l. What is the purpose of paragraph 15 besides concluding the essay? How would you describe the speaker's tone in this paragraph? Does it differ from the tone she uses in other parts of the essay?

## ENGAGING THE TEXT

a. Write a dictionary definition of *poverty* without using a dictionary. Then look up the word and compare your definition with the dictionary's. How specific were you or the dictionary able to get? Compare your definition to Parker's.

b. Describe your emotional response to Parker's essay as you read it.

## SUGGESTIONS FOR SUSTAINED WRITING

a. The speaker tells us about material poverty. Are there other kinds of poverty that are less frequently talked about—intellectual, spiritual, or moral poverty, for instance? Try to define one of these less commonly discussed types of poverty by using concrete details and illustrations as Parker does in this selection. If this assignment doesn't interest you, think about another abstract term that describes a human reality with which you are thoroughly familiar: power, personal ambition, grief, hunger, physical pain, or pride, for example. Following Parker's example, explain what that term means to you. Use your own personal experiences as concrete illustrations.

b. Read the essays by Barbara Ehrenreich and Garrett Hardin in Chapter 10. Then write an essay explaining how either or both of these authors might respond to Parker's essay. You might also want to consider what Jonathan Kozol has to say in Chapter 11. Make direct reference to Parker's "What Is Poverty?" as well as to the other essay or essays you are considering.

c. Parker creates a definition of poverty in 1971. Is this picture still accurate, or do people have more opportunities to lift themselves out of poverty than they did before? Using library and/or Internet research, focus on the plight of single mothers in America today. Explain the major economic and social problems they face. Is their situation materially different from what Parker's was? If it isn't, in what ways is it similar? If it is, discuss the kinds of opportunities, including public and private assistance, available today that would have improved Parker's life.

# Faith of the Father

Sam Pickering

*A graduate of the University of the South, Cambridge University, and Princeton University, Sam Pickering (b. 1941) has taught at Dartmouth College and is now a full professor at the University of Connecticut, where he teaches courses in nature writing and children's literature. He has written numerous scholarly books and articles on eighteenth- and nineteenth-century English literature and children's literature. A prolific writer, he regularly publishes familiar and critical essays in* College English, *the* Kenyon Review, National Review, *the* Virginia Quarterly Review, Sewanee Review, *and other prestigious journals. Pickering was the recipient of Fulbright Lectureships in both Lebanon and Syria. He has published several essay collections, including* The Right Distance, A Continuing Education, *and* May Days. *In some ways, "Faith of the Father" contrasts markedly with the other essays in this chapter, for it is, as Pickering might say, "more concerned with people than ideas." "Faith of the Father" first appeared in the* Southwest Review *in 1985.*

1    On weekdays Campbell's store was the center of life in the little Virginia town in which I spent summers and Christmas vacations. The post office was in a corner of the store, and the train station was across the road. In the morning men gathered on Campbell's porch and drank coffee while they waited for the train to Richmond. Late in the afternoon, families appeared. While waiting for their husbands, women bought groceries, mailed letters, and visited with one another. Children ate cups of ice cream and played in the woods behind the store. Sometimes a work train was on the siding, and the engineer filled his cab with children and took them for short trips down the track. On weekends life shifted from the store to St. Paul's Church. Built in a grove of pine trees in the nineteenth century, St. Paul's was a small, white clapboard building. A Sunday School wing added to the church in the 1920s jutted out into the graveyard. Beyond the graveyard was a field in which picnics were held and, on the Fourth of July, the yearly Donkey Softball Game was played.

2    St. Paul's was familial and comfortable. Only a hundred people attended regularly, and everyone knew everyone else and his business. What was private became public after the service as people gathered outside and talked for half an hour before going home to lunch. Behind the altar inside the church was a stained glass window showing Christ's ascension to heaven. A red carpet ran down the middle aisle, and worn, gold cushions covered the pews. On the walls were plaques in memory of parishioners killed in foreign wars or who had made large donations to the building fund. In summer the minister put fans out on the pews. Donated by a local undertaker, the fans were shaped like spades. On them, besides the undertaker's name and telephone number, were pictures of Christ per-

**132**

forming miracles: Walking on water, healing the lame, and raising Lazarus from the dead.

Holidays and funerals were special at St. Paul's. Funerals were occa- ₃ sions for reminiscing and telling stories. When an irascible old lady died and her daughter had "Gone to Jesus" inscribed on her tombstone, her son-in-law was heard to say "poor Jesus"—or so the tale went at the funeral. Christmas Eve was always cold and snow usually fell. Inside the church at midnight, though, all was cheery and warm as the congregation sang the great Christmas hymns: "O Come, All Ye Faithful," "The First Noel," "O Little Town of Bethlehem," and "Hark! The Herald Angels Sing." The last hymn was "Silent Night." The service did not follow the prayer book; inspired by Christmas and eggnog, the congregation came to sing, not to pray. Bourbon was in the air, and when the altar boy lit the candles, it seemed a miracle that the first spark didn't send us all to heaven in a blue flame.

Easter was almost more joyous than Christmas. Men stuck greenery ₄ into their lapels and women blossomed in bright bonnets, some ordering hats not simply from Richmond but from Baltimore and Philadelphia. On a farm outside town lived Miss Emma and Miss Ida Catlin. Miss Emma was the practical sister, running the farm and bringing order wherever she went. Unlike Miss Emma, Miss Ida was shy. She read poetry and raised guinea fowl and at parties sat silently in a corner. Only on Easter was she outgoing; then like a day lily she bloomed triumphantly. No one else's Easter bonnet ever matched hers, and the congregation eagerly awaited her entrance which she always made just before the first hymn.

One year Miss Ida found a catalogue from a New York store which ad- ₅ vertised hats and their accessories. For ten to twenty-five cents ladies could buy artificial flowers to stick into their bonnets. Miss Ida bought a counter full, and that Easter her head resembled a summer garden in bloom. Daffodils, zinnias, and black-eyed Susans hung yellow and red around the brim of her hat while in the middle stood a magnificent pink peony.

In all his glory Solomon could not have matched Miss Ida's bonnet. The ₆ congregation could not take its eyes off it; even the minister had trouble concentrating on his sermon. After the last hymn, everyone hurried out of the church, eager to get a better look at Miss Ida's hat. As she came out, the altar boy began ringing the bell. Alas, the noise frightened pigeons who had recently begun to nest and they shot out of the steeple. The congregation scattered, but the flowers on Miss Ida's hat hung over her eyes, and she did not see the pigeons until it was too late and the peony had been ruined.

Miss Ida acted like nothing had happened. She greeted everyone and ₇ asked about their healths and the healths of absent members of families. People tried not to look at her hat but were not very successful. For two Sundays Miss Ida's "accident" was the main subject of after-church conversation; then it was forgotten for almost a year. But, as Easter approached again, people remembered the hat. They wondered what Miss Ida would wear to church. Some people speculated that since she was a shy, poetic person, she wouldn't come. Even the minister had doubts. To reassure Miss Ida, he and his sons borrowed ladders two weeks before Easter, and climbing to the top of the steeple, chased the pigeons away and sealed off their nesting place with chicken wire.

8      Easter Sunday seemed to confirm the fears of those who doubted Miss Ida would appear. The choir assembled in the rear of the church without her. Half-heartedly the congregation sang the processional hymn, "Hail Thee, Festival Day." Miss Ida's absence had taken something bright from our lives, and as we sat down after singing, Easter seemed sadly ordinary.

9      We were people of little faith. Just as the minister reached the altar and turned to face us, there was a stir at the back of the church. Silently the minister raised his right hand and pointed toward the door. Miss Ida had arrived. She was wearing the same hat she wore the year before; only the peony was missing. In its place was a wonderful sunflower; from one side hung a black and yellow garden spider building a web while fluttering above was a mourning cloak, black wings, dotted with blue and a yellow border running around the edges. Our hearts leaped up, and at the end of the service people in Richmond must have heard us singing "Christ the Lord Is Risen Today."

10     St. Paul's was the church of my childhood, that storied time when I thought little about religion but knew that Jesus loved me, yes, because the Bible told me so. In the Morning Prayer of life I mixed faith and fairy tale, thinking God a kindly giant, holding in his hands, as the song put it, the corners of the earth and the strength of the hills. Thirty years have passed since I last saw St. Paul's, and I have come down from the cool upland pastures and the safe fold of childhood to the hot lowlands. Instead of being neatly tucked away in a huge hand, the world now seems to bound erratically, smooth and slippery, forever beyond the grasp of even the most magical deity. Would that it were not so, and my imagination could find a way through his gates, as the prayer says, with thanksgiving. Often I wonder what happened to the "faith of our fathers." Why if it endured dungeon, fire, and sword in others, did it weaken so within me?

11     For me religion is a matter of story and community, a congregation rising together to look at an Easter Bonnet, unconsciously seeing it as an emblem of hope and vitality, indeed of the Resurrection itself. For me religion ought to be more concerned with people than ideas, creating soft feeling rather than sharp thought. Often I associate religion with small, backwater towns in which tale binds folk one to another. Here in a university in which people are separated by idea rather than linked by story, religion doesn't have a natural place. In the absence of community, ceremony becomes important. Changeable and always controversial, subject to dispassionate analysis, ceremony doesn't tie people together like accounts of pi-

geons and peonies and thus doesn't promote good feeling and finally love for this world and hope for the next. Often when I am discouraged, I turn for sustenance, not to formal faith with articled ceremony but to memory, a chalice winey with story.

Not long ago I thought about Beagon Hackett, a Baptist minister in Carthage, Tennessee. Born in Bagdad in Jackson County, Beagon answered the call early in life. Before he was sixteen, he had preached in all the little towns in Jackson County: Antioch, Nameless, McCoinsville, Liberty, and Gum Springs. Although popular in country churches, Beagon's specialty was the all-day revival, picnic, and baptizing, usually held back in the woods near places like Seven Knobs, Booger Hill, Backbone Ridge, Chigger Hollow, and Twelve Corners. Beagon made such a name that the big Baptist church in Carthage selected him as minister. Once in Carthage, Beagon tempered his faith to suit the mood of the county seat. Only once a year did he hold a meeting out of doors. For his first four or five years in Carthage, he led a revival near Dripping Rock Bluff across Hell Bend on the Caney Fork River, the spot being selected for name not location.

The narrows of the river were swift and deep, and crossing Hell Bend was dangerous, a danger Beagon celebrated, first reminding the faithful that Jesus was a fisher of men and then buoying their spirits up on a raft of watery Christian song: "Shall We Gather at the River," "The Rock That Is Higher Than I," and "Sweet By and By." Beagon's meetings across the Caney Fork were a success with people traveling from as far as Macon and Trousdale counties to be baptized. But then one spring Gummert Capron or Doodlebug Healy, depending on whose memory is accurate, became frightened in mid-river and tipping over a rowboat changed "Throw Out the Life-Line" from word to deed. If Homer Nye had not grabbed Clara Jakeways by the hair, the dark waters, as the hymn puts it, would have swept her to eternity's shore. As it turned out Clara's salvation turned into romance, and three months later she and Nye were married, much to the disappointment of Silas Jakeways who owned a sawmill and the Eagle Iron Works and who disapproved of Nye, until that time an itinerant bricklayer. Clara, Silas was reported to have said, would "have been better off if love hadn't lifted her from the deep to become the wife of a no-account." Whatever the case, however, Beagon never led another revival across Hell Bend; instead he stayed dry on the Carthage side of the Caney Fork, once a year holding a temperate affair, more Sunday outing than revival, on Myers Bottom.

After Beagon had been in Carthage for twenty years, he grew heavy and dignified. No longer would he preside at river baptizings. In his church he erected, as Silas Jakeways said "a marble birdbath," a baptismal font, copied from one he saw in an Episcopal Church at Monteagle. In Carthage, though, pretension was always liable to be tipped over, if not by simple-minded folk like Gummert Capron or Doodlebug Healy, then by

daily life. Addicted to drink, Horace Armitage, the disreputable brother of
Benbow Armitage, occasionally cut hair at King's Barber Shop. One morning after a long night of carousing at Enos Mayfield's in South Carthage,
Horace was a bit shaky, and while shaving Beagon cut him slightly on the
chin. "That's what comes of taking too much to drink," said Beagon, holding a towel to his chin. "Yes, sir, Reverend," Horace replied, "Alcohol does
make the skin tender."

*1985*

## QUESTIONS FOR DISCUSSION

### Content

a. Explain the allusion at the beginning of paragraph 6. (Look up Solomon
   in a dictionary, an encyclopedia, or the Old Testament if you have to.)
   To what end does Pickering make this allusion?
b. How does the question at the end of paragraph 10 relate to the author's
   purpose and intent?
c. What does Pickering mean when he writes that "religion ought to be
   more concerned with people than ideas, creating soft feeling rather than
   sharp thought" (paragraph 11)? How might this idea serve as his thesis?
d. What is his purpose in mentioning that on Christmas Eve at St. Paul's,
   "Bourbon was in the air" (paragraph 3)?
e. Why is the congregation so elated at the return of Miss Ida and her hat
   (paragraph 9)? In what ways is the story of Miss Ida related to the Easter
   theme and to the essay's thesis?
f. How has the author's faith—his vision of God and the world changed
   in the 30 years since he attended St. Paul's?
g. Why does Pickering believe that "religion doesn't have a natural place"
   in a university (paragraph 11)?
h. "In Carthage," we are told, "pretension was always liable to be tipped
   over" (paragraph 14). How is this point illustrated?
i. How might Pickering defend the notion that humor can be used to define something as serious as religious faith?

### Strategy and Style

j. What details about St. Paul's in the first paragraph make that paragraph
   an appropriate introduction?

k. Find examples of irony in this piece.
l. The essay might have ended with paragraph 11. Why, then, does the author tell the story of Beagon Hackett?
m. Pickering mentions the titles of several Christian hymns. What does that accomplish other than helping to create atmosphere and establish the setting?
n. This selection is in three parts. What is the function of each? Is this organization appropriate?
o. Pickering's thesis appears in paragraph 11. Would the essay have been more effective if paragraph 11 had come at the essay's very beginning or at its very end?

## ENGAGING THE TEXT

a. "Faith of the Father" makes use of humorous anecdotes to illustrate the human quality in even the most serious and spiritual of ceremonies. Choose one of these anecdotes and explain why you like it and why it makes sense in this essay.
b. In paragraph 10, Pickering tells us that his childhood vision of religion was a mixture of "faith and fairy tale." How is it possible to combine the concepts of faith and fairy tale? Explain how Pickering does it.

## SUGGESTIONS FOR SUSTAINED WRITING

a. Note that Pickering's essay contrasts his childhood vision of Christianity with what he now experiences as an adult. Take your lead from this author; write an essay that compares and contrasts your childhood vision of religion with the way you see religion today.
b. We each worship in a different way. If you believe in a supreme being or in a spiritual power that controls the universe, write an essay explaining how you worship, recognize, or communicate with that being or power.
c. Easter is the most important of Christian holidays. Discuss a ritual or ceremony used in the celebration of a holiday important to your faith. Using information from personal observation, develop your essay with details that are specific and vivid. Use description, narration, and dialogue if appropriate. In addition, rely on secondary sources in your library or on the Internet for information that relates to the sources, purposes, and/or development of this ceremony and that explains the religious belief(s) it manifests.

# Erotica and Pornography

Gloria Steinem

*Born in Toledo, Ohio, Gloria Steinem (b. 1934) took her BA at Smith College and then stud-*
*ied at the University of Delhi and the University of Calcutta in India. Early in her career,*
*she was a television news writer for NBC's "That Was the Week That Was." She went*
*on to write for a number of America's most important magazines, including* Vogue, Life,
Cosmopolitan, *and* Glamour, *and served as an editorial consultant to* Seventeen *and*
Show. *One of the founders and leaders of the contemporary American feminist movement,*
*Steinem went undercover for* Show *magazine in 1963 to write "I Was a Playboy Bunny,"*
*an article that brought her journalistic acclaim. However, she is best known for her work as*
*cofounder of and contributing editor to* New York *and* Ms. *magazines. Today she is among*
*the most influential women in American public life, and her work has brought her numer-*
*ous awards and honors, including the United Nations Ceres Medal and the Front Page*
*Award. Among her full-length works are* Outrageous Acts and Everyday Rebellions
*(1983),* Marilyn: Norma Jean *(1986),* A Revolution from Within *(1993), and* Moving
Beyond Words *(1994).*
    *"Erotica and Pornography" was first published in 1978 in* Ms. *The essay uses con-*
*trast to define two important terms that are often confused and to present the sociopolitical*
*ideology of one of the founders of modern American feminism.*

1    Human beings are the only animals that experience the same sex drive at
times when we can—and cannot—conceive.

2    Just as we developed uniquely human capacities for language, planning, memory, and invention along our evolutionary path, we also developed sexuality as a form of expression, a way of communicating that is
separable from our need for sex as a way of perpetuating ourselves. For
humans alone, sexuality can be and often is primarily a way of bonding,
of giving and receiving pleasure, bridging differentness, discovering
sameness, and communicating emotion.

3    We developed this and other human gifts through our ability to
change our environment, adapt physically, and in the long run, to affect
our own evolution. But as an emotional result of this spiraling path away
from other animals, we seem to alternate between periods of exploring our
unique abilities to change new boundaries and feelings of loneliness in the
unknown that we ourselves have created; a fear that sometimes sends us
back to the comfort of the animal world by encouraging us to exaggerate
our sameness.

4    The separation of "play" from "work," for instance, is a problem only
in the human world. So is the difference between art and nature, or an intellectual accomplishment and a physical one. As a result, we celebrate
play, art, and invention as leaps into the unknown; but any imbalance can
send us back to nostalgia for our primate past and the conviction that the

**138**

basics of work, nature, and physical labor are somehow more worthwhile or even moral.

In the same way, we have explored our sexuality as separable from conception: A pleasurable, empathetic bridge to strangers of the same species. We have even invented contraception—a skill that has probably existed in some form since our ancestors figured out the process of birth— in order to extend this uniquely human difference. Yet we also have times of atavistic suspicion that sex is not complete—or even legal or intended- by-god—if it cannot end in conception.

No wonder the concepts of "erotica" and "pornography" can be so crucially different, and yet so confused. Both assume that sexuality can be separated from conception, and therefore can be used to carry a personal message. That's a major reason why, even in our current culture, both may be called equally "shocking" or legally "obscene," a word whose Latin de- rivative means "dirty, containing filth." This gross condemnation of all sexuality that isn't harnessed to childbirth and marriage has been in- creased by the current backlash against women's progress. Out of fear that the whole patriarchal structure might be upset if women really had the au- tonomous power to decide our reproductive futures (that is, if we con- trolled the most basic means of production), right-wing groups are not only denouncing pro-choice abortion literature as "pornographic," but are trying to stop the sending of all contraceptive information through the mails by invoking obscenity laws. In fact, Phyllis Schlafly recently de- nounced the entire Women's Movement as "obscene."

Not surprisingly, this religious, visceral backlash has a secular, intel- lectual counterpart that relies heavily on applying the "natural" behavior of the animal world to humans. That is questionable in itself, but these Li- onel Tigerish studies make their political purpose even more clear in the particular animals they select and the habits they choose to emphasize. The message is that females should accept their "destiny" of being sexu- ally dependent and devote themselves to bearing and rearing their young.

Defending against such reaction in turn leads to another temptation: To merely reverse the terms, and declare that *all* nonprocreative sex is good. In fact, however, this human activity can be as constructive or de- structive, moral or immoral, as any other. Sex as communication can send messages as different as life and death; even the origins of "erotica" and "pornography" reflect that fact. After all, "erotica" is rooted in *eros* or pas- sionate love, and thus in the idea of positive choice, free will, the yearning for a particular person. (Interestingly, the definition of erotica leaves open the question of gender.) "Pornography" begins with a root meaning "pros- titution" or "female captives," thus letting us know that the subject is not mutual love, or love at all, but domination and violence against women. (Though, of course, homosexual pornography may imitate this violence by

putting a man in the "feminine" role of victim.) It ends with a root meaning "writing about" or "description of" which puts still more distance between subject and object, and replaces a spontaneous yearning for closeness with objectification and a voyeur.

9      The difference is clear in the words. It becomes even more so by example.

10     Look at any photo or film of people making love; really making love.
The images may be diverse, but there is usually a sensuality and touch and
warmth, an acceptance of bodies and nerve endings. There is always a
spontaneous sense of people who are there because they *want* to be, out of
shared pleasure.

11     Now look at any depiction of sex in which there is clear force, or an unequal power that spells coercion. It may be very blatant, with weapons or
torture or bondage, wounds and bruises, some clear humiliation, or an
adult's sexual power being used over a child. It may be much more subtle:
A physical attitude of conqueror and victim, the use of race or class difference to imply the same thing, perhaps a very unequal nudity, with one person exposed and vulnerable while the other is clothed. In either case, there
is no sense of equal choice or equal power.

12     The first is erotic: A mutually pleasurable, sexual expression between
people who have enough power to be there by positive choice. It may or
may not strike the sense-memory in the viewer, or be creative enough to
make the unknown seem real; but it doesn't require us to identify with a
conqueror or a victim. It is truly sensuous, and may give us a contagion of
pleasure.

13     The second is pornographic: Its message is violence, dominance, and
conquest. It is sex being used to reinforce some inequality, or to create one,
or to tell us the lie that pain and humiliation (ours or someone else's) are
really the same as pleasure. If we are to feel anything, we must identify
with conqueror or victim. That means we can only experience pleasure
through the adoption of some degree of sadism or masochism. It also
means that we may feel diminished by the role of conqueror, or enraged,
humiliated, and vengeful by sharing identity with the victim.

14     Perhaps one could simply say that erotica is about sexuality, but
pornography is about power and sex-as-weapon—in the same way we
have come to understand that rape is about violence, and not really about
sexuality at all.

15     Yes, it's true that there are women who have been forced by violent
families and dominating men to confuse love with pain; so much so that
they have become masochists. (A fact that in no way excuses those who administer such pain.) But the truth is that, for most women—and for men
with enough humanity to imagine themselves into the predicament of
women—true pornography could serve as aversion therapy for sex.

16     Of course, there will always be personal differences about what is and
is not erotic, and there may be cultural differences for a long time to come.

Many women feel that sex makes them vulnerable and therefore may continue to need more sense of personal connection and safety before allowing any erotic feelings. We now find competence and expertise erotic in men, but that may pass as we develop those qualities in ourselves. Men, on the other hand, may continue to feel less vulnerable, and therefore more open to such potential danger as sex with strangers. As some men replace the need for submission from childlike women with the pleasure of cooperation from equals, they may find a partner's competence to be erotic, too.

Such group changes plus individual differences will continue to be reflected in sexual love between people of the same gender, as well as between women and men. The point is not to dictate sameness, but to discover ourselves and each other through sexuality that is an exploring, pleasurable, empathetic part of our lives; a human sexuality that is unchained both from unwanted pregnancies and from violence. 17

But that is a hope, not a reality. At the moment, fear of change is increasing both the indiscriminate repression of all nonprocreative sex in the religious and "conservative" male world, and the pornographic vengeance against women's sexuality in the secular world of "liberal" and "radical" men. It's almost futuristic to debate what is and is not truly erotic, when many women are again being forced into compulsory motherhood, and the number of pornographic murders, tortures, and womanhating images are on the increase in both popular culture and real life. 18

It's a familiar division: Wife or whore, "good" woman who is constantly vulnerable to pregnancy or "bad" woman who is unprotected from violence. *Both* roles would be upset if we were to control our own sexuality. And that's exactly what we must do. 19

In spite of all our atavistic suspicions and training for the "natural" role of motherhood, we took up the complicated battle for reproductive freedom. Our bodies had borne the health burden of endless births and poor abortions, and we had a greater motive for separating sexuality and conception. 20

Now we have to take up the equally complex burden of explaining that all nonprocreative sex is *not* alike. We have a motive: Our right to a uniquely human sexuality, and sometimes even to survival. As it is, our bodies have too rarely been enough our own to develop erotica in our own lives, much less in art and literature. And our bodies have too often been the objects of pornography and the womanhating, violent practice that it preaches. Consider also our spirits that break a little each time we see ourselves in chains or full labial display for the conquering male viewer, bruised or on our knees, screaming a real or pretended pain to delight the sadist, pretending to enjoy what we don't enjoy, to be blind to the images of our sisters that really haunt us—humiliated often enough ourselves by the truly obscene idea that sex and the domination of women must be combined. 21

22      Sexuality *is* human, free, separate—and so are we.

23      But until we untangle the lethal confusion of sex with violence, there will be more pornography and less erotica. There will be little murders in our beds—and very little love.

*1978*

## QUESTIONS FOR DISCUSSION

### Content

a. What is the distinction between *erotica* and *pornography?*

b. What place does the notion of choice have in that distinction?

c. Why is Steinem's separation of the notions of sexuality and conception important to this essay?

d. This selection was published in 1978. What does Steinem mean by "the current backlash against women's progress" (paragraph 6)?

e. Strong opinions are voiced in paragraphs 6 and 7. To what extent do you agree or disagree with them?

f. What, according to Steinem, is the danger in declaring "that *all* nonprocreative sex is good" (paragraph 8)?

g. In paragraph 13, we read that only by adopting "some degree of sadism or masochism" can we derive pleasure from pornography. Why is this notion central to Steinem's distinction between *erotica* and *pornography?*

h. What changes does Steinem predict in the attitudes of women and men toward sex? To what extent do you believe those changes have been realized since the publication of this essay?

i. Summarize Steinem's arguments in paragraphs 18 and 19. Then explain to what extent you agree or disagree.

j. How do you interpret the phrase "little murders" (paragraph 23)?

### Strategy and Style

k. Steinem sometimes uses etymology, the study of word origins. In what way does her explanation of the origins of *erotica* and *pornography* help her differentiate them (paragraph 8)?

l. As you know, this essay first appeared in *Ms.*, a magazine whose readership consists largely of women. What in the essay's content also reveals that Steinem is addressing women?

m. Based on the language used in this piece, what else can you say about Steinem's audience?

n. Analyze the vocabulary in paragraphs 6 and 7. Regardless of the opinions stated, how would you characterize Steinem's tone in those paragraphs?

o. What use does the author make of illustration in this definition essay?

p. How does she use contrast and analysis?

q. Where do you find an example of descriptive writing?

r. In what way is Steinem's conclusion (paragraphs 21–23) a call to action?

## ENGAGING THE TEXT

a. Paraphrase paragraphs 3 through 5. Then explain the function of those paragraphs in Steinem's essay. How do they relate to or help further her thesis?

b. Summarize Steinem's distinction between *erotica* and *pornography*.

## SUGGESTIONS FOR SUSTAINED WRITING

a. Pretend that this is 1978 and that you have just read "Erotica and Pornography" in *Ms.* magazine. Write a letter to the editor of this periodical in which you defend or attack Steinem's thesis. Begin by identifying key points in her definition of *pornography*. Then support or deny each of those points with facts and opinions of your own.

b. Read the essays by Camille Paglia and Susan Jacoby in Chapter 10. Then write an essay that explains how each of those authors might respond to Steinem's essay. Quote directly and paraphrase from all three essays.

c. Steinem's essay hinges on the distinction between two terms that are often confused. It is successful because the author is able to make that distinction clear. Choose two other terms that are often confused and write a paper that uses contrast to define them. Here are terms like those you might choose to distinguish: sensuous/sensual, ideology/philosophy, art/craft, love/infatuation, discipline/denial, intelligence/cleverness, democracy/republicanism, knowledge/wisdom, leadership/intimidation, faith/orthodoxy, criticism/disapproval, naïveté/gullibility, stupidity/ignorance, tragic/disastrous. You may want to discuss each concept by making reference to people or events about which you have read or learned through personal experience. However, this assignment provides a good opportunity to incorporate research from sources found in your library or on the Internet.

# Fire in the Sky

Claudia Glenn Dowling

*Two years after taking a degree in Chinese at Vassar College, Dowling began working for* People *magazine, where she became a senior writer and editor of the movie column. She then became a staff writer for* Life, *covering a variety of subjects from the Gulf War to space exploration to treatments for breast cancer. Her years with* Life *have been exciting, taking her around the world and giving her the opportunity to race a Porsche through Mexico, visit with the Cofan Indians in the Amazon, and tour Kyrgyzstan with Al Gore. She even climbed part of the way up Mount Everest with a British Special Forces team and got her passport taken away in China. Dowling is a fellow of the world-famous explorer's club and a winner of several awards for excellence in journalism.*

*"Fire in the Sky," which was first published in* Life *in 1994, uses language even a layperson can understand to explain a fascinating natural phenomenon. When we consider Dowling's intended audience, we realize that her writing is proof that even the most technical and specialized subject can be rendered understandable, interesting, and meaningful even to nonspecialists.*

1   Nights are long and bitter in the polar winters, but the compensations can be spectacular: The skies blaze in a display of energy called the aurora borealis in the Arctic, aurora australis in the Antarctic. Ancient tribes who saw the lights believed they were caused by the bonfires of spirits; today we know that awe-inspiring physical forces create the heavenly arrays. And we're about to know more: A hardy breed of scientists—who don't mind odd hours or sub-zero temperatures—are investigating the powerful magnetic storms hidden within the aurora's glory. A few years ago some of these researchers put up a sign outside their University of Alaska lab near the tiny village of Poker Flats. It said it all: "Center for the Study of Something which, on the face of it, might seem trivial, but on closer examination takes on Global Significance."

2       Auroras are born on the sun, where thermonuclear storms tear apart hydrogen atoms, blasting protons and electrons toward earth at up to 1,000 miles per second. As this solar wind approaches Earth's magnetic field, particles are drawn to the poles like iron filings to the ends of a bar magnet. When the particles collide with gases in the Earth's atmosphere, they create electrical discharges that glow purple, green, red and white. The effect is similar to the collision of electrons and gases inside a color television tube.

3       The beauty of an auroral storm hides its violence—the release of millions of amperes of electricity, 20 times that found in a bolt of lightning. Surges within auroras, called substorms, tap energy trapped by the Earth's

**144**

magnetic field on the side of the planet away from the sun. One physicist poetically calls this energy pool Earth's "electromagnetic soul."

A series of such storms knocked out power in all of Quebec as well as 4 several U.S. states in 1989. Earlier this year surges damaged two communications satellites. NASA researchers theorize that the substorms, which produce nitrogen oxides, may also damage the ozone layer above the poles. No one knows what effect the electrical charge may have on human beings, although Japanese travel agencies book tours to the Arctic specifically for couples who believe that their chances of conceiving a child are better under the aurora.

Lately, interest in mapping and predicting substorms has led to in- 5 creased government spending. (That may be why, not long ago, the sign at Poker Flats was changed to read: "This facility is uniquely dedicated to studies of the aurora borealis and other atmospheric research studies for the paying customer such as the National Aeronautics and Space Administration, the United States Air Force. . . .") Last month NASA launched a satellite—dubbed Wind—to monitor the solar wind as it howls toward Earth. Another, called Polar, the size of a school bus, is planned to orbit closer to the planet, photographing auroras with sensitive cameras. Next year Russia will launch two similar probes. And in November a consortium of European nations will open a radar installation in Spitsbergen, Norway, with high-powered dishes that will collect information about the velocity, density and temperature of solar particles. A European satellite that is designed to circle the Arctic will collect similar data from above.

Still, a nonscientific observer need only be in the right place at the right 6 time to study this natural wonder. A jargon-filled recorded message from the National Oceanic and Atmospheric Administration in Boulder, Colo. (303-497-3235), tells aficionados when conditions are favorable for a good show. Although the aurora can be seen year-round—the atmosphere is always being bombarded by the solar wind—and is sometimes visible as far away as the equator, it occurs most often in the extreme north and south and is easiest to see on a clear, dark winter night. Photographer Norbert Rosing's favorite site is Churchill, Manitoba, where winter skies are cloudless 80 percent of the time. There, every February and March, he waits in the cold, warming his film with his car heater so it won't crack. "When you see the northern lights," he says, "you're in love."

*1994*

## QUESTIONS FOR DISCUSSION

### Content

a. How would you define the term *aurora?*
b. What are some of the effects scientists have attributed to auroral sub-storms?
c. What advice does Dowling give amateur astronomers who want to see the northern lights?
d. Besides definition, for what purposes was this essay intended?

### Strategy and Style

e. Analyze Dowling's introduction. What about the first paragraph makes the reader want to continue?
f. Besides the fact that this essay was first published in *Life* magazine, how can we tell that Dowling is addressing a general audience?
g. This essay makes excellent use of figurative language to explain natural phenomena. Identify at least two examples of such language.

## ENGAGING THE TEXT

a. Summarize the ideas in paragraph 3.
b. Reread the essay, noting how Dowling conveys excitement about viewing an aurora. Using her description of an aurora as a model, write a brief description of a natural phenomenon you have experienced.

## SUGGESTIONS FOR SUSTAINED WRITING

a. Dowling conveys the excitement and fascination that many professional and amateur stargazers experience when viewing the aurora. Think about a natural phenomenon that arouses your interest. Then, following Dowling's lead, explain that phenomenon to an audience of nonspecialists like the one she addresses. Rely on your own observations and knowledge, but don't hesitate to research your topic if you need to. In fact, you might interview a science professor at your college or university for additional information.
b. In Chapter 9, James C. Rettie explains the origins of the universe. Like Dowling, he uses terminology that appeals to a lay audience. Unlike Dowling, he uses analogy rather than straightforward exposition. Write an essay that begins by explaining how and why the approaches each of these authors took fit their purposes. Continue developing your es-

say by discussing additional comparisons (and/or contrasts) between the two essays.

c. Dowling mentions both ancient and contemporary human reactions to the aurora. Do some library or Internet research on a natural phenomenon—such as an earthquake, a lightning storm, or a solar eclipse—and report on the folklore associated with it. Discuss one or two ways in which people have accounted for, explained, or reacted to this phenomenon.

# On Being a Cripple

Nancy Mairs

*Nancy Mairs (b. 1943) took an MFA and a Ph.D. at the University of Arizona. She has been a college teacher, an editor, and a professional writer. She writes fiction, essays, and poetry. Among her most recent books are* Remembering the Bone House *(1989),* Carnal Acts *(1990),* Ordinary Time *(1993),* Voice Lessons *(1994), and* Waist-High in the World: A Life *among the Nondisabled (1997). In 1984, the Western States Arts Foundation awarded Mairs a Poetry Prize for* In All the Rooms of the Yellow House *(1984).*

*Having suffered from anorexia and agoraphobia as a youngster, Mairs learned to deal with multiple sclerosis, a neurological disease, shortly after beginning adulthood. In addition to her family, her writing and her Roman Catholicism—a faith to which she converted—have proved to be sources of strength for Mairs. This essay, first published in* Plaintext *in 1986, details the long struggle she endured in coming to terms with the physical, psychological, and spiritual effects of her illness.*

> *To escape is nothing. Not to escape is nothing.*
>
> —Louise Bogan

The other day I was thinking of writing an essay on being a cripple. I was   1 thinking hard in one of the stalls of the women's room in my office building, as I was shoving my shirt into my jeans and tugging up my zipper. Preoccupied, I flushed, picked up my book bag, took my cane down from the hook, and unlatched the door. So many movements unbalanced me, and as I pulled the door open I fell over backward, landing fully clothed on the toilet seat with my legs splayed in front me: the old beetle-on-its-back routine. Saturday afternoon, the building deserted, I was free to laugh aloud as I wriggled back to my feet, my voice bouncing off the yellowish tiles from all directions. Had anyone been there with me, I'd have been still and faint and hot with chagrin. I decided that it was high time to write the essay.

2    First, the matter of semantics. I am a cripple. I choose this word to name me. I choose from among several possibilities, the most common of which are "handicapped" and "disabled." I made the choice a number of years ago, without thinking, unaware of my motives for doing so. Even now, I'm not sure what those motives are, but I recognize that they are complex and not entirely flattering. People—crippled or not—wince at the word "cripple," as they do not at "handicapped" or "disabled." Perhaps I want them to wince. I want them to see me as a tough customer, one to whom the fates/gods/viruses have not been kind, but who can face the brutal truth of her existence squarely. As a cripple, I swagger.

3    But, to be fair to myself, a certain amount of honesty underlies my choice. "Cripple" seems to me a clean word, straightforward and precise. It has an honorable history, having made its first appearance in the Lindisfarne Gospel in the tenth century. As a lover of words, I like the accuracy with which it describes my condition: I have lost the full use of my limbs. "Disabled," by contrast, suggests an incapacity, physical or mental. And I certainly don't like "handicapped," which implies that I have deliberately been put at a disadvantage, by whom I can't imagine (my God is not a Handicapper General), in order to equalize chances in the great race of life. These words seem to me to be moving away from my condition, to be widening the gap between word and reality. Most remote is the recently coined euphemism "differently abled," which partakes of the same semantic hopefulness that transformed countries from "undeveloped" to "underdeveloped," then to "less developed," and finally to "developing" nations. People have continued to starve in those countries during the shift. Some realities do not obey the dictates of language.

4    Mine is one of them. Whatever you call me, I remain crippled. But I don't care what you call me, so long as it isn't "differently abled," which strikes me as pure verbal garbage designed, by its ability to describe anyone, to describe no one. I subscribe to George Orwell's thesis that "the slovenliness of our language makes it easier for us to have foolish thoughts." And I refuse to participate in the degeneration of the language to the extent that I deny that I have lost anything in the course of this calamitous disease; I refuse to pretend that the only differences between you and me are the various ordinary ones that distinguish any one person from another. But call me "disabled" or "handicapped" if you like. I have long since grown accustomed to them; and if they are vague, at least they hint at the truth. Moreover, I use them myself. Society is no readier to accept crippledness than to accept death, war, sex, sweat, or wrinkles. I would never refer to another person as a cripple. It is the word I use to name only myself.

5    I haven't always been crippled, a fact for which I am soundly grateful. To be whole of limb is, I know from experience, infinitely more pleasant and useful than to be crippled; and if that knowledge leaves me open to

bitterness at my loss, the physical soundness I once enjoyed (though I did not enjoy it half enough) is well worth the occasional stab of regret. Though never any good at sports, I was a normally active child and young adult. I climbed trees, played hopscotch, jumped rope, skated, swam, rode my bicycle, sailed. I despised team sports, spending some of the wretchedest afternoons of my life sweaty and humiliated, behind a field-hockey stick and under a basketball hoop. I tramped alone for miles along the bridle paths that webbed the woods behind the house I grew up in. I swayed through countless dim hours in the arms of one man or another under the scattered shot of light from mirrored balls, and gyrated through countless more as Tab Hunter and Johnny Mathis gave way to the Rolling Stones, Creedence Clearwater Revival, Cream. I walked down the aisle. I pushed baby carriages, changed tires in the rain, marched for peace.

When I was twenty-eight I started to trip and drop things. What at first 6 seemed my natural clumsiness soon became too pronounced to shrug off. I consulted a neurologist, who told me that I had a brain tumor. A battery of tests, increasingly disagreeable, revealed no tumor. About a year and a half later I developed a blurred spot in one eye. I had, at last, the episodes "disseminated in space and time" requisite for a diagnosis: multiple sclerosis. I have never been sorry for the doctor's initial misdiagnosis, however. For almost a week, until the negative results of the tests were in, I thought that I was going to die right away. Every day for the past nearly ten years, then, has been a kind of gift. I accept all gifts.

Multiple sclerosis is a chronic degenerative disease of the central ner- 7 vous system, in which the myelin that sheathes the nerves is somehow eaten away and scar tissue forms in its place, interrupting the nerves' signals. During its course, which is unpredictable and uncontrollable, one may lose vision, hearing, speech, the ability to walk, control of bladder and/or bowels, strength in any or all extremities, sensitivity to touch, vibration, and/or pain, potency, coordination of movements—the list of possibilities is lengthy and yes, horrifying. One may also lose one's sense of humor. That's the easiest to lose and the hardest to survive without.

In the past ten years, I have sustained some of these losses. Character- 8 istic of MS are sudden attacks, called exacerbations, followed by remissions, and these I have not had. Instead, my disease has been slowly progressive. My left leg is now so weak that I walk with the aid of a brace and a cane; and for distances I use an Amigo, a variation on the electric wheelchair that looks rather like an electrified kiddie car. I no longer have much use of my left hand. Now my right side is weakening as well. I still have the blurred spot in my right eye. Overall, though, I've been lucky so far. My world has, of necessity, been circumscribed by my losses, but the terrain left me has been ample enough for me to continue many of the activities that absorb me: writing, teaching, raising children and cats and plants and snakes, reading, speaking publicly about MS and depression, even playing bridge with people patient and honorable enough to let me scatter cards every which way without sneaking a peek.

9    Lest I begin to sound like Pollyanna, however, let me say that I don't like having MS. I hate it. My life holds realities—harsh ones, some of them—that no right-minded human being ought to accept without grumbling. One of them is fatigue. I know of no one with MS who does not complain of bone-weariness; in a disease that presents an astonishing variety of symptoms, fatigue seems to be a common factor. I wake up in the morning feeling the way most people do at the end of a bad day, and I take it from there. As a result, I spend a lot of time *in extremis* and, impatient with limitation, I tend to ignore my fatigue until my body breaks down in some way and forces rest. Then I miss picnics, dinner parties, poetry readings, the brief visits of old friends from out of town. The offspring of a puritanical tradition of exceptional venerability, I cannot view these lapses without shame. My life often seems a series of small failures to do as I ought.

10    I lead, on the whole, an ordinary life, probably rather like the one I would have led had I not had MS. I am lucky that my predilections were already solitary, sedentary, and bookish—unlike the world-famous French cellist I have read about, or the young woman I talked with one long afternoon who wanted only to be a jockey. I had just begun graduate school when I found out something was wrong with me, and I have remained, interminably, a graduate student. Perhaps I would not have if I'd thought I had the stamina to return to a full-time job as a technical editor; but I've enjoyed my studies.

11    In addition to studying, I teach writing courses. I also teach medical students how to give neurological examinations. I pick up freelance editing jobs here and there. I have raised a foster son and sent him into the world, where he has made me two grandbabies, and I am still escorting my daughter and son through adolescence. I go to Mass every Saturday. I am a superb, if messy, cook. I am also an enthusiastic laundress, capable of sorting a hamper full of clothes into five subtly differentiated piles, but a terrible housekeeper. I can do italic writing and, in an emergency, bathe an oil-soaked cat. I play a fiendish game of Scrabble. When I have the time and the money, I like to sit on my front steps with my husband, drinking Amaretto and smoking a cigar, as we imagine our counterparts in Leningrad and make sure that the sun gets down once more behind the sharp childish scrawl of the Tucson Mountains.

12    This lively plenty has its bleak complement, of course, in all the things I can no longer do. I will never run again, except in dreams, and one day I may have to write that I will never walk again. I like to go camping, but I can't follow George and the children along the trails that wander out of a campsite through the desert or into the mountains. In fact, even on the level I've learned never to check the weather or try to hold a coherent conversation: I need all my attention for my wayward feet. Of late, I have be-

gun to catch myself wondering how people can propel themselves without one usable hand, I have to select my clothing with care not so much for style as for ease of ingress and egress, and even so, dressing can be laborious. I can no longer do fine stitchery, pick up babies, play the piano, braid my hair. I am immobilized by acute attacks of depression, which may or may not be physiologically related to MS but are certainly its logical concomitant.

These two elements, the plenty and the privation, are never pure, nor     13
are the delight and wretchedness that accompany them. Almost every pickle that I get into as a result of my weakness and clumsiness—and I get into plenty—is funny as well as maddening and sometimes painful. I recall one May afternoon when a friend and I were going out for a drink after finishing up at school. As we were climbing into opposite sides of my car, chatting, I tripped and fell, flat and hard, onto the asphalt parking lot, my abrupt departure interrupting him in mid-sentence. "Where'd you go?" he called as he came around the back of the car to find me hauling myself up by the door frame. "Are you all right?" Yes, I told him, I was fine, just a bit rattly, and we drove off to find a shady patio and some beer. When I got home an hour or so later, my daughter greeted me with "What have you done to yourself?" I looked down. One elbow of my white turtleneck with the green froggies, one knee of my white trousers, one white kneesock were blood-soaked. We peeled off the clothes and inspected the damage, which was nasty enough but not alarming. That part wasn't funny: The abrasions took a long time to heal, and one got a little infected. Even so, when I think of my friend talking earnestly, suddenly, to the hot thin air while I dropped from his view as though through a trap door, I find the image as silly as something from a Marx Brothers movie.

I may find it easier than other cripples to amuse myself because I live     14
propped by the acceptance and the assistance and, sometimes, the amusement of those around me. Grocery clerks tear my checks out of my checkbook for me, and sales clerks find chairs to put into dressing rooms when I want to try on clothes. The people I work with make sure I teach at times when I am least likely to be fatigued, in places I can get to, with the materials I need. My students, with one anonymous exception (in an end-of-the-semester evaluation), have been unperturbed by my disability. Some even like it. One was immensely cheered by the information that I paint my own fingernails; she decided, she told me, that if I could go to such trouble over fine details, she could keep on writing essays. I suppose I became some sort of bright-fingered muse. She wrote good essays, too.

The most important struts in the framework of my existence, of course,     15
are my husband and children. Dismayingly few marriages survive the MS test, and why should they? Most twenty-two and nineteen-year-olds, like George and me, can vow in clear conscience, after a childhood of chicken-pox and summer colds, to keep one another in sickness and in health so

long as they both shall live. Not many are equipped for catastrophe: the dismay, the depression, the extra work, the boredom that a degenerative disease can insinuate into a relationship. And our society, with its emphasis on fun and its association of fun with physical performance, offers little encouragement for a whole spouse to stay with a crippled partner. Children experience similar stresses when faced with a crippled parent, and they are more helpless, since parents and children can't usually get divorced. They hate, of course, to be different from their peers, and the child whose mother is tacking down the aisle of a school auditorium packed with proud parents like a Cape Cod dinghy in stiff breeze jolly well stands out in a crowd. Deprived of legal divorce, the child can at least deny the mother's disability, even her existence, forgetting to tell her about recitals and PTA meetings, refusing to accompany her to stores or church or the movies, never inviting friends to the house. Many do.

16      But I've been limping along for ten years now, and so far George and the children are still at my left elbow, holding tight. Ann and Matthew vacuum floors and dust furniture and haul trash and rake up dog droppings and button my cuffs and bake lasagna and Toll House cookies with just enough grumbling so I know that they don't have brain fever. And far from hiding me, they're forever dragging me by racks of fancy clothes or through teeming school corridors, or welcoming gaggles of friends while I'm wandering through the house in Anne's filmy pink babydoll pajamas. George generally calls before he brings someone home, but he does just as many dumb thankless chores as the children. And they all yell at me, laugh at some of my jokes, write me funny letters when we're apart—in short, treat me as an ordinary human being for whom they have some use. I think they like me. Unless they're faking. . . .

17      Faking. There's the rub. Tugging at the fringes of my consciousness always is the terror that people are kind to me only because I'm a cripple. My mother almost shattered me once, with that instinct mothers have— blind, I think, in this case, but unerring nonetheless—for striking blows along the fault-lines of their children's hearts, by telling me, in an attack on my selfishness, "We all have to make allowances for you, of course, because of the way you are." From the distance of a couple of years, I have to admit that I haven't any idea just what she meant, and I'm not sure that she knew either. She was awfully angry. But at the time, as the words thudded home, I felt my worst fear, suddenly realized. I could bear being called selfish: I am. But I couldn't bear the corroboration that those around me were doing in fact what I'd always suspected them of doing, professing fondness while silently putting up with me because of the way I am. A cripple. I've been a little cracked ever since.

18      Along with this fear that people are secretly accepting shoddy goods comes a relentless pressure to please—to prove myself worth the burdens I impose, I guess, or to build a substantial account of goodwill against

which I may write drafts in times of need. Part of the pressure arises from social expectations. In our society, anyone who deviates from the norm had better find some way to compensate. Like fat people, who are expected to be jolly, cripples must bear their lot meekly and cheerfully. A grumpy cripple isn't playing by the rules. And much of the pressure is self-generated. Early on I vowed that, if I had to have MS, by God I was going to do it well. This a class act, ladies and gentlemen. No tears, no recriminations, no faint-heartedness.

One way and another, then, I wind up feeling like Tiny Tim, peering   19
over the edge of the table at the Christmas goose, waving my crutch, piping down God's blessing on us all. Only sometimes I don't want to play Tiny Tim. I'd rather be Caliban, a most scurvy monster. Fortunately, at home no one much cares whether I'm a good cripple or a bad cripple as long as I make vichyssoise with fair regularity. One evening several years ago, Anne was reading at the dining-room table while I cooked dinner. As I opened a can of tomatoes, the can slipped in my left hand and juice spattered me and the counter with bloody spots. Fatigued and infuriated, I bellowed, "I'm so sick of being crippled!" Anne glanced at me over the top of her book. "There now," she said, "do you feel better?" "Yes," I said, "yes, I do." She went back to her reading. I felt better. That's about all the attention my scurviness ever gets.

Because I hate being crippled, I sometimes hate myself for being a crip-   20
ple. Over the years I have come to expect—even accept—attacks of violent self-loathing. Luckily, in general our society no longer connects deformity and disease directly with evil (though a charismatic once told me that I have MS because a devil is in me) and so I'm allowed to move largely at will, even among small children. But I'm not sure that this revision of attitude has been particularly helpful. Physical imperfection, even free of moral disapprobation, still defies and violates the ideal, especially for women, whose confinement in their bodies as objects of desire is far from over. Each age, of course, has its ideal, and I doubt that ours is any better or worse than any other. Today's ideal woman, who lives on the glossy pages of dozens of magazines, seems to be between the ages of eighteen and twenty-five; her hair has body, her teeth flash white, her breath smells minty, her underarms are dry; she has a career but is still a fabulous cook, especially of meals that take less than twenty minutes to prepare; she does not ordinarily appear to have a husband or children; she is trim and deeply tanned; she jogs, swims, plays tennis, rides a bicycle, sails, but does not bowl; she travels widely, even to out-of-the-way places like Finland and Samoa, always in the company of the ideal man, who possesses a nearly identical set of characteristics. There are a few exceptions. Though usually white and often blonde, she may be black, Hispanic, Asian, or Native American, so long as she is unusually sleek. She may be old, provided she is selling a laxative or is Lauren Bacall. If she is selling a detergent, she may

be married and have a flock of strikingly messy children. But she is never a cripple.

21      Like many women I know, I have always had an uneasy relationship with my body. I was not a popular child, largely, I think now, because I was peculiar: intelligent, intense, moody, shy, given to unexpected actions and inexplicable notions and emotions. But as I entered adolescence, I believed myself unpopular because I was homely: my breasts too flat, my mouth too wide, my hips too narrow, my clothing never quite right in fit or style. I was not, in fact, particularly ugly, old photographs inform me, though I was well off the ideal; but I carried this sense of self-alienation with me into adulthood, where it regenerated in response to the depredations of MS. Even with my brace I walk with a limp so pronounced that, seeing myself on the videotape of a television program on the disabled, I couldn't believe that anything but an inchworm could make progress humping along like that. My shoulders droop and my pelvis thrusts forward as I try to balance myself upright, throwing my frame into a bony S. As a result of contractures, one shoulder is higher than the other and I carry one arm bent in front of me, the fingers curled into a claw. My left arm and leg have wasted into pipe-stems, and I try always to keep them covered. When I think about how my body must look to others, especially to men, to whom I have been trained to display myself, I feel ludicrous, even loathsome.

22      At my age, however, I don't spend much time thinking about my appearance. The burning egocentricity of adolescence, which assures one that all the world is looking all the time, has passed, thank God, and I'm generally too caught up in what I'm doing to step back, as I used to, and watch myself as though upon a stage. I'm also too old to believe in the accuracy of self-image. I know that I'm not a hideous crone, that in fact, when I'm rested, well dressed, and well made up, I look fine. The self-loathing I feel is neither physically nor intellectually substantial. What I hate is not me but a disease.

23      I am not a disease.

24      And a disease is not—at least not singlehandedly—going to determine who I am, though at first it seemed to be going to. Adjusting to a chronic incurable illness, I have moved through a process similar to that outlined by Elizabeth Kübler-Ross in *On Death and Dying*. The major difference— and it is far more significant than most people recognize—is that I can't be sure of the outcome, as the terminally ill cancer patient can. Research studies indicate that, with proper medical care, I may achieve a "normal" life span. And in our society, with its vision of death as the ultimate evil, worse even than decrepitude, the response to such news is, "Oh well, at least you're not going to *die*," Are there worse things than dying? I think that there may be.

25      I think of two women I know, both with MS, both enough older than I to have served as models. One took to her bed several years ago and has

been there ever since. Although she can sit in a high-backed wheelchair, because she is incontinent she refuses to go out at all, even though incontinence pants, which are readily available at any pharmacy, could protect her from embarrassment. Instead, she stays at home and insists that her husband, a small quiet man, a retired civil servant, stay there with her except for a quick weekly foray to the supermarket. The other woman, whose illness was diagnosed when she was eighteen, a nursing student engaged to a young doctor, finished her training, married her doctor, accompanied him to Germany when he was in the service, bore three sons and a daughter, now grown and gone. When she can, she travels with her husband; she plays bridge, embroiders, swims regularly; she works, like me, as a symptomatic-patient instructor of medical students in neurology. Guess which woman I hope to be.

At the beginning, I thought about having MS almost incessantly. And  26 because of the unpredictable course of the disease, my thoughts were always terrified. Each night I'd get into bed wondering whether I'd get out again the next morning, whether I'd be able to see, to speak, to hold a pen between my fingers. Knowing that the day might come when I'd be physically incapable of killing myself, I thought perhaps I ought to do so right away, while I still had the strength. Gradually I came to understand that the Nancy who might one day lie inert under a bedsheet, arms and legs paralyzed, unable to feed or bathe herself, unable to reach out for a gun, a bottle of pills, was not the Nancy I was at present, and that I could not presume to make decisions for that future Nancy, who might well not want in the least to die. Now the only provision I've made for the future Nancy is that when the time comes—and it is likely to come in the form of pneumonia, friend to the weak and the old—I am not to be treated with machines and medications. If she is unable to communicate by then, I hope she will be satisfied with these terms.

Thinking all the time about having MS grew tiresome and intrusive,  27 especially in the large and tragic mode in which I was accustomed to considering my plight. Months and even years went by without catastrophe (at least without one related to MS), and really I was awfully busy, what with George and children and snakes and students and poems, and I hadn't the time, let alone the inclination, to devote myself to being a disease. Too, the richer my life became, the funnier it seemed, as though there were some connection between largesse and laughter, and so my tragic stance began to waver until, even with the aid of a brace and cane, I couldn't hold it for very long at a time.

After several years I was satisfied with my adjustment. I had suffered  28 my grief and fury and terror, I thought, but now I was at ease with my lot. Then one summer day I set out with George and the children across the desert for a vacation in California. Part way to Yuma I became aware that my right leg felt funny. "I think I've had an exacerbation," I told George.

"What shall we do?" he asked. "I think we'd better get the hell to California," I said, "because I don't know whether I'll ever make it again." So we went on to San Diego and then to Orange, and up the Pacific Coast Highway to Santa Cruz, across to Yosemite, down to Sequoia and Joshua Tree, and so back over the desert to home. It was a fine two-week trip, filled with friends and fair weather, and I wouldn't have missed it for the world, though I did in fact make it back to California two years later. Nor would there have been any point in missing it, since in MS, once the symptoms have appeared, the neurological damage has been done, and there's no way to predict or prevent that damage.

29      The incident spoiled my self-satisfaction, however. It renewed my grief and fury and terror, and I learned that one never finishes adjusting to MS. I don't know now why I thought one would. One does not, after all, finish adjusting to life, and MS is simply a fact of my life—not my favorite fact, of course—but as ordinary as my nose and my tropical fish and my yellow Mazda station wagon. It may at any time get worse, but no amount of worry or anticipation can prepare me for a new loss. My life is a lesson in losses. I learn one at a time.

30      And I had best be patient in the learning, since I'll have to do it like it or not. As any rock fan knows, you can't always get what you want. Particularly when you have MS. You can't, for example, get cured. In recent years researchers and the organizations that fund research have started to pay MS some attention even though it isn't fatal; perhaps they have begun to see that life is something other than a quantitative phenomenon, that one may be very much alive for a very long time in a life that isn't worth living. The researchers have made some progress toward understanding the mechanism of the disease: It may well be an autoimmune reaction triggered by a slow-acting virus. But they are nowhere near its prevention, control, or cure. And most of us want to be cured. Some, unable to accept incurability, grasp at one treatment after another, no matter how bizarre: megavitamin therapy, gluten-free diet, injections of cobra venom, hypothermal suits, lymphocytopharesis, hyberbaric chambers. Many treatments are probably harmless enough, but none are curative.

31      The absence of a cure often makes MS patients bitter toward their doctors. Doctors are, after all, the priests of modern society, the new shamans, whose business is to heal, and many an MS patient roves from one to another, searching for the "good" doctor who will make him well. Doctors too think of themselves as healers, and for this reason many have trouble dealing with MS patients, whose disease in its intransigence defeats their aims and mocks their skills. Too few doctors, it is true, treat their patients as whole human beings, but the reverse is also true. I have always tried to be gentle with my doctors, who often have more at stake in terms of ego than I do. I may be frustrated, maddened, depressed by the incurability of my disease, but I am not diminished by it, and they are. When I push my-

self up from my seat in the waiting room and stumble toward them, I incarnate the limitation of their powers. The least I can do is refuse to press on their tenderest spots.

This gentleness is part of the reason that I'm not sorry to be a cripple. 32 I didn't have it before. Perhaps I'd have developed it anyway—how could I know such a thing?—and I wish I had more of it, but I'm glad of what I have. It has opened and enriched my life enormously, this sense that my frailty and need must be mirrored in others, that in searching for and shaping a stable core in a life wrenched by change and loss, change and loss, I must recognize the same process, under individual conditions, in the lives around me. I do not deprecate such knowledge, however I've come by it.

All the same, if a cure were found, would I take it? In a minute. I may 33 be a cripple, but I'm only occasionally a loony and never a saint. Anyway, in my brand of theology God doesn't give bonus points for a limp. I'd take a cure; I just don't need one. A friend who also has MS startled me once by asking, "Do you ever say to yourself, 'Why me, Lord?' " "No, Michael, I don't," I told him, "because whenever I try, the only response I can think of is 'Why not?' " If I could make a cosmic deal, who would I put in my place? What in my life would I give up in exchange for sound limbs and a thrilling rush of energy? No one. Nothing. I might as well do the job myself. Now that I'm getting the hang of it.

*1986*

## QUESTIONS FOR DISCUSSION

### Content

a. What does Mairs intend by prefacing her essay with a quotation from Louise Bogan? What does this quotation mean?
b. What does the quotation by George Orwell in paragraph 4 contribute to this essay?
c. Why does Mairs use the word *cripple* to refer only to herself?
d. What are the physical effects of multiple sclerosis as Mairs explains them? What are some of the emotional effects?
e. Why, as the author explains, can she not view certain "lapses without shame" (paragraph 9)?
f. Who were the Marx Brothers, and why does Mairs mention them in paragraph 13?
g. Why does Mairs fear that people are kind to her only because of her illness?

h. How has Mairs's family helped her come to terms with her illness?
i. In what ways has Mairs been able to deal with attacks of "self-loathing," which she mentions in paragraphs 20 and 21? What does her ability to deal with this emotion tell us about her?
j. How would you assess the speaker's character, her attitude about her illness, and her vision of life? In what ways does she see herself as a person without an illness?
k. What provision has she made for her death? What does her explanation of these plans reveal about her?
l. In what ways has MS shaped the author's vision of doctors?
m. What one sentence most explicitly states the thesis of this essay? For what purpose did Mairs write this selection?

## Strategy and Style

n. Are Mairs's introduction and conclusion appropriate to her thesis and purpose?
o. Is Mairs's tone consistent, or does it shift at different times in the essay? If so, are these shifts appropriate?
p. Where in this essay do you find examples of description, cause and effect, and contrast?
q. This is a rather lengthy essay. Could Mairs have left out material and still have defined the illness and its effects as well? If so, find such material. If not, why is the length appropriate?

## ENGAGING THE TEXT

a. Read paragraph 29 again. In your own words, and using the insights the author presents in this paragraph, summarize what she means by "One does not, after all, finish adjusting to life, and MS is simply a fact of my life." How might the first part of that statement relate to you?
b. Respond to the various synonyms for *crippled* that Mairs discusses at the beginning of this essay.

## SUGGESTIONS FOR SUSTAINED WRITING

a. Mairs contrasts the ways two other MS patients have responded to their illness. Write an essay in which you contrast the ways in which two people with the same or similar problems or illnesses have dealt with their situations. One of your subjects might be yourself.

b. Read the essay by William Lutz in Chapter 5. How might Lutz respond to Mairs? Although Lutz's essay discusses the use and abuse of language, it provides insight into what Mairs is getting at. After finishing with Lutz, turn to another seemingly unrelated essay: Norman Cousins's "Pain Is Not the Ultimate Enemy" in Chapter 8. What might Cousins say about Mairs's essay?

c. Read paragraph 29 again. In your own words, and using the insights the author presents in this paragraph, summarize what she means by saying: "One does not, after all, finish adjusting to life, and MS is simply a fact of my life." Now, expand your work into a full-length essay on the topic of a disease that has affected your life or the life of a friend or loved one. In addition to relying on your own observations about the causes and effects of the disease, search the Internet or various print sources to provide an even more authoritative rendering of the disease under discussion.

# Classification and Division

Classification and division are attempts to explain the nature and connections between bits of information that may at first seem unrelated and confusing. Writers often find it useful to identify like qualities or characteristics among various facts, ideas, people, or things so as to create related categories or classes by which the material can be divided logically and discussed systematically.

If you are a people watcher, you know that public places—a bus station, a sports stadium, and even a college library—offer a variety of subjects. Let's say that two days before a math midterm, you resolve to study hard in the library. As you walk into the main reading room, you hear the giggles of young lovers seated in a corner. A few yards beyond, you spot one of the college's maintenance workers who is spending her lunch hour noisily turning the pages of a large newspaper. To your right, you begin to eavesdrop on a few students discussing a fraternity party, and you realize that their chatter is annoying a woman trying to take notes for a term paper. In a less-crowded part of the room, two of your friends are killing time by browsing through a few magazines they found lying about. After a while, you decide that the reading room offers too many distractions, so you find a corner in the basement where you can hide. It is no coincidence that other members of your math class had the same idea, so you sit down quietly and begin studying.

The decision to join your classmates and not stay in the reading room resulted from dividing the group of people you found at the library into three smaller categories: fun-seekers, browsers, and serious students. Your analysis may have been quick and informal, but it was effective. What's more, it revealed something important about the nature and function of classification: You began by observing similarities among individuals; you created categories based on those similarities and placed each individual you observed into one of them; and you made a decision—to study in one place and not another—based on what your classification revealed.

Classification is a versatile tool. It can be used to explain stages in human development as in Gail Sheehy's "Predictable Crises of Adulthood" or to discuss the manipulation of language in business and politics as in William Lutz's "Doublespeak" and Donna Woolfolk Cross's "Politics: The Art of Bamboozling." In "Growing Up Asian in America," Kesaya E.

Noda uses classification as a tool for self-analysis as she explores various aspects—ethnic, cultural, and sexual—of her identity. As we read her work, we cannot help thinking that she may be shedding light on aspects of our own personalities. Finally, Donald Hall shows in "Four Kinds of Reading" that classification can become a way to analyze and understand the processes and motivations behind the way we read, think, and comprehend.

The success of a classification paper depends on how logically an author divides the material and how thoroughly and concretely he or she develops each category. Among the most effective methods to develop such an essay is illustration. Examples like those in Judith Viorst's "The Truth about Lying" are often essential to the writer's purpose. Without them, an essay might remain a list of ill-defined labels and abstractions. The essay by Lutz, though different in style and approach, also contains examples to support important points. But good writers use a variety of techniques to keep readers interested. For example, Sheehy makes excellent use of definition; Noda relies on definition, contrast, and anecdote; and Cross uses narration, illustration, contrast, and analogy. Cross also quotes extensively from a variety of sources to drive home her point.

As you read the selections that follow, remember that almost any conglomeration of seemingly unrelated information can be classified to reveal patterns of meaning that readers will find valuable and interesting. The perspectives from which you view a subject and the choices you make to impose order on the material should be determined only by your purpose. Read the Suggestions for Sustained Writing after each selection. They describe activities that will help you use classification to accomplish a well-defined purpose. But even if you approach a writing assignment without a clear notion of purpose—something not uncommon even among experienced writers—you may still want to use classification in the early stages of your project to review the raw information you have collected; to group facts, ideas, and insights logically; and ultimately to improve your understanding both of the material and of your purpose.

# Predictable Crises of Adulthood

## Gail Sheehy

*Born in New York City and educated at the University of Vermont and Columbia University, Gail Sheehy (b. 1937) has been a contributing editor for* New York Magazine *and has written for* Paris Match, *the* London Sunday Telegraph, *the* New York Times Magazine, Cosmopolitan, *and* Glamour. *Sheehy's first sustained work was* Lovesounds

*(1970), a novel, which was followed by several pieces of nonfiction, including* Hustling: Prostitution in Our Wide Open Society *(1973),* Character: America's Search for Leadership *(1988), and* Gorbachev: The Man Who Changed the World *(1990). In 1986, Sheehy published* Spirit of Survival, *the story of a Cambodian girl she found and later adopted as a result of a journalistic assignment on refugee children in Southeast Asia. Her most recent works include* New Passages: Mapping Your Life across Time *(1995);* Passages for Men *(1998), which advises men to find new ways to demonstrate masculinity in an ever-changing social landscape; and* Hillary's Choice *(1999), which was written in the aftermath of the revelations about the Bill Clinton–Monica Lewinsky scandal.*

Passages *(1976), from which "Predictable Crises of Adulthood" is taken, discusses several natural crises through which everyone must pass and which, if understood and handled properly, can lay the foundation for a stable and fulfilling life.*

1   We are not unlike a particularly hardy crustacean. The lobster grows by developing and shedding a series of hard, protective shells. Each time it expands from within, the confining shell must be sloughed off. It is left exposed and vulnerable until, in time, a new covering grows to replace the old.

2   With each passage from one stage of human growth to the next we, too, must shed a protective structure. We are left exposed and vulnerable—but also yeasty and embryonic again, capable of stretching in ways we hadn't known before. These sheddings may take several years or more. Coming out of each passage, though, we enter a longer and more stable period in which we can expect relative tranquility and a sense of equilibrium regained. . . .

3   As we shall see, each person engages the steps of development in his or her own characteristic *step-style*. Some people never complete the whole sequence. And none of us "solves" with one step—by jumping out of the parental home into a job or marriage, for example—the problems in separating from the caregivers of childhood. Nor do we "achieve" autonomy once and for all by converting our dreams into concrete goals, even when we attain those goals. The central issues or tasks of one period are never fully completed, tied up, and cast aside. But when they lose their primacy and the current life structure has served its purpose, we are ready to move on to the next period.

4   Can one catch up? What might look to others like listlessness, contrariness, a maddening refusal to face up to an obvious task may be a person's own unique detour that will bring him out later on the other side. Developmental gains won can later be lost—and rewon. It's plausible, though it can't be proven, that the mastery of one set of tasks fortifies us for the next period and the next set of challenges. But it's important not to think too mechanistically. Machines work by units. The bureaucracy (supposedly) works step by step. Human beings, thank God, have an individual inner dynamic that can never be precisely coded.

Although I have indicated the ages when Americans are likely to go  5
through each stage, and the differences between men and women where
they are striking, do not take the ages too seriously. The stages are the
thing, and most particularly the sequence.

Here is the briefest outline of the developmental ladder.                  6

## PULLING UP ROOTS

Before 18, the motto is loud and clear: "I have to get away from my par-  7
ents." But the words are seldom connected to action. Generally still safely
part of our families, even if away at school, we feel our autonomy to be
subject to erosion from moment to moment.

After 18, we begin Pulling Up Roots in earnest. College, military ser-  8
vice, and short-term travels are all customary vehicles our society provides
for the first round trips between family and a base of one's own. In the attempt to separate our view of the world from our family's view, despite
vigorous protestations to the contrary—"I know exactly what I want!"—
we cast about for any beliefs we can call our own. And in the process of
testing those beliefs we are often drawn to fads, preferably those most
mysterious and inaccessible to our parents.

Whatever tentative memberships we try out in the world, the fear  9
haunts us that we are really kids who cannot take care of ourselves. We
cover that fear with acts of defiance and mimicked confidence. For allies
to replace our parents, we turn to our contemporaries. They become con-
spirators. So long as their perspective meshes with our own, they are able
to substitute for the sanctuary of the family. But that doesn't last very long.
And the instant they diverge from the shaky ideals of "our group," they
are seen as betrayers. Rebounds to the family are common between the
ages of 18 and 22.

The tasks of this passage are to locate ourselves in a peer group role, a  10
sex role, an anticipated occupation, an ideology or world view. As a result,
we gather the impetus to leave home physically and the identity to *begin*
leaving home emotionally.

Even as one part of us seeks to be an individual, another part longs to  11
restore the safety and comfort of merging with another. Thus one of the
most popular myths of this passage is: We can piggyback our development
by attaching to a Stronger One. But people who marry during this time often prolong financial and emotional ties to the family and relatives that im-
pede them from becoming self-sufficient.

A stormy passage through the Pulling Up Roots years will probably  12
facilitate the normal progression of the adult life cycle. If one doesn't have
an identity crisis at this point, it will erupt during a later transition, when
the penalties may be harder to bear.

## THE TRYING TWENTIES

13   The Trying Twenties confront us with the question of how to take hold in the adult world. Our focus shifts from the interior turmoils of late adolescence—"Who am I?" "What is truth?"—and we become almost totally preoccupied with working out the externals. "How do I put my aspirations into effect?" "What is the best way to start?" "Where do I go?" "Who can help me?" "How did *you* do it?"

14   In this period, which is longer and more stable compared with the passage that leads to it, the tasks are as enormous as they are exhilarating: To shape a Dream, that vision of ourselves which will generate energy, aliveness, and hope. To prepare for a lifework. To find a mentor if possible. And to form the capacity for intimacy without losing in the process whatever consistency of self we have thus far mustered. The first test structure must be erected around the life we choose to try.

15   Doing what we "should" is the most pervasive theme of the twenties. The "shoulds" are largely defined by family models, the press of the culture, or the prejudices of our peers. If the prevailing cultural instructions are that one should get married and settle down behind one's own door, a nuclear family is born. If instead the peers insist that one should do one's own thing, the 25-year-old is likely to harness himself onto a Harley-Davidson and burn up Route 66 in the commitment to have no commitments.

16   One of the terrifying aspects of the twenties is the inner conviction that the choices we make are irrevocable. It is largely a false fear. Change is quite possible, and some alteration of our original choices is probably inevitable.

17   Two impulses, as always, are at work. One is to build a firm, safe structure for the future by making strong commitments, to "be set." Yet people who slip into a ready-made form without much self-examination are likely to find themselves *locked* in.

18   The other urge is to explore and experiment, keeping any structure tentative and therefore easily reversible. Taken to the extreme, these are people who skip from one trial job and one limited personal encounter to another, spending their twenties in the *transient* state.

19   Although the choices of our twenties are not irrevocable, they do set in motion a Life Pattern. Some of us follow the lock-in pattern, others the transient pattern, the wunderkind pattern, the caregiver pattern, and there are a number of others. Such patterns strongly influence the particular questions raised for each person during each passage. . . .

20   Buoyed by powerful illusions and belief in the power of the will, we commonly insist in our twenties that what we have chosen to do is the one true course in life. Our backs go up at the merest hint that we are like our parents, that two decades of parental training might be reflected in our current actions and attitudes.

21   "Not me," is the motto, "I'm different."

## CATCH-30

Impatient with devoting ourselves to the "shoulds," a new vitality 22
springs from within as we approach 30. Men and women alike speak of
feeling too narrow and restricted. They blame all sorts of things, but what
the restrictions boil down to are the outgrowth of career and personal
choices of the twenties. They may have been choices perfectly suited to
that stage. But now the fit feels different. Some inner aspect that was left
out is striving to be taken into account. Important new choices must be
made, and commitments altered or deepened. The work involves great
change, turmoil, and often crisis—a simultaneous feeling of rock bottom
and the urge to bust out.

One common response is the tearing up of the life we spent most of 23
our twenties putting together. It may mean striking out on a secondary
road toward a new vision or converting a dream of "running for president" into a more realistic goal. The single person feels a push to find a
partner. The woman who was previously content at home with children
chafes to venture into the world. The childless couple reconsiders children.
And almost everyone who is married, especially those married for seven
years, feels a discontent.

If the discontent doesn't lead to a divorce, it will, or should, call for a 24
serious review of the marriage and of each partner's aspirations in their
Catch-30 condition. The gist of that condition was expressed by a 29-year-
old associate with a Wall Street law firm:

"I'm considering leaving the firm. I've been there four years now; I'm 25
getting good feedback, but I have no clients of my own. I feel weak. If I
wait much longer, it will be too late, too close to that fateful time of decision on whether or not to become a partner. I'm success-oriented. But the
concept of being 55 years old and stuck in a monotonous job drives me
wild. It drives me crazy now, just a little bit. I'd say that 85 percent of the
time I thoroughly enjoy my work. But when I get a screwball case, I come
away from court saying, 'What am I doing here?' It's a *visceral* reaction
that I'm wasting my time. I'm trying to find some way to make a social
contribution or a slot in city government. I keep saying, 'There's something more.' "

Besides the push to broaden himself professionally, there is a wish to 26
expand his personal life. He wants two or three more children. "The concept of a home has become very meaningful to me, a place to get away
from troubles and relax. I love my son in a way I could not have anticipated. I never could live alone."

Consumed with the work of making his own critical lifesteering deci- 27
sions, he demonstrates the essential shift at this age: An absolute require-
ment to be more self-concerned. The self has new value now that his com-
petency has been proved.

28   His wife is struggling with her own age-30 priorities. She wants to go to law school, but he wants more children. If she is going to stay home, she wants him to make more time for the family instead of taking on even wider professional commitments. His view of the bind, of what he would most like from his wife, is this:

29   "I'd like not to be bothered. It sounds cruel, but I'd like not to have to worry about what she's going to do next week. Which is why I've told her several times that I think she should do something. Go back to school and get a degree in social work or geography or whatever. Hopefully that would fulfill her, and then I wouldn't have to worry about her line of problems. I want her to be decisive about herself."

30   The trouble with his advice to his wife is that it comes out of concern with *his* convenience, rather than with *her* development. She quickly picks up on this lack of goodwill: He is trying to dispose of her. At the same time, he refuses her the same latitude to be "selfish" in making an independent decision to broaden her horizons. Both perceive a lack of mutuality. And that is what Catch-30 is all about for the couple.

## ROOTING AND EXTENDING

31   Life becomes less provisional, more rational and orderly in the early thirties. We begin to settle down in the full sense. Most of us begin putting down roots and sending out new shoots. People buy houses and become very earnest about climbing career ladders. Men in particular concern themselves with "making it." Satisfaction with marriage generally goes downhill in the thirties (for those who have remained together) compared with the highly valued, vision-supporting marriage of the twenties. This coincides with the couple's reduced social life outside the family and the inturned focus on raising their children.

## THE DEADLINE DECADE

32   In the middle of the thirties we come upon a crossroads. We have reached the halfway mark. Yet even as we are reaching our prime, we begin to see there is a place where it finishes. Time starts to squeeze.

33   The loss of youth, the faltering of physical powers we have always taken for granted, the fading purpose of stereotyped roles by which we have thus far identified ourselves, the spiritual dilemma of having no absolute answers—any or all of these shocks can give this passage the character of crisis. Such thoughts usher in a decade between 35 and 45 that can be called the Deadline Decade. It is a time of both danger and opportunity. All of us have the chance to rework the narrow identity by which we de-

fined ourselves in the first half of life. And those of us who make the most
of the opportunity will have a full-out authenticity crisis.

To come through this authenticity crisis, we must reexamine our pur- 34
poses and reevaluate how to spend our resources from now on. "Why am
I doing all this? What do I really believe in?" No matter what we have been
doing, there will be parts of ourselves that have been suppressed and now
need to find expression. "Bad" feelings will demand acknowledgment
along with the good.

It is frightening to step off onto the treacherous footbridge leading to 35
the second half of life. We can't take everything with us on this journey
through uncertainty. Along the way, we discover that we are alone. We no
longer have to ask permission because we are the providers of our own
safety. We must learn to give ourselves permission. We stumble upon feminine or masculine aspects of our natures that up to this time have usually
been masked. There is grieving to be done because an old self is dying. By
taking in our suppressed and even our unwanted parts, we prepare at the
gut level for the reintegration of an identity that is ours and ours alone—
not some artificial form put together to please the culture or our mates. It
is a dark passage at the beginning. But by disassembling ourselves, we can
glimpse the light and gather our parts into a renewal.

Women sense this inner crossroads earlier than men do. The time 36
pinch often prompts a woman to stop and take an all-points survey at age
35. Whatever options she has already played out, she feels a "my last
chance" urgency to review those options she has set aside and those that
aging and biology will close off in the now *foreseeable* future. For all her
qualms and confusion about where to start looking for a new future, she
usually enjoys an exhilaration of release. Assertiveness begins rising.
There are so many firsts ahead.

Men, too, feel the time push in the mid-thirties. Most men respond by 37
pressing down harder on the career accelerator. It's "my last chance" to
pull away from the pack. It is no longer enough to be the loyal junior executive, the promising young novelist, the lawyer who does a little *pro bono*
work on the side. He wants now to become part of top management, to be
recognized as an established writer, or an active politician with his own
legislative program. With some chagrin, he discovers that he has been too
anxious to please and too vulnerable to criticism. He wants to put together
his own ship.

During this period of intense concentration on external advancement, 38
it is common for men to be unaware of the more difficult, gut issues that
are propelling them forward. The survey that was neglected at 35 becomes
a crucible at 40. Whatever rung of achievement he has reached, the man of
40 usually feels stale, restless, burdened, and unappreciated. He worries
about his health. He wonders, "Is this all there is?" He may make a series
of departures from well-established lifelong base lines, including mar-

riage. More and more men are seeking second careers in midlife. Some become self-destructive. And many men in their forties experience a major shift of emphasis away from pouring all their energies into their own advancement. A more tender, feeling side comes into play. They become interested in developing an ethical self.

## RENEWAL OR RESIGNATION

39  Somewhere in the mid-forties, equilibrium is regained. A new stability is achieved, which may be more or less satisfying.

40      If one has refused to budge through the midlife transition, the sense of staleness will calcify into resignation. One by one, the safety and supports will be withdrawn from the person who is standing still. Parents will become children; children will become strangers; a mate will grow away or go away; the career will become just a job—and each of these events will be felt as an abandonment. The crisis will probably emerge again around 50. And although its wallop will be greater, the jolt may be just what is needed to prod the resigned middle-ager toward seeking revitalization.

41      On the other hand . . .

42      If we have confronted ourselves in the middle passage and found a renewal of purpose around which we are eager to build a more authentic life structure, these may well be the best years. Personal happiness takes a sharp turn upward for partners who can now accept the fact: "I cannot expect *anyone* to fully understand me." Parents can be forgiven for the burdens of our childhood. Children can be let go without leaving us in collapsed silence. At 50, there is a new warmth and mellowing. Friends become more important than ever, but so does privacy. Since it is so often proclaimed by people past midlife, the motto of this stage might be "No more bullshit."

*1976*

## QUESTIONS FOR DISCUSSION

### Content

a. The author explains that each of us has his or her own "stepstyle." What does she mean?

b. Do any people you know—your parents, for example—fit neatly into Sheehy's ladder? Explain.

c. What qualifications does the author include in her introductory paragraphs to allow her to generalize?
d. Why should we not think "too mechanistically" (paragraph 4) when it comes to understanding how people move through life stages?
e. Why are "rebounds to the family" common between the ages of 18 and 21?
f. What, according to Sheehy, is the common response to approaching age 30?
g. How is establishing identity during the Deadline Decade different from establishing it during earlier years? What does Sheehy mean by "disassembling ourselves" (paragraph 35)?
h. In what way might reaching age 50 bring renewal? In what way might it bring resignation?

## Strategy and Style

i. Is the analogy in the introduction appropriate? Does it help prepare us for what is to follow?
j. Sheehy's approach is, for the most part, objective, even detached. At times, however, she does express her personal reaction to the material. Find places in which the author's personal voice can be heard.
k. Why are the explanations of the steps on the developmental ladder written in fairly generalized terms? Would it have been possible to be more specific? What are some of the strategies Sheehy uses to make these explanations seem specific?

## ENGAGING THE TEXT

a. Sheehy begins this passage with an analogy linking humans to lobsters. Explain why her analogy is an apt one. What other animals could you use in an analogy to describe human development? Make a list of two or three and explain the analogies you see.
b. Briefly explain to what extent your chosen "course in life" is different from that of your parents or other members of your family. Refer to Sheehy's essay in your response.

## SUGGESTIONS FOR SUSTAINED WRITING

a. Where are you on Sheehy's developmental ladder? Write a narrative essay, using specific examples from your life, to discuss how your life fits Sheehy's categories or how it does not. This essay can be extended to include other members of your family. If this assignment doesn't interest you, write an essay in which you discuss someone who has gone through the "middle passage" Sheehy discusses in paragraphs 39–42. Briefly tell the story of this passage and explain whether this individual experienced a "renewal" or a "resignation."

b. Read Sanders's "The Men We Carry in Our Minds" in Chapter 6 or Noda's "Growing Up Asian in America" in this chapter. Then write an essay that explains how what Sheehy says about life's passages might apply to either or both of the speakers in those essays.

c. For a research essay, find other theories of adult development. Categorize each of them by applying age groups as Sheehy has done. Then compare and contrast the theories, speculating on which most accurately describes adult development. Use your own experiences and your observations of your family and friends to form criteria for judging the theories.

# Four Kinds of Reading

## Donald Hall

*A prolific writer of prose and poetry, Donald Hall was born in New Haven, Connecticut, in 1928. He studied at Harvard, Stanford, and Oxford universities, and he has taught at both Stanford University and the University of Michigan. From 1953 to 1961, he was poetry editor for the* Paris Review, *a prestigious literary journal. He has twice won National Book Awards, in 1968 and 1992. Hall's books of poetry include* Exiles and Marriages *(1955),* A Roof of Tiger Lilies *(1963),* The One Day *(1988), and* The Museum of Clear Ideas *(1993). Among his essay collections are* To Keep Moving *(1980),* Fathers Playing Catch with Sons: Essays on Sport *(1985), and* Here at Eagle Pond *(1989). Hall has also written biography, short fiction, and drama, as well as several volumes of children's literature. Among his most recent work is* Without: Poems *(1998), a poignant collection in which he writes about the death of his wife.*

*"Four Kinds of Reading" was first published in the* New York Times *in 1969. Although this essay is now over thirty years old, it continues to provide writers who wish to master classification with a clear and successful model.*

1   Everywhere one meets the idea that reading is an activity desirable in itself. It is understandable that publishers and librarians—and even writers—should promote this assumption, but it is strange that the idea should have general currency. People surround the idea of reading with piety, and do not take into account the purpose of reading or the value of what is being read. Teachers and parents praise the child who reads, and praise themselves, whether the text be *The Reader's Digest* or *Moby Dick*. The ad-

vent of TV has increased the false values ascribed to reading, since TV provides a vulgar alternative. But this piety is silly; and most reading is no
more cultural nor intellectual nor imaginative than shooting pool or
watching *What's My Line.*

It is worth asking how the act of reading became something to value  2
in itself, as opposed for instance to the act of conversation or the act of taking a walk. Mass literacy is a recent phenomenon, and I suggest that the
aura which decorates reading is a relic of the importance of reading to our
great-great-grandparents. Literacy used to be a mark of social distinction,
separating a small portion of humanity from the rest. The farm laborer
who was ambitious for his children did not daydream that they would become schoolteachers or doctors; he daydreamed that they would learn to
read, and that a world would therefore open up to them in which they did
not have to labor in the fields fourteen hours a day for six days a week in
order to buy salt and cotton. On the next rank of society, ample time for
reading meant that the reader was free from the necessity to spend most of
his waking hours making a living. This sort of attitude shades into the contemporary man's boast of his wife's cultural activities. When he says that
his wife is interested in books and music and pictures, he is not only enclosing the arts in a female world, he is saying that he is rich enough to provide her with the leisure to do nothing. Reading is an inactivity, and therefore a badge of social class. Of course, these reasons for the piety attached
to reading are never acknowledged. They show themselves in the shape of
our attitudes toward books; reading gives off an air of gentility.

It seems to me possible to name four kinds of reading, each with a char-  3
acteristic manner and purpose. The first is reading for information—reading
to learn about a trade, or politics, or how to accomplish something. We read
a newspaper this way, or most textbooks, or directions on how to assemble
a bicycle. With most of this material, the reader can learn to scan the page
quickly, coming up with what he needs and ignoring what is irrelevant to
him, like the rhythm of the sentence, or the play of metaphor. Courses in
speed reading can help us read for this purpose, training the eye to jump
quickly across the page. If we read the *New York Times* with the attention we
should give a novel or a poem, we will have time for nothing else, and our
mind will be cluttered with clichés and dead metaphor. Quick eye-reading
is a necessity to anyone who wants to keep up with what's happening, or
learn much of what has happened in the past. The amount of reflection,
which interrupts and slows down the reading, depends on the material.

But it is not the same activity as reading literature. There ought to be an-  4
other word. If we read a work of literature properly, we read slowly, and we
*hear* all the words. If our lips do not actually move, it's only laziness. The
muscles in our throat move, and come together when we see the word
"squeeze." We hear the sounds so accurately that if a syllable is missing in a
line of poetry we hear the lack, though we may not know what we are lacking. In prose we accept the rhythms, and hear the adjacent sounds. We also

register a track of feeling through the metaphors and associations of words. Careless writing prevents this sort of attention, and becomes offensive. But the great writers reward it. Only by the full exercise of our powers to receive language can we absorb their intelligence and their imagination. This kind of reading goes through the ear—though the eye takes in the print, and decodes it into sound—to the throat and the understanding, and it can never be quick. It is slow and sensual, a deep pleasure that begins with touch and ends with the sort of comprehension that we associate with dream.

5    Too many intellectuals read in order to reduce images to abstractions. One reads philosophy slowly, as if it were literature, but much time must be spent with the eyes turned away from the page, reflecting on the text. To read literature this way is to turn it into something it is not—to concepts clothed in character, or philosophy sugar-coated. I think that most literary intellectuals read this way, including brighter professors of English, with the result that they miss literature completely, and concern themselves with a minor discipline called the history of ideas. I remember a course in Chaucer at my university in which the final exam required the identification of a hundred or more fragments of Chaucer, none as long as a line. If you like poetry, and read Chaucer through a couple of times slowly, you found yourself knowing them all. If you were a literary intellectual, well-informed about the great chain of being, chances are you had a difficult time. To read literature is to be intimately involved with the words on the page, and never to think of them as the embodiments of ideas which can be expressed in other terms. On the other hand, intellectual writing— closer to mathematics on a continuum that has at its opposite pole lyric poetry—requires intellectual reading, which is slow because it is reflective and because the reader must pause to evaluate concepts.

6    But most of the reading which is praised for itself is neither literary nor intellectual. It is narcotic. Novels, stories, and biographies—historical sagas, monthly regurgitations of book clubs, four- and five-thousand word daydreams of the magazines—these are the opium of the suburbs. The drug is not harmful except to the addict himself, and is no more injurious to him than Johnny Carson or a bridge club, but it is nothing to be proud of. This reading is the automated daydream, the mild trip of the housewife and the tired businessman, interested not in experience and feeling but in turning off the possibilities of experience and feeling. Great literature, if we read it well, opens us up to the world, and makes us more sensitive to it, as if we acquired eyes that could see through walls and ears that could hear the smallest sounds. But by narcotic reading, one can reduce great literature to the level of *The Valley of the Dolls*. One can read *Anna Karenina* passively and inattentively, and float down the river of lethargy as if one were reading a confession magazine: "I Spurned My Husband for a Count."

7    I think that everyone reads for narcosis occasionally, and perhaps most consistently in late adolescence, when great readers are born. I remember

reading to shut the world out, away at a school where I did not want to be; I invented a word for my disease: "Bibliolepsy," on the analogy of narcolepsy. But after a while the books became a window on the world, and not a screen against it. This change doesn't always happen. I think that late adolescent narcotic reading accounts for some of the badness of English departments. As a college student, the boy loves reading and majors in English because he would be reading anyway. Deciding on a career, he takes up English teaching for the same reason. Then in graduate school he is trained to be a scholar, which is painful and irrelevant, and finds he must write papers and publish them to be a Professor—and at about this time he no longer requires reading for narcosis, and he is left with nothing but a Ph.D. and the prospect of fifty years of teaching literature; and he does not even like literature.

Narcotic reading survives the impact of television, because this type of reading has even less reality than melodrama; that is, the reader is in control: Once the characters reach into the reader's feelings, he is able to stop reading, or glance away, or superimpose his own daydream. The trouble with television is that it embodies its own daydream. Literature is often valued precisely because of its distance from the tangible. Some readers prefer looking into the text of a play to seeing it performed. Reading a play, it is possible to stage it oneself by an imaginative act; but it is also possible to remove it from real people. Here is Virginia Woolf, who was lavish in her praise of the act of reading, talking about reading a play rather than seeing it: "Certainly there is a good deal to be said for reading *Twelfth Night* in the book if the book can be read in a garden, with no sound but the thud of an apple falling to the earth, or of the wind ruffling the branches of the trees." She sets her own stage; the play is called *Virginia Woolf Reads Twelfth Night in a Garden*. Piety moves into narcissism, and the high metaphors of Shakespeare's lines dwindle into the flowers of an English garden; actors in ruffles wither, while the wind ruffles branches.

*1969*

## QUESTIONS FOR DISCUSSION

### Content

a. What are the four types of reading discussed in this selection?
b. What assumption does Hall tell us about in paragraph 1? To what end does he do this?

c. Explain "the aura which decorates reading," which is mentioned in paragraph 2.

d. What, according to Hall, accounts for the "piety" that we attach to reading?

e. What does Hall imply about the role of a reader in appreciating literature?

f. To what end does Hall recommend taking courses in speed reading (paragraph 3)?

g. In what ways are reading for information and reading literature dissimilar?

h. What distinction does the author make between literature and the history of ideas in paragraph 5?

i. What fault does Hall find in television?

j. Write one sentence of your own that might serve as this essay's thesis.

## Strategy and Style

k. Is Hall's two-paragraph introduction appropriate to this essay? In what way?

l. What methods of development, other than classification, are used in this essay?

m. How does Hall support his argument that the fourth type of reading is "nothing to be proud of" (paragraph 6)?

n. Explain the order in which Hall chose to address the four types of reading. For example, why does he begin with informational reading and end with narcotic reading?

o. Describe the intended audience for this essay.

p. Hall's tone is formal, and his style is somewhat elevated. Could he have approached his subject using a lighter tone and more familiar language?

## ENGAGING THE TEXT

a. Write a paragraph explaining Hall's belief that books should be "a window on the world, and not a screen against it" (paragraph 7). Do you agree with this statement? Why or why not? Under what circumstances, if any, might you find it appropriate to use reading as a screen?

b. Make an outline of the four types of reading Hall discusses. Then list the titles of books, magazines, and other materials you have read under the appropriate categories. What does your list tell you about your reading habits? Should you change them?

## SUGGESTIONS FOR SUSTAINED WRITING

a. Using the selection by Hall as a model, write an essay that discusses at least four different reasons for pursuing a particular goal, activity, or pastime. For example, write about the different reasons for which you go to the movies, explain why people choose a particular college major, or discuss four different reasons why people have babies. If this assignment doesn't interest you, interview a few friends and classmates on the subject of study habits. Then write a paper in which you explain three or four good methods you might recommend to someone who is trying to become a successful student. If you want, include a discussion of study methods that you would not recommend in the last section of your paper.

b. Read Fox's "Gawk Shows" in Chapter 9. Use this satire as inspiration for an essay in which you satirize talk shows or other types of television programs. However, adapt the organization of your essay to the model you see in Hall's essay. In other words, classify and evaluate three or four types of shows, arranging your discussion by order of the quality and value that you ascribe to them.

c. "The trouble with television is that it embodies its own daydreams," Hall claims in paragraph 8. What does he mean? Write an essay in which you cite examples from your own television viewing that would support or oppose this notion. In addition, however, support your thesis with information taken from sources you have researched in the library or on the Internet.

# Growing Up Asian in America

Kesaya E. Noda

*Born in a Japanese community in California, Kesaya E. Noda (b. 1950) was raised in New England. She studied Japanese after graduating from high school and lived in Japan for a year and a half. Noda is the author of* Yamato Colony *(1981), a history of the California community where her grandparents settled after immigrating to America. She earned a master of divinity degree from Harvard University in 1987.*

*"Growing Up Asian in America" first appeared in a collection of essays entitled* Making Waves *(1989), which was published by Asian Women United in California. Although it is a clear model for students of classification, Noda's essay is also a poignant and intelligent rendering of a young woman's having to come of age in two cultures.*

Sometimes when I was growing up, my identity seemed to hurtle toward   1
me and paste itself right to my face. I felt that way, encountering the stereotypes of my race perpetuated by non-Japanese people (primarily white) who may or may not have had contact with other Japanese in America.

"You don't like cheese, do you?" someone would ask. "I know your people don't like cheese." Sometimes questions came making allusions to history. That was another aspect of the identity. Events that had happened quite apart from the me who stood silent in that moment connected my face with an incomprehensible past. "Your parents were in California? Were they in those camps during the war?" And sometimes there were phrases or nicknames: "Lotus Blossom." I was sometimes addressed or referred to as racially Japanese, sometimes as Japanese-American, and sometimes as an Asian woman. Confusions and distortions abounded.

2      How is one to know and define oneself? From the inside—within a context that is self-defined, from a grounding in community and a connection with culture and history that are comfortably accepted? Or from the outside—within terms of messages received from the media and people who are often ignorant? Even as an adult I can still see two sides of my face and past. I can see from the inside out, in freedom. And I can see from the outside in, driven by the old voices of childhood and lost in anger and fear.

## I AM RACIALLY JAPANESE

3  A voice from my childhood says: "You are other. You are less than. You are unalterably alien." This voice has its own history. We have indeed been seen as other and alien since the early years of our arrival in the United States. The very first immigrants were welcomed and sought as laborers to replace the dwindling numbers of Chinese, whose influx had been cut off by the Chinese Exclusion Act of 1882. The Japanese fell natural heir to the same anti-Asian prejudice that had arisen against the Chinese. As soon as they began striking for better wages, they were no longer welcomed.

4      I can see myself today as a person historically defined by law and custom as being forever alien. Being neither "free white," nor "African," our people in California were deemed "aliens, ineligible for citizenship," no matter how long they intended to stay here. Aliens ineligible for citizenship were prohibited from owning, buying, or leasing land. They did not and could not belong here. The voice in me remembers that I am always a *Japanese*-American in the eyes of many. A third-generation German-American is an American. A third-generation Japanese-American is a Japanese-American. Being Japanese means being a danger to the country during the war and knowing how to use chopsticks. I wear this history on my face.

5      I move to the other side. I see a different light and claim a different context. My race is a line that stretches across ocean and time to link me to the shrine where my grandmother was raised. Two high, white banners lift in the wind at the top of the stone steps leading to the shrine. It is time for the summer festival. Black characters are written against the sky as boldly as the

clouds, as lightly as kites, as sharply as the big black crows I used to see above the fields in New Hampshire. At festival time there is liquor and food, ritual, discipline, and abandonment. There is music and drunkenness and invocation. There is hope. Another season has come. Another season has gone.

I am racially Japanese. I have a certain claim to this crazy place where  6 the prayers intoned by a neighboring Shinto priest (standing in for my grandmother's nephew who is sick) are drowned out by the rehearsals for the pop singing contest in which most of the villagers will compete later that night. The village elders, the priest, and I stand respectfully upon the immaculate, shining wooden floor of the outer shrine, bowing our heads before the hidden powers. During the patchy intervals when I can hear him, I notice the priest has a stutter. His voice flutters up to my ears only occasionally because two men and a woman are singing gustily into a microphone in the compound, testing the sound system. A pre-recorded tape of guitars, samisens, and drums accompanies them. Rock music and Shinto prayers. That night, to loud applause and cheers, a young man is given the award for the most *netsuretsu*—passionate, burning—rendition of a song. We roar our approval of the reward. Never mind that his voice had wandered and slid, now slightly above, now slightly below the given line of the melody. Netsuretsu. Netsuretsu.

In the morning, my grandmother's sister kneels at the foot of the stone  7 stairs to offer her morning prayers. She is too crippled to climb the stairs, so each morning she kneels here upon the path. She shuts her eyes for a few seconds, her motions as matter of fact as when she washes rice. I linger longer than she does, so reluctant to leave, savoring the connection I feel with my grandmother in America, the past, and the power that lives and shines in the morning sun.

Our family has served this shrine for generations. The family's need to  8 protect this claim to identity and place outweighs any individual claim to any individual hope. I am Japanese.

## I AM A JAPANESE-AMERICAN

"Weak." I hear the voice from my childhood years. "Passive," I hear. Our  9 parents and grandparents were the ones who were put into those camps. They went without resistance; they offered cooperation as proof of loyalty to America. "Victim," I hear. And, "Silent."

Our parents are painted as hard workers who were socially uncom-  10 fortable and had difficulty expressing even the smallest opinion. Clean, quiet, motivated, and determined to match the American way; that is us, and that is the story of our time here.

"Why did you go into those camps?" I raged at my parents, frightened  11 by my own inner silence and timidity. "Why didn't you do anything to resist? Why didn't you name it the injustice it was?" Couldn't our parents even think? Couldn't they? Why were we so passive?

12    I shift my vision and my stance. I am in California. My uncle is in the midst of the sweet potato harvest. He is pressed, trying to get the harvesting crews onto the field as quickly as possible, worried about the flow of equipment and people. His big pickup is pulled off to the side, motor running, door ajar. I see two tractors in the yard in front of an old shed; the flatbed harvesting platform on which the workers will stand has already been brought over from the other field. It's early morning. The workers stand loosely grouped and at ease, but my uncle looks as harried and tense as a police officer trying to unsnarl a New York City traffic jam. Driving toward the shed, I pull my car off the road to make way for an approaching tractor. The front wheels of the car sink luxuriously into the soft, white sand by the roadside and the car slides to a dreamy halt, tail still on the road. I try to move forward. I try to move back. The front bites contentedly into the sand, the back lifts itself at a jaunty angle. My uncle sees me and storms down the road, running. He is shouting before he is even near me.

13    "What's the matter with you?" he screams. "What the hell are you doing?" In his frenzy, he grabs his hat off his head and slashes it through the air across his knee. He is beside himself. "Don't you know how to drive in sand? What's the matter with you? You've blocked the whole roadway. How am I supposed to get my tractors out of here? Can't you use your head? You've cut off the whole roadway, and we've got to get out of here."

14    I stand on the road before him helplessly thinking. "No, I don't know how to drive in sand. I've never driven in sand."

15    "I'm sorry, uncle," I say, burying a smile beneath a look of sincere apology. I notice my deep amusement and my affection for him with great curiosity. I am usually devastated by anger. Not this time.

16    During the several years that follow I learn about the people and the place, and much more about what has happened in this California village where my parents grew up. The issei, our grandparents, made this settlement in the desert. Their first crops were eaten by rabbits and ravaged by insects. The land was so barren that men walking from house to house sometimes got lost. Women came here too. They bore children in 114-degree heat, then carried the babies with them into the fields to nurse when they reached the end of each row of grapes or other truck-farm crops.

17    I had had no idea what it meant to buy this kind of land and make it grow green. Or how, when the war came, there was no space at all for the subtlety of being who we were—Japanese-Americans. Either/or was the way. I hadn't understood that people were literally afraid for their lives then, that their money had been frozen in banks; that there was a five-mile travel limit; that when the early evening curfew came and they were inside their houses, some of them watched helplessly as people they knew went into their barns to steal their belongings. The police were patrolling the

road, interested only in violators of curfew. There was no help for them in the face of thievery. I had not been able to imagine before what it must have felt like to be an American—to know absolutely that one is an American—and yet to have almost everyone else deny it. Not only deny it, but challenge that identity with machine guns and troops of white American soldiers. In those circumstances it was difficult to say, "I'm a Japanese-American," "American" had to do.

But now I can say that I am a Japanese-American. It means I have a 18 place here in this country, too. I have a place here on the East Coast, where our neighbor is so much a part of our family that my mother never passes her house at night without glancing at the lights to see if she is home and safe; where my parents have hauled hundreds of pounds of rocks from fields and arduously planted Christmas trees and blueberries, lilacs, asparagus, and crab apples; where my father still dreams of angling a stream to a new bed so that he can dig a pond in the field and fill it with water and fish. "The neighbors already came for their Christmas tree?" he asks in December. "Did they like it? Did they like it?"

I have a place on the West Coast where my relatives still farm, where 19 I heard the stories of feuds and backbiting, and where I saw that people survived and flourished because fundamentally they trusted and relied upon one another. A death in the family is not just a death in a family; it is a death in the community. I saw people help each other with money, materials, labor, attention, and time. I saw men gather once a year, without fail, to clean the grounds of a ninety-year-old woman who had helped the community before, during, and after the war. I saw her remembering them with birthday cards sent to each of their children.

I come from a people with a long memory and a distinctive grace. We 20 live our thanks. And we are Americans. Japanese-Americans.

## I AM A JAPANESE-AMERICAN WOMAN

Woman. The last piece of my identity. It has been easier by far for me to 21 know myself in Japan and to see my place in America than it has been to accept my line of connection with my own mother. She was my dark self, a figure in whom I thought I saw all that I feared most in myself. Growing into womanhood and looking for some model of strength, I turned away from her. Of course, I could not find what I sought. I was looking for a black feminist or a white feminist. My mother is neither white nor black.

My mother is a woman who speaks with her life as much as with her 22 tongue. I think of her with her own mother. Grandmother had Parkinson's disease and it had frozen her gait and set her fingers, tongue, and feet jerking and trembling in a terrible dance. My aunts and uncles wanted her to be able to live in her own home. They fed her, bathed her, dressed her, awoke at midnight to take her for one last trip to the bathroom. My aunts (her daughters-in-law) did most of the care, but my mother went from New Hampshire to California each summer to spend a month living with Grandmother, because she wanted to and because she wanted to give my aunts at least a small rest. During those hot summer days, mother lay on the couch watching the television or reading, cooking foods that Grandmother liked, and speaking little. Grandmother thrived under her care.

23      The time finally came when it was too dangerous for Grandmother to live alone. My relatives kept finding her on the floor beside her bed when they went to wake her in the mornings. My mother flew to California to help clean the house and make arrangements for Grandmother to enter a local nursing home. On her last day at home, while Grandmother was sitting in her big, overstuffed armchair, hair combed and wearing a green summer dress, my mother went to her and knelt at her feet. "Here, Mamma," she said. "I've polished your shoes." She lifted Grandmother's legs and helped her into the shiny black shoes. My Grandmother looked down and smiled slightly. She left her house walking, supported by her children, carrying her pocket book, and wearing her polished black shoes. "Look, Mamma," my mom had said, kneeling. "I've polished your shoes."

24      Just the other day, my mother came to Boston to visit. She had recently lost a lot of weight and was pleased with her new shape and her feeling of good health. "Look at me, Kes," she exclaimed, turning toward me, front and back, as naked as the day she was born. I saw her small breasts and the wide, brown scar, belly button to pubic hair, that marked her because my brother and I were both born by Caesarean section. Her hips were small. I was not a large baby, but there was so little room for me in her that when she was carrying me she could not even begin to bend over toward the floor. She hated it, she said.

25      "Don't I look good? Don't you think I look good?"

26      I looked at my mother, smiling and as happy as she, thinking of all the times I have seen her naked. I have seen both my parents naked throughout my life, as they have seen me. From childhood through adulthood we've had our naked moments, sharing baths, idle conversations picked up as we moved between showers and closets, hurried moments at the beginning of days, quiet moments at the end of days.

27      I know this to be Japanese, this ease with the physical, and it makes me think of an old Japanese folk song. A young nursemaid, a fifteen-year-old girl, is singing a lullaby to a baby who is strapped to her back. The nursemaid has been sent as a servant to a place far from her own home. "We're the beggars," she says, "and they are the nice people. Nice people wear fine sashes. Nice clothes."

> If I should drop dead,
> bury me by the roadside!
> I'll give a flower
> to everyone who passes.
>
> What kind of flower?
> The cam-cam-camellia [tsun-tsun-tsubaki]
> watered by Heaven:
> alms water.

The nursemaid is the intersection of heaven and earth, the intersection  28
of the human, the natural world, the body, and the soul. In this song, with
clear eyes, she looks steadily at life, which is sometimes so very terrible
and sad. I think of her while looking at my mother, who is standing on the
red and purple carpet before me, laughing, without any clothes.

I am my mother's daughter. And I am myself.                    29
I am a Japanese-American woman.                                30

## EPILOGUE

I recently heard a man from West Africa share some memories of his child-  31
hood. He was raised Muslim, but when he was a young man, he found
himself deeply drawn to Christianity. He struggled against his inner impulse for years, trying to avoid the church yet feeling pushed to return to
it again and again. "I would have done anything to avoid the change," he
said. At last, he became Christian. Afterwards he was afraid to go home,
fearing that he would not be accepted. The fear was groundless, he discovered, when at last he returned—he had separated himself, but his family and friends (all Muslim) had not separated themselves from him.

The man, who is now a professor of religion, said that in the Africa he  32
knew as a child and a young man, pluralism was embraced rather than
feared. There was "a kind of tolerance that did not deny your particularity,"
he said. He alluded to zestful, spontaneous debates that would sometimes
loudly erupt between Muslims and Christians in the village's public spaces.
His memories of an atheist who harangued the villagers when he came to
visit them once a week moved me deeply. Perhaps the man was an agricultural advisor or inspector. He harassed the women. He would say: "Don't go
to the fields! Don't even bother to go to the fields. Let God take care of you.
He'll send you the food. If you believe in God, why do you need to work?
You don't need to work! Let God put the seeds in the ground. Stay home."

The professor said, "The women laughed, you know? They just laughed.  33
Their attitude was, 'Here is a child of God. When will he come home?' "

34      The storyteller, the professor of religion, smiled a most fantastic tender smile as he told this story. "In my country, there is a deep affirmation of the oneness of God," he said. "The atheist and the women were having quite different experiences in their encounter, though the atheist did not know this. He saw himself as quite separate from the women. But the women did not see themselves as being separate from him. 'Here is a child of God,' they said. 'When will he come home?' "

*1989*

## QUESTIONS FOR DISCUSSION

### Content

a. What function is served by the questions Noda asks in paragraph 2?
b. What is the distinction Noda draws between Japanese-Americans and other Americans (paragraph 4)?
c. What are the implications of the author's seeing herself "as a person historically defined by law and custom as being forever alien" (paragraph 4)?
d. Discuss this essay as an exercise in self-definition. In what way is classification appropriate to this exercise?
e. What was Noda's reaction to learning about the internment of Japanese-Americans during World War II? Why does she describe this reaction?
f. How does the story of the author's getting her car stuck in sand help define her as a Japanese-American? As an individual?
g. Explain what Noda sees when she looks at her mother. What role does the story of the nursemaid play in her defining herself as a Japanese-American woman?

### Strategy and Style

h. Is Noda's introduction (paragraph 1) appropriate to this classification essay? Explain.
i. In what ways are paragraphs 5, 12, and 24 alike? What function do they serve? What function do paragraphs 8, 20, 29–30 serve?
j. What light does the story of a West African Muslim in the epilogue shed on Noda's essay?
k. What role does narration play in this classification piece?
l. Noda divides her essay into three major sections and an epilogue. Describe the pattern she uses to organize her three major sections. What is the effect of her organizing all three sections the same way?

## ENGAGING THE TEXT

a. In paragraph 4, Noda says: "A third-generation German-American is an American. A third-generation Japanese-American is a Japanese-American." What can you infer from this statement about Noda's opinion of the "melting pot" concept? Can you name other ethnic groups that, after three or more generations, are still seen as "hyphenated Americans"?

b. Summarize each of the three subsections of this piece by explaining the three ways in which Noda sees herself: as racially Japanese, as a Japanese-American, and as a Japanese-American woman.

## SUGGESTIONS FOR SUSTAINED WRITING

a. There is a great deal of talk these days about cultural diversity. Unfortunately, some people are all too happy to define others as members of a particular group rather than as individuals. Yet members of ethnic, religious, economic, gender, or other groups can be very different from one another. Using classification as a method of organization, discuss various types of people you have encountered in a group to which you belong. In the process, explain how you are different from other members of your group. In essence, then, use your essay to define your group and yourself.

b. Noda defines herself by using ethnic categories. Yet we can define ourselves by using categories based on various principles. For example, you might define yourself by grouping your daily activities or responsibilities under various headings: "I am a student," "I am a bank teller," or "I am a parent." Then again, you might discuss various aspects of your emotional makeup: "I am a romantic," "I am an extrovert," or "I am family-oriented." Using the above as examples, list three or four categories that would help define your emotional makeup, lifestyle, value system, career aspirations, and so forth. For further inspiration, read Lydia Minatoya's "Discordant Fruit" in Chapter 6.

c. Define a particular religion, occupation, species of domestic animal, or other topic that lends itself to classification. After gathering information about your topic in the library or on the Internet, write an essay in which you explain various divisions of your subject so as to define it. For example, you might define the term *Muslim* by discussing Shiite Muslims, Sunni Muslims, and African-American Muslims. Or you might even limit your discussion to the term *Shiite* by discussing each of this Islamic branch's major sects, such as the Druses, Fatimids, Ismailis, Assassins, and Karmathians.

# The Truth about Lying

Judith Viorst

*A contributing editor at* Redbook *magazine, Judith Viorst (b. 1931) began her career as a poet in 1965 when she published* The Village Square. *This book of verse was followed by several other volumes of prose and poetry with intriguing titles. Among them are* It's Hard to Be Hip Over Thirty and Other Tragedies of Married Life *(1968),* People and Other Aggravations *(1971),* Yes, Married: A Saga of Love and Complaint *(1972), and* When Did I Stop Being Twenty and Other Injustices *(1987). Viorst has also published several works of children's fiction and nonfiction as well as a musical drama,* Birthday and Other Humiliations. *"The Truth about Lying" first appeared in* Redbook *in 1981. It shows that classification can be used for a variety of purposes. Here, Viorst produces an incisive social commentary that, although twenty years old, retains its full relevance today.*

1 I've been wanting to write on a subject that intrigues and challenges me: the subject of lying. I've found it very difficult to do. Everyone I've talked to has a quite intense and personal but often rather intolerant point of view about what we can—and can never *never*—tell lies about. I've finally reached the conclusion that I can't present any ultimate conclusions, for too many people would promptly disagree. Instead, I'd like to present a series of moral puzzles, all concerned with lying. I'll tell you what I think about them. Do you agree?

## SOCIAL LIES

2 Most of the people I've talked with say that they find social lying acceptable and necessary. They think it's the civilized way for folks to behave. Without these little white lies, they say, our relationships would be short and brutish and nasty. It's arrogant, they say, to insist on being so incorruptible and so brave that you cause other people unnecessary embarrassment or pain by compulsively assailing them with your honesty. I basically agree. What about you?

3 Will you say to people, when it simply isn't true, "I like your new hairdo," "You're looking much better," "It's so nice to see you," "I had a wonderful time"?

4 Will you praise hideous presents and homely kids?

5 Will you decline invitations with "We're busy that night—so sorry we can't come," when the truth is you'd rather stay home than dine with the So-and-sos?

6 And even though, as I do, you may prefer the polite evasion of "You really cooked up a storm" instead of "The soup"—which tastes like

warmed-over coffee—"is wonderful," will you, if you must, proclaim it wonderful?

There's one man I know who absolutely refuses to tell social lies. "I 7 can't play that game," he says; "I'm simply not made that way." And his answer to the argument that saying nice things to someone doesn't cost anything is, "Yes, it does—it destroys your credibility." Now, he won't, unsolicited, offer his views on the painting you just bought, but you don't ask his frank opinion unless you want *frank*, and his silence at those moments when the rest of us liars are muttering, "Isn't it lovely?" is, for the most part, eloquent enough. My friend does not indulge in what he calls "flattery, false praise and mellifluous comments." When others tell fibs he will not go along. He says that social lying is lying, that little white lies are still lies. And he feels that telling lies is morally wrong. What about you?


## PEACE-KEEPING LIES

Many people tell peace-keeping lies; lies designed to avoid irritation or ar- 8 gument; lies designed to shelter the liar from possible blame or pain; lies (or so it is rationalized) designed to keep trouble at bay without hurting anyone.

I tell these lies at times, and yet I always feel they're wrong. I under- 9 stand why we tell them, but still they feel wrong. And whenever I lie so that someone won't disapprove of me or think less of me or holler at me, I feel I'm a bit of a coward, I feel I'm dodging responsibility, I feel . . . guilty. What about you?

Do you, when you're late for a date because you overslept, say that 10 you're late because you got caught in a traffic jam?

Do you, when you forget to call a friend, say that you called several 11 times but the line was busy?

Do you, when you didn't remember that it was your father's birthday, 12 say that his present must be delayed in the mail?

And when you're planning a weekend in New York City and you're 13 not in the mood to visit your mother, who lives there, do you conceal—with a lie, if you must— the fact that you'll be in New York? Or do you have the courage—or is it the cruelty?—to say, "I'll be in New York, but sorry — I don't plan on seeing you"?

(Dave and his wife Elaine have two quite different points of view on 14 this very subject. He calls her a coward. She says she's being wise. He says she must assert her right to visit New York sometimes and not see her mother. To which she always patiently replies: "Why should we have useless fights? My mother's too old to change. We get along much better when I lie to her.")

15      Finally, do you keep the peace by telling your husband lies on the subject of money? Do you reduce what you really paid for your shoes? And in general do you find yourself ready, willing and able to lie to him when you make absurd mistakes or lose or break things?

16      "I used to have a romantic idea that part of intimacy was confessing every dumb thing that you did to your husband. But after a couple of years of that," says Laura, "have I changed my mind!"

17      And having changed her mind, she finds herself telling peace-keeping lies. And yes, I tell them too. What about you?

## PROTECTIVE LIES

18  Protective lies are lies folks tell—often quite serious lies—because they're convinced that the truth would be too damaging. They lie because they feel there are certain human values that supersede the wrong of having lied. They lie, not for personal gain, but because they believe it's for the good of the person they're lying to. They lie to those they love, to those who trust them most of all, on the grounds that breaking this trust is justified.

19      They may lie to their children on money or marital matters.

20      They may lie to the dying about the state of their health.

21      They may lie about adultery, and not—or so they insist—to save their own hide, but to save the heart and the pride of the men they are married to.

22      They may lie to their closest friend because the truth about her talents or son or psyche would be—or so they insist—utterly devastating.

23      I sometimes tell such lies, but I'm aware that it's quite presumptuous to claim I know what's best for others to know. That's called playing God. That's called manipulation and control. And we never can be sure, once we start to juggle lies, just where they'll land, exactly where they'll roll.

24      And furthermore, we may find ourselves lying in order to back up the lies that are backing up the lie we initially told.

25      And furthermore—let's be honest—if conditions were reversed, we certainly wouldn't want anyone lying to us.

26      Yet, having said all that, I still believe that there are times when protective lies must nonetheless be told. What about you?

27      If your Dad had a very bad heart and you had to tell him some bad family news, which would you choose: To tell him the truth or to lie?

28      If your former husband failed to send his monthly child-support check and in other ways behaved like a total rat, would you allow your children—who believed he was simply wonderful—to continue to believe that he was wonderful?

29      If your dearly beloved brother selected a wife whom you deeply disliked, would you reveal your feelings or would you fake it?

And if you were asked, after making love, "And how was that for 30
you?" would you reply, if it wasn't too good, "Not too good"?

Now, some would call a sex lie unimportant, little more than social ly- 31
ing, a simple act of courtesy that makes all human intercourse run
smoothly. And some would say all sex lies are bad news and unacceptably
protective. Because, says Ruth, "a man with an ego that fragile doesn't
need your lies—he needs a psychiatrist." Still others feel that sex lies are
indeed protective lies, more serious than simple social lying, and yet at
times they tell them on the grounds that when it comes to matters sexual,
everybody's ego is somewhat fragile.

"If most of the time things go well in sex," says Sue, "I think you're 32
allowed to dissemble when they don't. I can't believe it's good to say,
'Last night was four stars, darling, but tonight's performance rates only
a half.' "

I'm inclined to agree with Sue. What about you?                          33

## TRUST-KEEPING LIES

Another group of lies are trust-keeping lies, lies that involve triangulation, 34
with A (that's you) telling lies to B on behalf of C (whose trust you'd
promised to keep). Most people concede that once you've agreed not to betray a friend's confidence, you can't betray it, even if you must lie. But I've
talked with people who don't want you telling them anything that they
might be called on to lie about.

"I don't tell lies for myself," says Fran, "and I don't want to have to tell 35
them for other people." Which means, she agrees, that if her best friend is
having an affair, she absolutely doesn't want to know about it.

"Are you saying," her best friend asks, "that if I went off with a lover 36
and I asked you to tell my husband I'd been with you, that you wouldn't
lie for me, that you'd betray me?"

Fran is very pained but very adamant. "I wouldn't want to betray you, 37
so . . . don't ask me."

Fran's best friend is shocked. What about you?                           38

Do you believe you can have close friends if you're not prepared to re- 39
ceive their deepest secrets?

Do you believe you must always lie for your friends?                     40

Do you believe, if your friend tells a secret that turns out to be quite 41
immoral or illegal, that once you've promised to keep it, you must keep it?

And what if your friend were your boss—if you were perhaps one of 42
the President's men—would you betray or lie for him over, say, Watergate?

As you can see, these issues get terribly sticky.                        43

It's my belief that once we've promised to keep a trust, we must tell 44
lies to keep it. I also believe that we can't tell Watergate lies. And if these

two statements strike you as quite contradictory, you're right—they're quite contradictory. But for now they're the best I can do. What about you?

45    Some say that truth will out and thus you might as well tell the truth. Some say you can't regain the trust that lies lose. Some say that even though the truth may never be revealed, our lies pervert and damage our relationships. Some say . . . well, here's what some of them have to say.

46    "I'm a coward," says Grace, "about telling close people important, difficult truths. I find that I'm unable to carry it off. And so if something is bothering me, it keeps building up inside till I end up just not seeing them any more."

47    "I lie to my husband on sexual things, but I'm furious," says Joyce, "that he's too insensitive to know I'm lying."

48    "I suffer most from the misconception that children can't take the truth," says Emily. "But I'm starting to see that what's harder and more damaging for them is being told lies, is *not* being told the truth."

49    "I'm afraid," says Joan, "that we often wind up feeling a bit of contempt for the people we lie to."

50    And then there are those who have no talent for lying.

51    "Over the years, I tried to lie," a friend of mine explained, "but I always got found out and I always got punished. I guess I gave myself away because I feel guilty about any kind of lying. It looks as if I'm stuck with telling the truth."

52    For those of us, however, who are good at telling lies, for those of us who lie and don't get caught, the question of whether or not to lie can be a hard and serious moral problem. I liked the remark of a friend of mine who said, "I'm willing to lie. But just as a last resort—the truth's always better."

53    "Because," he explained, "though others may completely accept the lie I'm telling, I don't."

54    I tend to feel that way too.

55    What about you?

*1981*

## QUESTIONS FOR DISCUSSION

### Content

a. Is the essay's thesis explicit? What is it?

b. What arguments does the author offer to defend social lying? What arguments does she offer against social lying?

c. Why does Viorst believe that telling protective lies is a form of manipulation?

d. What else does she find objectionable or dangerous about protective lies?

e. Under what conditions does the author believe that telling protective lies is appropriate?

f. In what way is her position on trust-keeping lies contradictory? How does she respond to that contradiction?

## Strategy and Style

g. What is the introduction to this essay designed to do? Does it succeed?

h. To what end does Viorst address the reader directly?

i. What is the effect of her asking "What about you?" at the end of each section?

j. Where and to what end does Viorst use contrast? How does her creation of contrast relate to her thesis?

k. Viorst uses examples throughout this essay. What form do these examples take? Are they convincing?

l. Where in the essay does the author engage in definition?

m. Is Viorst's quoting of her friends an effective way to develop this essay? Why or why not?

n. What point does the author make in the conclusion? Does it bring closure to the essay, or is it simply another of the "moral puzzles" she mentions in her introduction?

## ENGAGING THE TEXT

a. Respond to Viorst by explaining how you react to what she says about one of the four kinds of lies she discusses. In other words, respond to the question with which she closes each section of this essay: "What about you?"

b. List examples of representative social, peace-keeping, protective, and trust-keeping lies that you tell or are told by others. Compare your examples to the examples in Viorst's essay.

## SUGGESTIONS FOR SUSTAINED WRITING

a. Write a letter to Viorst explaining why you tell lies like those discussed in her essay or why you refuse to tell such lies. If this doesn't interest you, think of another type of lie, one that Viorst does not discuss. Write an essay that explains that category. Like Viorst, include examples and direct quotations from others to develop your point.

b. Write a classification essay in which you develop three or four major categories relating to a type of human behavior or activity about which you have mixed feelings. For example, you might discuss "the truth about dieting," "the truth about gambling," "the truth about exercising," "the truth about being assertive," or "the truth about gossiping." For further inspiration, consult the two essays by Lutz and Cross, which follow in this chapter.

c. Using each of the categories Viorst presents and following the format she uses, write an essay in which you use your own examples of lies and liars. To gather information, read up on lies told by prominent historical or contemporary figures in politics, entertainment, the media, sports, and other high-profile professions. Incorporate this library or Internet research into your paper.

# Doublespeak

William Lutz

## BIOGRAPHY

*A professor of English at Rutgers University in New Jersey and a member of the Pennsylvania Bar, William Lutz (b. 1941) is America's premier critic of "doublespeak," the use of evasive, unnecessarily complex, and misleading language to manipulate or even deceive the reader. Doublespeak, Lutz believes, is most often encountered in U.S. government publications and announcements, followed by those of big business as a close second. Lutz edited the* National Council of Teachers of English Quarterly Review of Doublespeak *for fourteen years and chaired the Committee on Public Doublespeak for fifteen years. He has been a guest on television's* C-SPAN, Larry King Live, The Today Show, The MacNeil-Lehrer NewsHour, *and* The CBS Evening News. *His many books include* Doublespeak: From Revenue Enhancement to Terminal Living *(1989),* The New Doublespeak: Why No One Knows What Anyone's Saying Anymore *(1996), and* A Dictionary of Doublespeak *(1999). Lutz also collaborated on* A Plain English Handbook: How to Create Clear SEC Disclosure Documents, *published by the Securities and Exchange Commission. The essay that follows is Lutz's now classic definition of doublespeak. It first appeared in a book with the same title in 1989.*

1    There are no potholes in the streets of Tucson, Arizona, just "pavement deficiencies." The Reagan Administration didn't propose any new taxes, just "revenue enhancement" through new "user's fees." Those aren't bums on the street, just "non–goal oriented members of society." There are no more poor people, just "fiscal underachievers." There was no robbery of an au-

tomatic teller machine, just an "unauthorized withdrawal." The patient didn't die because of medical malpractice, it was just a "diagnostic misadventure of a high magnitude." The U.S. Army doesn't kill the enemy anymore, it just "services the target." And the doublespeak goes on.

Doublespeak is language that pretends to communicate but really 2 doesn't. It is language that makes the bad seem good, the negative appear positive, the unpleasant appear attractive or at least tolerable. Doublespeak is language that avoids or shifts responsibility, language that is at variance with its real or purported meaning. It is language that conceals or prevents thought; rather than extending thought, doublespeak limits it. . . .

## HOW TO SPOT DOUBLESPEAK

How can you spot doublespeak? Most of the time you will recognize dou- 3 blespeak when you see or hear it. But, if you have any doubts, you can identify doublespeak just by answering these questions: Who is saying what to whom, under what conditions and circumstances, with what intent, and with what results? Answering these questions will usually help you identify as doublespeak language that appears to be legitimate or that at first glance doesn't even appear to be doublespeak.

### First Kind of Doublespeak

There are at least four kinds of doublespeak. The first is the euphemism, 4 an inoffensive or positive word or phrase used to avoid a harsh, unpleasant, or distasteful reality. But a euphemism can also be a tactful word or phrase which avoids directly mentioning a painful reality, or it can be an expression used out of concern for the feelings of someone else, or to avoid directly discussing a topic subject to a social or cultural taboo.

When you use a euphemism because of your sensitivity for someone's 5 feelings or out of concern for a recognized social or cultural taboo, it is not doublespeak. For example, you express your condolences that someone has "passed away" because you do not want to say to a grieving person, "I'm sorry your father is dead." When you use the euphemism "passed away," no one is misled. Moreover, the euphemism functions here not just to protect the feelings of another person, but to communicate also your concern for that person's feelings during a period of mourning. When you excuse yourself to go to the "restroom," or you mention that someone is "sleeping with" or "involved with" someone else, you do not mislead anyone about your meaning, but you do respect the social taboos about discussing bodily functions and sex in direct terms. You also indicate your sensitivity to the feelings of your audience, which is usually considered a mark of courtesy and good manners.

However, when a euphemism is used to mislead or deceive, it becomes 6 doublespeak. For example, in 1984 the U.S. State Department announced that it would no longer use the word "killing" in its annual report on the status of human rights in countries around the world. Instead, it would use the phrase "unlawful or arbitrary deprivation of life," which the department claimed was more accurate. Its real purpose for using this phrase was simply to avoid discussing the embarrassing situation of government-sanctioned killings in countries that are supported by the United States and have been certified by the United States as respecting the human rights of their citizens. This use of a euphemism constitutes doublespeak, since it is designed to mislead, to cover up the unpleasant. Its real intent is at variance with its apparent intent. It is language designed to alter our perception of reality.

7      The Pentagon, too, avoids discussing unpleasant realities when it refers to bombs and artillery shells that fall on civilian targets as "incontinent ordnance." And in 1977 the Pentagon tried to slip funding for the neutron bomb unnoticed into an appropriations bill by calling it a "radiation enhancement device."

## Second Kind of Doublespeak

8  A second kind of doublespeak is jargon, the specialized language of a trade, profession, or similar group, such as that used by doctors, lawyers, engineers, educators, or car mechanics. Jargon can serve an important and useful function. Within a group, jargon functions as a kind of verbal shorthand that allows members of the group to communicate with each other clearly, efficiently, and quickly. Indeed, it is a mark of membership in the group to be able to use and understand the group's jargon.

9      But jargon, like the euphemism, can also be doublespeak. It can be—and often is—pretentious, obscure, and esoteric terminology used to give an air of profundity, authority, and prestige to speakers and their subject matter. Jargon as doublespeak often makes the simple appear complex, the ordinary profound, the obvious insightful. In this sense it is used not to express but impress. With such doublespeak, the act of smelling something becomes "organoleptic analysis," glass becomes "fused silicate," a crack in a metal support beam becomes a "discontinuity," conservative economic policies become "distributionally conservative notions."

10     Lawyers, for example, speak of an "involuntary conversion" of property when discussing the loss or destruction of property through theft, accident, or condemnation. If your house burns down or if your car is stolen, you have suffered an involuntary conversion of your property. When used by lawyers in a legal situation, such jargon is a legitimate use of language, since lawyers can be expected to understand the term.

11     However, when a member of a specialized group uses its jargon to communicate with a person outside the group, and uses it knowing that the nonmember does not understand such language, then there is doublespeak. For example, on May 9, 1978, a National Airlines 727 airplane

crashed while attempting to land at the Pensacola, Florida, airport. Three of the fifty-two passengers aboard the airplane were killed. As a result of the crash, National made an after-tax insurance benefit of $1.7 million, or an extra 18¢ a share dividend for its stockholders. Now National Airlines had two problems: It did not want to talk about one of its airplanes crashing, and it had to account for the $1.7 million when it issued its annual report to its stockholders. National solved the problem by inserting a footnote in its annual report which explained that the $1.7 million income was due to "the involuntary conversion of a 727." National thus acknowledged the crash of its airplane and the subsequent profit it made from the crash, without once mentioning the accident or the deaths. However, because airline officials knew that most stockholders in the company, and indeed most of the general public, were not familiar with legal jargon, the use of such jargon constituted doublespeak.

## Third Kind of Doublespeak

A third kind of doublespeak is gobbledygook or bureaucratese. Basically,   12
such doublespeak is simply a matter of piling on words, of overwhelming the audience with words, the bigger the words and the longer the sentences the better. Alan Greenspan, then chair of President Nixon's Council of Economic Advisors, was quoted in *The Philadelphia Inquirer* in 1974 as having testified before a Senate committee that "It is a tricky problem to find the particular calibration in timing that would be appropriate to stem the acceleration in risk premiums created by falling incomes without prematurely aborting the decline in the inflation-generated risk premiums."

Nor has Mr. Greenspan's language changed since then. Speaking to   13
the meeting of the Economic Club of New York in 1988, Mr. Greenspan, now Federal Reserve chair, said, "I guess I should warn you, if I turn out to be particularly clear, you've probably misunderstood what I've said." Mr. Greenspan's doublespeak doesn't seem to have held back his career.

Sometimes gobbledygook may sound impressive, but when the quote   14
is later examined in print it doesn't even make sense. During the 1988 presidential campaign, vice-presidential candidate Senator Dan Quayle explained the need for a strategic-defense initiative by saying, "Why wouldn't an enhanced deterrent, a more stable peace, a better prospect to denying the ones who enter conflict in the first place to have a reduction of offensive systems and an introduction to defense capability? I believe this is the route the country will eventually go."

The investigation into the *Challenger* disaster in 1986 revealed the dou-   15
blespeak of gobbledygook and bureaucratese used by too many involved in the shuttle program. When Jesse Moore, NASA's associate administrator, was asked if the performance of the shuttle program had improved with each launch or if it had remained the same, he answered, "I think our

performance in terms of the liftoff performance and in terms of the orbital performance, we knew more about the envelope we were operating under, and we have been pretty accurately staying in that. And so I would say the performance has not by design drastically improved. I think we have been able to characterize the performance more as a function of our launch experience as opposed to it improving as a function of time." While this language may appear to be jargon, a close look will reveal that it is really just gobbledygook laced with jargon. But you really have to wonder if Mr. Moore had any idea what he was saying.

### Fourth Kind of Doublespeak

16 The fourth kind of doublespeak is inflated language that is designed to make the ordinary seem extraordinary; to make everyday things seem impressive; to give an air of importance to people, situations, or things that would not normally be considered important; to make the simple seem complex. Often this kind of doublespeak isn't hard to spot, and it is usually pretty funny. While car mechanics may be called "automotive internists," elevator operators members of the "vertical transportation corps," used cars "pre-owned" or "experienced cars," and black-and-white television sets described as having "non-multicolor capability," you really aren't misled all that much by such language.

17 However, you may have trouble figuring out that, when Chrysler "initiates a career alternative enhancement program," it is really laying off five thousand workers; or that "negative patient care outcome" means the patient died; or that "rapid oxidation" means a fire in a nuclear power plant.

18 The doublespeak of inflated language can have serious consequences. In Pentagon doublespeak, "pre-emptive counterattack" means that American forces attacked first; "engaged the enemy on all sides" means American troops were ambushed; "backloading of augmentation personnel" means a retreat by American troops. In the doublespeak of the military, the 1983 invasion of Grenada was conducted not by the U.S. Army, Navy, Air Force, and Marines, but by the "Caribbean Peace Keeping Forces." But then, according to the Pentagon, it wasn't an invasion, it was a "predawn vertical insertion."

## THE DANGERS OF DOUBLESPEAK

19 These . . . examples of doublespeak should make it clear that doublespeak is not the product of carelessness or sloppy thinking. Indeed, most doublespeak is the product of clear thinking and is carefully designed and constructed to appear to communicate when in fact it doesn't. It is language designed not to lead but mislead. It is language designed to

distort reality and corrupt thought. . . . When a fire in a nuclear reactor building is called "rapid oxidation," an explosion in a nuclear power plant is called an "energetic disassembly," the illegal overthrow of a legitimate government is termed "destabilizing a government," and lies are seen as "inoperative statements," we are hearing doublespeak that attempts to avoid responsibility and make the bad seem good, the negative appear positive, something unpleasant appear attractive; and which seems to communicate but doesn't. It is language designed to alter our perception of reality and corrupt our thinking. Such language does not provide us with the tools we need to develop, advance, and preserve our culture and our civilization. Such language breeds suspicion, cynicism, distrust, and, ultimately, hostility.

*1989*

## QUESTIONS FOR DISCUSSION

### Content

a. Summarize Lutz's general definition of doublespeak.
b. What does the author advise those who wish to identify doublespeak?
c. According to Lutz, is it ever advisable to use euphemisms? When? When is it not?
d. The author claims that jargon can serve useful purposes. Explain.
e. When does jargon become doublespeak?
f. What does Lutz mean by "gobbledygook"? By "inflated language"? Why are they dangerous?
g. In what way does this essay's conclusion clarify Lutz's purpose?

### Strategy and Style

h. The organization of this classification essay is logical and easy to follow. Lutz simply labels and discusses four categories. Why does he also label his conclusion?
i. In what parts of this essay does Lutz use contrast, examples, and definition to support his thesis?
j. How would you characterize the tone of this essay? Does Lutz ever vary his tone? If so, to what end?

k. Lutz's writing style makes the essay easy to follow and appealing. Analyze one or two paragraphs to explain this statement.

l. How would you describe the intended audience for this piece?

## ENGAGING THE TEXT

a. Is higher education guilty of doublespeak? Summarize Lutz's definition of *doublespeak* and apply that definition to one, two, or three examples that you have noticed at your school.

b. Summarize the definition of each of the four types of doublespeak that Lutz includes. Then find or create at least one additional example for each of those four types.

## SUGGESTIONS FOR SUSTAINED WRITING

a. Write an essay in which you expose examples of doublespeak put forth by members of a particular industry or of several industries in an attempt to consciously deceive the public. For example, you might discuss several examples of doublespeak taken from the entertainment industry, or you might discuss one from that industry and one from the news media, one from the tobacco industry, and one from automobile manufacturers.

b. Lutz explains ways in which language is manipulated to deceive readers. Write an essay explaining other types of manipulation. For example, in what ways do movies, television sitcoms and commercials, highway billboards, musical recordings, music videos, and so on, try to manipulate us? Focus on one source of this manipulation, discuss its purpose, and explain how it works. For additional inspiration, read the essay by Cross, which follows.

c. This selection is more than a dozen years old. List and discuss examples of doublespeak used today, especially by people in government, big business, advertising, the news media, the entertainment industry, or another source of public information. You might also analyze doublespeak put forth by groups interested in advancing a particular political or social ideology. To gather information on this topic, rely on your own observations and reading, but consult library and Internet sources as well.

# Politics: The Art of Bamboozling

Donna Woolfolk Cross

## BIOGRAPHY

*Donna Woolfolk Cross (b. 1947) was born in New York City. She took a BA at the University of Pennsylvania and an MA in English at the University of California, Los Angeles. Now living in upstate New York, Cross teaches English at Onondaga Community College in Syracuse. An expert on how and to what ends language can be manipulated, she is the coauthor of* Speaking of Words *(1977) and the author of* Word Abuse *(1979) and* Mediaspeak: How Television Makes Up Your Mind *(1983). In 1996, she published* Pope Joan, *a historical novel about a woman who some historians say may have reigned as pope for two years during the ninth century. Although* Pope Joan *is Cross's first novel, it has enjoyed a great deal of interest and acclaim. "Politics: The Art of Bamboozling" first appeared in* Word Abuse.

> *Political language . . . is designed to make lies sound truthful and murder respectable, and to give an appearance of solidity to pure wind.*
> —George Orwell

Propaganda. How do we feel about it? If an opinion poll were taken tomorrow, nearly everyone would be against it. For one thing it *sounds* so bad. "Oh, that's just propaganda" means, to most people, "That's a pack of lies." 1

But propaganda doesn't have to be untrue—nor does it have to be the devil's tool. It can be used for good causes as well as for bad—to persuade people to give to charity, for example, or to love their neighbors, or to stop polluting the environment, or to treat the English language with more respect. 2

The real problem with propaganda is not the end it's used for, but the means it uses to achieve the end. Propaganda works by tricking us, by momentarily distracting the eye while the rabbit pops out from beneath the cloth. This is why propaganda always works best with an uncritical audience, one that will not stop to challenge or question. Most of us are bamboozled, at one time or another, because we simply don't recognize propaganda when we see it. 3

Here are some of the more common pitfalls for the unwary: 4

Name-calling is an obvious tactic but still amazingly effective. It's just what you would expect it to be—calling people names. The idea is to arouse our contempt so that we'll dismiss the "bad name" person or idea without examining the merits. 5

6      The old saw "Sticks and stones may break my bones but names will never hurt me" has always been nonsense. Names *do* hurt, and badly, as any child who has been called one can tell you. Name-calling can be devastating to a child's psychological development.

7      Bad names may wreak havoc with a child's ego, but they're even more dangerous when they're used against political opponents, policies, or belief. During the vice-presidential debates, when Senator Robert Dole denounced Senator Walter Mondale as "probably the most liberal Senator in the entire U.S. Senate," he wanted conservatives to react blindly, emotionally to the "liberal" label without stopping to consider Mondale's ideas. Name-calling is at work whenever a candidate for office is described as a "foolish idealist" or an incumbent's policies are denounced as "reckless," "reactionary," or just plain "stupid." Some of the most effective names a public figure may be called don't really mean anything at all: "Congresswoman Jane Doe is a *bleeding heart*" or "The Senator is a *tool of the military-industrial complex!*"

8      A variation of name-calling is **argumentum ad hominem,** which tries to discredit a particular issue or idea by attacking a person who supports it. For example, one of Phyllis Schlafly's supporters recently said that she was against the Equal Rights Amendment because "the women who support it are either fanatics or lesbians or frustrated old maids." Aside from the fact that the statistical probability of this being true is nil, it is also specious reasoning. The Equal Rights Amendment should be judged on its merits, not the alleged "personal problems" of its supporters. The fact that Alexander Hamilton was a bastard foreigner born to unmarried parents outside the continental limits of the United States does not reflect on the American Revolution nor on his policies as Secretary of the Treasury. And the fact that Thomas Jefferson had a black mistress who bore him several children does not diminish the eloquence of the Declaration of Independence. Issues are different from the people who support them, and deserve to be judged on their own merits.

9      Name-calling and *argumentum ad hominem* are sometimes done with style. In the nineteenth-century when Lord John Russell became leader of the House of Commons, Disraeli remarked, "Now man may well begin to comprehend how the Egyptians worshiped an insect." But the best practitioner of name-calling in recent times was Winston Churchill. He once described fellow statesman Clement Attlee as "a modest man with much to be modest about," and, on another occasion, as "a sheep in sheep's clothing." Of political rival Stanley Baldwin, Churchill remarked, "He occasionally stumbles over the truth, but he always hastily picks himself up and hurries on as if nothing had happened." He punctured an arrogant political rival by murmuring as the man left the room, "There, but for the grace of God, goes God."

Where name-calling tries to get us to *reject* or *condemn* someone or   10
something without examining the evidence, the **glittering generality** tries
to get us to *accept* and *agree* without examining the evidence. The Institute
for Propaganda Analysis calls glittering generalities "virtue words," and
adds that every society has certain "virtue words" it feels deeply about.
"Justice," "Motherhood," "The American Way," "Our Constitutional
Rights," "Our Christian Heritage," are words many people in our society
believe in, live by—and are willing to die for. "Let us fight to preserve our
American Birthright!" cries the Congressman, and the crowd roars its approval. We might not be in favor of war, but who wants to go on record as
being opposed to our "American Birthright"?

Glittering generalities have extraordinary power to move men. Con-   11
dorcet, the great French leader, went to the guillotine for "Liberty, Equality, Fraternity!" He might not have gone so willingly had he known that
the French Revolution was fought to establish the predominance of the
bourgeoisie over the aristocracies, of the new-emerging capitalism over
the surviving remnants of feudalism. Can anyone imagine Condorcet or
any of the others like him giving up their lives for a cause stated in such
terms? The struggle had to represent itself to men in glorious ringing terms
to win their hearts and minds.

A glittering generality is very seductive and appealing, but when you   12
open it up and look inside, it is usually empty. There is no specific, defin-
able meaning. If you doubt that, try getting definitions from a dozen people and discover for yourself how widely the interpretations differ. Just
what parts of the American society and culture does our "American
Birthright" include? The Bill of Rights? The free enterprise system? The
democratic process? The rights of citizens to bear arms? The rights of oil
companies to fix prices? The rights of coal companies to strip the land?
The rights of women to terminate their pregnancies? The rights of gays to
equal employment? The rights of the government to limit these rights? All
of the above?

These glittering generalities are slippery creatures, all right. They can   13
slide into almost any meaning. "We demand justice," say the workers, who
mean that they want more money and the right to join a union. "*We* want
justice" say the owners, who mean that they want the right to fire any
worker who demands more money or the right to join a union.

In his Inaugural Address, President Carter announced the beginning   14
of a "New Spirit" in the land, and asked us to dedicate ourselves to that
spirit. What exactly is this "New Spirit" that he proclaimed? Where can
one go to find it—much less dedicate one's self to it? Earlier, Carter also
said, "We can have an American President who does not govern with neg-
ativism and fear of the future, but with vigor and vision and aggressive
leadership—a President who is not isolated from our people, but who feels

your pain and shares your dreams, and takes his strength and wisdom and courage from you." Well, we're all in favor of that. Clearly, then-President Gerald Ford would have heartily endorsed the very same sentiments. He was, after all, not running on a platform that promised he would be isolated from the people, ignore their pain and laugh at their dreams, or take from them only their weakness, ignorance, and cowardice.

15        In his satirical book, *Our Gang*, Philip Roth has President "Trick E. Dixon" defend his decision to go to war with Denmark because of the eleventh-century "expansionist policies" of Eric the Red, which, President Dixon says, clearly are in "direct violation of the Monroe Doctrine." The speech is a perfect example of how glittering generalities can be used to support any course of action, no matter how inane:

> I am certain . . . that the great majority of Americans will agree that the actions I have taken in the confrontation between the United States of America and the sovereign state of Denmark are indispensable to our dignity, our honor, our moral and spiritual idealism, our credibility around the world, the soundness of the economy, our greatness, our dedication to the vision of our forefathers, the human spirit, the divinely inspired dignity of man, our treaty commitments, the principles of the United Nations, and the progress and peace for all people.
>
> Now no one is more aware than I am of the political consequences of taking bold and forthright action in behalf of our dignity, idealism and honor, to choose just three. But I would rather be a one-term President and take these noble, heroic measures against the state of Denmark, than be a two-term President by accepting humiliation at the hand of a tenth-rate military power. I want to make that perfectly clear.[1]

There are times when fiction pales before reality. Trick E. Dixon's speech bears a startling resemblance to Richard M. Nixon's speech on August 23, 1972, the day he accepted the Republican nomination for president the second time. Here is how he defended his policy of continuing the war in Vietnam:

> Let us reject . . . the policies of those who whine and whimper about our frustrations and call on us to turn inward. Let us not turn away from greatness. . . . With faith in God and faith in ourselves and faith in our country, let us have the vision and the courage to seize the moment and meet the challenge before it slips away.
>
> On your television screens last night, you saw the cemetery in Leningrad I visited on my trip to the Soviet Union where 300,000 people died . . . during World War II. At the cemetery I saw the picture of a 12-year-old girl. She was a beautiful child. Her name was Tanya. I read her diary. It tells the terrible story of war. In the simple words of a child, she wrote of the deaths of the members of her family—Senya in December,

---

[1]Philip Roth, *Our Gang* (New York. Random House, 1971).

Granny in January, then Yenka, then Uncle Basha, then Uncle Leosha, then Mama in May.

And finally, these were the words in her diary: "All are dead, only Tanya is left."

Let us think of Tanya and of the other Tanyas and their brothers and sisters everywhere in Russia and in China and in America as we proudly meet our responsibilities for leadership in the world in a way worthy of a great people.

I ask you, my fellow Americans, to join . . . in achieving a hope that mankind has had since the beginning of civilization.

Let us build a peace that our children and all the children of the world can enjoy for generations to come.

Tanya, touching as she is, has absolutely no relationship whatever to our former policy in Vietnam. But that doesn't matter. When it comes to politics, all that glitters is just gabble.

Both name-calling and glittering generalities work by stirring emotions to befog thinking. Another approach is to create a distraction, a **red herring** that will divert people's attention from the real issues. There are several different kinds of red herrings that can be used effectively. Most effective is the *plain folks* appeal. This is the verbal stratagem by which a speaker tries to win confidence and support by appearing to be "just one of the plain folks." "Wal, now, y'know I've been a farm boy all my life," says the millionaire cattle rancher to the crowd in Dallas. The same man speaking to a luncheon of Wall Street bankers might be heard saying, "Now, you know, I'm a businessman just like yourselves." Plain folks is a favorite on the campaign trail, a proven vote-getter, which is why so many candidates go around pumping factory workers' hands, kissing babies in supermarkets, and sampling pasta with Italians, fried chicken with Southerners, bagels and blintzes with Jews.

Crowds love plain-folks talk. When, during the Watergate hearings, Senator Sam Ervin remarked, "Well, I'm sorry Senator Gurney does not approve of my method of examining the witness. I'm an old country lawyer, and I don't know the finer ways to do it," the audience went wild and it took five minutes to restore order in the room. Obviously, the people must not have been aware of Lyndon Johnson's famous quip that "Whenever I hear someone say, 'I'm just an old country lawyer,' the first thing I reach for is my wallet to make sure it's still there."

In the 1978 South Carolina Senate race, Strom Thurmond's main campaign document was a leaflet of "Family Recipes." "Estill pumpkin bread" and "Orangeburg hand cookies" won an easy victory over Democratic opponent Charles Ravenel, whose family boasted no such "down-home" cooking.

Anybody can get into the plain folks act with no trouble at all:

> I understand only too well that a world-wide distance separates Roosevelt's ideas and my ideas. Roosevelt comes from a rich family and be-

longs to the class whose path is smoothed. . . . I was only the child of a
small, poor family and had to fight my way by work and industry. When
the Great War came Roosevelt occupied a position where he got to know
only its pleasant consequences, enjoyed by those who do business while
others bleed. I was only one of those who carried out orders as an ordinary soldier, and naturally returned from the war just as poor as I was in
the autumn of 1914. I shared the fate of millions, and Franklin Roosevelt
only the fate of the so-called Upper Ten Thousand. . . . After the war, Roosevelt tried his hand at financial speculations. He made profits out of inflation, out of the misery of others, while I . . . lay in a hospital. . . .

That's Adolf Hitler speaking to the Reichstag after Germany declared war
on America in 1941.

20     Another interesting red herring is *argumentum ad populum*, more popularly known as *stroking*. We all like to be liked, so it stands to reason that
we will get nice, warm feelings about anybody who "strokes" or compliments us. It's nice to hear that we are "hardworking taxpayers" or "the
most generous, free-spirited nation in the world." Farmers are told they
are the "backbone of the American economy" and college students are
hailed as the "leaders and policymakers of tomorrow." A truly gifted practitioner of *argumentum ad populum* can manage to stroke several different
groups of people in the same breath. Here is how Philip Roth's Trick E.
Dixon, in a speech that evokes memories of the famed "Checkers" television address, manages to cover as many bases as possible:

> When I was a young, struggling lawyer, and Pitter [his wife] and I were
> living on nine dollars a week out in Prissier, California . . . I would read
> through my lawbooks and study long into the night in order to help my
> clients, most of whom were wonderful young people. . . . At that time, by
> the way, I had the following debts outstanding:
>
> —$1,000    on our neat little house
>    200    to my dear parents
>    110    to my loyal and devoted brother
>     15    to our fine dentist, a warmhearted Jewish man for whom
>           we had the greatest respect
>   4.35    to our kindly grocer, an old Italian who always had a good
>           word for everybody. I still remember his name, Tony.
>      5    cents to our Chinese laundryman, a slightly-built fellow
>           who nonetheless worked long into the night over his
>           shirts, just as I did over my lawbooks, so that his children
>           might one day attend the college of their choice. I am sure
>           they have grown up to be fine and outstanding Chinese-
>           Americans.
>     60    cents to the Polish man, or polack, as the Vice-President
>           would affectionately call him, who delivered the ice for our

old-fashioned icebox. He was a strong man, with great pride in his native Poland.

We also owed monies amounting to $2.90 to a wonderful Irish plumber, a wonderful Japanese-American handyman and a wonderful couple from the deep South who happened to be of the same race as we were, and whose children played with ours in perfect harmony, despite the fact that they were from another region.[2]

A piquant variation of the stroking appeal is the "personal" letter which uses a computer to insert the recipient's name mechanically. The recipient is supposed to feel that the sender is saying all those nice things about him personally. Here's an interesting example: 21

Dear Mr. Hudgins:

The American Historical Society has created a flag in your honor. This flag commemorates the American Bicentennial and your Hudgins family name. Our research indicates that you are an affluent and achieving American family. You contribute to our society and pull your weight. . . . You are a winner. . . . You should see your Hudgins flag. We feel this flag finally gives your great name of Hudgins the recognition it so richly deserves. . . .

Presumably, the same compliments are being sent to people all over the United States. ("You should see your Kronkheit flag . . . " and "We feel this flag finally gives your great name of Ballsworth the recognition it so richly deserves.")

These advertise-by-mail manufacturers accurately pitch their sales to 22 the political and emotional makeup of the consumer. They do it by studying the profiles of the kind of people who read *Ladies' Home Journal* or *Reader's Digest* or *Ms.* magazines or whatever subscription list they get the recipient's name from. Here's an example of a "stroking appeal" I recently received:

Dear Mrs. Cross,

Frankly, you're someone magazines such as *Harper's*, *The New Yorker* and *Time* want as a subscriber. Judging from your neighborhood, you're far above average in means, intellect, and influence among those in the Syracuse and nearby areas.

. . . And when you think about it, Mrs. Cross, in just an hour or two a week, this is the most respected source for a busy, intelligent person like yourself to keep informed on the events and ideas that affect our lives. . . .

[2]Philip Roth, *Our Gang* (New York: Random House, 1971).

There's something unsettling about having a computer say all those nice things about me. I'd invite him (it?) for dinner, but my stuffed cabbage might gum up his (its?) gears. Of course, all those flattering assumptions about my neighborhood, my income, my intellect, and my influence are machine-tooled and calculated to stroke me into a mood of warm acceptance. Not just me, obviously, but everyone else winnowed out from those all-knowing mailing lists as the kind who will be most susceptible to this particular sales pitch.

23     Another device that almost everyone is susceptible to is the transfer device, also known as *guilt or glory by association*. In glory by association, the propagandist tries to "transfer" the positive feeling of something we love and respect over to the idea he wants us to accept. "Abraham Lincoln and Thomas Jefferson would have been proud of the Supreme Court decision to support school busing" is glory by association.

24     The process works equally well in reverse, when guilt by association is used to transfer dislike or disapproval of one thing to an idea or group that the propagandist wants us to reject. "John Doe says we need to make some changes in the way our government operates. That's exactly what the Symbionese Liberation Army wants!" There's no logical connection between John Doe and the Symbionese Liberation Army apart from the one the propagandist is trying to create in our minds.

25     In a recent issue of *American Opinion* magazine, columnist Gary Allen comes out in favor of censorship of school textbooks, saying,

> Parents have been asked to pay and pay, but are told to leave the education of their children "to the experts. . . ." Adolf Hitler had his experts, often brilliant scholars with impressive degrees after their names, who prescribed curricula and textbooks designed to fashion the Nazi mind. In Moscow, there is a Ministry of Education composed of equally brilliant educational experts whose job it is to manipulate the minds of Soviet youth. . . .

The implication is that Nazi storm troopers and Russian secret agents are leagued in a dastardly plot to overthrow America by infiltrating our third-grade readers and spelling workbooks.

26     To illustrate the last of the red herring devices, consider the *lemmings*. Lemmings are arctic rodents with a queer habit: periodically, for reasons no one entirely understands, they mass together in a large herd and commit group suicide by rushing into deep water and drowning themselves. They run in blindly, and not one has been observed to stop, scratch its little head, and ask, "*Why* am I doing this? This doesn't look like such a great idea," and thus save itself from destruction.

27     Obviously, lemmings are driven to perform this strange mass-suicide rite by common instinct. People also choose to "Follow the herd," perhaps for more complex reasons, yet just as blindly. The **bandwagon** appeal capitalizes on people's urge to merge with the crowd.

Basically, the bandwagon appeal gets us to support an action or an  28
opinion merely because it is popular—because "everyone else is doing it."
Advertising relies heavily on the bandwagon appeal ("join the Pepsi people") but so do politicians ("Thousands of people have already shown
their support by sending in a donation in the enclosed envelope. Won't
you become one of us and work together to build a great America?").

The great success of the bandwagon appeal is evident in the various  29
fashions and trends which capture the avid interest—and money—of thousands of people for a short time, then disappear utterly. "Oh, how I wish I
could keep up with all the latest fashions as they go rushing by me into
oblivion," English critic Max Beerbohm once wrote. Not so long ago, every
child in North America wanted a coonskin cap so he could be like Davy
Crockett. After that came the hula hoop and, more recently, the skateboard.
Children are not the only group susceptible to bandwagon buying. Not so
long ago, millions of adults rushed to the stores to buy their very own "pet
rocks"—a concept silly enough to set even a lemming atwitter.

The fallacy of the bandwagon appeal is obvious. Just because every-  30
one's doing something doesn't mean that it's worth doing. Large numbers
of people have supported actions we now condemn. Dictators have risen
to power in sophisticated and cultured countries with the support of millions of people who didn't want to be "left out" at the great historical moment. Once the bandwagon begins to move, momentum builds up dangerously fast.

If a propagandist can't reel you in by stirring your emotions or dis-  31
tracting your attention, he can always try a little faulty logic. This approach is more insidious than the other two because it gives the appearance of reasonable, fair argument. You have to look closely to see the holes
in the logical fiber. The most common kind of faulty logic is the *false-cause
and-effect fallacy*, also known as **post hoc, ergo propter hoc** ("after this,
therefore because of this").

A good example of false-cause-and-effect reasoning is the story of the  32
woman aboard the steamship *Andrea Doria*, who woke up from a nap and,
feeling seasick, looked around for a call button to summon the steward to
bring medication. She finally located a button on one of the walls of her
cabin and pushed it. A split second later, the *Andrea Doria* collided with the
*Stockholm* in the crash that was to send the ship to her destruction. "Oh
God, what have I done?" the woman screamed.

Her reasoning was understandable enough: a clear example of *post*  33
*hoc, ergo propter hoc*. False-cause-and-effect reasoning can be persuasive because it *seems* so logical, or is confirmed by our own experience. "I swal-
lowed X product—and my headache went away," says one woman. "We
elected Y official—and unemployment went down," says another. We conclude, "There *must* be a connection." Maybe it would be good to keep in
mind Harry Reasoner's remark, that "to call that cause and effect is to say

**206**

Chapter 5 Classification and Division

that sitting in the third row of burlesque theatres is what makes men bald." Cause and effect is an awfully complex phenomenon; you need a good deal of evidence to prove that one event following another in time is, in fact, "caused" by the first.

34    False cause and effect is used—and with great effect—by our ever-reliable politicians. During the final weeks of the 1976 campaign, Carter and Ford flooded the airwaves with their *post hoc, ergo propter hoc* messages. "Since I came to office," said Ford, "the inflation rate has dropped to 6%." "Since Gerald Ford took office," countered Carter, "the unemployment rate has risen 50% from 5.5% to 7.9%." Or how about this snip from a local political column for false-cause-and-effect reasoning:

> [Sex educators] loudly protest there is no relationship between their methods and promiscuity.
> Yet the facts are disheartening, to say the least.
> At a time when youngsters know more about sex than any preceding generation, we have more venereal disease, more teenage prostitution, more rape and generally, more sex-related problems than at any other time in history. If the advocates of sex education as now taught consider this an endorsement of their approach, then I think they're more in need of "instruction" than their childish charges.

Carry on with this reasoning and you can argue that the Boston Strangler, the Son of Sam, and the Zodiac Killer were all the monster creations of their ninth-grade hygiene classes. Of course, the writer blithely ignores all the multiple alternative possibilities for the phenomenon. It would be interesting to know whether the rate of venereal disease or of teenage pregnancies increased following the publication of this column. Then, by the same reasoning, we could argue that the "disheartening" rise was hardly an endorsement of such "irresponsible" attacks upon the methods of the "sex educators."

35    Another tricky use of false logic is the fallacy known as the **two-extremes dilemma.** Linguists have long noted that the English language tends to view reality in extreme or polar opposites. In English, things are either black or white, tall or short, up or down, front or back, left or right, good or bad, guilty or not guilty. "C'mon now, stop with all the talk—just give me a straightforward yes-or-no answer," we say, the understanding being that we will not accept anything in between. The problem is that there *are* things that can only be said in between: reality cannot always be dissected along strict lines. "Now, let's be fair," we say, "and listen to *both* sides of the argument." But who is to say that every argument has two sides? Can't there be a third—a fourth, fifth, or sixth—point of view? To say otherwise is to deny the nature of the world we live in, and accept the reality imposed by language.

36    In this statement by Lenin, the famed Marxist leader, we have a clear example of the two-extremes fallacy:

> You cannot eliminate one basic assumption, one substantial part of this
> philosophy of Marxism [it is as if it were a block of steel] without aban-
> doning truth, without falling into the arms of bourgeois-reactionary
> falsehood.

In other words, if you don't agree 100 percent with every premise of Marxism, you do not pass go, but move directly to jail for the ideological crime
of "bourgeois-reactionary falsehood"—the other extreme of the political
spectrum. There's no option to be 99 3/4 percent in favor of Marxism, with
perhaps a few quibbles about how a Communist state should be administered. If you're not with it, you're agin it, and that's that.

"Bourgeois reactionaries" are also capable of this kind of faulty rea- 37
soning. Texas Senator John Tower, in his 1978 reelection campaign, stated,
"I cast light on the issues: my opponent (conservative Democrat Robert
Krueger) plunges them into darkness." A recent advertisement against
gun control said, "If you're not helping to save hunting, you are helping to
outlaw it." There is no place between these polar opposites for the millions
of people in the world who might favor hunting, but oppose handguns or
Saturday night specials, or even for those who might favor guns and yet
oppose hunting, not to mention all the gradations of opinion in between.

A famous example of the two-extremes dilemma is the slogan "Amer- 38
ica: Love it or leave it." The implicit suggestion is that we must either accept *everything* in America today *just as it is*—or get out. Of course, there's
a whole range of action and belief between those two extremes which the
slogan entirely overlooks. The path of American history is littered with slogans that display the two-extremes dilemma—"Fifty-four forty or fight."
"Better dead than Red." "Millions for defense but not one cent for tribute."

There's one more propaganda technique that's the most under- 39
handed of them all. It's called **card stacking,** and means selecting only
those facts—or falsehoods—which support the propagandist's point of
view, ignoring all others. For example, a candidate could be made to look
like a legislative dynamo if you say, "Representative McNerd introduced
more new bills than any other member of Congress," and neglect to mention that most of them were so preposterous that they never got out of
committee.

When we feel deeply about something, it's difficult to resist the temp- 40
tation to stack the deck. Take this recent statement issued by an antiabor-
tion group:

> Why does this sin-sick society show leniency toward murderers, rapists,
> robbers, and other vicious criminals and then does an about-face by want-
> ing to destroy these little bundles of innocence through abortive murder:
> Let's face the truth. The majority of those who want to get rid of what God
> has created in their wombs are the unmarried who had a fling in the back
> seat of a parked automobile or some dingy motel room. Now when the

price for a night of adventure is beginning to manifest itself, they want to add to their wickedness by slaying this innocent little baby. . . .

41      The Second Amendment Foundation, a group opposing gun control and an affiliate of the national gun lobby, recently published a small pamphlet "warning Americans against the dangers of gun confiscation," which includes the following dire forecast:

> Even though you may not own or have any direct interest in firearms, I believe you must be informed of the terribly serious consequences of what the liberal press refers to as "gun control."
>
> My friend, they are not talking about *control*, they want complete and total confiscation. This will mean the elimination and removal of *all police revolvers, all sporting rifles* and *target pistols* owned by law-abiding citizens. Throughout our country a crime of violence, like murder, assault or rape, occurred once every 31 seconds in 1976. This means that over 1,026,280 men, women and children or elderly persons fell victims to thieves and hoodlums. . . .
>
> Tell me, how high would the crime rate be if the criminal knew our police were unarmed? . . . I don't believe we can sit back and allow the "gun confiscation" people in this country to pass laws that would set the stage for the most terrifying crime wave ever to occur in modern history. . . .

No mention here that England and Japan, where guns are banned, have a much lower crime rate than the United States, or that the rate of homicides is dramatically less. That wouldn't fit into this carefully stacked deck. Nor would a contrary argument citing only the English and Japanese experience pass any test. For there might be any number of other explanations (see the *post hoc* fallacy) for that phenomenon. But never mind these picky details—the big picture is clear enough in the gun lobby pamphlet: vote for gun control, and if the bill passes, the next day every pervert and gangster in the city will be scratching at your windows and jimmying your door, while the police stand by helplessly, swatting them with their hats.

42      Card stacking was used shamelessly throughout the 1976 election campaign. In the New York State [U.S. Senate] race, the "Democrats for Jim Buckley" came out with a campaign poster that announced:

> Two thirds of all Democrats who voted in the recent primary did not vote for Moynihan. He won with a one percent margin. That's not what we call a party mandate. . . . So, what is there about Moynihan that turns off so many members of his own party?

A cleverly loaded question. Since there were four strong candidates running in the Democratic primary, it was well-nigh impossible for *anyone* to get anything approaching a "mandate." And the fact that the vote was so widely split among the candidates did not necessarily mean that anyone was "turned off" to Moynihan, just that they were "turned on" to other people. In the last weeks of the presidential race, Carter's people took out an ad that stated, "Today's inflation rate of 6% is higher than it was at any time between the Korean War and the Inauguration of Richard Nixon." True enough. But they neglected to mention that the inflation rate actually *dropped* from 12 percent to 6 percent during Ford's Administration—not the kind of omission that's likely to be an unconscious oversight. For their part, the Ford people came up with the remark that "This administration doesn't believe the way to end unemployment is to go to war." Of course, no one is depraved enough to suggest that the way to end unemployment is to go to war, but somehow that remark suggests that this may be what Carter had in mind.

Card stacking isn't necessarily *untrue;* it just isn't the whole truth. It's a bit reminiscent of the story about the three blind men who encountered an elephant one day. The first blind man felt the elephant's trunk and concluded he was confronted with a snake; the second felt the elephant's leg and decided it must be a tree trunk; the third felt the tusk and was convinced it was the antler of a deer. A skillful card stacker can take *part* of the truth and use it to argue for a particular issue and take another part to argue against the very same issue he just argued for. When one of his constituents wrote to him complaining about federal spending, Arizona Congressman Morris Udall replied tongue in cheek with this tour de force of card stacking: 43

> If, when you say "federal spending," you mean the billions of dollars wasted on outmoded naval shipyards and surplus airbases in Georgia, Texas and New York; if you mean the billions of dollars lavished at Cape Kennedy and Houston on a "moondoggle" our nation cannot afford; if, sir, you mean the $2-billion wasted each year in wheat and corn price supports which rob midwestern farmers of their freedoms and saddle taxpayers with outrageous cost of storage in already bulging warehouses . . . if you mean the bloated federal aid to education schemes calculated to press federal educational controls down upon every student in this nation; if you mean the $2-billion misused annually by our Public Health Service and National Institutes of Health on activities designed to prostitute the medical profession and foist socialized medicine on every American; if, sir, you mean all these ill advised, unnecessary federal activities which have destroyed state's rights, created a vast, ever-growing, empire-building bureaucracy regimenting a once free people by illusory bait of cradle-to-grave security, and which indeed have taken us so far down the road to socialism that it may be, even at this hour, too late to retreat—then I am unyielding, bitter and foursquare in my opposition, regardless of the personal or political consequences.
>
> But, on the other hand, if when you say "federal spending," you mean those funds which maintain Davis Monthan Air Force Base, Fort Huachuca and other Arizona defense installations so vital to our nation's security, and which every year pour hundreds of millions of dollars into

our state's economy . . . if you mean those funds to send our brave astronauts voyaging, even as Columbus, into the unknown, in order to guarantee that no aggressor will ever threaten these great United States by nuclear blackmail from outer space; if you mean those sound farm programs which insure our hardy Arizona cotton farmers a fair price for their fiber, protect the sanctity of the family farm, ensure reasonable prices for consumers, and put to work for all the people of the world the miracle of American agricultural abundance . . . if you mean the federal education funds which built desperately needed college classrooms and dormitories for our local universities, provide little children in our Arizona schools with hot lunches (often their only decent meal of the day), furnish vocational training for our high school youth, and pay $10-million in impact funds to relieve the hard-pressed Arizona school property taxpayers from the impossible demands created by the presence of large federal installations; if you mean the federal medical and health programs which have eradicated the curse of malaria, smallpox, scarlet fever and polio from our country, and which even now enable dedicated teams of scientists to close in mercilessly on man's age-old enemies of cancer, heart disease, muscular dystrophy, multiple sclerosis, and mental retardation that afflict our little children, senior citizens and men and women in the prime years of life; if you mean all these federal activities by which a free people in the spirit of Jefferson, Lincoln, Teddy Roosevelt, Wilson and FDR, through a fair and progressive income tax, preserve domestic tranquility and promote the general welfare while preserving all our cherished freedoms and our self-reliant national character, then I shall support them with all the vigor at my command.[3]

44    Perhaps a good way to wind up is to show you how all these propaganda devices, from name-calling through card stacking, can be put to work together. Let's take a local candidate who doesn't have any very good reason why people should vote for him instead of his opponent, so he's going to have to rely on propaganda and not reasoned argument. Here, then, is State Senator Al Yakalot, running for reelection to the State Senate, addressing a crowd of his constituents on election day:

*Speech by Senator Yakalot to His Constituents*

45    My dear friends and fellow countrymen in this great and beautiful town of Gulliville, I stand before you today as your candidate for State Senator. And before I say anything else, I want to thank you wonderful people, you hard-working, right-living citizens that make our country great, for coming here today to hear me speak. Now, I'm at a disadvantage here because I don't have the gift of gab that a big-city fella like my opponent has—I'm just a small-town boy like you fine people—but I'm

[3]Morris Udall, *Preface to Critical Reading*. ed. Richard Altick (New York: Holt, Rinehart and Winston, 1969).

going to try, in my own simple way, to tell you why you should vote for me. Al Yakalot.

Now, my opponent may appear to you to be a pretty nice guy, but I'm here today to tell you that his reckless and radical policies represent a dire threat to all that we hold dear. He would tear down all that is great and good in America and substitute instead his own brand of creeping socialism.

For that's just what his ridiculous scheme to set up a hot meal program for the elderly in this town amounts to—socialism. Sure, *he* says our local citizens have expressed their willingness to donate some of their time and money to a so-called senior citizens' kitchen. But this kind of supposed "volunteer" work only undermines our local restaurants—in effect, our private enterprise system. The way I see it, in this world a man's either for private enterprise or he's for socialism. Mr. Stu Pott, one of the leading strategists of the hot meal campaign (a man who, by the way, sports a Fidel Castro beard) has said the program would be called the "Community Food Service." Well, just remember that the words "Community" and "Communism" look an awful lot alike!

After all, my friends, our forefathers who made this country great never had any free hot meal handouts. And look at what they did for our country! That's why I'm against the hot meal program. Hot meals will only make our senior citizens soft, useless, and dependent.

And that's not all you should know about my opponent, my fellow citizens. My pinko opponent has also called for a "consumers crusade" against what he terms "junk food" in school lunches. By "junk food," he means things like potato chips and hot dogs. Potato chips and hot dogs! My friends, I say that we've raised generations of patriotic American children on potato chips and hot dogs and we're not about to stop now! Potato chips have been praised by great Americans as well as by leading experts on nutrition.

What's more, potato chips are good for our children, too. A recent study shows that after children were given lunches that often included potato chips, their energy and attention spans improved by over ten percent. Obviously, potato chips have a beneficial effect on children's ability to learn. My opponent has tried to tell you that his attack on the venerable American custom of potato chip eating is just an attempt to improve our children's health and beauty. Yet this plan is supported by Congresswoman Doris Schlepp, who is no beauty herself!

My fellow taxpayers, I'm here today to tell you that this heartless plot to deprive our little ones of the food that they need most and love best won't work, because it's just plain unworkable. Trying to discourage children from eating potato chips is like trying to prevent people from voting—and the American people just aren't going to stand for it!

I'm mighty grateful to all of you wonderful folks for letting me speak what is in my heart. I know you for what you are—the decent, law-abiding citizens that are the great pulsing heart and the lifeblood of this, our beloved country. I stand for all that is good in America, for our American way and our American Birthright. More and more citizens are rallying to my cause every day. Won't you join them—and me—in our fight for America?

53          Thank you and May God Bless You All.

*1983*

## QUESTIONS FOR DISCUSSION

### Content

a. What, according to Cross, is propaganda? Can you define it in another way?

b. This essay refers to many people, issues, and organizations that made headlines in the 1970s as well as to those from earlier times. Make sure you know to whom and to what Cross is referring. For example, what is the Equal Rights Amendment? Who are Walter Mondale and Robert Dole? What is the Symbionese Liberation Army? Who were Benjamin Disraeli and Winston Churchill? If you are unsure about any of Cross's references, look them up in an encyclopedia, in a reference book, or on the Internet.

c. Pick out the "glittering generalities" in the examples Cross uses in paragraph 15.

d. What is a "red herring," and how does it work?

e. What is "glory by association"? Can it work in reverse? How?

f. Do you agree with Cross's arguments in paragraphs 25 and 26? Why or why not?

g. Analyze the examples concerning sex education in paragraph 34. What is Cross saying here? Are her examples effective, convincing, and easy to follow?

h. Why does Cross call "card stacking" the "most underhanded" propaganda technique of all?

i. Are the examples of card stacking in paragraphs 40 and 41 effective and appropriate? If so, why? If not, why not?

j. What is a loaded question (paragraph 42)?

k. Does this essay favor one political philosophy over another (say liberal versus conservative), or is it balanced?

### Strategy and Style

l. What about Cross's style is particularly effective? What does Cross's style tell you about her intended audience and purpose? How would you characterize Cross's tone? Is it appropriate to her purpose? What is her purpose?

m. What do you make of Cross's title? Is it effective? Should she have used more formal language in it?

n. Discuss the techniques Cross uses in her introduction. Do they entice the reader? Why?

o. In what way or ways does Cross develop paragraph 8? Paragraph 9? What other methods of development does this classification essay employ?

p. Why does Cross wait until the end of paragraph 19 to reveal the author of the quotation she includes?

q. What effect would omitting Senator Yakalot's speech have had on the essay's effectiveness?

## ENGAGING THE TEXT

a. Annotate the speech by Senator Yakalot to identify examples of the kinds of propaganda Cross discusses in this essay.

b. Write a summary of this essay, listing and defining in your own words each of the classes of propaganda that Cross covers.

## SUGGESTIONS FOR SUSTAINED WRITING

a. Find a speech by one or more contemporary political candidates who is running or has recently run for local, state, or national office. Based on what you read in Cross's essay, evaluate the extent to which the speech writer used propaganda to sway the audience.

b. Reread William Lutz's essay, which appears in this chapter. As you proceed, make a list of issues or points on which Cross and Lutz might agree. Then write a full-length essay based on the notes you made. Make frequent and direct reference to both Cross and Lutz. In addition, consider discussing issues or concerns on which these authors might disagree.

c. Pretend you are a speechwriter working for a candidate for local, state, or national office or for the leader of a group that is trying to advance a particular political or social ideology. Compose a speech for this person that contains at least one example of each of the classes of propaganda that Cross discusses. To complete this assignment, you will have to do some library and/or Internet research on the person for whom you are writing this speech.

Chapter

# 6

# Comparison and Contrast

The human tendency to measure one thing against another is so pervasive that it is only natural that it be used as a way to explore and explain complex ideas in writing. Comparison reveals similarities; contrast, differences. Both allow the writer to explain and explore new ideas by making reference to what the reader already knows. One way to begin describing a microwave oven to someone who has never seen one is to liken it to the oven in the conventional kitchen stove with which he or she is familiar. Both use energy to heat and cook food. Both are relatively easy to use, and both are no fun to clean! But there the similarities end. A microwave is quicker and more economical. And who ever heard of making popcorn in a conventional oven? Spend enough time explaining similarities and differences, and you are sure to give your reader at least a rudimentary acquaintance with this appliance.

As with all writing, the key to composing effective comparison/contrast papers is to collect important information—and plenty of it—before you begin. Look at your subjects long and hard, take careful notes, and gather the kinds of details that will help you reveal differences and similarities of the most telling kind.

You can use a variety of techniques to develop a comparison or contrast. As suits his purpose, Mark Twain relies heavily on description in "Two Views of the Mississippi," while Lydia Minatoya includes both narrative and descriptive details to create a complex essay about the relationships among cultures. Narration also informs Bruce Catton's brilliant study of Grant and Lee, May Sarton's commentary on loneliness and solitude, and Scott Russell Sanders's "The Men We Carry in Our Minds."

One of the major advantages of using comparison/contrast to explain ideas is that it can lend itself quite naturally to two easy-to-arrange and easy-to-follow patterns of organization. In the point-by-point method, writers address a series of characteristics or features shared by the two subjects; they compare or contrast the two subjects on one point and then move on to the next point. This is how the selection by Deborah Tannen is arranged. In the subject-by-subject method, one subject is discussed thoroughly before the writer moves on to the second. You can see good examples of the subject-by-subject method in the essay by Mark Twain. For example, Twain first describes the beautiful and poetic Mississippi before going on to the dangerous Mississippi.

But do not be misled. No writer represented in this chapter is content to follow a predetermined schema. Each author has a specific purpose in mind, and each draws on other organizational patterns to shape the essay. Indeed, Catton shifts from the point-by-point to the subject-by-subject arrangement so deftly that the reader hardly notices.

The selections in this chapter present a variety of subjects and purposes—from analyzing the psychological motivations behind the way men and women communicate to assessing the virtues of solitude. Carefully consider the Questions for Discussion, the items under Engaging the Text, and the Suggestions for Sustained Writing that follow each essay. They will lead you to many more insights about using comparison/contrast as a way to explore new ideas and make your writing more powerful no matter what your topic or purpose.

# The Rewards of Living a Solitary Life

May Sarton

*May Sarton (1912–1995) was born in Belgium, moving to the United States with her parents when she was 4 and becoming a U.S. citizen when she was 12. A writer with an extraordinary range (she wrote poetry, plays, film scripts, memoirs, novels, essays, and journals), she originally wanted to be an actor. From 1929 to 1933 she was an apprentice actor in New York, after which she formed and led her own theatrical group, the Associated Actors Theatre, from 1934 to 1937. She supplemented her income with literary reviews and essays about theater and literature, with teaching, and with writing scripts. She taught creative writing and choral speech at the Stuart School in Boston from 1937 to 1942 and wrote film scripts for the U.S. Office of War Information in 1943 and 1944. After the war, she lectured at various colleges, including Harvard University (1949–1952), Breadloaf Writer's Conference (1950, 1951, 1953), and Wellesley College (1960–1964), among others. In her prolific career, Sarton wrote about 50 books, including 12 novels. She wrote on themes of solitude, self-knowledge, and spiritual growth. Her later books also have feminist themes.*

*In 1968 she began publishing her journals, which she called "public diaries." These diaries were collections of reflective essays, and she published six of them between 1968 and 1993. It is for these reflective essays that Sarton is best known. "The Rewards of Living a Solitary Life," which was written for the* New York Times *in 1946, is typical of such essays. Here Sarton praises those who have the courage to voyage through their "own inner space, space as immense, unexplored and sometimes frightening as outer space to the astronaut."*

1    The other day an acquaintance of mine, a gregarious and charming man, told me he had found himself unexpectedly alone in New York for an hour or two between appointments. He went to the Whitney and spent the "empty" time looking at things in solitary bliss. For him it proved to be a shock nearly as great as falling in love to discover that he could enjoy himself so much alone.

2    What had he been afraid of, I asked myself? That, suddenly alone, he would discover that he bored himself, or that there was, quite simply, no self there to meet? But having taken the plunge, he is now on the brink of adventure; he is about to be launched into his own inner space, space as immense, unexplored and sometimes frightening as outer space to the astronaut. His every perception will come to him with a new freshness and, for a time, seem startlingly original. For anyone who can see things for himself with a naked eye becomes, for a moment or two, something of a genius. With another human being present vision becomes double vision, inevitably. We are busy wondering, what does my companion see or think of this, and what do I think of it? The original impact gets lost, or diffused.

3    "Music I heard with you was more than music." Exactly. And therefore music *itself* can only be heard alone. Solitude is the salt of personhood. It brings out the authentic flavor of every experience.

4    "Alone one is never lonely: The spirit adventures, walking / In a quiet garden, in a cool house, abiding single there."

5    Loneliness is most acutely felt with other people, for with others, even with a lover sometimes, we suffer from our differences of taste, temperament, mood. Human intercourse often demands that we soften the edge of perception, or withdraw at the very instant of personal truth for fear of hurting, or of being inappropriately present, which is to say naked, in a social situation. Alone we can afford to be wholly whatever we are, and to feel whatever we feel absolutely. That is a great luxury!

6    For me the most interesting thing about a solitary life, and mine has been that for the last twenty years, is that it becomes increasingly rewarding. When I can wake up and watch the sun rise over the ocean, as I do most days, and know that I have an entire day ahead, uninterrupted, in which to write a few pages, take a walk with my dog, lie down in the afternoon for a long think (why does one think better in a horizontal position?), read and listen to music, I am flooded with happiness.

7    I am lonely only when I am overtired, when I have worked too long without a break, when for the time being I feel empty and need filling up. And I am lonely sometimes when I come back home after a lecture trip, when I have seen a lot of people and talked a lot, and am full to the brim with experience that needs to be sorted out.

Then for a little while the house feels huge and empty, and I wonder ₈ where my self is hiding. It has to be recaptured slowly by watering the plants, perhaps, and looking again at each one as though it were a person, by feeding the two cats, by cooking a meal.

It takes a while, as I watch the surf blowing up in fountains at the end ₉ of the field, but the moment comes when the world falls away, and the self emerges again from the deep unconscious, bringing back all I have recently experienced to be explored and slowly understood, when I can converse again with my hidden powers, and so grow, and so be renewed, till death do us part.

*1946*

## QUESTIONS FOR DISCUSSION

### Content

a. What does Sarton mean by her sentence in paragraph 3, "Solitude is the salt of personhood"? What is the metaphor here?
b. Do you agree or disagree with Sarton's assessment of solitude?
c. To what does Sarton allude in the last phrase of the essay? What is her implication here?
d. What does Sarton use as examples to support her thesis that solitude is better than constant society? How effective are these examples?
e. What might be Sarton's purpose in including a passage of poetry as an entire paragraph (paragraph 4)?
f. Exactly what does Sarton compare and contrast in her essay?
g. Is this an argumentative essay? If so, what is her argument and with whom is she arguing? What does she hope to persuade them to do?
h. Have you ever found yourself in the same situation as Sarton's gregarious acquaintance? If so, were your reactions similar to his?

### Strategy and Style

i. Sarton begins her essay with an anecdote. What effect does this opening have on you? Does it draw you into the essay? Would the essay be better, or worse, without it?

j. How do you account for the brevity of the essay? Would it be a better essay if it were longer?

k. What allusions or metaphors does Sarton include?

## ENGAGING THE TEXT

a. Write your definitions of *loneliness* and of *solitude*. How do they compare to what Sarton says about loneliness and solitude?

b. What is your own experience of solitude? Describe a time when you were completely solitary. Compare your experience to Sarton's view of solitude.

## SUGGESTIONS FOR SUSTAINED WRITING

a. Write an essay in which you summarize Sarton's definition of *loneliness*. Explain whether you agree or disagree with it and explain how her definition differs from standard definitions.

b. Another essay—although quite different from Sarton's—in which the author tries to justify a particular lifestyle is Eighner's "On Dumpster Diving" in Chapter 11. Read that essay for additional inspiration. Then write an essay justifying your own lifestyle.

c. Contrast your lifestyle with that of someone of your sex, race, and economic class who lived a hundred years ago in the United States or Canada. As an alternative, you might even want to contrast your lifestyle with that of an ancestor, say a great-grandmother or great-grandfather, whatever part of the world he or she lived in. Rely on library and Internet research to gather information that will lend authority and accuracy to your discussion.

# Grant and Lee: A Study in Contrasts

Bruce Catton

*Born in Michigan, Bruce Catton (1899–1978) has come to be regarded as one of the most important historians of the American Civil War. Catton received the Pulitzer Prize and the National Book Award for* A Stillness at Appomattox *(1953). Among his other works are* This Hallowed Ground *(1956),* Mr. Lincoln's Army *(1951), and* Gettysburg: The Final Fury *(1974). The piece on Grant and Lee is one of the most frequently anthologized short selections on the subject of the Civil War. In it, Catton contrasts more than two men and two Civil War generals; he draws clear distinctions between two cultures, two eras, and two visions of life. "Grant and Lee: A Study in Contrasts" was first published in* The American Story *(1958).*

When Ulysses S. Grant and Robert E. Lee met in the parlor of a modest 1
house at Appomattox Court House, Virginia, on April 9, 1865, to work out
the terms for the surrender of Lee's Army of Northern Virginia, a great
chapter in American life came to a close, and a great new chapter began.

These men were bringing the Civil War to its virtual finish. To be sure, 2
other armies had yet to surrender, and for a few days the fugitive Confed-
erate government would struggle desperately and vainly, trying to find
some way to go on living now that its chief support was gone. But in effect
it was all over when Grant and Lee signed the papers. And the little room
where they wrote out the terms was the scene of one of the poignant, dramatic contrasts in American history.

They were two strong men, these oddly different generals, and they 3
represented the strengths of two conflicting currents that, through them,
had come into final collision.

Back of Robert E. Lee was the notion that the old aristocratic concept 4
might somehow survive and be dominant in American life.

Lee was tidewater Virginia, and in his background were family, cul- 5
ture, and tradition . . . the age of chivalry transplanted to a New World
which was making its own legends and its own myths. He embodied a
way of life that had come down through the age of knighthood and the
English country squire. America was a land that was beginning all over
again, dedicated to nothing much more complicated than the rather hazy
belief that all men had equal rights, and should have an equal chance in
the world. In such a land Lee stood for the feeling that it was somehow of
advantage to human society to have a pronounced inequality in the social
structure. There should be a leisure class, backed by ownership of land; in
turn, society itself should be keyed to the land as the chief source of wealth
and influence. It would bring forth (according to this ideal) a class of men
with a strong sense of obligation to the community; men who lived not to
gain advantage for themselves, but to meet the solemn obligations which
had been laid on them by the very fact that they were privileged. From
them the country would get its leadership; to them it could look for the
higher values—of thought, of conduct, of personal deportment—to give it
strength and virtue.

Lee embodied the noblest elements of this aristocratic ideal. Through 6
him, the landed nobility justified itself. For four years, the Southern states
had fought a desperate war to uphold the ideals for which Lee stood. In the
end, it almost seemed as if the Confederacy fought for Lee; as if he himself
was the Confederacy . . . the best thing that the way of life for which the
Confederacy stood could ever have to offer. He had passed into legend before Appomattox. Thousands of tired, underfed, poorly clothed Confeder-
ate soldiers, long-since past the simple enthusiasm of the early days of the
struggle, somehow considered Lee the symbol of everything for which they
had been willing to die. But they could not quite put this feeling into words.

If the Lost Cause, sanctified by so much heroism and so many deaths, had a living justification, its justification was General Lee.

7      Grant, the son of a tanner on the Western frontier, was everything Lee was not. He had come up the hard way, and embodied nothing in particular except the eternal toughness and sinewy fiber of the men who grew up beyond the mountains. He was one of a body of men who owed reverence and obeisance to no one, who were self-reliant to a fault, who cared hardly anything for the past but who had a sharp eye for the future.

8      These frontier men were the precise opposites of the tidewater aristocrats. Back of them, in the great surge that had taken people over the Alleghenies and into the opening Western country, there was a deep, implicit dissatisfaction with a past that had settled into grooves. They stood for democracy, not from any reasoned conclusion about the proper ordering of human society, but simply because they had grown up in the middle of democracy and knew how it worked. Their society might have privileges, but they would be privileges each man had won for himself. Forms and patterns meant nothing. No man was born to anything, except perhaps to a chance to show how far he could rise. Life was competition.

9      Yet along with this feeling had come a deep sense of belonging to a national community. The Westerner who developed a farm, opened a shop or set up in business as a trader, could hope to prosper only as his own community prospered—and his community ran from the Atlantic to the Pacific and from Canada down to Mexico. If the land was settled, with towns and highways and accessible markets, he could better himself. He saw his fate in terms of the nation's own destiny. As its horizons expanded, so did his. He had, in other words, an acute dollars-and-cents stake in the continued growth and development of his country.

10     And that, perhaps, is where the contrast between Grant and Lee becomes most striking. The Virginia aristocrat, inevitably, saw himself in relation to his own region. He lived in a static society which could endure almost anything except change. Instinctively, his first loyalty would go to the locality in which that society existed. He would fight to the limit of endurance to defend it, because in defending it he was defending everything that gave his own life its deepest meaning.

11     The Westerner, on the other hand, would fight with an equal tenacity for the broader concept of society. He fought so because everything he lived by was tied to growth, expansion, and a constantly widening horizon. What he lived by would survive or fall with the nation itself. He could not possibly stand by unmoved in the face of an attempt to destroy the Union. He would combat it with everything he had, because he could only see it as an effort to cut the ground out from under his feet.

12     So Grant and Lee were in complete contrast, representing two diametrically opposed elements in American life. Grant was the modern man emerging; beyond him, ready to come on the stage, was the great age of

steel and machinery, of crowded cities and a restless, burgeoning vitality. Lee might have ridden down from the old age of chivalry, lance in hand, silken banner fluttering over his head. Each man was the perfect champion of his cause, drawing both his strengths and his weaknesses from the people he led.

Yet it was not all contrast, after all. Different as they were—in background, in personality, in underlying aspiration—these two great soldiers had much in common. Under everything else, they were marvelous fighters. Furthermore, their fighting qualities were really very much alike. 13

Each man had, to begin with, the great virtue of utter tenacity and fidelity. Grant fought his way down the Mississippi Valley in spite of acute personal discouragement and profound military handicaps. Lee hung on in the trenches at Petersburg after hope itself had died. In each man there was an indomitable quality . . . the born fighter's refusal to give up as long as he can still remain on his feet and lift his two fists. 14

Daring and resourcefulness they had, too; the ability to think faster and move faster than the enemy. These were the qualities which gave Lee the dazzling campaigns of Second Manassas and Chancellorsville and won Vicksburg for Grant. 15

Lastly, and perhaps greatest of all, there was the ability, at the end, to turn quickly from war to peace once the fighting was over. Out of the way these two men behaved at Appomattox came the possibility of a peace of reconciliation. It was a possibility not wholly realized, in the years to come, but which did, in the end, help the two sections to become one nation again . . . after a war whose bitterness might have seemed to make such a reunion wholly impossible. No part of either man's life became him more than the part he played in their brief meeting in the McLean house at Appomattox. Their behavior there put all succeeding generations of Americans in their debt. Two great Americans, Grant and Lee—very different, yet under everything very much alike. Their encounter at Appomattox was one of the great moments of American history. 16

*1958*

## QUESTIONS FOR DISCUSSION

### Content

a. What does Catton mean in paragraph 5 when he says: "[Lee] embodied a way of life that had come down through the age of knighthood and the English country squire"?

b. Catton groups Grant with men who believed: "Forms and patterns meant nothing. No man was born to anything, except perhaps to a chance to show how far he could rise" (paragraph 8). Explain what he means by that.

c. Catton's thesis is stated rather early in the essay. What is it? How does it signal the pattern of organization that follows?

d. If this selection is "A Study in Contrasts," why does Catton spend the last four paragraphs discussing the similarities between Grant and Lee?

e. What are some of these similarities?

f. How would you explain the Westerner's "deep sense of belonging to a national community," which Catton mentions in paragraph 9? How does this idea differ from what tidewater aristocrats like Lee felt?

g. Discuss the other characteristics that Catton attributes to frontier men.

## Strategy and Style

h. What function do paragraphs 10 and 11 serve in the structure of this essay?

i. Catton organizes his prose by alternating the discussion from point to point rather than completing his discussion of one figure before moving on to the next. Is this method effective?

## ENGAGING THE TEXT

a. Describe what you consider to be the ideal general for today. In your opinion, do generals today share the same qualities as those in Grant and Lee's time?

b. Describe the meeting that might have occurred between Grant and Lee if the Confederacy had won the war. Refer to Catton's essay in your response.

## SUGGESTIONS FOR SUSTAINED WRITING

a. Choose two individuals with whom you have the same kind of relationship: two grandfathers, two aunts, two close friends. How do these individuals differ? List the major differences in their personalities or their outlooks on life. Is one a pessimist and the other an optimist? Is one an introvert and the other an extrovert? If you don't want to write about people you know personally, choose two figures from the world of politics, art, science, or business about whom you know a great deal. Write a well-developed essay that makes the contrast clear.

b. Catton characterized Lee as a "living justification" of the "Lost Cause." Do you see yourself as such an idealist? Do you espouse "lost causes" simply because you think they are right? Or are you more pragmatic and realistic in your approach to life? Whatever your answer, explain it in an essay; cite sufficient examples to be convincing and clear.

c. Select two rival candidates in an upcoming or recent political election (local, state, or national). Isolate and explain the major differences in their ideologies. Make sure to include information you have researched in newspapers, magazines, and journals or on the Internet.

# Talk in the Intimate Relationship: His and Hers

Deborah Tannen

*Deborah Tannen (b. 1945) is a professor of linguistics at Georgetown University. Although she has written articles for academic journals, she considers her "mission" to be "the presentation of linguistic research to a general audience." Her many popular nonfiction books do just that: make linguistic issues interesting and important to nonacademic readers. She draws on her experiences teaching English in Greece, studying gender-related language issues, and writing poetry and fiction to create books that are informal and engaging yet soundly researched. These books include* Conversational Style: Analyzing Talk Among Friends *(1984),* Talking 9 to 5 *(1944),* Gender and Conversational Interaction *(1993), and* The Argument Culture: Moving from Debate to Dialogue *(1998).*

*The following essay is from* That's Not What I Meant! How Conversational Style Makes or Breaks Your Relations with Others *(1986). In it, Tannen explains that women and men have "incongruent expectations" about interpersonal communications.*

Male-female conversation is cross-cultural communication. Culture is sim- 1 ply a network of habits and patterns gleaned from past experience, and women and men have different past experiences. From the time they're born, they're treated differently, talked to differently, and talk differently as a result. Boys and girls grow up in different worlds, even if they grow up in the same house. And as adults they travel in different worlds, reinforcing patterns established in childhood. These cultural differences include different expectations about the role of talk in relationships and how it fulfills that role.

Everyone knows that as a relationship becomes long-term, its terms 2 change. But women and men often differ in how they expect them to change. Many women feel, "After all this time, you should know what I want without my telling you." Many men feel, "After all this time, we should be able to tell each other what we want."

3      These incongruent expectations capture one of the key differences between men and women. Communication is always a matter of balancing
conflicting needs for involvement and independence. Though everyone
has both these needs, women often have a relatively greater need for involvement, and men a relatively greater need for independence. Being understood without saying what you mean gives a payoff in involvement,
and that is why women value it so highly.

4      If you want to be understood without saying what you mean explicitly in words, you must convey meaning somewhere else—in how words
are spoken, or by metamessages. Thus it stands to reason that women are
often more attuned than men to the metamessages of talk. When women
surmise meaning in this way, it seems mysterious to men, who call it
"women's intuition" (if they think it's right) or "reading things in" (if they
think it's wrong). Indeed, it could be wrong, since metamessages are not
on record. And even if it is right, there is still the question of scale: How
significant are the metamessages that are there?

5      Metamessages are a form of indirectness. Women are more likely to be
indirect, and to try to reach agreement by negotiation. Another way to understand this preference is that negotiation allows a display of solidarity,
which women prefer to the display of power (even though the aim may be
the same—getting what you want). Unfortunately, power and solidarity
are bought with the same currency: Ways of talking intended to create solidarity have the simultaneous effect of framing power differences. When
they think they're being nice, women often end up appearing deferential
and unsure of themselves or of what they want.

6      When styles differ, misunderstandings are always rife. As their differing styles create misunderstandings, women and men try to clear them up
by talking things out. These pitfalls are compounded in talks between men
and women because they have different ways of going about talking
things out, and different assumptions about the significance of going
about it.

7      Sylvia and Harry celebrated their fiftieth wedding anniversary at a
mountain resort. Some of the guests were at the resort for the whole weekend, others just for the evening of the celebration: a cocktail party followed
by a sit-down dinner. The manager of the dining room approached Sylvia
during dinner. "Since there's so much food tonight," he said, "and the hotel prepared a fancy dessert and everyone already ate at the cocktail party
anyway, how about cutting and serving the anniversary cake at lunch tomorrow?" Sylvia asked the advice of the others at her table. All the men
agreed: "Sure, that makes sense. Save the cake for tomorrow." All the
women disagreed: "No, the party is tonight. Serve the cake tonight." The
men were focusing on the message: The cake as food. The women were
thinking of the metamessage: Serving a special cake frames an occasion as
a celebration.

Why are women more attuned to metamessages? Because they are 8 more focused on involvement, that is, on relationships among people, and it is through metamessages that relationships among people are established and maintained. If you want to take the temperature and check the vital signs of a relationship, the barometers to check are its metamessages: What is said and how.

Everyone can see these signals, but whether or not we pay attention to 9 them is another matter—a matter of being sensitized. Once you are sensitized, you can't roll your antennae back in; they're stuck in the extended position.

When interpreting meaning, it is possible to pick up signals that 10 weren't intentionally sent out, like an innocent flock of birds on a radar screen. The birds are there—and the signals women pick up are there—but they may not mean what the interpreter thinks they mean. For example, Maryellen looks at Larry and asks, "What's wrong?" because his brow is furrowed. Since he was only thinking about lunch, her expression of concern makes him feel under scrutiny.

The difference in focus on messages and metamessages can give men 11 and women different points of view on almost any comment. Harriet complains to Morton, "Why don't you ask me how my day was?" He replies, "If you have something to tell me, tell me. Why do you have to be invited?" The reason is that she wants the metamessage of interest: Evidence that he cares how her day was, regardless of whether or not she has something to tell.

A lot of trouble is caused between women and men by, of all things, 12 pronouns. Women often feel hurt when their partners use "I" or "me" in a situation in which they would use "we" or "us." When Morton announces, "I think I'll go for a walk," Harriet feels specifically uninvited, though Morton later claims she would have been welcome to join him. She felt locked out by his use of "I" and his omission of an invitation: "Would you like to come?" Metamessages can be seen in what is not said as well as what is said.

It's difficult to straighten out such misunderstandings because each 13 one feels convinced of the logic of his or her position and the illogic—or irresponsibility—of the other's. Harriet knows that she always asks Morton how his day was, and that she'd never announce, "I'm going for a walk," without inviting him to join her. If he talks differently to her, it must be that he feels differently. But Morton wouldn't feel unloved if Harriet didn't ask about his day, and he would feel free to ask, "Can I come along?" if she announced she was taking a walk. So he can't believe she is justified in feeling responses he knows he wouldn't have.

These processes are dramatized with chilling yet absurdly amusing 14 authenticity in Jules Feiffer's play *Grown Ups*. To get a closer look at what happens when men and women focus on different levels of talk in talking things out, let's look at what happens in this play.

15      Jake criticizes Louise for not responding when their daughter, Edie, called her. His comment leads to a fight even though they're both aware that this one incident is not in itself important.

JAKE:  Look, I don't care if it's important or not, when a kid calls its mother the mother should answer.
LOUISE:  Now I'm a bad mother.
JAKE:  I didn't say that.
LOUISE:  It's in your stare.
JAKE:  Is that another thing you know? My stare?
Louise ignores Jake's message—the question of whether or not she responded when Edie called—and goes for the metamessage: His implication that she's a bad mother, which Jake insistently disclaims. When Louise explains the signals she's reacting to, Jake not only discounts them but is angered at being held accountable not for what he said but for how he looked—his stare.

16      As the play goes on, Jake and Louise replay and intensify these patterns:

LOUISE:  If I'm such a terrible mother, do you want a divorce?
JAKE:  I do not think you're a terrible mother and no, thank you, I do not want a divorce. Why is it that whenever I bring up any difference between us you ask me if I want a divorce?

The more he denies any meaning beyond the message, the more she blows it up, the more adamantly he denies it, and so on:

JAKE:  I have brought up one thing that you do with Edie that I don't think you notice that I have noticed for some time but which I have deliberately not brought up before because I had hoped you would notice it for yourself and stop doing it and also—frankly, baby, I have to say this—I knew if I brought it up we'd get into exactly the kind of circular argument we're in right now. And I wanted to avoid it. But I haven't and we're in it, so now, with your permission, I'd like to talk about it.
LOUISE:  You don't see how that puts me down?
JAKE:  What?
LOUISE:  If you think I'm so stupid why do you go on living with me?
JAKE:  *Dammit! Why can't anything ever be simple around here?!*

It can't be simple because Louise and Jake are responding to different levels of communication. As in Bateson's example of the dual-control electric blanket with crossed wires, each one intensifies the energy going to a different aspect of the problem. Jake tries to clarify his point by over-elaborating it, which gives Louise further evidence that he's condescending to her, making it even less likely that she will address his point rather than his condescension.

What pushes Jake and Louise beyond anger to rage is their different 17 perspectives on metamessages. His refusal to admit that his statements have implications and overtones denies her authority over her own feelings. Her attempts to interpret what he didn't say and put the metamessage into the message makes him feel she's putting words into his mouth—denying his authority over his own meaning.

The same thing happens when Louise tells Jake that he is being ma- 18 nipulated by Edie:

LOUISE: Why don't you ever make her come to see you? Why do you always go to her?
JAKE: You want me to play power games with a nine year old? I want her to know I'm interested in her. Someone around here has to show interest in her.
LOUISE: You love her more than I do.
JAKE: I didn't say that.
LOUISE: Yes, you did.
JAKE: You don't know how to listen. You have never learned how to listen. It's as if listening to you is a foreign language.

Again, Louise responds to his implication—this time, that he loves Edie more because he runs when she calls. And yet again, Jake cries literal meaning, denying he meant any more than he said.

Throughout their argument, the point to Louise is her feelings—that 19 Jake makes her feel put down—but to him the point is her actions—that she doesn't always respond when Edie calls:

LOUISE: You talk about what I do to Edie, what do you think you do to me?
JAKE: This is not the time to go into what we do to each other.

Since she will talk only about the metamessage, and he will talk only 20 about the message, neither can get satisfaction from their talk, and they end up where they started—only angrier:
JAKE: That's not the point!
LOUISE: It's my point!
JAKE: It's hopeless!
LOUISE: Then get a divorce.

American conventional wisdom (and many of our parents and English teachers) tell us that meaning is conveyed by words, so men who tend to be literal about words are supported by conventional wisdom. They may not simply deny but actually miss the cues that are sent by how words are spoken. If they sense something about it, they may nonetheless discount what they sense. After all, it wasn't said. Sometimes that's a dodge—a plausible defense rather than a gut feeling. But sometimes it is a sincere conviction. Women are also likely to doubt the reality of what they sense. If they don't doubt it in their guts, they nonetheless may lack the arguments to support their position and thus are reduced to repeating, "You said it. You did so." Knowing that metamessages are a real and fundamental part of communication makes it easier to understand and justify what they feel.

21    An article in a popular newspaper reports that one of the five most common complaints of wives about their husbands is "He doesn't listen to me anymore." Another is "He doesn't talk to me anymore." Political scientist Andrew Hacker noted that lack of communication, while high on women's lists of reasons for divorce, is much less often mentioned by men. Since couples are parties to the same conversations, why are women more dissatisfied with them than men? Because what they expect is different, as well as what they see as the significance of talk itself.

22    First, let's consider the complaint "He doesn't talk to me."

23    One of the most common stereotypes of American men is the strong silent type. Jack Kroll, writing about Henry Fonda on the occasion of his death, used the phrases "quiet power," "abashed silences," "combustible catatonia," and "sense of power held in check." He explained that Fonda's goal was not to let anyone see "the wheels go around," not to let the "machinery" show. According to Kroll, the resulting silence was effective on stage but devastating to Fonda's family.

24    The image of a silent father is common and is often the model for the lover or husband. But what attracts us can become flypaper to which we are unhappily stuck. Many women find the strong silent type to be a lure as a lover but a lug as a husband. Nancy Schoenberger begins a poem with the lines "It was your silence that hooked me, / so like my father's." Adrienne Rich refers in a poem to the "husband who is frustratingly mute." Despite the initial attraction of such quintessentially male silence, it may begin to feel, to a woman in a long-term relationship, like a brick wall against which she is banging her head.

25    In addition to these images of male and female behavior—both the result and the cause of them—are differences in how women and men view the role of talk in relationships as well as how talk accomplishes its purpose. These differences have their roots in the settings in which men and women learn to have conversations among their peers, growing up.

26    Children whose parents have foreign accents don't speak with accents. They learn to talk like their peers. Little girls and little boys learn how to have conversations as they learn how to pronounce words from their playmates. Between the ages of five and fifteen, when children are learning to have conversations, they play mostly with friends of their own sex. So it's not surprising that they learn different ways of having and using conversations.

Anthropologists Daniel Maltz and Ruth Borker point out that boys 27
and girls socialize differently. Little girls tend to play in small groups or,
even more common, in pairs. Their social life usually centers around a best
friend, and friendships are made, maintained, and broken by talk—especially "secrets." If a little girl tells her friend's secret to another little girl,
she may find herself with a new best friend. The secrets themselves may
or may not be important, but the fact of telling them is all-important. It's
hard for newcomers to get into these tight groups, but anyone who is admitted is treated as an equal. Girls like to play cooperatively; if they can't
cooperate, the group breaks up.

Little boys tend to play in larger groups, often outdoors, and they 28
spend more time doing things than talking. It's easy for boys to get into the
group, but not everyone is accepted as an equal. Once in the group, boys
must jockey for their status in it. One of the most important ways they do
this is through talk: Verbal display such as telling stories and jokes, challenging and sidetracking the verbal displays of other boys, and with-
standing other boys' challenges in order to maintain their own story—and
status. Their talk is often competitive talk about who is best at what.

Feiffer's play is ironically named *Grown Ups* because adult men and 29
women struggling to communicate often sound like children: "You said
so!" "I did not!" The reason is that when they grow up, women and men
keep the divergent attitudes and habits they learned as children—which
they don't recognize as attitudes and habits but simply take for granted as
ways of talking.

Women want their partners to be a new and improved version of a best 30
friend. This gives them a soft spot for men who tell them secrets. As Jack
Nicholson once advised a guy in a movie: "Tell her about your troubled childhood—that always gets 'em." Men expect to do things together and don't feel
anything is missing if they don't have heart-to-heart talks all the time.

If they do have heart-to-heart talks, the meaning of those talks may be 31
opposite for men and women. To many women, the relationship is working as long as they can talk things out. To many men, the relationship isn't
working out if they have to keep working it over. If she keeps trying to get
talks going to save the relationship, and he keeps trying to avoid them because he sees them as weakening it, then each one's efforts to preserve the
relationship appear to the other as reckless endangerment.

If talks (of any kind) do get going, men's and women's ideas about 32
how to conduct them may be very different. For example, Dora is feeling
comfortable and close to Tom. She settles into a chair after dinner and begins to tell him about a problem at work. She expects him to ask questions
to show he's interested; reassure her that he understands and that what
she feels is normal; and return the intimacy by telling her a problem of his.
Instead, Tom sidetracks her story, cracks jokes about it, questions her

interpretation of the problem, and gives her advice about how to solve it and avoid such problems in the future.

33      All of these responses, natural to men, are unexpected to women, who interpret them in terms of their own habits—negatively. When Tom comments on side issues or cracks jokes, Dora thinks he doesn't care about what she's saying and isn't really listening. If he challenges her reading of what went on, she feels he is criticizing her and telling her she's crazy, when what she wants is to be reassured that she's not. If he tells her how to solve the problem, it makes her feel as if she's the patient to his doctor—a metamessage of condescension, echoing male one-upmanship compared to the female etiquette of equality. Because he doesn't volunteer information about his problems, she feels he's implying he doesn't have any.

34      His way of responding to her bid for intimacy makes her feel distant from him. She tries harder to regain intimacy the only way she knows how—by revealing more and more about herself. He tries harder by giving more insistent advice. The more problems she exposes, the more incompetent she feels, until they both see her as emotionally draining and problem-ridden. When his efforts to help aren't appreciated, he wonders why she asks for his advice if she doesn't want to take it. . . .

35      When women talk about what seems obviously interesting to them, their conversations often include reports of conversations. Tone of voice, timing, intonation, and wording are all re-created in the telling in order to explain—dramatize, really—the experience that is being reported. If men tell about an incident and give a brief summary instead of recreating what was said and how, the women often feel that the essence of the experience is being omitted. If the woman asks, "What exactly did he say?," and "How did he say it?," the man probably can't remember. If she continues to press him, he may feel as if he's being grilled.

36      All these different habits have repercussions when the man and the woman are talking about their relationship. He feels out of his element, even one down. She claims to recall exactly what he said, and what she said, and in what sequence, and she wants him to account for what he said. He can hardly account for it since he has forgotten exactly what was said—if not the whole conversation. She secretly suspects he's only pretending not to remember, and he secretly suspects that she's making up the details.

37      One woman reported such a problem as being a matter of her boyfriend's poor memory. It is unlikely, however, that his problem was poor memory in general. The question is what types of material each person remembers or forgets.

38      Frances was sitting at her kitchen table talking to Edward, when the toaster did something funny. Edward began to explain why it did it. Frances tried to pay attention, but very early in his explanation, she realized she was completely lost. She felt very stupid. And indications were that he thought so too.

Later that day they were taking a walk. He was telling her about a dif-  39
ficult situation in his office that involved a complex network of interrela-
tionships among a large number of people. Suddenly he stopped and said,
"I'm sure you can't keep track of all these people." "Of course I can," she
said, and she retraced his story with all the characters in place, all the details right. He was genuinely impressed. She felt very smart.

How could Frances be both smart and stupid? Did she have a good  40
memory or a bad one? Frances's and Edward's abilities to follow, remember, and recount depended on the subject—and paralleled her parents'
abilities to follow and remember. Whenever Frances told her parents about
people in her life, her mother could follow with no problem, but her father
got lost as soon as she introduced a second character. "Now who was
that?" he'd ask. "Your boss?" "No, my boss is Susan. This was my friend."
Often he'd still be in the previous story. But whenever she told them about
her work, it was her mother who would get lost as soon as she mentioned
a second step: "That was your tech report?" "No, I handed my tech report
in last month. This was a special project."

Frances's mother and father, like many men and women, had honed  41
their listening and remembering skills in different arenas. Their experience
talking to other men and other women gave them practice in following different kinds of talk.

Knowing whether and how we are likely to report events later influ-  42
ences whether and how we pay attention when they happen. As women
listen to and take part in conversations, knowing they may talk about them
later makes them more likely to pay attention to exactly what is said and
how. Since most men aren't in the habit of making such reports, they are
less likely to pay much attention at the time. On the other hand, many
women aren't in the habit of paying attention to scientific explanations
and facts because they don't expect to have to perform in public by reciting them—just as those who aren't in the habit of entertaining others by
telling jokes "can't" remember jokes they've heard, even though they listened carefully enough to enjoy them.

So women's conversations with their women friends keep them in  43
training for talking about their relationships with men, but many men
come to such conversations with no training at all—and an uncomfortable
sense that this really isn't their event.

Most of us place enormous emphasis on the importance of a primary  44
relationship. We regard the ability to maintain such relationships as a
sign of mental health—our contemporary metaphor for being a good
person.

Yet our expectations of such relationships are nearly—maybe in fact—  45
impossible. When primary relationships are between women and men,
male-female differences contribute to the impossibility. We expect partners
to be both romantic interests and best friends. Though women and men

may have fairly similar expectations for romantic interests, obscuring their differences when relationships begin, they have very different ideas about how to be friends, and these are the differences that mount over time.

46      In conversations between friends who are not lovers, small misunderstandings can be passed over or diffused by breaks in contact. But in the context of a primary relationship, differences can't be ignored, and the pressure cooker of continued contact keeps both people stewing in the juice of accumulated minor misunderstandings. And stylistic differences are sure to cause misunderstandings—not, ironically, in matters such as sharing values and interests or understanding each other's philosophies of life. These large and significant yet palpable issues can be talked about and agreed on. It is far harder to achieve congruence—and much more surprising and troubling that it is hard—in the simple day-to-day matters of the automatic rhythms and nuances of talk. Nothing in our backgrounds or in the media (the present-day counterpart to religion or grandparents' teachings) prepares us for this failure. If two people share so much in terms of point of view and basic values, how can they continually get into fights about insignificant matters?

47      If you find yourself in such a situation and you don't know about differences in conversational style, you assume something's wrong with your partner, or you for having chosen your partner. At best, if you are forward thinking and generous minded, you may absolve individuals and blame the relationship. But if you know about differences in conversational style, you can accept that there are differences in habits and assumptions about how to have conversation, show interest, be considerate, and so on. You may not always correctly interpret your partner's intentions, but you will know that if you get a negative impression, it may not be what was intended—and neither are your responses unfounded. If he says he really is interested even though he doesn't seem to be, maybe you should believe what he says and not what you sense.

48      Sometimes explaining assumptions can help. If a man starts to tell a woman what to do to solve her problem, she may say, "Thanks for the advice but I really don't want to be told what to do. I just want you to listen and say you understand." A man might want to explain, "If I challenge you, it's not to prove you wrong; it's just my way of paying attention to what you're telling me." Both may try either or both to modify their ways of talking and to try to accept what the other does. The important thing is to know that what seem like bad intentions may really be good intentions expressed in a different conversational style. We have to give up our conviction that, as Robin Lakoff put it, "Love means never having to say 'What do you mean?' "

*1986*

## QUESTIONS FOR DISCUSSION

### Content

a. A key word in this essay is *metamessages* (paragraph 4). How does Tannen define this word? In the next few paragraphs, underline or point to phrases that illustrate what metamessages are.

b. Tannen asserts that "[a] lot of trouble is caused . . . by . . . pronouns" (paragraph 12). What kind of trouble is this? Why is it a problem?

c. Does the fact that Tannen is a woman influence how she analyzes men's and women's talk? If your answer is yes, point to several instances in the essay in which a gender bias seems apparent.

d. What are the specific kinds of communication that Tannen compares and contrasts?

e. Tannen occasionally blames stereotypes, such as the "strong silent" stereotype for men (paragraph 23), for causing misunderstandings between men and women. What are some other stereotypes of men and women that she cites? Why do these stereotypes cause misunderstandings?

f. According to Tannen, what do women value or notice as important in a conversation with a man? What do men value or notice as important?

g. Why are women better at remembering stories about people or events and men better at remembering stories about scientific explanations or facts? Do you think that the way men and women remember and tell stories is a factor of biology (i.e., women remember people/events better because they are female) or of cultural training (i.e., women remember people/events better because they have been taught to listen this way)?

### Strategy and Style

h. Tannen uses many examples to show how men and women miscommunicate. What is the effect on you as you read all these examples?

i. Does the author use too many examples? If so, what example(s) would you remove and why? How would the removal of the example(s) improve the logic or readability of the essay? If not, how do the examples work together to create a tightly controlled logic and structure?

j. Occasionally, Tannen uses a metaphor or simile to evoke an image. What are the images created and the effects of phrases such as "the barometers to check" (paragraph 8), "you can't roll your antennae back in" (paragraph 9), and "like an innocent flock of birds on a radar screen" (paragraph 10)?

k. Tannen uses simple, direct language and presents examples as anecdotes. What would happen if she had written this in the academic language of sociologists or linguists?

## ENGAGING THE TEXT

a. In paragraph 3, Tannen asserts that "women often have a relatively greater need for involvement, and men a relatively greater need for independence. Being understood without saying what you mean gives a payoff in involvement, and that is why women value it so highly." Explain how this statement applies or does not apply to you.

b. In your own experiences, what differences have you found in the ways men and women talk to each other? Describe a relationship you have with a member of the opposite sex in which there has been miscommunication. (While a romantic relationship may be the first thing you think of, you can also use a friendship or an acquaintance with a coworker, student, or teacher.) Compare your example to those used by Tannen to illustrate miscommunication.

## SUGGESTIONS FOR SUSTAINED WRITING

a. Write an analysis of a male/female conversation in a film, novel, or short story. Base your analysis on the metamessages in the conversation. As a first step in this assignment, reread Tannen's essay and make a list of the metamessages she describes. Use this list both to choose a suitable conversation and to analyze it. Then explain how these metamessages alter or make more complex the main message(s). You might also extend your analysis to an interpretation of the entire film or literary work.

b. Tannen talks about obstacles relating to the way in which men and women talk to each other. Pick two other groups that need to communicate better and explain what obstacles stand in their way. For example, you might explain what might hinder communication between a college student and a professor, an immigrant parent and a child born in this country, a member of the clergy and a layperson, a doctor and a patient, or a mechanic and a car owner. For more inspiration, read Minatoya's "Discordant Fruit" (this chapter) and/or Amy Tan's "Mother Tongue" (Chapter 11).

c. Find the book by Daniel Maltz and Ruth Borker referred to in paragraph 27. Read the book and write an extended response to it, citing both the book and Tannen's essay. Base your response on your general reaction to the book, on a particular passage that interests you, or on the question, "Do you think the differences in socialization are caused by biological differences or by environmental factors such as home life, school life, culture, etc.?"

# Two Views of the Mississippi

Mark Twain

*Mark Twain (1835–1910) was, of course, the pen name of Samuel Langhorne Clemens, the Missourian who learned to pilot Mississippi riverboats and who grew to become one of America's leading humorists, social critics, and men of letters. Twain recorded his experiences in numerous newspaper features and columns and in several books, including* Life on the Mississippi *(1883),* The Adventures of Tom Sawyer *(1876), and his masterpiece,* The Adventures of Huckleberry Finn *(1885). Indeed, for some literary historians, the true American novel has its beginnings in the work of Twain. In the selection that follows, Twain contrasts his views of the Mississippi first as a novice and then as an experienced river pilot.*

Now when I had mastered the language of this water, and had come to know every trifling feature that bordered the great river as familiarly as I knew the letters of the alphabet, I had made a valuable acquisition. But I had lost something, too. I had lost something which could never be restored to me while I lived. All the grace, the beauty, the poetry, had gone out of the majestic river! I still keep in mind a certain wonderful sunset which I witnessed when steamboating was new to me. A broad expanse of the river was turned to blood; in the middle distance the red hue brightened into gold, through which a solitary log came floating black and conspicuous; in one place a long, slanting mark lay sparkling upon the water; in another the surface was broken by boiling, tumbling rings, that were as many-tinted as an opal; where the ruddy flush was faintest, was a smooth spot that was covered with graceful circles and radiating lines, ever so delicately traced; the shore on our left was densely wooded, and the somber shadow that fell from this forest was broken in one place by a long, ruffled trail that shone like silver; and high above the forest wall a clean-stemmed dead tree waved a single leafy bough that glowed like a flame in the unobstructed splendor that was flowing from the sun. There were graceful curves, reflected images, woody heights, soft distances; and over the whole scene, far and near, the dissolving lights drifted steadily, enriching it every passing moment with new marvels of coloring. 1

I stood like one bewitched. I drank it in, in a speechless rapture. The world was new to me, and I had never seen anything like this at home. But as I have said, a day came when I began to cease from noting the glories and the charms which the moon and the sun and the twilight wrought upon the river's face; another day came when I ceased altogether to note them. Then, if that sunset scene had been repeated, I should have looked upon it without rapture, and should have commented upon it, inwardly, after this fashion: "This sun means that we are going to have wind tomorrow; that floating log means that the river is rising, small thanks to it; that 2

**235**

slanting mark on the water refers to a bluff reef which is going to kill some-body's steamboat one of these nights, if it keeps on stretching out like that; those tumbling 'boils' show a dissolving bar and a changing channel there; the lines and circles in the slick water over yonder are a warning that that troublesome place is shoaling up dangerously; that silver streak in the shadow of the forest is the 'break' from a new snag, and he has located himself in the very best place he could have found to fish for steamboats; that tall dead tree, with a single living branch, is not going to last long, and then how is a body ever going to get through this blind place at night with-out the friendly old landmark?"

3      No, the romance and beauty were all gone from the river. All the value any feature of it had for me now was the amount of usefulness it could fur-nish toward compassing the safe piloting of a steamboat. Since those days, I have pitied doctors from my heart. What does the lovely flush in a beauty's cheek mean to a doctor but a "break" that ripples above some deadly disease? Are not all her visible charms sown thick with what are to him the signs and symbols of hidden decay? Does he ever see her beauty at all, or doesn't he simply view her professionally, and comment upon her unwholesome condition all to himself? And doesn't he sometimes wonder whether he has gained most or lost most by learning his trade?

## QUESTIONS FOR DISCUSSION

### Content

a. Why does Twain pity doctors?
b. What purpose does paragraph 3 serve? Why does Twain compare the work of a steamboat pilot to that of a doctor? In what way is the con-duct of their work similar?
c. Twain fully describes his view of the river as a novice and then goes on to talk about his perception of it as a trained pilot. Does this pattern serve him better than discussing various aspects of the river point by point?
d. What details does Twain offer to prove that at one time in his life the river held grace, beauty, and poetry for him?

### Strategy and Style

e. Twain's thesis, which appears in paragraph 1, is presented in an obvi-ous and straightforward manner. How does it help determine the orga-nization of the rest of the piece?
f. The first paragraph is filled with descriptive language that captures a subjective, almost rhapsodic, view of the river. How would you charac-terize the language in paragraph 2?

g. What use does paragraph 2 make of the details Twain has already introduced in paragraph 1?

## ENGAGING THE TEXT

a. Brainstorm a list of metaphors and similes that Twain might have used to describe the Mississippi River. For example, "the Mississippi River is a _____," or "the Mississippi River is like a _____."
b. Summarize Twain's essay by dividing his comments about the Mississippi River into two columns, one column for each way the river can be viewed. Add your own items to the lists. Can the river be viewed only in two ways? In what other ways can it be seen?

## SUGGESTIONS FOR SUSTAINED WRITING

a. Twain's training as a pilot seems to have had a negative effect in that it took the romance out of his view of the river. However, learning more about a subject may enhance one's appreciation of it. Can you relate an instance from your own experience to illustrate this notion? For example, mastering the fundamentals of swimming may have given you the confidence you needed to try skin diving. Tuning your first engine may have motivated you to learn more about auto mechanics in general.
b. Scan the topics and titles of the essays in Chapter 10: Argument and Persuasion. Look for an essay that takes a position with which you disagree. After you have read that selection carefully, write an essay in which you explain whether and to what extent the argument you just read changed or modified your original opinion. If what you read changed your opinion only slightly or not at all, write an essay in which you explain why you continue to hold your original position.
c. As children, we become excited, enraptured, and even mystified by the rituals and customs associated with important religious or national holidays: Christmas, Yom Kippur, Thanksgiving, Halloween, the Fourth of July. Think about the holiday you found most exciting as a child. Has your view of it changed? Write an essay in which you define that holiday and explain why and how your vision of that holiday has or has not changed. To lend authority to your essay, include facts, ideas, and opinions from secondary sources found in your library or on the Internet.

# Discordant Fruit

Lydia Minatoya

## BIOGRAPHY

*Lydia Minatoya (b. 1950) was born in Albany, New York. Her parents had immigrated to the United States from Japan and had moved from the West Coast to New York. Growing up so far away from relatives in California and Japan made Minatoya curious about her family and its history, so, after earning a Ph.D. in psychology from the University of Maryland in 1981 and teaching briefly in Boston, she left to teach and travel in Japan, China, and Nepal. That trip prompted her to write* Talking to High Monks in the Snow: An Asian-American Odyssey *(1992), which won the 1991 PEN/Jerard Fund Award. In this memoir, Minatoya focuses on her experiences growing up in a predominantly European-ancestry area and on her travels in Asia. "Discordant Fruit" is a chapter from this book; in it, Minatoya describes the awkward cultural tension she experiences during dinner with her upper-class relatives in Japan.*

1   Once, in a cross-cultural training manual, I came across a riddle. In Japan, a young man and woman meet and fall in love. They decide they would like to marry. The young man goes to his mother and describes the situation. "I will visit the girl's family," says the mother. "I will seek their approval." After some time, a meeting between mothers is arranged. The boy's mother goes to the girl's ancestral house. The girl's mother has prepared tea. The women talk about the fine spring weather: Will this be a good year for cherry blossoms? The girl's mother serves a plate of fruit. Bananas are sliced and displayed in an exquisite design. Marriage never is mentioned. After the tea, the boy's mother goes home. "I am so sorry," she tells her son. "The other family has declined the match."

2       In the training manual, the following question was posed. How did the boy's mother know the marriage was unacceptable? That is easy, I thought when I read it. To a Japanese, the answer is obvious. Bananas do not go well with tea.

3       All of my life, I have been fluent in communicating through discordant fruit.

4       "You're not serious about applying to be a foreign exchange student!" exclaims a high school teacher. "The point is to sponsor an *American* kid." On my application, I deliberately misspell the teacher's name. I cross it out with an unsightly splotch. "Take that you mean narrow man," I gloat in triumph.

5       "Your mother is so deferential, so *quiet*," says a boyfriend. "Women like that drive me crazy." *His* mother is an attorney. That morning, I scorch his scrambled eggs. I hide the sports section of the Sunday news. "No insight, loudmouth fool," I mutter. Vengeance, I think, is mine.

The Japanese raise their daughters differently than their sons. *"Gam-* 6
*batte!"* they exhort their sons. "Have courage, be like the carp, swim upstream!" *"Kiotsukete,"* they caution their daughters. "Be careful, be modest,
keep safe."

In the old stories, men are warriors: Fierce and bold. But a lady never 7
lunges to slash the throat of an assailant. Instead, she writes a poem about
harsh winter; how it can snap a slender stalk. Then she kills *herself* in
protest. How the old stories galled me!

My mother was raised in a world such as this, in a house of tradition 8
and myth. And although she has traveled across continents, oceans, and
time, although she considers herself a modern woman—a believer in the
sunlight of science—it is a world that surrounds her still. Feudal Japan
floats around my mother. Like an unwanted pool of ectoplasm, it quivers
with supernatural might. It followed her into our American home and
governed my girlhood life.

And so, I was shaped. In that feudal code, all females were silent and 9
yielding. Even their possessions were accorded more rights. For, if mis-
treated, belongings were granted an annual holiday when they could
spring into life and complain.

And so, I was haunted. If I left my clothes on the floor, or my bicycle 10
in the rain; if I yanked on my comb with roughness; if it splintered and lost
its teeth (and I did these things often and deliberately, trying to challenge
their spell); then my misdeeds pursued me in dreams.

Emitting a hair-raising keening, my mittens would mourn for their 11
mates. The floors I had scuffed, the doors I had slammed, herded me into
the street. Broken dishes and dulled scissors joined them to form a large,
shrill, and reproachful parade of dutiful ill-treated items. How I envied
white children and the simple absolution of a spanking.

While other children were learning that in America you get what you 12
ask for, I was being henpecked by inanimate objects. While other children
were learning to speak their minds, I was locked in a losing struggle for
dominance with my clothing, my toys, and my tools.

The objects meant me no harm; they meant to humble and educate 13
me. "Ownership," they told me "means obligation, caretaking, reciproc-
ity." And although I was a resistant student, in time I was trained. Well-
maintained, my possessions live long, useful, and mercifully quiet lives
of service.

The consequence, however, is that I cannot view my belongings as 14
mere conveniences. They cannot serve as simple timesavers. For me, ac-
quisitiveness holds little allure. The indebtedness is much too great.

I am a woman who apologizes to her furniture. "Excuse me," I say 15
when I bump into a chair. My voice resonates with solicitude. In America,
such behavior is viewed as slightly loony.

16      I am a woman caught between standards of East and West. "I disagree," I say to elders, to the men in my life. My voice rises and cracks with shame. "Razor-tongue," relatives say with the pleasure of knowing. "No wonder she still is unmarried."

17      All these incongruities came flooding back while visiting my Japanese family. The pull to be deferent. The push to be bold. The tension and richness between.

18      In the evening, after we left the patriarch's house, Sachikosan prepared a feast. She kneeled before us, cooking a huge skillet of sukiyaki. She plucked plump morsels of tender beef from the pot and popped them onto my plate. Her teenaged daughters slipped shyly in and out of the room, bearing flasks of sake and platters of sushi.

19      Tadao-san, Yoshi, Mark, and I were seated at the table. Sachiko-san and the girls ate in the kitchen. "Where are the other women?" Mark asked Yoshi. "Yuri-chan is the guest," he replied. "She is being paid the house's high honor."

20      Loosened by the sake, chaffing from days of communicating only with me or through me, Mark bombarded Yoshi with questions. Did Yoshi like American rock and roll? Who were his favorite performers?

21      Uncomfortable with being the focus of attention, Yoshi attempted to generalize every query. "How familiar are Japanese youth with popular American music?" he translated for Tadao-san.

22      But Tadao-san was not fooled. Excluded in his own house, shunned in favor of his translator, Tadao-san grew increasingly irritable.

23      "How long has this one been riding autobikes?" he suddenly interjected. "Has he ever had an accident? Would he know how to make repairs should the autobike become disabled?"

24      At first, the American in me grinned. Clearly Tadao-san had grown weary of his subordinate role. He was asserting his authority. "How are you providing for Yuri-chan's safety?" his questions implied. "Do not forget you are welcome only in so far as you provide service to members of my house."

25      But quickly, the Japanese in me surfaced. The evening was not going smoothly and I was responsible.

26      "You're putting Yoshi on the spot!" I hissed into Mark's ear. "After all, he is not your host. Address your comments to the household head and try to act with more deference!"

27      "No kidding!" exclaimed Mark. He thought everything had been going along just fine.

28      I smiled apologetically at Yoshi and Tadao-san. My annoyance and
29  bossy instructiveness had not gone unnoticed. I flushed mightily. I knew my behavior was most unseemly for a lady.

30      "So Tadao-san," said Mark heartily, "what do you think about all these protests of American military presence in Japan?"

Yoshi reeled in horror. How could he translate, with delicacy, such an openly confrontational question?

"Don't you think it's a little, uhmmm, *ungrateful?*" continued Mark. 31 "After all, by picking up the bill for your country's defense, America has allowed Japan to become an economic competitor."

"How can you be so rude!" I croaked in anger. I staggered under the 32 responsibility of having brought a boor into the ancestral house.

"Relax. You're overreacting," snapped Mark. "Besides, this is my con- 33 versation." Mark was growing tired of my conduct coaching. I could hardly blame him. Only a few days earlier, as we sat in a coffee shop and I instructed him on the proper method of ordering, I had overheard a comment. *"Rimokon,"* a woman had murmured to her companion. She had nodded in Mark's direction. *Rimokon* is a shortened form of *rimoto-kontororu*. It is the Japanese pronunciation of remote control: Slang for a henpecked man.

Tadao-san looked questioningly at Yoshi. What was the meaning of all 34 this clamor? Yoshi rushed to translate.

"This is a most difficult question," said Tadao-san after hearing an 35 edited translation.

I cringed. When a Japanese says a question is difficult he is requesting 36 release from an uncomfortable situation.

"I work on a military base," said Mark, "and the sentiment is that 37 Japan is complaining about a free ride."

I wished we never had left the subject of rock and roll. I wished I were 38 not the honored guest. I wished I was with Sachiko-san, in the refuge of the kitchen.

Tadao-san and Yoshi caucused for a while. "Some Japanese believe 39 that America's motives are not fully benevolent," said Yoshi. His voice hesitated with the task of defusing the situation. "They say Americans do not fully view Asians as people. Japan and her people are expendable. Perhaps the point is not to defend Japan but rather to move the site of possible conflict. Asia may be a buffer zone. If war is based from Japan, South Korea, or the Philippines, the soil and civilians of these countries, not America, would be the first at risk."

"I don't know about that," muttered Mark.                                40

"In each country, there are prejudices," said Tadao-san. "We Japanese 41 are prejudiced against the Koreans. I have read your history. Has there not been discrimination against Japanese in America? Is there not discrimination today?"

"No," said Mark flatly.                                                  42

"Of course there is!" I cried. We argued hotly for a minute. Then, re- 43 membering that I was trying to act like a credit to my mother's upbringing, I demurred.

"Mark and I share slight disagreement about this point," I murmured 44 with sudden modesty.

45      Perhaps Mark was right. Perhaps I was overreacting. Perhaps among men, even in Japan, verbal confrontations and positioning for power are acceptable social forms. Perhaps when two samurai meet, they must engage in hostile sword play and find themselves well matched, before they can be friends.

46      The exchange of political opinions left me shaken, but Mark, Tadao-san, and Yoshi seemed unscathed. They raised their cups and had a seemingly splendid time.

47      But then again, perhaps I was right. Before the evening ended, Tadao-san slipped me an envelope. "In case you wish to leave the autobike, to continue, alone, by train," he said. Inside, was a staggering sum of money.

48      After midnight, Sachiko-san led me to her daughters' room. It was the room of teenagers, a sweet jumble of stuffed animals and pinups of popular singers. Several pencil sketches were carefully mounted on one wall. Through a window, I saw the crescent moon.

49      "Come Yuri-chan." Sachiko-san led me to the sketches. "Come and see your past."

50      The drawings were light, romantic renderings, of princesses all gowned and gloved.

51      "Your mother lived here briefly, when she was a girl," Sachiko-san explained. "These are her drawings. My daughters found them in storage and thought them pretty." She paused in reflection. "Your young mother's dreams have been rescued and honored, mounted here on my little ones' wall."

52      Through the open window came the sound of a bamboo flute. Sachiko-san looked at me with the warmth of a sister. She touched my hair gently and smiled. "The hearts of young girls," she whispered to me, "their visions, forever, the same."

## QUESTIONS FOR DISCUSSION

### Content

a. What does the title mean, and why is it appropriate?

b. In paragraph 3 Minatoya says that she has "been fluent in communicating through discordant fruit." What are some of the examples of this communication she includes?

c. According to Minatoya, how are Japanese sons and daughters raised differently?

d. What are the main attributes of a typical American girl that Minatoya finds appealing? How are these traits seen as negative in traditional Japanese culture?

e. Why does Minatoya feel a sense of obligation to her possessions?

f. What are the "American me" (paragraph 24) and the "Japanese me" (paragraph 25)? How are they in conflict?

## Strategy and Style

g. Why is the comparison/contrast format effective in this essay? What exactly is being compared and contrasted?
h. How does the example about her possessions (paragraphs 9–14) help Minatoya make a point about Japanese women?
i. Where does Minatoya use humor and irony to make a point? Identify specific paragraphs. What are the points she makes with humor?
j. What storytelling technique does Minatoya use to make this unlike a "typical" essay?
k. What is the purpose of the last section (paragraphs 48–52)? How does it comment on the rest of the essay?

## ENGAGING THE TEXT

a. Describe your relationship with your possessions. Do you feel responsible toward them? What do your possessions say about you? Refer to Minatoya's essay in your response.
b. Explain what Minatoya would say is the relationship of language—body language as well as words—to behavior. How is some language appropriate and some language inappropriate, depending on one's culture?

## SUGGESTIONS FOR SUSTAINED WRITING

a. Compare and contrast two cultures with which you are familiar. If your family recently emigrated to the United States, your choice is easy, but you can also compare and contrast more subtly different cultures, such as home to school, one block in your neighborhood to another block, a rural area to an urban area, or one part of the country to another. Try some of the techniques that Minatoya uses, such as dialogue, personal examples, and humor, to make your essay interesting. Whatever subjects you choose, limit your discussion by focusing on three or four of the same aspects of each culture.
b. Compare and contrast acceptable boys'/men's behavior and girls'/women's behavior as you have observed it in your family, neighborhood, and school. Define what you see as the rules for acceptable behavior for each sex. If you see any rules being challenged or changed,

discuss these changes. To gather more information and insights about your topic, look to the essays by Tannen and Sanders in this chapter and the one by Noda in Chapter 5.

c. Do we have different expectations for boys and girls as they are growing up? Do boys and girls attain maturity at different rates and in different ways? Making reference to research on child development found in your library or on the Internet, write an essay that explains three or four areas of difference concerning the rate and/or way boys and girls mature. For example, are boys or girls harder to toilet train? Are boys less sociable than girls, or is the opposite true? Which of the sexes seems to learn language faster?

# The Men We Carry in Our Minds

## Scott Russell Sanders

*Scott Russell Sanders (b. 1945) was born in Tennessee and is now a professor of English at Indiana University. Among his favorite subjects are nature and the American wilderness, about which he has written several books, including* Wilderness Plots: Tales about the Settlement of the American Land *(1983),* Audobon's Early Years *(1984), and* In Limestone Country *(1985). His most recent works include* Staying Put: Making a Home in a Restless World *(1993) and* Writing from the Center *(1995).*

*Sanders first published "The Men We Carry in Our Minds" in a periodical called the* Milkweed Chronicle *in 1984. It also has been anthologized in Sanders's* Paradise of Bombs, *a collection of essays on violence, which was published in 1987. In it, Sanders does more than contrast images of poor men and rich men, men and women. He comes to understand that no matter what the sex or class, people yearn "for a say over their future." In the process, he reveals much about himself.*

1   The first men, besides my father, I remember seeing were black convicts and white guards, in the cottonfield across the road from our farm on the outskirts of Memphis. I must have been three or four. The prisoners wore dingy gray-and-black zebra suits, heavy as canvas, sodden with sweat. Hatless, stooped, they chopped weeds in the fierce heat, row after row, breathing the acrid dust of boll-weevil poison. The overseers wore dazzling white shirts and broad shadowy hats. The oiled barrels of their shotguns flashed in the sunlight. Their faces in memory are utterly blank. Of course those men, white and black, have become for me an emblem of racial hatred. But they have also come to stand for the twin poles of my early vision of manhood—the brute toiling animal and the boss.

When I was a boy, the men I knew labored with their bodies. They were  2
marginal farmers, just scraping by, or welders, steel workers, carpenters;
they swept floors, dug ditches, mined coal, or drove trucks, their forearms
ropy with muscle; they trained horses, stoked furnaces, built tires, stood on
assembly lines wrestling parts onto cars and refrigerators. They got up before light, worked all day long whatever the weather, and when they came
home at night they looked as though somebody had been whipping them.
In the evenings and on weekends they worked on their own places, tilling
gardens that were lumpy with clay, fixing broken-down cars, hammering
on houses that were always too drafty, too leaky, too small.

The bodies of the men I knew were twisted and maimed in ways visi-  3
ble and invisible. The nails of their hands were black and split, the hands
tattooed with scars. Some had lost fingers. Heavy lifting had given many of
them finicky backs and guts weak from hernias. Racing against conveyor
belts had given them ulcers. Their ankles and knees ached from years of
standing on concrete. Anyone who had worked for long around machines
was hard of hearing. They squinted, and the skin of their faces was creased
like the leather of old work gloves. There were times, studying them, when
I dreaded growing up. Most of them coughed, from dust or cigarettes, and
most of them drank cheap wine or whiskey, so their eyes looked bloodshot
and bruised. The fathers of my friends always seemed older than the mothers. Men wore out sooner. Only women lived into old age.

As a boy I also knew another sort of men, who did not sweat and break  4
down like mules. They were soldiers, and so far as I could tell they scarcely
worked at all. During my early school years we lived on a military base,
an arsenal in Ohio, and every day I saw GIs in the guardshacks, on the
stoops of barracks, at the wheels of olive drab Chevrolets. The chief fact of
their lives was boredom. Long after I left the Arsenal I came to recognize
the sour smell the soldiers gave off as that of souls in limbo. They were all
waiting—for wars, for transfers, for leaves, for promotions, for the end of
their hitch—like so many braves waiting for the hunt to begin. Unlike the
warriors of older tribes, however, they would have no say about when the
battle would start or how it would be waged. Their waiting was broken
only when they practiced for war. They fired guns at targets, drove tanks
across the churned-up fields of the military reservation, set off bombs in
the wrecks of old fighter planes. I knew this was all play. But I also felt certain that when the hour for killing arrived, they would kill. When the real
shooting started, many of them would die. This was what soldiers were *for*,
just as a hammer was for driving nails.

Warriors and toilers: those seemed, in my boyhood vision, to be the  5
chief destinies for men. They weren't the only destinies, as I learned from
having a few male teachers, from reading books, and from watching television. But the men on television—the politicians, the astronauts, the generals, the savvy lawyers, the philosophical doctors, the bosses who gave

orders to both soldiers and laborers—seemed as remote and unreal to me as the figures in tapestries. I could no more imagine growing up to become one of these cool, potent creatures than I could imagine becoming a prince.

6        A nearer and more hopeful example was that of my father, who had escaped from a red-dirt farm to a tire factory, and from the assembly line to the front office. Eventually he dressed in a white shirt and tie. He carried himself as if he had been born to work with his mind. But his body, remembering the earlier years of slogging work, began to give out on him in his fifties, and it quit on him entirely before he turned sixty-five. Even such partial escape from man's fate as he had accomplished did not seem possible for most of the boys I knew. They joined the Army, stood in line for jobs in the smoky plants, helped build highways. They were bound to work as their fathers had worked, killing themselves or preparing to kill others.

7        A scholarship enabled me not only to attend college, a rare enough feat in my circle, but even to study in a university meant for the children of the rich. Here I met for the first time young men who had assumed from birth that they would lead lives of comfort and power. And for the first time I met women who told me that men were guilty of having kept all the joys and privileges of the earth for themselves. I was baffled. What privileges? What joys? I thought about the maimed, dismal lives of most of the men back home. What had they stolen from their wives and daughters? The right to go five days a week, twelve months a year, for thirty or forty years to a steel mill or a coal mine? The right to drop bombs and die in war? The right to feel every leak in the roof, every gap in the fence, every cough in the engine, as a wound they must mend? The right to feel, when the layoff comes or the plant shuts down, not only afraid but ashamed?

8        I was slow to understand the deep grievances of women. This was because, as a boy, I had envied them. Before college, the only people I had ever known who were interested in art or music or literature, the only ones who read books, the only ones who ever seemed to enjoy a sense of ease and grace were the mothers and daughters. Like the menfolk, they fretted about money, they scrimped and made-do. But, when the pay stopped coming in, they were not the ones who had failed. Nor did they have to go to war, and that seemed to me a blessed fact. By comparison with the narrow, ironclad days of fathers, there was an expansiveness, I thought, in the days of mothers. They went to see neighbors, to shop in town, to run errands at school, at the library, at church. No doubt, had I looked harder at their lives, I would have envied them less. It was not my fate to become a woman, so it was easier for me to see the graces. Few of them held jobs outside the home, and those who did filled thankless roles as clerks and waitresses. I didn't see, then, what a prison a house could be, since houses seemed to me brighter, handsomer places than any factory. I did not realize—because such things were never spoken of—how often women suffered from men's bullying. I did learn about the wretchedness of abandoned wives, single mothers, widows; but I also learned about the

wretchedness of lone men. Even then I could see how exhausting it was for a mother to cater all day to the needs of young children. But if I had been asked, as a boy, to choose between tending a baby and tending a machine, I think I would have chosen the baby. (Having now tended both, I know I would choose the baby.)

So I was baffled when the women at college accused me and my sex of having cornered the world's pleasures. I think something like my bafflement has been felt by other boys (and by girls as well) who grew up in dirt-poor farm country, in mining country, in black ghettos, in Hispanic barrios, in the shadows of factories, in Third World nations—any place where the fate of men is as grim and bleak as the fate of women. Toilers and warriors. I realize now how ancient these identities are, how deep the tug they exert on men, the undertow of a thousand generations. The miseries I saw, as a boy, in the lives of nearly all men I continue to see in the lives of many— the body-breaking toil, the tedium, the call to be tough, the humiliating powerlessness, the battle for a living and for territory. 9

When the women I met at college thought about the joys and privileges of men, they did not carry in their minds the sort of men I had known in my childhood. They thought of their fathers, who were bankers, physicians, architects, stockbrokers, the big wheels of the big cities. These fathers rode the train to work or drove cars that cost more than any of my childhood houses. They were attended from morning to night by female helpers, wives and nurses and secretaries. They were never laid off, never short of cash at month's end, never lined up for welfare. These fathers made decisions that mattered. They ran the world. 10

The daughters of such men wanted to share in this power, this glory. So did I. They yearned for a say over their future, for jobs worthy of their abilities, for the right to live at peace, unmolested, whole. Yes, I thought, yes yes. The difference between me and these daughters was that they saw me, because of my sex, as destined from birth to become like their fathers, and therefore as an enemy to their desires. But I knew better. I wasn't an enemy, in fact or in feeling. I was an ally. If I had known, then, how to tell them so, would they have believed me? Would they now? 11

*1984*

## QUESTIONS FOR DISCUSSION

### Content

a. In what ways did the soldiers Sanders observed in his youth resemble the laborers he knew? In what ways were they different?
b. Consider the essay's title. What other people does Sanders contrast in this essay?

c. How did Sanders's view of women change after he went to college? Why did it change?
d. Why was the author "slow to understand the deep grievances of women" (paragraph 8)?
e. What was the vision of men carried by the women the author met at college?
f. In what way or ways was the author like these women?
g. What are the purpose and thesis of this essay?

## Strategy and Style

h. How would you describe this essay's tone and its audience?
i. Where in this selection does the author use description? Classification?
j. The essay is enriched by Sanders's use of figurative language. Find examples of metaphor, simile, or other figures of speech and explain how they help the author make or develop a point.
k. Why does the author begin this piece with an image of "racial hatred"? Is his introduction effective? Why or why not?
l. Why does Sanders end this essay with a question? Does this question provide a logical conclusion to what has come before, or does it open up a new topic of discussion?

## ENGAGING THE TEXT

a. What is the first image of men or women that you held in your mind? Explain one way in which that image changed as you matured. Refer to Saunders's essay in your response.
b. Saunders says that the "bodies of men [he] knew were twisted and maimed in ways visible and invisible" (paragraph 3), and he provides examples of the "visible" ways. What might some of the "invisible" ways be?

## SUGGESTIONS FOR SUSTAINED WRITING

a. Have you ever misjudged a person and then realized your error after getting to know him or her better? List details or freewrite for 10 minutes to gather information that you then turn into an essay that contrasts your two perceptions of this individual. As an alternative, write an essay in which you contrast the way in which you now perceive or interact with members of the opposite sex with the way you perceived or interacted with them when you were an adolescent.

b. Attending college should teach us more than the facts, ideas, and skills contained within our academic coursework. It should change our vision and attitudes about other people. Explain a major change in attitude that you have adopted in regard to how you perceive, work with, or interact with others. For additional insight, read the essay by Leslie in Chapter 1 and the one by Staples in Chapter 7.

c. In paragraph 2, Sanders mentions men who worked at various types of physical labor. Do some research in the library or on the Internet about an occupation that requires or required hard physical labor in difficult conditions, whether in this country or abroad. For example, focus on contemporary coal miners, truck drivers, construction workers, or oil drillers. You might also discuss the immigrant dressmaker who worked in America's sweatshop factories in the 1920s or the Third World child who, at the dawn of the twenty-first century, still toils twelve hours a day in horrible conditions for less than a living wage. Write an essay that explains how hard these people work(ed) and/or the living standards they enjoy(ed) or endure(d).

# Example and Illustration

Illustration is a natural habit of mind. How often have we offered a "for example" or "for instance" when, as we try to make a point, our listeners respond quizzically or simply shake their heads in disbelief? "What's so unhealthy about my diet?" demands a good friend whose eating habits you have just impugned. "For starters," you respond, "you are a French-fry fanatic, stuffing your face with the greasy, salt-laden sticks at nearly every meal. You eat so much red meat, butter, ice cream, and candy that the *New England Journal of Medicine* ought to report your intake of cholesterol, calories, and fat. And you probably don't even remember what fruits and vegetables look like."

The three examples that explain what you meant by *unhealthy* are products of a powerful and effective technique common to all types of expository or persuasive prose. Good writers are rarely content to tell their readers what they mean; they want to show it. One way to do this is to fill your work with relevant, well-developed illustrations—concrete representations of abstract ideas.

Effective illustrations make possible the explanation of ideas that might otherwise remain vague because they enable the reader to grasp particular realities behind the abstraction, to see specific and pertinent instances of the generality. "My Aunt Tillie is the most unselfish person in town," you may exclaim. But consider how much more convincing your claim would become if you recalled the times she opened her home to folks who had no place to live, donated her savings to the hospital building fund, and took time off from work to help sick friends and relatives.

The clarity and strength illustration brings to your writing depend not on the number of examples you include—although sheer volume can be convincing—but on the degree to which each example is clear, well developed, and appropriate to your thesis. In "Black Men and Public Space," Brent Staples recalls only four brief anecdotes to explain the care with which young black men must conduct themselves in public. Each situation is narrated in such detail, however, that readers can picture themselves in his place, and they share his frustration, indignation, and sadness.

Depending on your purpose, you can choose from several kinds of examples to give your writing variety and power. Annie Dillard ranges widely and freely to gather illustrations from science, philosophy, and her own observations of nature as she considers the mystery that living things must die so that life can go on. Developments in the history of eating, each analyzed thoroughly, provide Peter Farb and George Armelagos with a trove of examples to show how changes in table manners "reflect fundamental changes in human relationships." Edward T. Hall uses many brief scenarios of intercultural communication to make his point about the necessity of learning about other cultures. And Barbara Huttman uses specific details gleaned from careful observation to recall an experience that explains the excruciating dilemma faced by many medical professionals.

Like most other methods of development, illustration is rarely used to the exclusion of other rhetorical techniques. In the selection by Robertson Davies, for instance, well-chosen examples develop categories (classification) through which the author sheds new and interesting light on the subject. Brent Staples makes excellent use of narration, Barbara Huttman draws on her powers of description, and Annie Dillard uses a powerful variety of techniques to build a profound argument for the necessity of mortality.

Enjoy the selections in this chapter. They vary significantly in purpose, tone, and subject. Each is effective, however, because it explains an abstract idea in terms that will allow the reader to experience the concrete realities for which that abstraction stands. Each shows us ways to grapple with even the most unwieldy notions in language that is clear, powerful, and convincing.

# A Few Kind Words for Superstition

Robertson Davies

*One of Canada's best-known satirists, novelists, and playwrights, Robertson Davies (1913–1995) was educated at Upper Canada College in Toronto, at Queen's University in Kingston, and at Oxford University in England. He began his career as an actor in London and then worked as an editor for* Saturday Night *in Toronto and for the* Examiner *in Petersborough, Ontario. He taught English at the University of Toronto and at Massey College and served as governor of the Stratford Shakespearean Festival in Stratford, Ontario. He was a fellow of the Royal Society of Canada and was a recipient of the Stephen Leacock Medal for Humor. He was also the first Canadian to become an honorary member of the American Academy and Institute of Arts and Letters. Davies published numerous plays and critical studies on drama and stagecraft and is known throughout Canada for the delightful satires he wrote under the pseudonym "Samuel Marchbanks." However, his reputation rests chiefly on his novels. The Salterton Trilogy, which includes* Tempest-Tost *(1951),* Leaven of Malice *(1954), and* A Mixture of Frailties *(1958), is a study of a fictional university town in Canada and its middle-class inhabitants. The Deptford Trilogy, which is made up of* Fifth Business *(1970),* The Manticore *(1972), and* World of Wonders *(1976), affirms the important role that the irrational plays in an individual's search for spiritual identity. Other popular books by Davies are* What's Bred in the Bone *(1985),* The Papers of Samuel Marchbanks *(1986), and* The Lyre of Orpheus *(1989).*

1    In grave discussions of "the renaissance of the irrational" in our time, superstition does not figure largely as a serious challenge to reason or science. Parapsychology, UFO's, miracle cures, transcendental meditation and all the paths to instant enlightenment are condemned, but superstition is merely deplored. Is it because it has an unacknowledged hold on so many of us?

2    Few people will admit to being superstitious; it implies naïveté or ignorance. But I live in the middle of a large university, and I see superstition in its four manifestations, alive and flourishing among people who are indisputably rational and learned.

3    You did not know that superstition takes four forms? Theologians assure us that it does. First is what they call Vain Observances, such as not walking under a ladder, and that kind of thing. Yet I saw a deeply learned professor of anthropology, who had spilled some salt, throwing a pinch of it over his left shoulder; when I asked him why, he replied, with a wink, that it was "to hit the Devil in the eye." I did not question him further about his belief in the Devil: but I noticed that he did not smile until I asked him what he was doing.

4    The second form is Divination, or consulting oracles. Another learned professor I know, who would scorn to settle a problem by tossing a coin (which is a humble appeal to Fate to declare itself), told me quite seriously that he had resolved a matter related to university affairs by consulting the I Ching. And why not? There are thousands of people on this continent who appeal to the I Ching, and their general level of education seems to absolve them of superstition. Almost, but not quite. The I Ching, to the embarrassment of rationalists, often gives excellent advice.

5    The third form is Idolatry, and universities can show plenty of that. If you have ever supervised a large examination room, you know how many jujus, lucky coins and other bringers of luck are placed on the desks of the candidates. Modest idolatry, but what else can you call it?

6    The fourth form is Improper Worship of the True God. A while ago, I learned that every day, for several days, a $2 bill (in Canada we have $2 bills, regarded by some people as unlucky) had been tucked under a candlestick on the altar of a college chapel. Investigation revealed that an engineering student, worried about a girl, thought that bribery of the Deity might help. When I talked with him, he did not think he was pricing God cheap, because he could afford no more. A reasonable argument, but perhaps God was proud that week, for the scientific oracle went against him.

Superstition seems to run, a submerged river of crude religion, below   7
the surface of human consciousness. It has done so for as long as we have
any chronicle of human behavior, and although I cannot prove it, I doubt
if it is more prevalent today than it has always been. Superstition, the theologians tell us, comes from the Latin *supersisto,* meaning to stand in terror
of the Deity. Most people keep their terror within bounds, but they cannot
root it out, nor do they seem to want to do so.

The more the teaching of formal religion declines, or takes a sociolog-   8
ical form, the less God appears to great numbers of people as a God of
Love, resuming his older form of a watchful, minatory power, to be pla-
cated and cajoled. Superstition makes its appearance, apparently unbid-
den, very early in life, when children fear that stepping on cracks in the
sidewalk will bring ill fortune. It may persist even among the greatly
learned and devout, as in the case of Dr. Samuel Johnson, who felt it necessary to touch posts that he passed in the street. The psychoanalysts have
their explanation, but calling a superstition a compulsion neurosis does
not banish it.

Many superstitions are so widespread and so old that they must have   9
risen from a depth of the human mind that is indifferent to race or creed.
Orthodox Jews place a charm on their door-posts; so do (or did) the Chinese. Some peoples of Middle Europe believe that when a man sneezes, his
soul, for that moment, is absent from his body, and they hasten to bless
him, lest the soul be seized by the Devil. How did the Melanesians come
by the same idea? Superstition seems to have a link with some body of belief that far antedates the religions we know—religions which have no
place for such comforting little ceremonies and charities.

People who like disagreeable historical comparisons recall that when   10
Rome was in decline, superstition proliferated wildly, and that something
of the same sort is happening in our Western world today. They point to
the popularity of astrology, and it is true that sober newspapers that would
scorn to deal in love philters carry astrology columns and the fashion magazines count them among their most popular features. But when has astrology not been popular? No use saying science discredits it. When has
the heart of man given a damn for science?

Superstition in general is linked to man's yearning to know his fate,   11
and to have some hand in deciding it. When my mother was a child, she
innocently joined her Roman Catholic friends in killing spiders on July 11,
until she learned that this was done to ensure heavy rain the day following, the anniversary of the Battle of Boyne, when the Orangemen would
hold their parade. I knew an Italian, a good scientist, who watched every
morning before leaving his house, so that the first person he met would not
be a priest or a nun, as this would certainly bring bad luck.

I am not one to stand aloof from the rest of humanity in this matter, for   12
when I was a university student, a gypsy woman with a child in her arms

used to appear every year at examination time, and ask a shilling of any-one who touched the Lucky Baby; that swarthy infant cost me four shillings altogether, and I never failed an examination. Of course, I did it merely for the joke—or so I thought then. Now, I am humbler.

*1978*

## QUESTIONS FOR DISCUSSION

### Content

a. What is Davies's thesis? Which paragraphs supply examples that sup-port this thesis?

b. Davies asserts in paragraph 11 that "superstition in general is linked to man's yearning to know his fate, and to have some hand in deciding it." Do you agree with this assertion? Is this a generalization?

c. What examples of superstitions does Davies include? What were his probable reasons for including them?

d. Are the examples of superstitions used as persuasive devices? If so, what are the readers being persuaded to do?

e. To what does the phrase " 'the renaissance of the irrational' " in the first sentence refer? What examples does Davies use? What examples can you add to the list?

f. What is Davies's answer to the last question in the first paragraph? How do you know? Why might Davies have used a question rather than a statement?

g. What are the four kinds of superstitions? Do you agree with Davies that these types of superstitions are still prevalent?

h. Do you believe in any of the superstitions that Davies describes? Do you know of people who do? How do you account for belief in superstitions?

i. In the last paragraph, Davies admits that what he did jokingly as a col-lege student to ensure passing his examinations was actually done in earnest. Have you had any similar experiences?

j. According to Davies, what is the relationship between superstition and religion? Between superstition and science? Between superstition and history?

### Strategy and Style

k. Why might Davies have first listed the four forms of superstitions and then gone on to a discussion of superstition in general? How do the four forms of superstitions establish expectations for the rest of the essay?

l. The author traces the word *superstition* to its Latin origin, *supersisto* (paragraph 7). Look up the origin of the words *divination, idolatry,* and any of the superstitions he lists. How do the origins of these words and superstitions help illustrate his thesis?

m. What is Davies's attitude toward superstition? How is his attitude revealed through the tone of the piece?

## ENGAGING THE TEXT

a. Describe the superstitions to which you or someone you know adheres. Into which of Davies's categories do they fall?

b. Are the several questions Davies asks merely rhetorical? Try writing an answer to one or more of them.

## SUGGESTIONS FOR SUSTAINED WRITING

a. Write a few unkind words about superstition. In what ways does belief in superstition harm society? Why should people try to divest themselves of superstitious beliefs?

b. Compare Davies's essay with "Patterns of Eating" by Farb and Armelagos in this chapter. What do the essays say about human behavior and cultural beliefs?

c. Interview friends and fellow students, asking them what superstitions they have and how strongly they believe in them. Using these examples as the raw material for your essay, analyze these superstitions, putting forth your theory of why people believe in them.

# Patterns of Eating

## Peter Farb and George Armelagos

*An anthropologist, naturalist, and acknowledged expert on the American Indian, Peter Farb (1929–1980) wrote numerous studies on the natural history of North America and its original inhabitants. He also published several introductions to scientific subjects for young readers. Farb was educated at Vanderbilt and Columbia Universities. He worked as feature editor for* Argosy *from 1950 to 1952 and as curator for the Riverside Museum in New York City from 1964 to 1971. He also held teaching positions at Yale University and Calhoun College and served as a consultant to the Smithsonian Institution in Washington, D.C. From 1959 to 1963, Farb wrote a column for* Better Homes and Gardens *and*

*contributed numerous articles on science and nature to many other popular American mag-
azines. Some of his best-known full-length works include* Living Earth *(1959),* The Forest *(1961),* Face of North America: The Natural History of a Continent *(1963), and*
Man's Rise to Civilization as Shown by the Indians of North America from
Primeval Times to the Coming of the Industrial State *(1968).*

*George Armelagos (b. 1936) received his Ph.D. in anthropology from the University
of Colorado and is now a professor of anthropology at the University of Massachusetts at
Amherst. He has completed extensive research on the relationship between nutrition and
human evolution.*

*Consuming Passions (1980), the book from which this selection was taken, is a fas-
cinating and extremely well-documented look at the development of eating habits through
the centuries. In it, Farb and Armelagos explain how the rituals we have come to associate
with food preparation, table manners, and dietary practices in general have helped both reveal and define our cultural identity. "The interrelation of men and menus," wrote one*
Time *book reviewer, "has filled hundreds of texts. But none of them has digested so many
facts so well."*

1   Among the important societal rules that represent one component of cuisine are table manners. As a socially instilled form of conduct, they reveal
the attitudes typical of a society. Changes in table manners through time,
as they have been documented for western Europe, likewise reflect fundamental changes in human relationships. Medieval courtiers saw their
table manners as distinguishing them from crude peasants; but by modern
standards, the manners were not exactly refined. Feudal lords used their
unwashed hands to scoop food from a common bowl and they passed
around a single goblet from which all drank. A finger or two would be extended while eating, so as to be kept free of grease and thus available for
the next course, or for dipping into spices and condiments—possibly accounting for today's "polite" custom of extending the finger while holding a spoon or small fork. Soups and sauces were commonly drunk by lifting the bowl to the mouth; several diners frequently ate from the same
bread trencher. Even lords and nobles would toss gnawed bones back into
the common dish, wolf down their food, spit onto the table (preferred conduct called for spitting under it), and blow their noses into the tablecloth.

2   By about the beginning of the sixteenth century, table manners began
to move in the direction of today's standards. The importance attached to
them is indicated by the phenomenal success of a treatise, *On Civility in
Children,* by the philosopher Erasmus, which appeared in 1530; reprinted
more than thirty times in the next six years, it also appeared in numerous
translations. Erasmus' idea of good table manners was far from modern,
but it did represent an advance. He believed, for example, that an upper
class diner was distinguished by putting only three fingers of one hand
into the bowl, instead of the entire hand in the manner of the lower class.
Wait a few moments after being seated before you dip into it, he advises.
Do not poke around in your dish, but take the first piece you touch. Do not

put chewed food from the mouth back on your plate; instead, throw it under the table or behind your chair.

By the time of Erasmus, the changing table manners reveal a fundamental shift in society. People no longer ate from the same dish or drank from the same goblet, but were divided from one another by a new wall of constraint. Once the spontaneous, direct, and informal manners of the Middle Ages had been repressed, people began to feel shame. Defecation and urination were now regarded as private activities; handkerchiefs came into use for blowing the nose; nightclothes were now worn, and bedrooms were set apart as private areas. Before the sixteenth century, even nobles ate in their vast kitchens; only then did a special room designated for eating come into use away from the bloody sides of meat, the animals about to be slaughtered, and the bustling servants. These new inhibitions became the essence of "civilized" behavior, distinguishing adults from children, the upper classes from the lower, and Europeans from the "savages" then being discovered around the world. Restraint in eating habits became more marked in the centuries that followed. By about 1800, napkins were in common use, and before long they were placed on the thighs rather than wrapped around the neck; coffee and tea were no longer slurped out of the saucer; bread was genteelly broken into small pieces with the fingers rather than cut into large chunks with a knife.

Numerous paintings that depict meals—with subjects such as the Last Supper, the wedding at Cana, or Herod's feast—show what dining tables looked like before the seventeenth century. Forks were not depicted until about 1600 (when Jacopo Bassano painted one in a Last Supper), and very few spoons were shown. At least one knife is always depicted—an especially large one when it is the only one available for all the guests—but small individual knives were often at each place. Tin disks or oval pieces of wood had already replaced the bread trenchers. This change in eating utensils typified the new table manners in Europe. (In many other parts of the world, no utensils at all were used. In the Near East, for example, it was traditional to bring food to the mouth with the fingers of the right hand, the left being unacceptable because it was reserved for wiping the buttocks.) Utensils were employed in part because of a change in the attitude toward meat. During the Middle Ages, whole sides of meat, or even an entire dead animal, had been brought to the table and then carved in view of the diners. Beginning in the seventeenth century, at first in France but later elsewhere, the practice began to go out of fashion. One reason was that the family was ceasing to be a production unit that did its own slaughtering; as that function was transferred to specialists outside the home, the family became essentially a consumption unit. In addition, the size of the family was decreasing, and consequently whole animals, or even large parts of them, were uneconomical. The cuisines of Europe reflected these social and economic changes. The animal origin of meat dishes was concealed by the arts of preparation. Meat itself became distasteful to look upon, and carving was moved out of sight to the kitchen. Comparable changes had already taken place in Chinese cuisine, with meat being cut up beforehand, unobserved by the diners. England was an exception to the change in Europe, and in its former colonies—the United States, Canada, Australia, and South Africa—the custom has persisted of bringing a joint of meat to the table to be carved.

5       Once carving was no longer considered a necessary skill among the well-bred, changes inevitably took place in the use of the knife, unquestionably the earliest utensil used for manipulating food. (In fact, the earliest English cookbooks were not so much guides to recipes as guides to carving meat.) The attitude of diners toward the knife, going back to the Middle Ages and the Renaissance, had always been ambivalent. The knife served as a utensil, but it offered a potential threat because it was also a weapon. Thus taboos were increasingly placed upon its use: It was to be held by the point with the blunt handle presented; it was not to be placed anywhere near the face; and most important, the uses to which it was put were sharply restricted. It was not to be used for cutting soft foods such as boiled eggs or fish, or round ones such as potatoes, or to be lifted from the table for courses that did not need it. In short, good table manners in Europe gradually removed the threatening aspect of the knife from social occasions. A similar change had taken place much earlier in China when the warrior was supplanted by the scholar as a cultural model. The knife was banished completely from the table in favor of chopsticks, which is why the Chinese came to regard Europeans as barbarians at their table who "eat with swords."

6       The fork in particular enabled Europeans to separate themselves from the eating process, even avoiding manual contact with their food. When the fork first appeared in Europe, toward the end of the Middle Ages, it was used solely as an instrument for lifting chunks from the common bowl. Beginning in the sixteenth century, the fork was increasingly used by members of the upper classes—first in Italy, then in France, and finally in Germany and England. By then, social relations in western Europe had so changed that a utensil was needed to spare diners from the "uncivilized" and distasteful necessity of picking up food and putting it into the mouth with the fingers. The addition of the fork to the table was once said to be for reasons of hygiene, but this cannot be true. By the sixteenth century people were no longer eating from a common bowl but from their own plates, and since they also washed their hands before meals, their fingers were now every bit as hygienic as a fork would have been. Nor can the reason for the adoption of the fork be connected with the wish not to soil the long ruff that was worn on the sleeve at the time, since the fork was also adopted in various countries where ruffs were not then in fashion.

7       Along with the appearance of the fork, all table utensils began to change and proliferate from the sixteenth century onward. Soup was no longer eaten directly from the dish, but each diner used an individual

spoon for that purpose. When a diner wanted a second helping from the serving dish, a ladle or a fresh spoon was used. More and more special utensils were developed for each kind of food: Soup spoons, oyster forks, salad forks, two-tined fondue forks, blunt butter knives, special utensils for various desserts and kinds of fruit, each one differently shaped, of a different size, with differently numbered prongs and with blunt or serrated edges. The present European pattern eventually emerged, in which each person is provided with a table setting of as many as a dozen utensils at a full-course meal. With that, the separation of the human body from the taking of food became virtually complete. Good table manners dictated that even the cobs of maize were to be held by prongs inserted in each end, and the bones of lamb chops covered by ruffled paper pantalettes. Only under special conditions—as when Western people consciously imitate an earlier stage in culture at a picnic, fish fry, cookout, or campfire—do they still tear food apart with their fingers and their teeth, in a nostalgic reenactment of eating behaviors long vanished.

Today's neighborhood barbecue recreates a world of sharing and hospitality that becomes rarer each year. We regard as a curiosity the behavior of hunters in exotic regions. But every year millions of North Americans take to the woods and lakes to kill a wide variety of animals—with a difference, of course: What hunters do for survival we do for sport (and also for proof of masculinity, for male bonding, and for various psychological rewards). Like hunters, too, we stuff ourselves almost whenever food is available. Nibbling on a roasted ear of maize gives us, in addition to nutrients, the satisfaction of participating in culturally simpler ways. A festive meal, however, is still thought of in Victorian terms, with the dominant male officiating over the roast, the dominant female apportioning vegetables, the extended family gathered around the table, with everything in its proper place—a revered picture, as indeed it was so painted by Norman Rockwell, yet one that becomes less accurate with each year that passes. 8

*1980*

## QUESTIONS FOR DISCUSSION

### Content

a. What were the Last Supper, the wedding at Cana, and Herod's feast? How do references to paintings of these events help illustrate important points about the history of table manners?

b. Summarize the illustrations Farb and Armelagos use to distinguish manners in the Renaissance from those of earlier eras. Does their treatment of the subject need to be as graphic as it is?

c. What illustrations do Farb and Armelagos use to explain the European's "ambivalent" attitude toward knives?

d. Who was Erasmus, and how did his ideas help advance table manners?

e. To what are Farb and Armelagos alluding when they tell us that the new table manners adopted by Europeans during the Renaissance distinguished them "from the 'savages' then being discovered around the world" (paragraph 3)? Why is the word *savages* in quotes?

f. This essay attempts to trace various developments that led to "the separation of "the human body from the taking of food." How would you interpret this statement?

g. The authors claim that early in the seventeenth century the family "was ceasing to be a production unit." What did this development have to do with the profound changes in the way Europeans prepared and served meat?

h. Explain the Chinese's opinion of European eating habits. Why did the Chinese banish knives from their tables, and how did their doing so affect the development of their cuisine?

i. Why did forks come into use? What other "special utensils" and instruments have since become common in table settings?

j. What accounts for the fact that in the United States and other English-speaking countries people still carve large cuts of meat at the table? Why do Farb and Armelagos consider this custom as well as the contemporary American cookout "a nostalgic reenactment of eating behaviors long vanished"?

k. How would you describe the work of Norman Rockwell, and why is one of his "revered pictures" mentioned in the conclusion?

## Strategy and Style

l. How would you define the terms *Middle Ages* and *Renaissance?* Why does this essay begin with the former? Should the authors have begun with an earlier period of history?

m. What are the "Victorian terms" to which the authors allude in the concluding paragraph?

n. To what extent are Farb and Armelagos making fun of people's eating habits? Point out instances where the tone becomes humorous.

## ENGAGING THE TEXT

a. Describe what you knew about the etiquette of eating before you read this essay. How did the essay corroborate or challenge your thinking? Did it change your mind about what is proper etiquette?

b. Describe the eating habits of your family, your roommates, or the students at the campus cafeteria. At which stage of the evolution of eating patterns would you say they belong? Refer to the essay in your response.

## SUGGESTIONS FOR SUSTAINED WRITING

a. Describe and evaluate the table manners people use in your college's dining hall or cafeteria. Like Farb and Armelagos, use as many concrete illustrations as you can to make your writing vivid.
b. What makes a meal "festive"? Using illustration as your dominant method of development, discuss how this term might apply to your favorite holiday dinner with family or friends. You need not focus on table manners exclusively. To illustrate your idea of "festive," describe place settings, table decorations, and any "rituals" that accompany the preparation of this meal. How are your family's festivities reflective of a wider culture? Use Edward T. Hall's "The Anthropology of Manners" in this chapter as a guide or model for your essay.
c. Describe one or more eating or cooking rituals from another country or culture. You might be able to gather many details about this topic from cookbooks, from personal experience, from conversations with the foreign students you meet in your classes, or from chats with people who have immigrated to this country but still follow the traditional culinary practices of their homelands. Address this essay to someone who knows very little about the culture you are discussing and be sure to include a sufficient number of examples and explanatory details.

# The Anthropology of Manners

Edward T. Hall

*Edward T. Hall (b. 1914) is a well-known anthropologist and an expert on cultural differences in communication, manners, and perception of time. He studied at Pomona College; the University of Denver, where he received an AB; the University of Arizona, where he received an MA in 1938; and Columbia University, where he received a Ph.D. in 1942. He did fieldwork from 1933 to 1942 with the Hopi and Navajo, some of which has reemerged in his book,* West of the Thirties *(1994). During World War I, Hall taught at the University of Denver and at Bennington College; after the war, he worked on the atoll of Truk (Micronesia), helping the Truks and U. S. Navy personnel understand each other's behavior and cultures. On his return to the United States, Hall became the director of the Point Four program in the Foreign Service Institute, part of the U.S. State Department, from 1950 to 1955. There he designed training programs for workers assigned to posts in Latin America and the Middle East. He has had an active career, bridging both the academic and the commercial worlds. From 1955 to 1960, he was president of Overseas Training and Research, Inc., in Washington, D.C.; he founded his own consulting firm in 1960; and he taught anthropology at the Illinois Institute of Technology from 1963 to 1967 and at Northwestern University from 1967 to 1977. Meanwhile, he was writing scholarly and popular books, only a few of which are* The Silent Language *(1959);* The Hidden Dimension *(1966);* Beyond Culture *(1976), from which "The Anthropology of Manners" is drawn; and* Dance of Life *(1983), which discusses time as a cultural concept.*

> The Goops they lick their fingers
>   and the Goops they lick their knives;
> They spill their broth on the table cloth—
>   Oh, they lead disgusting lives.
> The Goops they talk while eating,
>   and loud and fast they chew;
> And that is why I'm glad that I
>   am not a Goop—are you?

1   In Gelett Burgess' classic on the Goops we have an example of what anthropologists call "an enculturating device"—a means of conditioning the young to life in our society. Having been taught the lesson of the goops from childhood (with or without the aid of Mr. Burgess) Americans are shocked when they go abroad and discover whole groups of people behaving like goops—eating with their fingers, making noises and talking while eating. When this happens, we may (1) remark on the barbarousness or quaintness of the "natives" (a term cordially disliked all over the world) or (2) try to discover the nature and meaning of the differences in behavior. One rather quickly discovers that what is good manners in one context may be bad in the next. It is to this point that I would like to address myself.

2       The subject of manners is complex; if it were not, there would not be so many injured feelings and so much misunderstanding in international circles everywhere. In any society the code of manners tends to sum up the culture—to be a frame of reference for all behavior. Emily Post goes so far as to say: "There is not a single thing that we do, or say, or choose, or use, or even think, that does not follow or break one of the exactions of taste, or tact, or ethics of good manners, or etiquette—call it what you will." Unfortunately many of the most important standards of acceptable behavior in different cultures are elusive: They are intangible, undefined and unwritten.

3       An Arab diplomat who recently arrived in the U.S. from the Middle East attended a banquet which lasted several hours. When it was over, he met a fellow countryman outside and suggested they go get something to eat, as he was starving. His friend, who had been in this country for some time, laughed and said: "But, Habib, didn't you know that if you say, 'No,

thank you,' they think you really don't want any?" In an Arab country etiquette dictates that the person being served must refuse the proffered dish several times, while his host urges him repeatedly to partake. The other side of the coin is that Americans in the Middle East, until they learn better, stagger away from banquets having eaten more than they want or is good for them.

When a public-health movie of a baby being bathed in a bathinette was shown in India recently, the Indian women who saw it were visibly offended. They wondered how people could be so inhuman as to bathe a child in stagnant (not running) water. Americans in Iran soon learn not to indulge themselves in their penchant for chucking infants under the chin and remarking on the color of their eyes, for the mother has to pay to have the "evil eye" removed. We also learn that in the Middle East you don't hand people things with your left hand, because it is unclean. In India we learn not to touch another person, and in Southeast Asia we learn that the head is sacred.

In the interest of intercultural understanding various U.S. Government agencies have hired anthropologists from time to time as technical experts. The State Department especially has pioneered in the attempt to bring science to bear on this difficult and complex problem. It began by offering at the Foreign Service Institute an intensive four-week course for Point 4 technicians. Later these facilities were expanded to include other foreign service personnel.

The anthropologist's job here is not merely to call attention to obvious taboos or to coach people about types of thoughtless behavior that have very little to do with culture. One should not need an anthropologist to point out, for instance, that it is insulting to ask a foreigner: "How much is this in real money?" Where technical advice is most needed is in the interpretation of the unconscious aspects of a culture—the things people do automatically without being aware of the full implications of what they have done. For example, an ambassador who has been kept waiting for more than half an hour by a foreign visitor needs to understand that if his visitor "just mutters an apology" this is not necessarily an insult. The time system in the foreign country may be composed of different basic units, so that the visitor is not as late as he may appear to us. You must know the time system of the country to know at what point apologies are really due.

Twenty years of experience in working with Americans in foreign lands convinces me that the real problem in preparing them to work overseas is not with taboos, which they catch on to rather quickly, but rather with whole congeries of habits and attitudes which anthropologists have only recently begun to describe systematically.

Can you remember tying your shoes this morning? Could you give the rules for when it is proper to call another person by his first name? Could you describe the gestures you make in conversation? These examples illustrate how much of our behavior is "out of awareness," and how easy it is to get into trouble in another culture.

9    Nobody is continually aware of the quality of his own voice, the subtleties of stress and intonation that color the meaning of his words or the posture and distance he assumes in talking to another person. Yet all these are taken as cues to the real nature of an utterance, regardless of what the words say. A simple illustration is the meaning in the tone of voice. In the U.S. we raise our voices not only when we are angry but also when we want to emphasize a point, when we are more than a certain distance from another person, when we are concluding a meeting and so on. But to the Chinese, for instance, overloudness of the voice is most characteristically associated with anger and loss of self-control. Whenever we become really interested in something, they are apt to have the feeling we are angry, in spite of many years' experience with us. Very likely most of their interviews with us, however cordial, seem to end on a sour note when we exclaim heartily: "WELL, I'M CERTAINLY GLAD YOU DROPPED IN, MR. WONG."

10    The Latin Americans, who as a rule take business seriously, do not understand our mixing business with informality and recreation. We like to put our feet up on the desk. If a stranger enters the office, we take our feet down. If it turns out that the stranger and we have a lot in common, up go the feet again—a cue to the other fellow that we feel at ease. If the office boy enters, the feet stay up; if the boss enters and our relationship with him is a little strained at the moment, they go down. To a Latin American this whole behavior is shocking. All he sees in it is insult or just plain rudeness.

11    Differences in attitudes toward space—what would be territoriality in lower forms of life—raise a number of other interesting points. U.S. women who go to live in Latin America all complain about the "waste" of space in the houses. On the other hand, U.S. visitors to the Middle East complain about crowding, in the houses and on the streetcars and buses. Everywhere we go space seems to be distorted. When we see a gardener in the mountains of Italy planting a single row on each of six separate terraces, we wonder why he spreads out his crop so that he has to spend half his time climbing up and down. We overlook the complex chain of communication that would be broken if he didn't cultivate alongside his brothers and his cousin and if he didn't pass his neighbors and talk to them as he moves from one terrace to the next.

12    A colleague of mine was caught in a snowstorm while traveling with companions in the mountains of Lebanon. They stopped at the next house and asked to be put up for the night. The house had only one room. Instead of distributing the guests around the room, their host placed them next to the pallet where he slept with his wife—so close that they almost touched the couple. To have done otherwise in that country would have been unnatural and unfriendly. In the U.S. we distribute ourselves more evenly

than many other people. We have strong feelings about touching and being crowded; in a streetcar, bus or elevator we draw ourselves in. Toward a person who relaxes and lets himself come into full contact with others in a crowded place we usually feel reactions that could not be printed on this page. It takes years for us to train our children not to crowd and lean on us. We tell them to stand up, that it is rude to slouch, not to sit so close or not to "breathe down our necks." After a while they get the point. By the time we Americans are in our teens we can tell what relationship exists between a man and woman by how they walk or sit together.

In Latin America, where touching is more common and the basic units 13 of space seem to be smaller, the wide automobiles made in the U.S. pose problems. People don't know where to sit. North Americans are disturbed by how close the Latin Americans stand when they converse. "Why do they have to get so close when they talk to you?" "They're so pushy." "I don't know what it is, but it's something in the way they stand next to you." And so on. The Latin Americans, for their part, complain that people in the U.S. are distant and cold—*retraídos* (withdrawing and uncommunicative).

An analysis of the handling of space during conversations shows the 14 following: A U.S. male brought up in the Northeast stands 18 to 20 inches away when talking face to face to a man he does not know very well; talking to a woman under similar circumstances, he increases the distance about four inches. A distance of only eight to 13 inches between males is considered either very aggressive or indicative of a closeness of a type we do not ordinarily want to think about. Yet in many parts of Latin America and the Middle East distances which are almost sexual in connotation are the only ones at which people can talk comfortably. In Cuba, for instance, there is nothing suggestive in a man's talking to an educated woman at a distance of 13 inches. If you are a Latin American, talking to a North American at the distance he insists on maintaining is like trying to talk across a room.

To get a more vivid idea of this problem of the comfortable distance, 15 try starting a conversation with a person eight or 10 feet away or one separated from you by a wide obstruction in a store or other public place. Any normally enculturated person can't help trying to close up the space, even to the extent of climbing over benches or walking around tables to arrive within comfortable distance. U.S. businessmen working in Latin America try to prevent people from getting uncomfortably close by barricading themselves behind desks, typewriters or the like, but their Latin American office visitors will often climb up on desks or over chairs and put up with loss of dignity in order to establish a spatial context in which interaction can take place for them.

The interesting thing is that neither party is specifically aware of what 16 is wrong when the distance is not right. They merely have vague feelings of discomfort or anxiety. As the Latin American approaches and the North American backs away, both parties take offense without knowing why. When a North American, having had the problem pointed out to him, permits the Latin American to get close enough, he will immediately notice that the latter seems much more at ease.

17     My own studies of space and time have engendered considerable cooperation and interest on the part of friends and colleagues. One case recently reported to me had to do with a group of seven-year-olds in a crowded Sunday-school classroom. The children kept fighting. Without knowing quite what was involved, the teacher had them moved to a larger room. The fighting stopped. It is interesting to speculate as to what would have happened had the children been moved to a smaller room.

18     The embarrassment about intimacy in space applies also to the matter of addressing people by name. Finding the proper distance in the use of names is even more difficult than in space, because the rules for first-naming are unbelievably complex. As a rule we tend to stay on the "mister" level too long with Latins and some others, but very often we swing into first naming too quickly, which amounts to talking down to them. Whereas in the U.S. we use Mr. with the surname, in Latin America the first and last names are used together and señor (Sr.) is a title. Thus when one says, "My name is Sr. So-and-So," it is interpreted to mean, "I am the Honorable, his Excellency So-and-So." It is no wonder that when we stand away, barricade ourselves behind our desks (usually a reflection of status) and call ourselves mister, our friends to the south wonder about our so-called "good neighbor" policy and think of us as either high-hat or unbelievably rude. Fortunately most North Americans learn some of these things after living in Latin America for a while, but the aversion to being touched and to touching sometimes persists after 15 or more years of residence and even under such conditions as intermarriage.

19     The difference in sense of time is another thing of which we are not aware. An Iranian, for instance, is not taught that it is rude to be late in the same way that we in the U.S. are. In a general way we are conscious of this, but we fail to realize that their time system is structured differently from ours. The different cultures simply place different values on the time units.

20     Thus let us take as a typical case of the North European time system (which has regional variations) the situation in the urban eastern U.S. A middle-class businessman meeting another of equivalent rank will ordinarily be aware of being two minutes early or late. If he is three minutes late, it will be noted as significant but usually neither will say anything. If four minutes late, he will mutter something by way of apology; at five minutes he will utter a full sentence of apology. In other words, the major unit is a five-minute block. Fifteen minutes is the smallest significant period for all sorts of arrangements and it is used very commonly. A half hour of course is very significant, and if you spend three quarters of an hour or

an hour, either the business you transact or the relationship must be important. Normally it is an insult to keep a public figure or a person of significantly higher status than yourself waiting even two or three minutes, though the person of higher position can keep you waiting or even break an appointment.

Now among urban Arabs in the Eastern Mediterranean, to take an illustrative case of another time system, the unit that corresponds to our five-minute period is 15 minutes. Thus when an Arab arrives nearly 30 minutes after the set time, by his reckoning he isn't even "10 minutes" late yet (in our time units). Stated differently, the Arab's tardiness will not amount to one significant period (15 minutes in our system). An American normally will wait no longer than 30 minutes (two significant periods) for another person to turn up in the middle of the day. Thereby he often unwittingly insults people in the Middle East who want to be his friends.

How long is one expected to stay when making a duty call at a friend's house in the U.S.? While there are regional variations, I have observed that the minimum is very close to 45 minutes, even in the face of pressing commitments elsewhere, such as a roast in the oven. We may think we can get away in 30 minutes by saying something about only stopping for "a minute," but usually we discover that we don't feel comfortable about leaving until 45 minutes have elapsed. I am referring to afternoon social calls; evening calls last much longer and operate according to a different system. In Arab countries an American paying a duty call at the house of a desert sheik causes consternation if he gets up to leave after half a day. There a duty call lasts three days—the first day to prepare the feast, the second for the feast itself and the third to taper off and say farewell. In the first half day the sheik has barely had time to slaughter the sheep for the feast. The guest's departure would leave the host frustrated.

There is a well-known story of a tribesman who came to Kabul, the capital of Afghanistan, to meet his brother. Failing to find him, he asked the merchants in the marketplace to tell his brother where he could be found if the brother showed up. A year later the tribesman returned and looked again. It developed that he and his brother had agreed to meet in Kabul but had failed to specify what year! If the Afghan time system were structured similarly to our own, which it apparently is not, the brother would not offer a full sentence of apology until he was five years late.

Informal units of time such as "just a minute," "a while," "later," "a long time," "a spell," "a long, long time," "years" and so on provide us with the culturological equivalent of Evil-Eye Fleegle's "double-whammy" (in *Li'l Abner*). Yet these expressions are not as imprecise as they seem. Any American who has worked in an office with someone else for six months can usually tell within five minutes when that person will be back if he says, "I'll be gone for a while." It is simply a matter of learning from experience the individual's system of time indicators. A reader who is interested in communications theory can fruitfully speculate for a while on the very wonderful way in which culture provides the means whereby the receiver puts back all the redundant material that was stripped from such a message. Spelled out, the message might go somewhat as follows: "I am going downtown to see So-and-So about the Such-and-Such contract, but I don't know what the traffic conditions will be like or how long it will take me to get a place to park nor do I know what shape So-and-So will be in today, but taking all this into account I think I will be out of the office about an hour but don't like to commit myself, so if anyone calls you can say I'm not sure how long I will be; in any event I expect to be back before 4 o'clock."

25      Few of us realize how much we rely on built-in patterns to interpret messages of this sort. An Iranian friend of mine who came to live in the U.S. was hurt and puzzled for the first few years. The new friends he met and liked would say on parting: "Well, I'll see you later." He mournfully complained: "I kept expecting to see them, but the 'later' never came." Strangely enough we ourselves are exasperated when a Mexican can't tell us precisely what he means when he uses the expression *mañana*.

26      The role of the anthropologist in preparing people for service overseas is to open their eyes and sensitize them to the subtle qualities of behavior—tone of voice, gestures, space and time relationships—that so often build up feelings of frustration and hostility in other people with a different culture. Whether we are going to live in a particular foreign country or travel in many, we need a frame of reference that will enable us to observe and learn the significance of differences in manners. Progress is being made in this anthropological study, but it is also showing us how little is known about human behavior.

*1955*

## QUESTIONS FOR DISCUSSION

### Content

a. What are some of the differences between U.S. and Arab cultures and between U.S. and Latin American cultures?
b. What is the difference between "taboos" and "habits and attitudes" (paragraph 7)? Why do habits and attitudes cause more problems for outsiders than taboos cause?

c. In paragraph 8 Hall mentions the "rules for when it is proper to call another person by his first name." What are some of the rules that Hall includes in this essay? What other rules can you add to the list?

d. What are some of the ways in which people from different cultures deal with space, both personal and architectural space?

e. What do anthropologists like Hall do? Why are their skills important?

## Strategy and Style

f. Why is the "Goops" poem at the beginning of the essay so effective?

g. What is an "enculturating device" (paragraph 1)? Give some examples from the essay and from your own experience.

h. Go through the essay and mark or list the examples Hall uses. How many examples does he use for each point he makes?

i. Hall uses multiple examples to make his points, but he uses specific examples to represent a culture as a whole. In your opinion, are there any examples that might misrepresent the culture?

j. Hall writes quite informally. What might the essay sound like if he had written for an audience of scholars and other anthropologists? Why is the informal style more appropriate for general readers? What about Hall's style makes it informal?

## ENGAGING THE TEXT

a. Reread paragraph 18. Describe the movement from formal to informal address as it occurs in the culture with which you are most familiar.

b. How does Hall help you understand your own behavior? Choose one passage from the essay and discuss how it clarifies your understanding of yourself.

## SUGGESTIONS FOR SUSTAINED WRITING

a. What is "American culture"? Does the United States have a single, unchanging culture? Do you think the United States is a "melting pot" or a "patchwork" of distinctly different cultures? Write an opinion essay about these questions. If you think the United States is a melting pot, describe the American cultural traditions shared by everyone. If you think ethnic groups within the United States will always remain distinct and separate, explain, with examples, why this will be so.

b. Observe and record behavior in a study area, at a party, at a sports event, at a family gathering, and so forth. Try to find the rules that people are following but of which they are not conscious. Write an analytical essay in which you explain the rules, using specific examples from your observations. As a twist to this assignment, you could move from observer to participant, purposely break a rule, and record what happens. For example, in a nearly empty study area, break the rule of personal space by sitting next to a stranger to study. Use Horace Miner's "Body Ritual among the Nacirema" (Chapter 9) as a model for your essay.

c. List behaviors or other things from other cultures that puzzle you. Research—in the library but also by interviewing people from that culture—and write an essay explaining the culture to readers who are unfamiliar with the culture but are planning to visit that country or countries. Make your goal similar to Hall's: "to open their eyes and sensitize them to the subtle qualities of behavior—tone of voice, gestures, space and time relationships" (paragraph 26).

# Fecundity

Annie Dillard

*Born in Pittsburgh in 1945, Annie Dillard attended Hollins College, where she earned a BA in 1967 and an MA in 1968. She began her career as a columnist for the publication of the Wilderness Society,* The Living Wilderness, *from 1973 to 1975. She was also a contributing editor to* Harper's *magazine from 1973 to 1985. Before she was 30, she had won a Pulitzer Prize for* Pilgrim at Tinker Creek *(1974), a narrative about Virginia's Roanoke Valley, where she lived while attending Hollins College. She was scholar-in-residence at Western Washington University from 1975 to 1979 and currently teaches at Wesleyan University. She has served on the U.S. Cultural Delegation to the People's Republic of China and on the National Commission of U.S.-China Relations. From these experiences came* Encounters with Teaching a Stone to Talk *(1982). She also has published poetry, including* Tickets for a Prayer Wheel *(1974). Dillard's most recent books are* An American Childhood *(1988),* The Writing Life *(1992),* The Living: A Novel *(1993), and* Mornings Like This *(1995). "Fecundity" is taken from* Pilgrim at Tinker Creek.

1   I have to look at the landscape of the blue-green world again. Just think: In all the clean beautiful reaches of the solar system, our planet alone is a blot; our planet alone has death. I have to acknowledge that the sea is a cup of death and the land is a stained altar stone. We the living are survivors huddled on flotsam, living on jetsam. We are escapees. We wake in terror, eat in hunger, sleep with a mouthful of blood.

Death: W. C. Fields called death "the Fellow in the Bright Nightgown." 2
He shuffles around the house in all the corners I've forgotten, all the halls
I dare not call to mind or visit for fear I'll glimpse the hem of his shabby,
dazzling gown disappearing around a turn. This is the monster evolution
loves. How could it be?

The faster death goes, the faster evolution goes. If an aphid lays a mil- 3
lion eggs, several might survive. Now, my right hand, in all its human cun-
ning, could not make one aphid in a thousand years. But these aphid
eggs—which run less than a dime a dozen, which run absolutely free—can
make aphids as effortlessly as the sea makes waves. Wonderful things,
wasted. It's a wretched system. Arthur Stanley Eddington, the British
physicist and astronomer who died in 1944, suggested that all of "Nature"
could conceivably run on the same deranged scheme. "If indeed she has
no greater aim than to provide a home for her greatest experiment, Man, it
would be just like her methods to scatter a million stars whereof one might
haply achieve her purpose." I doubt very much that this is the aim, but it
seems clear on all fronts that this is the method.

Say you are the manager of the Southern Railroad. You figure that you 4
need three engines for a stretch of track between Lynchburg and Danville.
It's a mighty steep grade. So at fantastic effort and expense you have your
shops make nine thousand engines. Each engine must be fashioned just so,
every rivet and bolt secure, every wire twisted and wrapped, every needle
on every indicator sensitive and accurate.

You send all nine thousand of them out on the runs. Although there 5
are engineers at the throttles, no one is manning the switches. The engines
crash, collide, derail, jump, jam, burn . . . At the end of the massacre you
have three engines, which is what the run could support in the first place.
There are few enough of them that they can stay out of each others' paths.

You go to your board of directors and show them what you've done. 6
And what are they going to say? You know what they're going to say.
They're going to say: It's a hell of a way to run a railroad.

Is it a better way to run a universe?                                         7

Evolution loves death more than it loves you or me. This is easy to 8
write, easy to read, and hard to believe. The words are simple, the concept
clear—but you don't believe it, do you? Nor do I. How could I, when we're
both so lovable? Are my values then so diametrically opposed to those that
nature preserves? This is the key point.

Must I then part ways with the only world I know? I had thought to 9
live by the side of the creek in order to shape my life to its free flow. But I
seem to have reached a point where I must draw the line. It looks as though
the creek is not buoying me up but dragging me down. Look: Cock Robin
may die the most gruesome of slow deaths, and nature is no less pleased;
the sun comes up, the creek rolls on, the survivors still sing. I cannot feel

that way about your death, nor you about mine, nor either of us about the robin's—nor even the barnacles'. We value the individual supremely, and nature values him not a whit. It looks for the moment as though I might have to reject this creek life unless I want to be utterly brutalized. Is human culture with its values my only real home after all? Can it possibly be that I should move my anchor-hold to the side of a library? This direction of thought brings me abruptly to a fork in the road where I stand paralyzed, unwilling to go on, for both ways lead to madness.

10      Either this world, my mother, is a monster, or I myself am a freak.

11      Consider the former: The world is a monster. Any three-year-old can see how unsatisfactory and clumsy is this whole business of reproducing and dying by the billions. We have not yet encountered any god who is as merciful as a man who flicks a beetle over on its feet. There is not a people in the world who behaves as badly as praying mantises. But wait, you say, there is no right and wrong in nature; right and wrong is a human concept. Precisely: We are moral creatures, then, in an amoral world. The universe that suckled us is a monster that does not care if we live or die—does not care if it itself grinds to a halt. It is fixed and blind, a robot programmed to kill. We are free and seeing; we can only try to outwit it at every turn to save our skins.

12      This view requires that a monstrous world running on chance and death, careening blindly from nowhere to nowhere, somehow produced wonderful us. I came from the world, I crawled out of a sea of amino acids, and now I must whirl around and shake my fist at that sea and cry Shame! If I value anything at all, then I must blindfold my eyes when I near the Swiss Alps. We must as a culture dissemble our telescopes and settle down to back-slapping. We little blobs of soft tissue crawling around on this one planet's skin are right, and the whole universe is wrong.

13      Or consider the alternative.

14      Julian of Norwich, the great English anchorite and theologian, cited, in the manner of the prophets, these words from God: "See, I am God: See, I am in all things: See, I never lift my hands off my works, nor ever shall, without end . . . How should anything be amiss?" But now not even the simplest and best of us sees things the way Julian did. It seems to us that plenty is amiss. So much is amiss that I must consider the second fork in the road, that creation itself is blamelessly, benevolently askew by its very free nature, and that it is only human feeling that is freakishly amiss. The frog that the giant water bug sucked had, presumably, a rush of pure feeling for about a second, before its brain turned to broth. I, however, have been sapped by various strong feelings about the incident almost daily for several years.

15      Do the barnacle larvae care? Does the lacewing who eats her eggs care? If they do not care, then why am I making all this fuss? If I am a freak, then why don't I hush?

Our excessive emotions are so patently painful and harmful to us as  16
a species that I can hardly believe that they evolved. Other creatures manage to have effective matings and even stable societies without great emotions, and they have a bonus in that they need not ever mourn. (But some
higher animals have emotions that we think are similar to ours: Dogs, elephants, otters, and the sea mammals mourn their dead. Why do that to an
otter? What creator could be so cruel, not to kill otters, but to let them
care?) It would seem that emotions are the curse, not death—emotions
that appear to have devolved upon a few freaks as a special curse from
Malevolence.

All right then. It is our emotions that are amiss. We are freaks, the  17
world is fine, and let us all go have lobotomies to restore us to a natural
state. We can leave the library then, go back to the creek lobotomized, and
live on its banks as untroubled as any muskrat or reed. You first.

Of the two ridiculous alternatives, I rather favor the second. Although  18
it is true that we are moral creatures in an amoral world, the world's
amorality does not make it a monster. Rather, I am the freak. Perhaps I
don't need a lobotomy, but I could use some calming down, and the creek
is just the place for it. I must go down to the creek again. It is where I belong, although as I become closer to it, my fellows appear more and more
freakish, and my home in the library more and more limited. Imperceptibly at first, and now consciously, I shy away from the arts, from the human emotional stew. I read what the men with telescopes and micro-
scopes have to say about the landscape. I read about the polar ice, and I
drive myself deeper and deeper into exile from my own kind. But, since I
cannot avoid the library altogether—the human culture that taught me to
speak in its tongue—I bring human values to the creek, and so save myself from being brutalized.

What I have been after all along is not an explanation but a picture.  19
This is the way the world is, altar and cup, lit by the fire from a star that
has only begun to die. My rage and shock at the pain and death of individuals of my kind is the old, old mystery, as old as man, but forever fresh,
and completely unanswerable. My reservations about the fecundity and
waste of life among other creatures is, however, mere squeamishness. After all, I'm the one having the nightmares. It is true that many of the creatures live and die abominably, but I am not called upon to pass judgment.
Nor am I called upon to live in that same way, and those creatures who are
mercifully unconscious.

I don't want to cut this too short. Let me pull the camera back and look  20
at that fork in the road from a distance, in the larger context of the speck-
led and twining world. It could be that the fork will disappear, or that I will
see it to be but one of many interstices in a network, so that it is impossible to say which line is the main part and which is the fork.

21     The picture of fecundity and its excesses and of the pressures of growth and its accidents is of course no different from the picture I painted before of the world as an intricate texture of a bizarre variety of forms. Only now the shadows are deeper. Extravagance takes on a sinister, wastrel air, and exuberance blithers. When I added the dimension of time to the landscape of the world, I saw how freedom grew the beauties and horrors from the same live branch. This landscape is the same as that one, with a few more details added, and a different emphasis. I see squashes expanding with pressure and a hunk of wood rapt on the desert floor. The rye plant and the Bronx ailanthus are literally killing themselves to make seeds, and the animals to lay eggs. Instead of one goldfish swimming in its intricate bowl, I see tons and tons of goldfish laying and eating billions and billions of eggs. The point of all the eggs is of course to make goldfish one by one—nature loves the *idea* of the individual, if not the individual himself—and the point of a goldfish is pizzazz. This is familiar ground. I merely failed to mention that it is death that is spinning the globe.

22     It is harder to take, but surely it's been thought about. I cannot really get very exercised over the hideous appearance and habits of some deep-sea jellies and fishes, and I exercise easy. But about the topic of my own death I am decidedly touchy. Nevertheless, the two phenomena are two branches of the same creek, the creek that waters the world. Its source is freedom, and its network of branches is infinite. The graceful mockingbird that falls drinks there and sips in the same drop a beauty that waters its eyes and a death that fledges and flies. The petals of tulips are flaps of the same doomed water that swells and hatches in the ichneumon's gut.

23     That something is everywhere and always amiss is part of the very stuff of creation. It is as though each clay form had baked into it, fired into it, a blue streak of nonbeing, a shaded emptiness like a bubble that not only shapes its very structure but that also causes it to list and ultimately explode. We could have planned things more mercifully, perhaps, but our plan would never get off the drawing board until we agreed to the very compromising terms that are the only ones that being offers.

24     The world has signed a pact with the devil; it had to. It is a covenant to which every thing, even every hydrogen atom, is bound. The terms are clear: If you want to live, you have to die; you cannot have mountains and creeks without space, and space is a beauty married to a blind man. The blind man is Freedom, or Time, and he does not go anywhere without his great dog Death. The world came into being with the signing of the contract. A scientist calls it the Second Law of Thermodynamics. A poet says, "The force that through the green fuse drives the flower/Drives my green age." This is what we know. The rest is gravy.

*1974*

## QUESTIONS FOR DISCUSSION

### Content

a. What is Dillard's thesis? What is her purpose?

b. How does nature view the individual? How does this differ from the way human society views the individual?

c. What is Dillard saying in the railroad analogy in paragraph 5?

d. Who is Cock Robin (paragraph 9), and why does Dillard mention this figure?

e. Explain how Julius of Norwich "sees things" (paragraph 14)? To what end does the author quote this English theologian?

f. In what way, according to Dillard, is fecundity, a sign that there is something "amiss" in the world?

g. What does Dillard mean when she says that "the world has signed a pact with the devil; it had to" (paragraph 24)?

h. Why does the author's quoting of W. C. Fields help her develop this essay?

i. In the end, this essay is about a very specific concern: Dillard's own mortality. Trace the development of this essay and explain how the author manages to arrive at that idea.

### Strategy and Style

j. What illustrations does Dillard use to develop her essay? Why are they appropriate to her purpose?

k. What methods of development other than illustration does Dillard use?

l. Why is *Malevolence* capitalized in paragraph 16?

m. What use does the author make of figurative language? Where does she use analogy?

n. Reread the essay's introduction. What about it is so compelling?

o. How would you describe the author's tone? To what audience is she writing?

## ENGAGING THE TEXT

a. This essay is filled with a number of provocative statements, such as "Evolution loves death more than it loves you or me" (paragraph 8) and "Either this world, my mother, is a monster, or I myself am a freak" (paragraph 10). Find one such statement that interests you and interpret or explain it from your own point of view.

   b. For what do the creek and the library stand? Write a paragraph or two to explain the analogy Dillard creates by contrasting these two places. Use details from the text to develop your explanation.

## SUGGESTIONS FOR SUSTAINED WRITING

   a. Using Dillard's definition of fecundity as a starting point, explain your view of nature by using examples from your reading or experience. Is it a blind force that creates and destroys without plan or concern? Or is it more benevolent and purposeful? Do you agree or disagree with Dillard's notion that nature does not value the individual (paragraph 9)?

   b. Dillard seems to be trying to come to terms with her own mortality, something human beings have been trying to do for thousands of years. Using examples in any of the following essays to discuss ways in which people think about death: George Orwell's "A Hanging" (Chapter 1), Virginia Woolf's "The Death of the Moth" (Chapter 2), E. B. White's "Once More to the Lake" (Chapter 2), Jessica Mitford's "Behind the Formaldehyde Curtain" (Chapter 3), or Scott Russell Sanders's "The Men We Carry in Our Minds" (Chapter 6).

   c. Are right and wrong solely human concepts? Or are they present in nature as well? Defend your response by discussing examples of right and wrong drawn from history.

# A Crime of Compassion

Barbara Huttman

*Barbara Huttman (b. 1935) holds two degrees in nursing and has worked in that profession for more than thirty years. She has written a number of articles on the ethical dilemmas faced by medical professionals. In 1982, she published* Code Blue: A Nurse's True Life Story. *"A Crime of Compassion" was first published in* Newsweek *in 1983. When she told the story that year on the "Phil Donahue Show," she was called a murderer by some members of the audience.*

1    "Murderer," a man shouted. "God help patients who get *you* for a nurse."

2       "What gives you the right to play God?" another one asked.

3       It was the Phil Donahue show where the guest is a fatted calf and the audience a 200-strong flock of vultures hungering to pick up the bones. I had told them about Mac, one of my favorite cancer patients. "We resusci-

tated him 52 times in just one month. I refused to resuscitate him again. I simply sat there and held his hand while he died."

There wasn't time to explain that Mac was a young, witty, macho cop 4 who walked into the hospital with 32 pounds of attack equipment, looking as if he could single-handedly protect the whole city, if not the entire state. "Can't get rid of this cough," he said. Otherwise, he felt great.

Before the day was over, tests confirmed that he had lung cancer. And 5 before the year was over, I loved him, his wife, Maura, and their three kids as if they were my own. All the nurses loved him. And we all battled his disease for six months without ever giving death a thought. Six months isn't such a long time in the whole scheme of things, but it was long enough to see him lose his youth, his wit, his macho, his hair, his bowel and bladder control, his sense of taste and smell, and his ability to do the slightest thing for himself. It was also long enough to watch Maura's transformation from a young woman into a haggard, beaten old lady.

When Mac had wasted away to a 60-pound skeleton kept alive by liq- 6 uid food we poured down a tube, IV solutions we dripped into his veins, and oxygen we piped to a mask on his face, he begged us: "Mercy . . . for God's sake, please just let me go."

The first time he stopped breathing, the nurse pushed the button that 7 calls a "code blue" throughout the hospital and sends a team rushing to resuscitate the patient. Each time he stopped breathing, sometimes two or three times in one day, the code team came again. The doctors and technicians worked their miracles and walked away. The nurses stayed to wipe the saliva that drooled from his mouth, irrigate the big craters of bedsores that covered his hips, suction the lung fluids that threatened to drown him, clean the feces that burned his skin like lye, pour the liquid food down the tube attached to his stomach, put pillows between his knees to ease the bone-on-bone pain, turn him every hour to keep the bedsores from getting worse, and change his gown and linen every two hours to keep him from being soaked in perspiration.

At night I went home and tried to scrub away the smell of decaying flesh 8 that seemed woven into the fabric of my uniform. It was in my hair, the upholstery of my car—there was no washing it away. And every night I prayed that his agonized eyes would never again plead with me to let him die.

Every morning I asked the doctor for a "no code" order. Without that 9 order, we had to resuscitate every patient who stopped breathing. His doctor was one of the several who believe we must extend life as long as we have the means and knowledge to do it. To not do it is to be liable for negligence, at least in the eyes of many people, including some nurses. I thought about what it would be like to stand before a judge, accused of murder, if Mac stopped breathing and I didn't call a code.

And after the 52nd code, when Mac was still lucid enough to beg for 10 death again, and Maura was crumbled in my arms again, and when no amount of pain medication stilled his moaning and agony, I wondered about a spiritual judge. Was all this misery and suffering supposed to be building character or infusing us all with the sense of humility that comes from impotence?

11      Had we, the whole medical community, become so arrogant that we believed in the illusion of salvation through science? Had we become so self-righteous that we thought meddling in God's work was our duty, our moral imperative, and our legal obligation? Did we really believe that we had the right to force "life" on a suffering man who had begged for the right to die?

12      Such questions haunted me more than ever early one morning when Maura went home to change her clothes and I was bathing Mac. He had been still for so long, I thought he at last had the blessed relief of coma. Then he opened his eyes and moaned, "Pain . . . no more . . . Barbara . . .do something . . . God, let me go."

13      The desperation in the eyes and voice riddled me with guilt. "I'll stop," I told him as I injected the pain medication.

14      I sat on the bed and held Mac's hands in mine. He pressed his bony fingers against my hand and muttered, "Thanks." Then there was the one soft sigh and I felt his hands go cold in mine. "Mac?" I whispered, as I waited for his chest to rise and fall again.

15      A clutch of panic banded my chest, drew my finger to the code button, urged me to do something, anything . . . but sit there alone with death. I kept one finger on the button, without pressing it, as a waxen pallor slowly transformed his face from person to empty shell. Nothing I've ever done in my 47 years has taken so much effort as it took *not* to press that code button.

16      Eventually, when I was as sure as I could be that the code team would fail to bring him back, I entered the legal twilight zone and pushed the button. The team tried. And while they were trying, Maura walked in the room and shrieked, "No . . . don't let them do this to him . . .for God's sake . . . please, no more."

17      Cradling her in my arms was like cradling myself, Mac, and all those patients and nurses who had been in this place before who do the best they can in a death-denying society.

So a TV audience accused me of murder. Perhaps I am guilty. If a doctor had written a no-code order, which is the only *legal* alternative, would he have felt any less guilty? Until there is legislation making it a criminal act to code a patient who has requested the right to die, we will all of us risk the same fate as Mac. For whatever reason, we developed the means to prolong life, and now we are forced to use it. We do not have the right to die.

*1983*

## QUESTIONS FOR DISCUSSION

### Content

a. What is Huttman's purpose? Where in this essay does she state her thesis?

b. To what does the term "fatted calf" (paragraph 2) refer? What is the source of this metaphor, and how does it serve to advance the purpose of this essay?

c. What does Huttman mean by a "spiritual judge" in paragraph 10?

d. What is the "moral imperative" that the author mentions in paragraph 11?

e. Reread paragraphs 10 and 16. What are the legal implications of Huttman's decision?

### Strategy and Style

f. The author establishes her authority as an expert in her field early in this essay. How does she do this?

g. Huttman frames her essay by recalling her appearance on a television talk show. How do beginning and ending her essay this way advance her purpose?

h. The author is a capable observer who strengthens her writing by piling detail upon detail. Find a paragraph in which this practice is especially evident.

i. Why does Huttman tell us so much about her patient and his family?

j. This essay uses only one example to support its thesis. Would it have been more successful if it had used other examples as well? Why or why not?

## ENGAGING THE TEXT

a. Read this essay again. As you proceed, write down questions you might want to ask the author about her experiences with this or with other terminal patients. Choose one of your questions and answer it as Huttman might.

b. List three or more moral or ethical dilemmas college students might face during their academic careers. (One such dilemma might be how to react when you learn that someone in a class has cheated on exams or plagiarized papers.) Reread Huttman's essay before responding and compare your response to her comments.

## SUGGESTIONS FOR SUSTAINED WRITING

a. Have you or has someone you know ever had to choose between obeying a law or rule and doing what you think is morally correct? Write an

essay in which you explain how you or that person resolved this
dilemma, if at all.

b. Think about the profession you are preparing for or are considering.
Write an essay in which you try to predict the kinds of important moral,
ethical, or legal decisions with which you will be faced. Provide three or
four concrete examples. Compare your ideas with one or more essays
from the following list:

Mass Communication: *Gloria Steinem's "Erotica and Pornography"
(Chapter 4), Nicols Fox's "Gawk Shows" (Chapter 9), Mike Wallace's
"The Press Needs a National Monitor" (Chapter 10), Don Hewitt's "Mea
Culpa? Not Mea!" (Chapter 10).*

Public Service: *Ellen Goodman's "Watching the Grasshopper Get the Good-
ies" (Chapter 8), Barbara Ehrenreich's "A Step Back to the Workhouse?"
(Chapter 10), Garrett Hardin's "Lifeboat Ethics" (Chapter 10), Jonathan
Kozol's "Distancing the Homeless" (Chapter 11).*

Education: *Nat Hentoff's "Should This Student Have Been Expelled?"
(Chapter 10), Richard Rodriguez's "Bilingual Education" (Chapter 10).*

Law: *Nat Hentoff's "Should This Student Have Been Expelled?" (Chapter
10), Alan M. Dershowitz's "Shouting 'Fire!' " (Chapter 10), Camille
Paglia's "Rape" (Chapter 10), Susan Jacoby's "Common Decency" (Chapter 10).*

c. Do you agree with Huttman's thesis? Should we have laws "making it
a criminal act to code a patient who has requested the right to die?"
Write an essay using, in part, your own experience to support or attack
this proposal. After you have written your first draft, search the Internet or print materials on the "right to die" for other arguments that you
might use or that you might refute in later drafts.

# Black Men and Public Space

## Brent Staples

*Brent Staples (b. 1951) was born in Chester, Pennsylvania, the oldest of nine children. His
father was a truck driver who lost his job along with 40,000 other workers in the 1960s because of plant closings in the area. The family was reduced to poverty. Staples had never
considered college until a college professor took an interest in him and encouraged him to
apply to a program that recruited black students. He was enrolled at Widener University
(BA 1973), where he excelled and received a Danforth Fellowship for graduate study. He
took a Ph.D. in behavioral psychology at the University of Chicago in 1977. From 1977 to
1981 he taught psychology at several colleges in Pennsylvania and Illinois, but a job as re-*

*porter for the* Chicago Sun-Times *in 1982 and 1983 began his shift to journalism. He began writing for the* New York Times *in 1983 and has served on the editorial board of that newspaper, for which he writes opinion pieces on race, social problems, politics, and contemporary culture. In 1994, Staples published the autobiographical* Parallel Time: Growing Up in Black and White, *in which "Black Men and Public Space" appears.*

My first victim was a woman—white, well dressed, probably in her late  1
twenties. I came upon her late one evening on a deserted street in Hyde
Park, a relatively affluent neighborhood in an otherwise mean, impoverished section of Chicago. As I swung onto the avenue behind her, there
seemed to be a discreet, uninflammatory distance between us. Not so. She
cast back a worried glance. To her, the youngish black man—a broad six
feet two inches with a beard and billowing hair, both hands shoved into
the pockets of a bulky military jacket—seemed menacingly close. After a
few more quick glimpses, she picked up her pace and was soon running in
earnest. Within seconds, she disappeared into a cross street.

That was more than a decade ago. I was twenty-two years old, a grad-  2
uate student newly arrived at the University of Chicago. It was in the echo
of that terrified woman's footfalls that I first began to know the unwieldy
inheritance I'd come into—the ability to alter public space in ugly ways. It
was clear that she thought herself the quarry of a mugger, a rapist, or worse.
Suffering a bout of insomnia, however, I was stalking sleep, not defenseless
wayfarers. As a softy who is scarcely able to take a knife to a raw chicken—
let alone hold one to a person's throat—I was surprised, embarrassed, and
dismayed all at once. Her flight made me feel like an accomplice in tyranny.
It also made it clear that I was indistinguishable from the muggers who occasionally seeped into the area from the surrounding ghetto. That first encounter, and those that followed, signified that a vast, unnerving gulf lay
between nighttime pedestrians—particularly women—and me. And I soon
gathered that being perceived as dangerous is a hazard in itself. I only
needed to turn a corner into a dicey situation, or crowd some frightened,
armed person in a foyer somewhere, or make an errant move after being
pulled over by a policeman. Where fear and weapons meet—and they often do in urban America—there is always the possibility of death.

In that first year, my first away from my hometown, I was to become  3
thoroughly familiar with the language of fear. At dark, shadowy intersec-
tions, I could cross in front of a car stopped at a traffic light and elicit the
*thunk*, thunk, thunk, thunk of the driver—black, white, male, or female—
hammering down the door locks. On less traveled streets after dark, I grew
accustomed to but never comfortable with people crossing to the other
side of the street rather than pass me. Then there were the standard un-
pleasantries with policemen, doormen, bouncers, cabdrivers, and others
whose business it is to screen out troublesome individuals *before* there is
any nastiness.

4      I moved to New York nearly two years ago and I have remained an avid night walker. In central Manhattan, the near-constant crowd cover minimizes tense one-on-one street encounters. Elsewhere—in SoHo, for example, where sidewalks are narrow and tightly spaced buildings shut out the sky—things can get very taut indeed.

5      After dark, on the warrenlike streets of Brooklyn where I live, I often see women who fear the worst from me. They seem to have set their faces on neutral, and with their purse straps strung across their chests bandolier-style, they forge ahead as though bracing themselves against being tackled. I understand, of course, that the danger they perceive is not a hallucination. Women are particularly vulnerable to street violence, and young black males are drastically overrepresented among the perpetrators of that violence. Yet these truths are no solace against the kind of alienation that comes of being ever the suspect, a fearsome entity with whom pedestrians avoid making eye contact.

6      It is not altogether clear to me how I reached the ripe old age of twenty-two without being conscious of the lethality nighttime pedestrians attributed to me. Perhaps it was because in Chester, Pennsylvania, the small, angry industrial town where I came of age in the 1960s, I was scarcely noticeable against a backdrop of gang warfare, street knifings, and murders. I grew up one of the good boys, had perhaps a half-dozen fistfights. In retrospect, my shyness of combat has clear sources.

7      As a boy, I saw countless tough guys locked away; I have since buried several, too. They were babies, really—a teenage cousin, a brother of twenty-two, a childhood friend in his mid-twenties—all gone down in episodes of bravado played out in the streets. I came to doubt the virtues of intimidation early on. I chose, perhaps unconsciously, to remain a shadow—timid, but a survivor.

8      The fearsomeness mistakenly attributed to me in public places often has a perilous flavor. The most frightening of these confusions occurred in the late 1970s and early 1980s, when I worked as a journalist in Chicago. One day, rushing into the office of a magazine I was writing for with a deadline story in hand, I was mistaken for a burglar. The office manager called security and, with an ad hoc posse, pursued me through the labyrinthine halls, nearly to my editor's door. I had no way of proving who I was. I could only move briskly toward the company of someone who knew me.

9      Another time I was on assignment for a local paper and killing time before an interview. I entered a jewelry store on the city's affluent Near North Side. The proprietor excused herself and returned with an enormous red Doberman pinscher straining at the end of a leash. She stood, the dog extended toward me, silent to my questions, her eyes bulging nearly out of her head. I took a cursory look around, nodded, and bade her good night.

Relatively speaking, however, I never fared as badly as another black 10
male journalist. He went to nearby Waukegan, Illinois, a couple of summers ago to work on a story about a murderer who was born there. Mis-
taking the reporter for the killer, police officers hauled him from his car at
gunpoint and but for his press credentials would probably have tried to
book him. Such episodes are not uncommon. Black men trade tales like
this all the time.

Over the years, I learned to smother the rage I felt at so often being 11
taken for a criminal. Not to do so would surely have led to madness. I now
take precautions to make myself less threatening. I move about with care,
particularly late in the evening. I give a wide berth to nervous people on
subway platforms during the wee hours, particularly when I have ex-
changed business clothes for jeans. If I happen to be entering a building
behind some people who appear skittish, I may walk by, letting them clear
the lobby before I return, so as not to seem to be following them. I have
been calm and extremely congenial on those rare occasions when I've been
pulled over by the police.

And on late-evening constitutionals I employ what has proved to be 12
an excellent tension-reducing measure: I whistle melodies from Beethoven
and Vivaldi and the more popular classical composers. Even steely New
Yorkers hunching toward nighttime destinations seem to relax, and occasionally they even join in the tune. Virtually everybody seems to sense that
a mugger wouldn't be warbling bright, sunny selections from Vivaldi's
*Four Seasons*. It is my equivalent of the cowbell that hikers wear when they
know they are in bear country.

*1986*

## QUESTIONS FOR DISCUSSION

### Content

a. What does Staples mean in paragraph 2 by "the ability to alter public
   space"?
b. What does he learn from the encounter with a white woman that is recalled in paragraphs 1 and 2?
c. What other anecdotes does Staples use to illustrate the problem of
   "black men and public space"?
d. What is the essay's thesis?
e. What dilemma does the author explain in paragraph 5, and how does
   this explanation help him advance his thesis?

f.  In paragraph 10, the author claims, "Black men trade tales like this all the time." To what kinds of tales is he referring? How does including that sentence help him accomplish his purpose?

g.  Why has he forced himself "to smother the rage [he] felt at so often being taken for a criminal" (paragraph 11)?

h.  Who are Beethoven and Vivaldi? Why does Staples whistle their music?

## Strategy and Style

i.  Besides illustration, what methods of development does this essay employ?

j.  Staples begins with an anecdote. Discuss the effectiveness of this story as an introductory device.

k.  The thesis of the essay is implied. Would the essay have been more effective if it had been explicit?

l.  Staples's tone is remarkably subdued. Discuss the reason(s) behind his adopting such a tone. Should he have expressed more emotion?

## ENGAGING THE TEXT

a.  Reread paragraphs 8, 9, and 10. Then try to remember being wrongly accused of something. Write a paragraph or two briefly narrating this incident and explaining how you tried to establish your innocence or resolve the misunderstanding. Compare your response to Staples's essay.

b.  Have you ever acted like the white women in paragraphs 1 and 2, like the office manager in paragraph 8, or like the jewelry store proprietor in paragraph 9 by seriously misjudging someone's motives or intent? Can you justify your behavior? If so, on what grounds? If not, have you attempted to understand your behavior and amend your thinking? How have you done that? Compare your response to Staples's essay.

## SUGGESTIONS FOR SUSTAINED WRITING

a.  Read what you wrote in response to item *a* in Engaging the Text. Expand this material by discussing two or three more incidents of a similar nature. In the process, explain what these experiences taught you about human nature and what your reactions to them taught you about yourself and your ability to solve problems, deal with others, and/or cope with stress.

b.  Write an essay in which you explain the reaction of a particular race or group of people to an "outsider" or "outsiders" who might accidentally enter its "space." Use your own experiences, observations, and reading as sources of information. For example, how might a black community react to seeing a Pakistani family move in? How might a white suburban neighborhood react upon seeing a group of black teenage girls walking along its streets at dusk? Compare your essay to the ideas in Edward T. Hall's "The Anthropology of Manners" (Chapter 7) or Shelby Steele's "White Guilt" (Chapter 8).

c. At the beginning of paragraph 2, Staples remarks: "Where fear and weapons meet—and they often do in urban America—there is always the possibility of death." Using the Internet or materials in your college library, find information about recent events reported by the media that have a bearing on Staples's idea. Then turn your notes into a short research paper that explains how extensive and/or serious this problem is. There are several ways to approach this topic: one is to discuss incidents involving police shootings of armed and/or unarmed residents of the inner city; another is to discuss accidental shootings of innocent citizens by other innocent citizens; still another is to write about the shootings of children who got caught in the crossfire of gang warfare. Choose your own topic; just be sure to limit and focus it as much as possible.

# 8

# Cause and Effect

If you read Chapter 3, you know that explaining causes and effects is similar to analyzing a process. While the latter explains how something happens, however, the former seeks to reveal why it happens. Causal analysis often is used to explore questions in science, history, economics, and the social sciences. If you have taken courses in those subjects you may have written papers or essay exams that discuss the major causes of World War I, explain changes in the U.S. banking system brought on by the Great Depression, or predict the environmental consequences of uncontrolled pollution.

Causal analysis is so natural an activity that it appears in the earliest of stages of mental awareness. It is a tool by which we reflect upon and learn from our past: the child who burns her hand knows why she should stay away from the stove. But it is also a common way to anticipate the future. Peering into metaphorical crystal balls, we create elaborate plans, theorize about the consequences of our actions, and make appropriate changes in the way we live. "If I graduate in four years and get a fellowship to law school," dreams the ambitious college freshman, "I might land a job with Biddle and Biddle and even run for city council by the time I'm thirty. But first, I'd better improve my grades, which will mean studying harder and spending less time socializing."

The student's thinking illustrates an important point about the connection between causes and effects: it is often more complex than we imagine. For example, in "If Hitler Asked You to Electrocute a Stranger, Would You? Probably," Philip Meyer cannot theorize about people's willingness to obey authorities until he thoroughly explains Stanley Milgram's experiment and discusses Milgram's conclusions.

Keep this example in mind as you begin to use causal analysis as a way to develop ideas. More often than not, each cause and effect you discuss will require a thorough explanation using details that are carefully chosen and appropriate to your purpose. Remember, too, that you can call on a variety of skills and techniques to help you develop your analysis. For example, Ellen Goodman joins illustration with cause and effect, a brilliant combination that reveals the irony behind why planners and nonplanners reap the same rewards.

An important question any time you use cause and effects where to place your emphasis. Will you discuss what caused a particular phenomenon or will you focus on its effects? Shelby Steele discusses the relationship between "black power" and "white guilt" and the effects these two forces have had on American attitudes and political policy. Marya Mannes, on the other hand, spends most of her time explaining what causes so many people to "deny the existence of any valid criteria" for judging the arts. Of course, you may decide to strike a balance, as does Norman Cousins when he discusses both the reasons for the effects of our "becoming a nation of pill-grabbers and hypochondriacs."

As with the other kinds of writing in this text, purpose determines content and strategy. You read earlier that causal analysis is used frequently to explain historical or scientific phenomena. Such writing is often objective and dispassionate, but causal analysis has many applications. Because it is an especially powerful tool for persuasion, you might even want to use it to express a strong voice in regard to issues to which you are firmly committed. Take your lead from Mannes, for example, who addresses her readers directly and encourages them to adopt aesthetic standards "timeless as the universe itself." Like Cousins, warn your readers about a medical danger. Express concern over the state of the family, as does Barbara Dafoe Whitehead in "Where Have All the Parents Gone?" You might even want to analyze your reactions to social, political, or other types of problems to see what they tell you about yourself.

# How Do You Know It's Good?

Marya Mannes

*Marya Mannes (1904–1990) was born in New York City into a family of musicians. Her father, David Mannes, conducted the New York Symphony from 1898 to 1912 and was the founder of the Mannes College of Music. Her mother, Clara Mannes, was a professional pianist. Her brother, Leopold, was both a musician and a chemist; along with another musician/chemist, he invented Kodachrome. Marya, however, became a professional writer, editor, and televison commentator. She was a feature editor at* Vogue, *a columnist for* McCall's, *the* New York Times, *and United Features Syndicate; and a commentator for Channel 13, a public broadcasting station in New York. She also contributed frequently to several national magazines and was the author of two novels,* Message from a Stranger *(1948) and* They *(1968), and an autobiography,* Out of My Time *(1971). She was best known, however, for her essays, which have been collected in several books, including* But Will It Sell? *(1964), in which "How Do You Know It's Good?" appears.*

1 Suppose there were no critics to tell us how to react to a picture, a play, or a new composition of music. Suppose we wandered innocent as the dawn into an art exhibition of unsigned paintings. By what standards, by what values would we decide whether they were good or bad, talented or untalented, successes or failures? How can we ever know that what we think is right?

2 For the last fifteen or twenty years the fashion in criticism or appreciation of the arts has been to deny the existence of any valid criteria and to make the words "good" or "bad" irrelevant, immaterial, and inapplicable. There is no such thing, we are told, as a set of standards, first acquired through experience and knowledge and later imposed on the subject under discussion. This has been a popular approach, for it relieves the critic of the responsibility of judgment and the public of the necessity of knowledge. It pleases those resentful of disciplines, it flatters the empty-minded by calling them open-minded, it comforts the confused. Under the banner of democracy and the kind of equality which our forefathers did *not* mean, it says, in effect, "Who are you to tell us what *is* good or bad?" This is the same cry used so long and so effectively by the producers of mass media who insist that it is the public, not they, who decides what it wants to hear and see, and that for a critic to say that *this* program is bad and *this* program is good is purely a reflection of personal taste. Nobody recently has expressed this philosophy more succinctly than Dr. Frank Stanton, the highly intelligent president of CBS television. At a hearing before the Federal Communications Commission, this phrase escaped him under questioning: "One man's mediocrity is another man's good program."

3 There is no better way of saying "No values are absolute." There is another important aspect to this philosophy of *laissez faire:* It is the fear, in all observers of all forms of art, of guessing wrong. This fear is well come by, for who has not heard of the contemporary outcries against artists who later were called great? Every age has its arbiters who do not grow with their times, who cannot tell evolution from revolution or the difference between frivolous faddism, amateurish experimentation, and profound and necessary change. Who wants to be caught *flagrante delicto* with an error of judgment as serious as this? It is far safer, and certainly easier, to look at a picture or a play or a poem and to say "This is hard to understand, but it may be good," or simply to welcome it as a new form. The word "new"—in our country especially—has magical connotations. What is new must be good; what is old is probably bad. And if a critic can describe the new in language that nobody can understand, he's safer still. If he has mastered the art of saying nothing with exquisite complexity, nobody can quote him later as saying anything.

4 But all these, I maintain, are forms of abdication from the responsibility of judgment. In creating, the artist commits himself; in appreciating, you have a commitment of your own. For after all, it is the audience which

makes the arts. A climate of appreciation is essential to its flowering, and the higher the expectations of the public, the better the performance of the artist. Conversely, only a public ill-served by its critics could have accepted as art and as literature so much in these last years that has been neither. If anything goes, everything goes; and at the bottom of the junkpile lie the discarded standards too.

But what are these standards? How do you get them? How do you 5 know they're the right ones? How can you make a clear pattern out of so many intangibles, including that greatest one, the very private I?

Well for one thing, it's fairly obvious that the more you read and see 6 and hear, the more equipped you'll be to practice that art of association which is at the basis of all understanding and judgment. The more you live and the more you look, the more aware you are of a consistent pattern—as universal as the stars, as the tides, as breathing, as night and day—underlying everything. I would call this pattern and this rhythm an order. Not order—*an* order. Within it exists an incredible diversity of forms. Without it lies chaos—the wild cells of destruction—sickness. It is in the end up to you to distinguish between the diversity that is health and the chaos that is sickness, and you can't do this without a process of association that can link a bar of Mozart with the corner of a Vermeer painting, or a Stravinsky score with a Picasso abstraction; or that can relate an aggressive act with a Franz Kline painting and a fit of coughing with a John Cage composition.

There is no accident in the fact that certain expressions of art live for all 7 time and that others die with the moment, and although you may not always define the reasons, you can ask the questions. What does an artist say that is timeless; how does he say it? How much is fashion, how much is merely reflection? Why is Sir Walter Scott so hard to read now, and Jane Austen not? Why is baroque right for one age and too effulgent for another?

Can a standard of craftsmanship apply to art of all ages, or does each 8 have its own, and different, definitions? You may have been aware, inadvertently, that craftsmanship has become a dirty word these years because, again, it implies standards—something done well or done badly. The result of this convenient avoidance is a plenitude of actors who can't project their voices, singers who can't phrase their songs, poets who can't communicate emotion, and writers who have no vocabulary—not to speak of painters who can't draw. The dogma now is that craftsmanship gets in the way of expression. You can do better if you don't know how you do it, let alone *what* you're doing.

I think it is time you helped reverse this trend by trying to rediscover 9 craft: The command of the chosen instrument, whether it is a brush, a word, or a voice. When you begin to detect the difference between freedom and sloppiness, between serious experimentation and egotherapy, between skill and slickness, between strength and violence, you are on your way to separating the sheep from the goats, a form of segregation denied us for quite a while. All you need to restore it is a small bundle of standards and a Geiger counter that detects fraud, and we might begin our tour of the arts in an area where both are urgently needed: Contemporary painting.

10      I don't know what's worse: To have to look at acres of bad art to find the little good, or to read what the critics say about it all. In no other field of expression has so much double-talk flourished, so much confusion prevailed, and so much nonsense been circulated: Further evidence of the close interdependence between the arts and the critical climate they inhabit. It will be my pleasure to share with you some of this double-talk so typical of our times.

11      Item one: Preface for a catalogue of an abstract painter:

12      "Time-bound meditation experiencing a life; sincere with plastic piety at the threshold of hallowed arcana; a striving for pure ideation giving shape to inner drive; formalized patterns where neural balances reach a fiction." End of quote. Know what this artist paints like now?

13      Item two: A review in the *Art News:*

14      ". . . a weird and disparate assortment of material, but the monstrosity which bloomed into his most recent cancer of aggregations is present in some form everywhere. . . ." Then, later, "A gluttony of things and processes terminated by a glorious constipation."

15      Item three, same magazine, review of an artist who welds automobile fragments into abstract shapes:

16      "Each fragment . . . is made an extreme of human exasperation, torn at and fought all the way, and has its rightness of form as if by accident. *Any technique that requires order or discipline would just be the human ego.* No, these must be egoless, uncontrolled, undesigned and different enough to give you a bang—fifty miles an hour around a telephone pole. . . ."

17      "Any technique that requires order or discipline would just be the human ego." What does he mean—"just be"? What are they really talking about? Is this journalism? Is it criticism? Or is it that other convenient abdication from standards of performance and judgment practiced by so many artists and critics that they, like certain writers who deal only in sickness and depravity, "reflect the chaos about them"? Again, whose chaos? Whose depravity?

18      I had always thought that the prime function of art was to create order *out* of chaos—again, not the order of neatness or rigidity or convention or artifice, but the order of clarity by which one will and one vision could draw the essential truth out of apparent confusion. I still do. It is not enough to use parts of a car to convey the brutality of the machine. This is as slavishly representative, and just as easy, as arranging dried flowers under glass to convey nature.

19      Speaking of which, i.e., the use of real materials (burlap, old gloves, bottletops) in lieu of pigment, this is what one critic had to say about an exhibition of Assemblage at the Museum of Modern Art last year:

Spotted throughout the show are indisputable works of art, accounting for a quarter or even a half of the total display. But the remainder are works of non-art, anti-art, and art substitutes that are the aesthetic counterparts of the social deficiencies that land people in the clink on charges of vagrancy. These aesthetic bankrupts . . . have no legitimate ideological roof over their heads and not the price of a square intellectual meal, much less a spiritual sandwich, in their pockets.

I quote these words of John Canaday of the *New York Times* as an exam- 20 ple of the kind of criticism which puts responsibility to an intelligent public above popularity with an intellectual coterie. Canaday has the courage to say what he thinks and the capacity to say it clearly: Two qualities notably absent from his profession.

Next to art, I would say that appreciation and evaluation in the field 21 of music is the most difficult. For it is rarely possible to judge a new com-position at one hearing only. What seems confusing or fragmented at first might well become clear and organic a third time. Or it might not. The only salvation here for the listener is, again, an instinct born of experience and association which allows him to separate intent from accident, design from experimentation, and pretense from conviction. Much of contemporary music is, like its sister art, merely a reflection of the composer's own frag-mentation: An absorption in self and symbols at the expense of communi-cation with others. The artist, in short, says to the public: If you don't un-derstand this, it's because you're dumb. I maintain that you are not. You may have to go part way or even halfway to meet the artist, but if you must go the whole way, it's his fault, not yours. Hold fast to that. And remem-ber it too when you read new poetry, that estranged sister of music.

> A multitude of causes, unknown to former times, are now acting with a combined force to blunt the discriminating powers of the mind, and, un-fitting it for all voluntary exertion, to reduce it to a state of almost savage torpor. The most effective of these causes are the great national events which are daily taking place and the increasing accumulation of men in cities, where the uniformity of their occupations produces a craving for extraordinary incident, which the rapid communication of intelligence hourly gratifies. To this tendency of life and manners, the literature and theatrical exhibitions of the country have conformed themselves.

This startlingly applicable comment was written in the year 1800 by 22 William Wordsworth in the preface to his "Lyrical Ballads"; and it has been cited by Edwin Muir in his recently published book "The Estate of Poetry." Muir states that poetry's effective range and influence have di-minished alarmingly in the modern world. He believes in the inherent and indestructible qualities of the human mind and the great and per-manent objects that act upon it, and suggests that the audience will in-crease when "poetry loses what obscurity is left in it by attempting greater themes, for great themes have to be stated clearly." If you keep that firmly in mind and resist, in Muir's words, "the vast dissemination of secondary objects that isolate us from the natural world," you have gone a long way toward equipping yourself for the examination of any work of art.

23   When you come to theatre, in this extremely hasty tour of the arts, you can approach it on two different levels. You can bring to it anticipation and innocence, giving yourself up, as it were, to the life on the stage and reacting to it emotionally, if the play is good, or listlessly, if the play is boring; a part of the audience organism that expresses its favor by silence or laughter and its disfavor by coughing and rustling. Or you can bring to it certain critical faculties that may heighten, rather than diminish, your enjoyment.

24   You can ask yourselves whether the actors are truly in their parts or merely projecting themselves; whether the scenery helps or hurts the mood; whether the playwright is honest with himself, his characters, and you. Somewhere along the line you can learn to distinguish between the true creative act and the false arbitrary gesture; between fresh observation and stale cliché; between the avant-garde play that is pretentious drivel and the avant-garde play that finds new ways to say old truths.

25   Purpose and craftsmanship—end and means—these are the keys to your judgment in all the arts. What is this painter trying to say when he slashes a broad band of black across a white canvas and lets the edges dribble down? Is it a statement of violence? Is it a self-portrait? If it is *one* of these, has he made you believe it? Or is this a gesture of the ego or a form of therapy? If it shocks you, what does it shock you into?

26   And what of this tight little painting of bright flowers in a vase? Is the painter saying anything new about flowers? Is it different from a million other canvases of flowers? Has it any life, any meaning, beyond its statement? Is there any pleasure in its forms or texture? The question is not whether a thing is abstract or representational, whether it is "modern" or conventional. The question, inexorably, is whether it is good. And this is a decision which only you, on the basis of instinct, experience, and association, can make for yourself. It takes independence and courage. It involves, moreover, the risk of wrong decision and the humility, after the passage of time, of recognizing it as such. As we grow and change and learn, our attitudes can change too, and what we once thought obscure or "difficult" can later emerge as coherent and illuminating. Entrenched prejudices, obdurate opinions are as sterile as no opinions at all.

27   Yet standards there are, timeless as the universe itself. And when you have committed yourself to them, you have acquired a passport to that elusive but immutable realm of truth. Keep it with you in the forests of bewilderment. And never be afraid to speak up.

*1962*

## QUESTIONS FOR DISCUSSION

### Content

a.  What are the responsibilities of the audience? Do you feel qualified (based on Mannes's idea of responsibility) to "make the arts"? Do you think Mannes is asking too much, or not enough, of the audience?

b.  Mannes bemoans what she considers to be a lack of quality, craftsmanship, and so on, in the contemporary arts and gives reasons for this lack. But what other causes might explain the state of recent art? What reasons might Mannes have overlooked or conveniently left out of her essay?

c.  In paragraphs 8 Mannes implies that recent art is in the poor state it is because people no longer care about craftsmanship. Do you agree with Mannes's explanation of this cause-and-effect relationship?

d.  Can you infer from the first paragraph what Mannes thinks of critics? Where else in her essay does she reveal her opinion of them?

e.  Does she believe that "good" and "bad" can be defined? Does she define those terms? How do you define those terms? Can they be defined?

f.  In paragraph 2, Mannes uses televison programming as an example of the difficulty of defining *good* and *bad*. Which televison programs do you consider good, and which bad? What are your criteria for judgment?

g.  In paragraph 4, Mannes states that "it is the audience which makes the arts," an opinion that is implied repeatedly in the essay. Do you agree with this opinion? What effects do you feel an audience has on the arts or on other products?

h.  What are the steps Mannes recommends to acquire the standards necessary to determine what is good and what is bad?

i.  Mannes focuses her discussion on literature, fine arts, music, and the performing arts. Would her essay apply to other things just as well (for example, architecture, fashion, furniture, even products such as appliances)? If not, do these things require entirely different standards of judgment?

j.  Mannes wrote this essay in 1962. Does what she says hold true today as well?

k.  How would you answer the question posed by the title?

### Strategy and Style

l.  Mannes addresses the reader as "you," and her tone is quite authoritative. (See, for example, lines such as this one in paragraph 9: "I think it is time you helped reverse this trend. . . .")To whom is she speaking, and why might she want to sound authoritative? What does she want "you" to do?

m. How effective are the examples of critical "double-talk" that Mannes includes in paragraphs 11 through 17? Have you ever come across similar
double-talk in magazines, newspapers, or textbooks?

n. Mannes coins a new term in paragraph 9: "egotherapy." What is her implied definition of this word?

## ENGAGING THE TEXT

a. Go through Mannes's essay and make a list of her suggestions for answering the question posed by the title.

b. Select a work of art in a museum or gallery and write your responses to the
questions Mannes suggests in paragraphs 25 and 26. Rephrase her questions to fit the work you have chosen; for example, "What is this artist trying to say when she/he _____?" "Is this a statement of _____?" and so forth.

## SUGGESTIONS FOR SUSTAINED WRITING

a. Using Mannes's suggestions for evaluating the arts, write a review of an
art exhibit, play, novel, and so on.

b. Write an essay in which you extend to student essays Mannes's suggestions for creating one's own standards of bad and good. Do the same
standards fit? Does the "audience" determine the standards? Compare
the standards Mannes sets forth with standards stated or implied in any
of the following essays: Richard Marius's "Writing Drafts" (Chapter 3),
Gloria Steinem's "Erotica and Pornography" (Chapter 4), William
Lutz's "Doublespeak" (Chapter 5), Donna Woolfolk Cross's "Politics"
(Chapter 5), or Nicols Fox's "Gawk Shows" (Chapter 9).

c. Find a professional review you believe is especially full of meaningless
double-talk and rewrite it in ordinary English. What happens to the authority and to the meaning of the review when it is "translated"? Such
reviews can often be found in art or literature journals that your school
library carries or that can be found online.

# Pain Is Not the Ultimate Enemy

Norman Cousins

*Norman Cousins (1915–1990) served as editor of the prestigious* Staturday Review *for
more than four decades. After 1978, he was chairman of the editorial board of that journal*

*and senior lecturer at the Medical School of the University of California at Los Angeles. Always interested in international affairs, Cousins was twice president of the World Association of Federalists and the World Federalist Association. In 1963, he won the Eleanor Roosevelt Peace Award. Shortly thereafter, Cousins was stricken with a disease that left him almost totally paralyzed. His doctors advised him that there was no chance of recovery and that he would remain an invalid for the rest of his life. Despite their gloomy predictions, he fought back, often prescribing his own treatment, the foundation of which was an unswerving conviction that he could beat the disease. He wrote two books about his experience,* The Celebration of Life *(1974) and* The Anatomy of an Illness *(1979), in which this selection first appeared. Among Cousins's other well-known works are* Talks with Nehru *(1951),* Who Speaks for Man? *(1953),* Present Tense *(1967),* Albert Schweitzer's Mission *(1985),* The Pathology of Power *(1987), and* Head First *(1990).*

Americans are probably the most pain-conscious people on the face of the  1
earth. For years we have had it drummed into us—in print, on radio, over
television, in everyday conversation—that any hint of pain is to be banished as though it were the ultimate evil. As a result, we are becoming a
nation of pill-grabbers and hypochondriacs, escalating the slightest ache
into a searing ordeal.

We know very little about pain and what we don't know makes it hurt  2
all the more. Indeed, no form of illiteracy in the United States is so widespread or costly as ignorance about pain—what it is, what causes it, how
to deal with it without panic. Almost everyone can rattle off the names of
at least a dozen drugs that can deaden pain from every conceivable
cause—all the way from headaches to hemorrhoids. There is far less
knowledge about the fact that about 90 percent of pain is self-limiting, that
it is not always an indication of poor health, and that, most frequently, it is
the result of tension, stress, worry, idleness, boredom, frustration, suppressed rage, insufficient sleep, overeating, poorly balanced diet, smoking, excessive drinking, inadequate exercise, stale air, or any of the other
abuses encountered by the human body in modern society.

The most ignored fact of all about pain is that the best way to eliminate  3
it is to eliminate the abuse. Instead, many people reach almost instinctively
for the painkillers—aspirins, barbiturates, codeines, tranquilizers, sleeping pills, and dozens of other analgesics or desensitizing drugs.

Most doctors are profoundly troubled over the extent to which the  4
medical profession today is taking on the trappings of a pain-killing industry. Their offices are overloaded with people who are morbidly but mistakenly convinced that something dreadful is about to happen to them. It is all
too evident that the campaign to get people to run to a doctor at the first
sign of pain has boomeranged. Physicians find it difficult to give adequate
attention to patients genuinely in need of expert diagnosis and treatment
because their time is soaked up by people who have nothing wrong with
them except a temporary indisposition or a psychogenic ache.

5    Patients tend to feel indignant and insulted if the physician tells them he can find no organic cause of pain. They tend to interpret the term "psychogenic" to mean that they are complaining of nonexistent symptoms. They need to be educated about the fact that many forms of pain have no underlying physical cause but are the result, as mentioned earlier, of tension, stress, or hostile factors in the general environment. Sometimes a pain may be a manifestation of "conversion hysteria" . . . the name given by Jean Charcot to physical symptoms that have their origins in emotional disturbances.

6    Obviously, it is folly for an individual to ignore symptoms that could be a warning of a potentially serious illness. Some people are so terrified of getting bad news from a doctor that they allow their malaise to worsen, sometimes past the point of no return. Total neglect is not the answer to hypochondria. The only answer has to be increased education about the way the human body works, so that more people will be able to steer an intelligent course between promiscuous pill-popping and irresponsible disregard of genuine symptoms.

7    Of all forms of pain, none is more important for the individual to understand than the "threshold" variety. Almost everyone has a telltale ache that is triggered whenever tension or fatigue reaches a certain point. It can take the form of a migraine-type headache or a squeezing pain deep in the abdomen or cramps or a pain in the lower back or even pain in the joints. The individual who has learned how to make the correlation between such threshold pains and their cause doesn't panic when they occur; he or she does something about relieving the stress and tension. Then, if the pain persists despite the absence of apparent cause, the individual will telephone the doctor.

8    If ignorance about the nature of pain is widespread, ignorance about the way pain-killing drugs work is even more so. What is not generally understood is that many of the vaunted pain-killing drugs conceal the pain without correcting the underlying condition. They deaden the mechanism in the body that alerts the brain to the fact that something may be wrong. The body can pay a high price for suppression of pain without regard to its basic cause.

9    Professional athletes are sometimes severely disadvantaged by trainers whose job it is to keep them in action. The more famous the athlete, the greater the risk that he or she may be subjected to extreme medical measures when injury strikes. The star baseball pitcher whose arm is sore because of a torn muscle or tissue damage may need sustained rest more than anything else. But his team is battling for a place in the World Series; so the trainer or team doctor, called upon to work his magic, reaches for a strong dose of Butazolidine or other powerful pain suppressants. Presto, the pain disappears! The pitcher takes his place on the mound and does superbly. That could be the last game, however, in which he is able to throw a ball

with full strength. The drugs didn't repair the torn muscle or cause the damaged tissue to heal. What they did was to mask the pain, enabling the pitcher to throw hard, further damaging the torn muscle. Little wonder that so many star athletes are cut down in their prime, more the victims of overzealous treatment of their injuries than of the injuries themselves.

The king of all painkillers, of course, is aspirin. The U.S. Food and 10 Drug Administration permits aspirin to be sold without prescription, but the drug, contrary to popular belief, can be dangerous and, in sustained doses, potentially lethal. Aspirin is self-administered by more people than any other drug in the world. Some people are aspirin-poppers, taking ten or more a day. What they don't know is that the smallest dose can cause internal bleeding. Even more serious perhaps is the fact that aspirin is antagonistic to collagen, which has a key role in the formation of connective tissue. Since many forms of arthritis involve disintegration of the connective tissues, the steady use of aspirin can actually intensify the underlying arthritic condition.

Aspirin is not the only pain-killing drug, of course, that is known to 11 have dangerous side effects. Dr. Daphne A. Roe, of Cornell University, at a medical meeting in New York City in 1974, presented startling evidence of a wide range of hazards associated with sedatives and other pain suppressants. Some of these drugs seriously interfere with the ability of the body to metabolize food properly, producing malnutrition. In some instances, there is also the danger of bone-marrow depression, interfering with the ability of the body to replenish its blood supply.

Pain-killing drugs are among the greatest advances in the history of 12 medicine. Properly used, they can be a boon in alleviating suffering and in treating disease. But their indiscriminate and promiscuous use is making psychological cripples and chronic ailers out of millions of people. The un remitting barrage of advertising for pain-killing drugs, especially over television, has set the stage for a mass anxiety neurosis. Almost from the moment children are old enough to sit upright in front of a television screen, they are being indoctrinated into the hypochondriac's clamorous and morbid world. Little wonder so many people fear pain more than death itself.

It might be a good idea if concerned physicians and educators could 13 get together to make knowledge about pain an important part of the regular school curriculum. As for the populace at large, perhaps some of the same techniques used by public-service agencies to make people cancer-conscious can be used to counteract the growing terror of pain and illness in general. People ought to know that nothing is more remarkable about the human body than its recuperative drive, given a modicum of respect. If our broadcasting stations cannot provide equal time for responses to the pain-killing advertisements, they might at least set aside a few minutes each day for common-sense remarks on the subject of pain. As for the Food and Drug Administration, it might be interesting to know why an agency that has energetically warned the American people against taking vitamins without prescriptions is doing so little to control over-the-counter sales each year of billions of pain-killing pills, some of which can do more harm than the pain they are supposed to suppress.

*1979*

## QUESTIONS FOR DISCUSSION

### Content

a. Why does Cousins believe that aspirin is a dangerous drug? How does his use of aspirin serve as an illustration of his thesis?
b. Paragraph 8 may very well be the most important paragraph in this selection. Why?
c. Cousins sometimes refers to medical authorities. What purpose do such references serve? Are they effective?
d. How would you describe the audience Cousins is addressing? Analyze the details, vocabulary, and illustrations he uses as clues.
e. What can you infer about Cousins's opinions of the medical profession, the pharmaceutical industry, and the FDA?
f. Who or what does Cousins imply is mainly at fault for causing or worsening pain?
g. According to Cousins, what are some typical causes of pain? What does he mean when he claims that "90 percent of pain is self-limiting"?
h. What are some of the indications that the "medical profession . . . is taking on the trappings of the pain-killing industry"?

### Strategy and Style

i. What are the solutions Cousins suggests for remedying ignorance about pain and painkillers? Why might he have decided to end rather than to begin his essay with them?
j. How does Cousins define "threshold" pain?
k. Describe Cousins's tone in this essay. What is his attitude toward painkillers, and how is that attitude conveyed by his language?

## ENGAGING THE TEXT

a. Write about a time when you overcame pain of some sort. How did you overcome it? Compare your response to Cousins's essay.

b. Write a letter to Cousins, responding informally to his ideas. Tell him, referring to his essay, what you particularly liked or disliked about his essay.

## SUGGESTIONS FOR SUSTAINED WRITING

a. You may know a hypochondriac—someone who has convinced himself or herself that he or she is, has been, or will be afflicted by a variety of serious illnesses. Describe such a person and explain his or her thinking. In doing so, try to demonstrate the fact that hypochondria is itself a dangerous disease. Illustrate some of its more adverse effects, whether physical or emotional, on the "patient." Assume that your reader knows very little about the subject and provide sufficient explanatory detail to make your point clear.

b. Write a counterargument to Cousins's essay in which you try to convince him, or readers who would agree with him, that painkillers are not as dangerous as he says they are. Read any pair of essays in the Argument section of Chapter 10 to see how counterarguments can be written.

c. Cousins warns us about our overreliance on medication to relieve pain. Research the field of alternative medicine to find ways other than medication in which people cope with pain. Illustrate these methods as completely as you can. It would be wise to remember that some readers of your paper might be skeptical of pain-relieving methods that do not require the taking of medication, so be as convincing as you can without exaggerating.

# Watching the Grasshopper Get the Goodies

Ellen Goodman

*Ellen Goodman was born in Newton, Massachusetts, in 1941. She received a BA from Radcliffe College in 1963 and attended Harvard University on a Nieman Fellowship. Goodman began her journalistic career with* Newsweek, *where she was a researcher and reporter, and then moved to the* Detroit Free Press, *where she was a feature writer. She has been a feature writer and columnist for the* Boston Globe *since 1967. Her syndicated column, "At Large," appears in more than 200 newspapers across the country. Her first book,* Turning Points *(1979), was based on interviews she conducted about current changes in society. She has won several awards for her commentary, including a Pulitzer Prize in 1980. Many of her columns have been collected in* Close to Home *(1979),* At Large *(1981),* Keeping in Touch *(1985),* Making Sense *(1989), and* Value Judgments *(1993).*

*"Watching the Grasshopper" is reprinted from* At Large. *Her most recent book is* I Know Just What You Mean: The Power of Friendship in Women's Lives *(2000).*

1    I don't usually play the great American game called Categories. There are already too many ways to divide us into opposing teams, according to age, race, sex and favorite flavors. Every time we turn around, someone is telling us that the whole country is made up of those who drive pick-up trucks and those who do not, and then analyzing what this means in terms of the Middle East.

2    Still, it occurs to me that if we want to figure out why people are angry right now, it's not a bad idea to see ourselves as a nation of planners and nonplanners. It's the planners these days who are feeling penalized, right down to their box score at the bank.

3    The part of us which is most visibly and vocally infuriated by inflation, for example, isn't our liberal or conservative side but, rather, our planning side. Inflation devastates our attempts to control our futures—to budget and predict and expect. It particularly makes fools out of the people who saved then to buy now. To a certain extent, it rewards instant gratification and makes a joke out of our traditional notions of preparation.

4    It is no news bulletin that the people who dove over their heads into the real-estate market a few years ago are now generally better off than those who dutifully decided to save up for a larger down payment. With that "larger down payment" they can now buy two double-thick rib lamb-chops and a partridge in a pear tree.

5    But inflation isn't the only thing that leaves the planners feeling betrayed. There are other issues that find them actively pitched against the nonplanners.

6    We all know families who saved for a decade to send their kids to college. A college diploma these days costs about the same amount as a Mercedes-Benz. Of course, the Mercedes lasts longer and has a higher trade-in value. But the most devoted parent can be infuriated to discover that a neighboring couple who spent its income instead of saving is now eligible for college financial aid, while they are not. To the profligate go the spoils.

7    This can happen anywhere on the economic spectrum. There is probably only one mother in the annals of the New York welfare rolls to save up a few thousand dollars in hopes of getting off aid. But she would have been better off spending it. When she was discovered this year, the welfare department took the money back. She, too, was penalized for planning.

8    In these crimped times, the Planned Parents of the Purse are increasingly annoyed at other parents—whether they are unwed or on welfare or just prolific. For the first time in my own town, you can hear families with few children complaining out loud at the tax bill for the public schooling of families with many children.

One man I heard even suggested charging tuition for the third child.  9
He admitted, "It's not a very generous attitude, I know. But I'm not feeling
very generous these days." He is suffering from planner's warts.

At the same time I've talked with friends whose parents prepared, of-  10
ten with financial difficulty, for their "old age" and illness. They feel sad
when this money goes down a nursing home drain, but furious when
other people who didn't save get this same care for free.

Now we are all aware that if many people don't plan their economic  11
lives, it may be because they can't. It does no one any good to keep the
cashless out of college, to stash the old and poor into elderly warehouses,
to leave the "extra" children illiterate. We do want to help others, but we
also want our own efforts to make a difference.

There is nothing that grates a planner more than seeing a nonplanner  12
profit. It's as if the ant had to watch the grasshopper get the goodies.

Our two notions about what's fair end up on opposite sides. It isn't fair  13
if the poor get treated badly, and it isn't fair if those who work and save,
plan and postpone aren't given a better shake. We want the winners to be
the deserving. Only there is no divining rod for the deserving.

The hard part is to create policies that are neither unkind nor insane.  14
It is, after all, madness not to reward the kind of behavior we want to encourage. If we want the ranks of the planners to increase in this massive
behavior-modification program called society, we have to give them the
rewards, instead of the outrage.

*1981*

## QUESTIONS FOR DISCUSSION

### Content

a. What purpose might Goodman have had in starting her essay with a
   criticism of categorizing and then turning around and categorizing people into "planners and nonplanners"? Into which category does she implicitly place herself?
b. According to the author, what happens when you make long-range
   plans? Is she suggesting that people should never plan?
c. What might be her motives for writing this essay?
d. To whom is Goodman probably writing? How would you describe the
   ideal reader of this essay (age, occupation, level of education, opinions, etc.)?

was a remarkable loss of authority. And what whites lost in authority, blacks gained. You cannot feel guilty about anyone without giving away power to them. Suddenly, this huge vulnerability had opened up in whites and, as a black, you had the power to step right into it. In fact, black power all but demanded that you do so. What shocked me in the late 1960s, after the helplessness I had felt in the fifties, was that guilt had changed the nature of the white man's burden from the administration of inferiors to the uplift of equals—from the obligations of dominance to the urgencies of repentance.

3      I think what made the difference between the fifties and sixties, at least as far as white guilt was concerned, was that whites underwent an archetypal Fall. Because of the immense turmoil of the civil rights movement, and later the black-power movement, whites were confronted for more than a decade with their willingness to participate in, or comply with, the oppression of blacks, their indifference to human suffering and denigration, their capacity to abide evil for their own benefit and in the defiance of their own sacred principles. The 1964 Civil Rights Bill that bestowed equality under the law on blacks was also, in a certain sense, an admission of white guilt. Had white society not been wrong, there would have been no need for such a bill. In this bill the nation acknowledged its fallenness, its lack of racial innocence, and confronted the incriminating self-knowledge that it had rationalized for many years a flagrant injustice. Denial is a common way of handling guilt, but in the 1960s there was little will left for denial except in the most recalcitrant whites. With this defense lost there was really only one road back to innocence—through actions and policies that would bring redemption.

4      In the 1960s the need for white redemption from racial guilt became the most powerful, yet unspoken, element in America's social-policy-making process, first giving rise to the Great Society and then to a series of programs, policies, and laws that sought to make black equality and restitution a national mission. Once America could no longer deny its guilt, it went after redemption, or at least the look of redemption, and did so with a vengeance. Yet today, some twenty years later, study after study tells us that by many measures the gap between blacks and whites is widening rather than narrowing. A University of Chicago study indicates that segregation is more entrenched in American cities today than ever imagined. A National Research Council study notes the "status of blacks relative to whites (in housing and education) has stagnated or regressed since the early seventies." A follow-up to the famous Kerner Commission Report warns that blacks are as much at risk today of becoming a "nation within a nation" as we were twenty years ago, when the original report was made.

5      I think the white need for redemption has contributed to this tragic situation by shaping our policies regarding blacks in ways that may deliver

the look of innocence to society and its institutions but that do very little actually to uplift blacks. The specific effect of this hidden need has been to bend social policy more toward reparation for black oppression than toward the much harder and more mundane work of black uplift and development. Rather than facilitate the development of blacks to achieve parity with whites, these programs and policies—affirmative action is a good example—have tended to give blacks special entitlements that in many cases are of no use because blacks lack the development that would put us in a position to take advantage of them. I think the reason there has been more entitlement than development is (along with black power) the unacknowledged white need for redemption—not true redemption, which would have concentrated policy on black development, but the appearance of redemption, which requires only that society, in the name of development, seem to be paying back its former victims with preferences. One of the effects of entitlements, I believe, has been to encourage in blacks a dependency both on entitlements and on the white guilt that generates them. Even when it serves ideal justice, bounty from another man's guilt weakens. While this is not the only factor in black "stagnation" and "regression," I believe it is one very potent factor.

It is easy enough to say that white guilt too often has the effect of bend- 6 ing social policies in the wrong direction. But what exactly is this guilt, and how does it work in American life?

I think white guilt, in its broad sense, springs from a knowledge of ill- 7 gotten advantage. More precisely, it comes from the juxtaposition of this knowledge with the inevitable gratitude one feels for being white rather than black in America. Given the moral instincts of human beings, it is all but impossible to enjoy an ill-gotten advantage, much less to feel at least secretly grateful for it, without consciously or unconsciously experiencing guilt. If, as Kierkegaard writes, "innocence is ignorance," then guilt must always involve knowledge. White Americans *know* that their historical advantage comes from the subjugation of an entire people. So, even for whites today for whom racism is anathema, there is no escape from the knowledge that makes for guilt. Racial guilt simply accompanies the condition of being white in America.

I do not believe that this guilt is a crushing anguish for most whites, 8 but I do believe it constitutes a continuing racial vulnerability—an openness to racial culpability—that is a thread in white life, sometimes felt, sometimes not, but ever present as a potential feeling. In the late 1960s almost any black could charge this vulnerability with enough current for a white person to feel it. I had a friend who had developed this activity into a sort of specialty. I don't think he meant to be mean, though certainly he was mean. I think he was, in that hyperbolic era, exhilarated by the discovery that his race, which had long been a liability, now gave him a certain edge—that white guilt was the true force behind black power. To feel this power he would sometimes set up what he called "race experiments." Once I watched him stop a white businessman in the men's room of a large hotel and convince him to increase his tip to the black attendant from one to twenty dollars.

9      My friend's tactic was very simple, even corny. Out of the attendant's earshot he asked the man simply to look at the attendant, a frail, elderly, and very dark man in a starched white smock that made the skin on his neck and face look as leathery as a turtle's. He sat listlessly, pathetically, on a straight-backed chair next to a small table on which sat a stack of hand towels and a silver plate for tips. Since the attendant offered no service whatever beyond the handing out of towels, one could only conclude the hotel management offered his lowly presence as flattery to their patrons, as an opportunity for that easy noblesse oblige that could reassure even the harried and weary traveling salesman of his superior station. My friend was quick to make this point to the businessman and to say that no white man would do this job. But when the businessman put the single back in his wallet and took out a five, my friend only sneered. Did he understand the tragedy of a life spent this way, of what it must be like to earn one's paltry living as a symbol of inferiority? And did he realize that his privilege as an affluent white businessman (ironically he had just spent the day trying to sell a printing press to the Black Muslims for their newspaper *Mohammed Speaks*) was connected to the deprivation of this man and others like him?

10      But then my friend made a mistake that ended the game. In the heat of argument, which until then had only been playfully challenging, he inadvertently mentioned his father. This stopped the victim cold and his eyes turned inward. "What about your father?" the businessman asked. My friend replied, "He had a hard life, that's all." "How did he have a hard life?" the businessman asked. Now my friend was on the defensive. I knew he did not get along with his father, a bitter man who worked nights in a factory and demanded that the house be dark and silent all day. My friend blamed his father's bitterness on racism, but I knew he had not meant to exploit his own pain in this silly "experiment." Things had gotten too close to home, but he didn't know how to get out of the situation without losing face. Now, caught in his own trap, he did what he least wanted to do. He gave forth the rage he truly felt to a white stranger in a public men's room. "My father never had a chance," he said with the kind of anger that could easily turn to tears. "He never had a freakin' chance. Your father had all the goddamn chances, and you know he did. You sell printing presses to black people and make thousands and your father probably lives down in Fat City, Florida, all because you're white." On and on he went in this vein, using—against all that was honorable in him—his own profound racial pain to extract a flash of guilt from a white man he didn't even know.

He got more than a flash. The businessman was touched. His eyes be-  11
came mournful, and finally he simply said, "You're right. Your people got
a raw deal." He took a twenty dollar bill from his wallet and walked over
and dropped it in the old man's tip plate. When he was gone my friend and
I could not look at the old man, nor could we look at each other.

It is obvious that this was a rather shameful encounter for all con-  12
cerned—my friend and I, as his silent accomplice, trading on our racial
pain, tampering with a stranger for no reason, and the stranger then buying his way out of the situation for twenty dollars, a sum that was generous by one count and cheap by another. It was not an encounter of people
but of historical grudges and guilts. Yet, when I think about it now twenty
years later, I see that it had all the elements of a paradigm that I believe
has been very much at the heart of racial policy-making in America since
the 1960s.

My friend did two things that made this businessman vulnerable to  13
his guilt—that brought his guilt into the situation as a force. First he put
this man in touch with his own knowledge of his ill-gotten advantage as a
white. The effect of this was to disallow the man any pretense of racial innocence, to let him know that, even if he was not the sort of white who
used the word *nigger* around the dinner table, he still had reason to feel
racial guilt. But, as disarming as this might have been, it was too abstract
to do much more than crack open this man's vulnerability, to expose him
to the logic of white guilt. This was the five-dollar, intellectual sort of guilt.
The twenty dollars required something more visceral. In achieving this,
the second thing my friend did was something he had not intended to do,
something that ultimately brought him as much shame as he was doling
out: He made a display of his own racial pain and anger. (What brought
him shame was not the pain and anger, but his trading on them for what
turned out to be a mere twenty bucks.) The effect of this display was to reinforce the man's knowledge of ill-gotten advantage, to give credibility
and solidity to it by putting a face on it. Here was human testimony, a
young black beside himself at the thought of his father's racially con-
stricted life. The pain of one man evidenced the knowledge of the other.
When the businessman listened to my friend's pain, his racial guilt—normally only one source of guilt lying dormant among others—was called
out like a neglected debt he would finally have to settle. An ill-gotten advantage is not hard to bear—it can be marked up to fate—until it touches
the genuine human pain it has brought into the world. This is the pain that
hardens guilty knowledge.

Such knowledge is a powerful influence when it becomes conscious.  14
What makes it so powerful is the element of fear that guilt always carries,
the fear of what the guilty knowledge says about us. Guilt makes us afraid
for ourselves, and thus generates as much self-preoccupation as concern

for others. The nature of this preoccupation is always the redemption of innocence, the reestablishment of good feeling about oneself.

15     In this sense, the fear for the self that is buried in all guilt is a pressure toward selfishness. It can lead us to put our own need for innocence above our concern for the problem that made us feel guilt in the first place. But this fear for the self does not only inspire selfishness; it also becomes a pressure to *escape* the guilt-inducing situation. When selfishness and escapism are at work, we are no longer interested in the source of our guilt and, therefore, no longer concerned with an authentic redemption from it. Then we only want the look of redemption, the gesture of concern that will give us the appearance of innocence and escape from the situation. Obviously the businessman did not put twenty dollars in the tip plate because he thought it would uplift black Americans. He did it selfishly for the appearance of concern and for the escape it afforded him.

16     This is not to say that guilt is never the right motive for doing good works or showing concern, only that it is a very dangerous one because of its tendency to draw us into self-preoccupation and escapism. Guilt is a civilizing emotion when the fear for the self that it carries is contained—a containment that allows guilt to be more selfless and that makes genuine concern possible. I think this was the kind of guilt that, along with the other forces, made the 1964 Civil Rights Bill possible. But since then I believe too many of our social policies related to race have been shaped by the fearful underside of guilt.

17     Black power evoked white guilt and made it a force in American institutions, very much in the same way as my friend brought it to life in the businessman. Few people volunteer for guilt. Usually others make us feel it. It was the expression of black anger and pain that hardened the guilty knowledge of white ill-gotten advantage. And black power—whether from militant fringe groups, the civil rights establishment, or big city political campaigns—knew exactly the kind of white guilt it was after. It wanted to trigger the kind of white guilt in which whites fear for their own decency and innocence; it wanted the guilt of white self-preoccupation and escapism. Always at the heart of black power, in whatever form, has been a profound anger at what was done to blacks and an equally profound feeling that there should be reparations. But a sober white guilt (in which fear for the self is still contained) seeks a strict fairness—the 1964 Civil Rights Bill that guaranteed equality under the law. It is of little value when one is after more than fairness. So black power made its mission to have whites fear for their innocence, to feel a visceral guilt from which they would have to seek a more profound redemption. In such redemption was the possibility of black reparation. Black power upped the ante on white guilt.

18     With black power, all of the elements of the hidden paradigm that shape America's race-related social policy were in place. Knowledge of ill-gotten advantage could now be shown and deepened by black power into

the sort of guilt from which institutions could only redeem themselves by offering more than fairness—by offering forms of reparation and compensation for past injustice. I believe this bent our policies toward racial entitlements at the expense of racial development. In 1964, one of the assurances Senator Hubert Humphrey and others had to give Congress to get the landmark Civil Rights Bill passed was that the bill would not in any way require employers to use racial preferences to rectify racial imbalances. But this was before the explosion of black power in the late 1960s, before the hidden paradigm was set in motion. After black power, racial preferences became the order of the day.

If this paradigm brought blacks entitlements, it also brought the contin- 19 uation of the most profound problem in American society, the invisibility of blacks as a people. The white guilt that this paradigm elicits is the kind of guilt that preoccupies whites with their own innocence and pressures them toward escapism—twenty dollars in the plate and out the door. With this guilt, as opposed to the contained guilt of genuine concern, whites tend to see only their own need for quick redemption. Blacks then become a means to this redemption and, as such, they must be seen as generally "less than" others. Their needs are "special," "unique," "different." They are seen exclusively along the dimension of their victimization, so that they become "different" people with whom whites can negotiate entitlements but never fully see as people like themselves. Guilt that preoccupies people with their own innocence blinds them to those who make them feel guilty. This, of course, is not racism, and yet it has the same effect as racism since it makes blacks something of a separate species for whom normal standards and values do not automatically apply.

Nowhere is this more evident today than in American universities. At 20 some of America's most elite universities administrators have granted concessions in response to black student demands (black power) that all but sanction racial separatism on campus—black "theme" dorms, black student unions, black yearbooks, homecoming dances, and so forth. I don't believe administrators sincerely believe in these separatist concessions. Most of them are liberals who see racial separatism as wrong. But black student demands pull administrators into the paradigm of self-preoccupied white guilt, whereby they seek a quick redemption by offering special entitlements that go beyond fairness. As a result, black students become all but invisible to them. Though blacks have the lowest grade point average of any racial group in American universities, administrators never sit down with them and "demand" in kind that black students bring their grades up to par. The paradigm of white guilt makes the real problems of black students secondary to the need for white redemption. It also cuts administrators off from their own values, which would most certainly discourage racial separatism and encourage higher academic performance for black students. Lastly, it makes for escapist policies. There is no difference between giving black students a separate lounge and leaving twenty dollars in the tip plate on the way out the door.

*1990*

## QUESTIONS FOR DISCUSSION

### Content

a. According to Steele, what has caused white guilt? Trace the causal links he describes.
b. At the end of paragraph 6, Steele asks, "But what exactly is this guilt, and how does it work in American life?" How does he answer this question?
c. What does he mean when he says that "white guilt was the true force behind black power" (paragraph 8)?
d. What happened in the men's room between Steele's friend and the white businessman (paragraphs 8–13)? What was Steele's friend's "racial experiment"? What went "wrong" and why?
e. Why does the businessman put the twenty dollar bill in the tip plate?
f. How does Steele define *guilt*? What is the difference between the general term *guilt* and the specific term *white guilt*?
g. According to Steele, what effects does white guilt have on society? What are its positive and its negative effects?
h. What is the relationship between black power and white guilt?
i. According to Steele, what did the Civil Rights Act of 1964 cause?

### Strategy and Style

j. Look up *visceral*, a key word in paragraphs 13 and 17. What does this word mean in the context of these paragraphs? What other words does Steele use in these paragraphs to help define the word? Why was being visceral a problem?
k. What is the effect on you of the example of the "racial experiment"? Is it more of a "visceral" effect or an intellectual effect? What effect might Steele have intended by using this example?
l. Look up *paradigm* (paragraph 20). What does the word mean by itself? What does it mean in the phrase "paradigm of white guilt"?
m. How would you characterize the tone of this essay? Does Steele sound calm, angry, impassioned, and so forth?

## ENGAGING THE TEXT

a. In paragraph 2 Steele writes, "You cannot feel guilty about anyone without giving away power to them." Describe an event or two from your own life that illustrates this statement.

b. Summarize this essay in the form of a letter to your parents telling them about the reading you are doing for this class. Besides your summary, mention the one or two things that strike you as most important in the essay.

## SUGGESTIONS FOR SUSTAINED WRITING

a. By the end of the essay Steele begins to suggest ways to solve the problem of racial separatism; however, he does not elaborate on his suggestions. Write an essay in which you pick up on the points raised in paragraph 20 and present a detailed solution to the problem.

b. Compare Steele's essay to "Black Men and Public Space" by Brent Staples in Chapter 7. What does each essay say about stereotypes, anger, and racism?

c. Do some research into a particular period or event mentioned by Steele—the black power movement of the late 1960s or the 1964 Civil Rights Act, for example. Do not merely summarize your research but use it to come to an understanding of Steele's essay. You may wish to write the paper as a comparison of how you understood the essay on a first reading to how you understand it after your research.

# Where Have All the Parents Gone?

Barbara Dafoe Whitehead

*Barbara Dafoe Whitehead (b. 1944) was born in Rochester, Minnesota. She received a BA in 1966 from the University of Wisconsin and an MA in 1972 and a Ph.D. in 1976 from the University of Chicago. Whitehead is a social historian who heads the Family in American Culture Project for the Institute of American Values and also codirects the National Marriage Project. She became an overnight celebrity for her article "Dan Quayle Was Right" (published in* Atlantic Monthly *in 1993) supporting Quayle's criticism of the television show "Murphy Brown," which had broadcast an episode applauding single-parent families. Since then, Whitehead has been interested in how American culture allows such a high rate of divorce, an interest that formed the basis for her recent book* The Divorce Culture *(1997). She has written many articles about family issues, including "Where Have All the Parents Gone?" which originally appeared in* New Perspectives Quarterly *in 1990.*

1   "Invest in kids," George Bush mused during his 1988 presidential campaign, "I like it." Apparently so do others. A growing number of corporate CEOs and educators, elected officials and child-welfare advocates have embraced the same language. "Invest in kids" is the bumper-sticker for an important new cause, aptly tagged the *kids as capital* argument. It runs as follows:

2   America's human capital comes in two forms: The active work force and the prospective work force. The bulk of tomorrow's workers are to-day's children, of course. So children make up much of the stockpile of America's potential human capital.

3   If we look at them as tomorrow's workers, we begin to appreciate our stake in today's children. They will determine when we can retire, how well we can live in retirement, how generous our health insurance will be, how strong our social safety net, how orderly our society. What's more, to-day's children will determine how successfully we compete in the global economy. They will be going head-to-head against Japanese, Korean, and West German children.

4   Unfortunately, American children aren't prepared to run the race, let alone win it. Many are illiterate, undernourished, impaired, unskilled, poor. Consider the children who started first grade in 1986: 14 percent were illegitimate; 15 percent were physically or emotionally handicapped; 15 percent spoke a language other than English; 28 percent were poor; and fully 40 percent could be expected to live in a single-parent home before they reached eighteen. Given falling birth rates, this future work force is small—all the more reason to worry about its poor quality. So "invest in kids" is not the cry of the soft-hearted altruist but the call of the hard-headed realist.

5   *Kids as capital* has caught on because it responds to a broad set of national concerns. Whether one is worried about the rise of the under-class, the decline of the family, our standing in the global economy, the nation's level of educational performance, or intergenerational conflict, kids as capital seems to offer an answer.

6   Further, *kids as capital* offers the rationale for a new coalition for child-welfare programs. The argument reaches beyond the community of tradi-tional children's advocates and draws business into the child-saving fold. American corporations clearly have a stake in tomorrow's work force as they don't have in today's children. *Kids as capital* gives the toughminded, fifty-five-year-old CEO a reason to "care" about the eight-year-old, His-panic school girl.

7   Nevertheless, the argument left unchallenged could easily become yet another "feel-good" formula that doesn't work. Worse, it could end up be-traying those it seeks to save—the nation's children.

8   First, *kids as capital* departs from a classic American vision of the future. Most often, our history has been popularly viewed as progressive, with each generation breaking with and improving on the past. As an immi-

grant nation, we have always measured our progress through the progress of our children; they have been the bearers of the dream.

*Kids as capital* turns this optimistic view on its head. It conjures up a pic-  9
ture of a dark and disorderly future. Essentially, kids as capital is dystopic—closer to the spirit of *Blade Runner* and *Black Rain* than *Wizard of Oz* or *It's a Wonderful Life.* Children, in this view, do not bear the dream. They carry the seeds of our destruction. In short, *kids as capital* plays on our fears, rather than our hopes. It holds out the vision of a troubled future in order to secure a safer and more orderly present.

There is something troubling, too, in such an instrumental view of chil-  10
dren. To define them narrowly as tomorrow's wonders is to strip them of their full status as humans, as children: Kids can't be kids; they can only be embryonic workers. And treating *kids as capital* makes it easier to measure them solely through IQ tests, class standing, SAT scores, drop-out ratios, physical fitness tests. This leaves no place in the society for the slow starter, the handicapped, the quirky, and the nonconforming.

Yet *kids as capital* has an even more serious flaw. It evades the central  11
fact of life for American children: They have parents.

As we all know, virtually every child in America grows up in a family  12
with one or more parents. Parents house children. Parents feed children. Parents clothe children. Parents nurture and protect children. Parents instruct children in everything from using a fork to driving a car. To be sure, there have been vast changes in family life, and, increasingly, parents must depend on teachers, doctors, day-care workers, and technology to help care for and educate their children. Even so, these changes haven't altered one fundamental fact: In American society, parents still bear the primary responsibility for the material and spiritual welfare of children. As our teachers and counselors and politicians keep reminding us, everything begins at home. So, if today's children are in trouble, it's because today's parents are in trouble.

As recently as a dozen years ago, it was the central argument of an am-  13
bitious report by the Carnegie Council on Children. The Council put it plainly: "The best way to help children tomorrow is to support parents today." Yet, that view has been lost. The *kids as capital* argument suppresses the connection between parents and children. It imagines that we can improve the standing of children without improving the standing of the parents. In the new rhetoric, it is hard even to find the word "parent." Increasingly, kids are portrayed as standing alone out there somewhere, cosmically parent-free.

As a result, *kids as capital* ignores rather than addresses one of the most  14
important changes in American life: The decline in the power and standing of the nation's parents.

Only a generation ago, parents stood at the center of society. First of  15
all, there were so many of them—fully half the nation's households in 1960 were parent households with one or more children under eighteen. More-

workdays great enough to make up for the loss of sleep and leisure-time? Where did the mother of a feverish child belong—at the crib or at her desk?

26      On the whole, the first-stage critique was a sympathetic critique. In its view, parents might be affected by stress and guilt, but they weren't yet afflicted by serious pathology. After all, in the seventies, the nation's most suspect drug was laetrile, not crack or ice. Divorce was still viewed as a healthy alternative to an unhappy family life. But as the eighties began, a darker image of parents appeared. In the second-stage critique, . . . parents became toxic.

27      Day after day, throughout the eighties, Americans confronted an ugly new reality. Parents were hurting and murdering their children. Day after day, the newspapers brought yet another story of a child abandoned or battered. Day after day, the local news told of a child sexually abused by a father or a stepfather or a mother's boyfriend. Week by week, the national media brought us into courtrooms where photographs of battered children were held up to the camera. The sheer volume of stories suggested an epidemic of historic proportion. In even the most staid publications, the news was sensational. The *New York Times* carried bizarre stories usually found only in tabloids: A father who tortured his children for years; a mother who left her baby in a suitcase in a building she then set on fire; parents who abandoned babies dead or alive, in toilets, dumpsters, and alleyways.

28      Drug use among parents was one clear cause of abuse. And, increasingly child abuse and drug abuse were linked in the most direct way possible. Pregnant women were battering their children in the womb, delivering drugs through their umbilical cords. Nightly images of crack-addicted babies in neonatal units destroyed any lingering public sympathy for mothers of the underclass. And as the highly publicized Joel Steinberg case made clear, middle-class parents, too, took drugs and killed babies. Even those parents who occasionally indulged were causing their children harm. The Partnership for Drug-Free America ran ads asking: "With millions of parents doing drugs, is it any wonder their kids are too?"

29      More than drugs, it was divorce that lay at the heart of middle-class parental failure. It wasn't the crackhouse but the courthouse that was the scene of their collapse. Parents engaged in bitter custody battles. Parents kidnapped their own children. Parents used children as weapons against each other or simply walked away from their responsibilities. In an important new study on the long-term effects of divorce, Judith Wallerstein challenged the earlier notion that divorce is healthy for kids. She studied middle-class families for fifteen years after divorce and came up with some startling findings: Almost half of the children in the study entered adulthood as worried, underachieving, self-deprecating, and sometimes angry young men and women; one in four experienced

a severe and enduring drop in their standard of living; three in five felt rejected by at least one parent. Her study concluded: "Divorce is almost always more devastating for children than for their parents. . . . [W]hile divorce can rescue a parent from an intolerable situation, it can fail to rescue the children."

As a group, today's parents have been portrayed as selfish and un-   30 caring: Yuppie parents abandon the children to the au pair; working parents turn their kids over to the mall and the video arcade; single parents hang a key around their kids' necks and a list of emergency numbers on the refrigerator. Even in the healthiest families, parents fail to put their children first.

The indictment of parents is pervasive. In a survey by the Carnegie   31 Foundation, 90 percent of a national sample of public school teachers say a lack of parental support is a problem in their classrooms. Librarians gathered at a national convention to draft a new policy to deal with the problem of parents who send unattended children to the library after school. Day-care workers complain to Ann Landers that all too often parents hand over children with empty stomachs and full diapers. Everywhere, parents are flunking the most basic tests.

Declining demographically, hard-pressed economically, and disar-   32 rayed politically, parents have become part of the problem. For proponents of the *kids as capital* argument, the logic is clear: Why try to help parents— an increasingly marginal and unsympathetic bunch—when you can rescue their children?

To blame parents for larger social changes is nothing new. In the past,   33 child-saving movements have depended on building a public consensus that certain parents have failed. Child reformers in the Progressive Era, for example, were able to expand the scope of public sector responsibility for the welfare of children by exploiting mainstream fears about immigrant parents and their child-rearing practices. But what is new is the sense that the majority of parents—up and down the social ladder—are failing. Even middle-class parents, once solid, dependable caretakers of the next generation, don't seem to be up to the job.

By leaving parents out of the picture, *kids as capital* conjures up the im-   34 age of our little workers struggling against the little workers of Germany and the little workers of Japan. But this picture is obviously false. For the little workers of Germany and Japan have parents too. The difference is that their parents are strongly valued and supported by the society for their contributions *as parents*. We won't be facing up to reality until we are ready to pit our parents against their parents, and thus our family policy against theirs.

*1990*

# QUESTIONS FOR DISCUSSION

## Content

a. What is the "kids as capital" argument (paragraphs 2–6)?
b. What is Dafoe Whitehead's initial response to this argument (paragraphs 7–14)?
c. Though this essay is in part a cause/effect analysis, it is also an argument. What is Dafoe Whitehead arguing?
d. What is the main cause/effect relationship on which this argument is based?
e. Paraphrase and elaborate on paragraph 9. What is Dafoe Whitehead's point in this paragraph? Do you agree with her?
f. In paragraph 17, the author refers to a "pronatal ideology." What does she mean?
g. What are the stages in the shift from the rosy view of parenthood in the 1950s to the dark view of parenthood now? What has happened at each stage to further harm the image of parents?

## Strategy and Style

h. Writers who use the cause/effect approach often use particular words or phrases to signal the cause/effect relationships. Some of these words/phrases that Dafoe Whitehead uses are "as a result," "thus," "behind this," "then," "gave way to," and "lay at the heart of." Find these and other clues in this essay and explain what the cause/effect relationships are.
i. Dafoe Whitehead begins her essay with several paragraphs (2–6) that present the other side of the argument; she then presents her own argument (paragraph 7–14). What might have been her reasons for giving the other side so much attention?
j. Paragraph 7 is a transition between the two arguments. How does it link the two arguments? What are the key words that link the "kids as capital" argument with Dafoe Whitehead's argument?
k. Look at the transition words and phrases that frequently begin paragraphs (for example, "unfortunately" in paragraph 4, "further" in paragraph 6, "nevertheless" in paragraph 7, and "as we all know" in paragraph 12). What job do these words and phrases perform?

# ENGAGING THE TEXT

a. List the points of the "kids as capital" argument (paragraphs 2–6) that Whitehead summarizes before she presents her own argument. Then list the points of her own argument (paragraphs 7–14). Write a brief comparison of the two arguments. Which seems stronger?

b. Look up the Joel Steinberg case (mentioned in paragraph 28) in the *New York Times Index* and/or in a periodicals database. Find and summarize one or two articles about the case.

## SUGGESTIONS FOR SUSTAINED WRITING

a. Write a counterargument to Whitehead's argument. Before you begin drafting your paper, outline her essay so that you can clearly see its logic and main points. Then brainstorm a list of points that you could make against her points. Also mark places in your argument where facts and statistics would strengthen it.

b. Whitehead does not provide a plan for solving the problem she has described because her intention in this essay is merely to convince us of what the real problem is. She does imply, however, in her conclusion that we must find a way to value parents and to create stability in parenting. Write an essay in which you present a specific plan to achieve this. Bring in ideas from one or more of the following essays: N. Scott Momaday's "The Way to Rainy Mountain" (Chapter 2), Sam Pickering's "Faith of the Father" (Chapter 4), Gail Sheehy's "Predictable Crises of Adulthood" (Chapter 5), Scott Russell Sanders's "The Men We Carry in Our Minds" (Chapter 6), Barbara Ehrenreich's "A Step Back to the Workhouse?" (Chapter 10), Debra Dickerson's "Who Shot Johnny?" (Chapter 10).

c. Conversely, agree with Whitehead's argument and write an essay that expands upon it. Look up in the library the surveys and studies she cites. Use at least one of these studies as the basis for your essay.

# If Hitler Asked You to Electrocute a Stranger, Would You? Probably

Philip Meyer

*Philip Meyer (b. 1930) earned a BS in 1952 from Kansas State University and an MA in 1963 from the University of North Carolina and did graduate work at Harvard University in 1966 and 1967. While attending college, he worked as the assistant state editor of the* Topeka Daily Capital *and as a reporter for the* Miami Herald. *From 1962 to 1978 he was the Washington, D.C., correspondent for Knight-Ridder Newspapers, and from 1978 to*

*1982 he was Knight-Ridder's director of news and circulation research in Miami. Since then he as taught journalism at the University of North Carolina at Chapel Hill. In 1968 he shared a Pulitzer Prize with the staff of the* Detroit Free Press *for covering the Detroit riots in 1967. He has written several books about journalism, including* Precision Journalism, *which was first published in 1973 and has reappeared in subsequent editions;* To Keep the Republic, *written in collaboration with David Olson in 1975; and* Editors, Publishers, and Newspaper Ethics *(1983). He also contributes regularly to* Public Opinion Quarterly *and* Esquire. *"If Hitler Asked You . . ." was first published in* Esquire *in 1970.*

1    In the beginning, Stanley Milgram was worried about the Nazi problem. He doesn't worry much about the Nazis anymore. He worries about you and me, and, perhaps, himself a little bit too.

2    Stanley Milgram is a social psychologist, and when he began his career at Yale University in 1960 he had a plan to prove, scientifically, that Germans are different. The Germans-are-different hypothesis has been used by historians, such as William L. Shirer, to explain the systematic destruction of the Jews by the Third Reich.

3    The appealing thing about this theory is that it makes those of us who are not Germans feel better about the whole business. Obviously, you and I are not Hitler, and it seems equally obvious that we would never do Hitler's dirty work for him. But now, because of Stanley Milgram, we are compelled to wonder. Milgram developed a laboratory experiment which provided a systematic way to measure obedience. His plan was to try it out in New Haven on Americans and then go to Germany and try it out on Germans. He was strongly motivated by scientific curiosity, but there was also some moral content in his decision to pursue this line of research, which was, in turn, colored by his own Jewish background. If he could show that Germans are more obedient than Americans, he could then vary the conditions of the experiment and try to find out just what it is that makes some people more obedient than others. With this understanding, the world might, conceivably, be just a little bit better.

4    But he never took his experiment to Germany. He never took it any farther than Bridgeport. The first finding, also the most unexpected and disturbing finding, was that we Americans are an obedient people: Not blindly obedient, and not blissfully obedient, just obedient. "I found so much obedience," says Milgram softly, a little sadly, "I hardly saw the need for taking the experiment to Germany."

5    There is something of the theatre director in Milgram, and his technique, which he learned from one of the old masters in experimental psychology, Solomon Asch, is to stage a play with every line rehearsed, every prop carefully selected, and everybody an actor except one person. That one person is the subject of the experiment. The subject, of course, does not know he is in a play. He thinks he is in real life.

The experiment worked like this: If you were an innocent subject in Mil-  6
gram's melodrama, you read an ad in the newspaper or received one in the
mail asking for volunteers for an educational experiment. The job would
take about an hour and pay $4.50. So you make an appointment and go to
an old Romanesque stone structure on High Street with the imposing name
of The Yale Interaction Laboratory. It looks something like a broadcasting
studio. Inside, you meet a young, crew-cut man in a laboratory coat who
says he is Jack Williams, the experimenter. There is another citizen, fiftyish,
Irish face, an accountant, a little overweight, and very mild and harmless-
looking. This other citizen seems nervous and plays with his hat while the
two of you sit in chairs side by side and are told that the $4.50 checks are
yours no matter what happens. Then you listen to Jack Williams explain the
experiment.

It is about learning, says Jack Williams in a quiet, knowledgeable way.  7
Science does not know much about the conditions under which people
learn and this experiment is to find out about negative reinforcement.
Negative reinforcement is getting punished when you do something
wrong, as opposed to positive reinforcement which is getting rewarded
when you do something right. The negative reinforcement in this case is
electric shock.

Then Jack Williams takes two pieces of paper, puts them in a hat, and  8
shakes them up. One piece of paper is supposed to say, "Teacher" and the
other, "Learner." Draw one and you will see which you will be. The mild-
looking accountant draws one, holds it close to his vest like a poker player,
looks at it, and says, "Learner." You look at yours. It says, "Teacher." You do
not know that the drawing is rigged, and both slips say "Teacher." The experimenter beckons to the mild-mannered "learner."

"Want to step right in here and have a seat, please?" he says. "You can  9
leave your coat on the back of that chair . . . roll up your right sleeve,
please. Now what I want to do is strap down your arms to avoid excessive
movement on your part during the experiment. This electrode is connected to the shock generator in the next room.

"And this electrode paste," he says, squeezing some stuff out of a plas-  10
tic bottle and putting it on the man's arm, "is to provide a good contact and
to avoid a blister or burn. Are there any questions now before we go into
the next room?"

You don't have any, but the strapped-in "learner" does.  11

"I do think I should say this," says the learner. "About two years ago,  12
I was at the veterans' hospital . . . they detected a heart condition. Nothing
serious, but as long as I'm having these shocks, how strong are they—how
dangerous are they?"

Williams, the experimenter, shakes his head casually. "Oh, no," he says.  13
"Although they may be painful, they're not dangerous. Anything else?"

14       Nothing else. And so you play the game. The game is for you to read
a series of word pairs: For example, blue-girl, nice-day, fat-neck. When you
finish the list, you read just the first word in each pair and then a multiple-
choice list of four other words, including the second word of the pair. The
learner, from his remote, strapped-in position, pushes one of four switches
to indicate which of the four answers he thinks is the right one. If he gets
it right, nothing happens and you go on to the next one. If he gets it wrong,
you push a switch that buzzes and gives him an electric shock. And then
you go to the next word. You start with 15 volts and increase the number
of volts by 15 for each wrong answer. The control board goes from 15 volts
on one end to 450 volts on the other. So that you know what you are doing, you get a test shock yourself, at 45 volts. It hurts. To further keep you
aware of what you are doing to that man in there, the board has verbal descriptions of the shock levels, ranging from "Slight Shock" at the left-hand
side, through "Intense Shock" in the middle, to "Danger: Severe Shock" toward the far right. Finally, at the very end, under 435- and 450-volt
switches, there are three ambiguous X's. If, at any point, you hesitate, Mr.
Williams calmly tells you to go on. If you still hesitate, he tells you again.

15       Except for some terrifying details, which will be explained in a moment, this is the experiment. The object is to find the shock level at which
you disobey the experimenter and refuse to pull the switch.

16       When Stanley Milgram first wrote this script, he took it to fourteen
Yale psychology majors and asked them what they thought would happen. He put it this way: Out of one hundred persons in the teacher's
predicament, how would their breakoff points be distributed along the 15-
to-450-volt scale? They thought a few would break off very early, most
would quit someplace in the middle and a few would go all the way to the
end. The highest estimate of the number out of one hundred who would
go all the way to the end was three. Milgram then informally polled some
of his fellow scholars in the psychology department. They agreed that very
few would go to the end. Milgram thought so too.

17       "I'll tell you quite frankly," he says, "before I began this experiment,
before any shock generator was built, I thought that most people would
break off at 'Strong Shock' or 'Very Strong Shock.' You would get only a
very, very small proportion of people going out to the end of the shock
generator, and they would constitute a pathological fringe."

18       In his pilot experiments, Milgram used Yale students as subjects. Each
of them pushed the shock switches, one by one, all the way to the end of
the board.

19       So he rewrote the script to include some protests from the learner. At
first, they were mild, gentlemanly, Yalie protests, but, "it didn't seem to
have as much effect as I thought it would or should," Milgram recalls. "So
we had more violent protestation on the part of the person getting the

shock. All of the time, of course, what we were trying to do was not to create a macabre situation, but simply to generate disobedience. And that was one of the first findings. This was not only a technical deficiency of the experiment, that we didn't get disobedience. It really was the first finding: That obedience would be much greater than we had assumed it would be and disobedience would be much more difficult than we had assumed."

As it turned out, the situation did become rather macabre. The only 20 meaningful way to generate disobedience was to have the victim protest with great anguish, noise, and vehemence. The protests were tape-recorded so that all the teachers ordinarily would hear the same sounds and nuances, and they started with a grunt at 75 volts, proceeded through a "Hey, that really hurts," at 125 volts, got desperate with, "I can't stand the pain, don't do that," at 180 volts, reached complaints of heart trouble at 195, an agonized scream at 285, a refusal to answer at 315, and only heart-rending, ominous silence after that.

Still, sixty-five percent of the subjects, twenty- to fifty-year-old American 21 males, everyday, ordinary people, like you and me, obediently kept pushing those levers in the belief that they were shocking the mild-mannered learner, whose name was Mr. Wallace, and who was chosen for the role because of his innocent appearance, all the way up to 450 volts.

Milgram was now getting enough disobedience so that he had some- 22 thing he could measure. The next step was to vary the circumstances to see what would encourage or discourage obedience.

He put the learner in the same room with the teacher. He stopped 23 strapping the learner's hand down. He rewrote the script so that at 150 volts the learner took his hand off the shock plate and declared that he wanted out of the experiment. He rewrote the script some more so that the experimenter then told the teacher to grasp the learner's hand and physically force it down on the plate to give Mr. Wallace his unwanted electric shock.

"I had the feeling that very few people would go on at that point, if 24 any," Milgram says. "I thought that would be the limit of obedience that you would find in the laboratory."

It wasn't. 25

Although seven years have now gone by, Milgram still remembers the 26 first person to walk into the laboratory in the newly rewritten script. He was a construction worker, a very short man. "He was so small," says Milgram, "that when he sat on the chair in front of the shock generator, his feet didn't reach the floor. When the experimenter told him to push the victim's hand down and give the shock, he turned to the experimenter, and he turned to the victim, his elbow went up, he fell down on the hand of the victim, his feet kind of tugged to one side, and he said, 'Like this, boss?' Zzumph!"

27    The experiment was played out to its bitter end. Milgram tried it with forty different subjects. And thirty percent of them obeyed the experimenter and kept on obeying.

28    "The protests of the victim were strong and vehement, he was screaming his guts out, he refused to participate, and you had to physically struggle with him in order to get his hand down on the shock generator," Milgram remembers. But twelve out of forty did it.

29    Milgram took his experiment out of New Haven. Not to Germany, just twenty miles down the road to Bridgeport. Maybe, he reasoned, the people obeyed because of the prestigious setting of Yale University.

30    The new setting was a suite of three rooms in a run-down office building in Bridgeport. The only identification was a sign with a fictitious name: "Research Associates of Bridgeport." Questions about professional connections got only vague answers about "research for industry."

31    Obedience was less in Bridgeport. Forty-eight percent of the subjects stayed for the maximum shock, compared to sixty-five percent at Yale. But this was enough to prove that far more than Yale's prestige was behind the obedient behavior.

32    For more than seven years now, Stanley Milgram has been trying to figure out what makes ordinary American citizens so obedient. The most obvious answer—that people are mean, nasty, brutish and sadistic—won't do. The subjects who gave the shocks to Mr. Wallace to the end of the board did not enjoy it. They groaned, protested, fidgeted, argued, and in some cases, were seized by fits of nervous, agitated giggling.

33    "They even try to get out of it," says Milgram, "but they are somehow engaged in something from which they cannot liberate themselves. They are locked into a structure, and they do not have the skills or inner resources to disengage themselves."

34    Milgram's theory assumes that people behave in two different operating modes as different as ice and water. He does not rely on Freud or sex or toilet-training hang-ups for this theory. All he says is that ordinarily we operate in a state of autonomy, which means we pretty much have and assert control over what we do. But in certain circumstances, we operate under what Milgram calls a state of agency (after agent, *n* . . . one who acts for or in the place of another by authority from him; a substitute; a deputy—*Webster's Collegiate Dictionary*). A state of agency, to Milgram, is nothing more than a frame of mind.

35    "There's nothing bad about it, there's nothing good about it," he says. "It's a natural circumstance of living with other people. . . . I think of a state of agency as a real transformation of a person; if a person has different properties when he's in that state, just as water can turn to ice under certain conditions of temperature, a person can move to the state of mind that I call agency . . . the critical thing is that you see yourself as the instrument of the execution of another person's wishes. You do not see yourself as act-

ing on your own. And there's a real transformation, a real change of properties of the person."

So, for most subjects in Milgram's laboratory experiments, the act of 36 giving Mr. Wallace his painful shock was necessary, even though unpleasant, and besides they were doing it on behalf of somebody else and it was for science.

Stanley Milgram has his problems, too. He believes that in the labora- 37 tory situation, he would not have shocked Mr. Wallace. His professional critics reply that in his real-life situation he has done the equivalent. He has placed innocent and naïve subjects under great emotional strain and pressure in selfish obedience to his quest for knowledge. When you raise this issue with Milgram, he has an answer ready. There is, he explains patiently, a critical difference between his naïve subjects and the man in the electric chair. The man in the electric chair (in the mind of the naïve subject) is helpless, strapped in. But the naïve subject is free to go at any time.

Immediately after he offers this distinction, Milgram anticipates the 38 objection.

"It's quite true," he says, "that this is almost a philosophic position, be- 39 cause we have learned that some people are psychologically incapable of disengaging themselves. But that doesn't relieve them of the moral responsibility."

The parallel is exquisite. "The tension problem was unexpected," says 40 Milgram in his defense. But he went on anyway. The naïve subjects didn't expect the screaming protests from the strapped-in learner. But they went on.

"I had to make a judgment," says Milgram. "I had to ask myself, was 41 this harming the person or not? My judgment is that it was not. Even in the extreme cases, I wouldn't say that permanent damage results."

Sound familiar? "The shocks may be painful," the experimenter kept 42 saying, "but they're not dangerous."

After the series of experiments was completed, Milgram sent a report 43 of the results to his subjects and a questionnaire, asking whether they were glad or sorry to have been in the experiment. Eighty-three and seven-tenths percent said they were glad and only 1.3 percent were sorry; 15 percent were neither sorry nor glad. However, Milgram could not be sure at the time of the experiment that only 1.3 percent would be sorry.

Kurt Vonnegut Jr. put one paragraph in the preface to *Mother Night*, in 44 1966, which pretty much says it for the people with their fingers on the shock-generator switches, for you and me, and maybe even for Milgram. "If I'd been born in Germany," Vonnegut said, "I suppose I would have *been* a Nazi, bopping Jews and gypsies and Poles around, leaving boots sticking out of snowbanks, warming myself with my sweetly virtuous insides. So it goes."

Just so. One thing that happened to Milgram back in New Haven dur- 45 ing the days of the experiment was that he kept running into people he'd watched from behind the one-way glass. It gave him a funny feeling, seeing those people going about their everyday business in New Haven and knowing what they would do to Mr. Wallace if ordered to. Now that his research results are in and you've thought about it, you can get this funny feeling too. You don't need one-way glass. A glance in your own mirror may serve just as well.

*1970*

## QUESTIONS FOR DISCUSSION

### Content

a. Originally, what did Stanley Milgram intend his experiments to test? What unexpected turns did the experiment take?

b. Why did Milgram change the location and the details of the situation after the first experiment?

c. What are the probable reasons for the "teachers" in Milgram's experiments continued to administer shocks to the "learners"? List the reasons Milgram gives plus any other reasons you think are likely.

d. What does Milgram conclude about people's willingness to obey?

e. In your opinion, what other changes to the experiment would have made the results different? What might these other results have been?

### Strategy and Style

f. The use of "you," starting in paragraph 6, puts you directly into the action, into the role of the "teacher." What effect does this have on you? What is your reaction to the experimenter's requests?

g. What do the startling title and the bluntly worded first paragraph make you think the article will be about? Are your expectations met? Are the title and the opening effective?

h. What techniques does Meyer use to make this nonfiction article read like a fictional story?

i. Meyer wrote this article for *Esquire*, a magazine aimed primarily at college-educated, fashion-conscious men. How would the effect of the article change if it were written for radically different audiences, such as scholars, psychiatrists, or young children?

j. How does the reference to Kurt Vonnegut's novel *Mother Night* (paragraph 44) interpret Milgram's experiment? What is Meyer's opinion, as expressed in paragraphs 44 and 45? Do you agree with his take on Milgram's findings?

## ENGAGING THE TEXT

a. Describe what you would have done as a "teacher" in the experiment. Try to be as truthful as you can.
b. Do you think that Milgram's experiment was ethical? In other words, was it right of him to put his subjects in such a situation? Write a paragraph to explain your opinion about this.

## SUGGESTIONS FOR SUSTAINED WRITING

a. Continue the response you wrote for item *b* in Engaging the Text. Write an expanded definition of *ethical* in which you reflect on the meaning of this word in your own life.
b. Do you agree with Meyer's and Vonnegut's opinion that if you had been born in Germany, you would have become a Nazi (paragraphs 44 and 45)? Write an argumentative essay in which you expand that basic opinion, explaining why you agree or disagree with the opinion and defending your answer against possible counterarguments. Read any pair of essays in the Argument section of Chapter 10 to see how counterarguments can be written.
c. Do you think that continual exposure to violence (on television, on the news, in movies) desensitizes viewers to violence or even makes viewers violent themselves? Write a cause/effect essay in which you argue that, yes, exposure to violence has a direct relationship to increased violent crimes or, no, exposure to violence does not lead to violent behavior. You will need to do some research to support your opinion.

9

# Analogy

Have you ever taken a test that requires you to evaluate relationships between pairs of items or ideas? A typical question might go something like this:

Truck is to driver as horse is to _____.

When used to develop ideas in writing, analogies take the form of well-developed comparisons that reveal particular similarities between members of the same class or different classes. Like other forms of comparison, analogy introduces new subjects or ideas by referencing and drawing parallels to information with which the reader is already familiar. Writers often use analogy to create unexpected and startling comparisons between items from very different classes. Consider Loren Eiseley's discussion of our earthly environment as a kind of cosmic prison and his startling revelation that our perspective on this planet may be as limited as that of a white blood cell traveling through the body of a cat. Nonetheless, the beauty of analogy is that it can be used effectively to shed new light even on items from the same class.

Analogies, then, bring to light important relationships that can help define a term; describe a person, place, or object; or even argue an important point. Scientific writers rely on analogy to make their descriptions of complex mechanisms or obscure phenomena both interesting and accessible to lay readers. Analogy also can be used to emphasize the significance of particular scientific phenomena or issues. The fact that human beings evolved only relatively recently in the history of the planet will not be news to readers of James C. Rettie's "But a Watch in the Night." Nonetheless, charting the history of the Earth on a twelve-month clock helps the author underscore the fact that "we have just arrived. . . ."

Philosophical concepts, by their very nature abstract, also benefit from explanation through analogy. Plato's "The Myth of the Cave" is a cornerstone in the history of ideas; Camus' recounting of the Sisphus myth illuminates his definition of the absurd and explains why fate is a "human matter." Analogy is indeed a versatile tool. Consider the brilliant social commentary of Nicols Fox in "Gawk Shows" and of Horace Miner in "Body Ritual among the Nacirema." Consider too the personal portrait of a writer's anguish in Alice Walker's "Am I Blue?"

The items under Engaging the Text and Suggestions for Sustained Writing that follow each selection should help you create and develop interesting analogies of your own. But the essays themselves are so provocative, they might even help you come to grips with problems, issues, or concerns that play a significant role in your daily life. Can you compare your current social environment to a prison? Is taking fifteen credits and working twenty hours a week like trying to roll a boulder uphill? Does the way modern college students date resemble courtship rituals among "primitive" peoples (real or fictitious)? If questions like these pop into your mind as you read this chapter, write them down and show them to your instructor; they might make good topics for an essay. At the very least, they will help you begin using analogy as a tool for thinking and for writing.

# The Myth of the Cave

Plato

*The great Athenian philosopher of the fourth century B.C., Plato was the student of Socrates, whom he made the principal speaker in his dialogues. "The Myth of the Cave" appears in Book VII of* The Republic. *In it, Socrates addresses a series of questions to Glaucon in an attempt to explain that the world in which we live is a world of illusions and shadows—a mere reflection of the "real world" of the intellect. He explains that the "idea of the good" is the "universal author of all things beautiful and right, the parent of light . . . in this visible world, and the immediate source of reason and truth in the intellectual. . . ."*

And now, I said, let me show in a figure how far our nature is enlightened    1
or unenlightened:—Behold! human beings living in an underground den, which has a mouth open toward the light and reaching all along the den; here they have been from their childhood, and have their legs and necks chained so that they cannot move, and can only see before them, being prevented by the chains from turning round their heads. Above and behind them a fire is blazing at a distance, and between the fire and the prisoners there is a raised way; and you will see, if you look, a low wall built along the way, like the screen which marionette players have in front of them, over which they show the puppets.

I see.                                                                        2

And do you see, I said, men passing along the wall carrying all sorts    3
of vessels, and statues and figures of animals made of wood and stone and various materials, which appear over the wall? Some of them are talking, others silent.

You have shown me a strange image, and they are strange prisoners.    4

Like ourselves, I replied; and they see only their own shadows, or the shad-   5
ows of one another, which the fire throws on the opposite wall of the cave?

True, he said; how could they see anything but the shadows if they    6
were never allowed to move their heads?

7      And of the objects which are being carried in like manner they would only see the shadows?

8      Yes, he said.

9      And if they were able to converse with one another, would they not suppose that they were naming what was actually before them?

10     Very true.

11     And suppose further that the prison had an echo which came from the other side, would they not be sure to fancy when one of the passers-by spoke that the voice which they heard came from the passing shadow?

12     No question, he replied.

13     To them, I said, the truth would be literally nothing but the shadows of the images.

14     That is certain.

15     And now look again, and see what will naturally follow if the prisoners are released and disabused of their error. At first, when any of them is liberated and compelled suddenly to stand up and turn his neck round and walk and look toward the light, he will suffer sharp pains; the glare will distress him, and he will be unable to see the realities of which in his former state he had seen the shadows; and then conceive someone saying to him, that what he saw before was an illusion, but that now, when he is approaching nearer to being and his eye is turned toward more real existence, he has a clearer vision—what will be his reply? And you may further imagine that his instructor is pointing to the objects as they pass and requiring him to name them—will he not be perplexed? Will he not fancy that the shadows which he formerly saw are truer than the objects which are now shown to him?

16     Far truer.

17     And if he is compelled to look straight at the light, will he not have a pain in his eyes which will make him turn away to take refuge in the objects of vision which he can see, and which he will conceive to be in reality clearer than the things which are now being shown to him?

18     True, he said.

19     And suppose once more, that he is reluctantly dragged up a steep and rugged ascent, and held fast until he is forced into the presence of the sun himself, is he not likely to be pained and irritated? When he approaches the light his eyes will be dazzled, and he will not be able to see anything at all of what are now called realities.

20     Not all in a moment, he said.

21     He will require to grow accustomed to the sight of the upper world. And first he will see the shadows best, next the reflections of men and other objects in the water, and then the objects themselves; then he will gaze upon the light of the moon and the stars and the spangled heaven; and he will see the sky and the stars by night better than the sun or the light of the sun by day?

22     Certainly.

Last of all he will be able to see the sun, and not mere reflections of him   23
in the water, but he will see him in his own proper place, and not in another; and he will contemplate him as he is.

Certainly.   24

He will then proceed to argue that this is he who gives the season and   25
the years, and is the guardian of all that is in the visible world, and in a certain way the cause of all things which he and his fellows have been accustomed to behold?

Clearly, he said, he would first see the sun and then reason about him.   26

And when he remembered his old habitation, and the wisdom of the   27
den and his fellow-prisoners, do you not suppose that he would felicitate
himself on the change, and pity them?   28

Certainly, he would.   29

And if they were in the habit of conferring honors among themselves
on those who were quickest to observe the passing shadows and to remark
which of them went before, and which followed after, and which were together; and who were therefore best able to draw conclusions as to the future, do you think that he would care for such honors and glories, or envy
the possessors of them? Would he not say with Homer,

> Better to be the poor servant of a poor master,

and to endure anything, rather than think as they do and live after their
manner?

Yes, he said, I think that he would rather suffer anything than enter-   30
tain these false notions and live in this miserable manner.

Imagine once more, I said, such a one coming suddenly out of the sun to   31
be replaced in his old situation; would he not be certain to have his eyes full
of darkness?

To be sure, he said.   32

And if there were a contest, and he had to compete in measuring the   33
shadows with the prisoners who had never moved out of the den, while his
sight was still weak, and before his eyes had become steady (and the time
which would be needed to acquire this new habit of sight might be very considerable), would he not be ridiculous? Men would say of him that up he
went and down he came without his eyes; and that it was better not even to
think of ascending and if any one tried to loose another and lead him up to
the light, let them only catch the offender, and they would put him to death.

No question, he said.   34

This entire allegory, I said, you may now append, dear Glaucon, to the   35
previous argument; the prison-house is the world of sight, the light of the
fire is the sun, and you will not misapprehend me if you interpret the journey upwards to be the ascent of the soul into the intellectual world according to my poor belief, which, at your desire, I have expressed—
whether rightly or wrongly God knows. But, whether true or false, my
opinion is that in the world of knowledge the idea of good appears last of

all, and is seen only with an effort; and, when seen, is also inferred to be the universal author of all things beautiful and right, parent of light and of the lord of light in this visible world, and the immediate source of reason and truth in the intellectual; and that this is the power upon which he who would act rationally either in public or private life must have his eye fixed.

36      I agree, he said, as far as I am able to understand you.

37      Moreover, I said, you must not wonder that those who attain to this beatific vision are unwilling to descend to human affairs; for their souls are ever hastening into the upper world where they desire to dwell; which desire of theirs is very natural, if our allegory may be trusted.

38      Yes, very natural.

39      And is there anything surprising in one who passes from divine contemplations to the evil state of man, misbehaving himself in a ridiculous manner; if, while his eyes are blinking and before he has become accustomed to the surrounding darkness, he is compelled to fight in courts of law, or in other places, about the images or the shadows of images of justice, and is endeavoring to meet the conceptions of those who have never yet seen absolute justice?

40      Anything but surprising, he replied.

41      Anyone who has common sense will remember that the bewilderments of the eyes are of two kinds, and arise from two causes, either from coming out of the light or from going into the light, which is true of the mind's eye, quite as much as of the bodily eye; and he who remembers this when he sees anyone whose vision is perplexed and weak, will not be too ready to laugh; he will first ask whether that soul of man has come out of the brighter life, and is unable to see because unaccustomed to the dark, or having turned from darkness to the day is dazzled by excess of light. And he will count the one happy in his condition and state of being, and he will pity the other; or, if he have a mind to laugh at the soul which comes from below into the light, there will be more reason in this than in the laugh which greets him who returns from above out of the light into the den.

42      That, he said, is a very just distinction.

*ca. 373* BC

## QUESTIONS FOR DISCUSSION

### Content

a.  Why does Plato refer to "the world of sight" as a "prison-house"?

b. Does the fact that Plato has cast this extended analogy into a dialogue make it more effective than it would be if he had written it in conventional essay form?
c. What does the sun represent in Plato's analogy?
d. Consult an unabridged dictionary, encyclopedia, or reference book on ancient literature or civilization. Who was Homer? Why does Plato allude to him?
e. What is the "beatific" vision that Socrates describes to Glaucon? Why is it important that one "who would act rationally" experience this vision?
f. How does Plato account for the fact that honorable people who are able to see the truth and relate it to others often experience scorn and ridicule?
g. What has Glaucon learned by the end of the dialogue?

## Strategy and Style

h. How effective is the dialogue form used in this selection? What is the function of Glaucon's brief responses? Of Socrates' questions?
i. How do Socrates' questions help determine the organization?
j. What is Plato's role in this selection? Is he invisible, a mere transcriber of the dialogue, or is his voice heard in some way?

## ENGAGING THE TEXT

a. Write a short dialogue between yourself and Plato or between yourself and one of the dwellers in the cave.
b. This is an especially difficult selection. Try to capture the essence of Plato's ideas in a summary of one or two paragraphs.

## SUGGESTIONS FOR SUSTAINED WRITING

a. Describe the human condition by using an analogy other than the cave.
b. Do you believe that whatever is spiritual in a person can prevail? Write an essay in which you illustrate (from your own experiences, from those of people you know well, or from those you have read about) that people will deny themselves physical or material gratification in order to preserve the ethical principles or moral codes in which they believe. Compare your ideas with the ideas in Maya Angelou's "Grandmother's Victory" (Chapter 1), David Quammen's "Alias Benowitz Shoe Repair" (Chapter 2), or Barbara Huttman's "Crime of Compassion" (Chapter 7).
c. Do you believe that we are prisoners of the material world as Plato suggests? If so, write an essay based on research in which you illustrate

how people let their appetites (for food, money, sex, material possessions, for example) determine the course of their lives.

# The Myth of Sisyphus

Albert Camus

*Born in what was then the French colony of Algeria, Albert Camus (1913–1966) was edu-
cated at the University of Algeria. He began his career as an actor and playwright, but he
soon gave up the theater for journalism and began writing for* Alger Republican *and for*
Paris-Soir *in France. During World War II, Camus was very active in the French resistance and contributed regularly to* Combat, *an important underground newspaper. He is
remembered as a leading existentialist, a proponent of the modern philosophical movement
(if it can be termed that) that defines the individual as utterly free and totally responsible
for his or her own destiny. For many existentialists, God does not exist, and the world is
devoid of meaning except for that which the individual is able to create for himself or herself. Unlike the literature of many of his contemporaries, however, the works of Camus expose a view of life that, while hardly optimistic, encourages a belief in the inherent nobility
and courage of the human character even in the face of a hostile universe. Though clearly
evident in his famous novels,* The Stranger *(1942),* The Plague *(1947), and* The Rebel
*(1951), nowhere is this belief expressed more eloquently than in "The Myth of Sisyphus."*

1    The gods had condemned Sisyphus to ceaselessly rolling a rock to the top
of a mountain, whence the stone would fall back of its own weight. They
had thought with some reason that there is no more dreadful punishment
than futile and hopeless labor.

2    If one believes Homer, Sisyphus was the wisest and most prudent of
mortals. According to another tradition, however, he was disposed to practice the profession of highwayman. I see no contradiction in this. Opinions
differ as to the reasons why he became the futile laborer of the underworld.
To begin with, he is accused of a certain levity in regard to the gods. He stole
their secrets. Aegina, the daughter of Aesopus, was carried off by Jupiter. The
father was shocked by that disappearance and complained to Sisyphus. He,
who knew of the abduction, offered to tell about it on condition that Aesopus
would give water to the citadel of Corinth. To the celestial thunderbolts he
preferred the benediction of water. He was punished for this in the underworld. Homer tells us also that Sisyphus had put Death in chains. Pluto could
not endure the sight of his deserted, silent empire. He dispatched the god of
war, who liberated Death from the hands of her conqueror.

3    It is said also that Sisyphus, being near to death, rashly wanted to test
his wife's love. He ordered her to cast his unburied body into the middle

of the public square. Sisyphus woke up in the underworld. And there, annoyed by an obedience so contrary to human love, he obtained from Pluto permission to return to earth in order to chastise his wife. But when he had seen again the face of this world, enjoyed water and sun, warm stones and the sea, he no longer wanted to go back to the infernal darkness. Recalls, signs of anger, warnings were of no avail. Many years more he lived facing the curve of the gulf, the sparkling sea, and the smiles of earth. A decree of the gods was necessary. Mercury came and seized the impudent man by the collar and, snatching him from his joys, led him forcibly back to the underworld, where his rock was ready for him.

You have already grasped that Sisyphus is the absurd hero. He is, as 4 much through his passions as through his torture. His scorn of the gods, his hatred of death, and his passion for life won him that unspeakable penalty in which the whole being is exerted toward accomplishing nothing. This is the price that must be paid for the passions of this earth. Nothing is told us about Sisyphus in the underworld. Myths are made for the imagination to breathe life into them. As for this myth, one sees merely the whole effort of a body straining to raise the huge stone, to roll it and push it up a slope a hundred times over; one sees the face screwed up, the cheek tight against the stone, the shoulder bracing the clay-covered mass, the foot wedging it, the fresh start with arms outstretched, the wholly human security of two earth-clotted hands. At the very end of his long effort measured by skyless space and time without depth, the purpose is achieved. Then Sisyphus watches the stone rush down in a few moments toward that lower world whence he will have to push it up again toward the summit. He goes back down to the plain.

It is during that return, that pause, that Sisyphus interests me. A face that 5 toils so close to stones is already stone itself! I see that man going back down with a heavy yet measured step toward the torment of which he will never know the end. That hour like a breathing-space which returns as surely as his suffering, that is the hour of consciousness. At each of those moments when he leaves the heights and gradually sinks toward the lairs of the gods, he is superior to his fate. He is stronger than his rock.

If this myth is tragic, that is because its hero is conscious. Where would 6 his torture be, indeed, if at every step the hope of succeeding upheld him? The workman of today works every day in his life at the same tasks, and this fate is no less absurd. But it is tragic only at the rare moments when it becomes conscious. Sisyphus, proletarian of the gods, powerless and rebellious, knows the whole extent of his wretched condition: it is what he thinks of during his descent. The lucidity that was to constitute his torture at the same time crowns his victory. There is no fate that cannot be surmounted by scorn.

If the descent is thus sometimes performed in sorrow, it can also take 7 place in joy. This word is not too much. Again I fancy Sisyphus returning toward his rock, and the sorrow was in the beginning. When the images of earth cling too tightly to memory, when the call of happiness becomes too insistent, it happens that melancholy rises in man's heart: this is the rock's victory, this is the rock itself. The boundless grief is too heavy to bear. These are our nights of Gethsemane. But crushing truths perish from being acknowledged. Thus, Oedipus at the outset obeys fate without knowing it. But from the moment he knows, his tragedy begins. Yet at the same moment, blind and desperate, he realizes that the only bond linking him to the world is the cool hand of a girl. Then a tremendous remark rings out: "Despite so many ordeals, my advanced age and the nobility of my soul make me conclude that all is well." Sophocles' Oedipus, like Dostoevsky's Kirilov, thus gives the recipe for the absurd victory. Ancient wisdom confirms modern heroism.

8       One does not discover the absurd without being tempted to write a manual of happiness. "What! by such narrow ways—?" There is but one world, however. Happiness and the absurd are two sons of the same earth. They are inseparable. It would be a mistake to say that happiness necessarily springs from the absurd discovery. It happens as well that the feeling of the absurd springs from happiness. "I conclude that all is well," says Oedipus, and that remark is sacred. It echoes in the wild and limited universe of man. It teaches that all is not, has not been, exhausted. It drives out of this world a god who had come into it with dissatisfaction and a preference for futile sufferings. It makes of fate a human matter, which must be settled among men.

9       All Sisyphus' silent joy is contained therein. His fate belongs to him. His rock is his thing. Likewise, the absurd man, when he contemplates his torment, silences all the idols. In the universe suddenly restored to its silence, the myriad wondering little voices of the earth rise up. Unconscious, secret calls, invitations from all the faces, they are the necessary reverse and price of victory. There is no sun without shadow, and it is essential to know the night. The absurd man says yes and his effort will henceforth be unceasing. If there is a personal fate, there is no higher destiny, or at least there is but one which he concludes is inevitable and despicable. For the rest, he knows himself to be the master of his days. At that subtle moment when man glances backward over his life, Sisyphus returning toward his rock, in that slight pivoting he contemplates that series of unrelated actions which becomes his fate, created by him, combined under his memory's eye and soon sealed by his death. Thus, convinced of the wholly human origin of all that is human, a blind man eager to see who knows that the night has no end, he is still on the go. The rock is still rolling.

10      I leave Sisyphus at the foot of the mountain! One always finds one's burden again. But Sisyphus teaches the higher fidelity that negates the gods and raises rocks. He too concludes that all is well. This universe henceforth without a master seems to him neither sterile nor futile. Each atom of that stone, each mineral flake of that night-filled mountain, in itself forms a world. The struggle itself toward the heights is enough to fill a man's heart. One must imagine Sisyphus happy.

*1955*

## QUESTIONS FOR DISCUSSION

### Content

a. Who exactly was Sisyphus, and what does Camus mean when he calls him an "absurd hero"?

b. How do the various explanations behind his condemnation contribute to his portrayal as an "absurd hero"? In what way does the nature of Sisyphus' punishment help define that term?

c. Who was Pluto, and what does Camus mean by the "underworld"? Why are Sisyphus' efforts in that place "measured by skyless space and time without depth"?

d. What is Camus driving at when he tells us that "There is no fate that cannot be surmounted by scorn" (paragraph 6) and that we "must imagine Sisyphus happy" (paragraph 10)?

e. Does Camus succeed in comparing Sisyphus with a modern human being? Discuss this analogy and explain in what way a modern human might also be called absurd.

f. In order for Sisyphus to qualify as a "tragic hero," the author tells us, he must know the "whole extent of his wretched condition." In what way does this "lucidity" ennoble Sisyphus?

g. In what works do the famous literary characters Oedipus and Kirilov appear? How do their stories help illustrate "the recipe for the absurd victory"? What is "Gethsemane," which Camus mentions in paragraph 7?

h. What, for Camus, is "sacred" about Oedipus' conclusion that "'all is well'"? In what way does this remark make "of fate a human matter, which must be settled among men" (paragraph 8)?

i. Discuss the "higher fidelity that negates the gods and raises rocks" (paragraph 10).

### Strategy and Style

j. Camus uses the pronouns "you," "I," "one," and "he." To whom does each of these pronouns refer? In what ways do they create a persona for Camus?

k. What does Camus, or at least the persona of the essay, think of Sisyphus?

## ENGAGING THE TEXT

a. Why does Sisyphus continue to roll the rock uphill? Briefly explain his motivation.

b. Sketch the image that this essay evokes. Then write a description of the scene and speculate about why Camus may have chosen to create this scene in your mind's eye.

## SUGGESTIONS FOR SUSTAINED WRITING

a. Through a skillful use of analogy, Camus reveals the relevance of a
   classical myth to the modern world. Recall an ancient myth, parable
   from the Bible, folktale, or children's story that has special significance for you. Why is it still meaningful, and what does it tell us
   about life and people today? In short, what lesson(s) does it offer the
   modern reader?
b. In paragraph 6, Camus tells us, "The workman of today works every
   day in his life at the same tasks, and this fate is no less absurd [than that
   of Sisyphus]." Do you agree? In what way is a worker's "fate" similar
   to that of Camus' mythical hero? Would it be accurate to describe a
   worker, or any ordinary person, as a "tragic hero"? In what way is she
   or he "tragic"? In what way a "hero"? Use as examples the people described in other essays in this book: Maya Angelou's grandmother in
   "Grandmother's Victory" (Chapter 1), Maxine Hong Kingston's aunt in
   "No Name Woman" (Chapter 1), George Ochenski in David Quammen's "Alias Benowitz Shoe Repair" (Chapter 2), or Grant and Lee in
   Bruce Catton's "Grant and Lee" (Chapter 6).
c. Find out something about existentialism. What are the basic existential
   ideas? Explain how these ideas are reflected in "The Myth of Sisyphus"
   and/or other essays, stories, or novels by Camus.

# "But a Watch in the Night": A Scientific Fable

James C. Rettie

*James C. Rettie (1904–1968) was educated at the University of Oregon, Yale University,
and the University of London, where he studied economics. Employed by the U.S. Forest
Service for many years, Rettie was able to indulge his love for the outdoors and his interest
in conservation. During the Kennedy and Johnson administrations, he served as an adviser
to Secretary of the Interior Stuart Udall. Rettie published often in his field, but this is the
only essay for which he is widely remembered by the general public. It first appeared in 1948
in a publication of the Department of Agriculture. Rettie wrote it while serving at a Forest
Service station in Pennsylvania.*

Out beyond our solar system there is a planet called Copernicus. It came  1
into existence some four or five billion years before the birth of our Earth.
In due course of time it became inhabited by a race of intelligent men.

About 750 million years ago the Copernicans had developed the mo-  2
tion picture machine to a point well in advance of the stage that we have
reached. Most of the cameras that we now use in motion picture work are
geared to take twenty-four pictures per second on a continuous strip of
film. When such film is run through a projector, it throws a series of images on the screen and these change with a rapidity that gives the visual
impression of normal movement. If a motion is too swift for the human eye
to see it in detail, it can be captured and artificially slowed down by means
of the slow-motion camera. This one is geared to take many more shots per
second—ninety-six or even more than that. When the slow motion film is
projected at the normal speed of twenty-four pictures per second, we can
see just how the jumping horse goes over a hurdle.

What about motion that is too slow to be seen by the human eye? That  3
problem has been solved by the use of the time-lapse camera. In this one,
the shutter is geared to take only one shot per second, or one per minute,
or even one per hour—depending upon the kind of movement that is being photographed. When the time-lapse film is projected at the normal
speed of twenty-four pictures per second, it is possible to see a bean sprout
growing up out of the ground. Time-lapse films are useful in the study of
many types of motion too slow to be observed by the unaided, human eye.

The Copernicans, it seems, had time-lapse cameras some 757 million  4
years ago and they also had superpowered telescopes that gave them a
clear view of what was happening upon this Earth. They decided to make
a film record of the life history of Earth and to make it on the scale of one
picture per year. The photography has been in progress during the last 757
million years.

In the near future, a Copernican interstellar expedition will arrive  5
upon our Earth and bring with it a copy of the time-lapse film. Arrangements will be made for showing the entire film in one continuous run. This
will begin at midnight of New Year's Eve and continue day and night
without a single stop until midnight of December 31. The rate of projection
will be twenty-four pictures per second. Time on the screen will thus seem
to move at the rate of twenty-four years per second; 1440 years per minute;
86,400 years per hour; approximately two million years per day; and sixty-
two million years per month. The normal life-span of individual man will
occupy about three seconds. The full period of Earth history that will be
unfolded on the screen (some 757 million years) will extend from what the
geologists call Pre-Cambrian times up to the present. This will, by no
means, cover the full time-span of the Earth's geological history but it will
embrace the period since the advent of living organisms.

6       During the months of January, February, and March the picture will be desolate and dreary. The shape of the land masses and the oceans will bear little or no resemblance to those that we know. The violence of geological erosion will be much in evidence. Rains will pour down on the land and promptly go booming down to the seas. There will be no clear streams anywhere except where the rains fall upon hard rock. Everywhere on the steeper ground the stream channels will be filled with boulders hurled down by rushing waters. Raging torrents and dry stream beds will keep alternating in quick succession. High mountains will seem to melt like so much butter in the sun. The shifting of land into the seas, later to be thrust up as new mountains, will be going on at a grand scale.

7       Early in April there will be some indication of the presence of single-celled living organisms in some of the warmer and sheltered coastal waters. By the end of the month it will be noticed that some of these organisms have become multicellular. A few of them, including the Trilobites, will be encased in hard shells.

8       Toward the end of May, the first vertebrates will appear, but they will still be aquatic creatures. In June about 60 per cent of the land area that we know as North America will be under water. One broad channel will occupy the space where the Rocky Mountains now stand. Great deposits of limestone will be forming under some of the shallower seas. Oil and gas deposits will be in process of formation—also under shallow seas. On land there will still be no sign of vegetation. Erosion will be rampant, tearing loose particles and chunks of rock and grinding them into sand and silt to be sped out by the streams into bays and estuaries.

9       About the middle of July the first land plants will appear and take up the tremendous job of soil building. Slowly, very slowly, the mat of vegetation will spread, always battling for its life against the power of erosion. Almost foot by foot, the plant life will advance, lacing down with its root structures whatever pulverized rock material it can find. Leaves and stems will be giving added protection against the loss of the soil foothold. The increasing vegetation will pave the way for the land animals that will live upon it.

10      Early in August the seas will be teeming with fish. This will be what geologists call the Devonian period. Some of the races of these fish will be breathing by means of lung tissue instead of through gill tissues. Before the month is over, some of the lung fish will go ashore and take on a crude lizard-like appearance. Here are the first amphibians.

11      In early September the insects will put in their appearance. Some will look like huge dragonflies and will have a wing spread of 24 inches. Large portions of the land masses will now be covered with heavy vegetation that will include the primitive spore-propagating trees. Layer upon layer of this plant growth will build up, later to appear as the coal deposits. About the middle of this month, there will be evidence of the first seed-

bearing plants and the first reptiles. Heretofore, the land animals will have been amphibians that could reproduce their kind only by depositing a soft egg mass in quiet waters. The reptiles will be shown to be freed from the aquatic bond because they can reproduce by means of a shelled egg in which the embryo and its nurturing liquids are sealed and thus protected from destructive evaporation. Before September is over, the first dinosaurs will be seen—creatures destined to dominate the animal realm for about 140 million years and then to disappear.

In October there will be series of mountain uplifts along what is now   12 the eastern coast of the United States. A creature with feathered limbs— half bird and half reptile in appearance—will take itself into the air. Some small and rather unpretentious animals will be seen to bring forth their young in a form that is a miniature replica of the parents and to feed these young on milk secreted by mammary glands in the female parent. The emergence of this mammalian form of animal life will be recognized as one of the great events in geologic time. October will also witness the high water mark of the dinosaurs—creatures ranging in size from that of the modern goat to monsters like Brontosaurus that weighed some 40 tons. Most of them will be placid vegetarians, but a few will be hideous-looking carnivores, like Allosaurus and Tyrannosaurus. Some of the herbivorous dinosaurs will be clad in bony armor for protection against their flesh-eating comrades.

November will bring pictures of a sea extending from the Gulf of Mex-   13 ico to the Arctic in space now occupied by the Rocky Mountains. A few of the reptiles will take to the air on bat-like wings. One of these, called Pteranodon, will have a wingspread of 15 feet. There will be a rapid development of the modern flowering plants, modern trees, and modern insects. The dinosaurs will disappear. Toward the end of the month there will be a tremendous land disturbance in which the Rocky Mountains will rise out of the sea to assume a dominating place in the North American landscape.

As the picture runs on into December it will show the mammals in   14 command of the animal life. Seed-bearing trees and grasses will have covered most of the land with a heavy mantle of vegetation. Only the areas newly thrust up from the sea will be barren. Most of the streams will be crystal clear. The turmoil of geologic erosion will be confined to localized areas. About December 25 will begin the cutting of the Grand Canyon of the Colorado River. Grinding down through layer after layer of sedimentary strata, this stream will finally expose deposits laid down in Pre-Cambrian times. Thus in the walls of that canyon will appear geological formations dating from recent times to the period when the Earth had no living organisms upon it.

The picture will run on through the latter days of December and   15 even up to its final day with still no sign of mankind. The spectators will become alarmed in the fear that man has somehow been left out. But not so; sometime about noon on December 31 (one million years ago) will appear a stooped, massive creature of man-like proportions. This will be Pithecanthropus, the Java ape man. For tools and weapons he will have nothing but crude stone and wooden clubs. His children will live a precarious existence threatened on the one side by hostile animals and on the other by tremendous climatic changes. Ice sheets—in places 4,000 feet deep—will form in the northern parts of North America and Eurasia. Four times this glacial ice will push southward to cover half the continents. With each advance the plant and animal life will be swept under or pushed southward. With each recession of the ice, life will struggle to reestablish itself in the wake of the retreating glaciers. The woolly mammoth, the musk ox, and the caribou all will fight to maintain themselves near the ice line. Sometimes they will be caught and put into cold storage—skin, flesh, blood, bones and all.

16    The picture will run on through supper time with still very little evidence of man's presence on the earth. It will be about 11 o'clock when Neanderthal man appears. Another half hour will go by before the appearance of Cro-Magnon man living in caves and painting crude animal pictures on the walls of his dwelling. Fifteen minutes more will bring Neolithic man, knowing how to chip stone and thus produce sharp cutting edges for spears and tools. In a few minutes more it will appear that man has domesticated the dog, the sheep and, possibly, other animals. He will then begin the use of milk. He will also learn the arts of basket weaving and the making of pottery and dugout canoes.

17    The dawn of civilization will not come until about five or six minutes before the end of the picture. The story of the Egyptians, the Babylonians, the Greeks, and the Romans will unroll during the fourth, the third, and the second minute before the end. At 58 minutes and 43 seconds past 11:00 PM (just 1 minute and 17 seconds before the end) will come the beginning of the Christian era. Columbus will discover the new world 20 seconds before the end. The Declaration of Independence will be signed just 7 seconds before the final curtain comes down.

18    In those few moments of geologic time will be the story of all that has happened since we became a nation. And what a story it will be! A human swarm will sweep across the face of the continent and take it away from the . . . red men. They will change it far more radically than it has ever been changed before in a comparable time. The great virgin forests will be seen going down before ax and fire. The soil, covered for eons by its protective mantle of trees and grasses, will be laid bare to the ravages of water and wind erosion. Streams that had been flowing clear will, once again, take up a load of silt and push it toward the seas. Humus and mineral salts, both vital elements of productive soil, will be seen to vanish at a terrifying rate. The railroads and highways and cities that will spring up may divert attention, but they cannot cover up the blight of man's recent activities. In

great sections of Asia, it will be seen that man must utilize cow dung and every scrap of available straw or grass for fuel to cook his food. The forests that once provided wood for this purpose will be gone without a trace. The use of these agricultural wastes for fuel, in place of returning them to the land, will be leading to increasing soil impoverishment. Here and there will be seen a dust storm darkening the landscape over an area a thousand miles across. Man-creatures will be shown counting their wealth in terms of bits of printed paper representing other bits of a scarce but comparatively useless yellow metal that is kept buried in strong vaults. Meanwhile, the soil, the only real wealth that can keep mankind alive on the face of this earth is savagely being cut loose from its ancient moorings and washed into the seven seas.

We have just arrived upon this earth. How long will we stay?    19

*1950*

## QUESTIONS FOR DISCUSSION

### Content

a. What is the moral of this "scientific fable"?

b. Why does Rettie label this essay a fable? In what ways is it similar to other fables you may have read?

c. Given the fact that this essay was written in the 1940s, is it appropriate for Rettie to spend so much time introducing it with the story of the Copernicans and their invention of an advanced movie camera? Why does he go to such great lengths to explain time-lapse photography?

d. What is the obvious basis upon which Rettie constructs his analogy?

e. Rettie takes his title from Psalm 90:4 of the King James Version of the Bible. What do you make of this title? Does the last line of the essay shed any light on it? Look up Psalm 90. How does it relate to this selection?

### Strategy and Style

f. Does using an analogy aid Rettie in structuring his essay? Explain how Rettie has organized this piece and describe his use of transitions.

g. Consult an unabridged dictionary or encyclopedia to identify the following:

| | | |
|---|---|---|
| *Copernicus* | *Pre-Cambrian* | *Devonian* |
| *Babylonians* | *Cro-Magnon man* | *Neanderthal man* |
| *Java ape man* | *Mammoth* | |

h. Rettie makes use of scientific language and allusions to develop his essay. Are such terms and references bothersome to a reader without scientific training? Explain. Why does Rettie make it a point to include them?

i. Rettie writes in the future tense. What effect does that have on the narrative? On his argument?

j. Is there a difference in tone between Rettie's treatment of human history and his discussion of geological events? Where does he think we are heading?

## ENGAGING THE TEXT

a. Write a brief review of Rettie's "film."

b. Continue Rettie's film into the future, writing an extra paragraph that describes, depending on how you foresee it, either the Earth's destruction or its preservation.

## SUGGESTIONS FOR SUSTAINED WRITING

a. Analogy helps us grasp and order difficult concepts by enabling us to compare them to objects, processes, events, or other ideas with which we are more familiar. Compare an experience you are now going through or a problem you are now facing with something with which most readers might already be familiar. Some examples of such analogies are

- Working at XYZ Company is very much like living in a zoo.
- Driving Route 1 every morning is like gambling in Las Vegas.
- By the end of my day, I feel like I've just run a marathon.
- Having dinner at Aunt Tessie's is like eating at an Italian gourmet restaurant.

b. How would you answer the question Rettie asks at the very end of the essay? Describe the evidence you see in the world around you that humanity will continue to build, grow, and flourish—that it will prevail over the forces of doom. Then describe the evidence pointing to the very opposite conclusion. Some examples might be found in David Quammen's "Alias Benowitz Shoe Repair" (Chapter 2), Annie Dillard's "Fecundity" (Chapter 7), or Stephen Jay Gould's "Sex, Drugs, Disasters, and the Extinction of Dinosaurs" (Chapter 11).

c. Rettie's essay is essentially a listing of a number of important events in the history of the Earth and its inhabitants. He singles out several developments as particularly important, including the rise of the mam-

mals, the development of the Rocky Mountains, and the appearance of
Java man. Discuss an event or development (within the last fifteen
years) that you believe will have an enormous effect on the history of
the world. Explain the consequences of that event or development as
fully as you can. Bring in outside sources.

# Am I Blue?

Alice Walker

*Born in Eatontown, Georgia, Alice Walker (b. 1944) attended Spelman College on a scholarship; however, her active involvement in civil rights demonstrations led to her dismissal from that school. Fortunately, another scholarship, to Sarah Lawrence College, was soon offered, and Walker earned her BA in 1965. Although she was then offered a writing fellowship to study in Senegal, she decided to stay in the United States, working for the New York City Department of Welfare and with the civil rights movement in the South, registering voters. She has taught at Jackson State University, Tougaloo University, and Wellesley College and has been a writer-in-residence at several prestigious American colleges and universities. Among her many literary awards are a Pulitzer Prize and an American Book Award for* The Color Purple *(1982), which was turned into a major film. Walker's other major fiction includes* In Love and Trouble: Stories of Black Women *(1973),* The Temple of My Familiar *(1989), and* By the Light of My Father's Smile *(1998). She is also a well-known activist, literary critic, biographer, and essayist. She has recently written the memoirs* The Same River Twice: Honoring the Difficult *(1996)  and* Anything We Love Can Be Saved: A Writer's Activism *(1997). "Am I Blue?" first appeared in* Ms. *magazine in 1986.*

For about three years my companion and I rented a small house in the
country that stood on the edge of a large meadow that appeared to run
from the end of our deck straight into the mountains. The mountains, however, were quite far away, and between us and them there was, in fact, a
town. It was one of the many pleasant aspects of the house that you never
really were aware of this.

It was a house of many windows, low, wide, nearly floor to ceiling in
the living room, which faced the meadow, and it was from one of these that
I first saw our closest neighbor, a large white horse, cropping grass, flip-
ping its mane, and ambling about—not over the entire meadow, which
stretched well out of sight of the house, but over the five or so fenced-in
acres that were next to the twenty-odd that we had rented. I soon learned
that the horse, whose name was Blue, belonged to a man who lived in another town, but was boarded by our neighbors next door. Occasionally,
one of the children, usually a stocky teenager, but sometimes a much
younger girl or boy, could be seen riding Blue. They would appear in the

meadow, climb up on his back, ride furiously for ten or fifteen minutes, then get off, slap Blue on the flanks, and not be seen again for a month or more.

3    There were many apple trees in our yard, and one by the fence that Blue could almost reach. We were soon in the habit of feeding him apples, which he relished, especially because by the middle of summer the meadow grasses—so green and succulent since January—had dried out from lack of rain, and Blue stumbled about munching the dried stalks half-heartedly. Sometimes he would stand very still just by the apple tree, and when one of us came out he would whinny, snort loudly, or stamp the ground. This meant, of course: I want an apple.

4    It was quite wonderful to pick a few apples, or collect those that had fallen to the ground overnight, and patiently hold them, one by one, up to his large, toothy mouth. I remained as thrilled as a child by his flexible dark lips, huge, cubelike teeth that crunched the apples, core and all, with such finality, and his high, broad-breasted *enormity;* beside which, I felt small in-deed. When I was a child, I used to ride horses, and was especially friendly with one named Nan until the day I was riding and my brother deliberately spooked her and I was thrown, head first, against the trunk of a tree. When I came to, I was in bed and my mother was bending worriedly over me; we silently agreed that perhaps horseback riding was not the safest sport for me. Since then I have walked, and prefer walking to horseback riding—but I had forgotten the depth of feeling one could see in horses' eyes.

5    I was therefore unprepared for the expression in Blue's. Blue was lonely. Blue was horribly lonely and bored. I was not shocked that this should be the case; five acres to tramp by yourself, endlessly, even in the most beauti-ful of meadows—and his was—cannot provide many interesting events, and once rainy season turned to dry that was about it. No, I was shocked that I had forgotten that human animals and nonhuman animals can com-municate quite well; if we are brought up around animals as children we take this for granted. By the time we are adults we no longer remember. However, the animals have not changed. They are in fact *completed* creations (at least they seem to be, so much more than we) who are not likely to change; it is their nature to express themselves. What else are they going to express? And they do. And, generally speaking, they are ignored.

6    After giving Blue the apples, I would wander back to the house, aware that he was observing me. Were more apples not forthcoming then? Was that to be his sole entertainment for the day? My partner's small son had decided he wanted to learn how to piece a quilt; we worked in silence on our re-spective squares as I thought . . .

7    Well, about slavery: About white children, who were raised by black people, who knew their first all-accepting love from black women, and then, when they were twelve or so, were told they must "forget" the deep levels of communication between themselves and "mammy" that they

knew. Later they would be able to relate quite calmly, "My old mammy was sold to another good family." "My old mammy was ——— ———." Fill in the blank. Many more years later a white woman would say: "I can't understand these Negroes, these blacks. What do they want? They're so different from us."

And about the Indians, considered to be "like animals" by the "set-   8 tlers" (a very benign euphemism for what they actually were), who did not understand their description as a compliment.

And about the thousands of American men who marry Japanese, Ko-   9 rean, Filipina, and other non-English-speaking women and of how happy they report they are, *"blissfully,"* until their brides learn to speak English, at which point the marriages tend to fall apart. What then did the men see, when they looked into the eyes of the women they married, before they could speak English? Apparently only their own reflections.

I thought of society's impatience with the young. "Why are they playing  10 the music so loud?" Perhaps the children have listened to much of the music of oppressed people their parents danced to before they were born, with its passionate but soft cries for acceptance and love, and they have wondered why their parents failed to hear.

I do not know how long Blue had inhabited his five beautiful, boring  11 acres before we moved into our house; a year after we had arrived—and had also traveled to other valleys, other cities, other worlds—he was still there.

But then, in our second year at the house, something happened in  12 Blue's life. One morning, looking out the window at the fog that lay like a ribbon over the meadow, I saw another horse, a brown one, at the other end of Blue's field. Blue appeared to be afraid of it, and for several days made no attempt to go near. We went away for a week. When we returned, Blue had decided to make friends and the two horses ambled or galloped along together, and Blue did not come nearly as often to the fence underneath the apple tree.

When he did, bringing his new friend with him, there was a different  13 look in his eyes. A look of independence, of self-possession, of inalienable *horseness*. His friend eventually became pregnant. For months and months there was, it seemed to me, a mutual feeling between me and the horses of justice, of peace. I fed apples to them both. The look in Blue's eyes was one of unabashed "this is *itness*."

It did not, however, last forever. One day, after a visit to the city, I went  11 out to give Blue some apples. He stood waiting, or so I thought, though not beneath the tree. When I shook the tree and jumped back from the shower of apples, he made no move. I carried some over to him. He managed to half-crunch one. The rest he let fall to the ground. I dreaded looking into his eyes—because I had of course noticed that Brown, his partner, had gone—but I did look. If I had been born into slavery, and my partner had been sold or killed, my eyes would have looked like that. The children next door explained that Blue's partner had been "put with him" (the same expression that old people used, I had noticed, when speaking of an ancestor during slavery who had been impregnated by her owner) so that they could mate and she conceive. Since that was accomplished, she had been taken back by her owner, who lived somewhere else.

15  Will she be back? I asked.

16  They didn't know.

17  Blue was like a crazed person. Blue *was*, to me, a crazed person. He galloped furiously, as if he were being ridden, around and around his five beautiful acres. He whinnied until he couldn't. He tore at the ground with his hooves. He butted himself against his single shade tree. He looked always and always toward the road down which his partner had gone. And then, occasionally, when he came up for apples, or I took apples to him, he looked at me. It was a look so piercing, so full of grief, a look so *human*, I almost laughed (I felt too sad to cry) to think there are people who do not know that animals suffer. People like me who have forgotten, and daily forget, all that animals try to tell us. "Everything you do to us will happen to you; we are your teachers, as you are ours. We are one lesson" is essentially it, I think. There are those who never once have even considered animals' rights: Those who have been taught that animals actually want to be used and abused by us, as small children "love" to be frightened, or women "love" to be mutilated and raped. . . . They are the great-grandchildren of those who honestly thought, because someone taught them this: "Women can't think," and "niggers can't faint." But most disturbing of all, in Blue's large brown eyes was a new look more painful than the look of despair: The look of disgust with human beings, with life; the look of hatred. And it was odd what the look of hatred did. It gave him, for the first time, the look of a beast. And what that meant was that he had put up a barrier within to protect himself from further violence; all the apples in the world wouldn't change that fact.

18  And so Blue remained, a beautiful part of our landscape, very peaceful to look at from the window, white against the grass. Once a friend came to visit and said, looking out on the soothing view: "And it *would* have to be a *white* horse; the very image of freedom." And I thought, yes, the animals are forced to become for us merely "images" of what they once so beautifully expressed. And we are used to drinking milk from containers showing "contented" cows, whose real lives we want to hear nothing about, eating eggs and drumsticks from "happy" hens, and munching hamburgers advertised by bulls of integrity who seem to command their fate.

19  As we talked of freedom and justice one day for all, we sat down to steaks. I am eating misery, I thought, as I took the first bite. And spit it out.

*1986*

## QUESTIONS FOR DISCUSSION

### Content

a. To what is Blue analogous?

b. In paragraph 5 Walker writes that animals are "completed creations." What does she mean by this? Is she saying that humans are incomplete?

c. According to Walker, what is the usual relationship between animals and humans? What is the relationship that ought to exist?

d. What connections does Walker make between the treatment of animals and slavery?

e. What does Walker assume we will see if we really look into an animal's eyes? What would we see if we really looked into a person's eyes?

f. What is it that animals are trying to tell us?

### Strategy and Style

g. Although this essay primarily uses the strategy of analogy, it is also an argument. What is Walker arguing for or against? Is she making more than one argument?

h. The author projects human feelings onto Blue. What mood or tone does this create for the essay? How does it affect the argumentative nature of the essay? Does it make the essay seem less or more convincing?

i. The essay gets increasingly emotional as it progresses. How effective is this strategy?

j. At what point does Walker explicitly mention cruelty to animals? At what point does she mention cruelty to people?

k. Why is the childhood memory described in paragraph 4 necessary? What does it tell us that is essential to understanding the entire essay?

## ENGAGING THE TEXT

a. What is this essay mainly about? Slavery? Animal rights? Vegetarianism? Another subject? Decide what the main subject of the essay is and write a brief explanation of your choice. Cite examples from the essay to illustrate your explanation.

b. Describe the enclosed pasture from Blue's point of view. What does he think about his life? What does he think of Walker?

## SUGGESTIONS FOR SUSTAINED WRITING

a. Write an extended response to Walker's essay. Analyze her use of childhood memories, description, personification, and emotional appeals to create a unified argument. Include your own reactions as you read her essay, both what you felt and what you thought as you read. Finally, explain whether you find her use of memories, description, and so on, effective. In other words, do her strategies help her to persuade you?

b. Compare "Am I Blue?" to Joseph Pace's "Let's Go Veggie!" (Chapter 10) or Annie Dillard's "Fecundity" (Chapter 7). What does each writer say about the relationship between humans and animals?

c. Use analogy to write an argument. Begin by listing several possible analogies. In Walker's essay, for example, the life of Blue is analogous to the lives of slaves, Native Americans, and women and to those of other animals. In creating your analogy, think of things that are microcosms, that is, miniature versions of a larger world or of an important issue. Consider what you could argue by using such analogies. Use Walker's essay as a model for organization and as a guide for generating the kinds of examples to include. Draw on your own experiences and observations as well as on documented information you find in the library or on the Internet.

# Gawk Shows

Nicols Fox

*Nicols Fox is a commentator on media, culture, and the visual arts. Once an editor at the* Washington Journalism Review, *she is now a contributing editor at the* New Art Examiner *and a correspondent for the* Economist. *She also contributes to several other publications, such as the* Christian Science Monitor *and* Newsweek. *In 1993, covering the story of four children killed by E. coli from undercooked hamburgers, Fox became obsessed with the story and began researching the issue. That research led to the best-selling books* Spoiled: The Dangerous Truth about a Food Chain Gone Haywire *(1997) and* It Was Probably Something You Ate: A Practical Guide to Avoiding and Surviving Food-Borne Disease *(1999). Fox lives in Maine. "Gawk Shows" was first published in* Lear's *magazine in July 1991.*

1    I remember the dusty heat of late summer, the yellow and white tent, and the barker strutting on the platform. His voice rose above the sounds of the carnival, hinting of the wonders within the tent, wonders painted in cheap colors on the cracked backdrop: The two-headed baby, the world's fattest man, the bearded woman. I remember the sideshows. I thought they were long behind us.

2        I turn on the television and see an astonishing sight: A woman. Her soul is beautiful. It penetrates the atmosphere, even across airwaves. Her body is not. It is covered with the lumps and bumps of Elephant Man dis-

ease. Sally Jessy Raphael, wearing her trademark red spectacles, cocks her blond head and asks what the woman's life is like. A window is opened into pain. There are more victims of the disease sitting in the audience. We are treated to its various manifestations. We are horrified and amazed: We gawk.

Phil Donahue interviews tiny, wizened children. They have progeria, "the aging disease." With their outsize, hairless heads and huge eyes imparting solemnity and even wisdom, they offer us themselves as a sacrifice to our curiosity. We are compelled into silence, fascinated. We are back in the tent. 3

While I was living in Europe in the late sixties and early seventies, friends often asked me to tell them what to expect when they visited America. "Think of America as a carnival," I would tell them. "An unending carnival." This was the only way I knew to explain my country. Not just the quality of light and landscape but the excess, the enthusiasm, the love of excitement. We want no limitations on what we can have, on what we can do. We deny ourselves nothing—no objects, no sensations. "The pursuit of happiness": What other nation has made it an absolute right? 4

The carnival plays on, and we have returned to the sideshows—minus the honesty that made no pretense about what lay behind the curtain, the honesty that divided the world into those who were able to resist satisfying their curiosity at the expense of others and those who were not. Gawking is painted in shades of solicitude now. We justify much in the name of compassion, but we are in fact being entertained in the same ancient tradition. Gawk shows sell. 5

"I offer no apology," says Donahue. "These children have been unmercifully pressured by their very distinctive appearance." The purpose of the show? "To humanize people who have suffered. It becomes a vehicle for examining our prejudices. Just because it may be true that this kind of show draws a crowd does not condemn it," he says. 6

For Sally Jessy Raphael the rationale is the same: "Teaching the lessons of compassion. Man's triumph over adversity." 7

These are noble thoughts, and not entirely hypocritical. Compassion and understanding are always in short supply. There is an outside chance that some of each might be spread around in this exercise. We may also be witnessing exploitation. "These children are risking their lives to be here," says Sally, introducing children who will die if exposed to light. What may *she* be risking if they don't appear? As Donahue says, "If I don't draw a crowd, I could be parking cars for a living." 8

Donahue is open about the dilemma: "Americans are more interested in Madonna than Managua. The country suffers, in my opinion, from the diminished interest in serious news. Whichever way you look at it we have a culture of decay." It's tricky playing two sides at once. "It's like walking on eggs. I don't want to be a dead hero," he says. 9

10    We watch our cultural demise in living color.

11    Do you find yourself addicted to sex with prostitutes? Tell Oprah Winfrey and her audience all about it. Did you engage in an affair with your priest? Have your breast implants started slipping? Geraldo Rivera wants to know. Do you wish you could reverse your sex-change operation? Are you a celebrity subject to diarrhea at odd moments? Does your mother keep stealing your boyfriends? We care, we are interested. Whatever your problem, there's a television talk show that will accommodate you.

12    Donahue, Oprah, Sally, Geraldo: They are the virtuosos of voyeurism, lifting the skirts of our culture, peering into the closets, airing the national soiled linen. Sally thinks of her program as a kind of updated town meeting—the modern version of something we no longer have. Electronic gossip, in other words—the national back fence. Wishful thinking.

13    As Americans we've been indulging in an orgy of self-analysis and self-revelation—coupled with a natural curiosity now totally unbridled. We've become a society hooked on the bizarre and the astonishing—living in a perpetual state of "Can you top this?" Transvestite men marry women on Sally's show, thus proving an important point, one we all needed to know: Sixty-five percent of all transvestites are not homosexual.

14    Nothing is sacred. There are no memories, no mysteries too precious to reveal. A woman discusses her husband's sexual addiction. Geraldo asks the husband for details—and gets them. There is nothing we won't share, or watch someone else share, with a million strangers.

15    We have invented a new social contract on the talk shows: Lay bare your body, your bed, your soul, your emotions, your worst fears, your innermost secrets, and we will give you a moment or two of fame. Every sacrifice can and should be made to the video god.

16    Are there topics too hot to talk about?

17    "How to blow up your local post office," says Donahue. He'd draw the line there.

18    There is no topic Sally wouldn't consider if it "concerns the human condition." She draws the line only at being boring. We have to want to watch it. So we set the agenda.

19    Donahue, a man obviously in conflict between his natural honesty and better instincts and his ambition, admits that his audience calls the shots. Devoting a recent show to strippers—both male and female—he says, "It must be ratings week. I don't want to do these shows . . . they make me." Sure they do. But who is making us watch?

20    Freedom of expression is not the issue here. Nobody's suggesting censorship or even paternalistic decisions based on what someone else thinks is good for us. The issue is honesty—honesty about why we watch. The talk shows are merely giving us what we want. The question is, Why do we want it?

In some cultures it was thought that illness or bad luck could be trans-  21
ferred from one person to another by magic. James G. Frazer, in his classic
work *The Golden Bough*, told of one example: "To get rid of warts, take a
string and make as many knots in it as you have warts. Then lay the string
under a stone. Whoever treads upon the stone will get the warts, and you
will be rid of them." Something like that draws us to the tent. We confirm
our own normalcy because our worst fears have been manifested in someone else—the visual equivalent of burying the string. Or, if we see ourselves in someone who has survived our common plight, we are reassured;
we are not alone.

There is no slouching into the tent today. We walk in shamelessly, cast-  22
ing off inhibitions in the name of openness.

The new openness has, in fact, turned out to be an empty promise. Are  23
things any better than they were two decades ago? Has drug abuse or wife
abuse or child abuse declined as we have learned more? Are we any hap-
pier thinking that a friend who takes a drink is a potential alcoholic, that
every stranger is a child-snatcher?

How has this new compassion we are teaching been made evident?  24
Ask the parents who have three HIV-positive sons and found their
house burned down because of it. Ask the people who cluster over the
grates of subways in our largest cities. If you were a trapped whale or a
little girl down a well, solicitude would flow your way in great waves.
It still helps to be cute or little or white or furry or totally nonthreaten-
ing when you're looking for compassion—or pretty, when you want a
bone marrow transplant.

The potential is there on the TV talk shows for real entertainment—  25
and for service. Oprah scored with a terrific show on female comics. Programs on health matters or economic questions are valuable. During the
first days of the war in the Persian Gulf, Donahue aired shows that were
serious and important contributions to our understanding of the conflict.
"I do have a conscience," he says.

Geraldo, however, ever subject to the temptations of the flesh,  26
spoiled what could have been a serious discussion of breast implants by
having Jessica Hahn as the honored guest and by fondling examples of
the implants interminably. Does he have it right? Are we a people who
need to watch breast implants being fondled?

What happens when we set aside our last taboo? What happens when  27
we've finally been titillated to a terminal numbness, incapable of shock, on
the prowl for a new high? What manner of stimulation will we need next?
Are we addicted? Talk show codependent?

Which topic affects us more: the discussion of the S & L crisis Donahue  28
did last summer or the interviews with the strippers? Which do you think
got the better ratings?

29    In a free society we get what we want. We shouldn't be surprised when we end up with what we deserve. But we can't transfer blame. It's not the hosts' fault—it's the viewers'.

*1991*

## QUESTIONS FOR DISCUSSION

### Content

a. According to Fox, in what ways are carnival sideshows and television talk shows similar?
b. In what important way are carnival sideshows different from television talk shows?
c. Reread paragraph 5. In what way does the point Fox is making here relate to her thesis? What is her thesis, and where is it most succinctly expressed?
d. Explain the point made in paragraph 4. How does this idea relate to the essay's thesis?
e. How do talk-show hosts such as Sally Jessy Raphael justify the content of their shows?
f. What "dilemma" do talk-show hosts face? How does Fox react to this problem?
g. How does Fox answer those who might say that her essay is an attack on free speech? In what way does her response relate to her thesis?
h. What potential for constructive social discourse does the author see in television talk shows? Does her discussion of this potential weaken or strengthen her argument?
i. How does Fox respond to hosts who claim their shows teach valuable lessons?
j. In paragraph 15, the author says, "We have invented a new social contract on the talk shows." What does she mean? What was the "old" social contract?
k. What theory does Fox offer to explain the reasons why audiences are drawn to talk shows?

### Strategy and Style

l. The essay begins with a description of a carnival sideshow. Where in the essay do we find direct comparisons between the sideshow and the television talk show?
m. What does the fact that Fox chose to create an extended analogy tell you about her point of view?

n. How does Fox's citing James G. Fraser affect her argument?
o. Where does the author use irony? What is the effect of this device? How would you describe her tone overall?
p. The last few paragraphs criticize the viewing public. Why didn't Fox begin her essay with these comments?


## ENGAGING THE TEXT

a. "Nothing is sacred," Fox claims in paragraph 14. If you were a talk-show producer, would you consider certain topics off-limits? Which ones? Make a list of them and explain your reasons.
b. Is the title of this essay appropriate? Why or why not?


## SUGGESTIONS FOR SUSTAINED WRITING

a. In reference to television talk shows, Fox asks, "Are we addicted?" What's your opinion? Write an essay in which you argue one or the other side of this question.
b. Write an essay in which you use analogy to discuss a common "addiction" other than one to drugs or alcohol. For example, discuss America's addiction to fast food, sports, exercise, fast cars, television, the movies, or sex.
c. Is Fox criticizing a great majority of American television viewers in paragraphs 12, 13, 14, and 15? If so, do you agree with such an indictment or can such criticism be limited to a relatively small portion of the viewing public? Research the viewing trends of the American public. Sources could include scholarly journals, Internet articles, or a survey you conduct yourself. Include your research findings in an opinion essay in answer to these questions.


# Body Ritual among the Nacirema

Horace Miner

*Horace Miner (b. 1912) is a social anthropologist who studied at the University of Kentucky and the University of Chicago, where he earned a doctorate in 1937. In 1953, Miner wrote* The Primitive City of Timbuctoo, *a seminal study of primitive urban culture. His expertise in African culture is well known, and he has received several awards for his scholarship in that field. Most recently, Miner was a professor of social anthropology at the*

*University of Michigan. In "Body Ritual among the Nacirema," Miner departs from his serious scholarly style to write a parody that throws an interesting light on certain rituals practiced by a certain contemporary society. This essay first appeared as a "serious" article in 1959 in a professional journal, the* American Anthropologist. *It was and continues to be one of the most popular satires of American society; there is even a Web site devoted to it: http://www.beadsland.com/nacirema/*

1   The anthropologist has become so familiar with the diversity of ways in which different peoples behave in similar situations that he is not apt to be surprised by even the most exotic customs. In fact, if all of the logically possible combinations of behavior have not been found somewhere in the world, he is apt to suspect that they must be present in some yet undescribed tribe. This point has, in fact, been expressed with respect to clan organization by Murdock.[1] In this light, the magical beliefs and practices of the Nacirema present such unusual aspects that it seems desirable to describe them as an example of the extremes to which human behavior can go.

2       Professor Linton first brought the ritual of the Nacirema to the attention of anthropologists twenty years ago, but the culture of this people is still very poorly understood. They are a North American group living in the territory between the Canadian Cree, the Yaqui and Tarahumare of Mexico, and the Carib and Arawak of the Antilles.[2] Little is known of their origin, although tradition states that they came from the east. . . .

3       Nacirema culture is characterized by a highly developed market economy which has evolved in a rich natural habitat. While much of the people's time is devoted to economic pursuits, a large part of the fruits of these labors and a considerable portion of the day are spent in ritual activity. The focus of this activity is the human body, the appearance and health of which loom as a dominant concern in the ethos of the people. While such a concern is certainly not unusual, its ceremonial aspects and associated philosophy are unique.

4       The fundamental belief underlying the whole system appears to be that the human body is ugly and that its natural tendency is to debility and disease. Incarcerated in such a body, man's only hope is to avert these characteristics through the use of the powerful influences of ritual and ceremony. Every household has one or more shrines devoted to this purpose. The more powerful individuals in the society have several shrines in their houses and, in fact, the opulence of a house is often referred to in terms of the number of such ritual centers it possesses. Most houses are of wattle

---

[1]American anthropologist George Peter Murdock (b. 1897), authority on primitive cultures.
[2]Native American tribes formerly inhabiting the Saskatchewan region of Canada, the Sonora region of Mexico, and the West Indies.

and daub construction, but the shrine rooms of the more wealthy are walled with stone. Poorer families imitate the rich by applying pottery plaques to their shrine walls.

While each family has at least one such shrine, the rituals associated 5 with it are not family ceremonies but are private and secret. The rites are normally only discussed with children, and then only during the period when they are being initiated into these mysteries. I was able, however, to establish sufficient rapport with the natives to examine these shrines and to have the rituals described to me.

The focal point of the shrine is a box or chest which is built into the 6 wall. In this chest are kept the many charms and magical potions without which no native believes he could live. These preparations are secured from a variety of specialized practitioners. The most powerful of these are the medicine men, whose assistance must be rewarded with substantial gifts. However, the medicine men do not provide the curative potions for their clients, but decide what the ingredients should be and then write them down in an ancient and secret language. This writing is understood only by the medicine men and by the herbalists who, for another gift, provide the required charm.

The charm is not disposed of after it has served its purpose, but is 7 placed in the charm-box of the household shrine. As these magical materials are specific for certain ills, and the real or imagined maladies of the people are many, the charm-box is usually full to overflowing. The magical packets are so numerous that people forget what their purposes were and fear to use them again. While the natives are very vague on this point, we can only assume that the idea in retaining all the old magical materials is that their presence in the charm-box, before which the body rituals are conducted, will in some way protect the worshipper.

Beneath the charm-box is a small font. Each day every member of the 8 family, in succession, enters the shrine room, bows his head before the charm-box, mingles different sorts of holy water in the font, and proceeds with a brief rite of ablution. The holy waters are secured from the Water Temple of the community, where the priests conduct elaborate ceremonies to make the liquid ritually pure.

In the hierarchy of magical practitioners, and below the medicine men 9 in prestige, are specialists whose designation is best translated "holy-mouth-men." The Nacirema have an almost pathological horror of and fascination with the mouth, the condition of which is believed to have a supernatural influence on all social relationships. Were it not for the rituals of the mouth, they believe that their teeth would fall out, their gums bleed, their jaws shrink, their friends desert them, and their lovers reject them. They also believe that a strong relationship exists between oral and moral characteristics. For example, there is a ritual ablution of the mouth for children which is supposed to improve their moral fiber.

10    The daily body ritual performed by everyone includes a mouth-rite. Despite the fact that these people are so punctilious about care of the mouth, this rite involves a practice which strikes the uninitiated stranger as revolting. It was reported to me that the ritual consists of inserting a small bundle of hog hairs into the mouth, along with certain magical powders, and then moving the bundle in a highly formalized series of gestures.

11    In addition to the private mouth-rite, the people seek out a holy-mouth-man once or twice a year. These practitioners have an impressive set of paraphernalia, consisting of a variety of augers, awls, probes, and prods. The use of these objects in the exorcism of the evils of the mouth involves almost unbelievable ritual torture of the client. The holy-mouth-man opens the client's mouth and, using the above mentioned tools, enlarges any holes which decay may have created in the teeth. Magical materials are put into these holes. If there are not naturally occurring holes in the teeth, large sections of one or more teeth are gouged out so that the supernatural substance can be applied. In the client's view, the purpose of these ministrations is to arrest decay and to draw friends. The extremely sacred and traditional character of the rite is evident in the fact that the natives return to the holy-mouth-men year after year, despite the fact that their teeth continue to decay.

12    It is to be hoped that, when a thorough study of the Nacirema is made, there will be careful inquiry into the personality structure of these people. One has but to watch the gleam in the eye of a holy-mouth-man, as he jabs an awl into an exposed nerve, to suspect that a certain amount of sadism is involved. If this can be established, a very interesting pattern emerges, for most of the population shows definite masochistic tendencies. It was to these that Professor Linton referred in discussing a distinctive part of the daily body ritual which is performed only by men. This part of the rite involves scraping and lacerating the surface of the face with a sharp instrument. Special women's rites are performed only four times during each lunar month, but what they lack in frequency is made up in barbarity. As part of this ceremony, women bake their heads in small ovens for about an hour. The theoretically interesting point is that what seems to be a preponderantly masochistic people have developed sadistic specialists.

13    The medicine men have an imposing temple, or latipso, in every community of any size. The more elaborate ceremonies required to treat very sick patients can only be performed at this temple. These ceremonies involve not only the thaumaturge but a permanent group of vestal maidens who move sedately about the temple chambers in distinctive costume and headdress.

14    The latipso ceremonies are so harsh that it is phenomenal that a fair proportion of the really sick natives who enter the temple even recover. Small children whose indoctrination is still incomplete have been known to resist attempts to take them to the temple because "that is where you go

to die." Despite this fact, sick adults are not only willing but eager to undergo the protracted ritual purification, if they can afford to do so. No matter how ill the supplicant or how grave the emergency, the guardians of many temples will not admit a client if he cannot give a rich gift to the custodian. Even after one has gained admission and survived the ceremonies, the guardians will not permit the neophyte to leave until he makes still another gift.

The supplicant entering the temple is first stripped of all his or her  15 clothes. In everyday life the Nacirema avoids exposure of his body and its natural functions. Bathing and excretory acts are performed only in the secrecy of the household shrine, where they are ritualized as part of the body-rites. Psychological shock results from the fact that body secrecy is suddenly lost upon entry into the latipso. A man, whose own wife has never seen him in an excretory act, suddenly finds himself naked and assisted by a vestal maiden while he performs his natural functions into a sacred vessel. This sort of ceremonial treatment is necessitated by the fact that the excreta are used by a diviner to ascertain the course and nature of the client's sickness. Female clients, on the other hand, find their naked bodies are subjected to the scrutiny, manipulation and prodding of the medicine men.

Few supplicants in the temple are well enough to do anything but lie  16 on their hard beds. The daily ceremonies, like the rites of the holy-mouth-men, involve discomfort and torture. With ritual precision, the vestals awaken their miserable charges each dawn and roll them about on their beds of pain while performing ablutions, in the formal movements of which the maidens are highly trained. At other times they insert magic wands in the supplicant's mouth or force him to eat substances which are supposed to be healing. From time to time the medicine men come to their clients and jab magically treated needles into their flesh. The fact that these temple ceremonies may not cure, and may even kill the neophyte, in no way decreases the people's faith in the medicine men.

There remains one other kind of practitioner, known as a "listener."  17 This witchdoctor has the power to exorcise the devils that lodge in the heads of people who have been bewitched. The Nacirema believe that parents bewitch their own children. Mothers are particularly suspected of putting a curse on children while teaching them the secret body rituals. The counter-magic of the witchdoctor is unusual in its lack of ritual. The patient simply tells the "listener" all his troubles and fears, beginning with the earliest difficulties he can remember. The memory displayed by the Nacirema in these exorcism sessions is truly remarkable. It is not uncommon for the patient to bemoan the rejection he felt upon being weaned as a babe, and a few individuals even see their troubles going back to the traumatic effects of their own birth.

In conclusion, mention must be made of certain practices which have  18 their base in native esthetics but which depend upon the pervasive aversion to the natural body and its functions. There are ritual fasts to make fat people thin and ceremonial feasts to make thin people fat. Still other rites are used to make women's breasts larger if they are small, and smaller if they are large. General dissatisfaction with breast shape is symbolized in the fact that the ideal form is virtually outside the range of human variation. A few women afflicted with almost inhuman hypermammary development are so idolized that they make a handsome living by simply going from village to village and permitting the natives to stare at them for a fee.

19      Reference has already been made to the fact that excretory functions are ritualized, routinized, and relegated to secrecy. Natural reproductive functions are similarly distorted. Intercourse is taboo as a topic and scheduled as an act. Efforts are made to avoid pregnancy by the use of magical materials or by limiting intercourse to certain phases of the moon. Conception is actually very infrequent. When pregnant, women dress so as to hide their condition. Parturition takes place in secret, without friends or relatives to assist, and the majority of women do not nurse their infants.

20      Our review of the ritual life of the Nacirema has certainly shown them to be a magic-ridden people. It is hard to understand how they have managed to exist so long under the burdens which they have imposed upon themselves. But even such exotic customs as these take on real meaning when they are viewed with the insight provided by Malinowski when he wrote:

21      "Looking from far and above, from our high places of safety in the developed civilization, it is easy to see all the crudity and irrelevance of magic. But without its power and guidance early man could not have mastered his practical difficulties as he has done, nor could man have advanced to the higher stages of civilization."

*1956*

## QUESTIONS FOR DISCUSSION

### Content

a. What is Miner's purpose?

b. What is the essay's thesis? What is the author's opinion of the behavior of the Nacirema? What is his relationship to them?

c. At which point in the essay do you begin to realize who the Nacirema are? What clues to their identity does Miner provide?

d. What do you learn about the Nacirema that you never knew before?

e. In paragraph 4, Miner says that "the fundamental belief underlying the whole system appears to be that the human body is ugly . . . ." In paragraph 20, he comments that the Nacirema are "magic-ridden people." Do you agree with his assessment of his subject?

## Strategy and Style

f. Comment on the sophistication of Miner's style. Is it appropriate to a parody? Explain why or why not.
g. To whom is the author writing? What reaction might his readers have to this essay?
h. Why did Miner use an analogy to write this piece? Was it fair to present his observations in this form?
i. Look up the words *parody* and *satire* in a dictionary or glossary of literary terms. In what ways is this essay a parody? In what ways is it a satire? Do you think it is effective as either? Why or why not?
j. What is the effect of Miner's including references to actual anthropologists and tribes?
k. Choose any paragraph and paraphrase it using ordinary language. What patterns does Miner use in transforming terms for bathroom activities into "body rituals"?
l. Discuss Miner's tone at different levels of meaning in this essay. How do the differences in tone reflect his attitude toward his subject?

## ENGAGING THE TEXT

a. Describe one of the Nacirema based on what you have learned about these people from Miner. You might discuss your subject's physical, emotional, behavioral, or intellectual characteristics. In what way is your subject different from you or from people you know well? In what way is he or she the same?
b. Using Miner's approach, write a humorous explanation of the activities in a particular room in a house or in a garage, studio, workshop, or office.

## SUGGESTIONS FOR SUSTAINED WRITING

a. Write a descriptive report of some aspect of contemporary society from the point of view of an animal that has been transformed into an anthropologist. For example, consider how a cat or dog might think of a human family's behavior if it were sent to study one as an anthropologist.
b. Compare Miner's essay to the one or more of the following essays: Jessica Mitford's "Behind the Formaldehyde Curtain" in Chapter 3,

Deborah Tannen's "Talk in the Intimate Relationship" in Chapter 6, Peter Farb and George Armelagos's "Patterns of Eating" in Chapter 7, Edward T. Hall's "The Anthropology of Manners" in Chapter 7. How do the writers of these essays study their subjects? What similar kinds of conclusions do they reach about human behavior?

c. Closely observe a particular group of people or the people in a particular area and write an anthropological analysis of those people. You might study the "tribe" on your floor of the dorm, write about the character of the people in a club or group to which you belong, or observe the culture in a particular part of town, park, or neighborhood. Include outside sources to support or illustrate your analysis.

# The Cosmic Prison

Loren Eiseley

*An anthropologist, educator, and poet, Loren Eiseley (1907–1977) was one of the most highly respected and prolific scientific writers of the twentieth century. Born in Lincoln, Nebraska, Eiseley was educated at the University of Pennsylvania, where he later became a professor of anthropology and of the history of science. His other teaching assignments included appointments to the faculties of the University of Kansas and of Oberlin College. The recipient of numerous honors and awards for public service, Eiseley was also known for his work as a conservationist and nature lover. He contributed scores of scientific studies and articles to scholarly journals but also authored two books of poetry, a genre he found difficult to escape even when writing highly "technical" prose. Eiseley will probably be best remembered for the unique, eloquent, and sometimes verselike style with which he treats subject matter that would otherwise seem cold, abstract, and esoteric. In short, his work represents the best of the worlds of both poetry and science: perceptiveness, accuracy, insight, and, above all, an ability to make profound contact with the reader. Eiseley's major works include* The Immense Journey *(1957),* Darwin's Century *(1959),* The Firmament of Time *(1960),* The Unexpected Universe *(1969), and* The Invisible Pyramid *(1970), from which this selection is taken.*

1   "A name is a prison, God is free," once observed the Greek poet Nikos Kazantzakis. He meant, I think, that valuable though language is to man, it is by very necessity limiting, and creates for man an invisible prison. Language implies boundaries. A word spoken creates a dog, a rabbit, a man. It fixes their nature before our eyes; henceforth their shapes are, in a sense, our own creation. They are no longer part of the unnamed shifting architecture of the universe. They have been transfixed as if by sorcery,

frozen into a concept, a word. Powerful though the spell of human language has proven itself to be, it has laid boundaries upon the cosmos.

No matter how far-ranging some of the mental probes that man has ₂ philosophically devised, by his own created nature he is forced to hold the specious and emerging present and transform it into words. The words are startling in their immediate effectiveness, but at the same time they are always finally imprisoning because man has constituted himself a prison keeper. He does so out of no conscious intention, but because for immediate purposes he has created an unnatural world of his own, which he calls the cultural world, and in which he feels at home. It defines his needs and allows him to lay a small immobilizing spell upon the nearer portions of his universe. Nevertheless, it transforms that universe into a cosmic prison house which is no sooner mapped than man feels its inadequacy and his own.

He seeks then to escape, and the theory of escape involves bodily ₃ flight. Scarcely had the first moon landing been achieved before one U.S. senator boldly announced: "We are the masters of the universe. We can go anywhere we choose." This statement was widely and editorially acclaimed. It is a striking example of the comfort of words, also of the covert substitutions and mental projections to which they are subject. The cosmic prison is not made less so by a successful journey of some two hundred and forty thousand miles in a cramped and primitive vehicle.

To escape the cosmic prison man is poorly equipped. He has to drag ₄ portions of his environment with him, and his life span is that of a mayfly in terms of the distances he seeks to penetrate. There is no possible way to master such a universe by flight alone. Indeed such a dream is a dangerous illusion. This may seem a heretical statement, but its truth is self-evident if we try seriously to comprehend the nature of time and space that I sought to grasp when held up to view the fiery messenger that flared across the zenith in 1910. "Seventy-five years," my father had whispered in my ear, "seventy-five years and it will be racing homeward. Perhaps you will live to see it again. Try to remember."

And so I remembered. I had gained a faint glimpse of the size of our ₅ prison house. Somewhere out there beyond a billion miles in space, an entity known as a comet had rounded on its track in the black darkness of the void. It was surging homeward toward the sun because it was an eccentric satellite of this solar system. If I lived to see it it would be but barely, and with the dimmed eyes of age. Yet it, too, in its long traverse, was but a flitting mayfly in terms of the universe the night sky revealed.

So relative is the cosmos we inhabit that, as we gaze upon the outer ₆ galaxies available to the reach of our telescopes, we are placed in about the position that a single white blood cell in our bodies would occupy, if it were intelligently capable of seeking to understand the nature of its own universe, the body it inhabits. The cell would encounter rivers ramifying into miles of distance seemingly leading nowhere. It would pass through gigantic structures whose meaning it could never grasp—the brain, for example. It could never know there was an outside, a vast being on a scale it could not conceive of and of which it formed an infinitesimal part. It would know only the pouring tumult of the creation it inhabited, but of the nature of that great beast, or even indeed that it was a beast, it could have no conception whatever. It might examine the liquid in which it floated and decide, as in the case of the fall of Lucretius's atoms, that the pouring of obscure torrents had created its world.

7    It might discover that creatures other than itself swam in the torrent. But that its universe was alive, had been born and was destined to perish, its own ephemeral existence would never allow it to perceive. It would never know the sun; it would explore only through dim tactile sensations and react to chemical stimuli that were borne to it along the mysterious conduits of the arteries and veins. Its universe would be centered upon a great arborescent tree of spouting blood. This, at best, generations of white blood cells by enormous labor and continuity might succeed, like astronomers, in charting.

8    They could never, by any conceivable stretch of the imagination, be aware that their so-called universe was, in actuality, the prowling body of a cat or the more time-enduring body of a philosopher, himself engaged upon the same quest in a more gigantic world and perhaps deceived proportionately by greater vistas. What if, for example, the far galaxies man observes make up, across void spaces of which even we are atomically composed, some kind of enormous creature or cosmic snowflake whose exterior we will never see? We will know more than the phagocyte in our bodies, but no more than that limited creature can we climb out of our universe, or successfully enhance our size or longevity sufficiently to thrust our heads through the confines of the universe that terminates our vision.

9    Some further "outside" will hover elusively in our thought, but upon its nature, or even its reality, we can do no more than speculate. The phagocyte might observe the salty turbulence of an eternal river system, Lucretius the fall of atoms creating momentary living shapes. We suspiciously sense, in the concept of the expanding universe derived from the primordial atom—the monobloc—some kind of oscillating universal heart. At the instant of its contraction we will vanish. It is not given us, nor can our science recapture, the state beyond the monobloc, nor whether we exist in the diastole of some inconceivable being. We know only a little more extended reality than the hypothetical creature below us. Above us may lie realms it is beyond our power to grasp.

*1970*

## QUESTIONS FOR DISCUSSION

### Content

a. What is Eiseley saying in the last two sentences of this essay, and how do they relate to the analogy he has created? Would it be accurate to say that these ideas constitute his thesis?

b. What is the "fiery messenger" to which Eiseley alludes in paragraph 4? How does it and the analogy of the human life span to that of a mayfly help him convey the immensity of time and space?

c. How would you explain the analogy between humans and the white blood cell that forms the basis of this essay? What makes the analogy logical and consistent?

d. Who was Lucretius, and what was his "atomic theory"? How does mentioning this theory help Eiseley develop the central analogy of his essay?

e. What does Eiseley mean when he says that "some further 'outside' will hover elusively in our thought" (paragraph 9)? Why can we only "speculate" on "its nature, or even its reality"?

f. In paragraph 4, the author tells us that the dream of escaping from the "cosmic prison" is a "dangerous illusion." What does he mean by this curious statement, and why would someone like the U.S. senator quoted in paragraph 3 find it "heretical"?

g. What is "the oscillating universal heart" (paragraph 9) that we can only "suspiciously sense"? How would you define a "monobloc"?

### Strategy and Style

h. How do the quote from Nikos Kazantzakis and the explanation that proceeds from it serve as an appropriate introduction to this selection?

i. Define "the cosmic prison" that Eiseley describes in this selection. Why does he call it a prison? How does his use of the term *prison* relate to Plato's use of the word in the phrase *prison-house?*

j. How would you characterize Eiseley's tone in this piece? What image of Eiseley himself does the tone project?

## ENGAGING THE TEXT

a. Find a passage (a sentence or a paragraph) that has meaning for your own life and write about the connections you see between Eiseley's words and your life.

b. Eiseley writes of humankind's condition from an earthbound position; writing from a position outside the Earth, describe what you see as humankind's relation to the rest of the cosmos. You might try writing from the point of view of Halley's Comet.

## SUGGESTIONS FOR SUSTAINED WRITING

a. Eiseley has created a startling comparison between the existence of a human being in the universe and the life of a white blood cell in the human body. Create your own analogy by comparing yourself or someone you know well to a fictional character, to a famous historical figure, or even, for that matter, to an animal whose habits would be easily recognized by your audience. Incidentally, the analogy you develop need not be complimentary.
b. Compare Eiseley's ideas with those of Annie Dillard in "Fecundity" (Chapter 7) and/or Virginia Woolf in "The Death of the Moth" (Chapter 2). What does each writer say about humankind's limited perspective on the world?
c. Do research into the life and works of Loren Eiseley. Write an essay in which you make clear what Eiseley means by "the cosmic prison." Compare the essay "The Cosmic Prison" to one or more other essays by Eiseley. Discuss how his ideas about the cosmos are reflected in those other essays.

# 10

# Argument and Persuasion

Strictly speaking, argument is a rhetorical technique used to support or deny a proposition by offering detailed evidence for or against it in a logically connected fashion. Classical argument relies on deductive and inductive thinking; it appeals to reason and reason alone. Deduction proceeds from a general truth or principle to a more specific instance based on that principle. You would be using deduction if you argued:

All full-time students are permitted to use the college weight room free of charge;

I am a full-time student;

I am permitted to use the weight room free of charge.

Inductive reasoning, on the other hand, proceeds from several specific occurrences to one general truth. Let's say you come down with a bad case of food poisoning—fever, cramps, vomiting, the works! When you feel better, you call up the five people with whom you had dinner; each of them claims to have suffered the same symptoms. It is probably safe to infer that all six of you ate contaminated food.

Sometimes, of course, one's purpose may go beyond simply proving a point. The writer may feel a need to *persuade, that is,* to convert the audience, or even to convey a sense of urgency that will convince readers that they should act and act quickly. In such cases, pure logic may not suffice. Thus, while grounding the paper in logic and well-developed evidence, a writer may also wish to appeal to the emotions.

Both methods are legitimate forms studied under the general category of argumentation, and both are represented, to varying degrees, in the essays that follow. Indeed, it is often hard to draw a line. Jonathan Swift's "A Modest Proposal," a model of deductive reasoning expressed in language that is cool, clear, and eminently logical, is couched in a bitter irony that expresses the author's rage over Britain's treatment of the Irish.

Argument lends itself naturally to debate on matters scientific, social, and political. Five pairs of essays in this chapter take various sides on media ethics, welfare reform, free speech, diet, and rape. As you will see Mike Wallace and Don Hewitt give conflicting opinions on monitoring the press; Barbara Ehrenreich and Garrett Hardin debate society's responsibility to the poor; Nat Hentoff and Alan Dershowitz discuss matters relevant to the First Amendment; Joseph Pace and Alan Herscovici argue the pros and cons of vegetarianism; and Camille Paglia and Susan Jacoby present two views on rape. It is important to note that, as reasoned and clear as these ten selections are, each remains unique, varying in tone and urgency according to the proximity from which its author views the subject.

The six selections listed under Persuasion illustrate techniques you might use when trying to move your readers or convince them that they should act. Make sure to read "I Have a Dream" by Martin Luther King, Jr.; it is a classic. However, Richard Rodriguez's "Bilingual Education: Outdated and Unrealistic" and Debra Dickerson's "Who Shot Johnny?" also offer excellent insight into the workings of persuasion, and they are sure to interest and even move you. Finally, the essays by Ann N. Martin and Judy Brady might help you see some familiar subjects in a very new light.

Even though the essays in this chapter are examples of well-written and well-reasoned arguments, you might wish to take issue with the positions they advocate and write a rebuttal to one or two of them. Keep in mind, however, that the essential ingredient in building an effective argument is a thorough knowledge of your subject. Without it, your readers will remain unconvinced despite your ability to stir their emotions. Think of yourself as an attorney. You will have difficulty defending your client unless you know all the facts. Anything less will jeopardize your credibility with the jury. This idea also applies to your role as a writer. Good readers will approach your thesis with a healthy skepticism. They may be open to persuasion—some may even want to be convinced—but most will insist that you provide reasonable, well-developed, and convincing evidence before they give you their trust!

## ARGUMENT

### Media Ethics

# The Press Needs a National Monitor

#### Mike Wallace

*Mike Wallace (b. 1918) is an internationally known journalist who is now a coeditor and correspondent for CBS's television news magazine* 60 Minutes. *Wallace graduated from the University of Michigan and served in the U.S. Navy during World War II. He has worked as a radio and television reporter, interviewer, and commentator for more than fifty years and is the recipient of numerous journalistic honors, including 18 Emmy awards, several George Foster Peabody awards, and two DuPont Columbia Journalism awards. He was inducted into the Television Academy Hall of Fame in 1991. His full-length works in-* clude Mike Wallace Asks *(1958) and* Close Encounters *(1984).*

*Don Hewitt (b. 1922) is the executive producer of* 60 Minutes, *which he created in 1968. He attended New York University for one year before he began his career as head copy boy for the* New York Herald Tribune *in 1942. During World War II he was a war correspondent. With Douglas Edwards, Hewitt produced the first television network news show, which appeared in 1948. He also collaborated with Edward R. Morrow to create* See it Now, *and he directed the first televised presidential debates between John F. Kennedy and Richard M. Nixon in 1960, as well as the television coverage of the coronation of Queen Elizabeth II in 1953 and the installation of Pope John XXIII in 1958. Hewitt has received numerous awards, including eight Emmy Awards, two George Foster Peabody Awards, and the 1980 Broadcaster of the Year Award. He was inducted into the Television Academy Hall of Fame in 1990. His memoir* Minute by Minute *was published in 1985.*

*The point-counterpoint essays appears in the* Wall Street Journal *in December 1996.*

"You arrogant journalists, you spend your lives looking down our throats 1 and holding us up to public obloquy, but you cry foul (or First Amendment) when we want to look down yours!"

That's the plaint of hundreds of thousands of businessmen, doctors, 2 lawyers, politicians and other public figures who have lost confidence in what we report and in our professed journalistic objectivity.

And how do we respond? Too often too many of us shrug our shoul- 3 ders and dismiss the criticism as an occupational hazard, one that comes with the territory, or we suggest a letter to the editor. And if someone really feels his ox has been unfairly gored, his attorney may remind him that he can file a libel suit.

Is there no better way?                                                            4

As we reported recently on "60 Minutes," for the past 26 years an or- 5 ganization called the Minnesota News Council has been taking on these complaints and resolving them with some success.

Any individual, business or public institution in the state that feels its 6 integrity or reputation has been traduced in a news report may file a complaint with the council. If the council decides the complaint is worth its attention, it'll study the news report, hear from both sides in private and in public, and come to a decision. Either the council's members vote that the complaint is valid, or that the news report in question told its story fairly.

The Minnesota News Council consists of 24 members, half of them 7 journalists and half of them public members—businessmen, lawyers, teachers, other interested citizens. A state Supreme Court justice presides over their public hearings. These 24, chosen over the years by previous council members, study the article or broadcast in question. Then they read written arguments prepared by the news organization and the complainant and sit for a public session, amply covered by all the media, at which each side argues its case. Questions are asked and answered, opinions and rebuttals aired, and finally a vote is taken.

8    And what happens if the journalists are found wanting? No one goes to jail, no one is put out of business, no money is awarded. Instead, the journalists suffer the same kind of humiliation the objects of our scrutiny are bound to feel when our searching spotlight uncovers their flaws or malfeasances.

9    Over the past quarter-century, about half the cases filed with the Minnesota News Council have been decided in favor of the journalists. The Minnesota group is not the only such news council currently operating. There is one more, just one, the Honolulu Community Media Council. But there are suggestions that perhaps several regional councils or a national news council should be established.

10   Back in the 1970s and into the early 1980s, there was just such a national body, spawned by a group of journalists led by Richard Salant, who was president of CBS News. He believed the public should have some means to bring their complaints to someone with the competence and authority to give a public "thumbs up" or "thumbs down" as to the accuracy and the fairness of certain troubling news reports. Something, he felt, more defining than a letter to the editor and less onerous than a libel suit, with its attendant huge legal fees and interminable court procedures.

11   That early effort to establish a national news council was hampered by a struggle for funding, and by catcalls from inside the hypersensitive journalistic community. It sputtered after a few years and eventually it died, killed off mainly because two heavy hitters, Abe Rosenthal, then the executive editor of the *New York Times*, and Walter Cronkite, then the trusted anchor of "The CBS Evening News," were dead set against it—as was my colleague Don Hewitt, who heads up "60 Minutes." All three felt they didn't need anyone looking over their editorial shoulders; they were professionals, they said, and if not infallible surely they needed no help from unqualified outsiders.

12   Today Abe Rosenthal, no longer the man who runs the *Times* but whose columns appear regularly on the paper's op-ed page, hasn't changed his mind one whit. And Walter Cronkite? At a memorial service for Dick Salant a couple of years ago, this was Walter's take: "In the 1970s, I thought it was the worst idea I ever heard in my life, that we should put judgment as to the kind of job we do in the hands of another, somewhere outside our profession, outside our immediate workplace. But I think now, as I look back at it, that Dick was probably right."

13   At a time when the public trust in us may be even lower than it was in Dick Salant's time, I've come to the reluctant conclusion that Walter's change of mind is right.

*1996*

# Mea Culpa? Not Mea!

Don Hewitt

As I've said to my close friend and esteemed colleague Mike Wallace, bias, 1
like beauty, is in the eye of the beholder. And while I behold bias from time
to time in news coverage, I would rather leave it to a good editor to weed
it out than to a news council made up of a bunch of guys named Joe (as in
Kennedy, who wanted to ride Mike out of town on a rail for giving his son
Jack a hard time). Or Henry (as in Kissinger, who wanted to tar and feather
Mike because the story he aired about him wasn't as flattering as he
thought it should be). Or Alfonse (as in D'Amato, who wanted to take
Mike to the woodshed because he didn't like what Mike said about him).
Or L. Ron (as in Hubbard, whose Church of Scientology disciples threatened to "get" Mike for what he reported about them). Or Howard (as in
Squadron, of the Council of Presidents of Jewish Organizations, who
wanted Mike drawn and quartered for reporting that the Jerusalem police
were not as innocent as they said they were in the recent temple mount
massacre). Or Reed (as in Irvine, of Accuracy in Media, who is convinced
to this day that Mike is conspiring with the Clintons to cover up the murder of Vince Foster).

And that doesn't even include what a news council sitting in judgment 2
of my esteemed colleague would have said about him if some old soldiers
who refused to die or fade away showed up at a news council to join in the
fun after Mike's famous Westmoreland broadcast.

Are journalists as good as they think they are at avoiding bias? No, 3
nobody is. But at least journalists are trained to report fairly—unlike
corporate executives, academics, PR types and assorted members of the
citizenry who have the time and the inclination to sit on a news council. If anyone thinks certain journalists are unfair, he or she can always
complain to, or boycott, the advertisers who pay the reporters' salaries.
Or turn them off or tune them out or go buy or watch another news
magazine.

It has been my experience that what viewers and readers are most un- 4
happy about is not that journalists slant the news, but that we don't slant
it their way. And it's those readers and viewers who would sit on the news
councils in Mike's brave new world.

On paper, it may not be a bad idea. But in practice? Whoa there, Mikey, 5
slow down. Where in the world are you going to find the saints to sit in
judgment of us sinners? Mea culpa? Not mea.

*1996*

# QUESTIONS FOR DISCUSSION

## Content

a. What are Wallace's reasons for supporting the creation of a "National Monitor"? What are Hewitt's reasons for opposing it?

b. How does Wallace answer the argument of would-be opponents who claim that people who are wronged by journalists can always write letters to the editor or file lawsuits?

c. How might Wallace respond to someone arguing that submitting complaints to a group like the Minnesota News Council would intimidate journalists?

d. Who are each of the following: Joe Kennedy, Henry Kissinger, Alfonse D'Amato, L. Ron Hubbard, Howard Squadron, Irvine Reed, and (William) Westmoreland?

e. Explain the "brave new world" allusion in Hewitt's fourth paragraph.

f. What does Hewitt's title mean? Is it effective?

## Strategy and Style

g. Contrast Wallace's tone (his attitude toward his subject) and his style (the kind of vocabulary and sentence structure he uses) with what we see in Hewitt's essay.

h. How does Wallace begin his essay? Is his introduction successful? Why or why not?

i. Comment on Wallace's conclusion. What can you learn from it about how to close an essay?

j. To what end does Wallace tell us about the positions held by Salant, Rosenthal, Cronkite, and Hewitt?

k. Why does Wallace spend so much time (paragraphs 5–9) discussing the Minnesota News Council?

l. Evaluate Hewitt's introduction. What does he accomplish in the opening lines of his essay?

m. Why does Hewitt cite various incidents from Wallace's career in paragraph 1? How does recalling them help him advance his argument?

n. What use does Wallace make of evocative language? What about Hewitt?

o. What use does Wallace make of rhetorical questions? What about Hewitt?

# ENGAGING THE TEXT

a. Reread both selections. Then write notes in the margins that question or contradict the ideas and/or opinions each writer puts forth.

b. Write a paragraph in which you state several reasons for disagreeing with either Wallace or Hewitt.

## SUGGESTIONS FOR SUSTAINED WRITING

a. Write an essay that expands and develops the ideas in the paragraph you wrote when you responded to item *b* in Engaging the Text, above.
b. Read or reread the essays by Nat Hentoff and Alan M. Dershowitz (Chapter 10). Then write an essay in which you explain how each of these men might respond to the arguments put forth by Wallace and Hewitt. This assignment is not as easy as it might seem, for you will have to go beyond explaining whose side Dershowitz and Hentoff would take. You will also have to provide evidence that explains why the writer would take that side.
c. Write an essay in which you take a position on censoring or controlling the contents of a particular communications or entertainment medium, such as talk radio, the Internet, cable television, adult movies, rap music, or rock videos. Like Wallace and Hewitt, address your essay to the audience of a newspaper, perhaps your own college paper. Use information you collect from the library or the Internet to support and illustrate your ideas.

### Welfare Reform

# A Step Back to the Workhouse?

Barbara Ehrenreich

*Barbara Ehrenreich (b. 1941) earned her BA from Reed College in 1963 and her Ph.D. from Rockefeller University in 1968. A noted feminist and socialist, she is a contributing editor for* Ms. *but frequently writes for other magazines, such as the* Nation, *the* Utne Reader, *the* New Republic, *and* Time. *One of her central concerns is women's status in social institutions such as the health care system, politics, and, as in this article reprinted from* Ms., *the welfare system. The many books she has authored or coauthored deal with these and related concerns; they include* Complaints and Disorders: The Sexual Politics of Sickness *(1973),* Remaking Love: The Feminization of Sex *(1986), and* Fear of Falling: The Inner Life of the Middle Class *(1989). Two collections of articles critical of American culture that first appeared in* Time *and other magazines are* The Worst Years of Our Lives: Irreverent Notes from a Decade of Greed *(1990) and* The Snarling Citizen: Essays *(1995). She has been the recipient of several awards, including a National Magazine Award in 1980, a Ford Foundation Award for Humanistic Perspectives on Contemporary Issues in 1981, and a Guggenheim Fellowship in 1987.*

1    The commentators are calling it a "remarkable consensus." Workfare, as programs to force welfare recipients to work are known, was once abhorred by liberals as a step back toward the 17th-century workhouse or—worse— slavery. But today no political candidate dares step outdoors without some plan for curing "welfare dependency" by putting its hapless victims to work—if necessary, at the nearest Burger King. It is as if the men who run things, or who aspire to run things (and we are, unfortunately, talking mostly about men when we talk about candidates), had gone off and caucused for a while and decided on the one constituency that could be safely sacrificed in the name of political expediency and "new ideas," and that constituency is poor women.

2    Most of the arguments for workfare are simply the same indestructible stereotypes that have been around, in one form or another, since the first public relief program in England 400 years ago: That the poor are poor because they are lazy and dissolute, and that they are lazy and dissolute because they are suffering from "welfare dependency." Add a touch of modern race and gender stereotypes and you have the image that haunts the workfare advocates: A slovenly, over-weight, black woman who produces a baby a year in order to augment her welfare checks.

3    But there is a new twist to this season's spurt of welfare-bashing: Workfare is being presented as a kind of *feminist* alternative to welfare. As Senator Daniel Patrick Moynihan (D.–N.Y.) has put it, "A program that was designed to pay mothers to stay at home with their children [i.e., welfare, or Aid to Families with Dependent Children] cannot succeed when we now observe most mothers going out to work." Never mind the startling illogic of this argument, which is on a par with saying that no woman should stay home with her children because other women do not, or that a laid-off male worker should not receive unemployment compensation because most men have been observed holding jobs. We are being asked to believe that pushing destitute mothers into the work force (in some versions of workfare, for no other compensation than the welfare payments they would have received anyway) is consistent with women's strivings toward self-determination.

4    Now I will acknowledge that most women on welfare—like most unemployed women in general—would rather have jobs. And I will further acknowledge that many of the proponents of workfare, possibly including Senator Moynihan and the Democratic presidential candidates, have mounted the bandwagon with the best of intentions. Welfare surely needs reform. But workfare is not the solution, because "dependency"—with all its implications of laziness and depravity—is not the problem. The problem is poverty, which most women enter in a uniquely devastating way— with their children in tow.

Let me introduce a real person, if only because real people, as opposed 5
to imaginative stereotypes, never seem to make an appearance in the current rhetoric on welfare. "Lynn," as I will call her, is a friend and onetime
neighbor who has been on welfare for two years. She is also about as unlike
the stereotypical "welfare mother" as one can get—which is to say that she
is a fairly typical welfare recipient. She has only one child, which puts her
among the 74 percent of welfare recipients who have only one or two children. She is white (not that that should matter), as are almost half of welfare recipients. Like most welfare recipients, she is not herself the daughter
of a welfare recipient, and hence not part of anything that could be called
an "intergenerational cycle of dependency." And like every woman on welfare I have ever talked to, she resents the bureaucratic hassles that are the
psychic price of welfare. But, for now, there are no alternatives.

When I first met Lynn, she seemed withdrawn and disoriented. She 6
had just taken the biggest step of her 25 years; she had left an abusive husband and she was scared: Scared about whether she could survive on her
own and scared of her estranged husband. He owned a small restaurant;
she was a high school dropout who had been a waitress when she met him.
During their three years of marriage he had beaten her repeatedly. Only after he threw her down a flight of stairs had she realized that her life was in
danger and moved out. I don't think I fully grasped the terror she had
lived in until one summer day when he chased Lynn to the door of my
house with a drawn gun.

Gradually Lynn began to put her life together. She got a divorce and 7
went on welfare; she found a pediatrician who would accept Medicaid and
a supermarket that would take food stamps. She fixed up her apartment
with secondhand furniture and flea market curtains. She was, by my ad-
mittedly low standards, a compulsive housekeeper and an overprotective
mother; and when she wasn't waxing her floors or ironing her two-year-
old's playsuits, she was studying the help-wanted ads. She spent a lot of
her time struggling with details that most of us barely notice—the price of
cigarettes, mittens, or of a bus ticket to the welfare office—yet, somehow,
she regained her sense of humor. In fact, most of the time we spent together was probably spent laughing—over the foibles of the neighbors, the
conceits of men, and the snares of welfare and the rest of "the system."

Yet for all its inadequacies, Lynn was grateful for welfare. Maybe if she 8
had been more intellectually inclined she would have found out that she
was suffering from "welfare dependency," a condition that is supposed to
sap the will and demolish the work ethic. But "dependency" is not an issue when it is a choice between an abusive husband and an impersonal
government. Welfare had given Lynn a brief shelter in a hostile world, and
as far as she was concerned, it was her ticket to *independence*.

Suppose there had been no welfare at the time when Lynn finally 9
summoned the courage to leave her husband. Suppose she had gone for

help and been told she would have to "work off" her benefits in some menial government job (restocking the toilet paper in rest rooms is one such
"job" assigned to New York women in a current workfare program). Or
suppose, as in some versions of workfare, she had been told she would
have to take the first available private sector job, which (for a non-high
school graduate like Lynn) would have paid near the minimum wage, or
$3.35 an hour. How would she have been able to afford child care? What
would she have done for health insurance (as a welfare recipient she had
Medicaid, but most low-paying jobs offer little or no coverage)? Would she
have ever made the decision to leave her husband in the first place?

10      As Ruth Sidel points out in *Women and Children Last* (Viking), most
women who are or have been on welfare have stories like Lynn's. They go
onto welfare in response to a crisis—divorce, illness, loss of a job, the birth
of an additional child to feed—and they remain on welfare for two years or
less. They are not victims of any "welfare culture," but of a society that increasingly expects women to both raise and support children—and often
on wages that would barely support a woman alone. In fact, even some of
the most vociferous advocates of replacing welfare with workfare admit
that, in their own estimation, only about 15 percent of welfare recipients fit
the stereotype associated with "welfare dependency": Demoralization,
long-term welfare use, lack of drive, and so on.

11      But workfare will not help anyone, not even the presumed 15 percent
of "bad apples" for whose sake the majority will be penalized. First, it will
not help because it does not solve the problem that drives most women
into poverty in the first place: How to hold a job *and* care for children.
Child care in a licensed, professionally run center can easily cost as much
as $100 a week per child—more than most states now pay in welfare ben-
efits (for two children) and more than most welfare recipients could expect
to earn in the work force. Any serious effort to get welfare recipients into
the work force would require childcare provisions at a price that would
probably end up higher than the current budget for AFDC. But none of the
workfare advocates are proposing that sort of massive public commitment
to child care.

12      Then there is the problem of jobs. So far, studies show that existing
state workfare programs have had virtually no success in improving
their participants' incomes or employment rates. Small wonder: Nearly
half the new jobs generated in recent years pay poverty-level wages;
and most welfare recipients will enter jobs that pay near the minimum
wage, which is $6,900 a year—26 percent less than the poverty level for
a family of three. A menial, low-wage job may be character-building
(from a middle-class vantage point), but it will not lift anyone out of
poverty.

13      Some of my feminist activist friends argue that it is too late to stop the
workfare juggernaut. The best we can do, they say, is to try to defeat the

more pernicious proposals: Those that are over-coercive, that do not offer funds for child care, or that would relegate work clients to a "subemployee" status unprotected by federal labor and civil rights legislation. Our goal, the pragmatists argue, should be to harness the current enthusiasm for workfare to push for services welfare recipients genuinely need, such as child care and job training and counseling.

I wish the pragmatists well, but for me, it would be a betrayal of women 14 like Lynn to encourage the workfare bandwagon in any way. Most women, like Lynn, do not take up welfare as a career, but as an emergency measure in a time of personal trauma and dire need. At such times, the last thing they need is to be hustled into a low-wage job, and left to piece together child care, health insurance, transportation, and all the other ingredients of survival. In fact, the main effect of workfare may be to discourage needy women from seeking any help at all—a disastrous result in a nation already suffering from a child poverty rate of nearly 25 percent. Public policy should be aimed at giving impoverished mothers (and, I would add, fathers) the help they so urgently need—not only in the form of job opportunities, but sufficient income support to live on until a job worth taking comes along.

Besides, there is an ancient feminist principle at stake. The premise of 15 all the workfare proposals—the more humane as well as the nasty—is that single mothers on welfare are not *working*. But, to quote the old feminist bumper sticker, EVERY MOTHER IS A WORKING MOTHER. And those who labor to raise their children in poverty—to feed and clothe them on meager budgets and to nurture them in an uncaring world—are working the hardest. The feminist position has never been that all women must pack off their children and enter the work force, but that all women's work—in the home or on the job—should be valued and respected

*1987*

*Barbara Ehrenreich's essay stimulated a lively response from* Ms. *readers. The following letters were published in the February 1988 issue.*

I was absolutely thrilled when I read Barbara Ehrenreich's article on 16 workfare ("A Step Back to the Workhouse?" November 1987). As a single mother who received welfare for several years (with no child support) I'm against everything that workfare stands for. I belong to an organization called Women, Work, and Welfare, a group of current and former welfare recipients trying to empower ourselves and become a part of the decisions that affect our lives as poor women. It seems as if everybody but the welfare recipient herself has a hand in the decisions that are made.

CHERI HONKALA
*Minneapolis, Minn.*

17      I arrived in Chicago in 1952 with a husband and two children from a camp in Europe. I had another child in 1953, lost a newborn in 1954, had a miscarriage, a hysterectomy, and a divorce in 1955. I never received child support. My ex-husband was remarried within two months.

18      I *never* received welfare. I worked in another culture, while in very bad health. I found a two-room flat, had no furniture and slept for years on the floor. I even went back to school at night and had to contend with companies like Gulf Oil Corp., which did not believe in promoting women. But I just slugged on.

19      By the end of the sixties, I had two daughters in college, and I had bought a house. My total earnings for 1970 from three jobs came to a whopping $8,000.

20      A full-time minimum wage job *can* support one adult and one child. One just has to learn how to do it.

URRSULA SCHRAMM
*Hurley, Wis.*

21      I found myself agreeing with the problems that Barbara Ehrenreich outlines in the present workfare program.

22      Yet deep inside a protesting rumbling exploded when I read that impoverished mothers should receive sufficient income support to live on "until a job worth taking comes along." *Bullshit!* Sure, we all should have the right to only work a job we love, but how many of us can afford to wait for it? That we are often forced to work at jobs that are not fulfilling says a lot about our society in which more needs to be changed than just the welfare system!

23      My mother was forced to go to work when I was nine years old. Our family was in dire financial straits and at the age of 50 she took a job in a factory. Was that job "worth taking"? Did it utilize her unique talents? *No!* Did it bring her personal fulfillment? *No!* Did it prevent the bank from foreclosing on our home? *Yes!* Did it give my mother the power to overcome our financial crisis and maintain her autonomy? *Yes!* You tell me if it was "worth taking." That depends on what your self-respect is worth to you.

GAIL FREI
*Newtown Square, Pa.*

24      Barbara Ehrenreich omitted a major element in her discussion of the victimization of welfare families: The inability or unwillingness of the legal system to award *and enforce* realistic child support. Until it stops being

easier to abandon your children than to default on that car loan, women
and those who depend on them will be welfare/workfare victims.

SUSAN MARTIN RYNARD
*Durham, N.C.*

I went on welfare when my daughter was three, when I left my hus-    25
band. I had a high school education, but had always wanted to go to college. I was 25.

So, with the help of the government, I got my B.S. in nursing. I worked    26
for several years as an R.N. and then returned to school for my master's
degree. For graduate school, I lived on savings, loans, and grants. The
loans ($19,000 for undergrad and graduate in all) will be paid off in less
than a year, in time for my daughter to begin college!

KATHRYN REID
*Silverado, Calif.*

Although I share Barbara Ehrenreich's concerns about workfare and    27
the plight of her friend Lynn, the conclusions she draws strike me as misguided. We live in a society where the myths of the work ethic and self-
help are deeply embedded in the popular culture; where resort to the dole
is frowned upon unless the need is temporary or arises from disability;
where the middle-class majority feels inequitably taxed, as compared to
the wealthy, to support a system that directly benefits few of its members.

Feminists and other liberals should acknowledge the swelling demand    28
for welfare reform. Our support should be conditional upon the incorpora
tion in any welfare reform plan of provision for *quality* childcare facilities;
upon the minimization of coercion; and upon further efforts to compel ex-
spouses to pay their fair share of support. Nothing in this approach rules out
our going ahead simultaneously with other, parallel efforts to question the
mystique of work or to expose the links between welfare and poverty, on the
one hand, and capitalism and the subordination of women, on the other.

DAVID G. BECKER
*Hanover, N.H.*

California is serious about workfare, but we call it GAIN (Greater Av-    29
enues for Independence). It offers welfare recipients vocational counseling, up to two years of vocational training, and workshops in how to get
and hold a job.

30      GAIN also pays for child care and transportation. No job need be accepted by the recipient unless she/he will *net* at least as much as their AFDC grant, *including* child care, transportation, and medical insurance. And even then, they will receive funds to cover these costs for three months after they begin working to help them make the transition to the work force.

JANE KIRCHMAN
*Guerneville, Calif.*

## QUESTIONS FOR DISCUSSION

### Content

a. What does Ehrenreich mean when she writes: "We are being asked to believe that pushing destitute mothers into the work force . . . is consistent with women's strivings toward self-determination" (paragraph 3)? How is "self-determination" used in this context?

b. Where is Ehrenreich's thesis, her argument, in a nutshell? What are the two main points she uses to support this argument? Evaluate these points. Do you agree with the argument?

c. Discuss the stereotype of "welfare dependency" she tries to dispel in this essay.

d. What do the "pragmatists" she mentions in paragraph 13 want? Why won't she oblige them?

e. What, according to the author, are the benefits of the welfare system?

### Strategy and Style

f. Why does she begin by attacking opposing arguments? Is she strategy effective? In what other essays in this chapter is this strategy used?

g. In paragraph 5, Ehrenreich tells the story of a woman she knows. Why is narration a particularly effective strategy at this point in the essay?

h. Besides telling Lynn's story, the author uses many statistics. Which is more effective in convincing you? Why?

i. In what parts of this essay does the author use the opinions of authorities on the welfare system to support her arguments?

j. Why does she begin an essay on so serious a subject with sarcasm ("putting its hapless victims to work—if necessary, at the nearest Burger King," paragraph 1)? Does doing so make her argument more effective? If so, in what ways?

k. Point to other uses of irony and sarcasm. How would you characterize the overall tone of this essay?

## ENGAGING THE TEXT

a. Use freewriting to address Ehrenreich's point in paragraph 3. Do you agree with the author, with Senator Moynihan, or with neither? Explain your position.
b. Reread paragraph 15. Respond negatively or positively to Ehrenreich's premise that "every mother is a working mother."

## SUGGESTIONS FOR SUSTAINED WRITING

a. Write a letter in response to a recent newspaper or magazine article with which you find yourself strongly agreeing or disagreeing. Submit it as a letter to the editor of that newspaper or magazine.
b. Write a dialogue between Barbara Ehrenreich and Garrett Hardin. If you wish to make this a more complex discussion, bring in Jo Goodwin Parker ("What Is Poverty?" in Chapter 4) and Ellen Goodman ("Watching the Grasshopper Get the Goodies" in Chapter 8). This conversation could be written as a talk show script. Include at the end your comments about the conversation.
c. Write an argument for or against workfare in which you take into account the arguments cited in Ehrenreich's essay. Research the issue to back your claims and to illustrate the claims of those readers who would oppose you.

**Welfare Reform**

# Lifeboat Ethics: The Case Against Helping the Poor

Garrett Hardin

*Garrett Hardin (b. 1915) is professor emeritus of biology at the University of California–Santa Barbara. He is a human ecologist who writes, lectures, and teaches about this subject. Although his formal scientific training has been extensive (he was educated at the University of Chicago and at Stanford University, where he received a Ph.D. in biology) and he has written many academic articles, he has always been most interested in making the connections between science and society clear to a wide, nonacademic audience. His desire is to "explain science to the public," and his many books written for lay readers show this. His most famous essay is "The Tragedy of the Commons," published in 1968; the ideas in that essay resurface in "Lifeboat Ethics." Among his books are several on population growth, including* Population, Evolution and Birth Control *(1964),* The Limits of Altruism *(1977),* Filters Against Folly *(1985), and* Living Within Limits: Ecology, Economics, and Population Taboos *(1993). Among his recent books are* The Immigration Dilemma: Avoiding the Tragedy of the Commons *(1995) and* The Ostrich Factor: Our Population Myopia *(1999). Some of his essays are collected in* Naked Emperors: Essays of a Taboo-Stalker *(1982).*

1   Environmentalists use the metaphor of the Earth as a "spaceship" in trying to persuade countries, industries and people to stop wasting and polluting our natural resources. Since we all share life on this planet, they argue, no single person or institution has the right to destroy, waste, or use more than a fair share of its resources.

2   But does everyone on Earth have an equal right to an equal share of its resources? The spaceship metaphor can be dangerous when used by misguided idealists to justify suicidal policies for sharing our resources through uncontrolled immigration and foreign aid. In their enthusiastic but unrealistic generosity, they confuse the ethics of a spaceship with those of a lifeboat.

3   A true spaceship would have to be under the control of a captain, since no ship could possibly survive if its course were determined by committee. Spaceship Earth certainly has no captain; the United Nations is merely a toothless tiger, with little power to enforce any policy upon its bickering members.

4   If we divide the world crudely into rich nations and poor nations, two thirds of them are desperately poor, and only one third comparatively rich, with the United States the wealthiest of all. Metaphorically each rich nation can be seen as a lifeboat full of comparatively rich people. In the ocean outside each lifeboat swim the poor of the world, who would like to get in, or at least to share some of the wealth. What should the lifeboat passengers do?

5   First, we must recognize the limited capacity of any lifeboat. For example, a nation's land has a limited capacity to support a population and as the current energy crisis has shown us, in some ways we have already exceeded the carrying capacity of our land. So here we sit, say 50 people in our lifeboat. To be generous, let us assume it has room for 10 more, making a total capacity of 60. Suppose the 50 of us in the lifeboat see 100 others swimming in the water outside, begging for admission to our boat or for handouts. We have several options: We may be tempted to try to live by the Christian ideal of being "our brother's keeper," or by the Marxist ideal of "to each according to his needs." Since the needs of all in the water are the

same, and since they can all be seen as our "brothers," we could take them all into our boat, making a total of 150 in a boat designed for 60. The boat swamps; everyone drowns. Complete justice, complete catastrophe.

Since the boat has an unused excess capacity of 10 more passengers, 6 we could admit just 10 more to it. But which 10 do we let in? How do we choose? Do we pick the best 10, the neediest 10, "first come, first served"? And what do we say to the 90 we exclude? If we do let an extra 10 into our lifeboat, we will have lost our "safety factor," an engineering principle of critical importance. For example, if we don't leave room for excess capacity as a safety factor in our country's agriculture, a new plant disease or a bad change in the weather could have disastrous consequences.

Suppose we decide to preserve our small safety factor and admit no 7 more to the lifeboat. Our survival is then possible, although we shall have to be constantly on guard against boarding parties.

While this last solution clearly offers the only means of our survival, 8 it is morally abhorrent to many people. Some say they feel guilty about their good luck. My reply is simple: "Get out and yield your place to others." This may solve the problem of the guilt-ridden person's conscience, but it does not change the ethics of the lifeboat. The needy person to whom the guilt-ridden person yields his place will not himself feel guilty about his good luck. If he did, he would not climb aboard. The net result of conscience-stricken people giving up their unjustly held seats is the elimination of that sort of conscience from the lifeboat.

This is the basic metaphor within which we must work out our solu- 9 tions. Let us now enrich the image, step by step, with substantive additions from the real world, a world that must solve real and pressing problems of overpopulation and hunger.

The harsh ethics of the lifeboat become even harsher when we consider 10 the reproductive differences between the rich nations and the poor nations. The people inside the lifeboats are doubling in numbers every 87 years; those swimming around outside are doubling, on the average, every 35 years, more than twice as fast as the rich. And since the world's resources are dwindling, the difference in prosperity between the rich and the poor can only increase.

As of 1973, the United States had a population of 210 million people, 11 who were increasing by 0.8 percent per year. Outside our lifeboat, let us imagine another 210 million people (say the combined populations of Colombia, Ecuador, Venezuela, Morocco, Pakistan, Thailand, and the Philippines), increasing at a rate of 3.3 percent per year. Put differently, the doubling time for this aggregate population was 21 years, compared to 87 years for the United States.

Now suppose the United States agreed to pool its resources with those 12 seven countries, with everyone receiving an equal share. Initially the ratio of Americans to non-Americans in this model would be one-to-one. But consider what the ratio would be after 87 years, by which time the Americans would have doubled to a population of 420 million. By then, doubling every 21 years, the other group would have swollen to 3.54 billion. Each American would have to share the available resources with more than eight people.

13     But, one could argue, this discussion assumes that current population trends will continue, and they may not. Quite so. Most likely the rate of population increase will decline much faster in the United States than it will in the other countries, and there does not seem to be much we can do about it. In sharing with "each according to his needs," we must recognize that needs are determined by population size, which is determined by the rate of reproduction, which at present is regarded as a sovereign right of every nation, poor or not. This being so, the philanthropic load created by the sharing ethic of the spaceship can only increase.

14     The fundamental error of spaceship ethics, and the sharing it requires, is that it leads to what I call "the tragedy of the commons." Under a system of private property, people who own property recognize their responsibility to care for it, for if they don't they will eventually suffer. A farmer, for instance, will allow no more cattle in a pasture than its carrying capacity justifies. If he overloads it, erosion sets in, weeds take over, and he loses the use of the pasture.

15     If a pasture becomes a commons open to all, the right of each to use it may not be matched by a corresponding responsibility to protect it. Asking everyone to use it with discretion will hardly do, for the considerate herdsman who refrains from overloading the commons suffers more than a selfish one who says his needs are greater. If everyone would restrain himself, all would be well; but it takes only one less than everyone to ruin a system of voluntary restraint. In a crowded world of less than perfect human beings, mutual ruin is inevitable if there are no controls. This is the tragedy of the commons.

16     One of the major tasks of education today should be the creation of such an acute awareness of the dangers of the commons that people will recognize its many varieties. For example, the air and water have become polluted because they are treated as commons. Further growth in the population or per-capita conversion of natural resources into pollutants will only make the problem worse. The same holds true for the fish of the oceans. Fishing fleets have nearly disappeared in many parts of the world; technological improvements in the art of fishing are hastening the day of complete ruin. Only the replacement of the system of the commons with a responsible system of control will save the land, air, water and oceanic fisheries.

17     In recent years there has been a push to create a new commons called a World Food Bank, an international depository of food reserves to which nations would contribute according to their abilities and from which they

would draw according to their needs. This humanitarian proposal received support from many liberal international groups, and from such prominent citizens as Margaret Mead, the U.N. Secretary General, and Senator Edward Kennedy.

A world food bank appeals powerfully to our humanitarian impulses. 18 But before we rush ahead with such a plan, let us ask if such a program would actually do more good than harm, not only momentarily but also in the long run. Those who propose a food bank usually refer to a current "emergency" or "crisis" in terms of world food supply. But what is an emergency? Although they may be infrequent and sudden, everyone knows that emergencies will occur from time to time. A well-run family, company, organization or country prepares for the likelihood of accidents and emergencies. It expects them, it budgets for them, it saves for them.

What happens if some organizations or countries budget for accidents 19 and others do not? If each country is solely responsible for its own well-being, poorly managed ones will suffer. But they can learn from experience. They may mend their ways, and learn to budget for infrequent but certain emergencies. For example, the weather varies from year to year, and periodic crop failures are certain. A wise and competent government saves out of the production of the good years in anticipation of bad years to come. Joseph taught this policy to Pharaoh in Egypt more than 2,000 years ago. Yet the great majority of the governments in the world today do not follow such a policy. They lack either the wisdom or the competence, or both. Should those nations that do manage to put something aside be forced to come to the rescue each time an emergency occurs among the poor nations?

"But it isn't their fault!" some kind-hearted liberals argue. "How can 20 we blame the poor people who are caught in an emergency? Why must they suffer for the sins of their governments?" The concept of blame is simply not relevant here. The real question is, what are the operational consequences of establishing a world food bank? If it is open to every country every time a need develops, slovenly rulers will not be motivated to take Joseph's advice. Someone will always come to their aid. Some countries will deposit food in the world food bank, and others will withdraw it. There will be almost no overlap. As a result of such solutions to food shortage emergencies, the poor countries will not learn to mend their ways, and will suffer progressively greater emergencies as their populations grow.

On the average, poor countries undergo a 2.5 percent increase in pop- 21 ulation each year; rich countries, about 0.6 percent. Only rich countries have anything in the way of food reserves set aside, and even they do not have as much as they should. Poor countries have none. If poor countries received no food from the outside, the rate of their population growth would be periodically checked by crop failures and famines. But if they can always draw on a world food bank in time of need, their population can continue to grow unchecked, and so will their "need" for aid. In the short run, a world food bank may diminish that need, but in the long run it actually increases the need without limit.

22      Without some system of worldwide food sharing, the proportion of people in the rich and poor nations might eventually stabilize. The over-populated poor countries would decrease in numbers while the rich countries that had room for more people would increase. But with a well-meaning system of sharing, such as a world food bank, the growth differential between the rich and the poor countries will not only persist, it will increase. Because of the higher rate of population growth in the poor countries of the world, 88 percent of today's children are born poor, and only 12 percent rich. Year by year the ratio becomes worse as the fast-re-producing poor outnumber the slow-reproducing rich.

23      A world food bank is thus a commons in disguise. People will have more motivation to draw from it than to add to any common store. The less provident and less able will multiply at the expense of the abler and more provident, bringing eventual ruin upon all who share in the commons. Besides, any system of "sharing" that amounts to foreign aid from the rich nations to the poor nations will carry the taint of charity, which will contribute little to the world peace so devoutly desired by those who support the idea of a world food bank.

24      As past U.S. foreign-aid programs have amply and depressingly demonstrated, international charity frequently inspires mistrust and antagonism rather than gratitude on the part of the recipient nation.

25      The modern approach to foreign aid stresses the export of technology and advice, rather than money and food. As an ancient Chinese proverb goes: "Give a man a fish and he will eat for a day; teach him how to fish and he will eat for the rest of his days." Acting on this advice, the Rockefeller and Ford Foundations have financed a number of programs for improving agriculture in the hungry nations. Known as the "Green Revolution," these programs have led to the development of "miracle rice" and "miracle wheat," new strains that offer bigger harvests and greater resistance to crop damage.

26      Whether or not the Green Revolution can increase food production as much as its champions claim is a debatable but possibly irrelevant point. Those who support this well-intended humanitarian effort should first consider some of the fundamentals of human ecology. Ironically, one man who did was the late Alan Gregg, a vice president of the Rockefeller Foundation. Two decades ago he expressed strong doubts about the wisdom of such attempts to increase food production. He likened the growth and spread of humanity over the surface of the Earth to the spread of cancer in the human body, remarking that "cancerous growths demand food, but, as far as I know, they have never been cured by getting it."

Every human born constitutes a draft on all aspects of the environ- 27 ment: Food, air, water, forests, beaches, wildlife, scenery and solitude. Food can, perhaps, be significantly increased to meet a growing demand. But what about clean beaches, unspoiled forests, and solitude? If we satisfy a growing population's need for food, we necessarily decrease its per capita supply of the other resources needed by people.

India, for example, now has a population of 600 million, which in- 28 creases by 15 million each year. This population already puts a huge load on a relatively impoverished environment. The country's forests are now only a small fraction of what they were three centuries ago, and floods and erosion continually destroy the insufficient farmland that remains. Every one of the 15 million new lives added to India's population puts an additional burden on the environment, and increases the economic and social costs of crowding. However humanitarian our intent, every Indian life saved through medical or nutritional assistance from abroad diminishes the quality of life for those who remain, and for subsequent generations. If rich countries make it possible, through foreign aid, for 600 million Indians to swell to 1.2 billion in a mere 28 years, as their current growth rate threatens, will future generations of Indians thank us for hastening the destruction of their environment? Will our good intentions be sufficient excuse for the consequences of our actions?

Without a true world government to control reproduction and the use 29 of available resources, the sharing ethic of the spaceship is impossible. For the foreseeable future, our survival demands that we govern our actions by the ethics of a lifeboat, harsh though they may be. Posterity will be satisfied with nothing less.

*1974*

## QUESTIONS FOR DISCUSSION

### Content

a. What are ethics? How does Hardin use the term in the context of his essay?
b. Summarize Hardin's argument. What is his main point?
c. Hardin uses the lifeboat as the primary metaphor to create a lasting image in his readers' minds. Describe this lifeboat as you see it.
d. The other key metaphor is the spaceship. What is the difference between thinking of Earth as a lifeboat and as a spaceship?
e. What other metaphors does Hardin use?

f. Who are the people against whom Hardin positions himself? What is the main fault he finds with their thinking?

## Strategy and Style

g. Hardin asks questions occasionally as a way to guide our thinking (see paragraphs 2 and 6 for examples). What other questions could be asked to which Hardin would not have easy answers?
h. Does the lifeboat metaphor stand up under close scrutiny? If not, where do you think the metaphor is weak?
i. Where and how does Hardin use statistics? What kind of a writer's "voice" do these statistics create?
j. Hardin continually refers to "we." Who is "we"? Is Hardin necessarily included in this pronoun?
k. In paragraph 19 Hardin backs up his point with an allusion to the Bible: "Joseph taught this policy to Pharaoh in Egypt more than 2,000 years ago." In the next paragraph, he says that "slovenly rulers will not be motivated to take Joseph's advice." What does the biblical reference add to his argument? Who might be the slovenly rulers to whom he refers?

## ENGAGING THE TEXT

a. Reread the essay and mark passages that grab your interest because they puzzle, please, or irritate you or because they connect with things you are learning in another class. Choose one such passage and write a brief response to it, explaining why it puzzles, pleases, or irritates you.
b. Summarize the essay. Since the essay is complex, you may wish to do this summary in a creative way, perhaps in the form of a letter to someone outside the class.

## SUGGESTIONS FOR SUSTAINED WRITING

a. Continue with item *b* from Engaging the Text. Discuss the connections between Hardin's essay and ideas discussed in your other courses, past or present.
b. Find another metaphor that could be used to describe the Earth's current situation. Frame an argument around that metaphor. Some examples of metaphors: race car, leaky barge, tapestry, pond, house. Come up with your own metaphors, but for examples to get you started, refer to Joan Didion's "Marrying Absurd" (Chapter 2), James C. Rettie's " 'But

a Watch in the Night' " (Chapter 9), or Loren Eiseley's "The Cosmic Prison" (Chapter 9).

c. Write a counterargument to this selection. Present an alternative solution (or at least a first step in the solution) to the problems of overpopulation and hunger. Do library research to find statistics that will argue with Hardin's statistics. You may want to take a creative approach and write this paper as a letter to Hardin.

**Free Speech**

# Should This Student Have Been Expelled?

Nat Hentoff

*Nat Hentoff (b. 1925) writes a regular column for the* Village Voice, *a* New York City *weekly, and contributes frequently to the* Washington Post, *the* New Yorker, *and other major magazines, journals, and newspapers. Born in Boston, he took his BA at Northeastern University and attended Harvard University for postgraduate study. He also studied at the Sorbonne in Paris as a Fulbright fellow. He was associate editor at* Down Beat *magazine from 1953 to 1957. He has received a Guggenheim Fellowship in education and an American Bar Association Silver Gavel Award. In 1985 he was awarded an honorary doctorate by Northeastern University. Hentoff describes himself as an "advocacy writer," and his interests range from jazz to educational reform, subjects on which he has written several books and articles. He also has written several novels and biographies. However, Hentoff's reputation rests chiefly on his writings on the First Amendment to the U.S. Constitution. Indeed, he is among America's staunchest defenders of free speech and its most outspoken opponent of censorship. His recent book on this subject is* The First Freedom: The Tumultuous History of Free Speech in America *(1989). "Should This Student Have Been Expelled?" which first appeared in the* Village Voice *in 1991, responds to a letter to the* New York Times *by Vartan Gregorian, president of Brown University, and to a* Times *editorial supporting Brown's expulsion of Douglas Hann. Both the letter and the editorial appear after Hentoff's essay.*

> *The day that Brown denies any student freedom of speech is the day I give up my presidency of the university.*
> —Vartan Gregorian, president of Brown University,
> February 20, 1991

Doug Hann, a varsity football player at Brown, was also concentrating on   1
organizational behavior and management and business economics. On the

night of October 18, 1990, Hann, a junior, was celebrating his twenty-first birthday, and in the process had imbibed a considerable amount of spirits.

2      At one point, Hann shouted into the air, "Fuck you, niggers!" It was aimed at no one in particular but apparently at all black students at Brown. Or in the world. A freshman leaned out a dormitory window and asked him to stop being so loud and offensive.

3      Hann, according to reporters on the *Brown Daily Herald,* looked up and yelled, "What are you, a faggot?" Hann then noticed an Israeli flag in the dorm. "What are you, a Jew?" he shouted. "Fucking Jew!"

4      Hann had achieved the hat trick of bigotry. (In hockey, the hat trick is scoring three goals in a game.) In less than a minute, Hann had engaged in racist, anti-Semitic, and homophobic insults.

5      He wasn't through. As reported by Smita Nerula in the *Brown Daily Herald,* the freshman who had asked Hann to cool it recruited a few people from his dorm "and followed Hann and his friends."

6      "This resulted in a verbal confrontation outside of Wayland Arch. At this time, [Hann] was said to have turned to one of the freshman's friends, a black woman, and shouted, 'My parents own your people.' "

7      To the Jewish student, or the student he thought was Jewish, Hann said, "Happy Hanukkah."

8      There are reports that at this juncture Hann tried to fight some of the students who had been following him. But, the *Brown Daily Herald* reports, he "was held back by one of his friends, while [another] friend stretched his arm across the Wayland Gates to keep the students from following Hann."

9      John Howard Crouch—a student and Brown chapter secretary of the American Civil Liberties Union there—tells me that because Hann had friends restraining him, "nobody seriously expected fighting, regardless of anyone's words."

10      Anyway, there was no physical combat. Just words. Awful words, but nothing more than speech. (Nor were there any threats.)

11      This was not the first time Hann's disgraceful drunken language had surfaced at Brown. Two years before, in an argument with a black student at a fraternity bar, Hann had called the student a "nigger." Thereupon he had been ordered to attend a race relations workshop and to get counseling for possible alcohol abuse. Obviously, he has not been rehabilitated.

12      Months went by after Hann's notorious birthday celebration as Brown's internal disciplinary procedures cranked away. (To steal a phrase from Robert Sherrill, Brown's way of reaching decisions in these matters is to due process as military music is to music. But that's true of any college or university I know anything about.)

13      At last, the Undergraduate Disciplinary Council (five faculty or administration members and five students) ruled that Doug Hann was to leave the university forevermore. Until two years ago, it was possible for

a Brown student to be dismissed, which meant that he or she could reapply after a decent period of penance. But now, Brown has enshrined the sentence of expulsion. You may go on to assist Mother Teresa in caring for the dying or you may teach a course in feminism to 2 Live Crew, but no accomplishments, no matter how noble, will get you back into Brown once you have been expelled.

Doug Hann will wander the Earth without a Brown degree for the rest 14 of his days.

The president of Brown, Vartan Gregorian—formerly the genial head of 15 the New York Public Library—had the power to commute or even reverse the sentence. But the speech code under which Hann was thrown out had been proposed by Gregorian himself shortly after he was inaugurated in 1989, so he was hardly a detached magistrate.

On January 25, 1991, Vartan Gregorian affirmed, with vigor, the ex- 16 pulsion decision by the Undergraduate Disciplinary Council.

Hann became a historic figure. Under all the "hate speech" codes en- 17 acted around the country in recent years, he is the first student to actually be expelled for violating one of the codes.

The *New York Times* (February 12) reported that "Howard Ehrlich, the 18 research director of the National Institute Against Prejudice and Violence, said that he did not know of any other such expulsions, but that he was familiar with cases in which students who had harassed others were moved to other dormitories or ordered to undergo counseling."

But that takes place in *educational* institutions, whose presidents rec- 19 ognize that there are students who need help, not exile.

At first, there didn't seem to be much protest among the student body 20 at Brown on free speech grounds—except for members of the Brown chapter of the ACLU and some free thinkers on the student paper, as well as some unaffiliated objectors to expelling students for what they say, not for what they do. The number of these dissenters is increasing, as we shall see.

At the student paper, however, the official tone has changed from the 21 libertarian approach of Vernon Silver, who was editor-in-chief last semester. A February 13 *Brown Daily Herald* editorial was headed: "*Good Riddance.*"

It began: "Doug Hann is gone, and the university is well to be rid of 22 him."

But President Gregorian has been getting a certain amount of flack and 23 so, smiting his critics hip and thigh, he wrote a letter to the *New York Times*. Well, that letter (printed on February 21) was actually a press release, distributed by the Brown University News Bureau to all sorts of people, including me, on February 12. There were a few changes—and that *Brown Daily Herald* editorial was attached to it—but Gregorian's declaration was clearly not written exclusively for the *Times*.

Is this a new policy at the *Times*—taking public relations handouts for 24 the letters page?

25    Next week I shall include a relentlessly accurate analysis of President Gregorian's letter by the executive director of the Rhode Island ACLU. But first, an account of what Gregorian said in that letter to the *Times*.

26    President Gregorian indignantly denies that Brown has ever expelled "anyone for the exercise of free speech, nor will it ever do so." Cross his heart.

27    He then goes into self-celebration: "My commitment to free speech and condemnation of racism and homophobia are well known. . . .

28    "The university's code of conduct does not prohibit speech; it prohibits *actions*."

29    Now watch this pitiable curve ball:

30    "Offense III [of the Brown code]—which deals with harassment—prohibits inappropriate, abusive, threatening, or demeaning actions based on race, religion, gender, handicap, ethnicity, national origin, or sexual orientation."

31    In the original press release, Gregorian underlined the word *actions*. There, and in the letter to the *Times*—lest a dozing reader miss the point—Gregorian emphasizes that "The rules do not proscribe words, epithets, or slanders, they proscribe behavior." Behavior that "shows flagrant disrespect for the well-being of others or is unreasonably disruptive of the University community."

32    Consider the overbreadth and vagueness of these penalty-bearing provisions. What are the definitions of "harassment," "inappropriate," "demeaning," "flagrant," "disrespect," "well-being," "unreasonably"?

33    Furthermore, with regard to Brown's termination of Doug Hann with extreme prejudice, Gregorian is engaging in the crudest form of Orwellian newspeak. Hann was kicked out for *speech*, and only speech—not for *actions*, as Gregorian huffily insists. As for behavior, the prickly folks whose burning of the American flag was upheld by the Supreme Court were indeed engaged in behavior, but that behavior was based entirely on symbolic speech. So was Hann's. He didn't punch anybody or vandalize any property. He brayed.

34    Art Spitzer, legal director of the ACLU's National Capital Area affiliate, wrote a personal letter to Gregorian:

35    "There is a very simple test for determining whether a person is being punished for his actions or his speech. You just ask whether he would have received the same punishment if he had spoken different words while engaging in the same conduct."

36    "Thus, would your student have been expelled if he had gotten drunk and stood in the same courtyard at the same hour of the night, shouting at the same decibel level, 'Black is Beautiful!' 'Gay is Good!' or 'Go Brown! Beat Yale!' or even 'Nuke Baghdad! Kill Saddam!'?

37    "I am confident," Spitzer said, that "he would not have been expelled for such 'actions.' If that is correct, it follows that *he was expelled for the un-*

*savory content of his speech,* and not for his actions. I have no doubt that you can understand this distinction. (Emphasis added.)

"Now, you are certainly entitled to believe that it is appropriate to ex- 38 pel a student for the content of his speech when that content is sufficiently offensive to the 'university community.' ...

"If that is your position, why can't you deliver it forthrightly? Then the 39 university community can have an open debate about which opinions it finds offensive, and ban them. Perhaps this can be done once a year, so that the university's rules can keep pace with the tenor of the times—after all, it wouldn't do to have outmoded rules banning procommunist or blasphemous speech still on the books, now that it's 1991. Then students and teachers applying for admission or employment at Brown will know what they are getting into.

"Your recent statements, denying the obvious, are just hypocritical...." 40

And what did the *New York Times*—in a stunningly fatuous February 41 21 editorial—say of Vartan Gregorian's sending Doug Hann into permanent exile? "A noble attempt both to govern and teach."

The *Times* editorials should really be signed, so that the rest of the ed- 42 itorial board isn't blamed for such embarrassments.

*1991*

# How Much Hate to Tolerate

*New York Times* editorial, (February 21, 1991)

Free speech and human relations seemed to collide last month at Brown 1 University when it expelled a student for racial and religious harassment. In fact, however, to judge by all that is publicly known, the school walked a fine line with sensitivity toward its complex mission.

One mission of a university is to send into the world graduates who 2 are tolerant of many races, faiths and cultures. Another mission is to teach the value of free expression and tolerance even for hateful ideas. But should such tolerance cover racist, sexist or homophobic speech that makes the learning environment intolerable for racial and religious minorities, women and other targets of abuse? Brown found a reasonable basis for saying, clearly, no.

Douglas Hann, white, a junior and a varsity football player, had pre- 3 viously been disciplined for alcohol abuse and for racial insults against a black fellow student. Then, one evening last fall, he shouted racial insults in a university courtyard. A Jewish student who opened a dormitory window and called for quiet was answered with a religious insult. Later that evening Mr. Hann directed a racial insult at a black undergraduate.

4      The student–faculty discipline committee found him guilty of three violations of student rules, including another count of alcohol abuse. Vartan Gregorian, the university's president, upheld the student's expulsion last month. He had a sound basis for doing so. If the facts are reported correctly, Mr. Hann crossed the line between merely hateful speech and hateful speech that directly confronted and insulted other undergraduates.

5      Some courts have found that public universities are bound by the First Amendment's ban on state censorship and thus may not punish students for expressing politically incorrect or socially distasteful ideas. Brown, like other private schools, is less directly bound by the Constitution but committed to its precepts. It is trying to avoid censorship but draws a line between strong language and what the courts often call "fighting words."

6      In the adjacent Letters column today, Mr. Gregorian insists that Brown does not punish unruly speech as such but will decide case-by-case whether a student has passed "the point at which speech becomes behavior" that flagrantly disregards the well-being of others or "subjects someone to abusive or demeaning actions."

7      That formula is a noble attempt both to govern and teach. It offers a principled basis for disciplinary action against Mr. Hann for his direct, confrontational conduct.

8      The lines may not be so clearly drawn in other cases. There may also be more of them in the present climate of evidently increasing student intolerance. But when bigots attack other students with ugly invective, universities, whether public or private, need not remain silent. Their presidents, like Mr. Gregorian, may denounce indecency and, in so doing, protect tolerance.

# Brown Expulsion Not about Free Speech

*New York Times* letter to the editor, (February 21, 1991)

To the Editor:

1      "Student at Brown Is Expelled Under a Rule Barring 'Hate Speech' " (news article, Feb. 12) suggests I have instituted "hate-speech" prohibitions at Brown University and that the expulsion of a student who shouted racial and homophobic epithets on campus last October is the first such in the

nation based on restrictions of free speech. Brown University has never expelled anyone for free speech, nor will it ever do so.

My commitment to free speech and condemnation of racism and ho- 2
mophobia are well known. In April 1989, several students were subjected
to a cowardly attack of racial and homophobic graffiti. The words and slogans scrawled anonymously on doors in one of our dormitories were vicious attacks threatening the well-being and security of Brown students.

I condemned that anonymous poisoning of our community and said I 3
would prosecute vigorously and seek the expulsion of those who incite hatred or perpetuate such acts of vandalism. Nothing I said then or have
done since should be construed as limiting anyone's freedom of speech,
nor have I revised the university's code of conduct to that effect.

The university's code of conduct does not prohibit speech; it prohibits ac- 4
tions, and these include behavior that "shows flagrant disrespect for the well-
being of others or is unreasonably disruptive of the university community."

Offense III, which deals with harassment, prohibits inappropriate, 5
abusive, threatening or demeaning actions based on race, religion, gender, handicap, ethnicity, national origin or sexual orientation.

"The Tenets of Community Behavior," which outline community stan- 6
dards for acceptable behavior at Brown, have been read for more than 10
years by entering students, who agree in writing to abide by them.

The rules do not proscribe words, epithets or slanders; they proscribe be- 7
havior. The point at which speech becomes behavior and the degree to which
that behavior shows flagrant disrespect for the well-being of others (Offense
II), subjects someone to abusive or demeaning actions (Offense III) or is related to drug or alcohol use (Offense IV) is determined by a hearing to consider the circumstances of each case. The student is entitled to an appeal,
which includes review by a senior officer and a decision by the president.

I cannot and will not comment about any specific case. I regret the re- 8
lease of any student's name in connection with a disciplinary hearing and
the exposure any case may receive in *The Brown Herald*.

Freedom-of-speech questions lie at the heart of any academic commu- 9
nity. The very nature of the academic enterprise necessitates that universities remain partisans of heterodoxy, of a rich and full range of opinions,
ideas and expression. Imposed orthodoxies of all sorts, including what is
called "politically correct" speech, are anathema to our enterprise.

The university's most compelling challenge is to achieve a balance be- 10
tween the right of its individual members to operate and speak freely, and
fostering respect for and adherence to community values and standards of
conduct.

VARTAN GREGORIAN
President, Brown University
Providence, R.I., Feb. 21, 1991

## QUESTIONS FOR DISCUSSION

### Content

a. In a sentence or two, summarize Hentoff's argument against Hann's expulsion.
b. Explain the analogy the author uses in paragraph 12.
c. Why, according to Hentoff, wouldn't Vartan Gregorian "commute or
   even reverse" Hann's sentence (paragraph 15)?
d. What did Hentoff imply about Brown's president in paragraph 19?
e. What is "Orwellian newspeak" (paragraph 33)? According to Hentoff,
   in what way is Gregorian engaging in "newspeak"?
f. Explain the test "for determining whether a person is being punished
   for his actions or his speech" as articulated by Art Spitzer in paragraphs
   35–37.
g. Explain the advice Spitzer gave Gregorian as quoted form his letter in
   paragraph 39.
h. What purpose does Hentoff's conclusion serve? What is his point in the
   essay's very last paragraph?

### Strategy and Style

i. Why does Hentoff include paragraph 10? Is it really necessary?
j. Why does he characterize Gregorian's letter to the *Times* as a "public relations" handout (paragraph 24)? How would you describe Hentoff's
   attitude toward the newspaper's editorial board?
k. Analyze the structure of the essay. If necessary, write a brief outline that
   includes its key points and reveals its organization.
l. Where in this section does Hentoff appeal to authority by quoting expert testimony? Who are those experts? Is their testimony convincing?
m. What advantage does Hentoff achieve by quoting directly from Gregorian's letter to the *Times?* Other than directly attacking the letter's contents, how does he refute Gregorian?

### ENGAGING THE TEXT

a. Summarize the arguments made by the writer of the *New York Times* editorial "How Much Hate to Tolerate." Then do the same for Vartan Gregorian's letter to the editor.
b. Are you in favor of unlimited freedom of expression? If so, explain why.
   In an attempt to anticipate opposing arguments, explain how you
   would defend the right of others to express themselves in ways you

consider immoral, abhorrent, or even dangerous. If not, explain why freedom of expression should be limited in certain instances. Refer to Hentoff's essay in your response.

## SUGGESTIONS FOR SUSTAINED WRITING

a. In your own letter to the editor, attack or defend Hentoff's position on the expulsion of Doug Hann and on its implications vis-à-vis the exercise of free speech on college campuses. Whichever position you take, make reference to or quote from Hentoff's essay, the *New York Times* editorial, and/or Gregorian's letter. On the other hand, remember that this is *your* letter, so rely heavily on your own arguments and ideas.

b. Compare Hentoff's ideas with those in the essays by William Lutz and Donna Woolfolk Cross in Chapter 5. Write an essay in which you discuss how language is used to cover or to expose a person's "true" feelings. What does one's choice of words reveal about one's worldview?

c. The American college is a place where open and free debate should be encouraged. You probably know of several important issues—academic, political, cultural, scientific, theological, economic, and so on—being discussed by students and faculty at your college. Take a clear position on an issue that affects you as a student, that you have studied or read about, or that you have debated with others at your school. You need not choose an issue of universal significance. Interesting and effective arguments can be written on increasing scholarship aid, providing more parking spaces for college commuters, keeping the library open late at night and on Sundays, and giving students access to computer labs free of charge. Research your topic as thoroughly as you can through secondary and primary sources.

**Free Speech**

# Shouting "Fire!"

Alan M. Dershowitz

*A graduate of Brooklyn College and Yale Law School, Alan Dershowitz (b. 1938), was appointed to the law faculty at Harvard University in 1963, where he has taught courses on a variety of subjects, including criminal law, legal ethics, and civil liberties. He has written several books for the lay reader, some of which are discussions of criminal law, such as* Psychoanalysis, Psychiatry, and the Law *(coauthored with others, 1967). Other books discuss some of the controversial cases on which he has worked, such as* The Best Defense *(1982) and* Reversal of Fortune *(1982), on the Claus von Bulow case. In 1997, Dershowitz published* The Abuse Excuse, *a series of essays on personal responsibility and the law. From his experience as a member of the team that defended O. J. Simpson, Dershowitz wrote* Reasonable Doubts: The O. J. Simpson Case and the Criminal Justice System *(1996). His most recent books are* The Genesis of Justice *(2000) and* Just Revenge *(2001). "Shouting 'Fire!' " was first published in the* Atlantic Monthly *in 1989.*

1   When the Reverend Jerry Falwell learned that the Supreme Court had reversed his $200,000 judgment against *Hustler* magazine for the emotional distress that he had suffered from an outrageous parody, his response was typical of those who seek to censor speech: "Just as no person may scream 'Fire!' in a crowded theater when there is no fire, and find cover under the First Amendment, likewise, no sleazy merchant like Larry Flynt should be able to use the First Amendment as an excuse for maliciously and dishonestly attacking public figures, as he has so often done."

2   Justice Oliver Wendell Holmes's classic example of unprotected speech—falsely shouting "Fire!" in a crowded theater—has been invoked so often, by so many people, in such diverse contexts, that it has become part of our national folk language. It has even appeared—most appropriately—in the theater: In Tom Stoppard's play *Rosencrantz and Guildenstern Are Dead* a character shouts at the audience, "Fire!" He then quickly explains: "It's all right—I'm demonstrating the misuse of free speech." Shouting "Fire!" in the theater may well be the only jurisprudential analogy that has assumed the status of a folk argument. A prominent historian recently characterized it as "the most brilliantly persuasive expression that ever came from Holmes's pen." But in spite of its hallowed position in both the jurisprudence of the First Amendment and the arsenal of political discourse, it is and was an inapt analogy, even in the context in which it was originally offered. It has lately become—despite, perhaps even because of, the frequency and promiscuousness of its invocation—little more than a caricature of logical argumentation.

3   The case that gave rise to the "Fire!"-in-a-crowded-theater analogy, *Schenck v. United States*, involved the prosecution of Charles Schenck, who was the general secretary of the Socialist Party in Philadelphia, and Elizabeth Baer, who was its recording secretary. In 1917 a jury found Schenck and Baer guilty of attempting to cause insubordination among soldiers who had been drafted to fight in the First World War. They and other party members had circulated leaflets urging draftees not to "submit to intimidation" by fighting in a war being conducted on behalf of "Wall Street's chosen few."

4   Schenck admitted, and the Court found, that the intent of the pamphlets' "impassioned language" was to "influence" drafters to resist the draft. Interestingly, however, Justice Holmes noted that nothing in the pam-

phlet suggested that the draftees should use unlawful or violent means to oppose conscription: "In form at least [the pamphlet] confined itself to peaceful measures, such as petition for the repeal of the act" and an exhortation to exercise "your right to assert your opposition to the draft." Many of its most impassioned words were quoted directly from the Constitution.

Justice Holmes acknowledged that "in many places and in ordinary 5 times the defendants, in saying all that was said in the circular, would have been within their constitutional rights." "But," he added, "the character of every act depends upon the circumstances in which it is done." And to illustrate that truism he went on to say:

> The most stringent protection of free speech would not protect a man in falsely shouting fire in a theater, and causing panic. It does not even protect a man from an injunction against uttering words that may have all the effect of force.

Justice Holmes then upheld the convictions in the context of a wartime 6 draft, holding that the pamphlet created "a clear and present danger" of hindering the war effort while our soldiers were fighting for their lives and our liberty.

The example of shouting "Fire!" obviously bore little relationship to 7 the facts of the *Schenck* case. The Schenck pamphlet contained a substantive political message. It urged its draftee readers to *think* about the message and then—if they so chose—to act on it in a lawful and nonviolent way. The man who shouts "Fire!" in a crowded theater is neither sending a political message nor inviting his listener to think about what he has said and decide what to do in a rational, calculated manner. On the contrary, the message is designed to force action *without* contemplation. The message "Fire!" is directed not to the mind and the conscience of the listener but, rather, to his adrenaline and his feet. It is a stimulus to immediate *action*, not thoughtful reflection. It is—as Justice Holmes recognized in his follow-up sentence—the functional equivalent of "uttering words that may have all the effect of force."

Indeed, in that respect the shout of "Fire!" is not even speech, in any 8 meaningful sense of the term. It is a *clang* sound, the equivalent of setting off a nonverbal alarm. Had Justice Holmes been more honest about his example, he would have said that freedom of speech does not protect a kid who pulls a fire alarm in the absence of a fire. But that obviously would have been irrelevant to the case at hand. The proposition that pulling an alarm is not protected speech certainly leads to the conclusion that shouting the word "fire" is also not protected. But the core analogy is the nonverbal alarm, and the derivative example is the verbal shout. By cleverly substituting the derivative shout for the core alarm, Holmes made it possible to analogize one set of words to another—as he could not have done if he had begun with the self-evident proposition that setting off an alarm bell is not free speech.

9      The analogy is thus not only inapt but also insulting. Most Americans do not respond to political rhetoric with the same kind of automatic acceptance expected of schoolchildren responding to a fire drill. Not a single recipient of the Schenck pamphlet is known to have changed his mind after reading it. Indeed, one draftee, who appeared as a prosecution witness, was asked whether reading a pamphlet asserting that the draft law was unjust would make him "immediately decide that you must erase that law." Not surprisingly, he replied, "I do my own thinking." A theatergoer would probably not respond similarly if asked how he would react to a shout of "Fire!"

10     Another important reason why the analogy is inapt is that Holmes emphasizes the factual falsity of the shout "Fire!" The Schenck pamphlet, however, was not factually false. It contained political opinions and ideas about the causes of the war and about appropriate and lawful responses to the draft. As the Supreme Court recently reaffirmed (in *Falwell v. Hustler*), "The First Amendment recognizes no such thing as a 'false' idea." Nor does it recognize false opinions about the causes of or cures for war.

11     A closer analogy to the facts of the *Schenck* case might have been provided by a person's standing outside a theater, offering the patrons a leaflet advising them that in his opinion the theater was structurally unsafe, and urging them not to enter but to complain to the building inspectors. That analogy, however, would not have served Holmes's argument for punishing Schenck. Holmes needed an analogy that would appear relevant to Schenck's political speech but that would invite the conclusion that censorship was appropriate.

12     Unsurprisingly, a war-weary nation—in the throes of a know-nothing hysteria over immigrant anarchists and socialists—welcomed the comparison between what was regarded as a seditious political pamphlet and a malicious shout of "Fire!" Ironically, the "Fire!" analogy is nearly all that survives from the *Schenck* case; the ruling itself is almost certainly not good law. Pamphlets of the kind that resulted in Schenck's imprisonment have been circulated with impunity during subsequent wars.

13     Over the past several years I have assembled a collection of instances—cases, speeches, arguments—in which proponents of censorship have maintained that the expression at issue is "just like" or "equivalent to" falsely shouting "Fire!" in a crowded theater and ought to be banned, "just as" shouting "Fire!" ought to be banned. The analogy is generally invoked, often with self-satisfaction, as an absolute argument-stopper. It does, after all, claim the high authority of the great Justice Oliver Wendell Holmes. I have rarely heard it invoked in a convincing, or even particularly relevant, way. But that, too, can claim lineage from the great Holmes.

14     Not unlike Falwell, with his silly comparison between shouting "Fire!" and publishing an offensive parody, courts and commentators have

frequently invoked "Fire!" as an analogy to expression that is not an automatic stimulus to panic. A state supreme court held that "Holmes's aphorism . . . applies with equal force to pornography"—in particular to the exhibition of the movie *Carmen Baby* in a drive-in theater in close proximity to highways and homes. Another court analogized "picketing . . . in support of a secondary boycott" to shouting "Fire!" because in both instances "speech and conduct are brigaded." In the famous Skokie case one of the judges argued that allowing Nazis to march through a city where a large number of Holocaust survivors live "just might fall into the same category as one's 'right' to cry fire in a crowded theater."

Outside court the analogies become even more badly stretched. A 15 spokesperson for the New Jersey Sports and Exposition Authority complained that newspaper reports to the effect that a large number of football players had contracted cancer after playing in the Meadowlands—a stadium atop a landfill—were the "journalistic equivalent of shouting fire in a crowded theater." An insect researcher acknowledged that his prediction that a certain amusement park might become roach-infested "may be tantamount to shouting fire in a crowded theater." The philosopher Sidney Hook, in a letter to the *New York Times* bemoaning a Supreme Court decision that required a plaintiff in a defamation action to prove that the offending statement was actually false, argued that the First Amendment does not give the press carte blanche to accuse innocent persons "any more than the First Amendment protects the right of someone falsely to shout fire in a crowded theater."

Some close analogies to shouting "Fire!" or setting off an alarm are, of 16 course, available: Calling in a false bomb threat; dialing 911 and falsely describing an emergency; making a loud, gun-like sound in the presence of the President; setting off a voice-activated sprinkler system by falsely shouting "Fire!" In one case in which the "Fire!" analogy was directly to the point, a creative defendant tried to get around it. The case involved a man who calmly advised an airline clerk that he was "only here to hijack the plane." He was charged, in effect, with shouting "Fire!" in a crowded theater, and his rejected defense —as quoted by the court—was as follows: "If we built fire-proof theaters and let people know about this, then the shouting of 'Fire!' would not cause panic."

Here are some more-distant but still related examples: The recent inci- 17 dent of the police slaying in which some members of an onlooking crowd urged a mentally ill vagrant who had taken an officer's gun to shoot the officer; the screaming of racial epithets during a tense confrontation; shouting down a speaker and preventing him from continuing his speech.

Analogies are, by their nature, matters of degree. Some are closer to 18 the core example than others. But any attempt to analogize political ideas in a pamphlet, ugly parody in a magazine, offensive movies in a theater, controversial newspaper articles, or any of the other expressions and actions catalogued above to the very different act of shouting "Fire!" in a crowded theater is either self-deceptive or self-serving.

19       The government does, of course, have some arguably legitimate bases for suppressing speech which bear no relationship to shouting "Fire!" It may ban the publication of nuclear-weapon codes, of information about troop movements, and of the identity of undercover agents. It may criminalize extortion threats and conspiratorial agreements. These expressions may lead directly to serious harm, but the mechanisms of causation are very different from those at work when an alarm is sounded. One may also argue—less persuasively, in my view—against protecting certain forms of public obscenity and defamatory statements. Here, too, the mechanisms of causation are very different. None of these exceptions to the First Amendment's exhortation that the government "shall make no law . . . abridging the freedom of speech, or of the press" is anything like falsely shouting "Fire!" in a crowded theater; they all must be justified on other grounds.

20       A comedian once told his audience, during a stand-up routine, about the time he was standing around a fire with a crowd of people and got in trouble for yelling "Theater, theater!" That I think, is about as clever and productive a use as anyone has ever made of Holmes's flawed analogy.

*1989*

## QUESTIONS FOR DISCUSSION

### Content

a. Explain the connection between shouting "fire!" and censorship.
b. What is the false connection (analogy) with which Dershowitz finds fault? Why does he find fault with it?
c. What is the valid analogy?
d. Why is it important for us to see the difference between the false analogy and the valid one? What impact does this distinction have on your life?
e. Reread paragraph 8 and paraphrase it. What are the "core analogy" and the "derivative example"? How did Holmes make it "possible to analogize one set of words to another"?
f. Why is it necessary for Dershowitz to explain the concept of shouting "fire!" so thoroughly?

### Strategy and Style

g. What is a "folk argument" (paragraph 2)? What is the author's attitude toward folk arguments?

h. Why does the author end with the humorous example of shouting "theater!"?

i. Dershowitz relies heavily on quotations from the people and cases with which he finds fault. How does he use these quotations? Is it appropriate to use such material in an argumentative essay? Does this practice work here?

j. Dershowitz constructs sentences so that the quotes he uses seem to sound as if they were his own prose. What techniques does he use to accomplish this?

## ENGAGING THE TEXT

a. Write definitions of *free speech* and *censorship* as you understand them. Then write definitions of those terms as you believe Dershowitz understands them. Are there differences between your definitions and his? Explain those differences.

b. With two or three classmates, brainstorm a list of other examples of how the "shouting fire!" analogy would apply to your lives.

## SUGGESTIONS FOR SUSTAINED WRITING

a. What does Dershowitz's essay have to do with you and your world? Write an essay in which you first explain Dershowitz's thesis, main points, and purpose. Then, with examples drawn from your own experiences, observations, or reading, argue that Dershowitz's thesis has or does not have relevance to you or to the people with whom you associate.

b. Read or reread the essay by Nat Hentoff that appears in this chapter. Consider how Hentoff might have approached Dershowitz's topic in "Shouting 'Fire!' " Would he have engaged the topic by using analogy as Dershowitz did, or would he have used a different technique? In an essay explain how this topic might be treated in Hentoff's hands.

c. Should there be laws limiting free speech? If you believe that speech should be limited, write an essay in which you argue for such laws. What are the limitations you would impose and why? Explain your proposal in detail, and defend it by citing real or hypothetical cases in which your laws would be beneficial.

If you believe that speech should not be limited in any way, write an argument in which you show that limitations would have a detrimental effect on society. Again, be detailed and use real or hypothetical cases to illustrate your points.

Whichever position you take, consider doing some additional reading on this subject in print or electronic sources. A good piece with which to start is the essay by Nat Hentoff in this chapter.

# Let's Go Veggie!

Joseph Pace

*Joseph Pace (b. 1971) was born in Owen Sound, Ontario. He was a student at the University of Waterloo when he wrote this essay. He is now the author and project director of the forthcoming book* One Bite: Food and the Power to Change the World. *The book is a compilation of the work of a research team of more than 40 experts in the fields of nutrition, food safety, ecology, and animal welfare. Pace began his study of diet at age 16, when he realized that a meat diet is the cause of many diseases and environmental problems. He took on vegetarianism as a political cause, writing newspaper articles and speaking to local groups across Canada, for which he was awarded the Canadian Youth Citizenship Award. He spent the next several years organizing environmental speaking tours and other events before entering the university to study Canada's food system. Pace is a frequent speaker at conferences and symposiums throughout Canada.*

*Alan Herscovici (b. 1948) was born in Montreal. He received a BA in 1969 from McGill University and an MA in 1971 from the University of Sussex. He has worked as a broadcaster, editor, economic researcher, and even goat herder. He is now a consultant and writer. In 1983 he wrote the radio documentary* Men and Animals: Building a New Relationship with Nature; *this documentary inspired his books* Second Nature: The Animals Rights Controversy *(1984),* Furs: An Environmental Ethic *(1988), and* Food for Thought: Facts about Food and Farming in Canada *(1991). He argues that the goals of animals rights activism are neither environmentally nor economically sound and seeks to find a compromise. He has also written a novel,* The Tibetan Treasure *(1984), exposing human rights abuses in Tibet.*

*For the May 27 edition of the* Toronto Star *in 1998, Pace and Herscovici were asked to write point-counterpoint essays on the topic of vegetarianism.*

1   If there was a single act that would improve your health, cut your risk of food-borne illnesses, and help preserve the environment and the welfare of millions of animals, would you do it?

2   The act I'm referring to is the choice you make every time you sit down to a meal.

3   More than a million Canadians have already acted: They have chosen to not eat meat. And the pace of change has been dramatic.

4   Vegetarian food sales are showing unparalleled growth. Especially popular are meat-free burgers and hot dogs, and the plant-based cuisines of India, China, Mexico, Italy and Japan.

5   Even fast food chains are getting in on the act. Subway reports that its Number 1–selling sub worldwide is the Veggie Delite.

**404**

Fuelling the shift toward vegetarianism have been the health recommen-  6
dations of medical research. Study after study has uncovered the same basic
truth: Plant foods lower your risk of chronic disease; animal foods increase it.

The American Dietetic Association says: "Scientific data suggest posi-  7
tive relationships between a vegetarian diet and reduced risk for several
chronic degenerative diseases."

This past fall, after reviewing 4,500 studies on diet and cancer, the  8
World Cancer Research Fund flatly stated: "We've been running the human biological engine on the wrong fuel."

This "wrong fuel" has helped boost the cost of degenerative disease in  9
Canada to an estimated $400 billion a year, according to Bruce Holub, a
professor of nutritional science at the University of Guelph.

Animal foods have serious nutritional drawbacks: They are devoid of  10
fibre, contain far too much saturated fat and cholesterol, and may even
carry traces of hormones, steroids and antibiotics. It makes little difference
whether you eat beef, pork, chicken or fish.

Animal foods are also gaining notoriety as breeding grounds for *E.*  11
*coli,* campylobacter and other bacteria that cause illness. According to the
Canadian Food Inspection Agency, six out of ten chickens are infected with
salmonella. It's like playing Russian roulette with your health.

So why aren't governments doing anything about this? Unfortunately,  12
they have bowed to pressure from powerful lobby groups such as the Beef
Information Centre, the Canadian Egg Marketing Agency and the Dairy
Farmers of Canada. According to documents retrieved through the Freedom of Information Act, these groups forced changes to Canada's latest
food guide before it was released in 1993.

This should come as no surprise: Even a minor reduction in recom-  13
mended intakes of animal protein could cost these industries billions of
dollars a year.

While health and food safety are compelling reasons for choosing a  14
vegetarian lifestyle, there are also larger issues to consider. Animal-based
agriculture is one of the most environmentally destructive industries on
the face of the Earth.

Think for a moment about the vast resources required to raise, feed,  15
shelter, transport, process and package the 500 million Canadian farm animals slaughtered each year. Water and energy are used at every step of the
way. Alberta Agriculture calculates that it takes 10 to 20 times more energy
to produce meat than to produce grain.

Less than a quarter of our agricultural land is used to feed people di-  16
rectly. The rest is devoted to grazing and growing food for animals.
Ecosystems of forest, wetland and grassland have been decimated to fuel
the demand for land. Using so much land heightens topsoil loss, the use of
harsh fertilizers and pesticides, and the need for irrigation water from

dammed rivers. If people can shift away from meat, much of this land could be converted back to wilderness.

17       The problem is that animals are inefficient at converting plants to edible flesh. It takes, for example, 8.4 kilograms of grain to produce one kilogram of pork, the U.S. government estimates.

18       After putting so many resources into animals, what do we get out? Manure—at a rate of over 10,000 kilograms per second in Canada alone, according to the government. Environment Canada says cattle excrete 40 kilograms of manure for every kilogram of edible beef. A large egg factory can produce 50 to 100 tonnes of waste per week, the Ontario Ministry of Agriculture estimates.

19       And where does it go? In the 1992 Ontario Groundwater Survey, 43 per cent of tested wells were contaminated with agricultural run-off containing fecal coliform bacteria and nitrates. Earlier this month, charges were laid against a large Alberta feedlot operator for dumping 30 million litres of cattle manure into the Bow River, "killing everything in its path," as a news story described it.

20       And then there is methane, a primary contributing gas in global warming and ozone layer depletion. Excluding natural sources, 27 per cent of Canada's and 20 percent of the world's methane comes from livestock.

21       John Robbins, author of the Pulitzer prize–nominated book *Diet for a New America* (Group West), said it best when he stated: "Eating lower on the food chain is perhaps the most potent single act we can take to halt the destruction of our environment and preserve our natural resources."

22       Our environment also includes the animals killed for their meat. It has become an accepted fact that today's factory-farmed animals live short, miserable, unnatural lives.

23       As part of my research at the University of Waterloo, I toured some of the country's largest "processing" plants. The experience has left me with recurring nightmares.

24       I saw "stubborn" cows being beaten and squealing pigs chased around the killing floor with electric calipers.

25       I looked on in utter shock as a cow missed the stun gun and was hoisted fully conscious upside down by its hind leg and cut to pieces, thrashing until its last breath.

26       Noticing my shock, the foreman remarked: "Who cares? They're going to die anyway."

27       Because it can cost hundreds of dollars per minute to stop the conveyor line, animal welfare comes second to profit. Over 150,000 animals are "processed" every hour of every working day in Canada, according to Agriculture Canada.

28       The picture gets uglier still. En route to slaughter, farm animals may legally spend anywhere from 36 to 72 hours without food, water or rest.

They're not even afforded the "luxury" of temperature controlled trucks in extreme summer heat or sub-zero cold.

Agriculture Canada has estimated that more than 3 million Canadian 29 farm animals die slow and painful deaths en route to slaughter each year.

I've also visited typical Canadian farms. Gone are the days when 30 piglets snorted and roosters strutted their way about the barnyard. Most of today's modernized farms have long, windowless sheds in which animals live like prisoners their entire lives. I have seen chickens crammed four to a cage, nursing pigs separated from their young by iron bars and veal calves confined to crates so narrow they couldn't turn around. Few of these animals ever experience sunlight or fresh air—and most of their natural urges are denied.

Although it is difficult to face these harsh realities, it is even more dif- 31 ficult to ignore them. Three times a day, you make a decision that not only affects the quality of your life, but the rest of the living world. We hold in our knives and forks the power to change this world.

Consider the words of Albert Einstein: "Nothing will benefit human 32 health and increase the chances for survival of life on Earth as the Evolution to a vegetarian diet."

Bon appetite.                                                                    33

*1998*

# Where's the Beef?

Alan Herscovici

With summer comes that most wonderful of North American traditions, the 1 backyard barbecue. The succulent aroma of fresh grilled steak, sausages, chicken and fish draws family, friends and neighbours together for a communal feast. Inevitably, in these politically correct times, the conversation may drift to the question of whether we really ought to be eating meat at all.

The following guide should help see you through until the burgers are 2 done.

Appealing to self-interest, a common opening line for proselytizing 3 vegetarians is to claim that "eating meat is bad for us." They have trouble explaining, however, why human health and longevity have improved steadily as animal products became more readily available throughout this century. In fact, meat is an excellent source of 12 essential nutrients, including protein, iron, zinc and B vitamins.

4      It is true that excessive fats can be harmful, but today's meats are lean. Based on equal-size servings, tofu has more fat than a sirloin steak and only half the protein. (Tofu also makes a mess of the grill.)

5      With the exception of certain religious sects, people have rarely been vegetarian by choice. Most often, vegetarianism is the unfortunate result of poverty. Yet the veggie crowd also claims that "humans are not natural meat-eaters." Our teeth are not as sharp and our intestinal tracts not as short as those of cats and other pure carnivores. But we are not equipped to be herbivores, either. Like other omnivores (such as bears or racoons), our digestive equipment allows us to tackle a wide range of foods.

6      If we were not designed to eat meat, why do we produce large quantities of the enzymes required to break down such foods? Why is vitamin $B_{12}$ (found only in animal products) essential to human life? If we were not natural meat-eaters, or at least bug and grub eaters, our species would have died out long ago. If we did not develop as hunters, why are our eyes in the front of our heads like those of other predators (tigers, wolves or owls)? Why does the mere smell of a sizzling steak set my saliva glands watering?

7      Shifting their ground, animal activists now charge that livestock threatens the environment. But much of the world's arable land is best suited to be used as pasture. It is too hilly, fragile, dry or cold for cultivation. Cattle convert grass into nutrients that can be digested by humans. Those who promote organic agriculture understand that livestock completes the nutrient cycle by returning organic matter to the soil with manure.

8      Other anti-meat myths can also be dismissed. For example:

- Whatever you may think about fast food hamburgers, eating them does *not* encourage the destruction of Amazon rainforests. Because of disease-control measures, no unprocessed South American beef products at all may be imported into Canada.
- Livestock do *not* use up grains that could otherwise feed starving people in Third World countries. The main diet of cattle is grass and hay. Pigs, chickens and other farm animals are generally fed corn and barley, while people eat mainly wheat and rice. Animals also consume pest- and weather-damaged grains, crop residues (corn stalks and leaves) and by-products from food-processing, such as unusable grains (or parts of grains) left over from producing breakfast cereals and other human foods. Raising livestock in Canada does not prevent us from shipping emergency supplies to people in need. Hunger today, however, is usually the result of political, economic and distribution problems, not a lack of production capacity.

- The production of methane gas by livestock is *not* a major contributor to global warming. Methane gas is only one of many possible "greenhouse" gases. It is produced by all sorts of decomposition of organic matter, including normal digestion (even by vegetarians). Main sources of greenhouse gases include wetlands, forest fires, landfills, rice paddies, the extraction of gas, oil and coal—and even termites.
- Meat does *not* contain harmful pesticide, antibiotic or other residues. This is assured by stringent Agriculture Canada and Health Canada regulations and inspection. Concerns about dangerous bacteria are easily addressed by cooking your meat well. (Fruit and raw vegetables, in fact, present a more difficult problem.)

One study that is not often cited by animal activists is a recent report 9 by the Centre for Energy and the Environment at the University of Exeter in England. David Coley and his associates analyzed how much fuel energy is used to produce and process different foods. Burning fuel releases carbon into the atmosphere, the major suspected cause of global warming.

To the dismay of the politically correct set, meat scores far better than 10 vegetables on this environmental-impact scale. It requires eight megajoules of fuel energy to produce enough beef or burgers to provide one megajoule of food energy. The fuel energy costs of chicken and lamb are seven megajoules and six megajoules respectively. Typical salad vegetables, however, require as much as 45 megajoules of fuel energy for each energy unit of food intake provided.

"Meat does well because it is not highly processed, provides a lot of 11 calories and is often produced locally." Coley reported in *New Scientist* last December.

It would require more ink than is available to us here to respond to all 12 the claims animal activists have made about the supposed evils of modern livestock husbandry methods, what they misleadingly label "factory farming." For example, they criticize the caging of laying hens, while ignoring the fact that such systems improve hygiene, preventing disease and reducing the need for antibiotics.

Detailed responses to animal-welfare concerns are provided in *Food* 13 *For Thought: Facts about Food and Farming*, published by the Ontario Farm Animal Council (7195 Millcreek Dr., Mississauga, Ont. L5N 4H1).

For debate around the barbecue, suffice it to say that animals cannot be 14 productive unless they receive excellent nutrition and care. Farmers who do not provide good care for their animals will not remain in business for long.

Once fallacious claims about health, environment and animal welfare 15 are stripped away, the heart of the animal-rights argument is exposed. What right, they ask, do we have to use animals at all?

The central fallacy of this argument is that it ignores basic principles 16 of biology and ecology. Every plant and animal species naturally produces far more offspring than their environment can support to maturity. This "surplus" provides food for other species. Aboriginal people called this "the cycle of life." We now usually call it "the food chain." We are part of this cycle, like every other living organism on the planet. The domestication of livestock has been a very successful survival strategy, not only for humans, but also for the other species involved.

17    The squeamishness some people now feel about eating animals does not represent a more evolved sensitivity to nature. It is a symptom of how cut off some people have become from nature.

18    Thanks to modern agriculture, many city people now take our abundant food supply for granted. We forget that all our food must still be wrested from the land. Even our vegetables must be protected from other creatures. Even a carrot clings to the soil with all its strength. Like other animals, we kill to eat. But because we are human, we can also give thanks and treat the animals that feed us with respect.

19    I think those burgers should be ready about now . . .

*1998*

## QUESTIONS FOR DISCUSSION

### Content

a. What is each writer's main point? What would Pace like his readers to do? What would Herscovici like his readers to do?
b. What reasons does Pace give for not eating meat? What other reasons could he have included but did not?
c. According to or implied by Pace, what benefits would universal vegetarianism have? What might be Herscovici's reply?
d. What reasons does Herscovici give for eating meat? What other reasons could he have included but did not?
e. According to or implied by Herscovici, what negative effects would universal vegetarianism have? How would Pace reply?
f. To what extent would Pace's and Herscovici's arguments apply to the United States or other countries?

### Strategy and Style

g. Which essay strikes you as better argued? Why?

h. What are your own opinions on this issue? How does your opinion influence how you react to each essay?

i. What sources seem most credible? What sources seem lease credible? Why?

j. Sources are not cited, as is typical of newspaper writing. What information would need to be cited if these essays were college research papers?

k. What features—sentence structure, writing style, vocabulary, and so forth—mark these two essays as newspaper articles? How do these articles differ from typical college essays?

l. How does each writer employ statistics? What is the message sent by using statistics in general? What is the message sent by the statistics Pace and Herscovici choose?

## ENGAGING THE TEXT

a. Identify flaws in the arguments of Pace and Herscovici. First list the main and supporting points that each writer makes; then list the points that each writer overlooks, whether intentionally or unintentionally.

b. Write a response based on emotion to either or both essays. Then write a response based on reason. This prompt can be used as prewriting for Suggestions for Sustained Writing b or c.

## SUGGESTIONS FOR SUSTAINED WRITING

a. Write an argument on a similarly controversial topic, such as the World Trade Organization's mission or the increase in the number of heavily polluting vehicles such as SUVs. Work in pairs, with each student choosing a side and writing an essay aiming to convince the other student.

b. Analyze Pace's and Herscovici's arguments. Begin with item a in Engaging the Text and then write a critique in which you both summarize and evaluate the arguments. What are the strengths of each argument? What are the weaknesses of each argument? What logical errors do both writers make? (For help in answering this last question, read "Politics: The Art of Bamboozling" by Donna Woolfolk Cross in Chapter 5.)

c. Check out facts or statistics proferred by either Pace or Herscovici to make a case. Expand on, clarify, or refute Pace's or Herscovici's argument, based on what you uncover.

# Rape and Modern Sex War

Camille Paglia

*Camille Paglia (b. 1947) was born in Endicott, New York. She received a BA in 1968 from the State University of New York–Binghampton and an M.Phil. in 1971 and then a Ph.D. in 1974 from Yale University. Her dissertation became the book* Sexual Personae: Art and Decadence from Nefertiti to Emily Dickinson, *which, when it was published in 1991, catapulted her to international fame. In that book Paglia categorizes female archetypes in Western art and literature, archetypes that she argues have been ignored by historians and critics. She has taught at Wesleyan University and at Yale University; since 1984 she has been professor of humanities at the University of the Arts in Philadelphia. Her other works include* Sex, Art, and American Culture *(1992) and* Vamps and Tramps: New Essays *(1994), as well as numerous critical essays on film and the arts. "Rape: A Bigger Danger Than Feminists Know" was first published in* Long Island Newsday.

1    Rape is an outrage that cannot be tolerated in civilized society. Yet feminism, which has waged a crusade for rape to be taken more seriously, has put young women in danger by hiding the truth about sex from them.

2    In dramatizing the pervasiveness of rape, feminists have told young women that before they have sex with a man, they must give consent as explicit as a legal contract's. In this way, young women have been convinced that they have been the victims of rape. On elite campuses in the Northeast and on the West Coast, they have held consciousness-raising sessions, petitioned administrations, demanded inquests. At Brown University, outraged, panicky "victims" have scrawled the names of alleged attackers on the walls of women's rest rooms. What marital rape was to the '70s, "date rape" is to the '90s.

3    The incidence and seriousness of rape do not require this kind of exaggeration. Real acquaintance rape is nothing new. It has been a horrible problem for women for all of recorded history. Once, father and brothers protected women from rape. Once, the penalty for rape was death. I come from a fierce Italian tradition where, not so long ago in the motherland, a rapist would end up knifed, castrated, and hung out to dry.

4    But the old clans and small rural communities have broken down. In our cities, on our campuses far from home, young women are vulnerable and defenseless. Feminism has not prepared them for this. Feminism keeps saying the sexes are the same. It keeps telling women they can do

**412**

anything, go anywhere, say anything, wear anything. No, they can't. Women will always be in sexual danger.

One of my male students recently slept overnight with a friend in a pas-  5 sageway of the Great Pyramid in Egypt. He described the moon and sand, the ancient silence and eerie echoes. I will never experience that. I am a woman. I am not stupid enough to believe I could ever be safe there. There is a world of solitary adventure I will never have. Women have always known these somber truths. But feminism, with its pie-in-the-sky fantasies about the perfect world, keeps young women from seeing life as it is.

We must remedy social injustice whenever we can. But there are some  6 things we cannot change. There are sexual differences that are based in biology. Academic feminism is lost in a fog of social constructionism. It believes we are totally the product of our environment. This idea was invented by Rousseau. He was wrong. Emboldened by dumb French language theory, academic feminists repeat the same hollow slogans over and over to each other. Their view of sex is naive and prudish. Leaving sex to the feminists is like letting your dog vacation at the taxidermist's.

The sexes are at war. Men must struggle for identity against the over-  7 whelming power of their mothers. Women have menstruation to tell them they are women. Men must do or risk something to be men. Men become masculine only when other men say they are. Having sex with a woman is one way a boy becomes a man.

College men are at their hormonal peak. They have just left their moth-  8 ers and are questing for their male identity. In groups, they are dangerous. A woman going to a fraternity party is walking into Testosterone Flats, full of prickly cacti and blazing guns. If she goes, she should be armed with resolute alertness. She should arrive with girlfriends and leave with them. A girl who lets herself get dead drunk at a fraternity party is a fool. A girl who goes upstairs alone with a brother at a fraternity party is an idiot. Feminists call this "blaming the victim." I call it common sense.

For a decade, feminists have drilled their disciples to say, "Rape is a  9 crime of violence but not of sex." This sugar-coated Shirley Temple nonsense has exposed young women to disaster. Misled by feminism, they do not expect rape from the nice boys from good homes who sit next to them in class.

Aggression and eroticism are deeply intertwined. Hunt, pursuit and  10 capture are biologically programmed into male sexuality. Generation after generation, men must be educated, refined, and ethically persuaded away from their tendency toward anarchy and brutishness. Society is not the enemy, as feminism ignorantly claims. Society is woman's protection against rape. Feminism, with its solemn Carry Nation repressiveness, does not see what is for men the eroticism or fun element in rape, especially the wild, infectious delirium of gang rape. Women who do not understand rape cannot defend themselves against it.

11      The date-rape controversy shows feminism hitting the wall of its own broken promises. The women of my Sixties generation were the first respectable girls in history to swear like sailors, get drunk, stay out all night—in short, to act like men. We sought total sexual freedom and equality. But as time passed, we woke up to cold reality. The old double standard protected women. When anything goes, it's women who lose.

12      Today's young women don't know what they want. They see that feminism has not brought sexual happiness. The theatrics of public rage over date rape are their way of restoring the old sexual rules that were shattered by my generation. Because nothing about the sexes has really changed. The comic film *Where the Boys Are* (1960), the ultimate expression of Fifties man-chasing, still speaks directly to our time. It shows smart, lively women skillfully anticipating and fending off the dozens of strategies with which horny men try to get them into bed. The agonizing date-rape subplot and climax are brilliantly done. The victim, Yvette Mimieux, makes mistake after mistake, obvious to the other girls. She allows herself to be lured away from her girlfriends and into isolation with boys whose character and intentions she misreads. *Where the Boys Are* tells the truth. It shows courtship as a dangerous game in which the signals are not verbal but subliminal.

13      Neither militant feminism, which is obsessed with politically correct language, nor academic feminism, which believes that knowledge and experience are "constituted by" language, can understand preverbal or nonverbal communication. Feminism, focusing on sexual politics, cannot see that sex exists in and through the body. Sexual desire and arousal cannot be fully translated into verbal terms. This is why men and women misunderstand each other.

14      Trying to remake the future, feminism cut itself off from sexual history. It discarded and suppressed the sexual myths of literature, art and religion. Those myths show us the turbulence, the mysteries and passions of sex. In mythology we see men's sexual anxiety, their fear of women's dominance. Much sexual violence is rooted in men's sense of psychological weakness toward women. It takes many men to deal with one woman. Woman's voracity is a persistent motif. Clara Bow, it was rumored, took on the USC football team on weekends. Marilyn Monroe, singing "Diamonds Are a Girl's Best Friend," rules a conga line of men in tuxes. Half-clad Cher, in the video for "If I Could Turn Back Time," deranges a battleship of screaming sailors and straddles a pink-lit cannon. Feminism, coveting social power, is blind to woman's cosmic sexual power.

15      To understand rape, you must study the past. There never was and never will be sexual harmony. Every woman must take personal responsibility for her sexuality, which is nature's red flame. When she makes a mistake, she must accept the consequences and, through self-criticism, resolve never to make that mistake again. Running to Mommy and Daddy on the

campus grievance committee is unworthy of strong women. Posting lists of guilty men in the toilet is cowardly, infantile stuff.

The Italian philosophy of life espouses high-energy confrontation. A 16 male student makes a vulgar remark about your breasts? Don't slink off to whimper with the campus shrinking violets. Deal with it. On the spot. Say, "Shut up, you jerk! And crawl back to the barnyard where you belong!" In general, women who project this take-charge attitude toward life get harassed less often. I see too many dopey, immature, self-pitying women walking around like melting sticks of butter. It's the Yvette Mimieux syndrome: make me happy. And listen to me weep when I'm not.

The date-rape debate is already smothering in propaganda churned out 17 by the expensive Northeastern colleges and universities, with their over-concentration of boring, uptight academic feminists and spoiled, affluent students. Beware of the deep manipulativeness of rich students who were neglected by their parents. They love to turn the campus into hysterical psychodramas of sexual transgression, followed by assertions of parental authority and concern. And don't look for sexual enlightenment from academe, which spews out mountains of books but never looks at life directly.

As a fan of football and rock music, I see in the simple, swaggering 18 masculinity of the jock and in the noisy posturing of the heavy-metal guitarist certain fundamental, unchanging truths about sex. Masculinity is aggressive, unstable, combustible. It is also the most creative cultural force in history. Women must reorient themselves toward the elemental powers of sex, which can strengthen or destroy.

The only solution to date rape is female self-awareness and self- 19 control. A woman's number-one line of defense against rape is herself. When a real rape occurs, she should report it to the police. Complaining to college committees because the courts "take too long" is ridiculous. College administrations are not a branch of the judiciary. They are not equipped or trained for legal inquiry. Colleges must alert incoming students to the problems and dangers of adulthood. Then colleges must stand back and get out of the sex game.

*1988*

## QUESTIONS FOR DISCUSSION

### Content

a. If asked, how would Paglia define rape?
b. To what extent do you agree with Paglia that women will never be able to do the things men can do, such as sleep outdoors in Egypt (paragraph 5)?

the nation. What seems clear to me is that those who place acquaintance rape in a different category from "stranger rape"—those who excuse friendly social rapists on grounds that they are too dumb to understand when "no" means no—are being even more insulting to men than to women.

4      These apologists for date rape—and some of them are women—are really saying that the average man cannot be trusted to exercise any impulse control. Men are nasty and men are brutes—and a woman must be constantly on her guard to avoid giving a man any excuse to give way to his baser instincts.

5      If this view were accurate, few women would manage to get through life without being raped, and few men would fail to commit rape. For the reality is that all of us, men as well as women, send and receive innumerable mixed signals in the course of our sexual lives—and that is as true in marital beds at age fifty as in the back seats of cars at age fifteen.

6      Most men somehow manage to decode these signals without using superior physical strength to force themselves on their partners. And most women manage to handle conflicting male signals without, say, picking up carving knives to demonstrate their displeasure at sexual rejection. This is called civilization.

7      Civilized is exactly what my old boyfriend was being when he didn't use my muddleheaded emotional distress as an excuse to rape me. But I don't owe him excessive gratitude for his decent behavior—any more than he would have owed me special thanks for not stabbing him through the heart if our situations had been reversed. Most date rapes do not happen because a man honestly mistakes a woman's "no" for a "yes" or a "maybe." They occur because a minority of men—an ugly minority, to be sure—can't stand to take "no" for an answer.

8      This minority behavior—and a culture that excuses it on grounds that boys will be boys—is the target of the movement against date rape that has surfaced on many campuses during the past year.

9      It's not surprising that date rape is an issue of particular importance to college-age women. The campus concentration of large numbers of young people, in an unsupervised environment that encourages drinking and partying, tends to promote sexual aggression and discourage inhibition. Drunken young men who rape a woman at a party can always claim they didn't know what they were doing—and a great many people will blame the victim for having been there in the first place.

10     That is the line adopted by antifeminists like Camille Paglia, author of the controversial *Sexual Personae: Art and Decadence from Nefertiti to Emily Dickinson*. Paglia, whose views strongly resemble those expounded twenty years ago by Norman Mailer in *The Prisoner of Sex*, argues that feminists have deluded women by telling them they can go anywhere and do anything without fear of rape. Feminism, in this view, is both naïve and anti-

sexual because it ignores the power of women to incite uncontrollable male passions.

Just to make sure there is no doubt about a woman's place, Paglia also  11
links the male sexual aggression that leads to rape with the creative energy of art. "There is no female Mozart," she has declared, "because there is no female Jack the Ripper." According to this "logic," one might expect to discover the next generation of composers in fraternity houses and dorms that have been singled out as sites of brutal gang rapes.

This type of unsubtle analysis makes no distinction between sex as an  12
expression of the will to power and sex as a source of pleasure. When domination is seen as an inevitable component of sex, the act of rape is defined not by a man's actions but by a woman's signals.

It is true, of course, that some women (especially the young) initially  13
resist sex not out of real conviction but as part of the elaborate persuasion and seduction rituals accompanying what was once called courtship. And it is true that many men (again, especially the young) take pride in the ability to coax a woman a step further than she intended to go.

But these mating rituals do not justify or even explain date rape. Even  14
the most callow youth is capable of understanding the difference between resistance and genuine fear; between a halfhearted "no, we shouldn't" and tears or screams; between a woman who is physically free to leave a room and one who is being physically restrained.

The immorality and absurdity of using mixed signals as an excuse  15
for rape is cast in high relief when the assault involves one woman and a group of men. In cases of gang rape in a social setting (usually during or after a party), the defendants and their lawyers frequently claim that group sex took place but no force was involved. These upright young men, so the defense invariably contends, were confused because the girl had voluntarily gone to a party with them. Why, she may have even displayed sexual interest in *one* of them. How could they have been expected to understand that she didn't wish to have sex with the whole group?

The very existence of the term "date rape" attests to a slow change in  16
women's consciousness that began with the feminist movement of the late 1960s. Implicit in this consciousness is the conviction that a woman has the right to say no at any point in the process leading to sexual intercourse—and that a man who fails to respect her wishes should incur serious legal and social consequences.

The other, equally important half of the equation is respect for men. If  17
mixed signals are the real cause of sexual assault, it behooves every woman to regard every man as a potential rapist.

In such a benighted universe, it would be impossible for a woman  18
(and, let us not forget, for a man) to engage in the tentative emotional and physical exploration that eventually produces a mature erotic life. She

would have to make up her mind right from the start in order to prevent a rampaging male from misreading her intentions.

19      Fortunately for everyone, neither the character of men nor the general quality of relations between the sexes is that crude. By censuring the minority of men who use ordinary socializing as an excuse for rape, feminists insist on sex as a source of pure pleasure rather than as a means of social control. Real men want an eager sexual partner—not a woman who is quaking with fear or even one who is ambivalent. Real men don't rape.

*1991*

## QUESTIONS FOR DISCUSSION

### Content

a. How does Jacoby define *rape* and *date rape?* How are they similar? How do they differ?

b. Why does Jacoby dislike Paglia's ideas so much? Are there other possible reasons that Jacoby does not mention?

c. Why does Jacoby call Paglia an "antifeminist" (paragraph 10)? What does she mean by "antifeminist"? If Paglia is an antifeminist, does that make Jacoby a feminist?

d. Jacoby claims that Paglia "makes no distinction between sex as an expression of the will to power and sex as a source of pleasure" (paragraph 12). What does she mean by this? Is she right in her assessment of Paglia?

e. Has Jacoby addressed all of Paglia's points? If so, how well has she addressed them? If not, what points has she overlooked?

### Strategy and Style

f. What was the effect on you of reading the personal story as an introduction to the essay? Why might Jacoby have started with a story, especially one that shows her in an unflattering light?

g. Where does Jacoby's argument seem flawed? How would you describe the flaws? Could she have avoided these flaws?

h. Jacoby's tone is less passionate than Paglia's. Does this tone help or hinder Jacoby's purpose?

i. What persuasive techniques does Jacoby use to get you to believe her? How do the persuasive techniques blend with her reasoned argument?

j. Jacoby ends with two sentences that begin with the well-known cliché "real men." Is this phrase effective in emphasizing her points? If so, how?

## ENGAGING THE TEXT

a. Outline Jacoby's argument, including her main and secondary points. List the evidence she used to support her points. Compare her argument to Paglia's.

b. Choose and write a brief response to one or two sentences from Jacoby's essay that delight or anger you. If none provoke delight or anger, respond to one of the following sentences: "Most date rapes do not happen because a man honestly mistakes a woman's 'no' for a 'yes' or a 'maybe.' They occur because a minority a men—an ugly minority, to be sure—can't stand to take 'no' for an answer" (paragraph 7) or "Real men want an eager sexual partner—not a woman who is quaking with fear or even one who is ambivalent" (paragraph 19).

## SUGGESTIONS FOR SUSTAINED WRITING

a. Write a detailed critique of Jacoby's essay, evaluating her argument paragraph by paragraph or point by point. For an expanded essay, compare Jacoby to Paglia. Which is the stronger argument?

b. Write a dialogue between Jacoby and Paglia, the author of the previous selection. If desired, expand the dialogue to a discussion among Jacoby, Paglia, and Susan Sontag (Chapter 4), Gloria Steinem (Chapter 4), and Deborah Tannen (Chapter 6).

c. Write an essay on the topic of rape. You can use the strategy of division and classification by discussing types of rape; you can use the strategy of narrative by looking at several rape cases; you can use the strategy of definition by discussing legal and personal definitions of rape; or you can use a combination of these strategies. Whichever approach you choose, do research to find actual cases and discussions of the topic.

**PERSUASION**

# A Modest Proposal

Jonathan Swift

*Jonathan Swift (1667–1745) was born in Dublin, Ireland; studied at Trinity College, Dublin; and took an MA at Oxford. Ordained an Anglican priest, eventually he was made Dean of St. Patrick's Cathedral in Dublin. He is remembered chiefly for his satires, the most famous of which are* A Tale of a Tub *(1704), a vicious satire on government abuses in education and religion, and* Gulliver's Travels *(1726). After the death of Queen Anne in 1714, Swift remained almost the rest of his life in Ireland. There he wrote many essays defending the Irish against English oppression. "A Modest Proposal" is one of a series of satirical essays that exposed English cruelties in Ireland. It demonstrates Swift's keen sensitivity to the problems of the poor in his native country as well as his ability to create satire that is both ironic and incisive.*

1   It is a melancholy object to those who walk through this great town or travel in the country, when they see the streets, the roads, and cabin doors, crowded with beggars of the female sex, followed by three, four, or six children, all in rags and importuning every passenger for an alms. These mothers, instead of being able to work for their honest livelihood, are forced to employ all their time in strolling to beg sustenance for their helpless infants: Who as they grow up either turn thieves for want of work, or leave their dear native country to fight for the Pretender in Spain, or sell themselves to the Barbadoes.

2       I think it is agreed by all parties that this prodigious number of children in the arms, or on the backs, or at the heels of their mothers, and frequently of their fathers, is in the present deplorable state of the kingdom a very great additional grievance; and, therefore, whoever could find out a fair, cheap, and easy method of making these children sound, useful members of the commonwealth, would deserve so well of the public as to have his statue set up for a preserver of the nation.

3       But my intention is very far from being confined to provide only for the children of professed beggars; it is of a much greater extent, and shall take in the whole number of infants at a certain age who are born of parents in effect as little able to support them as those who demand our charity in the streets.

4       As to my own part, having turned my thoughts for many years upon this important subject, and maturely weighed the several schemes of our projectors, I have always found them grossly mistaken in their computation. It is true, a child just dropped from its dam may be supported by her milk for a solar year, with little other nourishment; at most not above the value of 2s., which the mother may certainly get, or the value in scraps, by her lawful occupation of begging; and it is exactly at one year old that I propose to provide for them in such a manner as instead of being a charge upon their parents or the parish, or wanting food and raiment for the rest of their lives, they shall on the contrary contribute to the feeding, and partly to the clothing, of many thousands.

5       There is likewise another great advantage in my scheme, that it will prevent those voluntary abortions, and that horrid practice of women murdering their bastard children, alas! too frequent among us! sacrificing the poor innocent babes I doubt more to avoid the expense than the

shame, which would move tears and pity in the most savage and inhuman breast.

The number of souls in this kingdom being usually reckoned one million and a half, of these I calculate there may be about 200,000 couples whose wives are breeders; from which number I subtract 30,000 couples who are able to maintain their own children (although I apprehend there cannot be so many, under the present distress of the kingdom); but this being granted, there will remain 170,000 breeders. I again subtract 50,000 for those women who miscarry, or whose children die by accident or disease within the year. There only remain 120,000 children of poor parents annually born. The question therefore is, how this number shall be reared and provided for? which, as I have already said, under the present situation of affairs, is utterly impossible by all the methods hitherto proposed. For we can neither employ them in handicraft or agriculture; we neither build houses (I mean live in the country) nor cultivate land; they can very seldom pick up a livelihood by stealing, till they arrive at six years old, except where they are of towardly parts; although I confess they learn the rudiments much earlier; during which time they can, however, be properly looked upon only as probationers; as I have been informed by a principal gentleman in the county of Cavan, who protested to me that he never knew above one or two instances under the age of six, even in a part of the kingdom so renowned for the quickest proficiency in that art. 6

I am assured by our merchants, that a boy or a girl before twelve years old is no saleable commodity; and even when they come to this age they will not yield above 3l. or 3l.2s. 6d. at most on the exchange; which cannot turn to account either to the parents or kingdom, the charge of nutriment and rags having been at least four times that value. 7

I shall now therefore humbly propose my own thoughts, which I hope will not be liable to the least objection. 8

I have been assured by a very knowing American of my acquaintance in London, that a young healthy child well nursed is at a year old a most delicious, nourishing, and wholesome food, whether stewed, roasted, baked, or broiled; and I make no doubt that it will equally serve in a fricassee or a ragout. 9

I do therefore humbly offer it to public consideration that of the 120,000 children already computed, 20,000 may be reserved for breed, whereof only one-fourth part to be males; which is more than we allow to sheep, black cattle, or swine; and my reason is, that these children are seldom the fruits of marriage, a circumstance not much regarded by our savages; therefore one male will be sufficient to serve four females. That the remaining 100,000 may, at a year old, be offered in sale to the persons of quality and fortune through the kingdom; always advising the mother to let them suck plentifully in the last month, so as to render them plump and fat for a good table. A child will make two dishes at an entertainment for friends; and when the family dines 10 alone, the fore or hind quarter will make a reasonable dish, and seasoned with a little pepper or salt will be very good boiled on the fourth day, especially in winter.

11    I have reckoned upon a medium that a child just born will weigh 12 pounds, and in a solar year, if tolerably nursed, will increase to 28 pounds.

12    I grant this food will be somewhat dear, and therefore very proper for landlords, who, as they have already devoured most of the parents, seem to have the best title to the children.

13    Infant's flesh will be in season throughout the year, but more plentiful in March, and a little before and after; for we are told by a grave author, an eminent French physician, that fish being a prolific diet, there are more children born in Roman Catholic countries about nine months after Lent than at any other season; therefore, reckoning a year after Lent, the markets will be more glutted than usual, because the number of popish infants is at least three to one in this kingdom: and therefore it will have one other collateral advantage, by lessening the number of papists among us.

14    I have already computed the charge of nursing a beggar's child (in which list I reckon all cottagers, laborers, and four-fifths of the farmers) to be about 2s. per annum, rags included; and I believe no gentleman would repine to give 10s. for the carcass of a good fat child, which, as I have said, will make four dishes of excellent nutritive meat, when he has only some particular friend or his own family to dine with him. Thus the squire will learn to be a good landlord, and grow popular among the tenants; the mother will have 8s. net profit, and be fit for work till she produces another child.

15    Those who are more thrifty (as I must confess the times require) may flay the carcass; the skin of which artificially dressed will make admirable gloves for ladies, and summer boots for fine gentlemen.

16    As to our city of Dublin, shambles may be appointed for this purpose in the most convenient parts of it, and butchers we may be assured will not be wanting: although I rather recommend buying the children alive, and dressing them hot from the knife as we do roasting pigs.

17    A very worthy person, a true lover of his country, and whose virtues I highly esteem, was lately pleased in discoursing on this matter to offer a refinement upon my scheme. He said that many gentlemen of this kingdom, having of late destroyed their deer, he conceived that the want of venison might be well supplied by the bodies of young lads and maidens, not exceeding fourteen years of age nor under twelve; so great a number of both sexes in every country being now ready to starve for want of work and service; and these to be disposed of by their parents, if alive, or otherwise by their nearest relations. But with due deference to so excellent a friend and so deserving a patriot, I cannot be altogether in his sentiments; for as to the males, my American acquaintance assured me from frequent experience that their flesh was generally tough and lean, like that of our schoolboys by continual exercise, and their taste disagreeable; and to fatten them would not an-

swer the charge. Then as to the females, it would, I think, with humble submission be a loss to the public, because they soon would become breeders themselves; and besides, it is not improbable that some scrupulous people might be apt to censure such a practice (although indeed very unjustly), as a little bordering upon cruelty; which, I confess, has always been with me the strongest objection against any project, how well so-ever intended.

But in order to justify my friend, he confessed that this expedient was 18 put into his head by the famous Psalmanazar, a native of the island Formosa, who came from thence to London about twenty years ago: And in conversation told my friend, that in his country when any young person happened to be put to death, the executioner sold the carcass to persons of quality as a prime dainty; and that in his time the body of a plump girl of fifteen, who was crucified for an attempt to poison the emperor, was sold to his imperial majesty's prime minister of state, and other great mandarins of the court, in joints from the gibbet, at 400 crowns. Neither indeed can I deny, that if the same use were made of several plump young girls in this town, who without one single groat to their fortunes cannot stir without a chair, and appear at the playhouse and assemblies in foreign fineries which they never will pay for, the kingdom would not be the worse.

Some persons of a desponding spirit are in great concern about that 19 vast number of poor people, who are aged, diseased, or maimed, and I have been desired to employ my thoughts what course may be taken to ease the nation of so grievous an encumbrance. But I am not in the least pain upon that matter, because it is very well known that they are every day dying and rotting by cold and famine, and filth and vermin, as fast as can be reasonably expected. And as to the young laborers, they are now in as hopeful a condition: they cannot get work, and consequently pine away for want of nourishment, to a degree that if at any time they are accidentally hired to common labor, they have not strength to perform it; and thus the country and themselves are happily delivered from the evils to come.

I have too long digressed, and therefore shall return to my subject. I 20 think the advantages by the proposal which I have made are obvious and many, as well as of the highest importance.

For first, as I have already observed, it would greatly lessen the num- 21 ber of papists, with whom we are yearly overrun, being the principal breeders of the nation as well as our most dangerous enemies; and who stay at home on purpose to deliver the kingdom to the Pretender, hoping to take their advantage by the absence of so many good Protestants, who have chosen rather to leave their country than stay at home and pay tithes against their conscience to an Episcopal curate.

Secondly, the poor tenants will have something valuable of their own, 22 which by law may be made liable to distress and help to pay their landlord's rent, their corn and cattle being already seized, and money a thing unknown.

23    Thirdly, whereas the maintenance of 100,000 children from two years old and upward, cannot be computed at less than 10s. apiece per annum, the nation's stock will be thereby increased £50,000 per annum, beside the profit of a new dish introduced to the tables of all gentlemen of fortune in the kingdom who have any refinement in taste. And the money will circulate among ourselves, the goods being entirely of our own growth and manufacture.

24    Fourthly, the constant breeders beside the gain of 8s. sterling per annum by the sale of their children, will be rid of the charge of maintaining them after the first year.

25    Fifthly, this food would likewise bring great custom to taverns, where the vintners will certainly be so prudent as to procure the best recipes for dressing it to perfection, and consequently have their houses frequented by all the fine gentlemen, who justly value themselves upon their knowledge in good eating; and a skilful cook who understands how to oblige his guests, will contrive to make it as expensive as they please.

26    Sixthly, this would be a great inducement to marriage, which all wise nations have either encouraged by rewards or enforced by laws and penalties. It would increase the care and tenderness of mothers toward their children, when they were sure of a settlement for life to the poor babes, provided in some sort by the public, to their annual profit instead of expense. We should see an honest emulation among the married women, which of them would bring the fattest child to the market. Men would become as fond of their wives during the time of their pregnancy as they are now of their mares in foal, their cows in calf, their sows when they are ready to farrow; nor offer to beat or kick them (as is too frequent a practice) for fear of a miscarriage.

27    Many other advantages might be enumerated. For instance, the addition of some thousand carcasses in our exportation of barreled beef, the propagation of swine's flesh, and improvement in the art of making good bacon, so much wanted among us by the great destruction of pigs, too frequent at our table; which are no way comparable in taste or magnificence to a well-grown, fat, yearling child, which roasted whole will make a considerable figure at a lord mayor's feast or any other public entertainment. But this and many others I omit, being studious of brevity.

28    Supposing that 1,000 families in this city would be constant customers for infants' flesh, besides others who might have it at merry-meetings, particularly at weddings and christenings, I compute that Dublin would take off annually about 20,000 carcasses; and the rest of the kingdom (where probably they will be sold somewhat cheaper) the remaining 80,000.

29    I can think of no one objection that will possibly be raised against this proposal, unless it should be urged that the number of people will be thereby much lessened in the kingdom. This I freely own, and it was indeed one principal design in offering it to the world. I desire the reader will

observe, that I calculate my remedy for this one individual kingdom of Ireland and for no other than ever was, is, or I think ever can be upon Earth. Therefore let no man talk to me of other expedients: Of taxing our absentees at 5s. a pound: Of using neither clothes nor household furniture except what is of our own growth and manufacture: Of utterly rejecting the materials and instruments that promote foreign luxury: Of curing the expensiveness of pride, vanity, idleness, and gaming in our women: Of introducing a vein of parsimony, prudence, and temperance: Of learning to love our country, in the want of which we differ even from Laplander and the inhabitants of Topinamboo: Of quitting our animosities and factions, nor acting any longer like the Jews, who were murdering one another at the very moment their city was taken: Of being a little cautious not to sell our country and conscience for nothing: Of teaching landlords to have at least one degree of mercy toward their tenants: Lastly, of putting a spirit of honesty, industry, and skill into our shopkeepers; who, if a resolution could now be taken to buy only our native goods, would immediately unite to cheat and exact upon us in the price, the measure, and the goodness, nor could ever yet be brought to make one fair proposal of just dealing, though often and earnestly invited to it.

Therefore I repeat, let no man talk to me of these and the like expedi- 30 ents, till he has at least some glimpse of hope that there will be ever some hearty and sincere attempt to put them in practice.

But as to myself, having been wearied out for many years with offer- 31 ing vain, idle, visionary thoughts, and at length utterly despairing of success, I fortunately fell upon this proposal; which, as it is wholly new, so it has something solid and real, of no expense and little trouble, full in our own power, and whereby we can incur no danger in disobliging England. For this kind of commodity will not bear exportation, the flesh being of too tender a consistence to admit a long continuance in salt, although perhaps I could name a country which would be glad to eat up our whole nation without it.

After all, I am not so violently bent upon my own opinion as to reject 32 any offer proposed by wise men, which shall be found equally innocent, cheap, easy, and effectual. But before something of that kind shall be advanced in contradiction to my scheme, and offering a better, I desire the author or authors will be pleased maturely to consider two points. First, as things now stand, how they will be able to find food and raiment for 100,000 useless mouths and backs. And secondly, there being a round million of creatures in human figure throughout this kingdom, whose subsistence put into a common stock would leave them in debt 2,000,000*l*. sterling, adding those who are beggars by profession to the bulk of farmers, cottagers, and laborers, with the wives and children who are beggars in effect; I desire those politicians who dislike my overture, and may perhaps be so bold as to attempt an answer, that they will first ask the parents of cramming for exams rather than studying for them systematically. You can also use one of the societal problems described in any of the following essays: Jo Goodwin Parker's "What Is Poverty?" (Chapter 4), Barbara Huttman's "Crime of Compassion" (Chapter 7), Ellen Goodman's "Watching the Grasshopper Get the Goodies" (Chapter 8), Barbara Dafoe Whitehead's "Where Have All the Parents Gone?" (Chapter 8), Nicols Fox's "Gawk Shows" (Chapter 9), Jonathan Kozol's "Distancing the Homeless" (Chapter 11), Lars Eighner's "On Dumpster Diving" (Chapter 11), or any of the other essays in Chapter 10. Write a proposal, "modest" or realistic, to solve the problem.

c. One aspect of Swift's proposal focuses on the relationship between tenants and landlords. This is still an important issue. Using information you find in the library or on the Internet, write an essay that argues for the enactment of

- Laws that keep rents at reasonable levels and protect tenants from unscrupulous landlords.
- Laws that help landlords make a fair profit and protect their properties from irresponsible tenants.

# I Have a Dream

Martin Luther King, Jr.

*Martin Luther King, Jr. (1929–1968) had at first planned to become a doctor or a lawyer, but when he graduated from Morehouse College in Atlanta at the age of 19, he abandoned those ambitions and went into the seminary. After seminary, he went to Boston University, where he received his Ph.D. in 1955. He was ordained as a Baptist minister in his father's church, the Ebenezer Baptist Church in Atlanta, a church he copastored with his father from 1960 to 1968. He was also the founder and director of the Southern Christian Leadership Conference from 1957 to 1968 and a member of the Montgomery Improvement Association, an activist group protesting racial segregation. Inspired by Mahatma Gandhi's principles of nonviolent protest, King led this group in several demonstrations. In May 1963, he was arrested and imprisoned in Birmingham for demonstrating against segregation in hotels and restaurants. It was while in jail that he wrote his famous "Letter from Birmingham Jail," a work that was published in 1963 and expanded and republished in 1968. It was also in 1963 that King made the speech entitled "I Have a Dream" to over 200,000 people at the March on Washington. King received numerous awards for his work for human rights, including the Nobel Prize for Peace in 1964. On April 4, 1968, while talking with other human rights activists on a motel balcony in Memphis, King was assassinated.*

Five score years ago, a great American, in whose symbolic shadow we   1
stand, signed the Emancipation Proclamation. This momentous decree
came as a great beacon light of hope to millions of Negro slaves who had
been seared in the flames of withering injustice. It came as a joyous day-
break to end the long night of captivity.

But one hundred years later, we must face the tragic fact that the Ne-   2
gro is still not free. One hundred years later, the life of the Negro is still
sadly crippled by the manacles of segregation and the chains of discrimination. One hundred years later, the Negro lives on a lonely island of
poverty in the midst of a vast ocean of material prosperity. One hundred
years later, the Negro is still languishing in the corners of American society and finds himself an exile in his own land. So we have come here today to dramatize an appalling condition.

In a sense we have come to our nation's capital to cash a check. When   3
the architects of our republic wrote the magnificent words of the Constitution and the Declaration of Independence, they were signing a promissory
note to which every American was to fall heir. This note was a promise that
all men would be guaranteed the unalienable rights of life, liberty, and the
pursuit of happiness.                                                    4

It is obvious today that America has defaulted on this promissory note
insofar as her citizens of color are concerned. Instead of honoring this sacred obligation, America has given the Negro people a bad check; a check
which has come back marked "insufficient funds." But we refuse to believe
that the bank of justice is bankrupt. We refuse to believe that there are insufficient funds in the great vaults of opportunity of this nation. So we
have come to cash this check—a check that will give us upon demand the
riches of freedom and the security of justice We have also come to this hallowed spot to remind America of the fierce urgency of *now*. This is no time
to engage in the luxury of cooling off or to take the tranquilizing drugs of
gradualism. *Now* is the time to make real the promises of Democracy. *Now*
is the time to rise from the dark and desolate valley of segregation to the
sunlit path of racial justice. *Now* is the time to open the doors of opportunity to all of God's children. *Now* is the time to lift our nation from the
quicksands of racial injustice to the solid rock of brotherhood.

It would be fatal for the nation to overlook the urgency of the moment   5
and to underestimate the determination of the Negro. This sweltering
summer of the Negro's legitimate discontent will not pass until there is an
invigorating autumn of freedom and equality. 1963 is not an end, but a beginning. Those who hope that the Negro needed to blow off steam and will
now be content will have a rude awakening if the nation returns to business as usual. There will be neither rest nor tranquillity in America until
the Negro is granted his citizenship rights. The whirlwinds of revolt will
continue to shake the foundations of our nation until the bright day of justice emerges.

6    But there is something that I must say to my people who stand on the warm threshold which leads into the palace of justice. In the process of gaining our rightful place we must not be guilty of wrongful deeds. Let us not seek to satisfy our thirst for freedom by drinking from the cup of bitterness and hatred. We must forever conduct our struggle on the high plane of dignity and discipline. We must not allow our creative protest to degenerate into physical violence. Again and again we must rise to the majestic heights of meeting physical force with soul force. The marvelous new militancy which has engulfed the Negro community must not lead us to a distrust of all white people, for many of our white brothers, as evidenced by their presence here today, have come to realize that their destiny is tied up with our destiny and their freedom is inextricably bound to our freedom. We cannot walk alone.

7    And as we walk, we must make the pledge that we shall march ahead. We cannot turn back. There are those who are asking the devotees of civil rights, "When will you be satisfied?" We can never be satisfied as long as the Negro is the victim of the unspeakable horrors of police brutality. We can never be satisfied as long as our bodies, heavy with the fatigue of travel, cannot gain lodging in the motels of the highways and the hotels of the cities. We cannot be satisfied as long as the Negro's basic mobility is from a smaller ghetto to a larger one. We can never be satisfied as long as a Negro in Mississippi cannot vote and a Negro in New York believes he has nothing for which to vote. No, no, we are not satisfied, and we will not be satisfied until justice rolls down like waters and righteousness like a mighty stream.

8    I am not unmindful that some of you have come here out of great trials and tribulations. Some of you have come fresh from narrow jail cells. Some of you have come from areas where your quest for freedom left you battered by the storms of persecution and staggered by the winds of police brutality. You have been the veterans of creative suffering. Continue to work with the faith that unearned suffering is redemptive.

9    Go back to Mississippi, go back to Alabama, go back to South Carolina, go back to Georgia, go back to Louisiana, go back to the slums and ghettos of our northern cities, knowing that somehow this situation can and will be changed. Let us not wallow in the valley of despair.

10   I say to you today, my friends, that in spite of the difficulties and frustrations of the moment I still have a dream. It is a dream deeply rooted in the American dream.

11   I have a dream that one day this nation will rise up and live out the true meaning of its creed: "We hold these truths to be self-evident; that all men are created equal."

12   I have a dream that one day on the red hills of Georgia the sons of former slaves and the sons of former slaveowners will be able to sit down together at the table of brotherhood.

I have a dream that one day even the state of Mississippi, a desert state  13
sweltering with the heat of injustice and oppression, will be transformed
into an oasis of freedom and justice.

I have a dream that my four little children will one day live in a nation  14
where they will not be judged by the color of their skin but by the content
of their character.

I have a dream today.                                                     15

I have a dream that one day the state of Alabama, whose governor's  16
lips are presently dripping with the words of interposition and nullifica-
tion, will be transformed into a situation where little black boys and black
girls will be able to join hands with little white boys and white girls and
walk together as sisters and brothers.

I have a dream today.                                                     17

I have a dream that one day every valley shall be exalted, every hill  18
and mountain shall be made low, the rough places will be made plain,
and the crooked places will be made straight, and the glory of the Lord
shall be revealed, and all flesh shall see it together.

This is our hope. This is the faith with which I return to the South. With  19
this faith we will be able to hew out of the mountain of despair a stone of
hope. With this faith we will be able to transform the jangling discords of
our nation into a beautiful symphony of brotherhood. With this faith we
will be able to work together, to pray together, to struggle together, to go to
jail together, to stand up for freedom together, knowing that we will be free
one day.

This will be the day when all of God's children will be able to sing with  20
new meaning

> My country, 'tis of thee,
> Sweet land of liberty,
>     Of thee I sing:
> Land where my fathers died,
> Land of the pilgrims' pride,
> From every mountain-side
>     Let freedom ring.

And if America is to be a great nation this must become true. So let free-  21
dom ring from the prodigious hilltops of New Hampshire. Let freedom ring
from the mighty mountains of New York. Let freedom ring from the height-
ening Alleghenies of Pennsylvania!

Let freedom ring from the snowcapped Rockies of Colorado!              22
Let freedom ring from the curvaceous peaks of California!             23
But not only that; let freedom ring from Stone                        24
    Mountain of Georgia!

25   Let freedom ring from Lookout Mountain of Tennessee!
26   Let freedom ring from every hill and molehill of Mississippi.
        From every mountainside, let freedom ring.

27       When we let freedom ring, when we let it ring from every village and
     every hamlet, from every state and every city, we will be able to speed up
     that day when all of God's children, black men and white men, Jews and
     Gentiles, Protestants and Catholics, will be able to join hands and sing in the
     words of the old Negro spiritual, "Free at last! free at last! thank God
     almighty, we are free at last!"

                                                                                    *1963*


## QUESTIONS FOR DISCUSSION

### Content

a.  What does King hope to evoke in his audience by mentioning various
    historical documents (the Emancipation Proclamation, the Declaration
    of Independence, the Constitution)?
b.  King makes it a point to address issues that are of particular interest to
    white listeners and readers. What might have been his reasons for do-
    ing this?
c.  Why might King have decided to quote all of the first seven lines of "My
    Country 'Tis of Thee"? Why did he not stop at "Of thee I sing"?
d.  What effect does King create when he makes reference to specific places,
    events, and public figures?
e.  King makes reference to the Bible and to the faith that has sustained him
    throughout his struggle for civil rights. What effect is created with such
    references?


### Strategy and Style

f.  King's speech is especially moving because he succeeds in creating em-
    phasis through parallelism. Find a few examples of this technique.
g.  What does King mean when he says: "America has given the Negro
    people a bad check" (paragraph 4)? Identify other metaphors that he
    uses and explain why they are effective.
h.  Why does King use the term *marvelous* to describe the "new militancy
    which has engulfed the Negro community"?
i.  How would you describe King's tone? Controlled? Angry? Impas-
    sioned?

## ENGAGING THE TEXT

a. Choose one of the metaphors that King uses in this essay, the metaphor that strikes you as most or least effective. Explain why you chose the metaphor and what makes it effective or ineffective.

b. What is King's dream? Summarize it in a paragraph.

## SUGGESTIONS FOR SUSTAINED WRITING

a. Do you have a "dream" that in the future some social or political injustice will be eliminated, that a cure will be found for a disease, that war and famine will cease? Describe your "dream" and propose ways in which to make it a reality.

b. Has King's dream of equality and opportunity for African-Americans been fulfilled in the decades since he spoke at the Lincoln Memorial? Has the situation of black Americans changed, or not changed, since King gave this speech? Explain by using as much specific detail as possible. Bring in comments from Brent Staples' "Black Men and Public Space" (Chapter 7), Shelby Steele's "White Guilt" (Chapter 8), and Debra Dickerson's "Who Shot Johnny?" (Chapter 10).

c. Do some research in your college library by reading several newspaper or magazine articles that chronicle the events leading up to King's address at the Lincoln Memorial. Summarize those events and try to comment on their significance to the civil rights movement of the 1960s. Be certain to footnote or in some way cite the authorship of material you quote or paraphrase.

# Who Shot Johnny?

Debra Dickerson

*Debra Dickerson (b. 1955) is a journalist working in Washington, D.C. Currently, she is Senior Fellow at the New America Foundation, where she writes articles on race and poverty and produces panel discussions on those topics. She is a graduate of Harvard Law School and was an officer in the U.S. Air Force, on active duty from 1980 to 1992. In 1989 and 1990 she was chief of intelligence at the Ankara (Turkey) Air Station. She has also been a lawyer for the NAACP Legal Defense Fund, a senior editor for* U.S. News and World Report, *and a national correspondent for the online magazine* Salon. *Her articles have appeared in* U.S. News and World Report, *the* Nation, *the* Village Voice, *and the* New Republic. *She has just published a memoir,* An American Story *(2000). "Who Shot Johnny?" was first published on January 1, 1996 in the* New Republic.

1   Given my level of political awareness, it was inevitable that I would come to view the everyday events of my life through the prism of politics and the national discourse. I read *The Washington Post, The New Republic, The New Yorker, Harper's, The Atlantic Monthly, The Nation, National Review, Black Enterprise,* and *Essence* and wrote a weekly column for the Harvard Law School *Record* during my three years just ended there. I do this because I know that those of us who are not well-fed white guys in suits must not yield the debate to them, however well-intentioned or well-informed they may be. Accordingly, I am unrepentant and vocal about having gained admittance to Harvard through affirmative action; I am a feminist, stoic about my marriage chances as a well-educated, thirty-six-year-old black woman who won't pretend to need help taking care of herself. My strength flags, though, in the face of the latest role assigned to my family in the national drama. On July 27, 1995, my sixteen-year-old nephew was shot and paralyzed.

2   Talking with friends in front of his house, Johnny saw a car he thought he recognized. He waved boisterously—his trademark—throwing both arms in the air in a full-bodied, hip-hop Y. When he got no response, he and his friends sauntered down the walk to join a group loitering in front of an apartment building. The car followed. The driver got out, brandished a revolver, and fired into the air. Everyone scattered. Then he took aim and shot my running nephew in the back.

3   Johnny never lost consciousness. He lay in the road, trying to understand what had happened to him, why he couldn't get up. Emotionlessly, he told the story again and again on demand, remaining apologetically firm against all demands to divulge the missing details that would make sense of the shooting but obviously cast him in a bad light. Being black, male, and shot, he must apparently be involved with gangs or drugs. Probably both. Witnesses corroborate his version of events.

4   Nearly six months have passed since that phone call in the night and my nightmarish headlong drive from Boston to Charlotte. After twenty hours behind the wheel, I arrived haggard enough to reduce my mother to fresh tears and to find my nephew reassuring well-wishers with an eerie sang-froid.

5   I take the day shift in his hospital room; his mother and grandmother, a clerk and cafeteria worker, respectively, alternate nights there on a cot. They don their uniforms the next day, gaunt after hours spent listening to Johnny moan in his sleep. How often must his subconscious replay those events and curse its host for saying hello without permission, for being carefree and young while a would-be murderer hefted the weight of his uselessness and failure like Jacob Marley's chains? How often must he watch himself lying stubbornly immobile on the pavement of his nightmares while the sound of running feet syncopate his attacker's taunts?

I spend these days beating him at gin rummy and Scrabble, holding a  6
basin while he coughs up phlegm and crying in the corridor while he
catheterizes himself. There are children here much worse off than he. I
should be grateful. The doctors can't, or won't, say whether he'll walk again.

I am at once repulsed and fascinated by the bullet, which remains  7
lodged in his spine (having done all the damage it can do, the doctors say).
The wound is undramatic—small, neat, and perfectly centered—an impossibly pink pit surrounded by an otherwise undisturbed expanse of ma-
hogany. Johnny has asked me several times to describe it but politely declines to look in the mirror I hold for him.

Here on the pediatric rehab ward, Johnny speaks little, never cries,  8
never complains, works diligently to become independent. He does whatever he is told; if two hours remain until the next pain pill, he waits quietly. Eyes bloodshot, hands gripping the bed rails. During the week of his
intravenous feeding, when he was tormented by the primal need to mas-
ticate, he never asked for food. He just listened while we counted down
the days for him and planned his favorite meals. Now required to dress
himself unassisted, he does so without demur, rolling himself back and
forth valiantly on the bed and shivering afterward, exhausted. He
"ma'am"s and "sir"s everyone politely. Before his "accident," a simple re-
quest to take out the trash could provoke a firestorm of teenage attitude.
We, the women who have raised him, have changed as well; we've finally
come to appreciate those boxer-baring, oversized pants we used to hate—
it would be much more difficult to fit properly sized pants over his diaper.

He spends a lot of time tethered to rap music still loud enough to break  9
my concentration as I read my many magazines. I hear him try to sound-
lessly mouth the obligatory "mothafuckers" overlaying the funereal dirge
of the music tracks. I do not normally tolerate disrespectful music in my or
my mother's presence, but if it distracts him now . . .

"Johnny," I ask later, "do you still like gangster rap?" During the long  10
pause I hear him think loudly, I'm paralyzed, Auntie, not stupid. "I mostly
just listen to hip-hop," he says evasively into his *Sports Illustrated.*

Miserable though it is, time passes quickly here. We always seem to be  11
jerking awake in our chairs just in time for the next pill, his every-other-
night bowel program, the doctor's rounds. Harvard feels a galaxy away—
the world revolves around Family Members Living with Spinal Cord Injury class, Johnny's urine output, and strategizing with my sister to find
affordable, accessible housing. There is always another long-distance uncle in need of an update, another church member wanting to pray with us,
or Johnny's little brother in need of some attention.

We Dickerson women are so constant a presence the ward nurses and  12
cleaning staff call us by name and join us for cafeteria meals and cigarette
breaks. At Johnny's birthday pizza party, they crack jokes and make fun of

each other's husbands (there are no men here). I pass slices around and try not to think, seventeen with a bullet.

13     Oddly, we feel little curiosity or specific anger toward the man who shot him. We have to remind ourselves to check in with the police. Even so, it feels pro forma, like sending in those $2 rebate forms that come with new pantyhose: You know your request will fall into a deep, dark hole somewhere, but still, it's your duty to try. We push for an arrest because we owe it to Johnny and to ourselves as citizens. We don't think about it otherwise—our low expectations are too ingrained. A Harvard aunt notwithstanding, for people like Johnny, Marvin Gaye was right that only three things are sure: Taxes, death, and trouble. At least it wasn't the second.

14     We rarely wonder about or discuss the brother who shot him because we already know everything about him. When the call came, my first thought was the same one I'd had when I'd heard about Rosa Parks's beating: A brother did it. A non-job-having, middle-of-the-day malt-liquor-drinking, crotch-clutching, loud-talking brother with many neglected children born of many forgotten women. He lives in his mother's basement with furniture rented at an astronomical interest rate, the exact amount of which he does not know. He has a car phone, an $80 monthly cable bill, and every possible phone feature but no savings. He steals Social Security numbers from unsuspecting relatives and assumes their identities to acquire large TV sets for which he will never pay. On the slim chance that he is brought to justice, he will have a colorful criminal history and no coherent explanation to offer for his act. His family will raucously defend him and cry cover-up. Some liberal lawyer just like me will help him plea-bargain his way to yet another short stay in a prison pesthouse that will serve only to add another layer to the brother's sociopathology and formless, mindless nihilism. We know him. We've known and feared him all our lives.

15     As a teenager, he called, "Hey, baby, gimme somma that boodie!" at us from car windows. Indignant at our lack of response, he followed up with, "Fuck you, then, 'ho!" He called me a "white-boy-lovin' nigger bitch oreo" for being in the gifted program and loving it. At twenty-seven, he got my seventeen-year-old sister pregnant with Johnny and lost interest without ever informing her that he was married. He snatched my widowed mother's purse as she waited in predawn darkness for the bus to work and then broke into our house while she soldered on an assembly line. He chased all the small entrepreneurs from our neighborhood with his violent thievery and put bars on our windows. He kept us from sitting on our own front porch after dark and laid the foundation for our periodic bouts of self-hating anger and racial embarrassment. He made our neighborhood a ghetto. He is the poster fool behind the maddening community knowledge that there are still some black mothers who raise their daughters but merely love their sons. He and his cancerous carbon copies

eclipse the vast majority of us who are not sociopaths and render us invisible. He is the Siamese twin who has died but cannot be separated from his living, vibrant sibling; which of us must attract more notice? We despise and disown this anomalous loser, but for many he *is* black America. We know him, we know that he is outside the fold, and we know that he will only get worse. What we didn't know is that, because of him, my little sister would one day be the latest hysterical black mother wailing over a fallen child on TV.

Alone, lying in the road bleeding and paralyzed but hideously conscious, Johnny had lain helpless as he watched his would-be murderer come to stand over him and offer this prophecy: "Betch'ou won't be doin' nomo' wavin', mothafucker." 16

Fuck you, asshole. He's fine from the waist up. You just can't do anything right, can you? 17

*1996*


## QUESTIONS FOR DISCUSSION

### Content

a. What is Dickerson's relationship to Johnny? How does she feel about him? What in her words and actions shows us how she feels?
b. How does Dickerson describe herself? How does she differ from Johnny's mother and grandmother?
c. What is Dickerson's attitude toward Johnny's mother and grandmother?
d. What upsets Dickerson most about Johnny's shooting?
e. Who is Jacob Marley, and why does Dickerson compare Johnny to him?
f. At the beginning of paragraph 14 Dickerson writes, "We rarely wonder about or discuss the brother who shot him because we already know everything about him." What does she mean by this?


### Strategy and Style

g. What are some of the words Dickerson uses to describe Johnny and the man who shot him? Why are these words effective choices?
h. Dickerson shifts her style from telling a fairly straightforward story in paragraphs 1 to 13 to a hypothetical, generalized, and stereotypical description in paragraphs 14 and 15 of the man who shot Johnny. What might have been her reasons for doing that?

i.  Dickerson uses obscenities several times in the essay, especially at the end when addressing the man who shot Johnny. Why is it important for her to use these words and not words that are less harsh? How do these words affect you?

j.  Where does Dickerson use irony? What might be her purpose for using irony?

k.  What persuasive techniques does Dickerson use? In your opinion, how effective are they? What could she have added to the essay to make it even more persuasive?

l.  What does this essay teach you about narrative as a strategy for making experiences meaningful?


## ENGAGING THE TEXT

a.  Choose two or three words from the essay that you do not already know. Look them up in a dictionary and write out their definitions. Then speculate about what they mean in the context of Dickerson's essay.

b.  Summarize what happened to Johnny as Dickerson describes it. Then summarize it from Johnny's point of view and/or the point of view of the shooter.


## SUGGESTIONS FOR SUSTAINED WRITING

a.  In a journal or as a first draft, describe an event in which a family member was wronged and that angered you, including an explanation of how you dealt with the situation. Then write a persuasive essay in which you try to convey the same sense of anger to your readers.

b.  Who shot Johnny? Using Dickerson's essay as a springboard, write a reflective essay in which you discuss Dickerson's answer to this question. Consider Dickerson's comments in paragraphs 14 and 15 about the tragic nature of the attacker, both the real person and the stereotyped image. Questions you might want to address in your essay: Do you agree with Dickerson's implication that Johnny's attacker represents "black America" for most people? How does your own experience relate to this essay? Compare Dickerson with Brent Staples's ideas in "Black Men and Public Space" (Chapter 7). Discuss the stereotyped images evoked by the phrase "young black man."

c. Research the topic of violent crime in the United States. Is it increasing or decreasing?: Have the types of violent crimes changed? Write a report to your classmates about what you find out.

# Bilingual Education: Outdated and Unrealistic

## Richard Rodriguez

*The son of Mexican immigrants, Richard Rodriguez (b. 1944) was born in San Francisco. He received a BA in 1967 from Stanford University and an MA in 1969 from Columbia University and did graduate study at the University of California–Berkeley and at the Warburg Institute in London, where he studied English Renaissance literature on a Fulbright Fellowship. In 1982, Rodriguez published* Hunger of Memory: The Education of Richard Rodriguez, *a collection of autobiographical essays in which he describes the challenges of growing up in an immigrant household and of enduring the process of assimilation that eventually led him into the American mainstream. A second book,* Days of Obligation: An Argument with My Mexican Father *(1992), continues with the same theme. Rodriguez writes regularly for the* American Scholar, Saturday Review, *and other widely read periodicals and is a regular commentator on the* "News Hour with Jim Lehrer."

How shall we teach the dark-eyed child *ingles?* The debate continues much as it did two decades ago. 1

Bilingual education belongs to the 1960s, the years of the black civil rights movement. Bilingual education became the official Hispanic demand; as a symbol, the English-only classroom was intended to be analogous to the segregated lunch counter; the locked school door. Bilingual education was endorsed by judges and, of course, by politicians well before anyone knew the answer to the question: Does bilingual education work? 2

Who knows? *Quien sabe?* 3

The official drone over bilingual education is conducted by educationalists with numbers and charts. Because bilingual education was never simply a matter of pedagogy, it is too much to expect educators to resolve the matter. Proclamations concerning bilingual education are weighted at bottom with Hispanic political grievances and, too, with middle-class romanticism. 4

No one will say it in public; in private, Hispanics argue with me about bilingual education and every time it comes down to memory. Everyone remembers going to that grammar school where students were slapped for
5  speaking Spanish. Childhood memory is offered as parable; the memory is meant to compress the gringo's long history of offenses against Spanish, Hispanic culture, Hispanics.

It is no coincidence that, although all of America's ethnic groups are implicated in the policy of bilingual education, Hispanics, particularly Mexican-Americans, have been its chief advocates. The English words
6  used by Hispanics in support of bilingual education are words such as "dignity," "heritage," "culture." Bilingualism becomes a way of exacting from gringos a grudging admission of contrition—for the 19th-century theft of the Southwest, the relegation of Spanish to a foreign tongue, the injustice of history. At the extreme, Hispanic bilingual enthusiasts demand that public schools "maintain" a student's sense of separateness.

Hispanics may be among the last groups of Americans who still believe in the 1960s. Bilingual-education proposals still serve the romance of that decade, especially of the late 60s, when the heroic black civil rights
7  movement grew paradoxically wedded to its opposite—the ethnic revival movement. Integration and separatism merged into twin, possible goals.

With integration, the black movement inspired middle-class Americans to imitations—the Hispanic movement; the Gray Panthers; feminism; gay rights. Then there was withdrawal, with black glamour leading a ro-
8  mantic retreat from the anonymous crowd.

Americans came to want it both ways. They wanted in and they wanted out. Hispanics took to celebrating their diversity, joined other Americans in dancing rings around the melting pot.

9

## MYTHIC METAPHORS

10  More intently than most, Hispanics wanted the romance of their dual cultural allegiance backed up by law. Bilingualism became proof that one could have it both ways, could be a full member of public America and yet also separate, privately Hispanic. "Spanish" and "English" became mythic metaphors like country and city, describing separate islands of private and public life.

11  Ballots, billboards, and, of course, classrooms in Spanish. For nearly two decades now, middle-class Hispanics have had it their way. They have foisted a neat ideological scheme on working-class children. What they want to believe about themselves, they wait for the child to prove, that it is possible to be two, that one can assume the public language (the public life) of America, even while remaining what one was, existentially separate.

Adulthood is not so neatly balanced. The tension between public and  12
private life is intrinsic to adulthood—certainly middle-class adulthood.
Usually the city wins because the city pays. We are mass people for more
of the day than we are with our intimates. No Congressional mandate or
Supreme Court decision can diminish the loss.

I was talking the other day to a carpenter from Riga, in the Soviet  13
Republic of Latvia. He has been here six years. He told me of his having
to force himself to relinquish the "luxury" of reading books in Russian
or Latvian so he could begin to read books in English. And the books he
was able to read in English were not of a complexity to satisfy him. But
he was not going back to Riga.

Beyond any question of pedagogy there is the simple fact that a lan-  14
guage gets learned as it gets used, fills one's mouth, one's mind, with the
new names for things.

The civil rights movement of the 1960s taught Americans to deal with  15
forms of discrimination other than economic—racial, sexual. We forget
class. We talk about bilingual education as an ethnic issue; we forget to notice that the program mainly touches the lives of working-class immigrant
children. Foreign-language acquisition is one thing for the upper-class
child in a convent school learning to curtsy. Language acquisition can only
seem a loss for the ghetto child, for the new language is psychologically
awesome, being, as it is, the language of the bus driver and Papa's em-
ployer. The child's difficulty will turn out to be psychological more than
linguistic because what he gives up are symbols of home.

## PAIN AND GUILT

I was that child! I faced the stranger's English with pain and guilt and fear.  16
Baptized to English in school, at first I felt myself drowning—the ugly
sounds forced down my throat—until slowly, slowly (held in the tender
grip of my teachers), suddenly the conviction took; English was my language to use.

What I yearn for is some candor from those who speak about bilin-  17
gual education. Which of its supporters dares speak of the price a child
pays—the price of adulthood—to make the journey from a working-class
home into a middle-class schoolroom? The real story, the silent story of
the immigrant child's journey is one of embarrassments in public; betrayal of all that is private; silence at home; and at school the hand tentatively raised.

Bilingual enthusiasts bespeak an easier world. They seek a linguistic  18
solution to a social dilemma. They seem to want to believe that there is an
easy way for the child to balance private and public, in order to believe
that there is some easy way for themselves.

19      Ten years ago, I started writing about the ideological implications of bilingual education. Ten years from now some newspaper may well invite me to contribute another Sunday supplement essay on the subject. The debate is going to continue. The bilingual establishment is now inside the door. Jobs are at stake. Politicians can only count heads; growing numbers of Hispanics will ensure the compliance of politicians.

20      Publicly, we will continue the fiction. We will solemnly address this issue as an educational question, a matter of pedagogy. But privately, Hispanics will still seek from bilingual education an admission from the gringo that Spanish has value and presence. Hispanics of middle class will continue to seek the romantic assurance of separateness. Experts will argue. Dark-eyed children will sit in the classroom. Mute.

*1985*

## QUESTIONS FOR DISCUSSION

### Content

a. Summarize Rodriguez's argument. To what extent do you agree with him?
b. What is bilingual education?
c. What is "middle-class romanticism" (paragraph 4)? What is its relationship to bilingual education?
d. Why does Rodriguez say that "every time it comes down to memory" when Hispanics argue with him about bilingual education?
e. What are "mythic metaphors" (paragraph 15), and what do they have to do with bilingual education?
f. How does Rodriguez describe the groups of people to which he refers in this essay—Hispanics, the middle class in general (paragraph 4), Mexican-Americans (Paragraph 6), and middle-class Hispanics (paragraph 11)? In Rodrigeuz's mind, how are these groups different from each other?
g. What is Rodriguez's solution to the problems bilingual education creates?

### Strategy and Style

h. Rodriguez begins his essay with a question. Does he answer it? If so, where and how? If not, why not?
i. Where does Rodriguez go beyond argument to use persuasive techniques? What persuasive techniques does he use in this essay?

j. What is the purpose of the Spanish terms *ingles* (paragraph 1) and *quien sabe* (paragraph 3)?

k. What effect do the personal examples have on how you read the essay? Why does Rodriguez use so few? Would more personal examples make the essay more persuasive? Why or why not?

l. Rodriguez's tone is one of a professional and an authority. Why might this tone be more effective than an angry, complaining, or pleading tone?

m. What is the effect of the many short sentences in the concluding paragraph?

## ENGAGING THE TEXT

a. Divide a sheet of paper into two columns. In the left column, list the points that Rodriguez makes to persuade you that bilingual education is outdated and unrealistic. In the right column, list as many counterpoints as you can think of to challenge or refute Rodriguez.

b. Quickly write down your first response to this essay. What did you like or dislike about it? How did you react to particular paragraphs? Where did you find yourself nodding in agreement, and where shaking your head in disagreement?

## SUGGESTIONS FOR SUSTAINED WRITING

a. Reply to Rodriguez. If you agree with him, write an extension or follow-up to his essay. If your disagree with him, write an essay in which you challenge him. Or write an essay in which you point out where you think he is right and where he is wrong. Whatever option you choose, Engaging the Text's item *b* can get you started.

b. Compare Rodriguez's essay with the ideas in Kesaya E. Noda's "Growing Up Asian in America" (Chapter 5) and/or Amy Tan's "Mother Tongue" (Chapter 11). What experiences did the writers have in common? How did their formal education help or hinder them?

c. Find out more about the history or controversies of bilingual education in the United States. Summarize your findings, but also include a discussion of both Rodriguez's essay and your own opinions.

   Or propose a plan that will address the problems of teaching children who don't speak English or whose first language is not English. Back up your plan with details, examples, and statistics or other information from primary or secondary sources.

# Food Pets Die For

Ann N. Martin

*Ann N. Martin (b. 1944) is an animal rights activist who lives in London, Ontario. She researches and reports on pet nutrition and the pet food industry, writing articles for* Natural Pet, Earth Island Journal, *and similar magazines. She also lectures widely and appeared in a Canadian television documentary,* An Evening with Ann Martin *(1997). Her findings can be found in her book* Food Pets Die For: Shocking Facts about Pet Food *(1997), from which this essay is exerpted.*

1    Pets in pet food? No, you say? Be assured that this is happening. Rendered companion animals are just another source of protein used in both pet foods and livestock feeds.

2    Rendering is a cheap, viable means of disposal. Pets are mixed with other material from slaughterhouse facilities that has been condemned for human consumption—rotten meat from supermarket shelves, restaurant grease and garbage, "4-D" (dead, diseased, dying and disabled) animals, roadkill and even zoo animals [Summer '96 *EIJ*].

3    In 1990, *San Francisco Chronicle* reporter John Eckhouse wrote a two-part exposé on the rendering of companion animals in California. While the pet food companies vehemently denied that this was happening, a rendering plant employee told Eckhouse that "it was common practice for his company to process dead pets into products sold to pet food manufacturers."

4    Eckhouse's informant, upset that some of the most disturbing information was left out of the *Chronicle* article, subsequently brought his story to *Earth Island Journal*. (After the *Journal* published this insider's extensive report ["The Dark Side of Recycling," Fall 1990], the author placed a frantic call to the *Journal* to say that he was "going underground" because he feared for his safety.)

## A SEARCH FOR THE TRUTH

5    I had always assumed that deceased pets were either buried or cremated. I had never heard of rendering. In early 1992, I decided to find out what was happening to the euthanized pets in London, Ontario.

6    Veterinary clinics advised me that dead pets were incinerated by a local disposal company. After hearing U.S. horror stories, I was skeptical. I obtained the name of the company that was picking up the pets, a dead-stock removal operation. Classified as "recollectors," these companies—along with "receiving plants," "brokers," and "rendering plants"—are licensed by Canada's Ministry of Agriculture.

7    I asked the ministry how the recollector disposed of the dogs and cats that it picked up. Two months later, I received a letter along with a document from the dead-stock removal company. This document, addressed to

the investigator, was stamped with the warning that the information in the document was "not to be made known to any other agency or person without the written permission of the Chief Investigator."

Small wonder. The document confirmed that dead pets were, in fact, 8 disposed of by rendering (unless cremation was "specially requested" and "paid [for] . . . by their owners or by the veterinary clinic").

The dead animals were shipped to a broker located about 300 miles 9 away who sold the bodies to a rendering plant in Quebec. When I contacted the rendering plant, the owner admitted that cats and dogs were rendered along with livestock and roadkill. "Do pet food companies purchase this rendered material?" I asked. Again, his reply was, "Yes."

I was numb. How had this barbaric practice gone undetected all these 10 years?

When I advised the veterinarians in my city about what was happen- 11 ing, most of them immediately ceased using the dead-stock company and began using the local humane society where the animals are cremated.

In the United States and Canada, the rendering of companion animals 12 is not illegal. Millions of pets are disposed of by rendering each year. According to the Eckhouse article, an employee and ex-employee of Sacramento Rendering, a plant in California, stated that their company "rendered somewhere between 10,000 and 30,000 pounds of dogs and cats a day out of a total of 250,000 to 500,000 pounds of cattle, poultry, butcher shop scraps and other material." The rendering plant in Quebec was rendering 11 tons of dogs and cats per week—from one province alone.

## THE SITUATION IN THE U.S.

If this was the case in Canada, I wondered if the U.S. government was 13 aware of what was happening?

The Food and Drug Administration's Center for Veterinary Medicine 14 (CVM) responded to my query regarding the disposal of pets, stating: "In recognizing the need for disposal of a large number of unwanted pets in this country, CVM has not acted to specifically prohibit the rendering of pets. However, that is not to say that the practice of using this material in pet food is condoned by CVM."

The U.S. Department of Agriculture's (USDA) Food Safety and Inspec- 15 tion Services (FSIS) informed me that dog and cat cadavers are excluded as an ingredient in pet foods under FSIS regulations. But, when I asked the USDA if it could provide me with a list of the companies that were using this inspection service, I was told that only two small facilities were licensed for this service and neither had subscribed to the service for four years.

Pet food companies advertise that only quality meats are being used 16 in their products. As of 1996, however, not one of the major pet food companies was using the USDA's inspection service.

## WHAT'S IN THE CAN?

17   Television commercials and magazine advertisements for pet food would have us believe that the meats, grains, and fats used in these foods could grace our dining tables. Over seven long years, I have been able to unearth information about what actually is contained in most commercial pet food. My initial shock has turned to anger as I've realized how little consumers are told about the actual contents of pet food.

18        Animal slaughterhouses strip the flesh and send the remains—heads, feet, skin, toenails, hair, feathers, carpal and tarsal joints, and mammary glands—to rendering plants. Also judged suitable for rendering: Animals who have died on their way to slaughter; cancerous tissue or tumors and worm-infested organs; injection sites, blood clots, bone splinters or extraneous matter; contaminated blood; stomach and bowels.

19        At the rendering plant, slaughterhouse material, restaurant and supermarket refuse (including Styrofoam trays and Shrink-wrap), deadstock, roadkill, and euthanized companion animals are dumped into huge containers. A grinding machine slowly pulverizes the entire mess. After it is chipped or shredded, it is cooked at temperatures between 220°F and 270°F (104.4 to 132.2°C) for 20 minutes to one hour. The grease or tallow that rises to the top is used as a source of animal fat in pet foods. The remaining material is put into a press where the moisture is squeezed out to produce meat and bone meal.

20        The Association of American Feed Control Officials describes "meat meal" as the rendered product from mammal tissue exclusive of blood, hair, hoof, hide, trimmings, manure, stomach, and rumen (the first stomach of a cud-chewing animal) contents—except in such amounts as may occur unavoidably in "good processing" practices. In his article, "Animal Disposal: Fact and Fiction," David C. Cooke asks, "Can you imagine trying to remove the hair and stomach contents from 600,000 tons of dogs and cats prior to cooking them?"

## DRUGS, METAL, PESTICIDES

21   Pet food labels only provide half the story. Labels do not indicate the hidden hazards that lurk in most pet food. Hormones, pesticides, pathogens, heavy metals, and drugs are just a few of the hidden contaminants.

22        Sodium pentobarbital and Fatal Plus™ are barbiturates used to euthanize companion animals. When animals eat pet food that has gone through the rendering process, it is likely that they are ingesting one of these euthanizing drugs.

23        Almost 50 percent of the antibiotics manufactured in the United States are dumped into animal feed, according to the 1996 Consumer Alert

brochure, "The Dangers of Factory Farming." Pigs, cows, veal calves, turkeys, and chickens are continually fed antibiotics (primarily penicillin and tetracycline) in an attempt to eradicate the many ills that befall factory-farmed animals—pneumonia, intestinal disease, stress, rhinitis, *e-coli* infections and mastitis.

While this high-level application of antibiotics means millions of dollars for the pharmaceutical companies, the U.S. Centers for Disease Control, National Resources Defense Council and the U.S. Food and Drug Administration (FDA) all warn that these "levels of antibiotics and other contaminants in commercially raised meat constitute a serious threat to the health of the consumer."     24

Zinc, copper, and iron are listed on most pet food labels. But the metals in pet foods that do *not* need to be listed on the label include: Silver, beryllium, cadmium, bismuth, cobalt, manganese, barium, molybdenum, nickel, lead, strontium, vanadium, phosphorus, titanium, chromium, aluminum, selenium, and tungsten.     25

The U.S. FDA and Health and Welfare Canada would be very concerned if the level of lead found in pet food were found in the human food chain. For the dog food I had tested, for example, a dog ingesting 15 ounces would receive .43 to 2.4 mg of lead per day. Three mg per day is considered hazardous for a child. But when it comes to pet food, no testing is undertaken by state officials for heavy metals, pathogens, pesticides or drugs.     26

Although the pet food industry is not regulated in the United States and Canada, we as consumers have been lulled into believing that government and voluntary organizations are overseeing every ingredient stuffed into a container of pet food. What is required is government-enforced regulation of the industry. Only state legislatures can turn the tide, but it will be a long and difficult battle to persuade our representatives to take up the fight.     27

In the meantime, let the buyer beware!     28

*1997*

## QUESTIONS FOR DISCUSSION

### Content

a. What is Martin's answer to the question she asks to open her essay?
b. What is the process of rendering? Why is it done?
c. According to Martin, why should pet owners be concerned about the ingredients in pet food?

d. Summarize Martin's research. What were her first questions, and how did she go about getting the answers to them? Where did each stage of the research lead her? How long did it take her to find the answers?
e. What obstacles did Martin encounter in her research? Why were they obstacles? How did she deal with them?
f. What questions does Martin still have?
g. What points does Martin make that she supports with statistics or evidence?'
h. What points does Martin make that she does *not* support with statistics or evidence?
i. How might a pet food company respond to Martin's claims?

## Strategy and Style

j. What images does Martin create to instill in readers a negative image of rendering companies?
k. What is the effect of phrases such as "rendered companion animals" (paragraph 1), "euthanized pets" (paragraph 6), "horror stories" (paragraph 6), and other emotionally laden phrases?
l. What is Martin's tone? How might her background as an animal rights activist influence both her tone and the kind of information she chose to include in the essay?

## ENGAGING THE TEXT

a. Describe your first, "gut" reactions to this essay. How did it affect you as you read it?
b. Write down the list of ingredients on a can of pet food. Look up ingredients you don't know to find out what they are. Write a brief commentary on this list and refer to Martin's essay in your response.

## SUGGESTIONS FOR SUSTAINED WRITING

a. Analyze Martin's essay, pointing out the flaws in its argument. For example, where are claims made that are not supported with evidence? Where does she use persuasive techniques unfairly?
b. Compare Martin's essay to Alice Walker's "Am I Blue?" (Chapter 9). What are the authors' attitudes toward animals? What do they think should be humans' relationship with animals? What role do or should animals have?

c. Using Martin's essay as a starting point and reference, do further research about either the practice of rendering animals or pet food ingredients. Report on your findings to your classmates.

# Why I Want a Wife

Judy Brady

*Born in San Francisco, Judy Brady (b. 1937) took her bachelor's degree at the University of Iowa, where she majored in fine arts. An author and editor, Brady has worked to support the principles of modern feminism and the other contemporary political and social movements to which she is committed. This essay, which has been anthologized many times, was first published in* Ms. *magazine's inaugural issue in 1971. A follow-up essay, "Why I Still Want a Wife," was published in* Ms. *in the July/August 1990 issue.*

I belong to that classification of people known as wives. I am A Wife. And, 1 not altogether incidentally, I am a mother.

Not too long ago a male friend of mine appeared on the scene fresh 2 from a recent divorce. He had one child, who is, of course, with his ex-wife. He is looking for another wife. As I thought about him while I was ironing one evening, it suddenly occurred to me that I, too, would like to have a wife. Why do I want a wife?

I would like to go back to school so that I can become economically in- 3 dependent, support myself, and, if need be, support those dependent upon me. I want a wife who will work and send me to school. And while I am going to school I want a wife to take care of my children. I want a wife to keep track of the children's doctor and dentist appointments. And to keep track of mine, too. I want a wife to make sure my children eat properly and are kept clean. I want a wife who will wash the children's clothes and keep them mended. I want a wife who is a good nurturant attendant to my children, who arranges for their school, makes sure that they have an adequate social life with their peers, takes them to the park, the zoo, etc. I want a wife who takes care of the children when they are sick, a wife who arranges to be around when the children need special care, because, of course, I cannot miss classes at school. My wife must arrange to lose time at work and not lose the job. It may mean a small cut in my wife's income from time to time, but I guess I can tolerate that. Needless to say, my wife will arrange and pay for the care of the children while my wife is working.

4       I want a wife who will take care of *my* physical needs. I want a wife who will keep my house clean. A wife who will pick up after my children, a wife who will pick up after me. I want a wife who will keep my clothes clean, ironed, mended, replaced when need be, and who will see to it that my personal things are kept in their proper place so that I can find what I need the minute I need it. I want a wife who cooks the meals, a wife who is a *good* cook. I want a wife who will plan the menus, do the necessary grocery shopping, prepare the meals, serve them pleasantly, and then do the cleaning up while I do my studying. I want a wife who will care for me when I am sick and sympathize with my pain and loss of time from school. I want a wife to go along when our family takes a vacation so that someone can continue to care for me and my children when I need a rest and change of scene.

5       I want a wife who will not bother me with rambling complaints about a wife's duties. But I want a wife who will listen to me when I feel the need to explain a rather difficult point I have come across in my course of studies. And I want a wife who will type my papers for me when I have written them.

6       I want a wife who will take care of the details of my social life. When my wife and I are invited out by my friends, I want a wife who will take care of the babysitting arrangements. When I meet people at school that I like and want to entertain, I want a wife who will have the house clean, will prepare a special meal, serve it to me and my friends, and not interrupt when I talk about things that interest me and my friends. I want a wife who will have arranged that the children do not bother us. I want a wife who takes care of the needs of my guests so that they feel comfortable, who makes sure that they have an ashtray, that they are passed the hors d'oeuvres, that they are offered a second helping of the food, that their wine glasses are replenished when necessary, that the coffee is served to them as they like it. And I want a wife who knows that sometimes I need a night out by myself.

7       I want a wife who is sensitive to my sexual needs, a wife who makes love passionately and eagerly when I feel like it, a wife who makes sure that I am satisfied. And, of course, I want a wife who will not demand sexual attention when I am not in the mood for it. I want a wife who assumes the complete responsibility for birth control, because I do not want more children. I want a wife who will remain sexually faithful to me so that I do not have to clutter up my intellectual life with jealousies. And I want a wife who understands that *my* sexual needs may entail more than strict adherence to monogamy. I must, after all, be able to relate to people as fully as possible.

8       If, by chance, I find another person more suitable as a wife than the wife I already have, I want the liberty to replace my present wife with an-

other one. Naturally, I will expect a fresh, new life; my wife will take the children and be solely responsible for them so that I am left free.

When I am through with school and have a job, I want my wife to quit 9 working and remain at home so that my wife can more fully and completely take care of a wife's duties.

My God, who *wouldn't* want a wife?

10

*1970*

## QUESTIONS FOR DISCUSSION

### Content

a. List the reasons Brady offers for wanting a wife.
b. Define the word *wife* as portrayed in this essay. Do you agree with this definition?
c. What does Brady imply in the first paragraph when she says: "And not altogether incidentally, I am a mother"? How does this statement predict the contents and/or organization of the rest of the essay?
d. In what ways is the role that Brady assigned to wives in 1970 similar to the role you think wives play today? In what ways is it different?
e. Might husbands also look for their mothers when they choose wives? What examples of motherly behavior do you find in this essay?

### Strategy and Style

f. What technique(s) does Brady use to introduce her essay? Comment on their effectiveness.
g. How does Brady conclude? Is her conclusion long enough for this essay?
h. *Ms.* is a popular publication, as opposed to a scholarly journal. In light of this, describe Brady's style and explain why she uses the level of vocabulary and the sentence structure she does.
i. How would you describe Brady's tone? Does it change or evolve as we get nearer to her conclusion?
j. To what audience is Brady writing? How do you know?
k. Is the length of the essay appropriate? Should Brady have extended it? Why or why not?
l. What role does illustration play in this persuasive essay? What other methods does Brady use to develop her argument?

## ENGAGING THE TEXT

a. If you are female, list a few additional reasons why you might want a "wife." If you are male, list a few reasons you might want a "husband."
b. What to you is an ideal wife? What is an ideal husband? What is an ideal mother? What is an ideal father? Write a short definition of one or more of these people using a serious or an ironic approach.

## SUGGESTIONS FOR SUSTAINED WRITING

a. Is Brady attacking marriage itself? Write an essay in which you explain why marriage is right or wrong for you now or at any time.

   Or is Brady simply trying to expose the double standard applied to husbands and wives? Write an essay in which you argue that the double standard for husbands and wives still exists, is disappearing, or has disappeared since Brady's essay was first published.
b. Is Brady's view of the typical husband extreme? If you believe it is, write an essay rebutting her views or offering a more balanced view. If you believe Brady's view is accurate, write an essay supporting her opinion by citing examples of husbands you know or about which you have read. Bring in ideas from Deborah Tannen's "Talk in the Intimate Relationship" (Chapter 6) and/or Gretel Ehrlich's "The Rules of the Game: Rodeo" (Chapter 11) to support or illustrate your ideas.
c. Write an essay in which you expand upon the notes you made when responding to item *b* under Engaging the Text.

# Mixed Strategies

As the title of this chapter indicates, the essays contained in it do not rely on a predominant method of development, technique, or strategy to make their point. Instead they are models of the kind of writing that draws widely and freely on various approaches and that blends them naturally and seamlessly. They have been collected in this chapter to provide you with additional readings on a variety of subjects. Each one is a model of effective writing. Moreover, while they differ in terms of the subjects they address and the methods they use to develop those topics, each selection makes a clear statement in a strong authorial voice. Like the other essays in this text, they were written by people highly committed to the art of communication and to the subjects they chose to write about.

Steven Jay Gould's "Sex, Drugs, Disasters, and the Extinction of Dinosaurs" is an example of clear, accurate, and interesting scientific writing intended for an audience of nonspecialists. Gould's essay is essentially an argument, but it makes good use of techniques ordinarily associated with narrative, definition, process analysis, and cause-and-effect essays. Jonathan Kozol's "Distancing the Homeless" relies heavily on examples and illustrations. Nonetheless, its purpose is to argue a point, and it does that by making use of strategies found in essays listed under narration, description, and cause-effect analysis as well as illustration.

In "The Rules of the Game: Rodeo," Gretel Ehrlich explains a process. However, she also engages in description, comparison, definition, and illustration. Unlike most writers of process analysis, Ehrlich also quotes directly from the people who inhabit her essay's world, thereby lending authority and immediacy to what she is explaining. In this way, in fact, her writing is much like Kozol's, a fact you might want to remember if you choose to write a paper comparing writing styles used in essays on disparate subjects.

Amy Tan's "Mother Tongue" aims at definition, but she also makes excellent use of direct quotations. In addition, her writing relies on narration and illustration. Narration and lush description play a major role in the introspective "On Seeing England for the First Time," but this brilliant essay by Jamaica Kincaid can also be considered a comparison/contrast piece.

The last essay in the text, Lars Eighner's "On Dumpster Diving," appears to be a narrative on first inspection. But this is a far more complex piece. Indeed, like the other selections in this chapter, it is a rich tapestry. Eighner's purpose is to defend a distinctive—if not odd—lifestyle choice.

But first he must define this lifestyle, establish his authority on the subject through the narration of personal experience, provide specific details of his observations through concrete and vivid description, explain the process of "diving," and, when appropriate, apply a pinch of irony and sardonic humor.

Pay especially close attention to the items under Engaging the Text and Suggestions for Sustained Writing, which follow each selection in this chapter. They provide guidance and inspiration on writing essays enriched by the use of varied strategies and approaches. In addition, consider making your own connections between these essays and those appearing earlier in the text. Doing so will help you exercise skills important to the analysis of language and the synthesis of ideas. In fact, it might also lead you to design unique approaches to discussing the subjects you find most interesting and important.

# Sex, Drugs, Disasters, and the Extinction of Dinosaurs

## Stephen Jay Gould

*Stephen Jay Gould (b. 1941) is a professor of biology, geology, and the history of science at Harvard University, where he has taught since 1967. He was born in New York City and attended Antioch College (A.B., 1963) and Columbia University (Ph.D., 1967). He was an adviser to the Children's Television Workshop from 1978 to 1987 and to "Nova" from 1980 to 1992. He is currently a professor of geology and zoology at Harvard University, where his research specialties are paleontology, evolutionary biology, and the history of science. A prolific writer, he publishes a monthly column in* National History *magazine and has contributed well over a hundred articles to scientific journals across the United States. Among numerous full-length works are several collections of essays first published in* Natural History. *They include* Ever Since Darwin *(1978),* The Panda's Thumb *(1980),* Hen's Teeth and Horses' Toes *(1983),* The Flamingo's Smile *(1985), and* Bully for Brontosaurus *(1991). He is also the author of* The Mismeasure of Man *(1980),* Wonderful Life *(1990), and* Full House: The Spread of Excellence from Plato to Darwin *(1996), which argue against the theory of biological determinism and explain the notion of chance in evolution. Like James C. Rettie in Chapter 9, Gould makes scientific fact and theory appetizing even to readers with no scientific training. John Noble Wilford, science editor of the* New York Times, *has called him "one of the most spirited essayists of our time." Indeed, his common sense and delightful wit make it seem as if we are reading an article in a popular magazine rather than a reasoned and thoroughly researched scientific study.*

Science, in its most fundamental definition, is a fruitful mode of inquiry, 1 not a list of enticing conclusions. The conclusions are the consequence, not the essence.

My greatest unhappiness with most popular presentations of science 2 concerns their failure to separate fascinating claims from the methods that scientists use to establish the facts of nature. Journalists, and the public, thrive on controversial and stunning statements. But science is, basically, a way of knowing—in P. B. Medawar's apt words, "the art of the soluble." If the growing corps of popular science writers would focus on *how* scientists develop and defend those fascinating claims, they would make their greatest possible contribution to public understanding.

Consider three ideas, proposed in perfect seriousness to explain that 3 greatest of all titillating puzzles—the extinction of dinosaurs. Since these three notions invoke the primally fascinating themes of our culture—sex, drugs, and violence—they surely reside in the category of fascinating claims. I want to show why two of them rank as silly speculation, while the other represents science at its grandest and most useful.

Science works with testable proposals. If, after much compilation and 4 scrutiny of data, new information continues to affirm a hypothesis, we may accept it provisionally and gain confidence as further evidence mounts. We can never be completely sure that a hypothesis is right, though we may be able to show with confidence that it is wrong. The best scientific hypotheses are also generous and expansive: They suggest extensions and implications that enlighten related, and even far distant, subjects. Simply consider how the idea of evolution has influenced virtually every intellectual field.

Useless speculation, on the other hand, is restrictive. It generates no 5 testable hypothesis, and offers no way to obtain potentially refuting evidence. Please note that I am not speaking of truth or falsity. The speculation may well be true; still, if it provides, in principle, no material for affirmation or rejection, we can make nothing of it. It must simply stand forever as an intriguing idea. Useless speculation turns in on itself and leads nowhere; good science, containing both seeds for its potential refutation and implications for more and different testable knowledge, reaches out. But, enough preaching. Let's move on to dinosaurs, and the three proposals for their extinction.

1. *Sex:* Testes function only in a narrow range of temperature (those of mammals hang externally in a scrotal sac because internal body temperatures are too high for their proper function). A worldwide rise in temperature at the close of the Cretaceous period caused the testes of dinosaurs to stop functioning and led to their extinction by sterilization of males.

2. *Drugs:* Angiosperms (flowering plants) first evolved toward the end of the dinosaurs' reign. Many of these plants contain psychoactive agents, avoided by mammals today as a result of their bitter taste. Dinosaurs had neither means to taste the bitterness nor livers effective enough to detoxify the substances. They died of massive overdoses.

3. *Disasters:* A large comet or asteroid struck the Earth some 65 million years ago, lofting a cloud of dust into the sky and blocking sunlight, thereby suppressing photosynthesis and so drastically lowering world temperatures that dinosaurs and hosts of other creatures became extinct.

6      Before analyzing these three tantalizing statements, we must establish a basic ground rule often violated in proposals for the dinosaurs' demise. *There is no separate problem of the extinction of dinosaurs.* Too often we divorce specific events from their wider contexts and systems of cause and effect. The fundamental fact of dinosaur extinction is its synchrony with the demise of so many other groups across a wide range of habitats, from terrestrial to marine.

7      The history of life has been punctuated by brief episodes of mass extinction. A recent analysis by University of Chicago paleontologists Jack Sepkoski and Dave Raup, based on the best and most exhaustive tabulation of data ever assembled, shows clearly that five episodes of mass dying stand well above the "background" extinctions of normal times (when we consider all mass extinctions, large and small, they seem to fall in a regular 26-million-year cycle). The Cretaceous debacle, occurring 65 million years ago and separating the Mesozoic and Cenozoic eras of our geological time scale, ranks prominently among the five. Nearly all the marine plankton (single-celled floating creatures) died with geological suddenness; among marine invertebrates, nearly 15 percent of all families perished, including many previously dominant groups, especially the ammonites (relatives of squids in coiled shells). On land, the dinosaurs disappeared after more than 100 million years of unchallenged domination.

8      In this context, speculations limited to dinosaurs alone ignore the larger phenomenon. We need a coordinated explanation for a system of events that includes the extinction of dinosaurs as one component. Thus it makes little sense, though it may fuel our desire to view mammals as inevitable inheritors of the Earth, to guess that dinosaurs died because small mammals ate their eggs (a perennial favorite among untestable speculations). It seems most unlikely that some disaster peculiar to dinosaurs befell these massive beasts—and that the debacle happened to strike just when one of history's five great dyings had enveloped the Earth for completely different reasons.

9      The testicular theory, an old favorite from the 1940s, had its root in an interesting and thoroughly respectable study of temperature tolerances in

the American alligator, published in the staid *Bulletin of the American Museum of Natural History* in 1946 by three experts on living and fossil reptiles—E. H. Colbert, my own first teacher in paleontology; R. B. Cowles; and C. M. Bogert.

The first sentence of their summary reveals a purpose beyond alligators: 10 "This report describes an attempt to infer the reactions of extinct reptiles, especially the dinosaurs, to high temperatures as based upon reactions observed in the modern alligator." They studied, by rectal thermometry, the body temperatures of alligators under changing conditions of heating and cooling. (Well, let's face it, you wouldn't want to try sticking a thermometer under a 'gator's tongue.) The predictions under test go way back to an old theory first stated by Galileo in the 1630s—the unequal scaling of surfaces and volumes. As an animal, or any object, grows (provided its shape doesn't change), surface areas must increase more slowly than volumes—since surfaces get larger as length squared, while volumes increase much more rapidly, as length cubed. Therefore, small animals have high ratios of surface to volume, while large animals cover themselves with relatively little surface.

Among cold-blooded animals lacking any physiological mechanism 11 for keeping their temperatures constant, small creatures have a hell of a time keeping warm—because they lose so much heat through their relatively large surfaces. On the other hand, large animals, with their relatively small surfaces, may lose heat so slowly that, once warm, they may maintain effectively constant temperatures against ordinary fluctuations of climate. (In fact, the resolution of the "hot-blooded dinosaur" controversy that burned so brightly a few years back may simply be that, while large dinosaurs possessed no physiological mechanism for constant temperature, and were not therefore warm-blooded in the technical sense, their large size and relatively small surface area kept them warm.)

Colbert, Cowles, and Bogert compared the warming rates of small and 12 large alligators. As predicted, the small fellows heated up (and cooled down) more quickly. When exposed to a warm sun, a tiny 50-gram (1.76-ounce) alligator heated up one degree Celsius every minute and a half, while a large alligator, 260 times bigger at 13,000 grams (28.7 pounds), took seven and a half minutes to gain a degree. Extrapolating up to an adult 10-ton dinosaur, they concluded that a one-degree rise in body temperature would take eighty-six hours. If large animals absorb heat so slowly (through their relatively small surfaces), they will also be unable to shed any excess heat gained when temperatures rise above a favorable level.

The authors then guessed that large dinosaurs lived at or near their 13 optimum temperatures; Cowles suggested that a rise in global temperatures just before the Cretaceous extinction caused the dinosaurs to heat up beyond their optimal tolerance—and, being so large, they couldn't shed the unwanted heat. (In a most unusual statement within a scientific paper,

Colbert and Bogert then explicitly disavowed this speculative extension of their empirical work on alligators.) Cowles conceded that this excess heat probably wasn't enough to kill or even to enervate the great beasts, but since testes often function only within a narrow range of temperature, he proposed that this global rise might have sterilized all the males, causing extinction by natural contraception.

14      The overdose theory has recently been supported by UCLA psychiatrist Ronald K. Siegel. Siegel has gathered, he claims, more than 2,000 records of animals who, when given access, administer various drugs to themselves— from a mere swig of alcohol to massive doses of the big H. Elephants will swill the equivalent of twenty beers at a time, but do not like alcohol in concentrations greater than seven percent. In a silly bit of anthropocentric speculation, Siegel states that "elephants drink, perhaps, to forget . . . the anxiety produced by shrinking rangeland and the competition for food."

15      Since fertile imaginations can apply almost any hot idea to the extinction of dinosaurs, Siegel found a way. Flowering plants did not evolve until late in the dinosaurs' reign. These plants also produced an array of aromatic, amino-acid-based alkaloids—the major group of psychoactive agents. Most mammals are "smart" enough to avoid these potential poisons. The alkaloids simply don't taste good (they are bitter); in any case, we mammals have livers happily supplied with the capacity to detoxify them. But, Siegel speculates, perhaps dinosaurs could neither taste the bitterness nor detoxify the substances once ingested. He recently told members of the American Psychological Association: "I'm not suggesting that all dinosaurs OD'd on plant drugs, but it certainly was a factor." He also argued that death by overdose may help explain why so many dinosaur fossils are found in contorted positions. (Do not go gentle into that good night.)

16      Extraterrestrial catastrophes have long pedigrees in the popular literature of extinction, but the subject exploded again in 1979, after a long lull, when the father-son, physicist-geologist team of Luis and Walter Alvarez proposed that an asteroid, some 10 km in diameter, struck the Earth 65 million years ago (comets, rather than asteroids, have since gained favor. Good science is self-corrective).

17      The force of such a collision would be immense, greater by far than the megatonnage of all the world's nuclear weapons. In trying to reconstruct a scenario that would explain the simultaneous dying of dinosaurs on land and so many creatures in the sea, the Alvarezes proposed that a gigantic dust cloud, generated by particles blown aloft in the impact, would so darken the Earth that photosynthesis would cease and temperatures drop precipitously. (Rage, rage against the dying of the light.) The single-celled photosynthetic oceanic plankton, with life cycles measured in weeks, would perish outright, but land plants might survive through the dormancy of their seeds (land plants were not much affected by the Creta-

ceous extinction, and any adequate theory must account for the curious pattern of differential survival). Dinosaurs would die by starvation and freezing; small, warm-blooded mammals, with more modest requirements for food and better regulation of body temperature, would squeak through. "Let the bastards freeze in the dark," as bumper stickers of our chauvinistic neighbors in sunbelt states proclaimed several years ago during the Northeast's winter oil crisis.

All three theories, testicular malfunction, psychoactive overdosing, 18 and asteroidal zapping, grab our attention mightily. As pure phenomenology, they rank about equally high on any hit parade of primal fascination. Yet one represents expansive science, the others restrictive and untestable speculation. The proper criterion lies in evidence and methodology; we must probe behind the superficial fascination of particular claims.

How could we possibly decide whether the hypothesis of testicular 19 frying is right or wrong? We would have to know things that the fossil record cannot provide. What temperatures were optimal for dinosaurs? Could they avoid the absorption of excess heat by staying in the shade, or in caves? At what temperatures did their testicles cease to function? Were late Cretaceous climates ever warm enough to drive the internal temperatures of dinosaurs close to this ceiling? Testicles simply don't fossilize, and how could we infer their temperature tolerances even if they did? In short, Cowles's hypothesis is only an intriguing speculation leading nowhere. The most damning statement against it appeared right in the conclusion of Colbert, Cowles, and Bogert's paper, when they admitted: "It is difficult to advance any definite arguments against the hypothesis." My statement may seem paradoxical—isn't a hypothesis really good if you can't devise any arguments against it? Quite the contrary. It is simply untestable and unusable.

Siegel's overdosing has even less going for it. At least Cowles ex- 20 trapolated his conclusion from some good data on alligators. And he didn't completely violate the primary guideline of siting dinosaur extinction in the context of a general mass dying—for rise in temperature could be the root cause of a general catastrophe, zapping dinosaurs by testicular malfunction and different groups for other reasons. But Siegel's speculation cannot touch the extinction of ammonites or oceanic plankton (diatoms make their own food with good sweet sunlight; they don't OD on the chemicals of terrestrial plants). It is simply a gratuitous, attention-grabbing guess. It cannot be tested, for how can we know what dinosaurs tasted and what their livers could do? Livers don't fossilize any better than testicles.

The hypothesis doesn't even make any sense in its own context. An- 21 giosperms were in full flower ten million years before dinosaurs went the way of all flesh. Why did it take so long? As for the pains of a chemical death recorded in contortions of fossils, I regret to say (or rather I'm pleased to note for the dinosaurs' sake) that Siegel's knowledge of geology must be a bit deficient: Muscles contract after death and geological strata rise and fall with motions of the Earth's crust after burial—more than enough reason to distort a fossil's pristine appearance.

22      The impact story, on the other hand, has a sound basis in evidence. It can be tested, extended, refined, and, if wrong, disproved. The Alvarezes did not just construct an arresting guess for public consumption. They proposed their hypothesis after laborious geochemical studies with Frank Asaro and Helen Michael had revealed a massive increase of iridium in rocks deposited right at the time of extinction. Iridium, a rare metal of the platinum group, is virtually absent from indigenous rocks of the Earth's crust; most of our iridium arrives on extraterrestrial objects that strike the Earth.

23      The Alvarez hypothesis bore immediate fruit. Based originally on evidence from two European localities, it led geochemists throughout the world to examine other sediments of the same age. They found abnormally high amounts of iridium everywhere—from continental rocks of the western United States to deep sea cores from the South Atlantic.

24      Cowles proposed his testicular hypothesis in the mid-1940s. Where has it gone since then? Absolutely nowhere, because scientists can do nothing with it. The hypothesis must stand as a curious appendage to a solid study of alligators. Siegel's overdose scenario will also win a few press notices and fade into oblivion. The Alvarezes' asteroid falls into a different category altogether, and much of the popular commentary has missed this essential distinction by focusing on the impact and its attendant results, and forgetting what really matters to a scientist—the iridium. If you talk just about asteroids, dust, and darkness, you tell stories no better and no more entertaining than fried testicles or terminal trips. It is the iridium—the source of testable evidence—that counts and forges the crucial distinction between speculation and science.

25      The proof, to twist a phrase, lies in the doing. Cowles's hypothesis has generated nothing in thirty-five years. Since its proposal in 1979, the Alvarez hypothesis has spawned hundreds of studies, a major conference, and attendant publications. Geologists are fired up. They are looking for iridium at all other extinction boundaries. Every week exposes a new wrinkle in the scientific press. Further evidence that the Cretaceous iridium represents extraterrestrial impact and not indigenous volcanism continues to accumulate. As I revise this essay in November 1984 (this paragraph will be out of date when the book is published), new data include chemical "signatures" of other isotopes indicating unearthly provenance, glass spherules of a size and sort produced by impact and not by volcanic eruptions, and high-pressure varieties of silica formed (so far as we know) only under the tremendous shock of impact.

My point is simply this: Whatever the eventual outcome (I suspect it 26 will be positive), the Alvarez hypothesis is exciting, fruitful science because it generates tests, provides us with things to do, and expands outward. We are having fun, battling back and forth, moving toward a resolution, and extending the hypothesis beyond its original scope.

As just one example of the unexpected, distant cross-fertilization that 27 good science engenders, the Alvarez hypothesis made a major contribution to a theme that has riveted public attention in the past few months—so-called nuclear winter. In a speech delivered in April 1982, Luis Alvarez calculated the energy that a ten-kilometer asteroid would release on impact. He compared such an explosion with a full nuclear exchange and implied that all-out atomic war might unleash similar consequences.

This theme of impact leading to massive dust clouds and falling tem- 28 peratures formed an important input to the decision of Carl Sagan and a group of colleagues to model the climatic consequences of nuclear holocaust. Full nuclear exchange would probably generate the same kind of dust cloud and darkening that may have wiped out the dinosaurs. Temperatures would drop precipitously and agriculture might become impossible. Avoidance of nuclear war is fundamentally an ethical and political imperative, but we must know the factual consequences to make firm judgments. I am heartened by a final link across disciplines and deep concerns—another criterion, by the way, of science at its best. A recognition of the very phenomenon that made our evolution possible by exterminating the previously dominant dinosaurs and clearing a way for the evolution of large mammals, including us, might actually help to save us from joining those magnificent beasts in contorted poses among the strata of the Earth.

*1984*

## QUESTIONS FOR DISCUSSION

### Content

a. In paragraph 1, Gould claims that science is a "fruitful mode of inquiry," not a set of "conclusions." What does he mean, and how does this assertion help explain his argument? Where is this assertion illustrated in his essay?
b. Why can we "never be completely sure" that a hypothesis is correct (paragraph 4)?
c. Summarize the three hypotheses on the extinction of dinosaurs. What is the main element in each that makes it testable or untestable?

d. What distinctions does the author make between scientific hypothesis and speculation? Explain his assertion that the "proper criterion lies in evidence and methodology" (paragraph 18).

e. Why, according to Gould, is a hypothesis suspect if one cannot mount arguments against it?

f. What does he mean when he implies that science should be fun (paragraph 26)? In what way does the Alvarez hypothesis meet this criterion? Why are the other two theories not fun?

## Strategy and Style

g. In paragraph 9, Gould reports that the "testicular theory" had its origins in a respectable scientific study. Why does he say this if he wishes to discredit that theory?

h. What are his views of the various scientists whose studies he cites? Compare his opinions of the team of Colbert, Cowles, and Bogert (paragraphs 9–13); of Siegel (paragraphs 14 and 15); and of the Alvarezes (paragraphs 16 and 17). What words does he use to describe each? How do these words provide foreshadowing?

i. In paragraph 6, Gould writes, "Too often we divorce specific events." Who is "we"?

j. Is Gould's intended audience limited to scientists or people interested in science? How do you know?

k. What is the effect of quoting the poet Dylan Thomas in paragraph 17 ("Rage, rage against the dying of the light")?

l. What rhetorical strategies does Gould use, and where are they most apparent in the essay? What might be his reasons for choosing these strategies?

## ENGAGING THE TEXT

a. Read through the essay once more, writing questions in the margins that you would ask the author if you had the chance to meet with him. For example, you might inquire why he believes it is "silly" to think that elephants might experience anxiety (paragraph 14).

b. Look around your town or college. Briefly "speculate" about what it or the land it sits on might have looked like 50, 100, or even 1,000 years ago. Use Gould's style of speculation as a guide.

## SUGGESTIONS FOR SUSTAINED WRITING

a. In paragraphs 15 and 17, Gould quotes from "Do Not Go Gentle into That Good Night" by Dylan Thomas. Find a copy of the poem in your

library and read it. Then write an essay in which you explain the significance of the lines that Gould takes from it.
b. Compare Gould's essay to James C. Rettie's "'But a Watch in the Night'"
(Chapter 9). Comment on the theories about the evolution of life forms
on Earth. How does studying the era of the dinosaurs help us understand humans' comparatively short time on Earth?
c. When he brings in the idea of nuclear war in his concluding paragraphs, Gould suggests that the Alvarezes' theory has implications beyond the scope of paleontology. What other implications might their
theory have? Do research to write an essay in which you speculate on
these implications.

# Distancing the Homeless

Jonathan Kozol

*Teacher, author, and recipient of two National Book Awards, Jonathan Kozol (b. 1936) took
his bachelor's degree at Harvard University and did graduate work at Magdalen College,
Oxford. He writes extensively on the problems of homelessness, illiteracy, and poverty, especially as they affect children. Kozol's best-known works,* Death at an Early Age *(1967),*
Illiterate America *(1995),* Rachel and Her Children: Homeless Families in America
*(1988), and* Savage Inequalities: Children in American's Schools *(1992), have helped
arouse the conscience of a generation to problems that an affluent society supposedly solved.
His book* Amazing Grace *(1995) focuses on the effects of poverty in New York City's
Harlem, Washington Heights, and the South Bronx. His most recent book is* Ordinary
Resurrections *(2000). Matthew Rothschild, editor of the* Progressive *magazine, describes
Kozol as someone who "has spent more than three decades shining the spotlight on injus-
tice in our society, especially the injustice of poverty." "Distancing the Homeless" attacks
many popular notions about homelessness and the homeless.*

It is commonly believed by many journalists and politicians that the [1]
homeless of America are, in large part, former patients of large mental
hospitals who were deinstitutionalized in the 1970s— the consequence, it
is sometimes said, of misguided liberal opinion, which favored the treatment of such persons in community-based centers. It is argued that this
policy, and the subsequent failure of society to build such centers or to
provide them in sufficient number, is the primary cause of homelessness
in the United States.

Those who work among the homeless do not find that explanation sat- [2]
isfactory. While conceding that a certain number of the homeless are, or
have been, mentally unwell, they believe that, in the case of most unsheltered people, the primary reason is economic rather than clinical. The

cause of homelessness, they say with disarming logic, is the lack of homes and of income with which to rent or acquire them.

3      They point to the loss of traditional jobs in industry (2,000,000 every year since 1980) and to the fact that half of those who are laid off end up in work that pays a poverty-level wage. They point to the parallel growth of poverty in families with children, noting that children, who represent one quarter of our population, make up 40 percent of the poor; since 1968, the number of children in poverty has grown by 3,000,000, while welfare benefits to families with children have declined by 35 percent.

4      And they note, too, that these developments have coincided with a time in which the shortage of low-income housing has intensified as the gentrification of our major cities has accelerated. Half a million units of low-income housing have been lost each year to condominium conversion as well as to arson, demolition, or abandonment. Between 1978 and 1980, median rents climbed 30 percent for people in the lowest income sector, driving many of these families into the streets. After 1980, rents rose at even faster rates. In Boston, between 1982 and 1984, over 80 percent of the housing units renting below $300 disappeared, while the number of units renting above $600 nearly tripled.

5      Hard numbers, in this instance, would appear to be of greater help than psychiatric labels in telling us why so many people become homeless. Eight million American families now pay half or more of their income for rent or a mortgage. Six million more, unable to pay rent at all, live doubled up with others. At the same time, federal support for low-income housing dropped from $30 billion (1980) to $9 billion (1986). Under Presidents Ford and Carter, 500,000 subsidized private housing units were constructed. By President Reagan's second term, the number had dropped to 25,000. "We're getting out of the housing business, period," said a deputy assistant secretary of the Department of Housing and Urban Development in 1985.

6      One year later, the *Washington Post* reported that the number of homeless families in Washington, D.C., had grown by 500 percent over the previous 12 months. In New York City, the waiting list for public housing now contains 200,000 names. The waiting is 18 years.

7      Why, in the face of these statistics, are we impelled to find a psychiatric explanation for the growth of homelessness in the United States?

8      A misconception, once it is implanted in the popular imagination, is not easy to uproot, particularly when it serves a useful social role. The notion that the homeless are largely psychotics who belong in institutions, rather than victims of displacement at the hands of enterprising realtors, spares us from the need to offer realistic solutions to the fact of deep and widening extremes of wealth and poverty in the United States. It also enables us to tell ourselves that the despair of homeless people bears no inti-

mate connection to the privileged existence we enjoy—when, for example, we rent or purchase one of those restored townhouses that once provided shelter for people now huddled in the street.

But there may be another reason to assign labels to the destitute. 9 Terming economic victims "psychotic" or "disordered" helps to place them at a distance. It says that they aren't quite like us—and, more important, that we could not be like them. The plight of homeless families is a nightmare. It may not seem natural to try to banish human beings from our midst, but it is natural to try to banish nightmares from our minds.

So the rituals of clinical contamination proceed uninterrupted by the 10 economic facts described above. Research that addresses homelessness as an *injustice* rather than as a medical *misfortune* does not win the funding of foundations. And the research which is funded, defining the narrowed borders of permissible debate, diverts our attention from the antecedent to the secondary cause of homelessness. Thus it is that perfectly ordinary women whom I know in New York City—people whose depression or anxiety is a realistic consequence of months and even years in crowded shelters or the streets—are interrogated by invasive research scholars in an effort to decode their poverty, to find clinical categories for their despair and terror, to identify the secret failing that lies hidden in their psyche.

Many pregnant women without homes are denied prenatal care be- 11 cause they constantly travel from one shelter to another. Many are anemic. Many are denied essential dietary supplements by recent federal cuts. As a consequence, some of their children do not live to see their second year of life. Do these mothers sometimes show signs of stress? Do they appear disorganized, depressed, disordered? Frequently. They are immobilized by pain, traumatized by fear. So it is no surprise that when researchers enter the scene to ask them how they "feel," the resulting reports tell us that the homeless are emotionally unwell. The reports do not tell us we have *made* these people ill. They do not tell us that illness is a natural response to intolerable conditions. Nor do they tell us of the strength and the resilience that so many of these people still retain despite the miseries they must endure. They set these men and women apart in capsules labeled "personality disorder" or "psychotic," where they no longer threaten our complacence.

I visited Haiti not many years ago, when the Duvalier family was still 12 in power. If an American scholar were to have made a psychological study of the homeless families living in the streets of Port-au-Prince—sleeping amidst rotten garbage, bathing in open sewers—and if he were to return to the United States to tell us that the reasons for their destitution were "behavioral problems" or "a lack of mental health," we would be properly suspicious. Knowledgeable Haitians would not merely be suspicious. They would be enraged. Even to initiate such research when economic and political explanations present themselves so starkly would appear grotesque. It is no less so in the United States.

13      One of the more influential studies of this nature was carried out in 1985 by Ellen Bassuk, a psychiatrist at Harvard University. Drawing upon interviews with eight homeless parents, Dr. Bassuk contends, according to the *Boston Globe,* that "90 percent [of these people] have problems other than housing and poverty that are so acute they would be unable to live successfully on their own." She also precludes the possibility that illness, where it does exist, may be provoked by destitution. "Our data," she writes, "suggest that mental illness tends to precede homelessness." She concedes that living in the streets can make a homeless person's mental illness worse; but she insists upon the fact of prior illness.

14      The executive director of the Massachusetts Commission on Children and Youth believes that Dr. Bassuk's estimate is far too high. The staff of Massachusetts Human Services Secretary Phillip Johnston believes the appropriate number is closer to 10 percent.

15      In defending her research, Bassuk challenges such critics by claiming that they do not have data to refute her. This may be true. Advocates for the homeless do not receive funds to defend the sanity of the people they represent. In placing the burden of proof upon them, Dr. Bassuk has created an extraordinary dialectic: How does one prove that people aren't unwell? What homeless mother would consent to enter a procedure that might "prove" her mental health? What overburdened shelter operator would divert scarce funds to such an exercise? It is an unnatural, offensive, and dehumanizing challenge.

16      Dr. Bassuk's work, however, isn't the issue I want to raise here; the issue is the use or misuse of that work by critics of the poor. For example, in a widely syndicated essay published in 1986, the newspaper columnist Charles Krauthammer argued that the homeless are essentially a deranged segment of the population and that we must find the "political will" to isolate them from society. We must do this, he said, "whether they like it or not." Arguing even against the marginal benefits of homeless shelters, Krauthammer wrote: "There is a better alternative, however, though no one dares speak its name." Krauthammer dares: That better alternative, he said, is "asylum."

17      One of Mr. Krauthammer's colleagues at the *Washington Post,* the columnist George Will, perceives the homeless as a threat to public cleanliness and argues that they ought to be consigned to places where we need not see them. "It is," he says, "simply a matter of public hygiene" to put them out of sight. Another journalist, Charles Murray, writing from the vantage point of a social Darwinist, recommends the restoration of the almshouses of the 1800s. "Granted Dickensian horror stories about almshouses," he begins, there were nonetheless "good almshouses"; he proposes "a good correctional 'halfway house'" as a proper shelter for a mother and child with no means of self-support.

18      In the face of such declarations, the voices of those who work with and know the poor are harder to hear.

Manhattan Borough President David Dinkins made the following ob- 19
servation on the basis of a study commissioned in 1986: "No facts support
the belief that addiction or behavioral problems occur with more frequency
in the homeless family population than in a similar socioeconomic population. Homeless families are not demographically different from other public assistance families when they enter the shelter system . . . Family homelessness is typically a housing and income problem: The unavailability of
affordable housing and the inadequacy of public assistance income."

In a "hypothetical world," write James Wright and Julie Lam of the 20
University of Massachusetts, "where there were no alcoholics, no drug addicts, no mentally ill, no deinstitutionalization, . . . indeed, no personal social pathologies at all, there would still be a formidable homelessness
problem, simply because at this stage in American history, there is not
enough low-income housing" to accommodate the poor.

New York State's respected commissioner of social services, Cesar 21
Perales, makes the point in fewer words: "Homelessness is less and less a
result of personal failure, and more and more is caused by larger forces.
There is no longer affordable housing in New York City for people of poor
and modest means."

Even the words of medical practitioners who care for homeless people 22
have been curiously ignored. A study published by the Massachusetts
Medical Society, for instance, has noted that the most frequent illnesses
among a sample of the homeless population, after alcohol and drug use, are
trauma (31 percent), upper respiratory disorders (28 percent), limb disorders (19 percent), mental illness (16 percent), skin diseases (15 percent), hy-
pertension (14 percent), and neurological illnesses (12 percent). (Excluded
from this tabulation are lead poisoning, malnutrition, acute diarrhea, and
other illnesses especially common among homeless infants and small children.) Why, we may ask, of all these calamities, does mental illness command so much political and press attention? The answer may be that the label of mental illness places the destitute outside the sphere of ordinary life.
It personalizes an anguish that is public in its genesis; it individualizes a
misery that is both general in cause and general in application.

The rate of tuberculosis among the homeless is believed to be 10 times 23
that of the general population. Asthma, I have learned in countless interviews, is one of the most common causes of discomfort in the shelters.
Compulsive smoking, exacerbated by the crowding and the tension, is
more common in the shelters than in any place that I have visited except
prison. Infected and untreated sores, scabies, diarrhea, poorly set limbs,
protruding elbows, awkwardly distorted wrists, bleeding gums, im-
pacted teeth, and other untreated dental problems are so common among
children in the shelters that one rapidly forgets their presence. Hunger
and emaciation are everywhere. Children as well as adults can bring to
mind the photographs of people found in camps for refugees of war in

1945. But these miseries bear no stigma, and mental illness does. It conveys a stigma in the Soviet Union. It conveys a stigma in the United States. In both nations the label is used, whether as a matter of deliberate policy or not, to isolate and treat as special cases those who, by deed or word or sheer presence, represent a threat to national complacence. The two situations are obviously not identical, but they are enough alike to give Americans reason for concern.

24    Last summer, some 28,000 homeless people were afforded shelter by the city of New York. Of this number, 12,000 were children and 6,000 were parents living together in families. The average child was six years old, the average parent 27. A typical homeless family included a mother with two or three children, but in about one-fifth of these families two parents were present. Roughly 10,000 single persons, then, made up the remainder of the population of the city's shelters.

25    These proportions vary somewhat from one area of the nation to another. In all areas, however, families are the fastest-growing sector of the homeless population, and in the Northeast they are by far the largest sector already. In Massachusetts, three-fourths of the homeless now are families with children; in certain parts of Massachusetts—Attleboro and Northampton, for example—the proportion reaches 90 percent. Two-thirds of the homeless children studied recently in Boston were less than five years old.

26    Of an estimated two to three million homeless people nationwide, about 500,000 are dependent children, according to Robert Hayes, counsel to the National Coalition for the Homeless. Including their parents, at least 750,000 homeless people in America are family members.

27    What is to be made, then, of the supposition that the homeless are primarily the former residents of mental hospitals, persons who were carelessly released during the 1970s? Many of them are, to be sure. Among the older men and women in the streets and shelters, as many as one-third (some believe as many as one-half) may be chronically disturbed, and a number of these people were deinstitutionalized during the 1970s. But in a city like New York, where nearly half the homeless are small children with an average age of six, to operate on the basis of such a supposition makes no sense. Their parents, with an average age of 27, are not likely to have been hospitalized in the 1970s, either.

28    Nor is it easy to assume, as was once the case, that single men—those who come closer to fitting the stereotype of the homeless vagrant, the drifting alcoholic of an earlier age—are the former residents of mental hospitals. The age of homeless men has dropped in recent years; many of them are only 21 to 28 years old. Fifty percent of homeless men in New York City shelters in 1984 were there for the first time. Most had previously had homes and jobs. Many had never before needed public aid.

A frequently cited set of figures tells us that in 1955, the average daily  29
census of nonfederal psychiatric institutions was 677,000, and that by 1984,
the number had dropped to 151,000. Subtract the second number from the
first, conventional logic tells us, and we have an explanation for the homelessness of half a million people. A closer look at the same number offers
us a different lesson.

The sharpest decline in the average daily census of these institutions  30
occurred prior to 1978, and the largest part of that decline, in fact, appeared
at least a decade earlier. From 677,000 in 1955, the census dropped to
378,000 in 1972. The 1974 census was 307,000. In 1976 it was 230,000; in 1977
it was 211,000; and in 1978 it was 190,000. In no year since 1978 has the average daily census dropped by more than 9,000 persons, and in the six-year
period from 1978 to 1984, the total decline was 39,000 persons. Compared
with a decline of 300,000 from 1955 to 1972, and of nearly 200,000 more from
1972 to 1978, the number is small. But the years since 1980 are the period in
which the present homeless crisis surfaced. Only since 1983 have homeless
individuals overflowed the shelters.

If the large numbers of the homeless lived in hospitals before they  31
reappeared in subway stations and in public shelters, we need to ask
where they were and what they had been doing from 1972 to 1980. Were
they living under bridges? Were they waiting out the decade in the base-
ments of deserted buildings?

No. The bulk of those who had been psychiatric patients and were re-  32
leased from hospitals during the 1960s and early 1970s had been living in
the meantime in low-income housing, many in skid-row hotels or boarding
houses. Such housing—commonly known as SRO (single-room occu-
pancy) units—was drastically diminished by the gentrification of our cities
that began in 1970. Almost 50 percent of SRO housing was replaced by luxury apartments or by office buildings between 1970 and 1980, and the remaining units have been disappearing at even faster rates. As recently as
1986, after New York City had issued a prohibition against conversion of
such housing, a well-known developer hired a demolition team to destroy
a building in Times Square that had previously been home to indigent people. The demolition took place in the middle of the night. In order to avoid
imprisonment, the developer was allowed to make a philanthropic gift to
homeless people as a token of atonement. This incident, bizarre as it appears, reminds us that the profit motive for displacement of the poor is very
great in every major city. It also indicates a more realistic explanation for the
growth of homelessness during the 1980s.

Even for those persons who are ill and were deinstitutionalized during  33
the decades before 1980, the precipitating cause of homelessness in 1987 is
not illness but loss of housing. SRO housing, unattractive as it may have
been, offered low-cost sanctuaries for the homeless, providing a degree of

safety and mutual support for those who lived within them. They were a demeaning version of the community health centers that society had promised; they were the de facto "halfway houses" of the 1970s. For these people too, then—at most half of the homeless single persons in America—the cause of homelessness is lack of housing.

34    A writer in the *New York Times* describes a homeless woman standing on a traffic island in Manhattan. "She was evicted from her small room in the hotel just across the street," and she is determined to get revenge. Until she does, "nothing will move her from that spot. . . . Her argumentativeness and her angry fixation on revenge, along with the apparent absence of hallucinations, mark her as a paranoid." Most physicians, I imagine, would be more reserved in passing judgment with so little evidence, but this author makes his diagnosis without hesitation. "The paranoids of the street," he says, "are among the most difficult to help."

35    Perhaps so. But does it depend on who is offering the help? Is anyone offering to help this woman get back her home? Is it crazy to seek vengeance for being thrown into the street? The absence of anger, some psychiatrists believe, might indicate much greater illness.

36    The same observer sees additional symptoms of pathology ("negative symptoms," he calls them) in the fact that many homeless persons demonstrate a "gross deterioration in their personal hygiene" and grooming, leading to "indifference" and "apathy." Having just identified one woman as unhealthy because she is so far from being "indifferent" as to seek revenge, he now sees apathy as evidence of illness; so consistency is not what we are looking for in this account. But how much less indifferent might the homeless be if those who decide their fate were less indifferent themselves? How might their grooming and hygiene be improved if they were permitted access to a public toilet?

37    In New York City, as in many cities, homeless people are denied the right to wash in public bathrooms, to store their few belongings in a public locker, or, in certain cases, to make use of public toilets altogether. Shaving, cleaning of clothes, and other forms of hygiene are prohibited in the men's room of Grand Central Station. The terminal's three hundred lockers, used in former times by homeless people to secure their goods, were removed in 1986 as "a threat to public safety," according to a study made by the New York City Council.

38    At 1:30 every morning, homeless people are ejected from the station. Many once attempted to take refuge on the ramp that leads to Forty-Second Street because it was protected from the street by wooden doors and thus provided some degree of warmth. But the station management responded to this challenge in two ways. The ramp was mopped with a strong mixture of ammonia to produce a noxious smell, and when the people sleeping there brought cardboard boxes and newspapers to pro-

tect them from the fumes, the entrance doors were chained wide open. Temperatures dropped some nights to 10 degrees. Having driven these people to the streets, city officials subsequently determined that their willingness to risk exposure to cold weather could be taken as further evidence of mental illness

At Pennsylvania Station in New York, homeless women are denied the use of toilets. Amtrak police come by and herd them off each hour on the hour. In June 1985, Amtrak officials issued this directive to police: "It is the policy of Amtrak to not allow the homeless and undesirables to remain. . . . Officers are encouraged to eject all undesirables. . . . Now is the time to train and educate them that their presence will not be tolerated as cold weather sets in." In an internal memo, according to CBS, an Amtrak official asked flatly: "Can't we get rid of this trash?"

I have spent many nights in conversation with the women who are huddled in the corridors and near the doorway of the public toilets in Penn Station. Many are young. Most are cogent. Few are dressed in the familiar rags suggested by the term *bag ladies*. Unable to bathe or use the toilets in the station, almost all are in conditions of intolerable physical distress. The sight of clusters of police officers, mostly male, guarding a toilet from use by homeless women speaks volumes about the public conscience of New York.

Where do these women defecate? How do they bathe? What will we do when, in her physical distress, a woman finally disrobes in public and begins to urinate right on the floor? "Gross deterioration," someone will call it, evidence of mental illness. In the course of an impromptu survey in the streets last September, Mayor Koch observed a homeless woman who had soiled her own clothes. Not only was the woman crazy, said the mayor, but those who differed with him on his diagnosis must be crazy, too. "I am the number one social worker in this town—with sanity," said he.

It may be that this woman was psychotic, but the mayor's comment says a great deal more about his sense of revulsion and the moral climate of a decade in which words like these may be applauded than about her mental state.

A young man who had lost his job, then his family, then his home, all in the summer of 1986, spoke with me for several hours in Grand Central Station on the weekend following Thanksgiving. "A year ago," he said, "I never thought that somebody like me would end up in a shelter. Nothing you've ever undergone prepares you. You walk into the place [a shelter on the Bowery]—the smell of sweat and urine hits you like a wall. Unwashed bodies and the look of absolute despair on many, many faces there would make you think you were in Dante's Hell. . . . What you fear is that you will be here forever. You do not know if it is ever going to end. You think to yourself: It is a dream and I will awake. Sometimes I think: It's an experiment. They are watching you to find out how much you can take. . . . I was a pretty stable man. Now I tremble when I meet somebody in the ordinary world. I'm trembling right now. . . . For me, the loss of work and loss of wife had left me rocking. Then the welfare regulations hit me. I began to feel that I would be reduced to trash. . . . Half the people that I know are suffering from chest infections and sleep deprivation. The lack of sleep leaves you debilitated, shaky. You exaggerate your fears. If a psychiatrist came along he'd say that I was crazy. But I was an ordinary man. There was nothing wrong with me. I lost my kids. I lost my home. Now would you say that I was crazy if I told you I was feeling sad?"

44    "If the plight of homeless adults is the shame of America," writes Fred Hechinger in the *New York Times*, "the lives of homeless children are the nation's crime."

45    In November 1984, a fact already known to advocates for the homeless was given brief attention by the press. Homeless families, the *New York Times* reported, "mostly mothers and young children, have been sleeping on chairs, counters, and floors of the city's emergency welfare offices." Reacting to such reports, the mayor declared: "The woman is sitting on a chair or on a floor. It is not because we didn't offer her a bed. We provide a shelter for every single person who knocks on our door." On the same day, however, the city reported that in the previous 11 weeks it had been unable to give shelter to 153 families, and in the subsequent year, 1985, the city later reported that about 2,000 children slept in welfare offices because of lack of shelter space.

46    Some 800 homeless infants in New York City, reported the National Coalition for the Homeless, "routinely go without sufficient food, cribs, health care, and diapers." The lives of these children "are put at risk," while "high-risk pregnant women" are repeatedly forced to sleep in unsafe "barracks shelters" or welfare offices called Emergency Assistance Units (EAUs). "Coalition monitors, making sporadic random checks, found eight women in their *ninth* month of pregnancy sleeping in EAUs. . . . Two women denied shelter began having labor contractions at the EAU." In one instance, the Legal Aid Society was forced to go to court after a woman lost her child by miscarriage while lying on the floor of a communal bathroom in a shelter which the courts had already declared unfit to house pregnant women.

47    The coalition also reported numerous cases in which homeless mothers were obliged to choose between purchasing food or diapers for their infants. Federal guidelines issued in 1986 deepened the nutrition crisis faced by mothers in the welfare shelters by counting the high rent paid to the owners of the buildings as a part of family income, rendering their residents ineligible for food stamps. Families I interviewed who had received as much as $150 in food stamps monthly in June 1986 were cut back to $33 before Christmas.

48    "Now you're hearing all kinds of horror stories," said President Reagan, "about the people that are going to be thrown out in the snow to hunger and

[to] die of cold and so forth. . . . We haven't cut a single budget." But in the four years leading up to 1985, according to the *New Republic,* Aid to Families with Dependent Children had been cut by $4.8 billion, child nutrition programs by $5.2 billion, food stamps by $6.8 billion. The federal government's authority to help low-income families with housing assistance was cut from $30 billion to $11 billion in Reagan's first term. In his fiscal 1986 budget, the president proposed to cut that by an additional 95 percent.

"If even one American child is forced to go to bed hungry at night," the  49 president said on another occasion, "that is a national tragedy. We are too generous a people to allow this." But in the years since the president spoke these words, thousands of poor children in New York alone have gone to bed too sick to sleep and far too weak to rise the next morning to attend a public school. Thousands more have been unable to attend school at all because their homeless status compels them to move repeatedly from one temporary shelter to another. Even in the affluent suburbs outside New York City, hundreds of homeless children are obliged to ride as far as 60 miles twice a day in order to obtain an education in the public schools to which they were originally assigned before their families were displaced. Many of these children get to school too late to eat their breakfast; others are denied lunch at school because of federal cuts in feeding programs.

Many homeless children die—and others suffer brain damage—as a  50 direct consequence of federal cutbacks in prenatal programs, maternal nutrition, and other feeding programs. The parents of one such child shared with me the story of the year in which their child was delivered, lived, and died. The child, weighing just over four pounds at birth, grew deaf and blind soon after, and for these reasons had to stay in the hospital for several months. When he was released on Christmas Eve of 1984, his mother and father had no home. He lived with his parents in the shelters, subways, streets, and welfare offices of New York City for four winter months, and was readmitted to the hospital in time to die in May 1985.

When we met and spoke the following year, the father told me that his  51 wife had contemplated and even attempted suicide after the child's death, while he had entertained the thought of blowing up the welfare offices of New York City. I would tell him that to do so would be illegal and unwise. I would never tell him it was crazy.

"No one will be turned away," says the mayor of New York City, as  52 hundreds of young mothers with their infants are turned from the doors of shelters season after season. That may sound to some like denial of reality. "Now you're hearing all these stories," says the president of the United States as he denies that anyone is cold or hungry or unhoused. On another occasion he says that the unsheltered "are homeless, you might say, by choice." That sounds every bit as self-deceiving.

The woman standing on the traffic island screaming for revenge until  53 her room has been restored to her sounds relatively healthy by comparison.

If 3,000,000 homeless people did the same, and all at the same time, we might finally be forced to listen.

*1988*

## QUESTIONS FOR DISCUSSION

### Content

a. The author cites several examples of changes in public policy during the 1980s that contributed to increases in homelessness. Identify them.
b. What is the author's response to those who argue that mental illness precedes and is a major cause of homelessness?
c. How does he answer Dr. Ellen Bassuk's claim that advocates for the homeless have been unable to provide data to prove that these people are not "unwell" (paragraph 15)?
d. Summarize the arguments of those who advocate isolating the homeless from the rest of society. What do you think of such arguments? Do you agree or disagree? Why?
e. What examples does Kozol include to illustrate inconsistency in public policy and attitudes toward the homeless?
f. What examples of public denial does Kozol cite? Are these examples convincing? Why or why not?
g. Kozol has always been an advocate for children. In what way does this essay reflect that role?

### Strategy and Style

h. What use does Kozol make of rhetorical questions? Where can such questions be found in his essay?
i. Why does the author compare homelessness in America with homelessness in Haiti?
j. Why does Kozol compare the ways in which mental illness is viewed in the former Soviet Union and in the United States? What similarities does he note?
k. What elements or techniques associated with argumentation do you find in this essay? Where does Kozol use the cause-and-effect technique? Illustration?
l. Statistics can be powerful tools for writing. They make abstract ideas clearer and more convincing. Where in this essay does Kozol use statistical or numerical data?

m. Why does Kozol bring up the case of the young man he quotes in paragraph 43? Why does he tell us about the woman who stands in a traffic island in Manhattan (paragraph 34)? Would his essay have been more effective had he explained the effects of homelessness on the population as a whole?

## ENGAGING THE TEXT

a. "A misconception, once it is implanted in the popular imagination, is not easy to uproot, particularly when it serves a useful social role," Kozol says in paragraph 8. Explain how this statement might apply to any social problem other than homelessness.
b. In several instances, Kozol challenges the conventional perception of homelessness by picturing homeless people as sane while exposing the public policy governing them as quite the opposite. Find and discuss such instances.

## SUGGESTIONS FOR SUSTAINED WRITING

a. Isolate a section of this essay that argues a specific point about the nature of homelessness or about public policy toward the homeless. Then write an essay in which you defend or attack the opinion expressed in those paragraphs.
b. Read essays in this text by other authors who discuss poverty. For example, try Parker (Chapter 4), Ehrenreich and Hardin (Chapter 10), or Eighner (Chapter 11). Then explain how one or more of these authors might react to Kozol's arguments. What similarities or differences do you see in their ideas?
c. Using Kozol's organization as a general model, research a critical current issue about which you feel strongly. Begin by becoming familiar with the general background and parameters of the issue, making a list of questions you—and perhaps your readers—have about it. With your list as a guide, use library and Internet resources to find facts and statistics that answer those questions. Then, if possible, use the materials you have gathered thus far as the basis for interviews with local people involved in this issue. Finally, write your findings as a report with an argumentative bent.

# The Rules of the Game: Rodeo

Gretel Ehrlich

*Gretel Ehrlich (b. 1946) studied at Bennington College, UCLA Film School, and the New School for Social Research. She went to Wyoming to make a film documentary but stayed on and now lives there with her husband on a remote ranch, dividing her time between ranch work and writing. "I often write—notepad balanced on saddlehorn—gathering cattle," she says, "and when I'm in my writing room, . . . I often get up mid-sentence to fix a panel of fence or change an irrigation dam, or put a stray horse away. . . . Our ranch, and the entire ecosystem in which it lies, is my laboratory." For Ehrlich, this combination is essential to her writing, which is characterized by closely observed detail and moving images, a blending of the ordinary and the wondrous. A versatile writer, she has published poetry,* To Touch the Water *(1981); short stories,* Wyoming Stories *(1986) and* Drinking Dry Clouds *(1991); a novel,* Heart Mountain *(1988); a children's book,* A Blizzard Year: Timmy's Almanac of Seasons *(1999); a biography,* John Muir: Nature's Visionary *(2000); and essays,* The Solace of Open Spaces *(1986), from which "The Rules of the Game" is taken. Other essays by Ehrlich have appeared in the* New York Times, *the* Atlantic, Harper's, Sierra, *and* Antaeus.

1    Instead of honeymooning in Paris, Patagonia, or the Sahara as we had planned, my new husband and I drove through a series of blizzards to Oklahoma City. Each December the National Finals Rodeo is held in a modern, multistoried colosseum next to buildings that house banks and petroleum companies in a state whose flatness resembles a swimming pool filled not with water but with oil.

2    The National Finals is the "World Series of Professional Rodeo," where not only the best cowboys but also the most athletic horses and bucking stock compete. All year, rodeo cowboys have been vying for the honor to ride here. They've been to Houston, Las Vegas, Pendleton, Tucson, Cheyenne, San Francisco, Calgary; to as many as eighty rodeos in one season, sometimes making two or three on a day like the Fourth of July, and when the results are tallied up (in money won, not points) the top fifteen riders in each event are invited to Oklahoma City.

3    We climbed to our peanut gallery seats just as Miss Rodeo America, a lanky brunette swaddled in a lavender pantsuit, gloves, and cowboy hat, loped across the arena. There was a hush in the audience; all the hats swimming down in front of us, like buoys, steadied and turned toward the chutes. "Out of chute number three, Pat Linger, a young cowboy from Miles City, Montana, making his first appearance here on a little horse named Dillinger." And as fast as these words sailed across the colosseum, the first bareback horse bumped into the lights.

4    There's a traditional order to the four timed and three rough stock events that make up a rodeo program. Bareback riders are first, then steer

wrestlers, team ropers, saddle bronc riders, barrel racers, and finally, the bull riders.

After Pat Linger came Steve Dunham, J. C. Trujillo, Mickey Young, and    5
the defending champ, Bruce Ford on a horse named Denver. Bareback riders do just that: they ride a horse with no saddle, no halter, no rein, clutching only a handhold riveted into a girth that goes around the horse's belly. A bareback rider's loose style suggests a drunken, comic bout of love-making: he lies back on the horse and, with each jump and jolt, flops delightfully, like a libidinous Raggedy Andy, toes turned out, knees flexed, legs spread and pumping, back arched, the back of his hat bumping the horse's rump as if nodding, "Yes, let's do 'er again." My husband, who rode saddle broncs in amateur rodeos, explains it differently: "It's like riding a runaway bicycle down a steep hill and lying on your back; you can't see where you're going or what's going to happen next."

Now the steer wrestlers shoot out of the box on their own well-trained    6
horses: There is a hazer on the right to keep the steer running straight, the wrestler on the left, and the steer between them. When the wrestler is neck and neck with the animal, he slides sideways out of his saddle as if he's been stabbed in the ribs and reaches for the horns. He's airborne for a second; then his heels swing into the dirt, and with his arms around the horns, he skids to a stop twisting the steer's head to one side so the animal loses his balance and falls to the ground. It's a fast-paced game of catch with a thousand-pound ball of horned flesh.

The team ropers are next. Most of them hail from the hilly, oak-strewn    7
valleys of California where dally roping originated.[1] Ropers are the graceful technicians, performing their pas de deux (plus steer) with a precision that begins to resemble a larger clarity—an erudition. Header and heeler come out of the box at the same time, steer between them, but the header acts first: He ropes the horns of the steer, dallies up, turns off, and tries to position the steer for the heeler who's been tagging behind this duo, loop clasped in his armpit as if it were a hen. Then the heeler sets his generous, unsweeping loop free and double-hocks the steer. It's a complicated act which takes about six seconds. Concomitant with this speed and skill is a feminine grace: they don't clutch their stiff loop or throw it at the steer like a bag of dirty laundry the way I do, but hold it gently, delicately, as if it were a hoop of silk. One or two cranks and both arm and loop vault forward, one becoming an appendage of the other, as if the tendons and pulse that travel through the wrist had lengthened and spun forward like fishing line until the loop sails down on the twin horns, then up under the hocks like a repeated embrace that tightens at the end before it releases.

---

[1]The word dally is a corruption of the Spanish *da la vuelta,* meaning to take a turn, as with a rope around the saddle horn.

8        The classic event at rodeo is saddle bronc riding. The young men look as serious as academicians: They perch spryly on their high-kicking mounts, their legs flicking forward and back, "charging the point" "going back to the cantle" in a rapid, staccato rhythm. When the horse is at the high point of his buck and the cowboy is stretched out, legs spurring above the horse's shoulder, rein-holding arm straight as a board in front, and free hand lifted behind, horse and man look like a propeller. Even their dismounts can look aeronautical: springing off the back of the horse, they land on their feet with a flourish—hat still on—as if they had been ejected mechanically from a burning plane long before the crash.

9        Barrel racing is the one women's event. Where the men are tender in their movements, as elegant as if Balanchine had been their coach, the women are prodigies of Wayne Gretzky, all speed, bully, and grit. When they charge into the arena, their hats fly off; they ride brazenly, elbows, knees, feet fluttering, and by the time they've careened around the second of three barrels, the whip they've had clenched between their teeth is passed to a hand, and on the home stretch they urge the horse to the finish line.

10       Calf ropers are the whiz kids of rodeo: They're expert on the horse and on the ground, and their horses are as quick-witted. The cowboy emerges from the box with a loop in his hand, a piggin' string in his mouth, coils and reins in the other, and a network of slack line strewn so thickly over horse and rider, they look as if they'd run through a tangle of kudzu before arriving in the arena. After roping the calf and jerking the slack in the rope, he jumps off the horse, sprints down the length of nylon, which the horse keeps taut, throws the calf down, and ties three legs together with the piggin' string. It's said of Roy Cooper, the defending calf-roping champion, that "even with pins and metal plates in his arm, he's known for the fastest groundwork in the business; when he springs down his rope to flank the calf, the resulting action is pure rodeo poetry." The six or seven separate movements he makes are so fluid they look like one continual unfolding.

11       Bull riding is last, and of all the events it's the only one truly dangerous. Bulls are difficult to ride: They're broadbacked, loose-skinned, and powerful. They don't jump balletically the way a horse does; they jerk and spin, and if you fall off, they'll try to gore you with a horn, kick, or trample you. Bull riders are built like the animals they ride: Low to the ground and hefty. They're the tough men on the rodeo circuit, and the flirts. Two of the current champs are city men: Charlie Samson is a small, shy black from Watts, and Bobby Del Vecchio, a brash Italian from the Bronx who always throws the audience a kiss after a ride with a Catskill-like showmanship not usually seen here. What a bull rider lacks in technical virtuosity—you won't see the fast spurring action of a saddle bronc rider in this event—he makes up for in personal flamboyance, and because it's a deadlier game they're playing, you can see the belligerence rise up their necks and settle into their faces as the bull starts his

first spin. Besides the bull and the cowboy, there are three other men in the ring—the rodeo clowns—who aren't there to make children laugh but to divert the bull from some of his deadlier tricks, and, when the rider bucks off, jump between the two—like secret service men—to save the cowboy's life.

Rodeo, like baseball, is an American sport and has been around almost 12 as long. While Henry Chadwick was writing his first book of rules for the fledgling ball clubs in 1858, ranch hands were paying $25 a dare to a kid who would ride five outlaw horses from the rough string in a makeshift arena of wagons and carts. The first commercial rodeo in Wyoming was held in Lander in 1895, just nineteen years after the National League was formed. Baseball was just as popular as bucking and roping contests in the West, but no one in Cooperstown, New York, was riding broncs. And that's been part of the problem. After 124 years, rodeo is still misunderstood. Unlike baseball, it's a regional sport (although they do have rodeos in New Jersey, Florida, and other eastern states); it's derived from and stands for the western way of life and the western spirit. It doesn't have the universal appeal of a sport contrived solely for the competition and winning; there is no ball bandied about between opposing players.

Rodeo is the wild child of ranch work and embodies some of what 13 ranching is all about. Horsemanship—not gunslinging—was the pride of western men, and the chivalrous ethics they formulated, known as the western code, became the ground rules for every human game. Two great partnerships are celebrated in this Oklahoma arena: The indispensable one between man and animal that any rancher or cowboy takes on, enduring the joys and punishments of the alliance; and the one between man and man, cowboy and cowboy.

Though rodeo is an individualist's sport, it has everything to do with 14 teamwork. The cowboy who "covers" his bronc (stays on the full eight seconds) has become a team with that animal. The cowboys' competitive feelings amongst each other are so mixed with western tact as to appear ambivalent. When Bruce Ford, the bareback rider, won a go-round he said, "The hardest part of winning this year was taking it away from one of my best friends, Mickey Young, after he'd worked so hard all year." Stan Williamson, who'd just won the steer wrestling, said, "I just drew a better steer. I didn't want Butch to get a bad one. I just got lucky, I guess."

Ranchers, when working together, can be just as diplomatic. They'll 15 apologize if they cut in front of someone while cutting out a calf, and their thanks to each other at the end of the day has a formal sound. Like those westerners who still help each other out during branding and roundup, rodeo cowboys help each other in the chutes. A bull rider will steady the saddle bronc rider's horse, help measure out the rein or set the saddle, and a bareback rider might help the bull rider set his rigging and pull his rope. Ropers lend each other horses, as do barrel racers and steer wrestlers. This isn't a show they put on; they offer their help with the utmost goodwill and good-naturedness. Once, when a bucking horse fell over backward in the chute with my husband, his friend H. A., who rode bulls, jumped into the chute and pulled him out safely.

16    Another part of the "westernness" rodeo represents is the drifting cowboys do. They're on the road much of their lives the way turn-of-the-century cowboys were on the trail, but these cowboys travel in style if they can—driving pink Lincolns and new pickups with a dozen fresh shirts hanging behind the driver, and the radio on.

17    Some ranchers look down on the sport of rodeo; they don't want these "drugstore cowboys" getting all the attention and glory. Besides, rodeo seems to have less and less to do with real ranch work. Who ever heard of gathering cows on a bareback horse with no bridle, or climbing on a herd bull? Ranchers are generalists—they have to know how to do many things—from juggling the futures market to overhauling a tractor or curing viral scours (diarrhea) in calves—while rodeo athletes are specialists. Deep down, they probably feel envious of each other: The rancher for the praise and big money; the rodeo cowboy for the stay-at-home life among animals to which their sport only alludes.

18    People with no ranching background have even more difficulty with the sport. Every ride goes so fast, it's hard to see just what happened, and perhaps because of the Hollywood mythologizing of the West which distorted rather than distilled western rituals, rodeo is often considered corny, anachronistic, and cruel to animals. Quite the opposite is true. Rodeo cowboys are as sophisticated athletically as Bjorn Borg or Fernando Valenzuela. That's why they don't need to be from a ranch anymore, or to have grown up riding horses. And to undo another myth, rodeo is not cruel to animals. Compared to the arduous life of any "using horse" on a cattle or dude ranch, a bucking horse leads the life of Riley. His actual work load for an entire year, i.e., the amount of time he spends in the arena, totals approximately 4.6 minutes, and nothing done to him in the arena or out could in any way be called cruel. These animals aren't bludgeoned into bucking; they love to buck. They're bred to behave this way, they're athletes whose ability has been nurtured and encouraged. Like the cowboys who compete at the National Finals, the best bulls and horses from all the bucking strings in the country are nominated to appear in Oklahoma, winning money along with their riders to pay their own way.

19    The National Finals run ten nights. Every contestant rides every night, so it is easy to follow their progress and setbacks. One evening we abandoned our rooftop seats and sat behind the chutes to watch the saddle broncs ride. Behind the chutes two cowboys are rubbing rosin—part of their staying power—behind the saddle swells and on their Easter-egg-colored chaps which are pink, blue, and light green with white fringe. Up above, standing on the chute rungs, the stock contractors direct horse traf-

fic: "Velvet Drums" in chute #3, "Angel Sings" in #5, "Rusty" in #1. Rick Smith, Monty Henson, Bobby Berger, Brad Gjermudson, Mel Coleman, and friends climb the chutes. From where I'm sitting, it looks like a field hospital with five separate operating theaters, the cowboys, like surgeons, bent over their patients with sweaty brows and looks of concern. Horses are being haltered; cowboys are measuring out the long, braided reins, saddles are set: One cowboy pulls up on the swells again and again, repositioning his hornless saddle until it sits just right. When the chute boss nods to him and says, "Pull 'em up, boys," the ground crew tightens front and back cinches on the first horse to go, but very slowly so he won't panic in the chute as the cowboy eases himself down over the saddle, not sitting on it, just hovering there. "Okay, you're on." The chute boss nods to him again. Now he sits on the saddle, taking the rein in one hand, holding the top of the chute with the other. He flips the loose bottoms of his chaps over his shins, puts a foot in each stirrup, takes a breath, and nods. The chute gate swings open releasing a flood—not of water, but of flesh, groans, legs kicking. The horse lunges up and out in the first big jump like a wave breaking whose crest the cowboy rides, "marking out the horse," spurs well above the bronc's shoulders. In that first second under the lights, he finds what will be the rhythm of the ride. Once again he "charges the point," his legs pumping forward, then so far back his heels touch behind the cantle. For a moment he looks as though he were kneeling on air, then he's stretched out again, his whole body taut but released, free hand waving in back of his head like a palm frond, rein-holding hand thrust forward: *"En garde!"* he seems to be saying, but he's airborne; he looks like a wing that has sprouted suddenly from the horse's broad back. Eight seconds. The whistle blows. He's covered the horse. Now two gentlemen dressed in white chaps and satin shirts gallop beside the bucking horse. The cowboy hands the rein to one and grabs the waist of the other—the flank strap on the bronc has been undone, so all three horses move at a run—and the pickup man from whom the cowboy is now dangling slows almost to a stop, letting him slide to his feet on the ground.

Rick Smith from Wyoming rides, looking pale and nervous in his 20 white shirt. He's bucked off and so are the brash Monty "Hawkeye" Henson, and Butch Knowles, and Bud Pauley, but with such grace and aplomb, there is no shame. Bobby Berger, an Oklahoma cowboy, wins the go-round with a score of 83.

By the end of the evening we're tired, but in no way as exhausted as 21 these young men who have ridden night after night. "I've never been so sore and had so much fun in my life," one first-time bull rider exclaims breathlessly. When the performance is over we walk across the street to the chic lobby of a hotel chock full of cowboys. Wives hurry through the crowd with freshly ironed shirts for tomorrow's ride, ropers carry their rope bags with them into the coffee shop, which is now filled with contestants, eating mild midnight suppers of scrambled eggs, their numbers hanging crookedly on their backs, their faces powdered with dust, and looking at this late hour prematurely old.

22      We drive back to the motel, where, the first night, they'd "never heard of us" even though we'd had reservations for a month. "Hey, it's our honeymoon," I told the night clerk and showed him the white ribbons my mother had tied around our duffel bag. He looked embarrassed, then surrendered another latecomer's room.

23      The rodeo finals in Oklahoma may be a better place to honeymoon than Paris. All week, we've observed some important rules of the game. A good rodeo, like a good marriage, or a musical instrument when played to the pitch of perfection, becomes more than what it started out to be. It is effort transformed into effortlessness; a balance becomes grace, the way love goes deep into friendship.

24      In the rough stock events such as the one we watched tonight, there is no victory over the horse or bull. The point of the match is not conquest but communion: The rhythm of two beings becoming one. Rodeo is not a sport of opposition; there is no scrimmage line here. No one bears malice— neither the animals, the stock contractors, nor the contestants; no one wants to get hurt. In this match of equal talents, it is only acceptance, surrender, respect, and spiritedness that make for the midair union of cowboy and horse. Not a bad thought when starting out fresh in a marriage.

*1985*

## QUESTIONS FOR DISCUSSION

### Content

a. What two great partnerships are celebrated in the rodeo arena?

b. Ehrlich uses two similes for bareback riding in paragraph 5. What is the main difference between the two? Why are they both apt similes?

c. Why is rodeo a particularly American sport? What is the "western code" mentioned in paragraph 13?

d. What myths about the rodeo does the author attempt to dispel? Are her arguments convincing?

e. The events she describes in paragraphs 5 through 11 happen in a matter of seconds, but they are slowed down by her description of each step in the process. Is she successful at recreating these brief events? Why or why not?

f. In the same paragraphs, Ehrlich describes only the parts of the events that actually get judged. For example, she leaves out what happens immediately after the steer wrestlers throw the steers to the ground. What does stopping these events in mid-action add to her essay?

g. In paragraph 10, what did the unidentified speaker mean when he called Roy Copper's skill "rodeo poetry"?

h. Why is rodeo a misunderstood sport (paragraph 12)? In what way do people misunderstand it?

i. What is the distinction Ehrlich makes between rodeo athletes and ranchers? How does this distinction help her explain rodeo?

## Strategy and Style

j. Why does Ehrlich include the names of so many actual rodeo cowboys?

k. What does the author mean by saying that an erudition is a "larger clarity" (paragraph 7)? What is it a larger clarity of?

l. Process writers often rely on analogies. Where in this essay do analogies appear, and in what way do they help Ehrlich achieve her purpose? What other methods of development does she use?

m. Do you find the essay's introduction appropriate? Why or why not?

## ENGAGING THE TEXT

a. Ehrlich's love for the rodeo and its people is obvious. Do about ten minutes of freewriting about a sport, game, or other activity you "love," such as baseball, soccer, tennis, chess, reading, acting, going to the movies, cooking, or repairing old cars. After you complete this assignment, write a sentence that explains the one thing you love most about this activity.

b. In Ehrlich's opinion, what do rodeo and marriages have in common? Explain why a trip to the National Rodeo Finals makes a particularly good honeymoon for Ehrlich and her husband.

## SUGGESTIONS FOR SUSTAINED WRITING

a. Explain a fast-moving, complicated sport or activity. Attempt to make your explanation evocative enough to recreate the event *in action* in your reader's mind.

b. Compare the views of marriage discussed or implied by Ehrlich as well as Maxine Hong Kingston in "No Name Woman" (Chapter 1), Joan Didion in "Marrying Absurd" (Chapter 2), Nancy Mairs in "On Being a

Cripple" (Chapter 4), Deborah Tannen in "Talk in the Intimate Relationship" (Chapter 6), or Judy Brady in "Why I Want a Wife" (Chapter 10).

c. Explain another quintessential American sport, communal activity, or job. Make sure to tell your readers what makes the sport "American." If you know of a related foreign sport or activity, compare and contrast it with your topic in order to point out its American elements.

Or dispel the myths about a sport or job. For example, explain one or two reasons that ballet is definitely not for weaklings, that football players can be sensitive, or that women can make good police officers.

# Mother Tongue

Amy Tan

*Amy Tan (b. 1952) studied at San Jose State University, earning a BA in 1973 and an MA in 1974, and did postgraduate work at the University of California–Berkeley from 1974 to 1976. From 1976 to 1987 she worked in San Francisco in various jobs: as a language consultant to programs for disabled children from 1976 to 1981; as the project director for the MORE Project in 1980 and 1981; as a reporter, managing editor, and associate publisher for* Emergency Room Reports *from 1981 to 1983; and as a freelance technical writer from 1983 to 1987. Realizing that she had become a "workaholic," Tan began therapy to deal with the problem. Unfortunately (or perhaps fortunately), her therapist tended to fall asleep during their sessions. Disgusted, Tan turned to herself for therapy, taking jazz piano lessons and beginning to write fiction as a way to slow down. Her enormously successful novel* The Joy Luck Club *(1989) was the result of this "therapy" and the start of a literary career. Since then, Tan has published novels—*The Kitchen God's Wife *(1991),* The Hundred Secret Senses *(1995),* The Year of the Flood *(1995), and* The Bonesetter's Daughter *(2001)—and children's books—*The Moon Lady *(1992) and* The Chinese Siamese Cat *(1994). In addition, she has written short stories and essays for various magazines.*

1   I am not a scholar of English or literature. I cannot give you much more than personal opinions on the English language and its variations in this country or others,

2      I am a writer. And by that definition, I am someone who has always loved language. I am fascinated by language in daily life. I spend a great deal of my time thinking about the power of language—the way it can evoke an emotion, a visual image, a complex idea, or a simple truth. Language is the tool of my trade. And I use them all—all the Englishes I grew up with.

Recently, I was made keenly aware of the different Englishes I do use. 3
I was giving a talk to a large group of people, the same talk I had already
given to half a dozen other groups. The nature of the talk was about my
writing, my life, and my book *The Joy Luck Club*. The talk was going along
well enough, until I remembered one major difference that made the
whole talk sound wrong. My mother was in the room. And it was perhaps
the first time she had heard me give a lengthy speech, using the kind of
English I have never used with her. I was saying things like, "The intersection of memory upon imagination" and "There is an aspect of my fiction that relates to thus-and-thus"—a speech filled with carefully wrought
grammatical phrases, burdened, it suddenly seemed to me, with nominal-
ized forms, past perfect tenses, conditional phrases, all the forms of standard English that I had learned in school and through books, the forms of
English I did not use at home with my mother.

Just last week, I was walking down the street with my mother, and I 4
again found myself conscious of the English I was using, the English I do
use with her. We were talking about the price of new and used furniture
and I heard myself saying this: "Not waste money that way." My husband
was with us as well, and he didn't notice any switch in my English. And
then I realized why. It's because over the twenty years we've been together
I've often used that same kind of English with him, and sometimes he even
uses it with me. It has become our language of intimacy, a different sort of
English that relates to family talk, the language I grew up with.

So you'll have some idea of what this family talk I heard sounds like, 5
I'll quote what my mother said during a recent conversation which I
videotaped and then transcribed. During this conversation, my mother
was talking about a political gangster in Shanghai who had the same last
name as her family's, Du, and how the gangster in his early years wanted
to be adopted by her family, which was rich by comparison. Later, the
gangster became more powerful, far richer than my mother's family, and
one day showed up at my mother's wedding to pay his respects. Here's
what she said in part:

"Du Yusong having business like fruit stand. Like off the street kind. 6
He is Du like Du Zong—but not Tsung-ming Island people. The local people call putong, the river east side, he belong to that side local people. That
man want to ask Du Zong father take him in like become own family. Du
Zong father wasn't look down on him, but didn't take seriously, until that
man big like become a mafia. Now important person, very hard to inviting him. Chinese way, came only to show respect, don't stay for dinner. Respect for making big celebration, he shows up. Mean gives lots of respect.
Chinese custom. Chinese social life that way. If too important won't have
to stay too long. He come to my wedding. I didn't see, I heard it. I gone to
boy's side, they have YMCA dinner. Chinese age I was nineteen."

7    You should know that my mother's expressive command of English belies how much she actually understands. She reads the *Forbes* report, listens to *Wall Street Week,* converses daily with her stockbroker, reads all of Shirley MacLaine's books with ease—all kinds of things I can't begin to understand. Yet some of my friends tell me they understand 50 percent of what my mother says. Some say they understand 80 to 90 percent. Some say they understand none of it, as if she was speaking pure Chinese. But to me, my mother's English is perfectly clear, perfectly natural. It's my mother tongue. Her language, as I hear it, is vivid, direct, full of observation and imagery. That was the language that helped shape the way I saw things, expressed things, made sense of the world.

8    Lately, I've been giving more thought to the kind of English my mother speaks. Like others, I have described it to people as "broken" or "fractured" English. But I wince when I say that. It has always bothered me that I can think of no way to describe it other than "broken," as if it were damaged and needed to be fixed, as if it lacked a certain wholeness and soundness. I've heard other terms used, "limited English," for example. But they seem just as bad, as if everything is limited, including people's perceptions of the limited English speaker.

9    I know this for a fact, because when I was growing up, my mother's "limited" English limited *my* perception of her. I was ashamed of her English. I believed that her English reflected the quality of what she had to say. That is, because she expressed them imperfectly her thoughts were imperfect. And I had plenty of empirical evidence to support me: the fact that people in department stores, at banks, and at restaurants did not take her seriously, did not give her good service, pretended not to understand her, or even acted as if they did not hear her.

10    My mother has long realized the limitations of her English as well. When I was fifteen, she used to have me call people on the phone to pretend I was she. In this guise, I was forced to ask for information or even to complain and yell at people who had been rude to her. One time it was a call to her stockbroker in New York. She had cashed out her small portfolio and it just so happened we were going to go to New York the next week, our very first trip outside California. I had to get on the phone and say in an adolescent voice that was not very convincing, "This is Mrs. Tan."

11    And my mother was standing in the back whispering loudly, "Why he don't send me check, already two weeks late. So mad he lie to me, losing me money."

12    And then I said in perfect English, "Yes, I'm getting rather concerned. You had agreed to send the check two weeks ago, but it hasn't arrived."

13    Then she began to talk more loudly. "What he want, I come to New York tell him front of his boss, you cheating me?" And I was trying to calm her down, make her be quiet, while telling the stockbroker, "I can't tolerate any

more excuses. If I don't receive the check immediately, I am going to have to speak to your manager when I'm in New York next week." And sure enough, the following week there we were in front of this astonished stockbroker, and I was sitting there red-faced and quiet, and my mother, the real Mrs. Tan, was shouting at his boss in her impeccable broken English.

We used a similar routine just five days ago, for a situation that was far 14 less humorous. My mother had gone to the hospital for an appointment, to find out about a benign brain tumor a CAT scan had revealed a month ago. She said she had spoken very good English, her best English, no mistakes. Still, she said, the hospital did not apologize when they said they had lost the CAT scan and she had come for nothing. She said they did not seem to have any sympathy when she told them she was anxious to know the exact diagnosis, since her husband and son had both died of brain tumors. She said they would not give her any more information until the next time and she would have to make another appointment for that. So she said she would not leave until the doctor called her daughter. She wouldn't budge. And when the doctor finally called her daughter, me, who spoke in perfect English—lo and behold—we had assurances the CAT scan would be found, promises that a conference call on Monday would be held, and apologies for any suffering my mother had gone through for a most regrettable mistake.

I think my mother's English almost had an effect on limiting my possi- 15 bilities in life as well. Sociologists and linguists probably will tell you that a person's developing language skills are more influenced by peers. But I do think that the language spoken in the family, especially in immigrant families which are more insular, plays a large role in shaping the language of the child. And I believe that it affected my results on achievements tests, IQ tests, and the SAT. While my English skills were never judged as poor, compared to math, English could not be considered my strong suit. In grade school I did moderately well, getting perhaps B's, sometimes B-pluses, in English and scoring perhaps in the sixtieth or seventieth percentile on achievement tests. But those scores were not good enough to override the opinion that my true abilities lay in math and science, because in those areas I achieved A's and scored in the ninetieth percentile or higher.

This was understandable. Math is precise; there is only one correct an- 16 swer. Whereas, for me at least, the answers on English tests were always a judgment call, a matter of opinion and personal experience. Those tests were constructed around items like fill-in-the-blank sentence completion, such as: "Even though Tom was _ _____, Mary thought he was _____." And the correct answer always seemed to be the most bland combinations of thoughts, for example, "Even though Tom was shy, Mary thought he was charming," with the grammatical structure "even though" limiting the correct answer to some sort of semantic opposites, so you wouldn't get answers like, "Even though Tom was foolish, Mary thought he was ridiculous." Well, according to my mother, there were very few limitations as to what Tom could have been and what Mary might have thought of him. So I never did well on tests like that.

17    The same was true with word analogies, pairs of words in which you were supposed to find some sort of logical, semantic relationship—for example, "*Sunset* is to *nightfall* as _____ is to _____." And here you would be presented with a list of our possible pairs, one of which showed the same kind of relationship: *red* is to *stoplight*, *bus* is to *arrival*, *chills* is to *fever*, *yawn* is to *boring*. Well, I could never think that way. I knew what the tests were asking, but I could not block out of my mind the images already created by the first pair, "*sunset* is to *nightfall*"—and I would see a burst of colors against a darkening sky, the moon rising, the lowering of a curtain of stars. And all the other pairs of words—red, bus, stoplight, boring—just threw up a mass of confusing images, making it impossible for me to sort out something as logical as saying: "A sunset precedes nightfall" is the same as "a chill precedes a fever." The only way I would have gotten that answer right would have been to imagine an associative situation, for example, my being disobedient and staying out past sunset, catching a chill at night, which turns into feverish pneumonia as punishment, which indeed did happen to me.

18    I have been thinking about all this lately, about my mother's English, about achievement tests. Because lately I've been asked, as a writer, why there are not more Asian Americans represented in American literature. Why are there few Asian Americans enrolled in creative writing programs? Why do so many Chinese students go into engineering? Well, these are broad sociological questions I can't begin to answer. But I have noticed in surveys—in fact, just last week—that Asian students, as a whole, always do significantly better on math achievement tests than in English. And this makes me think that there are other Asian-American students whose English spoken in the home might also be described as "broken" or "limited." And perhaps they also have teachers who are steering them away from writing and into math and science, which is what happened to me.

19    Fortunately, I happen to be rebellious in nature and enjoy the challenge of disproving assumptions made about me. I became an English major my first year in college, after being enrolled as premed. I started writing nonfiction as a freelancer the week after I was told by my former boss that writing was my worst skill and I should hone my talents toward account management.

20    But it wasn't until 1985 that I finally began to write fiction. And at first I wrote using what I thought to be wittily crafted sentences, sentences that would finally prove I had mastery over the English language. Here's an example from the first draft of a story that later made its way into *The Joy Luck Club*, but without this line: "That was my mental quandary in its nascent state." A terrible line, which I can barely pronounce.

Fortunately, for reasons I won't get into today, I later decided I should   21
envision a reader for the stories I would write. And the reader I decided
upon was my mother, because these were stories about mothers. So with
this reader in mind—and in fact she did read my early drafts—I began to
write stories using all the Englishes I grew up with: the English I spoke to
my mother, which for lack of a better term might be described as "simple";
the English she used with me, which for lack of a better term might be described as "broken"; my translation of her Chinese, which could certainly
be described as "watered down"; and what I imagined to be her translation of her Chinese if she could speak in perfect English, her internal language, and for that I sought to preserve the essence, but neither an English
nor a Chinese structure. I wanted to capture what language ability tests
can never reveal: her intent, her passion, her imagery, the rhythms of her
speech and the nature of her thoughts.

Apart from what any critic had to say about my writing, I knew I had   22
succeeded where it counted when my mother finished reading my book
and gave me her verdict: "So easy to read."

*1990*

## QUESTIONS FOR DISCUSSION

### Content

a. How does Tan define a *writer* (paragraph 2)? How does this definition
   compare with other definitions you have heard?
b. What are "the different Englishes" (paragraph 3) that Tan and her
   mother use in their public and private lives? What differentiates each
   type of English from the others?
c. In what ways does Tan's public English contrast with her mother's pub
   lic English? Why would two women so closely related have such different public "Englishes"?
d. What influence has her mother had on Tan's writing? Describe Tan's
   mother's type of English. Why does calling it "broken" (paragraph 8)
   make Tan wince?
e. Why did Tan not do well on language tests? How did her "mother
   tongue" contribute to her not doing well?
f. How did Tan train herself to write literary English?

## Strategy and Style

g. What rhetorical strategies does Tan use, and where are they most apparent in the essay? What might be her reason for choosing these strategies? How effectively does she use them?

h. How would you describe the style of this essay? What type of English is it? What terms or phrases illustrate the type of English it is?

i. Are the examples of her mother's Englishes effective ones? Why or why not?

j. "Mother Tongue" was first published in *Threepenny Review,* a literary journal. How does Tan craft her essay for the type of people who read literary journals? How would they respond to her essay? How might Tan's mother react to it?

## ENGAGING THE TEXT

a. Describe the Englishes (or other languages) that you grew up speaking or now use. How does the way you speak with your family differ from the way you speak with your teachers, coworkers, and friends? Refer to Tan's essay in your response.

b. Write your definition of *writer.* You can begin with Tan's definition and expand it, making it more specific, adding examples, and so forth.

## SUGGESTIONS FOR SUSTAINED WRITING

a. Write an essay combining the strategies of narrative and example or narrative and definition. Possible topics are stories about your family or friends, especially a difference between you and a family member or between you and a friend.

b. Compare Tan's essay to N. Scott Momaday's "The Way to Rainy Mountain" (Chapter 2). Discuss the relationship that the younger person has toward her and his elders and the attitudes they have toward the culture of their ancestors.

Or read Tan's novel *The Joy Luck Club,* or a part of it, and identify the Englishes used in the book that Tan describes in paragraph 21. Write an essay discussing how these Englishes help or hinder those who speak or write them.

c. Do research into another version or dialect of English, such as ebonics, Gullah, or Creole. Write an essay tracing the history and explaining the current status of this other type of English. Explore the historical and political relationship of the dialect to standard English.

# On Seeing England for the First Time

Jamaica Kincaid

*Jamaica Kincaid (b. 1949) was born Elaine Potter Richardson in St. John, Antigua. She emigrated to the United States in 1965, coming to Westchester, New York, where she worked as an au pair before studying photography at the New School for Social Research. Later, she studied at Franconia College in New Hampshire and then returned to New York, becoming a staff writer for the* New Yorker *in 1976 and continuing to work there until 1995. She changed her name in 1973 when her first articles were published, because her family did not approve of her writing. Her books include, among others,* At the Bottom of the River *(1983),* Annie John *(1985),* A Small Place *(1988),* Lucy *(1990),* Autobiography of My Mother *(1996), and* My Brother *(1997). She currently lives in Bennington, Vermont.*

When I saw England for the first time, I was a child in school sitting at a 1
desk. The England I was looking at was laid out on a map gently, beautifully, delicately, a very special jewel; it lay on a bed of sky blue—the background of the map—its yellow form mysterious, because though it looked like a leg of mutton, it could not really look like anything so familiar as a leg of mutton because it was England—with shadings of pink and green, unlike any shadings of pink and green I had seen before, squiggly veins of red running in every direction. England was a special jewel all right, and only special people got to wear it. The people who got to wear England were English people. They wore it well and they wore it everywhere: in jungles, in deserts, on plains, on top of the highest mountains, on all the oceans, on all the seas, in places where they were not welcome, in places they should not have been. When my teacher had pinned this map up on the blackboard, she said, "This is England"—and she said it with authority, seriousness, and adoration, and we all sat up. It was as if she had said, "This is Jerusalem, the place you will go to when you die but only if you have been good." We understood then—we were meant to understand then—that England was to be our source of myth and the source from which we got our sense of reality, our sense of what was meaningful, our sense of what was meaningless—and much about our own lives and much about the very idea of us headed that last list.

At the time I was a child sitting at my desk seeing England for the first 2
time, I was already very familiar with the greatness of it. Each morning before I left for school, I ate a breakfast of half a grapefruit, an egg, bread and butter and a slice of cheese, and a cup of cocoa; or half a grapefruit, a bowl of oat porridge, bread and butter and a slice of cheese, and a cup of cocoa. The can of cocoa was often left on the table in front of me. It had written on it the name of the company, the year the company was established, and the words "Made in England." Those words, "Made in England," were

written on the box the oats came in too. They would also have been written on the box the shoes I was wearing came in; a bolt of gray linen cloth
lying on the shelf of a store from which my mother had bought three yards
to make the uniform that I was wearing had written along its edge those
three words. The shoes I wore were made in England; so were my socks
and cotton undergarments and the satin ribbons I wore tied at the end of
two plaits of my hair. My father, who might have sat next to me at breakfast, was a carpenter and cabinet maker. The shoes he wore to work would
have been made in England, as were his khaki shirt and trousers, his un-
derpants and undershirt, his socks and brown felt hat. Felt was not the
proper material from which a hat that was expected to provide shade from
the hot sun should be made, but my father must have seen and admired a
picture of an Englishman wearing such a hat in England, and this picture
that he saw must have been so compelling that it caused him to wear the
wrong hat for a hot climate most of his long life. And this hat—a brown felt
hat—became so central to his character that it was the first thing he put on
in the morning as he stepped out of bed and the last thing he took off before he stepped back into bed at night. As we sat at breakfast a car might
go by. The car, a Hillman or a Zephyr, was made in England. The very idea
of the meal itself, breakfast, and its substantial quality and quantity was an
idea from England; we somehow knew that in England they began the day
with this meal called breakfast and a proper breakfast was a big breakfast.
No one I knew liked eating so much food so early in the day; it made us
feel sleepy, tired. But this breakfast business was Made in England like almost everything else that surrounded us, the exceptions being the sea, the
sky, and the air we breathed.

3       At the time I saw this map—seeing England for the first time—I did
not say to myself, "Ah, so that's what it looks like," because there was no
longing in me to put a shape to those three words that ran through every
part of my life, no matter how small; for me to have had such a longing
would have meant that I lived in a certain atmosphere, an atmosphere in
which those three words were felt as a burden. But I did not live in such an
atmosphere. My father's brown felt hat would develop a hole in its crown,
the lining would separate from the hat itself, and six weeks before he
thought that he could not be seen wearing it—he was a very vain man—
he would order another hat from England. And my mother taught me to
eat my food in the English way: the knife in the right hand, the fork in the
left, my elbows held still close to my side, the food carefully balanced on
my fork and then brought up to my mouth. When I had finally mastered
it, I overheard her saying to a friend, "Did you see how nicely she can eat?"
But I knew then that I enjoyed my food more when I ate it with my bare
hands, and I continued to do so when she wasn't looking. And when my
teacher showed us the map, she asked us to study it carefully, because no

test we would ever take would be complete without this statement: "Draw a map of England."

I did not know then that the statement "Draw a map of England"  4 was something far worse than a declaration of war, for in fact a flat-out declaration of war would have put me on alert, and again in fact, there was no need for war—I had long ago been conquered. I did not know then that this statement was part of a process that would result in my erasure, not my physical erasure, but my erasure all the same. I did not know then that this statement was meant to make me feel in awe and small whenever I heard the word "England": awe at its existence, small because I was not from it. I did not know very much of anything then— certainly not what a blessing it was that I was unable to draw a map of England correctly.

After that there were many times of seeing England for the first time.  5 I saw England in history. I knew the names of all the kings of England. I knew the names of their children, their wives, their disappointments, their triumphs, the names of people who betrayed them, I knew the dates on which they were born and the dates they died. I knew their conquests and was made to feel glad if I figured in them; I knew their defeats. I knew the details of the year 1066 (the Battle of Hastings, the end of the reign of the Anglo-Saxon kings) before I knew the details of the year 1832 (the year slavery was abolished). It wasn't as bad as I make it sound now; it was worse. I did like so much hearing again and again how Alfred the Great, traveling in disguise, had been left to watch cakes, and because he wasn't used to this the cakes got burned, and Alfred burned his hands pulling them out of the fire, and the woman who had left him to watch the cakes screamed at him. I loved King Alfred. My grandfather was named after him; his son, my uncle, was named after King Alfred; my brother is named after King Alfred. And so there are three people in my family named after a man they have never met, a man who died over ten centuries ago. The first view I got of England then was not unlike the first view received by the person who named my grandfather.

This view, though—the naming of the kings, their deeds, their disap-  6 pointments—was the vivid view, the forceful view. There were other views, subtler ones, softer, almost not there—but these were the ones that made the most lasting impression on me, these were the ones that made me really feel like nothing. "When morning touched the sky" was one phrase, for no morning touched the sky where I lived. The mornings where I lived came on abruptly, with a shock of heat and loud noises. "Evening approaches" was another, but the evening where I lived did not approach; in fact, I had no evening—I had night and I had day and they came and went in a mechanical way: on, off; on, off. And then there were gentle mountains and low blue skies and moors over which people took walks for nothing but pleasure, when where I lived a walk was an act of labor, a burden, something only death or the automobile could relieve. And there were things that a small turn of a head could convey—entire worlds, whole lives would depend on this thing, a certain turn of a head. Everyday life could be quite tiring, more tiring than anything I was told not to do. I was told not to gossip, but they did that all the time. And they ate so much food, violating another of those rules they taught me: do not indulge in gluttony. And the foods they ate actually: if only sometime I could eat cold cuts after theater, cold cuts of lamb and mint sauce, and Yorkshire pudding and scones, and clotted cream, and sausages that came from upcountry (imagine, "up-country"). And having troubling thoughts at twilight, a good time to have troubling thoughts, apparently; and ser-vants who stole and left in the middle of a crisis, who were born with a limp or some other kind of deformity, not nourished properly in their mother's womb (that last part I figured out for myself; the point was, oh to have an untrustworthy servant); and wonderful cobbled streets onto which solid front doors opened; and people whose eyes were blue and who had fair skins and who smelled only of lavender, or sometimes sweet pea or primrose. And those flowers with those names: delphiniums, fox-gloves, tulips, daffodils, floribunda, peonies; in bloom, a striking display, being cut and placed in large glass bowls, crystal, decorating rooms so large twenty families the size of mine could fit in comfortably but used only for passing through. And the weather was so remarkable because the rain fell gently always, only occasionally in deep gusts, and it colored the air various shades of gray, each an appealing shade for a dress to be worn when a portrait was being painted; and when it rained at twilight, won-derful things happened: people bumped into each other unexpectedly and that would lead to all sorts of turns of events—a plot, the mere weather caused plots. I saw that people rushed: they rushed to catch trains, they rushed toward each other and away from each other; they rushed and rushed and rushed. That word: rushed! I did not know what it was to do that. I was too hot to do that, and so I came to envy people who would rush, even though it had no meaning to me to do such a thing. But there they are again. They loved their children; their children were sent to their own rooms as a punishment, rooms larger than my entire house. They were special, everything about them said so, even their clothes; their clothes rustled, swished, soothed. The world was theirs, not mine; every-thing told me so.

7        If now as I speak of all this I give the impression of someone on the outside looking in, nose pressed up against a glass window, that is wrong. My nose was pressed up against a glass window all right, but there was an iron vise at the back of my neck forcing my head to stay in place. To avert my gaze was to fall back into something from which I had been rescued, a hole filled with nothing, and that was the word for everything about me,

nothing. The reality of my life was conquests, subjugation, humiliation, enforced amnesia. I was forced to forget. Just for instance, this: I lived in a part of St. John's, Antigua, called Ovals. Ovals was made up of five streets, each of them named after a famous English seaman—to be quite frank, an officially sanctioned criminal: Rodney Street (after George Rodney), Nelson Street (after Horatio Nelson), Drake Street (after Francis Drake), Hood Street, and Hawkins Street (after John Hawkins). But John Hawkins was knighted after a trip he made to Africa, opening up a new trade, the slave trade. He was then entitled to wear as his crest a Negro bound with a cord. Every single person living on Hawkins Street was descended from a slave. John Hawkins's ship, the one in which he transported the people he had bought and kidnapped, was called *The Jesus*. He later became the treasurer of the Royal Navy and rear admiral.

Again, the reality of my life, the life I led at the time I was being shown 8 these views of England for the first time, for the second time, for the one-hundred-millionth time, was this: the sun shone with what sometimes seemed to be a deliberate cruelty; we must have done something to deserve that. My dresses did not rustle in the evening air as I strolled to the theater (I had no evening, I had no theater; my dresses were made of a cheap cotton, the weave of which would give way after not too many washings). I got up in the morning, I did my chores (fetched water from the public pipe for my mother, swept the yard), I washed myself, I went to a woman to have my hair combed freshly every day (because before we were allowed into our classroom our teachers would inspect us, and children who had not bathed that day, or had dirt under their fingernails, or whose hair had not been combed anew that day, might not be allowed to attend class). I ate that breakfast. I walked to school. At school we gathered in an auditorium and sang a hymn, "All Things Bright and Beautiful," and looking down on us as we sang were portraits of the Queen of England and her husband; they wore jewels and medals and they smiled. I was a Brownie. At each meeting we would form a little group around a flagpole, and after raising the Union Jack, we would say, "I promise to do my best, to do my duty to God and the Queen, to help other people every day and obey the scouts' law."

Who were these people and why had I never seen them, I mean really 9 seen them, in the place where they lived? I had never been to England. No one I knew had ever been to England, or I should say, no one I knew had ever been and returned to tell me about it. All the people I knew who had gone to England had stayed there. Sometimes they left behind them their small children, never to see them again. England! I had seen England's representatives. I had seen the governor general at the public grounds at a ceremony celebrating the Queen's birthday. I had seen an old princess and I had seen a young princess. They had both been extremely not beautiful, but who of us would have told them that? I had never seen England, really seen it, I had only met a representative, seen a picture, read books, memorized its history. I had never set foot, my own foot, in it.

10      The space between the idea of something and its reality is always wide and deep and dark. The longer they are kept apart—idea of thing, reality of thing—the wider the width, the deeper the depth, the thicker and darker the darkness. This space starts out empty, there is nothing in it, but it rapidly becomes filled up with obsession or desire or hatred or love—sometimes all of these things, sometimes some of these things, sometimes only one of these things. The existence of the world as I came to know it was a result of this: idea of thing over here, reality of thing way, way over there. There was Christopher Columbus, an unlikable man, an unpleasant man, a liar (and so, of course, a thief) surrounded by maps and schemes and plans, and there was the reality on the other side of that width, that depth, that darkness. He became obsessed, he became filled with desire, the hatred came later, love was never a part of it. Eventually, his idea met the longed-for reality. That the idea of something and its reality are often two completely different things is something no one ever remembers; and so when they meet and find that they are not compatible, the weaker of the two, idea or reality, dies. That idea Christopher Columbus had was more powerful than the reality he met, and so the reality he met died.

11      And so finally, when I was a grown-up woman, the mother of two children, the wife of someone, a person who resides in a powerful country that takes up more than its fair share of a continent, the owner of a house with many rooms in it and of two automobiles, with the desire and will (which I very much act upon) to take from the world more than I give back to it, more than I deserve, more than I need, finally then, I saw England, the real England, not a picture, not a painting, not through a story in a book, but England, for the first time. In me, the space between the idea of it and its reality had become filled with hatred, and so when at last I saw it I wanted to take it into my hands and tear it into little pieces and then crumble it up as if it were clay, child's clay. That was impossible, and so I could only indulge in not-favorable opinions.

12      There were monuments everywhere; they commemorated victories, battles fought between them and the people who lived across the sea from them, all vile people, fought over which of them would have dominion over the people who looked like me. The monuments were useless to them now, people sat on them and ate their lunch. They were like markers on an old useless trail, like a piece of old string tied to a finger to jog the memory, like old decoration in an old house, dirty, useless, in the way. Their skins were so pale, it made them look so fragile, so weak, so ugly. What if I had the power to simply banish them from their land, send boat after boatload of them on a voyage that in fact had no destination, force them to live in a place where the sun's presence was a constant? This would rid them of their

pale complexion and make them look more like me, make them look more like the people I love and treasure and hold dear, and more like the people who occupy the near and far reaches of my imagination, my history, my geography, and reduce them and everything they have ever known to figurines as evidence that I was in divine favor, what if all this was in my power? Could I resist it? No one ever has.

And they were rude, they were rude to each other. They didn't like each   13
other very much. They didn't like each other in the way they didn't like me, and it occurred to me that their dislike for me was one of the few things they agreed on.

I was on a train in England with a friend, an English woman. Before   14
we were in England she liked me very much. In England she didn't like me at all. She didn't like the claim I said I had on England, she didn't like the views I had of England. I didn't like England, she didn't like England, but she didn't like me not liking it too. She said, "I want to show you my England, I want to show you the England that I know and love." I had told her many times before that I knew England and I didn't want to love it anyway. She no longer lived in England; it was her own country, but it had not been kind to her, so she left. On the train, the conductor was rude to her; she asked something, and he responded in a rude way. She became ashamed. She was ashamed at the way he treated her; she was ashamed at the way he behaved. "This is the new England," she said. But I liked the conductor being rude; his behavior seemed quite appropriate. Earlier this had happened: we had gone to a store to buy a shirt for my husband; it was meant to be a special present, a special shirt to wear on special occasions. This was a store where the Prince of Wales has his shirts made, but the shirts sold in this store are beautiful all the same. I found a shirt I thought my husband would like and I wanted to buy him a tie to go with it. When I couldn't decide which one to choose, the salesman showed me a new set. He was very pleased with these, he said, because they bore the crest of the Prince of Wales, and the Prince of Wales had never allowed his crest to decorate an article of clothing before. There was something in the way he said it; his tone was slavish, reverential, awed. It made me feel angry; I wanted to hit him. I didn't do that. I said, my husband and I hate princes, my husband would never wear anything that had a prince's anything on it. My friend stiffened. The salesman stiffened. They both drew themselves in, away from me. My friend told me that the prince was a symbol of her Englishness, and I could see that I had caused offense. I looked at her. She was an English person, the sort of English person I used to know at home, the sort who was nobody in England but somebody when they came to live among the people like me. There were many people I could have seen England with; that I was seeing it with this particular person, a person who reminded me of the people who showed me England long ago as I sat in church or at my desk, made me feel silent and afraid, for I wondered if, all

these years of our friendship, I had had a friend or had been in the thrall
of a racial memory.

15      I went to Bath—we, my friend and I, did this, but though we were together, I was no longer with her. The landscape was almost as familiar as
my own hand, but I had never been in this place before, so how could that
be again? And the streets of Bath were familiar, too, but I had never
walked on them before. It was all those years of reading, starting with Roman Britain. Why did I have to know about Roman Britain? It was of no
real use to me, a person living on a hot, drought-ridden island, and it is of
no use to me now, and yet my head is filled with this nonsense, Roman
Britain. In Bath, I drank tea in a room I had read about in a novel written
in the eighteenth century. In this very same room, young women wearing
those dresses that rustled and so on danced and flirted and sometimes
disgraced themselves with young men, soldiers, sailors, who were on
their way to Bristol or someplace like that, so many places like that where
so many adventures, the outcome of which was not good for me, began.
Bristol, England. A sentence that began "That night the ship sailed from
Bristol, England" would end not so good for me. And then I was driving
through the countryside in an English motorcar, on narrow winding
roads, and they were so familiar, though I had never been on them before;
and through little villages the names of which I somehow knew so well
though I had never been there before. And the countryside did have all
those hedges and hedges, fields hedged in. I was marveling at all the toil
of it, the planting of the hedges to begin with and then the care of it, all
that clipping, year after year of clipping, and I wondered at the lives of
the people who would have to do this, because wherever I see and feel the
hands that hold up the world, I see and feel myself and all the people who
look like me. And I said, "Those hedges" and my friend said that someone, a woman named Mrs. Rothchild, worried that the hedges weren't being taken care of properly; the farmers couldn't afford or find the help to
keep up the hedges, and often they replaced them with wire fencing. I
might have said to that, well if Mrs. Rothchild doesn't like the wire fencing, why doesn't she take care of the hedges herself, but I didn't. And then
in those fields that were now hemmed in by wire fencing that a privileged
woman didn't like was planted a vile yellow flowering bush that produced an oil, and my friend said that Mrs. Rothchild didn't like this either; it ruined the English countryside, it ruined the traditional look of the
English countryside.

16      It was not at that moment that I wished every sentence, everything
I knew, that began with England would end with "and then it all died;
we don't know how, it just all died." At that moment, I was thinking,

who are these people who forced me to think of them all the time, who forced me to think that the world I knew was incomplete, or without substance, or did not measure up because it was not England; that I was incomplete, or without substance, and did not measure up because I was not English. Who were these people? The person sitting next to me couldn't give me a clue; no one person could. In any case, if I had said to her, I find England ugly, I hate England; the weather is like a jail sentence, the English are a very ugly people, the food in England is like a jail sentence, the hair of English people is so straight, so dead looking, the English have an unbearable smell so different from the smell of people I know, real people of course, she would have said that I was a person full of prejudice. Apart from the fact that it is I—that is, the people who look like me—who made her aware of the unpleasantness of such a thing, the idea of such a thing, prejudice, she would have been only partly right, sort of right: I may be capable of prejudice, but my prejudices have no weight to them, my prejudices have no force behind them, my prejudices remain opinions, my prejudices remain my personal opinion. And a great feeling of rage and disappointment came over me as I looked at England, my head full of personal opinions that could not have public, my public, approval. The people I come from are powerless to do evil on grand scale.

The moment I wished every sentence, everything I knew, that began 17 with England would end with "and then it all died, we don't know how, it just all died" was when I saw the white cliffs of Dover. I had sung hymns and recited poems that were about a longing to see the white cliffs of Dover again. At the time I sang the hymns and recited the poems, I could really long to see them again because I had never seen them at all, nor had anyone around me at the time. But there we were, groups of people longing for something we had never seen. And so there they were, the white cliffs, but they were not that pearly majestic thing I used to sing about, that thing that created such a feeling in these people that when they died in the place where I lived they had themselves buried facing a direction that would allow them to see the white cliffs of Dover when they were resurrected, as surely they would be. The white cliffs of Dover, when finally I saw them, were cliffs, but they were not white; you would only call them that if the word "white" meant something special to you; they were dirty and they were steep; they were so steep, the correct height from which all my views of England, starting with the map before me in my classroom and ending with the trip I had just taken, should jump and die and disappear forever.

*1991*

## QUESTIONS FOR DISCUSSION

### Content

a. How would you describe Kincaid's attitude toward England in this essay? How do you account for her feelings?

b. How is Kincaid's view of England a result of her upbringing in Antigua, especially her schooling?

c. In paragraph 16, Kincaid admits that her friend would have called her "a person full of prejudice." But *is* she prejudiced? What does Kincaid say? What would you say?

d. What stereotypical images of England does Kincaid describe? In what way to these stereotypes symbolize England? How does Kincaid use these symbols?

e. In the last sentence, what does Kincaid mean by saying that she wished all her views of England would jump off the cliffs of Dover? Why does she choose the cliffs of Dover as the launching site?

f. In your opinion, would seeing England for a second or third time have a different effect on Kincaid? In what way?

### Strategy and Style

g. Kincaid's tone is often bitter. Why is she bitter, or why would she want to portray herself as bitter?

h. Kincaid's sentences are short and have a clipped sound; in addition, she frequently uses "and" to connect sentences and parts of sentences. How does this sentence style help convey her emotions? What other techniques does she use, and to what effect?

i. This essay has fairly easy vocabulary. What does the choice of vocabulary imply about the audience?

j. Although the essay has fairly easy vocabulary, it has long paragraphs and a rambling style. Do the paragraphs and style help or hinder your reading?

k. What rhetorical strategies does Kincaid use, and where are they most apparent in the essay? What might be her reason for choosing these strategies? How effectively does she use them?

## ENGAGING THE TEXT

a. Make a list of places—cities such as New York, Los Angeles, Paris, or Tokyo; or countries such as Afghanistan, South Africa, and Mexico. List the images that are evoked in your mind when you think of any one or two of these places. In one column, list the images you have (or, if you have been to that place, the images that you had before going there). In another column, list the probable realities (or, if you have been there, the realities).

b. Find a map of a place you have not been. What location on the map intrigues you? Briefly explain why that location intrigues you.

## SUGGESTIONS FOR SUSTAINED WRITING

a. Combine description and narration to tell the story about a place that has special meaning (negative or positive) for you. Try to recreate the place in the mind of your readers.

b. Compare Kincaid's essay with other essays about place in this textbook, such as James Baldwin's "Fifth Avenue, Uptown" (Chapter 2), E. B. White's "Once More to the Lake" (Chapter 2), Joan Didion's "Marrying Absurd" (Chapter 2), and Mark Twain's "Two Views of the Mississippi" (Chapter 6). What do the writers consider most important about their places? Why?

c. Begin with items in Engaging the Text and then write an essay in which you compare and contrast the stereotypical images to the realities of a particular place. Use both primary research (interviews, your own experience) and secondary research (books, articles).

# On Dumpster Diving

Lars Eighner

*A freelance writer living in Austin, Lars Eighner (b. 1948) was born in Corpus Christi, Texas, and attended the University of Texas from 1966 to 1969. He was an attendant and ward worker at the Austin State Hospital from 1980 to 1987 worked off and on for a drug crisis program and as a freelance writer. Eighner lived on the streets for several years, and his homeless experiences are recalled in* Travels with Lizbeth *(1993), which became a best-seller and from which "Dumpster Diving" is excerpted. Travels started as a series of letters to his friends describing life on the street. His sentence style has been compared to the style of the nineteenth-century English novel. "Dumpster Diving" was first anthologized in* The Pushcart Prize Best of the Small Presses *in 1992 and has been included in many anthologies since then. Among Eighner's other works are a novel,* Pawn to Queen Four *(1995), and* Elements of Arousal *(1994), advice to would-be authors of gay erotica.*

1   Long before I began Dumpster diving I was impressed with Dumpsters, enough so that I wrote the Merriam-Webster research service to discover what I could about the word *Dumpster*. I learned from them that it is a proprietary word belonging to the Dempster Dumpster company. Since then I have dutifully capitalized the word, although it was lowercased in almost all the citations Merriam-Webster photocopied for me. Dempster's word is too apt. I have never heard these things called anything but Dumpsters. I do not know anyone who knows the generic name for these objects. From time to time I have heard a wino or hobo give some corrupted credit to the original and call them Dipsy Dumpsters.

2   I began Dumpster diving about a year before I became homeless.

3   I prefer the word *scavenging* and use the word *scrounging* when I mean to be obscure. I have heard people, evidently meaning to be polite, use the word *foraging*, but I prefer to reserve that word for gathering nuts and berries and such, which I do also according to the season and the opportunity. *Dumpster diving* seems to me to be a little too cute and, in my case, inaccurate because I lack the athletic ability to lower myself into the Dumpsters as the true divers do, much to their increased profit.

4   I like the frankness of the word *scavenging*, which I can hardly think of without picturing a big black snail on an aquarium wall. I live from the refuse of others. I am a scavenger. I think it a sound and honorable niche, although if I could I would naturally prefer to live the comfortable consumer life, perhaps—and only perhaps—as a slightly less wasteful consumer, owing to what I have learned as a scavenger.

5   While Lizbeth [Eighner's dog] and I were still living in the shack on Avenue B as my savings ran out, I put almost all my sporadic income into rent. The necessities of daily life I began to extract from Dumpsters. Yes, we ate from them. Except for jeans, all my clothes came from Dumpsters. Boom boxes, candles, bedding, toilet paper, a virgin male love doll, medicine, books, a typewriter, dishes, furnishing, and change, sometimes amounting to many dollars—I acquired many things from the Dumpsters.

6   I have learned much as a scavenger. I mean to put some of what I have learned down here, beginning with the practical art of Dumpster diving and proceeding to the abstract.

7   What is safe to eat?

8   After all, the finding of objects is becoming something of an urban art. Even respectable employed people will sometimes find something tempting sticking out of a Dumpster or standing beside one. Quite a number of people, not all of them of the bohemian type, are willing to brag that they found this or that piece in the trash. But eating from Dumpsters is what separates the dilettanti from the professionals. Eating safely from the Dumpsters involves three principles: using the senses and common sense to evaluate the condition of the found materials, knowing the Dumpsters

of a given area and checking them regularly, and seeking always to answer the question "Why was this discarded?"

Perhaps everyone who has a kitchen and a regular supply of groceries  9 has, at one time or another, made a sandwich and eaten half of it before discovering mold on the bread or got a mouthful of milk before realizing the milk had turned. Nothing of the sort is likely to happen to a Dumpster diver because he is constantly reminded that most food is discarded for a reason. Yet a lot of perfectly good food can be found in Dumpsters.

Canned goods, for example, turn up fairly often in the Dumpsters I  10 frequent. All except the most phobic people would be willing to eat from a can, even if it came from a Dumpster. Canned goods are among the safest of foods to be found in Dumpsters but are not utterly foolproof.

Although very rare with modern canning methods, botulism is a pos-  11 sibility. Most other forms of food poisoning seldom do lasting harm to a healthy person, but botulism is almost certainly fatal and often the first symptom is death. Except for carbonated beverages, all canned goods should contain a slight vacuum and suck air when first punctured. Bulging, rusty, and dented cans and cans that spew when punctured should be avoided, especially when the contents are not very acidic or syrupy.

Heat can break down the botulin, but this requires much more cook-  12 ing than most people do to canned goods. To the extent that botulism occurs at all, of course, it can occur in cans on pantry shelves as well as in cans from Dumpsters. Need I say that home-canned goods are simply too risky to be recommended.

From time to time one of my companions, aware of the source of my  13 provisions, will ask, "Do you think these crackers are really safe to eat?" For some reason it is most often the crackers they ask about.

This question has always made me angry. Of course I would not offer  14 my companion anything I had doubts about. But more than that, I wonder why he cannot evaluate the condition of the crackers for himself. I have no special knowledge and I have been wrong before. Since he knows where the food comes from, it seems to me he ought to assume some of the responsibility for deciding what he will put in his mouth. For myself I have few qualms about dry foods such as crackers, cookies, cereal, chips, and pasta if they are free of visible contaminates and still dry and crisp. Most often such things are found in the original packaging, which is not so much a positive sign as it is the absence of a negative one.

Raw fruits and vegetables with intact skins seem perfectly safe to  15 me, excluding of course the obviously rotten. Many are discarded for minor imperfections that can be pared away. Leafy vegetables, grapes, cauliflower, broccoli, and similar things may be contaminated by liquids and may be impractical to wash.

Candy, especially hard candy, is usually safe if it has not drawn ants.  16 Chocolate is often discarded only because it has become discolored as the cocoa butter de-emulsified. Candying, after all, is one method of food preservation because pathogens do not like very sugary substances.

17    All of these foods might be found in any Dumpster and can be evaluated with some confidence largely on the basis of appearance. Beyond these are foods that cannot be correctly evaluated without additional information.

18    I began scavenging by pulling pizzas out of the Dumpster behind a pizza delivery shop. In general, prepared food requires caution, but in this case I knew when the shop closed and went to the Dumpster as soon as the last of the help left.

19    Such shops often get prank orders; both the orders and the products made to fill them are called *bogus*. Because help seldom stays long at these places, pizzas are often made with the wrong topping, refused on delivery for being cold, or baked incorrectly. The products to be discarded are boxed up because inventory is kept by counting boxes: A boxed pizza can be written off; an unboxed pizza does not exist.

20    I never placed a bogus order to increase the supply of pizzas and I believe no one else was scavenging in this Dumpster. But the people in the shop became suspicious and began to retain their garbage in the shop overnight. While it lasted I had a steady supply of fresh, sometimes warm pizza. Because I knew the Dumpster I knew the source of the pizza, and because I visited the Dumpster regularly I knew what was fresh and what was yesterday's.

21    The area I frequent is inhabited by many affluent college students. I am not here by chance; the Dumpsters in this area are very rich. Students throw out many good things, including food. In particular they tend to throw everything out when they move at the end of a semester, before and after breaks, and around midterm, when many of them despair of college. So I find it advantageous to keep an eye on the academic calendar.

22    Students throw food away around breaks because they do not know whether it has spoiled or will spoil before they return. A typical discard is a half jar of peanut butter. In fact, nonorganic peanut butter does not require refrigeration and is unlikely to spoil in any reasonable time. The student does not know that, and since it is Daddy's money, the student decides not want to take a chance. Opened containers require caution and some attention to the question, "Why was this discarded?" But in the case of discards from student apartments, the answer may be that the item was thrown out through carelessness, ignorance, or wastefulness. This can sometimes be deduced when the item is found with many others, including some that are obviously perfectly good.

23    Some students, and others, approach defrosting a freezer by chucking out the whole lot. Not only do the circumstances of such a find tell the story, but also the mass of frozen goods stays cold for a long time and items may be found still frozen or freshly thawed.

Yogurt, cheese, and sour cream are items that are often thrown out 24
while they are still good. Occasionally I find a cheese with a spot of mold,
which of course I just pare off, and because it is obvious why such a cheese
was discarded, I treat it with less suspicion than an apparently perfect
cheese found in similar circumstances. Yogurt is often discarded, still
sealed, only because the expiration date on the carton had passed. This is
one of my favorite finds because yogurt will keep for several days, even in
warm weather.

Students throw out canned goods and staples at the end of semesters 25
and when they give up college at midterm. Drugs, pornography, spirits,
and the like are often discarded when parents are expected—Dad's Day,
for example. And spirits also turn up after big party weekends, presumably discarded by the newly reformed. Wine and spirits, of course, keep
perfectly well even once opened, but the same cannot be said of beer.

My test for carbonated soft drinks is whether they still fizz vigorously. 26
Many juices or other beverages are too acidic or too syrupy to cause much
concern, provided they are not visibly contaminated. I have discovered
nasty molds in vegetable juices, even when the product was found under its
original seal; I recommend that such products be decanted slowly into a
clear glass. Liquids always require some care. One hot day I found a large
jug of Pat O'Brien's Hurricane mix. The jug had been opened but was still
ice cold. I drank three large glasses before it became apparent to me that
someone had added the rum to the mix, and not a little rum. I never tasted
the rum, and by the time I began to feel the effects I had already ingested a
very large quantity of the beverage. Some divers would have considered this
a boon, but being suddenly intoxicated in a public place in the early afternoon is not my idea of a good time.

I have heard of people maliciously contaminating discarded food and 27
even handouts, but mostly I have heard of this from people with vivid
imaginations who have had no experience with the Dumpsters themselves. Just before the pizza shop stopped discarding its garbage at night,
jalapeños began showing up on most of the thrown-out pizzas. If indeed
this was meant to discourage me, it was a wasted effort because I am a native Texan.

For myself, I avoid game, poultry, pork, and egg-based foods, whether 28
I find them raw or cooked. I seldom have the means to cook what I find,
but when I do I avail myself of plentiful supplies of beef, which is often in
very good condition. I suppose fish becomes disagreeable before it becomes dangerous. Lizbeth is happy to have any such thing that is past its
prime and, in fact, does not recognize fish as food until it is quite strong.

Home leftovers, as opposed to surpluses from restaurants, are very of- 29
ten bad. Evidently, especially among students, there is a common type of
personality that carefully wraps up even the smallest leftover and shoves
it into the back of the refrigerator for six months or so before discarding it.

**508**

Characteristic of this type are the reused jars and margarine tubs to which the remains are committed. I avoid ethnic foods I am unfamiliar with. If I do not know what it is supposed to look like when it is good, I cannot be certain I will be able to tell if it is bad.

30    No matter how careful I am I still get dysentery at least once a month, oftener in warm weather. I do not want to paint too romantic a picture. Dumpster diving has serious drawbacks as a way of life.

31    I learned to scavenge gradually, on my own. Since then I have initiated several companions into the trade. I have learned that there is a predictable series of stages a person goes through in learning to scavenge.

32    At first the new scavenger is filled with disgust and self-loathing. He is ashamed of being seen and may lurk around, trying to duck behind things, or he may try to dive at night. (In fact, most people instinctively look away from a scavenger. By skulking around, the novice calls attention to himself and arouses suspicion. Diving at night is ineffective and needlessly messy.)

33    Every grain of rice seems to be a maggot. Everything seems to stink. He can wipe the egg yolk off the found can, but he cannot erase from his mind the stigma of eating garbage.

34    That stage passes with experience. The scavenger finds a pair of running shoes that fit and look and smell brand-new. He finds a pocket calculator in perfect working order. He finds pristine ice cream, still frozen, more than he can eat or keep. He begins to understand: People throw away perfectly good stuff, a lot of perfectly good stuff.

35    At this stage, Dumpster shyness begins to dissipate. The diver, after all, has the last laugh. He is finding all manner of good things that are his for the taking. Those who disparage his profession are the fools, not he.

36    He may begin to hang on to some perfectly good things for which he has neither a use nor a market. Then he begins to take note of the things that are not perfectly good but are nearly so. He mates a Walkman with broken earphones and one that is missing a battery cover. He picks up things that he can repair.

37    At this stage he may become lost and never recover. Dumpsters are full of things of some potential value to someone and also of things that never have much intrinsic value but are interesting. All the Dumpster divers I have known come to the point of trying to acquire everything they touch. Why not take it, they reason, since it is all free? This is, of course, hopeless. Most divers come to realize that they must restrict themselves to items of relatively immediate utility. But in some cases the diver simply cannot control himself. I have met several of these pack-rat types. Their ideas of the values of various pieces of junk verge on the psychotic. Every bit of glass may be a diamond, they think, and all that glistens, gold.

38    I tend to gain weight when I am scavenging. Partly this is because I always find far more pizza and doughnuts than water-packed tuna, nonfat

yogurt, and fresh vegetables. Also I have not developed much faith in the reliability of Dumpsters as a food source, although it has been proven to me many times. I tend to eat as if I have no idea where my next meal is coming from. But mostly I just hate to see food go to waste and so I eat much more than I should. Something like this drives the obsession to collect junk.

As for collecting objects, I usually restrict myself to collecting one kind 39 of small object at a time, such as pocket calculators, sunglasses, or campaign buttons. To live on the street I must anticipate my needs to a certain extent: I must pick up and save warm bedding I find in August because it will not be found in Dumpsters in November. As I have no access to health care, I often hoard essential drugs, such as antibiotics and antihistamines. (This course can be recommended only to those with some grounding in pharmacology. Antibiotics, for example, even when indicated are worse than useless if taken in insufficient amounts.) But even if I had a home with extensive storage space, I could not save everything that might be valuable in some contingency.

I have proprietary feelings about my Dumpsters. As I have mentioned, 40 it is no accident that I scavenge from ones where good finds are common. But my limited experience with Dumpsters in other areas suggests to me that even in poorer areas, Dumpsters, if attended with sufficient diligence, can be made to yield a livelihood. The rich students discard perfectly good kiwifruit; poorer people discard perfectly good apples. Slacks and Polo shirts are found in the one place; jeans and T-shirts in the other. The population of competitors rather than the affluence of the dumpers most affects the feasibility of survival by scavenging. The large number of competitors is what puts me off the idea of trying to scavenge in places like Los Angeles.

Curiously, I do not mind my direct competition, other scavengers, so 41 much as I hate the can scroungers.

People scrounge cans because they have to have a little cash. I have 42 tried scrounging cans with an able-bodied companion. Afoot a can scrounger simply cannot make more than a few dollars a day. One can extract the necessities of life from the Dumpsters directly with far less effort than would be required to accumulate the equivalent value in cans. (These observations may not hold in places with container redemption laws.)

Can scroungers, then, are people who must have small amounts of 43 cash. These are drug addicts and winos, mostly the latter because the amounts are so small. Spirits and drugs do, like all other commodities, turn up in Dumpsters and the scavenger will from time to time have a half bottle of a rather good wine with his dinner. But the wino cannot survive on these occasional finds; he must have his daily dose to stave off the DTs. All the cans he can carry will buy about three bottles of Wild Irish Rose.

I do not begrudge them the cans, but can scroungers tend to tear up 44 the Dumpsters, mixing the contents and littering the area. They become so specialized that they can see only cans. They earn my contempt by passing up change, canned goods, and readily hockable items.

45      There are precious few courtesies among scavengers. But it is common practice to set aside surplus items: pairs of shoes, clothing, canned goods, and such. A true scavenger hates to see good stuff go to waste, and what he cannot use he leaves in good condition in plain sight.

46      Can scroungers lay waste to everything in their path and will stir one of a pair of good shoes to the bottom of a Dumpster, to be lost or ruined in the muck. Can scroungers will even go through individual garbage cans, something I have never seen a scavenger do.

47      Individual garbage cans are set out on the public easement only on garbage days. On other days going through them requires trespassing close to a dwelling. Going through individual garbage cans without scattering litter is almost impossible. Litter is likely to reduce the public's tolerance of scavenging. Individual cans are simply not as productive as Dumpsters; people in houses and duplexes do not move so often and for some reason do not tend to discard as much useful material. Moreover, the time required to go through one garbage can that serves one household is not much less than the time required to go through a Dumpster that contains the refuse of twenty apartments.

48      But my strongest reservation about going through individual garbage cans is that this seems to me a very personal kind of invasion to which I would object if I were a householder. Although many things in Dumpsters are obviously meant never to come to light, a Dumpster is somehow less personal.

49      I avoid trying to draw conclusions about the people who dump in the Dumpsters I frequent. I think it would be unethical to do so, although I know many people will find the idea of scavenger ethics too funny for words.

50      Dumpsters contain bank statements, correspondence, and other documents, just as anyone might expect. But there are less obvious sources of information. Pill bottles, for example. The labels bear the name of the patient, the name of the doctor, and the name of the drug. AIDS drugs and antipsychotic medicines, to name but two groups, are specific and are seldom prescribed for any other disorders. The plastic compacts for birth-control pills usually have complete label information.

51      Despite all of this sensitive information, I have had only one apartment resident object to my going through the Dumpster. In that case it turned out the resident was a university athlete who was taking bets and who was afraid I would turn up his wager slips.

52      Occasionally a find tells a story. I once found a small paper bag containing some unused condoms, several partial tubes of flavored sexual lubricants, a partially used compact of birth-control pills, and the torn pieces of a picture of a young man. Clearly she was through with him and planning to give up sex altogether.

Dumpster things are often sad—abandoned teddy bears, shredded  53
wedding books, despaired-of sales kits. I find many pets lying in state in
Dumpsters. Although I hope to get off the streets so that Lizbeth can have
a long and comfortable old age, I know this hope is not very realistic. So I
suppose when her time comes she too will go into a Dumpster. I will have
no better place for her. And after all, it is fitting, since for most of her life
her livelihood has come from the Dumpster. When she finds something I
think is safe that has been spilled from a Dumpster, I let her have it. She already knows the route around the best ones. I like to think that if she survives me she will have a chance of evading the dog catcher and of finding
her sustenance on the route.

Silly vanities also come to rest in the Dumpsters. I am a rather accom-  54
plished needleworker. I get a lot of material from the Dumpsters. Evidently sorority girls, hoping to impress someone, perhaps themselves,
with their mastery of a womanly art, buy a lot of embroider-by-number
kits, work a few stitches horribly, and eventually discard the whole mess.
I pull out their stitches, turn the canvas over, and work an original design.
Do not think I refrain from chuckling as I make gifts from these kits.

I find diaries and journals. I have often thought of compiling a book of  55
literary found objects. And perhaps I will one day. But what I find is hope-
lessly commonplace and bad without being, even unconsciously, camp. College students also discard their papers. I am horrified to discover the kind of
paper that now merits an A in an undergraduate course. I am grateful, however, for the number of good books and magazines the students throw out.

In the area I know best I have never discovered vermin in the Dump-  56
sters, but there are two kinds of kitty surprise. One is alley cats whom I
meet as they leap, claws first, out of Dumpsters. This is especially thrilling
when I have Lizbeth in tow. The other kind of kitty surprise is a plastic
garbage bag filled with some ponderous, amorphous mass. This always
proves to be used cat litter.

City bees harvest doughnut glaze and this makes the Dumpster at the  57
doughnut shop more interesting. My faith in the instinctive wisdom of animals is always shaken whenever I see Lizbeth attempt to catch a bee in her
mouth, which she does wherever bees are present. Evidently some birds
find Dumpsters profitable, for birdie surprise is almost as common as kitty
surprise of the first kind. In hunting season all kinds of small game turn
up in Dumpsters, some of it, sadly, not entirely dead. Curiously, summer
and winter, maggots are uncommon.

The worst of the living and near-living hazards of the Dumpsters are the  58
fire ants. The food they claim is not much of a loss, but they are vicious and
aggressive. It is very easy to brush against some surface of the Dumpster and
pick up half a dozen or more fire ants, usually in some sensitive area such as
the underarm. One advantage of bringing Lizbeth along as I make Dumpster rounds is that, for obvious reasons, she is very alert to ground-based fire

ants. When Lizbeth recognizes a fire-ant infestation around our feet, she does the Dance of the Zillion Fire Ants. I have learned not to ignore this warning from Lizbeth, whether I perceive the tiny ants or not, but to remove ourselves at Lizbeth's first pas de bourée. All the more so because the ants are the worst in the summer months when I wear flip-flops if I have them. (Perhaps someone will misunderstand this. Lizbeth does the Dance of the Zillion Fire Ants when she recognizes more fire ants than she cares to eat, not when she is being bitten. Since I have learned to react promptly, she does not get bitten at all. It is the isolated patrol of fire ants that falls in Lizbeth's range that deserves pity. She finds them quite tasty.)

59        By far the best way to go through a Dumpster is to lower yourself into it. Most of the good stuff tends to settle at the bottom because it is usually weightier than the rubbish. My more athletic companions have often demonstrated to me that they can extract much good material from a Dumpster I have already been over.

60        To those psychologically or physically unprepared to enter a Dumpster, I recommend a stout stick, preferable with some barb or hook at one end. The hook can be used to grab plastic garbage bags. When I find canned goods or other objects loose at the bottom of a Dumpster, I lower a bag into it, roll the desired object into the bag, and then hoist the bag out— a procedure more easily described than executed. Much Dumpster diving is a matter of experience for which nothing will do except practice.

61        Dumpster diving is outdoor work, often surprisingly pleasant. It is not entirely predictable; things of interest turn up every day and some days there are finds of great value. I am always very pleased when I can turn up exactly the thing I most wanted to find. Yet in spite of the element of chance, scavenging more than most other pursuits tends to yield returns in some proportion to the effort and intelligence brought to bear. It is very sweet to turn up a few dollars in change from a Dumpster that has just been gone over by a wino.

62        The land is now covered with cities. The cities are full of Dumpsters. If a member of the canine race is ever able to know what it is doing, then Lizbeth knows that when we go around to the Dumpsters, we are hunting. I think of scavenging as a modern form of self-reliance. In any event, after having survived nearly ten years of government service, where everything is geared to the lowest common denominator, I find it refreshing to have work that rewards initiative and effort. Certainly I would be happy to have a sinecure again, but I am no longer heartbroken that I left one.

63        I find from the experience of scavenging two rather deep lessons. The first is to take what you can use and let the rest go by. I have come to think that there is no value in the abstract. A thing I cannot use or make useful, perhaps by trading, has no value however rare or fine it may be. I mean useful in a broad sense—some art I would find useful and some otherwise.

64        I was shocked to realize that some things are not worth acquiring, but now I think it is so. Some material things are white elephants that eat up

the possessor's substance. The second lesson is the transcience of material being. This has not quite converted me to a dualist, but it has made some headway in that direction. I do not suppose that ideas are immortal, but certainly mental things are longer lived than other material things.

Once I was the sort of person who invests objects with sentimental 65 value. Now I no longer have those objects, but I have the sentiments yet.

Many times in our travels I have lost everything but the clothes I was 66 wearing and Lizbeth. The things I find in Dumpsters, the love letters and rag dolls of so many lives, remind me of this lesson. Now I hardly pick up a thing without envisioning the time I will cast it aside. This I think is a healthy state of mind. Almost everything I have now has already been cast out at least once, proving that what I own is valueless to someone.

Anyway, I find my desire to grab for the gaudy bauble has been largely 67 sated. I think this is an attitude I share with the very wealthy—we both know there is plenty more where what we have came from. Between us are the rat-race millions who nightly scavenge the cable channels looking for they know not what.

I am sorry for them.                                                   68

*1993*

## QUESTIONS FOR DISCUSSION

### Content

a. What is Eighner's thesis?

b. What is the purpose of this essay? Is it simply a guide to finding food while living on the streets? Or is there more involved? Explain.

c. What differences do you see in connotations of the words *scavenging, scrounging,* and *foraging* (paragraph 3)? Why does Eighner prefer to call what he does *scavenging?* How does this distinction affect the content and presentation of what is to come in this essay?

d. In what ways does the author determine whether something he finds in a Dumpster is safe to eat?

e. Other than how to spot edible food, what has Eighner learned from Dumpster diving?

f. What are the emotional drawbacks to Dumpster diving? What pleasures does the author take in this activity?

g. Why won't he scavenge in places like Los Angeles (paragraph 40)?

h. What does the author have against "can scroungers," and why does he bother to discuss them in such detail (paragraphs 42–47)?

i. Why does Eighner restrict his diving to Dumpsters and not search through individual garbage cans?

j. Who is Lizbeth, and why does the author mention her so often?

## Strategy and Style

k. In what ways is this essay an argument?

l. In what ways is it a process analysis? Where in the essay do you find classification and description?

m. How would you describe the author's tone, his attitude toward his subject?

n. What is the author's attitude toward the people who discard things in Dumpsters? Why is it important for him to reveal this attitude?

o. What is his attitude toward his audience?

p. Why does the author bother to tell us about the derivation of the word *Dumpster?*

q. Is this a balanced view of Dumpster diving? Explain.

r. Comment on Eighner's introduction and conclusion. Do you find them effective? Why?

# ENGAGING THE TEXT

a. The author reveals a great deal about himself in this essay. Reread "On Dumpster Diving" and make marginal notes in places that contain such detail. Then, write a paragraph or two that comment on Eighner's character.

b. In one or two well-developed paragraphs, explain Eighner's attitude toward college students. Make direct reference to his text and use direct quotations whenever appropriate.

# SUGGESTIONS FOR SUSTAINED WRITING

a. Explain what the contents of your garbage might reveal about you to anyone who cared to go through it.

b. Compare Eighner to the character of Charley Best in Naton Leslie's "Don't Get Comfortable" (Chapter 1). What do Eighner and Best have in common. How does each person make the best of what life hands him?

c. Do you agree with Eighner's vision of college students? Are they as spoiled and wasteful as he says? Write an essay in which you address this issue by agreeing with Eighner, rebutting him, or defending a third point of view. Do research to find statistical as well as anecdotal evidence to support your opinion.

# Permissions Acknowledgments

**515**

Jacoby, Susan. "Common Decency." First appeared in *The New York Times Magazine.* Copyright © 1991 Susan Jacoby.

Johnson, James Weldon. "Travelling South." From *The Autobiography of an Ex-Colored Man.* Public domain.

Kincaid, Jamaica. "On Seeing England for the First Time" from *Transitions.* Copyright © 1991 by Jamaica Kincaid. Reprinted by permission of the author.

King, Martin Luther, Jr. "I Have a Dream." Reprinted by arrangement with The Heirs to the Estate of Martin Luther King, Jr., c/o Writers House, Inc., as agent for the proprietor. Copyright © 1963 by Martin Luther King, Jr., copyright renewed 1991 by Coretta Scott King.

Kingston, Maxine Hong. "No Name Woman." From *The Woman Warrior.* Copyright © 1975, 1976 by Maxine Hong Kingston. Reprinted by permission of Alfred A. Knopf, a Division of Random House Inc.

Kozol, Jonathon. "Distancing the Homeless." Copyright © 1988. Reprinted by permission of the author.

Leslie, Naton. "Don't Get Comfortable." First published in *High Plains Literary Review,* and reprinted in *Best American Essays: 1997* (Houghton). Reprinted by permission of the author. Poet and essayist Naton Leslie teaches at Siena College in upstate New York.

Lutz, William. "Doublespeak." From *Doublespeak.* Copyright © 1989 by Blonde Bear, Inc. Reprinted by permission of HarperCollins Publishers, Inc.

Mairs, Nancy. "On Being a Cripple." From *Plaintext by Nancy Mairs.* Copyright © 1986 by The Arizona Board of Regents. Reprinted by permission of The University of Arizona Press.

Mannes, Marya. "How Do You Know It's Good?" Copyright 1962 by Marya Mannes, renewed 1990. Reprinted by permission of David J. Blow as Executor of the Estate of Marya Mannes.

Marius, Richard. "Writing Drafts." From *A Writer's Companion,* 2nd ed. Copyright © 1984, 1981. Reprinted by permission of the McGraw-Hill Companies.

Martin, Ann N. "Food Pets Die For." From *Earth Island Journal* (300 Broadway #28, San Francisco, CA 94133), published by NewSage Press (PO Box 607, Toutdale, OR 97060-0607). Reprinted by permission.

Meyer, Philip. "If Hitler Asked You to Electrocute a Stranger, Would You? Probably." Reprinted with permission of *Esquire* magazine. © Hearst Communications, Inc. *Esquire* is a trademark of Hearst Magazines Property, Inc. All Rights Reserved.

Minatoya, Lydia. "Discordant Fruit." From *Talking to High Monks in the Snow.* Copyright © 1992 by Lydia Minatoya. Reprinted by permission of HarperCollins Publishers, Inc.

Miner, Horace. "Body Ritual among the Nacirema." Reprinted by permission of the American Anthropological Association and Agnes Miller from *American Anthropologist* 58, no. 3 (June 1956).

Mitford, Jessica. "The American Way of Death." Reprinted by permission of Jessica Mitford. Copyright © 1963, 1978 by Jessica Mitford, all rights reserved.

Momaday, N. Scott. "The Way to Rainy Mountain." First published in *The Reporter,* January 26, 1967. Reprinted with permission from *The Way to Rainy Mountain* © 1969, The University of New Mexico Press.

Noda, Kesaya E. "Growing Up Asian in America." From *Making Waves,* by Asian Women United. © 1989 by Asian Women United. Reprinted by permission of the author.

Orwell, George. "A Hanging." From *Shooting an Elephant and Other Essays.* Copyright © 1950 by Sonia Brownell Orwell and renewed 1978 by Sonia Pitt-Rivers. Reprinted by permission of Harcourt, Inc.

Pace, Joseph. "Let's Go Veggie!" From *The Toronto Star,* May 27, 1988. Reprinted by permission from *The Toronto Star.*

Paglia, Camille. "Rape and Modern Sex War." From *Sex, Art, and American Culture.* Copyright © 1992. Reprinted by permission of Vintage Books.

Parker, Jo Goodwin. "What Is Poverty?" From *America's Other Children: Public Schools Outside Suburbia,* ed. George Henderson. Copyright © 1971 by the University of Oklahoma Press. Reprinted by permission.

Petrunkevitch, Alexander. "The Spider and the Wasp." *Scientific American,* August 1952. Reprinted with permission. Copyright © 1952 by Scientific American, Inc. All rights reserved.

Pickering, Samuel. "Faith of the Father." From *Still Life.* Copyright © 1990 by University Press of New England. Reprinted with permission.

Quammen, David. "Alias Benowitz Shoe Repair." From *Natural Acts.* Reprinted by permission of David Quammen. All rights reserved. Copyright © 1985 by David Quammen.

Rettie, James C. "But a Watch in the Night." From *Forever the Land* by Russell and Kate Lord. Copyright © 1950 by Harper & Brothers. Copyright renewed 1978 by Russell and Kate Lord. Reprinted by permission of HarperCollins Publishers, Inc.

Rodriguez, Richard. "Bilingual Education: Outdated and Unrealistic." Copyright © 1985 by Richard Rodriguez. Reprinted by permission of Georges Borchardt, Inc., for the author. Article originally appeared in *The New York Times.*

Sanders, Scott Russell. "The Men We Carry in Our Minds." From *Staying Put.* Copyright © 1993 by Scott Russell Sanders. Reprinted by permission of Beacon Press, Boston.

Sarton, May. "The Rewards of Living a Solitary Life." Copyright © 1974 by the New York Times Co. Reprinted by permission.

Sheehy, Gail. "Predictable Crises of Adulthood." From *Passages.* Copyright © 1974, 1976 by Gail Sheehy. Used by permission of Dutton, a division of Penguin Putnam Inc.

Sontag, Susan. "Women's Beauty: Put Down or Power Source?" Copyright © 1975 by Susan Sontag. Reprinted by permission of Farrar, Straus Giroux, LLC.

Staples, Brent. "Black Men in Public Spaces." Copyright © 1986. Reprinted by permission of the author.

Steele, Shelby. "White Guilt." First published in *The American Scholar,* Autumn 1990. Copyright © 1990 by Shelby Steele. Reprinted by permission of Carol Mann Agency.

Steinem, Gloria. "Erotica and Pornography." *Ms.,* November 1978. © 1978 by Gloria Steinem. Reprinted by permission of the author.

Tan, Amy. "Mother Tongue." Copyright © 1990 by Amy Tan. Reprinted by permission of the author.

Tannen, Deborah. "Talk in the Intimate Relationship: His and Hers." From *That's Not What I Meant.* Copyright © 1986 by Deborah Tannen. Reprinted by permission of HarperCollins Publishers, Inc. and William Morrow.

# Index

**521**